Lecture Notes in Comput9

Edited by G. Goos, J. Hartmanis and

Springer

Berlin
Heidelberg
New York
Barcelona
Hong Kong
London
Milan
Paris
Singapore
Tokyo

Lucas Chi-Kwong Hui   Dik Lun Lee (Eds.)

Internet Applications

5th International Computer Science Conference
ICSC'99
Hong Kong, China, December 13-15, 1999
Proceedings

Springer

Series Editors

Gerhard Goos, Karlsruhe University, Germany
Juris Hartmanis, Cornell University, NY, USA
Jan van Leeuwen, Utrecht University, The Netherlands

Volume Editors

Lucas Chi-Kwong Hui
The University of Hong Kong
Department of Computer Science and Information Systems
Pokfulam Road, Hong Kong, China
E-mail: hui@csis.hku.hk

Dik Lun Lee
Hong Kong University of Science and Technology
Department of Computer Science
Clear Water Bay, Hong Kong, China
E-mail: dlee@cs.ust.hk

Cataloging-in-Publication data applied for

Die Deutsche Bibliothek - CIP-Einheitsaufnahme

Internet applications : proceedings / 5th International Computer
Science Conference, ICSC '99, Hong Kong, China, December 13 - 15,
1999. Lucas Chi-Kwong Hui ; Dik Lun Lee (ed.). - Berlin ; Heidelberg ;
New York ; Barcelona ; Hong Kong ; London ; Milan ; Paris ; Singapore
; Tokyo : Springer, 1999
  (Lecture notes in computer science ; Vol. 1749)
  ISBN 3-540-66903-5

CR Subject Classification (1998): H.3, C.2, I.2, H.4.3, H.5, H.2

ISSN 0302-9743
ISBN 3-540-66903-5 Springer-Verlag Berlin Heidelberg New York

© Springer-Verlag Berlin Heidelberg 1999
Printed in Germany

Typesetting: Camera-ready by author
SPIN: 10750055   06/3142 – 5 4 3 2 1 0   Printed on acid-free paper

Message from the Chairman of the International Computer Congress 1999

Introduction

The International Computer Congress 1999 to be organized in Hong Kong from December 13-17, 1999, features four international conferences, namely the International Computer Science Conference (ICSC'99), the Sixth International Conference on Real-Time Computing Systems and Applications (RTCSA'99), the First International Conference on Mobile Data Access (MDA'99), and 1999 Pacific Rim International Symposium on Dependable Computing (PRDC 1999).

The International Computer Science Conference (ICSC) is the flagship conference of the IEEE Hong Kong Section Computer Chapter. ICSC'99 is the fifth in the series of conferences dedicated to the forefront of computer science. This is the 10th year of ICSC and every ICSC had a different theme reflecting the general interest of computer science at the time. The ICSC'97 was a joint conference with APSEC'97 featuring advanced topics on Software Engineering. For 1999, the theme is Internet Applications to celebrate the tremendous growth of the Internet.

RTCSA'99 will be the sixth in its series and will be held in Hong Kong for the first time. RTCSA has previously been held in Japan, Korea, and Taiwan. RTCSA'99 will bring together researchers and developers from academia and industry for advancing the technology of real-time computing systems and applications. The conference has the following goals:(1) to investigate advances in real-time systems and applications; (2) to promote interaction among real-time systems and applications; (3) to evaluate the maturity and directions of real-time system technology.

The First International Conference on Mobile Data Access is the successor of the workshop on Mobile Data Access held in Singapore in November 1998. Recognizing the success of the workshop and the importance of the area, the organizing team decided to transform it into an international conference to address the support of data access over hybrid wireless and wired networks. The scope of the conference includes but is not limited to information broadcast and filtering, data and location management, mobile networks, quality of service, and applications.

The Pacific Rim International Symposium on Dependable Computing (formerly the Pacific Rim International Symposium on Fault-Tolerant Systems) is a biennial symposium. This will be the sixth in the series of biennial symposia organized since 1989. The growing influence of computers and information technology on our lives calls into question several issues related to the dependability, safety, and security of computing systems and software. The objective of this symposium is to disseminate state-of-the-art research in dependable computing, with particular emphasis on systems and software.

The Computer Science Congress is structured to have ICSC'99 and RTCSA'99 running in parallel from December 13-15, 1999. MDA'99 will start on December 15 and run in parallel with PRDC 1999 from December 16-17, 1999.

Objectives and benefits of holding the four conferences in Hong Kong

The Hong Kong economy, and economies in the Asia-Pacific region in general are going through a painful recession and restructuring at the moment due to the widespread economic crisis. Leaders in the region are grappling with ways and means of coming to terms with the problems and leading these economies towards growth and success in the next millenium. The Chief Executive's Commission on Innovation and Technology, in its first report, has attempted to address these issues and has made recommendations for the future direction of Hong Kong. In the words of Tien Chang-Lin, the chairman of the commission (paraphrased from The Hong Kong Industrialist, December 1998):

> The commission envisages Hong Kong to be an innovation-led, technology-intensive economy in the 21st century, serving the region not only as a business and financial centre, but also as a leading city in the world for the development and use of information technology.

The Secretary for Information Technology and Broadcasting, The Hon. K. C. Kwong, outlines the government's IT strategy for Hong Kong (paraphrased from The Hong Kong Industrialist, December 1998) as:

> A healthy local IT industry is essential to the development of content and innovative applications in Hong Kong.

Rapid advances in information technology are evident in how it impacts our daily lives, personified by the explosive growth of the Internet. The widespread penetration of IT into our daily lives, be it in banking, financial services, real estate, transportation, manufacturing, government, and high technology areas, is unfathomable. Hong Kong, being a technology-savvy city, has been at the forefront of adopting information technology in all aspects of its economy and daily life. While the introduction of IT brings with it immense benefits, special attention should be devoted to addressing the problems of dependability arising from this growing dependance on IT.

This brings us to the focus and significance of holding the International Computer Congress 1999 in Hong Kong. ICSC'99, with its primary focus on Internet applications, focuses on an important and growth-oriented field. RTSCA'99, with its focus on real-time systems and their applications is very important for the local manufacturing and services industry. MDA'99 with its emphasis on the support of data access over hybrid wireless and wired networks, and PRDC 1999, with its focus on dependability issues, both address an important area of potential problems due to the widespread application of computer and information technology in our daily lives. The four conferences will enable researchers and industry participants from Hong Kong, China, and the rest of the world, to share their common knowledge, expertise, and ideas about various aspects of information technology.

Conference Plans

Each of the conferences featured in the International Computer Congress 1999 have formed very strong program committees whose members are experienced and internationally recognized researchers in their fields of expertise. We are pleased that we have attracted many high quality research paper submissions which will benefit all participants including many professionals and academics from Hong Kong, China, and the rest of the world. These papers will provide state-of-the-art information on engineering and information technology for developing possible applications in the local industry.

In addition to accepting high quality research papers, the congress has also accepted papers reflecting on industrial experience. There are special sessions for presenting such industry-oriented papers. This will provide a forum for the practitioners in industry to discuss their practical experience in applying engineering methodology and tools. This will also allow other researchers to learn from the first hand experience of the practitioners and to fuel their future research.

The conferences also feature keynote speeches by eminent and internationally renowned researchers in the respective fields. These speakers will provide their own vision of the future for their fields of expertise. This will greatly benefit both academics and industrial participants because the speeches will highlight new directions for future research and development.

Acknowledgements

We would like to thank all those who submitted papers to the conferences of this congress. We would also like to thank all program committee members who have devoted their valuable time to reviewing and selecting the papers, and all organization committee members of the ICC and the four conferences who have devoted their valuable time and effort to making this conference a success. Furthermore, we would like to thank the advisors for their firm support and valuable advice.

November 1999

Karl R.P.H. Leung

Committee of International Computer Congress 1999

Congress General Chair: Karl R.P.H. Leung (Chairman, IEEE Hong Kong Section Computer Chapter)

Conference General Co-chairs: K. P. Chan (The University of Hong Kong)
Jane Liu (University of Illinois at Urbana Champaign)
Yinghua Min (CAS, China)
Joseph Ng (Hong Kong Baptist University)
Hideyuki Tokuda (Keio University)
W. Zhao (Texa A&M University)

Conference Program Co-chairs: Dik Lee (Hong Kong University of Science and Technology)
Joseph Ng (Hong Kong Baptist University)
Heung-Kyu Lee (KAIST)
Michael Lyu (Chinese University of Hong Kong)
Jogesh Muppala (Hong Kong University of Science and Technology)

Secretary: M. W. Mak (Hong Kong Polytechnic University)

Treasurer: Wai Wong (Hong Kong Baptist University)

ICC Advisory Committee

Benjamin Wah (University of Illinois at Urbana-Champaign)
Franics Y. L. Chin (The University of Hong Kong)
Roland T. H. Chin (Hong Kong University of Science and Technology)
Horace H. S. Ip (City University of Hong Kong)
Ernest Lam (Hong Kong Baptist University)

Message from the ICSC General Chairman

The ICSC is the conference organized by the IEEE HK Section, Computer Chapter. This year's conference is not only the 5th conference, but also the last one before the Millenium. It therefore gives me great pleasure to welcome you all to Hong Kong, one of the 50 cities you have to visit at least once in your life. The theme - internet application - is a timely one, as the entire world becomes more closely linked by the Internet. I hope you will enjoy your stay in Hong Kong and look forward to seeing you at future conferences. Finally, I would like to thank the members of the organizing committee for their hard work, and Mr Ricky Tang for his help in compiling these proceedings.

November 1999   Kwok-Ping Chan

Organizing Committee of the
International Computer Science Conference 1999

General Chairman:	K. P. Chan (The University of Hong Kong)
General Co-chairman:	Joseph Ng (Hong Kong Baptist University)
Advisor:	Karl R. P. H. Leung (IEEE Hong Kong Section Computer Chapter)
Technical Program Chair:	Dik Lee (Hong Kong University of Science & Technology)
Secretary:	M. W. Mak (Hong Kong Polytechnic University)
Treasurer:	Wai Wong (Hong Kong Baptist University)
Publication:	L. Hui (The University of Hong Kong)
Local Arrangement:	P. K. Wong (Hong Kong Inst. of Vocational Training)
Registration:	J. Kwok (Hong Kong Baptist University)
Tutorial:	P. F. Sum (Hong Kong Baptist University)

Message from the
ICSC Program Committee Chairman

ICSC'99 is the fifth of a series of conferences organized by the IEEE Hong Kong Section, Computer Chapter. Each ICSC conference has a theme. This time, the theme "Internet Application" has been selected.

The tremendous growth of the Internet in the past decade has begun to impact us in almost every aspect we can imagine. We depend more and more on the Internet to communicate with each other (and even feel more comfortable about it than, say, telephones). Our education and economy are dependent more and more on the Internet – witness the boom of Internet-based retail and auction companies and the increasing use of Web-based distance learning. With the penetration of the Internet in Asia, ICSC'99 is a timely event for researchers and industrialists to get together and to share with each other problems, solutions, and new ideas.

What is special about ICSC'99 is that it is being held as part of the Federated 1999 International Computer Congress (ICC'99), a week-long event consisting of four conferences: the Fifth International Computer Science Conference (ICSC'99), the Sixth International Conference on Real-Time Computing Systems and Applications (RTCSA'99), the Pacific Rim International Symposium on Dependable Computing (PRDC'99), and the First International Conference on Mobile Data Access (MDA'99). While each conference maintains its own focus, I hope delegates to ICSC'99 will participate in and take advantage of the other conferences, and vice versa.

For ICSC'99, we received 80 papers and accepted 30 regular papers and 30 short papers. We aimed at balancing the technical quality and diversity, so that conference participants can interact with each other in a wide range of areas. As can be seen from the technical program, the papers cover a large number of topics relating to the Internet. The fact that the authors of these papers come from many different countries is perhaps equally important. I hope delegates to the conference will interact not only in the technical sessions but in coffee breaks, during lunches (arranged by the conference), and at the conference banquet as well.

This year, several paper sessions have been reserved for the AEARU Second Workshop of Computer Science. AEARU is an association of 17 major research universities in East Asia. Delegates from the member universities will join ICSC'99 and discuss their research and curriculum development activities.

Last but not least, I would like to take this opportunity to acknowledge the excellent work of the program committee and external reviewers in putting the technical program together.

October 1999

Dik Lun Lee

Program Committee of the
International Computer Science Conference 1999

External Reviewers

Amitabha Das (Singapore)
Anthony K. H. Tung (USA)
C.M. Lee (Hong Kong)
Chao-Chun Chen (USA)
Chih-Horng Ke (USA)
Chun Zeng (China)
Chun-Hung Cheng (Hong Kong)
Derek Munneke (USA)
Dickson K.W. Chiu (Hong Kong)
Dit-Yan Yeung (Hong Kong)
Jack Yiu-bun Lee (Hong Kong)
He Yong (Hong Kong)
Hongjun Lu (Hong Kong)
Honglan Jin (Hong Kong)
I-Fong Su (USA)
James Kwok (Hong Kong)
Jianliang Xu (Hong Kong)
K.S. Leung (Hong Kong)
Kazutoshi Sumiya (Japan)
Kok-Wee Gan (Hong Kong)
L.M. Cheng (Hong Kong)
Wing Pong Robert Luk (Hong Kong)
Lin Chi Wai (Hong Kong)

Manhoi Choy (Hong Kong)
Matt Robshaw (USA)
Mei Jie (Hong Kong)
Mengchi Liu (Singapore)
Nikos Mamoulis (Hong Kong)
P.F. Shum (Hong Kong)
Po-Shan Kam (Hong Kong)
S.S.M. Chan (Hong Kong)
Shiguang Qiu (Singapore)
Shing-Chi Cheung (Hong Kong)
Sin Yeung Lee (Singapore)
Vincent Ng (Hong Kong)
Wai-Ching Wong (Hong Kong)
Wai-Chiu Wong (Hong Kong)
Weijia Jia (Hong Kong)
Wenhu Tian (China)
Xiang Gao (China)
Xiaochun Yang (China)
Yipeng Shen (Hong Kong)
Yiqun Lisa Yin (USA)
Yoshiharu Ishikawa (Japan)
Yu-Chi Chung (USA)

Table of Contents

User Interface

Multimedia

Modeling

Information Retrieval

Workflow

Applications

Agent / Active Networks II

Mobility and Distributed Databases I

Protocol I

Distributed Systems

Applications

Information Retrieval and Filtering

Web Technologies

E-Commerce

Mobility and Distributed Databases II

Protocol II

A Study of Belief Revision in the Context of Adaptive Information Filtering

Raymond Lau[1], Arthur H.M. ter Hofstede[1], and Peter D. Bruza[2]

[1] Cooperative Information Systems Research Centre
Queensland University of Technology, Brisbane, Qld 4001, Australia
{raymond, arthur}@icis.qut.edu.au
[2] Distributed Systems Technology Centre, The University of Queensland
Brisbane, Qld 4072, Australia
bruza@dstc.edu.au

Abstract. The rapid growth of the Internet and the World Wide Web (*Web*) provides access to vast amounts of valuable information. However, the problem of information overload is an obstacle to the practical use of potentially useful information on the Web. Agent based information filtering alleviates the above problem by proactively scanning through the incoming stream of information on behalf of the users. However, users' information needs will change over time. To make intelligent information filtering effective, the agents must be *adaptive*. The *AGM* belief revision framework, a logic based revision paradigm, offers a sound and rigorous method of updating an agent's beliefs of users' information needs. This article examines the issues of applying the AGM belief revision framework to adaptive information filtering.

1 Introduction

With the explosive growth of the Internet and the World Wide Web *(Web)*, it becomes more and more difficult to locate relevant information on the Web. Though Internet search engines and meta-search engines have been developed to facilitate information retrieval, they cannot solve the problem of information overload on the Web. One of the reasons is that they are not tailor-made to the specific information retrieval requirements of an individual. Another reason is that users often have difficulties in translating their implicit information needs into corresponding Internet queries. Issuing an imprecise query to search engine such as AltaVista could lead to the retrieval of thousands of Web documents. It was observed that the average Internet query consisted of only 2.2 terms [11]. This figure implies that users' information needs are poorly represented as corresponding Internet queries. Consequently, too much irrelevant information is often delivered to the users.

Information Filtering (*IF*) and Information Retrieval (*IR*) are seen as two sides of the same coin [4]. However, IR often refers to short term queries in which the users take an active role to specify their queries, whereas IF concerns with the removal of irrelevant information from a stream of incoming information based on the users' long term and recurring retrieval goals stored in *user profiles*. Given the volume of information available on the Web, agent based information filtering is promising because agents support automatic and personalised information dissemination. Information agents [15] are *autonomous* and *proactive*. They can actively seek for and filter relevant information on behalf of the users. Information agents are also *adaptive* in the sense that they can learn the representations of the users' information needs, and continuously refine these representations by observing users' relevance feedback. Since timeliness is one of the significant factors in IF [4], agent based filtering systems should be *efficient* enough to give their users instant responses. When compared with quantitative approach of IF, one of the advantages of agent based IF is that the behavior of the filtering systems is *explanatory*. The reason why a particular document is presented can be explained by the formal deduction process. Above all, agent based filtering systems should present *precise* information to their users given accurate representations of users' information needs.

It is our belief that augmenting the Internet search engines with filtering agents can alleviate the problem of information overload on the Web. By considering the above features of agent based IF, an agent based adaptive information filtering system *(AIFS)* is proposed. Figure 1 depicts the proposed system architecture. Directed arrow lines in the diagram represent data flow.

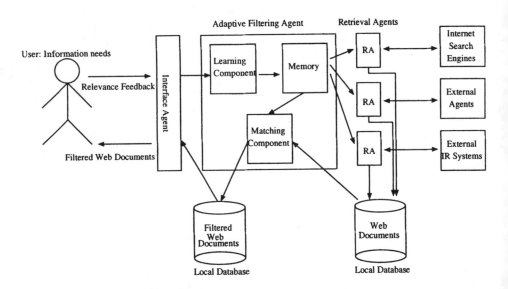

Fig. 1. The System Architecture of AIFS

The focus of our research is on the adaptive filtering agent. The filtering agent consists of two main functional components, namely the *learning* component and the document *matching* component. After receiving a user's relevance feedback [13] via the interface agent, the learning component can update the agent's memory where the beliefs about the user's information needs are stored. The AGM Belief Revision Framework [1] provides a sound and rigorous formalism for carrying out such operation. On the other hand, the document matching function is underpinned by a non-classical inference process with reference to a logic based approach [2]. The matching component can autonomously scan through the incoming web documents stored in the local database, and select the most relevant web documents for presentation.

In the proposed architecture, the retrieval agents *(RA)* act as wrappers to external information sources. After collecting the query results from external information sources, the retrieval agents will put the Web documents into a local database for filtering by the filtering agent. This article will focus on the discussion of applying the AGM belief revision framework to develop the learning component of the adaptive filtering agent.

2 Preliminaries of the AGM Belief Revision Framework

The AGM Belief Revision Framework [1] is a formalism for modeling the rational and minimal changes to an agent's beliefs. Intuitively, rational changes imply that the transition between belief states should not incur inconsistency. Minimal changes state that as many beliefs as possible should be retained during belief state transition. If a finite language $\mathcal{L}$, such as classical propositional logic, is chosen as the representation language, the initial belief state K, the new belief state K'_a, and the epistemic input a that triggers the belief state transition can be expressed as formulae. More specifically, the notion of *belief set* was employed to represent a belief state [9]. A belief set should satisfy the following conditions: (1) $K \nvdash \bot$, (2) $K \vdash a$ implies $a \in K$. The first property states that a belief set is consistent. The second property specifies that beliefs are closed under logical consequence. Technically, a belief set K is equivalent to a *theory* in classical logic. In the AGM framework, three types of belief state transitions are identified:

Expansion (K_a^+) : acceptance of a new belief that will not contradict existing beliefs in the belief set i.e. $a \notin K$, $\neg a \notin K$, $a \in K_a^+$
Contraction (K_a^-) : removal of a belief and all other beliefs that imply this belief i.e. $a \in K$, $a \notin K_a^-$
Revision (K_a^*) : acceptance of a belief that may contradict existing beliefs in the belief set i.e. $a \notin K$, $\neg a \in K$, $a \in K_a^*$

The concept of belief functions was proposed to model the above three processes. For instance, the belief contraction function (-) is a function from pairs of belief sets and formulae ($K \times \mathcal{L}$) to belief sets (K). Essentially, the AGM framework includes the sets of postulates to characterise the expansion, contraction, and revision functions such that these functions adhere to the rationales of consistent and minimal changes. In addition, the framework also illustrates the constructions of these functions based on different approaches such as selection functions, systems of spheres, safe contraction, and epistemic entrenchment. The focus of this paper is on epistemic entrenchment because it is more applicable to the domain of information filtering. For example, the preference orderings among documents with respect to a user's information needs can be represented as orderings of beliefs in a belief set.

Intuitively, epistemic entrenchment ($\leqslant$) is a preference ordering of beliefs according to importance in the face of change. When faced with a choice, beliefs with the lowest degree of epistemic entrenchment are given up. Epistemic entrenchment captures the notions of *firmness*, *significance*, or *defeasibility* of beliefs. Given a total preorder among the sentences in a belief set K such that the following properties are fulfilled, we can uniquely define a revision or contraction function [10].

(EE1): $\forall a, b, c \in K : a \leqslant b \leqslant c$ implies $a \leqslant c$ (transitivity)
(EE2): $\forall a, b \in K : a \vdash b$ implies $a \leqslant b$ (dominance)
(EE3): $\forall a, b \in K : a \leqslant a \wedge b$ or $b \leqslant a \wedge b$ (conjunctiveness)
(EE4): If $K \neq K_\perp$, $a \notin K$ iff $\forall b \in K : a \leqslant b$ (minimality)
(EE5): $\forall b \in K : b \leqslant a$ implies $\vdash a$ (maximality)

(EE1) simply states that an epistemic entrenchment ordering is transitive. (EE2) says that a logically weaker sentence is at least as entrenched as a logically stronger sentence. (EE3) tells us that a conjunction is at least as entrenched as its conjuncts. (EE4) says that sentences not in the belief set are minimal in the epistemic entrenchment ordering. (EE5) states that tautologies are maximal in the ordering.

3 Informational Fundamentals

This section illustrates some fundamental concepts in IR so that the assumptions of the AGM formalism can be evaluated in the context of IR.

Information Carriers: We propose the concept of information carriers (IC) to represent the content of information. Examples of ICs are documents, parts of documents (e.g., a section) and document descriptors, such as keywords. The lowercase letters such as i, j, etc. are used to represent information carriers. The elementary information carriers that can not be further decomposed are called atomic information carriers. From an application point of view, keywords or terms are elementary enough to be considered as atomic information carriers.

Information Composition: Information carriers can be composed to form more complex information carriers. For example, information carriers such as *river* and *pollution* can be composed as *river* $\oplus$ *pollution* which means the pollution about river. More formally, $i \oplus j$ is the smallest information carrier that precisely contains the information carried by information carriers i and j. There is difference between $\oplus$ described here and $\wedge$ used in Boolean retrieval models. The Boolean operator $\wedge$ assumes terms independence. However, it is assumed that $\oplus$ satisfies idempotentcy, but commutativity and associativity can not be taken for granted because they are dependent on the semantic meanings of associated information carriers. In general, an information language $\mathbb{L}_T$ which is built from a set of terms can be defined [6]: Let IC be a set of information carriers, then, (1) $IC \subset \mathbb{L}_T$; (2) if $i, j \in \mathbb{L}_T$ then $(i \oplus j) \in \mathbb{L}_T$.

Information Containment: As some information carriers convey more information about a situation(s) than others, it was suggested that information can be partially ordered with respect to information containment, denoted by $\rightarrow$ [3]. $i \rightarrow j$ iff information carrier i contains all the information carried by information carrier j.

Aboutness: Information retrieval is driven by a process which decides whether a document is about a query. Abstracting from documents and queries renders the IR process as one which decides whether one information carrier is about another. "Aboutness" has recently come under scrutiny as a by product of research into logic-based information retrieval [12]. Early attempts viewed aboutness as being a model-theoretic relation, that is a document was considered as a sort of model in which the query was interpreted [7]. More recent investigations have shown that aboutness is similar in many ways to nonmonotonic consequence [8, 6, 2]. Generally speaking, an information carrier i is deemed to be about information carrier j, denoted $i \models_a j$ if the information borne by j holds in i. In other words, information carrier j is a summary or an abstraction of information carrier i.

Information Preclusion: Not all information carriers can be meaningfully composed because the information that they carry is contradictory. In general, information carriers i and j are said to preclude each other, denoted $i \perp j$ [7]. It is natural to assume that any fact precludes its negation (i.e. $i \perp \neg i$). This is the concept of logical consistency in classical logic. However, information preclusion not only deals with syntactic consistency but also semantic consistency. For example, *flying* $\perp$ *dog* is true in most contexts. Sometimes, information carriers preclude each other with respect to the information need of a user [6]. For instance, *apple* $\perp_N$ *orange* if the user just wants to retrieve information about *apple* rather than *orange* or vice versa.

4 Belief Revision for Adaptive Information Filtering

The intuition of applying the AGM belief revision formalism to develop the learning component of the adaptive filtering agent is that an agent's memory is modelled as a belief set and its content is modified by means of either the revision, or the contraction function. Initially, the AIFS system will deliver a random set of Web documents to a user via the interface agent. The user decides whether a document is relevant or not, and notifies the system about her judgment by clicking corresponding buttons on the interface. This is the relevance feedback process. Conceptually, the set of relevant documents can be denoted as D_+, and the set of irrelevant documents can be denoted as D_-. After receiving the relevance feedback from the user, the AIFS system can characterise a Web document by a term extraction process. This process is assumed to be based on traditional IR techniques [14]. Information carriers extracted from relevant documents will form the representation of the user's information needs i.e.

$K \subseteq IC_+ = \{i : i \in \chi(D_+)\}$ where K is a belief set, IC_+ is the set of relevant ICs, and $\chi(D_+)$ is the characterisation of the relevant documents. The AGM belief functions are applied to update the filtering agent's memory i.e. the belief set K.

As a user's information preferences will change over time, information carriers deemed relevant initially may become irrelevant later on. The filtering agent can detect this shift of information preferences by monitoring the user's relevance feedback. Conceptually, if an information carrier is from the irrelevant set i.e. $IC_- = \{j : j \in \chi(D_-)\}$, the corresponding belief will be removed from the belief set by the contraction function. On the other hand, if new information carriers are deemed relevant, they will be added to the filtering agent's memory by the revision function. As the filtering agent only deals with relevance feedback one at a time, the set of information carriers in a document is either added to or removed from its memory. Subsequently, the matching component of the filtering agent can use these beliefs to determine whether an incoming Web document should be delivered to the user.

An example can be used to illustrate the belief revision process. If a user is interested in Web documents about *Japanese*, *Buddhism*, and *Sushi*, her initial information needs can be extracted as the procedure described above and represented as: $K = \{$ Japanese, Buddhism, Sushi $\}$, where K is a belief set and each information carrier becomes the agent's belief (i.e. a propositional variable). If the user's information preference shifts from *Japanese* to *English* later on, noting that is *English* $\perp_N$ *Japanese*, this can be detected by observing a positive feedback from a document containing information carrier *English*, and a negative feedback from a document containing information carrier *Japanese*. Accordingly, the AIFS system will employ the belief revision function to insert the belief of *English* to its belief set i.e. $K^*_{English} = \{$ English, Japanese, Buddhism, Sushi $\}$. Then, a contraction function will be invoked to remove the belief of *Japanese* i.e. $K^-_{Japanese} = \{$ English, Buddhism, Sushi $\}$.

In general, to implement preferential preclusion ($\perp_N$), both the belief revision function and the belief contraction function are involved. However, it is believed that the sequence of invoking the belief functions is insignificant. In other words, the revision of *English*, and the contraction of *Japanese* can take place in any order. Our hypothesis is: $i \perp_N j \equiv (K^*_i)^-_j \equiv (K^-_j)^*_i$, where $i \in IC_+$ and $j \in IC_-$.

Nevertheless, one problem of the above approach is that it is too cumbersome for the users to give both the positive and the negative feedback in order to implement the general information preclusion ($\perp$). For instance, if a user's initial information needs are represented as: $K = \{$ flying, bird $\}$. After changing her interest to *dog* at a later stage i.e. ($dog \perp_N bird$), the resulting belief set will become: $K^*_{dog} = \{$ flying, dog $\}$. In this case, it is more desirable for the revision mechanism to automatically detect the semantic inconsistency between *flying* and *dog*, and remove *flying* accordingly. However, the AGM belief revision formalism can only detect logical inconsistency such as ($p \wedge \neg p$), where $p, \neg p$ are sentences of classical logic, but fails to resolve semantic inconsistency such as *flying* $\perp$ *dog*.

Recalling the definition of belief set in section 2, it is a consistent set of sentences that is closed under classical consequence operation. However, IR actually deals with information carriers rather than logical sentences. Therefore, the notion of *aboutness* was introduced to analyse the characteristics of information retrieval models [7]. Though both the aboutness relation ($\models_a$) and the logical derivability relation ($\vdash$) are kinds of deduction mechanisms, there is a difference between them. For example, based on logical implication ($\supset$), if we have $K = \{a, a \supset b, b \supset c, c \supset d\}$, the logical closure of this set of formulae will include d, that is $d \in K$. Nevertheless, if *information containment* ($\rightarrow$) is used to perform similar reasoning in the context of IR, given $K = \{$ *penguin* $\rightarrow$ *bird*, *bird* $\rightarrow$ *animal*, *animal* $\rightarrow$ *entity* $\}$, we still can not conclude that *penguin* $\models_a$ *entity* or *entity* $\in K$. According to [5], users' perception of document relevance along the information containment chain will be broken at a certain point (i.e. two semantic steps away from the original text). Therefore, it is generally considered that *penguin* $\not\models_a$ *entity*. This restriction makes the characteristic of the aboutness relation different from that of the logical derivability relation. It may be necessary for us to apply such restrictions to define the closure of the belief set if we want to use it to model a set of beliefs about information carriers. For instance, $C(K) = \{i \in \mathbb{L}_T : K \models_a i\}$, where C is defined as the closure of the set of information carriers K.

Apart from these differences, the rationale of minimal and consistent changes of the AGM belief revision framework is quite applicable in adaptive information filtering. With reference to our preceding example, after incorporating the new belief of information carrier *English*, certainly we do not want to lose the beliefs of *Sushi* and *Buddhism*. Moreover, if *English* is in the belief set, $\neg$ *English* should not be there. The AGM framework is able to guarantee such properties.

5   Interpreting Epistemic Entrenchment in IR

Since epistemic entrenchment is used to construct the AGM belief functions, its validity in the context of IR should be examined before applying this formalism to build the agent's learning component. The five epistemic entrenchment postulates are examined in the context of IR.

(EE1): $\forall a, b, c \in K : a \leqslant b \leqslant c$ implies $a \leqslant c$ (transitivity)

In IR, it is believed [8] that a user's information need imposes a preferential ordering on the underlying set of documents. Furthermore, it is assumed that the preference relation is irreflexive and transitive. For example, if one prefers document c over b, and document b over a, then it means that she prefers document c over a. As documents are in fact information carriers, it implies that a transitive preference relation exists among information carriers. Therefore, EE1 is valid in the context of IR.

(EE2): $\forall a, b \in K : a \vdash b$ implies $a \leqslant b$ (dominance)

To examine this property in the context of IR, we first need to interpret the ($\vdash$) derivability relation in terms of IR concepts. The aboutness relation ($\models_a$) in IR seems a counterpart of the derivability relation in logic. So, given an aboutness relation such as salmon $\models_a$ fish, is salmon $\leqslant$ fish? If we interpret $\leqslant$ in terms of defeasibility, will salmon be a more defeasible information carrier than fish? In a query situation, assuming that a user is interested in different kinds of fish, she may try out different information carriers like salmon, tuna, bream, etc. until she finally receives some relevant information from the IR system. In other words, her beliefs about the information carriers change from salmon to tuna, and from tuna to bream. Nevertheless, the information objects are still about fish. Therefore, the information carrier of fish is less defeasible than either salmon, tuna, or bream. So, in a query refinement situation, the aboutness relation demonstrates the characteristic as described by EE2.

Another interpretation of EE2 is that whenever an agent accepts sentence a, it must prepare to accept sentence b. Therefore, sentence b must be at least as entrenched or significant as sentence a. In the context of IR, if $a \models_a b$, it means that b is an abstraction of a. If the filtering system admits that information carrier a is the representation of a user's information need, it should also believe that information carrier b is an appropriate representation because of the nature of the aboutness relation. Therefore, in the context of IR, if $a \models_a b$, information carrier b is at least as significant as information carrier a. Based on the above discussion, EE2 seems characterising the relationships between information carriers in the context of IR.

(EE3): $\forall a, b \in K : a \leqslant a \wedge b$ or $b \leqslant a \wedge b$ \qquad (conjunctiveness)

This property can be linked to the concept of *specificity* in IR. From the IR point of view, more specific terms should generally produce higher precision results. Therefore, if given a choice of information carrier a or information carrier $a \oplus b$ for describing a user's information need, $a \oplus b$ should be the preferred representation of the user's information needs. So, $a \leqslant a \oplus b$ or $b \leqslant a \oplus b$ matches the characteristic of precision oriented IR. Nevertheless, in the context of IR, we must be careful about the semantic clash between information carriers. For example, if $a \perp b$, $a \oplus b$ certainly will not be more useful than a alone. So, it is necessary to add such a condition to the original EE3.

However, the combined result of (EE1) to (EE3) shows that $a = a \wedge b$ or $b = a \wedge b$. In general, the assumption that both information carrier a and the information carrier $a \oplus b$ are about a user's information need is difficult to establish since the user's information need is contingent. For example, if the user actually prefers more general information, either a or b will be a better representation of her need. Hence, in a recall oriented IR system, it is hard to state that $a \leqslant a \oplus b$ or $b \leqslant a \oplus b$. The property can only be generalised in that any information carrier a is as useful or entrenched as itself plus another arbitrary information carrier i.e. $a = a \oplus b$ as long as their meanings do not clash.

(EE4): If $K \neq K_\perp$, $a \notin K$ iff $\forall b \in K : a \leqslant b$ \qquad (minimality)

If a set of information carriers $K = \{$Japanese, Buddhism, Sushi $\}$ is used to represent a user's information needs, the information carrier *Japanese* should only be removed from this set if the user is no longer interested in information about Japanese. In other words, *Japanese* is the least preferred information carrier in the set. So, in general, an information carrier should only be contracted from a belief set if it is the least entrenched information carrier when compared with all other information carriers in the set. This conforms to the property of EE4.

(EE5): $\forall b \in K : b \leqslant a$ implies $\vdash a$ \qquad (maximality)

This is another property to handle the extreme case in belief revision. Validity ($\vdash a$) can be interpreted as information carrier a being true in all retrieval situations. The concept of validity can be used by the filtering agent to handle special information requirement from a user. For instance, if a user wants to specify a query that should not be discarded by the agent under all possible situations, she can set the corresponding information carriers as maximal elements in the epistemic entrenchment ordering. As these information carriers will be treated as valid formulae by the belief revision formalism, they will be retained in the belief set until the user makes an explicit request to delete them via the interface agent. So, (EE5) actually provides a very nice property to handle the special cases in IR.

In summary, the five postulates of epistemic entrenchment can be translated to the following counterparts which characterise the preference ordering among information carriers in the context of information filtering:

(IC-EE1): $\forall i, j, k \in \mathbb{L}_T : i \leqslant j \leqslant k$ implies $i \leqslant k$
(IC-EE2): $\forall i, j \in \mathbb{L}_T : i \models_a j$ implies $i \leqslant j$
(IC-EE3): $\forall i, j \in \mathbb{L}_T :$ if $i \not\perp j$, $i \leqslant i \oplus j$ or $j \leqslant i \oplus j$
(IC-EE4): If $K \neq K_\perp$, $i \notin K$ iff $\forall j \in \mathbb{L}_T : i \leqslant j$
(IC-EE5): $\forall j \in \mathbb{L}_T : j \leqslant i$ implies $\vdash i$

6 Conclusions

The rationales of consistent and minimal changes behind the AGM belief revision framework fulfill the general requirements of revising the representation of a user's information needs in the context of adaptive information filtering. Evaluation of the postulates of epistemic entrenchment shows that the preference ordering among information carriers demonstrates similar properties as the preference ordering among logical sentences. As a whole, the AGM belief revision framework is promising for the development of the adaptive mechanism of the information filtering agent. However, some deficiencies of the formalism in the context of information filtering need to be addressed before it can successfully be applied to adaptive information filtering in practice.

Acknowledgments The work reported in this paper has been funded in part by the Cooperative Research Centres Program through the Department of the Prime Minister and Cabinet of Australia.

References

1. C.E. Alchourrón, P. Gärdenfors, and D. Makinson. On the logic of theory change: partial meet contraction and revision functions. *Journal of Symbolic Logic*, 50:510–530, 1985.
2. G. Amati and K. Georgatos. Relevance as deduction: a Logical View of Information Retrieval. In F. Crestani and M. Lalmas, editors, *Proceedings of the Second Workshop on Information Retrieval, Uncertainty and Logic WIRUL'96*, pages 21–26. University of Glasgow, Glasgow, Scotland, 1996. Technical Report TR-1996-29.
3. J. Barwise. *The Situation in Logic*, volume 17 of *CSLI Lecture Note Series*. CSLI, Stanford, California, 1989.
4. N. Belkin and W. Croft. Information Filtering and Information Retrieval: Two sides of the same coin? *Communications of the ACM*, 35(12):29–38, 1992.
5. T.A. Brooks. People, Words, and Perceptions: A Phenomenological Investigation of Textuality. *American Society for Information Science*, 46(2):103–115, 1995.
6. P.D. Bruza. Intelligent Filtering using Nonmonotonic Inference. In *Proceedings of the 1st Australian Document Computing Symposium*, pages 1–7, Melbourne, Australia, March 1996. Department of Computer Science, RMIT.
7. P.D. Bruza and T.W.C. Huibers. Investigating Aboutness Axioms Using Information Fields. In W.B. Croft and C.J. van Rijsbergen, editors, *Proceedings of the 17th Annual International ACM SIGIR Conference on Research and Development in Information Retrieval*, pages 112–121, Dublin, Ireland, July 1994. Springer-Verlag.
8. P.D. Bruza and B. van Linder. Preferential Models of Query by Navigation. In F. Crestani, M. Lalmas, and C.J. van Rijsbergen, editors, *Information Retrieval: Uncertainty and Logics*, volume 4 of *The Kluwer International Series on Information Retrieval*, pages 73–96. Kluwer Academic Publishers, 1998.
9. P. Gärdenfors. *Knowledge in flux: modeling the dynamics of epistemic states*. The MIT Press, Cambridge, Massachusetts, 1988.
10. P. Gärdenfors. Belief revision: An introduction. In P. Gärdenfors, editor, *Belief Revision*, pages 1–28. Cambridge University Press, Cambridge, UK, 1992.
11. S. Kirsch. The future of Internet Search: Infoseek's experiences searching the Internet. *ACM SIGIR FORUM*, 32(2):3–7, 1998.
12. C.J. van Rijsbergen. Towards an Information Logic. In N.J. Belkin and C.J. van Rijsbergen, editors, *Proceedings of the 12th Annual International ACM SIGIR Conference on Research and Development in Information Retrieval*, pages 77–86, Cambridge, Massachusetts, June 1989. ACM Press.
13. J. Rocchio. Relevance Feedback in Information Retrieval. In G. Salton, editor, *The SMART retrieval system : experiments in automatic document processing*, pages 313–323. Prentice-Hall, Englewood Cliffs, N.J., 1971.
14. G. Salton and M.J. McGill. *Introduction to Modern Information Retrieval*. McGraw-Hill, New York, New York, 1983.
15. M. Wooldridge and N. Jennings. Intelligent Agents: Theory and Practice. *Knowledge Engineering Review*, 10(2):115–152, 1995.

Evaluating Performance Indicators
for Adaptive Information Filtering

Carsten Lanquillon

DaimlerChrysler Research and Technology
D-89013 Ulm, Germany
carsten.lanquillon@daimlerchrysler.com

Abstract. The task of information filtering is to classify documents from a stream as either relevant or non-relevant according to a particular user interest with the objective to reduce information load. When using an information filter in an environment that changes over time, methods for adapting the filter should be considered in order to retain classification performance. We favor a methodology that attempts to detect changes and adapts the information filter only if need be. Thus the amount of user feedback for providing new training data can be minimized. Nevertheless, detecting changes may also require expensive hand-labeling of documents. This paper explores two methods for assessing performance indicators without user feedback. The first is based on performance estimation and the second counts uncertain classification decisions. Empirical results for a simulated change scenario with real-world text data show that our adaptive information filter can perform well in changing domains.

1   Introduction

The task of *information filtering* is to reduce a user's information load with respect to his or her interest. The filter is supposed to remove all non-relevant documents from an incoming stream, such that only relevant documents are presented to the user. Thus, information filtering can be described as a binary classification problem. In this paper, we only consider text documents and regard information filtering as a specific instance of text classification. For a comparison of common text classifiers, see [3] and [13].

Classification problems can be solved by applying supervised learning techniques which learn from a set of given examples and can then be used to determine the class of new, unseen observations. This is based on the essential assumption that training data and new data come from at least similar distributions. In a long-term application, however, the distribution of new texts and thus their content may change over time. Then a classifier should be adapted in order to retain classification performance.

We favor a methodology that attempts to detect changes and adapts the information filter only if inevitable in order to minimize the amount of required user feedback. Alternatively, an information filter could be relearned in regular intervals no matter if changes really occur. This, however, requires the user to regularly provide new training texts and thus to read even many non-relevant texts. This hand-labeling is prohibitive since the task of information filtering is to reduce information load.

This paper proceeds as follows. The next section describes possible changes and explores ways of detecting them. In Section 3 we present empirical results for a simulated change scenario with real-world text data. Section 4 briefly covers some related work, and a discussion follows in Section 5.

2 Detecting Changes

This section describes possible changes and shows the need for continuously observing the performance of an information filter. We thus motivate the use of quality control charts for detecting changes. This requires indicators to be derived from the underlying process. The remainder of the section therefore describes several performance indicators.

2.1 Dynamic Aspects

We make the simplifying assumption that that each text can be uniquely associated with exactly one topic. Further, each topic must be either relevant or non-relevant with respect to a particular user interest. Looking at a stream of incoming texts, we may observe that either new topics arise, existing topics change over time or even disappear. Since a changing topic can be considered as the superposition of a new and a disappearing topic, we focus on changes due to new topics.

Formally, we can describe this by a parametric mixture model where each mixture component generates either relevant or non-relevant texts according to a probability distribution defined by a set of parameters. The dynamic aspects can then be characterized as changes in this parameter set. Note that this also includes a change in the number of mixture components.

Assuming forced recognition, two types of errors can occur. On the one hand, a text of a new non-relevant topic may be classified as relevant. This is easy to detect if feedback for texts presented to the user is given. On the other hand, a text of a new relevant topic may be erroneously kept from the user. This constitutes a crucial problem in information filtering. How can we be guaranteed that due to changes relevant texts are not permanently misclassified?

2.2 Statistical Quality Control

Obviously, we need a method for continuously observing classification performance. We propose to use techniques from statistical quality control to detect changes in terms of deviations from expected performance.

We assume that the text stream is divided into batches with respect to its chronological order. Even if information filtering is regarded as an on-line process where each text is classified as it arrives, constructing batches is quite natural since, for example, all texts arriving in the course of a day or a week can be grouped together. The value of any indicator being used to detect changes will then be calculated separately for each batch. Using batches offers the advantage to detect changes by observing the deviation from the indicator value of the current batch to the mean derived from indicator values of past batches. While averaging and thus reducing stochastic perturbations, less attention is given to single outliers.

A *cumulative sum (cusum) control chart* accumulates deviations from an expected value and can thus detect small changes which occur successively. By contrast, a *Shewhart control chart* tests whether only a single observation of the indicator is within acceptable variation and can thus better detect larger shifts. In the following we will use a combined *cusum-Shewhart control chart* for monitoring an indicator ν. For further details and an introduction to statistical quality control, see [9].

Let $\bar{\nu}$ be an estimate of the indicator mean and s_ν an estimate of the corresponding standard deviation. We define the one-sided upper cusum as $C_t^+ = \max[0, \nu_t - (\bar{\nu} + 0.5s_\nu) + C_{t-1}^+]$ for the batch at time t, starting with an initial value $C_0^+ = 0$. We assume that a change has occurred at time t if either $C_t^+ > \gamma s_\nu$ based on the cusum chart, or $\nu_t > \bar{\nu} + \alpha s_\nu$ according to the Shewhart control chart. In our approach, we set $\alpha = 2.33$. This corresponds to a one-sided 99% confidence interval for observing values smaller than the obtained bound, assuming that the indicator values approximately follow a normal distribution. Further, we set $\gamma = 3$. For example, this would suspect a change when two observations in a row deviated from the mean by at least twice the standard deviation. Note that there seems to be only a small basis for selecting γ in the literature.

2.3 Indicators for Text Classification

We consider two categories of indicators that can be derived during the text classification process:

- *Text properties*: The indicator characterizes a current subset (batch) of the text stream, e.g. class distribution or frequencies of words.
- *Classification properties*: The indicator is based on final or intermediate classification results, e.g. performance measures such as the error rate.

Indicators derived from text properties basically concern the preprocessing of texts. Natural texts are transformed into feature vectors which can then be handled by common classifiers. Observing text properties, there is a chance of detecting changes even before actually classifying any new texts and the user can be warned that the upcoming decisions may be uncertain. We are currently successfully exploring text properties for change detection. Here we focus on indicators bases on classification properties.

Table 1. Contingency table for $N = a + b + c + d$ relevance judgements.

	User Says Yes	User Says No
System Says Yes	a	b
System Says No	c	d

Recall that information filtering is a binary text classification problem. The decision is whether or not a text is relevant for a certain user. Assume that a set of N texts has been classified by a text classification system and the true class labels are given by the user. The relationship between the classification decisions and the true class labels can be summarized in a contingency table as shown in Table 1. For example, entry a is the number of texts that the information filter presents to the user and that are in fact relevant.

Common performance measures in information retrieval and machine learning are *recall*, *precision*, and *error rate*. In terms of the contingency table, they are defined for non-zero denominators as:

- recall $= a/(a + c)$
- precision $= a/(a + b)$
- error rate $= (b + c)/(a + b + c + d)$

In words, *precision* is an estimate of the probability that a text presented as relevant to the user is indeed relevant. Likewise, *recall* is an estimate of the probability that the filter lets through relevant texts to the user, and the *error rate* estimates the probability of misclassification.

Assuming feedback for all texts presented to the user is available, precision can be evaluated. Yet, it does not provide any information about relevant texts kept from the user. By contrast, in a real application, recall and error rate cannot be evaluated because the values for entries c and d are generally unknown.

2.4 Assessing Performance Indicators

As demonstrated above, evaluating performance measures is usually not feasible. In the following we describe two methods that try to overcome this evaluation problem, also see [6].

Estimation of Expected Performance In order to estimate the expected performance of a classifier on new data, Lewis [7] models the unknown user judgement (the true class labels) by a Bernoulli (0/1) random variable, Z_i, with parameter p_i for each classified text t_i giving the probability that Z_i will take on the value 1. The event $Z_i = 1$ occurs if the current text is actually relevant, and $Z_i = 0$ otherwise. The value of each p_i is assumed to be the classifier's estimate of the probability of class membership. Further, it is assumed that each document is judged independently of all others.

Lewis provides a general expression for an expected performance measure as the sum of performance values that would be obtained for each of the 2^N possible combinations of the user judgements for all texts of the current batch, weighted by the probability of each judgement as determined by the classifier. For large N, it is not feasible to directly evaluate this expression. For the expected error rate, for example, a simpler expression is given by

$$e_{\text{expected}} = \frac{1}{N} \sum_{i=1}^{N} ((1 - 2d_i)p_i + d_i) \tag{1}$$

where N is the current batch size and d_i is the classifier's decision for text t_i with $d_i = 1$ if t_i is classified as relevant, and 0 otherwise.

Note that this approach requires the classifier to respond to new texts with confidence scores that are probability estimates of class membership. However, note that many classifiers are not probabilistic. In that case the obtained expression no longer estimates the the expected performance measure as intended by Lewis. Yet it may still serve as an indicator for detecting changes.

Virtual Rejects The motivation of this approach is as follows. Let H be a classifier that explicitly models each relevance class and consequently responds to a new texts with a confidence score for each class. By individually thresholding the scores for the relevant and the non-relevant class, we could obtain two new classifiers H_{rel} and H_{non}, respectively. Now, the idea is to measure the disagreement between H and either H_{rel} or H_{non} depending on the decision of H. We call the texts on which the classifiers would disagree the set of *virtual rejects* V because H is still forced to decide whether or not to present a text to the user. The following describes how we derive an indicator based on V for detecting changes.

For all texts in the current batch, we observe the winning confidence scores, i.e. the confidence scores for the assigned class. V consists of all texts classified as relevant or non-relevant with a confidence score that is below a threshold θ_{rel} or θ_{non}, respectively. Let N be the current batch size and $\text{reject}(t_i) = 1$ if text $t_i \in V$, and 0 otherwise. The reject indicator is evaluated as

$$\nu_{\text{reject}} = \frac{1}{N} \sum_{i=1}^{N} \text{reject}(t_i) \tag{2}$$

The key challenge of this approach is to define the confidence thresholds θ_{rel} and θ_{non}. The objective is to find threshold values that best separate the distributions of confidence scores for each relevance class independent of the actual classification. This corresponds to finding the point of intersection of the density functions of two overlapping distributions. For approximating the value of the threshold θ_{non} (and likewise the value for θ_{rel}) we proceed as follows. We perform k-fold cross-validation on the training texts as for getting unbiased confidence scores. The scores obtained for the non-relevant class are split into two sets S_{rel} and S_{non} of size N_{rel} and N_{non} for texts actually being relevant and non-relevant, respectively. Let $n_{non}(\theta_{non})$ denote the number of scores in S_{non}

below θ_{non} and $n_{rel}(\theta_{non})$ the number of scores in S_{rel} above θ_{non} as functions of θ_{non}. We then determine θ_{non} such that

$$\frac{n_{rel}(\theta_{non})}{N_{rel}} \approx \frac{n_{non}(\theta_{non})}{N_{non}}. \tag{3}$$

3 Empirical Results

The experiments made for the evaluation of our adaptive information filters are based on a subset of the *Reuters-21578* collection. The data set consists of 21 578 news stories that have been assigned to one or more of a large number of categories (such as corporate acquisitions, earnings, money market, grain, and interest). Two large categories, namely *corporate acquisitions (ACQ)* with 2 429 texts and *earnings (EARN)* with 3 968 texts are selected as relevant topics. All other categories are combined to represent the non-relevant class.

Due to space limitations we present results from only one change scenario that is simulated as follows. The texts are randomly split into 41 batches, each containing roughly 500 texts. Throughout all batches a constant number of relevant texts of topic ACQ is present. Starting from batch 15, a gradually increasing number of texts of the relevant topic EARN is added. Texts of the non-relevant class are distributed among the batches such that the batch sizes are approximately equal. The first batch serves as the initial training set while the remaining 40 batches represent the temporal development. The texts of each batch are classified as if they were new texts of an incoming stream. Based on the texts in each batch, an indicator may be evaluated for the purpose of detecting changes. We assume that the examples of a batch are sufficient for learning and simply relearn the classifier from scratch with only the most recent batch of texts in case a change is detected. Experiments show that this assumptions holds for our setting. Generally, however, the performance of an adaptive information filter also depends on the updating strategy. See [8] and [10] for more elaborate ways of adapting classifiers in a long-term application.

We represent texts as vectors in the *bag-of-words* fashion. Stop words like "and", "or", etc. and words that occur fewer than five times in the training set are removed. From the remaining set word words, 1000 words per relevance class are selected according to average mutual information with the classes [3]. For the task of classification, a simple similarity-based classifier is applied which is a variant of Rocchio's method for relevance feedback [12] applied to text classification. The classifier models each of the two relevance classes with exactly one prototype. Each prototype is the average (centroid) of all vector representation of texts of the corresponding class. Even though this learning method is very simple, further experiments show that in our setting it performs well in comparison to other common methods like Naïve Bayes and kNN classification.

In the following, results of four approaches averaged over ten trials with different random seeds are presented. The first approach is learned based on the training texts of the first batch and is then left unchanged. Thus it cannot adapt to changes. The performance is shown in Figure 1. When the change starts

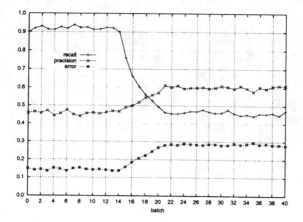

Fig. 1. Approach without adaptation to changes.

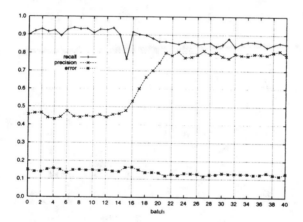

Fig. 2. Approach that relearns after each batch.

after batch 14, more and more relevant texts are kept from the user, and recall starts to decrease. Notice that precision increases because the total fraction of non-relevant and thus also the probability of presenting non-relevant texts to the user decreases.

As mentioned in the introduction, an alternative yet infeasible approach for coping with changes is to *relearn* the information filter in regular intervals no matter if there are any changes. Here, the classifier is updated after each batch which requires a prohibitive amount of new labeled training data. Note that interleaving batches with no adaptation or increasing the batch size to reduce the number of updates is actually no remedy for this problem. Generally it is unknown when changes occur and determining the right setup is hardly possible. Figure 2 shows the performance of this benchmark approach. Recall almost reaches the previous level and precision further increases. Obviously texts of the new topic help in separating between the existing topics.

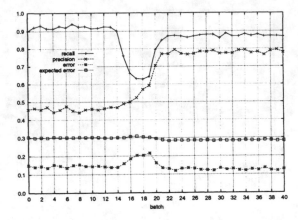

Fig. 3. Adaptive approach monitoring the expected error.

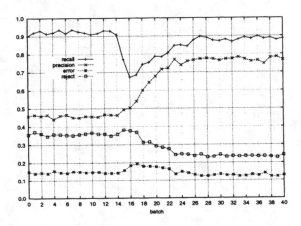

Fig. 4. Adaptive approach monitoring virtual rejects.

The first feasible adaptive approach monitors the expected error as defined in Equation 1. The results are shown in Figure 3. In each trial there is exactly one update between batches 16 and 21. This is indicated by the seemingly small but according to the control charts statistically significant increase of the indicator values, here denoted as *expected error*. After the adaptation, the average performance over all trials reaches about the same level as that of the relearn approach.

The other feasible adaptive approach is based on Equations 2 and 3. The performance of this approach and the reject indicator, denoted *reject*, are shown in Figure 4. This approach adapted the classifier 1.8 times per trial on average. The larger number of updates results from a couple of false alarms and the fact that in some trials a change is suspected twice while gradually adding texts of the new relevant topic. Again, the performance reaches about the level of the relearn approach. The results of all approaches are summarized in Table 2.

Table 2. Average values of recall, precision and error rate over all batches and the average number of adaptations (updates) performed in each trial.

Approach	Recall	Precision	Error	updates
No Adaptation	64.21%	54.14%	22.47%	0.0
Relearn	87.98%	64.69%	13.66%	40.0
Expected Error	86.11%	63.50%	14.20%	1.0
Virtual Rejects	86.78%	62.85%	14.49%	1.8

4   Related Work

Besides the work on autonomous text classification systems [7] mentioned in Section 2, there is some research about adaptive information filtering by Klinkenberg and Renz [4]. Notice that we examine changes in the content of a text stream while Klinkenberg focuses on changes in the user interest. The effect on the performance of an information filter is very similar, though. Klinkenberg also tries to cope with dynamic aspects by detecting changes first. He monitors indicators which are based on classification results and generally require the true class labels of the new texts in order to be evaluated. Although his adaptive approaches achieve promising results, in our setting they are not feasible because hand-labeling a large number of texts that have been kept the user is prohibitive.

Concerning the detection of changes, the objective of this paper is similar to the task of *Topic Detection and Tracking (TDT)*. Note, however, that TDT is generally defined as an unsupervised learning problem, the classes are not known or fixed in advance. Hence there are no relevance classes with respect to a particular user interest. Further, note the difference of detecting new events of a given topic defined as clusters in time as in TDT and determining whether or not the performance of a classifier is acceptable as in our work. Once new topics have been detected, the tracking of new topics in TDT and adapting a classifier have further similarities. For some interesting approaches, see [1] and [2].

5   Discussion

In previous work we show for similar approaches on different text data sets that shifts in the data can be reliably detected without user feedback [5] [6]. However, the approaches struggle when confronted with gradual changes. In this case, the applied Shewhart control chart reveals its weakness in detecting small changes. In this paper we use a combined cusum-Shewhart control chart and thus improve the change detection ability. This is demonstrated by some initial experiments presented in Section 3.

A further improvement of this approach might be achieved when evaluating an indicator after classifying each new text based on a constant number of the most recent texts in a moving window (rolling average) fashion. Another idea for improvement is to derive indicators by comparing the distribution of confidence scores over batches rather then looking at average scores or counting the number of classifications made with low confidence. Moreover, indicators based on text properties are studied in ongoing research.

So far only an adaptation strategy that relearns an information filter from scratch is applied. However, approaches that update existing classifiers based on some new training data should also be considered because they provide more potential for further reducing the amount of required user feedback. In a current project, we use text clustering as well as learning with labeled and unlabeled data to improve learning for text classification with only a small set of labeled training data.

References

1. J. Allan, J. Carbonell, G. Doddington, J. Yamron, and Y. Yang. Topic detection and tracking pilot study final report. In *Proceedings of the Broadcast News Transcription and Understranding Workshop (Sponsored by DARPA)*, 1998.
2. D. Baker, T. Hofmann, A. McCallum, and Y. Yang. A hierarchical probabilistic model for novelty detection in text. In *submitted*, 1999.
3. S. Dumais, J. Platt, D. Heckerman, and M. Sahami. Inductive learning algorithms and representation for text categorization. In *Proceedings of the Seventh International Conference on Information and Knowledge Management*, 1998.
4. R. Klinkenberg and I. Renz. Adaptive information filtering: Learning in the presence of concept drifts. In *Learning for Text Categorization*, pages 33–40, Menlo Park, California, 1998. AAAI Press.
5. C. Lanquillon. Information filtering in changing domains. In *Proceedings of the IJCAI'99 Workshop on Machine Learning for Information Filtering*, Stockholm, Sweden, 1999.
6. C. Lanquillon and I. Renz. Adaptive information filtering: Detecting changes in text streams. In *Proceedings of the Eighth International Conference on Information and Knowledge Management*, Kansas City, Missouri, 1999. To appear.
7. David D. Lewis. Evaluating and optimizing autonomous text classification systems. In *Proceedings of the Eighteenth Annual International ACM-SIGIR Conference on Research and Development in Information Retrieval*, pages 246–254, 1995.
8. M. Maloof and R. Michalski. Learning evolving concepts using partial memory approach. In *Working Notes of the 1995 AAAI Fall Symposium on Active Learning*, pages 70–73, Boston, MA, 1995.
9. D.C. Montgomery. *Introduction to Statistical Quality Control*. Wiley, New York, 3rd edition, 1997.
10. G. Nakhaeizadeh, C. Taylor, and C. Lanquillon. Evaluating usefulness for dynamic classification. In *Proceedings of The Fourth International Conference on Knowledge Discovery & Data Mining*, pages 87–93, New York, 1998.
11. Reuters-21578. This text categorization test collection from D. Lewis is publicly available at *http://www.research.att.com/~lewis/reuters21578.html*, 1997.
12. J.J. Jr. Rocchio. Relevance feedback in information retrieval. In G. Salton, editor, *The SMART Retrieval System: Experiments in Automatic Document Processing*, pages 313–323. Prentice Hall, 1971.
13. Y. Yang and X. Liu. A re-examination of text categorization methods. In *Proceeding of ACM SIGIR Conference on Research and Developement in Information Retrieval*, 1999.

Optimizing Data-Mining Processes: A CBR Based Experience Factory for Data Mining

Kai Bartlmae

DaimlerChrysler AG, Research and Technology FT3/KL, Ulm, Germany
kai.bartlmae@daimlerchrysler.com

Abstract. In this paper we introduce an integrated framework for Data Mining and Knowledge Management and show how Knowledge Management can complement Data Mining. Specifically, we examine methods how to improve the knowledge intensive and weak-structured process of Data Mining (DM) through the use of an Experience Factory and the method of Case Base Reasoning.

The paper is divided into two sections: In the first section, we explain how knowledge and experience made in Data Mining can be used for following DM-projects and why it is therefore important to manage the creation, capture, organization and reuse of Data Mining experience. We then analyze a DM-process model, here CRISP-DM [8], and identify how knowledge and experience of this process can be captured and reused. In the second step, we describe our approach to support the DM-process through methods of Case Based Reasoning within an Experience Factory.

1 Introduction

In order to support organizations to conduct Data Mining, many technologies and organizational methods have been created in the last years. So the use of process models give an explicit conceptional representation of phases or task to be conducted, which make the process of Data Mining more transparent and communicable. A major step to make Data Mining more structured and applicable in a business environment with larger teams has been the definition of generic Data Mining processes like CRISP-DM [8] or the approaches from Berry [5], Cabena [6] or Fayyad [10]. Here a framework has been put on what Data Mining steps should be taken, giving guidelines for a DM-initiative and setting quality-standards on the process-steps i.e. on deliverables.

However, in order to use these process models, they have to be tailored, mapped or revised on the specific application-domain and problem-characteristics[1]. Here experience plays the important part throughout the process of Data Mining. Further, through continuos feedback on Data Mining projects and continuos

---

[1] In CRISP-DM, this is called "mapping"

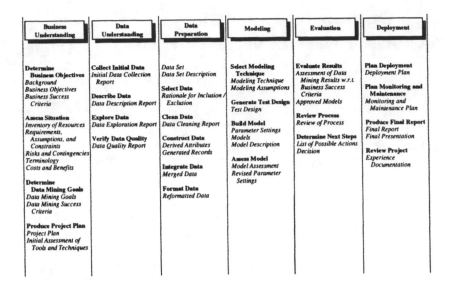

Fig. 1. The Crisp Reference Model: Phases, Generic Tasks (bold) and Outputs (italic) of the CRISP-DM Reference Model [8]

learning about a domain, DM-processes of a domain change incrementally and evolutionary.

Here we propose a method, that adds experience to the process of mapping DM-processes to applicable Data Mining tasks: It has been proposed, that experiential knowledge [7] is an important source of knowledge that can contribute to the ability of problem solving. Experiences can be used to respond to new situations in a similar way and to avoid similar failures. It is a form of continuos learning that the organization can improve on.

We propose an approach of reusing experience in Data Mining [3]: Using a former solution of a similar DM-problem as a basis will decrease the time and cost spent on the current problem. Further, the creation of an organization wide knowledge infrastructure including past experiences promotes the use of DM technology in practice.

In a first step we now explain, why it is important to collect and reuse experience and knowledge about DM in general and the CRISP-DM process in special in the context of a certain task and how this can be done. Further, we want to introduce methods and architectures of an integrated framework of Data Mining within an Experience Factory. Innovative knowledge management concepts and infrastructures are needed to provide the integrated support for the DM-teams.

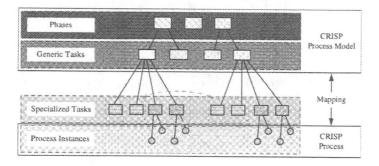

Fig. 2. The Crisp Mapping Model: Four Level Breakdown of the CRISP-DM Methodology, At the specialized task level, the same colored boxes belong to the same project: Since CRISP-DM is generic, different projects processes can be derived[8]

2 Applying the CRISP-DM model to a DM-problem

Here we understand under the Data Mining process model a general framework under which knowledge is created and used in a business environment. A generic strategy to do so is the CRISP-DM process model using Data Mining to solve this business problem. It formulates different phases, broken down to tasks and process-instances (see [8]). The process is divided into the phases *business understanding, data understanding, data preparation, modeling, evaluation, deployment* and requires for each phases task predefined outputs. All of them specify general steps that taken together help to structure DM and to fulfill quality standards (see figure 1 for an overview of CRISP-DM). Since the framework is generic, it is of no use in order to solve specific business-problems. Here all the information has to come from the Data Mining-specialists and business experts. Unfortunately, it will be the case, that neither the DM-expert will have worked on a similar problem nor the business analyst with Data Mining. Further, as far as we observed in Data Mining, the used algorithms often depend strongly on the domain (see Michie, Spiegelhalter, Taylor [12]). This means that even an experienced Data Mining expert can be clueless if confronted with a new problem or different domain.

Therefore, the CRISP-model is a guiding framework, but the model is brought to life by the DM-team. So, the process starts with a general DM-framework, that is more and more specialized for a specific problem by its users. In CRISP this is called "Mapping Generic Models to Specialized Models" (see figure 2). Based on this context, we see the DM-process as a knowledge intensive and weak-structured process, that has high need for innovation. Further, in each process step, the agent has to choose from a large variety of possible actions, which makes it difficult even for experts to choose the right one.

While CRISP-DM helpful to structure the process of Data Mining, it does not help on *how* to map this on a business problem like Credit Risk Management.

While on some steps, these mappings are straightforward, on others, this is not the case: these mappings are highly domain-depended, difficult to apply and can only be done with background-knowledge either from the technical side (DM-algorithms, data characteristics, etc.) or from the business-domain (i.e. attribute selection, data-availability and preprocessing).

In our opinion this mapping can be supported by using knowledge and experience from successfully completed similar DM-processes of similar business-problems[2]. In our opinion, experience is the major key for successful DM-projects and therefore it is very important that once experience in the context of Data Mining is acquired, it will never again leave the organization. Further, we believe that the problem can not be seen in a static context, but that knowledge about DM and the business problem is constantly changing.

This has consequences towards organizational support in Data Mining. First of all, all knowledge or experience encountered in the realization of a DM(-CRISP) process have to be captured in containers in the context of a problem, since it can be of use for future projects. However, plain reporting is not sufficient enough. The collected and saved experience must be in a form that is easily accessible, readable and understandable. We further believe that knowledge can not be created and collected in a single form. In order to make best use of it, different views on knowledge have to be used.

Second, users can constantly learn from other projects and other users. Therefore, collaboration with other DM- or business-experts, who work or have worked on similar problems should be part of such an approach. Means have to be found to capture their experience and knowledge on a problem.

Third, the problems will be business-driven rather than technology-driven. Customers are interested in DM results, but not in technology. DM-tools will therefore play a less important role and are exchangeable, but means to support the user to perform Data Mining on a certain domains problems have to be found.

Forth, supporting the user in DM can not be a static technology, but since business organizations and domains change, therefore will their knowledge about them. Procedures and methods for change of knowledge have to be included into any approach of team-support.

In general, mastering mappings of a DM-process model and successfully completing a DM-process for a specific business problem requires a long learning time and relies heavily on the experience and know-how of the people involved. In times of high personnel fluctuations in an organization, changing domains and high time-pressures, we see it as the most important issue on the Data Mining process to collect and preserve context-specific knowledge made in Data Mining

---

[2] but also general experience of different domains would be possible

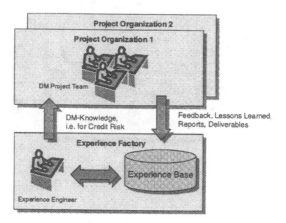

Fig. 3. The model for the management of Data Mining-knowledge through an Experience Factory: Data Mining teams collaborate, subscribe to and capture DM-knowledge in order to share experience through an Experience Factory (see also [4])

projects in order to give new projects a better start and a faster and better realization.

3 A Data Mining Experience Factory

Our approach of mapping a generic Data Mining Process Model, here CRISP-DM, on specific Data Mining steps is based on the use of past experiences with Data Mining and its distribution with an Experience Factory.

Our Data Mining Experience Factory is an organizational and technical infrastructure for the continuos build-up of knowledge derived from past experiences (see figure 3). Under an Data Mining Experience Factory we understand a common platform that captures and distributes different types of knowledge in many forms, from documents to reusable DM-programs, models, and data. Further, collaboration is made possible through the use of browsing and search mechanisms. This makes it possible to share, discuss and learn from knowledge through the whole organization, catalyzing continuos improvement. The concept of an Experience Factory has its basis in Software Engineering and has proven successful in this domain (see [4]).

The main product of such an experience factory is an *Experience Package*. Its content and structure varies based upon the kind of experience clustered in it. In this case, the DM-experience of a DM-task is memorized through special Data Mining packages that are characterized by context attributes and give information on how to solve a Data Mining step or give technological or methodological advice with lessons learned from past projects (see figure 4).

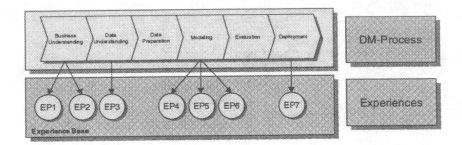

Fig. 4. The model of Data Mining knowledge and experience along the CRISP-DM Data Mining process. Experience packages (EP) of former DM-projects can be attached to appropriate steps and reused in new DM-tasks.

The Experience Factory approach is logically separated from project teams and has its own organizational structure. It is therefore more than user-guidance in Data Mining [9] or just technology. The major task of the Experience Factory is to capture experiences, represent and store knowledge in a reusable form and have means to efficiently reuse this knowledge in future Data Mining projects. As stated, newly gathered experience have to be continuously captured and integrated into the base.

4 Case Based Reasoning

Here we propose the approach of *Case Based Reasoning* (CBR)[3] for the realization of an Experience Base in Data Mining. The CBR approach is based on the method, that new problems can be solved by using similar solved problems. The approaches premise is that human tend to reason from experience. CBR consists hereby of the following steps (see figure 5):

- *Retrieve* the most similar case or cases to a new problem
- *Reuse* the information and knowledge in that case to solve the problem
- *Revise* the proposed solution
- *Retain* the parts of this experience likely to be useful for future problem solving

For a new problem, the most *similar* cases, defined by a predefined measure, are retrieved from the case-base and reused. With Case Based Reasoning, appropriate cases for an new problem can be retrieved using a similarity-based measure. The newly solved problem is then examined and appropriate cases stored in the case-base. Here cases in form of Experience Packages are captured and stored in a way that they can be reused best. In this way, incremental learning is an integral part of the reuse process.

---

[3] For an overview see [1]

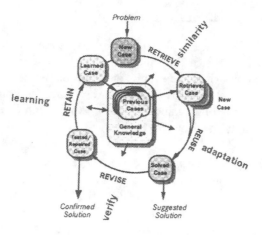

Fig. 5. The CBR Cycle (See [1]).

4.1 Case Based Reasoning for Capture and Reuse of Data Mining Experience

At DaimlerChrysler, the CRISP-DM process is being applied from different DM-teams in projects from Credit-Scoring to Customer Care. In order to organize and capture knowledge in these projects, we are building a CBR-based Experience Factory to take full advantage of the possibilities of an integrated knowledge infrastructure as a technological and organizational platform to exchange information between DM-projects.

Types of Experience

We distinguish between different kinds of experience, which is being reflected in the representation of the experience packages. We regard:

Lessons Learned Reports	Guidelines	Deliverables
External Information	Documentation	Best Practices Documents
Identified Success Factors, Mistakes	Critique	Process Models

as sources of knowledge and experience valuable to store into the experience base. So far, we are mapping these types of knowledge onto two different kinds of experience packages. We distinguish concepts that represent problem-solution pairs, where a solution to a specific problem is being presented, (i.e. Mistakes, Critique, Lessons Learned) and information-concepts, where information, methods and solutions are presented. This is the case i.e. for Data-Mining Process Models. Here information, tactics, procedures and rules not bound on a specific problem are stored.

Domain Model and Representation

In order to reuse experience in practice, the knowledge is captured and retrieved through the DM-Experience Base in DM-Experience Packages[4]. Here we use a semi-structured approach for the representation of the cases. On the one hand, we use a domain-model with attributes to represent the domain of experiences in Data Mining, on the other hand, we use textual components to represent the problem (if used) and a solution/experience.

Each of the packages is structured in a case-description of the occurred problem (if any), a method or solution and information about the rationale and the cause. Further, we use the domain model to describe the context for classification of the package (and for effective retrieval). Keywords allow for the introduction of additional context descriptions and an abstract with free-text help the user to identify useful packages. We use eight attributes to describe the context of a package. Here the dimensions are the Data-Mining phase or task, the application type, the package(experience)-type, the applied methods, the used tools, the life-cycle of the experience, the specialization of the experience and the perspective onto the experience. Through the use of taxonomies i.e. for Data-Mining phases and tasks, we are able to model dependencies like that the Data Description task belongs to the Data Understanding phase. Further we can use a key-word list of the domain in order to fill keyword-attributes representing the context on a specialized level.

Similarity Measures and Retrieval of DM-Experience

In order to implement an Experience Factory in practice, easy retrieval for each DM-project member is necessary. Since today's organizations rely on intranets and WWW-technology, the aggregation and distribution can be performed through these (see figure 6). In order to support efficient retrieval, search facilities have to be implemented. This is, where CBR-retrieval methods are used. Its search facilities implements a more advanced techniques on the case base than simple searches for equality or patterns like in basic IR.

Based on the given characteristics of the new problem, described by the context-variables, a set of possible reuse candidate can be retrieved. Here a similarity measure that measures the similarity using the domain model including taxonomies is used. In a first step, the similarity between each case attribute and the query attribute, in a second step the global similarity between each case and the query is computed. Through browsing and navigating through these resulting set, the best candidate can be chosen by the DM-team [2]. In order to retrieve meaningful cases, the measure of interestingness is to be defined, that sorts the set of reuse candidates. Here weights and measures have to be defined by the experience engineer of the domain.

---

[4] See [11] for a representation in the domain of software measurement

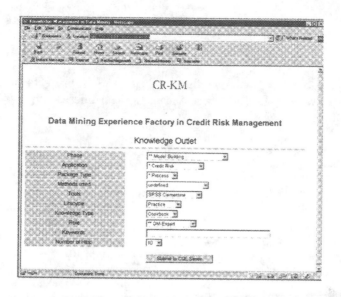

Fig. 6. Retrieval of an Experience Package. A new problems context is being categorized and the expected type of experience is selected. Further keywords allow a more specific description.

5 Conclusion

Systematic knowledge creation, capture, organization and use provides a new way to support the DM-process model CRISP-DM. We see the DM-process as a knowledge intensive and weak-structured process, where the agents have to choose on each step from a variety of options. This makes organizational team support an important topic in the case of Data Mining. At DaimlerChrysler, the CRISP-DM process is being applied from different DM-teams in projects from Credit-Scoring to Customer Care. We observed, that because of the repetitive application of Data Mining, experience can be used in successive projects. But until today no means were taken to support the agents to do DM in a business-problem context. We therefore identified sources of experiences that can improve DM-processes and show, how experience can be integrated using a CBR-based Experience Factory for Data Mining.

In a first step we used the process model of CRISP-DM to define the DM-process and to hold best requirements in documentation and quality. Through the use of CRISP-DM in all projects, we can derive comparable and reusable patterns on how to map the CRISP-DM process model on a specific business problems DM-process.

In a second step, we propose a CBR-based Experience Factory for Data Mining, capturing knowledge and experience when reviewing a step or process in CRISP-

DM. We use an integrated knowledge infrastructure within our organization to capture, organize and reuse this knowledge. This infrastructure is based on the Experience Factory approach by Basili.

Our further research will examine this approach on DM-projects and define measures of improvement. Further, own concepts for the different types of experiences will be defined.

References

1. Aamodt, A. Plaza, E.: "Case-based reasoning: Foundational issues, methodological variations, and system approaches". AI-Communications, 7(1), 39-59, 1994
2. Althoff, K.-D. and Nick, M. and Tautz, C. :"Concepts for reuse in the experience factory and their implementation for CBR system development". In Proceedings of the Eleventh German Workshop on Machine Learning, August 1998.
3. Bartlmae, K.: "An Experience Factory Approach for Data Mining". In Proceedings of the second Workshop: "Data Mining und Data Warehousing als Grundlage Entscheidungsunterstützender Systeme (DMDW99)", Univ. Magdeburg, September 1999.
4. Basili, V. R., Caldiera, G. , Rombach., H. D.: "Experience Factory". In John J. Marciniak, editor, Encyclopedia of Software Engineering, vol.1, pp.528-532. John Wiley and Sons, 1994.
5. Berry, M.J.A., Linhoff, G.: "Data Mining Techniques. For Marketing, Sales and Customer Support". Wiley Computer Publication, 1997
6. Cabena, P., Hadjinian, P., Stadler, R., Verhees, J, Zanasi, A.: "Discovering Data Mining. From Concept To Implementaion". Prentice Hall, Upper Saddle River, New Jeresey 07458, 1998
7. Cho, J.R., Mathews, R.C.:" Interactions Between Mental Models Used in Categorization and Experiential Knowledge of Specific Cases". The Journal of Experimental Psychology, 49A (3), 1996
8. CRISP-DM, March 1999, DaimlerChrysler, Forschung und Technologie, 1999, http://www.ncr.dk/CRISP
9. R. Engels, G. Lindner and R. Studer:"A Guided Tour through the Data Mining Jungle". In: Proceedings of the 3rd International Conference on Knowledge Discovery in Databases (KDD-97), August 1997, Newport Beach, CA.
10. Fayyad, U., Piatetsky-Shapiro, G., Smyth, P.: "Form Data Mining to Knowledge Discovery: An Overview". In: U.Fayyad, G. Piatetsky-Shapiro, P Smyth, and R. Uthurusamy editors, Advances in Knowledge Discovery and Data Mining. MIT Press, Cambrige, MA 1995
11. Gresse von Wangenheim, C., Moraes, A. R., Althoff, K.-D., Barcia, R. M., Weber, R. , Martins, A.: "Case-Based Reasoning Approach to Reuse of Experiential Knowledge in Software Measurement Programs". Proc. of the 6th German Workshop on Case-Based Reasoning, Berlin, Germany, 1998
12. D.Michie, D.J. Spiegelhalter, C.C.Taylor: "Machine Learning, neural and statistical Classification, Ellis Horwood", 1994

Analysing Warranty Claims of Automobiles

An Application Description Following the CRISP-DM Data Mining Process

Jochen Hipp[1] and Guido Lindner[2]

[1] Wilhelm Schickard Institute, University of Tübingen, 72076 Tübingen, Germany
jochen.hipp@informatik.uni-tuebingen.de
[2] DaimlerChrysler AG, Research & Technology FT3/KL, 89013 Ulm, Germany
guido.lindner@daimlerchrysler.com

Abstract. This paper describes a real world application of Data Mining methods for deviation detection. The goal is to analyse warranty claims in the automobile sector. Basically we want to support the technical engineers concerned with warranty issues in two ways: First of all we want to guide them during verification of their hypothesis and additionally we want to strengthen their creative and inspirational potentials.

For this purpose we accessed the Quality Information System (QUIS) of DaimlerChrysler. The whole project was carried through according to the CRISP-DM data mining process. The methods from Data Mining that we applied were: baysian nets, boolean association rules, generalised association rules, quantitative association rules and sequential patterns. We present some of the data mining results exemplarily, discuss the difficulties we encountered and finally give a short conclusion.

1 Introduction

Quality insurance is a major topic for the manufacturing of automobiles, especially in the upper segments where the products of DaimlerChrysler are positioned.

A prerequisite to establish an efficient quality control process is the systematic and careful collection of information about the sold vehicles and their fault behaviour. At DaimlerChrysler the Quality Information System (QUIS) is used for this purpose. In QUIS for each produced vehicle detailed information collected during the manufacturing process are stored together with all information about later warranty claims and garage visits. Currently, the database contains information about more than seven million vehicles and has a size of approximately 40 gigabytes.

The QUIS system is used for various tasks like

- prediction of warranty costs,
- analysis of customer complaints,
- generation of product surveys like quality reports,
- general quality monitoring

Based on techniques from the field of Data Mining, we developed new approaches to support such tasks. In this application paper we describe how to support the analysis of customer complaints during the warranty time. We employed methods that can be subsumed under deviation detection, that is baysian nets, association rules, and sequential patterns.

Our investigation follows the **CR**oss **I**ndustrie **S**tandard **P**rocess Model for **D**ata **M**ining (CRISP-DM) that was developed as on open standard by leading Data Mining appliers and a tool supplier [6]. In fact this standard model has already proven to be very useful in various Data Mining projects at Daimler-Chrysler, see e.g.[12].

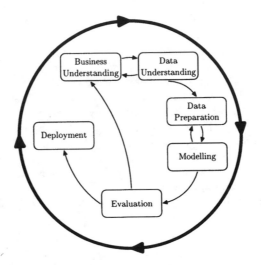

Fig. 1. CRISP Data Mining Process Model

The rest of the paper is structured according to the CRISP-DM–phases: Business Understanding, Data Understanding, Data Preparation, Modelling, Evaluation, and Deployment. We conclude with a brief summary of our experiences.

2 Business Understanding

For several reasons it is very important for DaimlerChrysler to learn about warranty claims. Not only the obvious goal to reduce the warranty costs counts, but also so called soft facts, e.g. image aspects and customer satisfaction, are to be taken into account. Such soft facts are difficult to measure but actually turn out to be crucial, especially in the automobile business.

The engineers at the plants are the experts concerning the technical aspects of vehicle manufacturing. Therefore the process to examine and analyse complaints is driven by their knowledge and experience. They define hypotheses about the reason of the claim and accordingly start queries to the QUIS system.

Our idea is to support this process with methods from the field of Data Mining. The goal is on the one hand to enable an engineer to quickly testify the hypothesis he has in mind. On the other hand we also want the results of the Data Mining step to inspire him to easily develop completely new ideas. That is, we want to relieve the engineers from the more or less annoying parts of their work and at the same time we want to strengthen their creative and inspirational potentials.

To give a real world example: Electric and electronic components and systems increasingly conquer modern vehicles. With the rising number of such devices an appropriate cabling becomes more and more a challenge. As one consequence, today problems somehow connected to the cabling occur much more frequently than in the past.

An engineer in the plant, who is confronted with a reported warranty claim that the garage classified and repaired as "cable problem", wants questions like the following ones to be answered:

- Is there a special type or variant of vehicle, which is significantly "more infected" by the claim?
- Are there any interdependencies between complaints?
- Are there some dependencies over time? That is, do claims from the past support the occurrence of other or the same claims in the future?
- Was there a true problem with the cabling? That is, was there really a defect or did the garage simply exchange the cables for reason of suspicion?
- Is there a remarkable dependency between the claim "cable problem" and some garages?

At the moment the QUIS system supports analysing such business questions mainly by means of directed search queries. Taking into consideration the detailed information collected in QUIS, this is already a mighty approach in the hands of skilled engineers, but with introducing Data Mining methods into QUIS we go far beyond.

3   Data Understanding

A very general overview on QUIS and its data sources is given in figure 2.[1] Basically the system contains exact information on how and where a vehicle was actually built. Also other production details, like sales codes, which describe the equipment of the vehicles, are included. Today, there are more than 700 sales codes possible and an average truck for example has between 30 and 50 of such sales codes.

In addition QUIS contains complete information on requested warranty claims. All garages, that are DaimlerChrysler service partners, are obliged to encode the

---

[1] For obvious reason we cannot go too much into detail when describing the actual layout of QUIS.

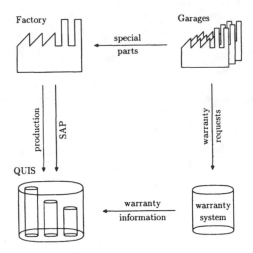

Fig. 2. Information Sources of QUIS

complaints with the help of a standardised code. Today there are more than 5000 components which are potential causes of a claim.

QUIS collects data from different sources and already in advance it became obvious that without the help of domain experts satisfyingly understanding the data was hardly feasible. So experts from different departments had to be located and consulted: in brief a task that turned out to be rather costly.

We experienced that this early phase of data mining is easily underestimated. That is, it is too tempting to simply accept a database like QUIS as being setup and "somehow" documented by competent experts and then quickly step further to the phases Modelling and Evaluation, that are the ones promising "pastime and honour" instead of laboriously walking through rows and columns.

Unfortunately shortcomings during Data Understanding phase already at the Data Preparation phase but at least at the Modelling and Evaluation phases inevitably make costly additional iterations of the data mining process necessary. An observation that cannot be stressed enough.

4   Data Preparation

Although QUIS offers a rather evolved access to the data, the Data Preparation step is still inevitable.

The information in QUIS is presented in a typical relational way. Nevertheless the users have no free SQL-access to the system, but rely on selecting the data using standard queries offered by the QUIS-system.

In fact as a first step we had to select the interesting rows and columns from the different views. After all not the whole information implicitly contained in QUIS was explicitly available. So we had to manually derive attributes, e.g. derive "Number of days from selling date until first claim" from the corresponding dates.

Finally we integrated the various collected and derived pieces of information into one all-including table.

After this first step the actual work began: Whereas we were able to use standard tools to do the information gathering and integration, in the following modelling phase we relied on proprietary implementations of data mining methods, originating from a former project at DaimlerChrysler. The main problem was that each of these algorithm implementations came together with its own data format.

For example our association rule algorithms do not directly work on relational tables with attributes names in clear but on sets of integer values the attribute names are mapped on. We therefore had to exhaustively preprocess the data.

To do such demanding Data Preparation tasks we helped ourselves with Perl [11], a scripting language that among other things was designed to do text preprocessing. This language offers in some way a very low-level functionality but actually turned out to be a powerful tool for our purposes.

In fact this part of the data preparation phase was much more time consuming than we anticipated and moreover turned out to be quite error prone.

5 Modelling

We subsumed our business questions under the general Data Mining goal of deviation detection. From the various methods available today we chose baysian nets, different kinds of association rules and sequential patterns.

5.1 Baysian Nets

As mentioned before we are interested in dependencies which lead to technical reasons or at least could serve as an indicator for a special claim. The main question is: Are there any combinations of construction details, that fundamentally increase the probability for a claim to be significantly higher than its a priori probability?

To answer such questions, we employed INES [4]. INES supports the directed and interactive search for dependencies. Actually the user starts with an initial set of dependencies. If he considers a dependency as being not relevant, he can delete it and restart the algorithm to search for further ("deeper") dependencies. In this way he moves step by step through the defined hypothesis space.

5.2 Boolean Association Rules

Association rules were introduced in [1] and today the mining of such rules can be seen as one of the key tasks of KDD. The intuitive meaning of an association rule $X \Rightarrow Y$, where X and Y are sets of so called items, is that a record containing X is likely to also contain Y. The prototypical application is the analysis of supermarket basket data where rules like "34% of all customers who buy fish also buy white wine" may be found. Obviously such rules exactly fit with our application. For our investigations we used the algorithm Apriori described in [2].

5.3 Generalised Association Rules

One shortcoming of boolean association rules is that they are restricted to mine rules between items of a fixed level of generality, see [9]. Especially in our domain, rules on the level of e.g. a special part of a window winder typically may be much too accurate but in some cases may be exactly what we want. To overcome this problem we make use of a taxonomy available on the considered sales codes and employ the algorithm Prutax described in [7] to mine generalised association rules.

5.4 Quantitative Association Rules

Boolean and generalised association rules cannot take quantities into consideration. So if e.g. frequent occurrences of claims connected to the alternator typically lead to a complete exchange of the corresponding cables but not already the first or second of such claims, this dependency might remain undetected. Quantitative association rules were first described in [10] and we use the algorithm Q2 from [5] to mine such rules.

5.5 Sequential Patterns

Some of the business questions aim on dependencies that take time into consideration. E.g. we want to know if repairs of special parts imply future claims of the same or other parts. So called sequential patterns are an extension of association rules that exactly model such dependencies. For mining we employ an algorithm that is implemented according to [3].

6 Evaluation

In this section we give some examples of the results we obtained. The details of course are confidential so we are only able to give a general idea of the kind of dependencies we found with the different methods. In addition we conclude with some general remarks on problems we encountered.

6.1 Dependencies between claims and construction details

With boolean association rules we were able to identify a special combination of construction details that doubles the likelihood of "cable problem" compared to its a priori probability. Our experts now take this dependency as a base for further technical driven investigations in order to identify the reasons behind the problem.

Another insight we had on customer complaints concerning problems with the justification of the headlights. The analysis with INES lead to a dependency between the occurrence of this claim and the distance of the axes, see figure 3. Only vehicles with a special distance between the front and the rear axe were

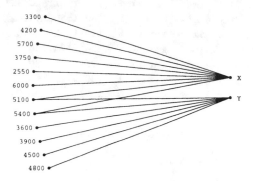

Fig. 3. Example of output from INES

rejected. When the engineers became aware of this dependency they took the level regulation as starting point for their further investigations.

6.2 Dependencies between claims and garages

Another point of interest are dependencies between claims and garages. Are there any garages that have more claims of a special type than the others have? To discover such dependencies we employed boolean association rules. Our results are partly shown in Figure 4[2].

For example the first association rule in the figure shows that from the 140 vehicles (corresponding to 1.3% of all vehicles) visiting garage "a" 20.1% had problems with the cables.

Obviously the example claim is not uniformly distributed over the different garages and immediately new questions arise: Are these garages placed in a special kind of area? Is there a special usage of the vehicles that visited the garage? Actually further analysis are needed to find appropriate answers.

6.3 Dependencies among claims

Concerning the dependencies among claims we are particularly interested in finding actionable sequences. We therefore expected results from the employment of sequential patterns for this analysis.

Unfortunately our investigations with sequential patterns suffer from a fundamental problem: The absolute support values of the found patterns are relatively

---

[2] Note that all values are pure fiction.

```
cable_claim <= garage_a (140:1.3%, 20.1%)
cable_claim <= garage_b (140:1.3%, 31.1%)
cable_claim <= garage_c (140:1.3%, 27.2%)
cable_claim <= garage_d (119:1.1%, 37.3%)
cable_claim <= garage_e (184:1.7%, 20.2%)
cable_claim <= garage_f (162:1.5%, 20.9%)
cable_claim <= garage_g (162:1.5%, 35.4%)
cable_claim <= garage_h (140:1.3%, 29.0%)
cable_claim <= garage_i (130:1.2%, 28.1%)
cable_claim <= garage_j (227:2.1%, 20.6%)
cable_claim <= garage_k (130:1.2%, 29.7%)
cable_claim <= garage_l (162:1.5%, 30.9%)
...
```

Fig. 4. Example rules

small, so that we cannot be sure about the degree of generality of our results. Anyway our analysis proved that the likelihood of a certain claim to reoccur after visiting a garage is fundamentally smaller than its a priori probability.

In addition running the sequential pattern algorithm and varying the time interval parameter lead to an insight that actually is not a sequential pattern but nevertheless is quite interesting: The garages submit cable claims that are either coded as general cable claims or as cable claims tied to a specific electronic system. Our analysis showed that approximately 20% of the general cable claims occur together with a specified cable claim or a claim concerning an electronic system, whereas "together" means together in an interval of seven days. These 20% then can be seen as an upper bound on the theoretically possible improvement when only considering the identified cable claims and electronic systems for enhancement.

6.4   General Remarks

The results from the baysian nets, the boolean association rules and partly from the sequential patterns were quite encouraging. In contrast, generalised and quantitative association rules did not prove to be useful in this special application. In fact we did not find any rule, that our domain experts would judge as interesting, at least at first sight.

Concerning the failure of generalised association rules we see the taxonomy we relied on as the main reason. Originally this taxonomy was not designed to implement data mining but to serve for completely different purposes at the garages and the production plants. E.g. parts were grouped according to historic or technical reasons that did not make sense in the context of association rule mining. Without carefully adapting and redesigning the taxonomy – involving both data mining and domain experts – mining generalised association rules on QUIS will hardly lead to any useful insights.

The problem when mining quantitative association rules is more subtle: On the one hand it turned out that in our data a claim very rarely occurs more than once or twice per vehicle. As a consequence the existence of associations between different quantities is rather unlikely and therefore it is not astonishing that we did not gain any deeper insights by mining quantitative association rules. On the other hand there are some quantitative attributes in the data, e.g. distances and weights. We think that probably further investigations that would have gone beyond the limited possibilities of our pilot project might have lead to insights based on quantitative association rules.

In our opinion the fundamental problem of association rule mining in contrast to other data mining methods is the enormous number of rules generated in one pass. E.g Baysian nets as implemented in INES offer a kind of stepwise search through the space of dependencies whereas when mining association rules we were confronted with sets of upto several hundred thousands of rules of which actually only very few turned out to be interesting.

Due to the lack of appropriate tools we accessed these sets by means of low-level operations, mainly employing regular expressions offered by the Unix command "grep". At least in the hands of experts working on a pilot application this is a mighty and flexibly approach but for obvious reasons not suitable to support the everyday work of our technical engineers.

7 Deployment

Beside the shown pilot application we have been carrying out further proofs of concept with comparable applications. The domain experts were impressed by our first results and now we are in the phase of developing strategies to integrate our techniques into the existing information technology environment at DaimlerChrysler.

As mentioned above our main goal is to efficiently support the technical engineers at the production plants during their everyday work. That is we want them to generate and access data mining results on their own without the interference of a data mining expert. For this purpose we plan an intranet based system that offers the ability to mine QUIS independent of any particular location.

The main component of this system will be a so called rule browser, that offers access to the generated data mining results. This browser is intended to be a visualisation and presentation tool that enables even non specialists to conveniently analyse the very large sets of association rules typically generated during the modelling phase.

8 Conclusion

Following the CRISP Data Mining process model we exemplarily showed how deviation detection could be used for the analysis of warranty claims in the automobile industry. Our pilot application aimed at efficiently supporting technical engineers concerned with warranty issues in their everyday work.

For this purpose we employed various different Data Mining methods. Whereas generalised and quantitative association rules did not yield to satisfactory outcomes the results from baysian nets, boolean association rules and sequential patterns were encouraging and considered as very useful by the domain experts.

We described the difficulties we encountered when applying the data mining algorithms developed by the scientific community to real-world problems at DaimlerChrysler. In addition we presented some general insights that we think may be useful also in other contexts than our special application.

Currently we are developing strategies to integrate our techniques into the existing information technology environment at DaimlerChrysler.

References

1. R. Agrawal, T. Imielinski, and A. Swami. Mining association rules between sets of items in large databases. In *Proceedings of the ACM SIGMOD International Conference on Management of Data (ACM SIGMOD '93)*, pages 207 – 216, Washington, USA, May 1993.
2. R. Agrawal and R. Srikant. Fast algorithms for mining association rules. In *Proceedings of the 20th International Conference on Very Large Databases (VLDB '94)*, Santiago, Chile, June 1994.
3. R. Agrawal and R. Srikant. Mining sequential patterns. In *Proceedings of the International Conference on Data Engineering (ICDE)*, Taipei, Taiwan, March 1995.
4. C. Borgelt, R. Kruse, and G. Lindner. Lernen probabilistischer und possibilistischer Netze aus Daten: Theorie und Anwendung. *KI Fachzeitschrift Themenheft Data Mining*, 1998.
5. O. Büchter and R. Wirth. Discovery of association rules over ordinal data: A new and faster algorithm and its application to basket analysis. In *Research and Development in Knowledge Discovery and Data Mining (Proceedings of the Second Pacific-Asia Conference on Knowledge Discovery and Data Mining, PAKDD-98)*, Melbourne, Australia, April 1998.
6. CRISP. The CRISP-DM process model. http://www.ncr.dk/CRISP/, 1999.
7. J. Hipp, A. Myka, R. Wirth, and U. Güntzer. A new algorithm for faster mining of generalized association rules. In *Proceedings of the 2nd European Symposium on Principles of Data Mining and Knowledge Discovery (PKDD '98)*, Nantes, France, September 1998.
8. G. Lindner and R. Studer. Forecasting the Fault Rate Behaviour of Cars. In *Workshop proceedings from the ICML 1999,*, March 1999.
9. R. Srikant and R. Agrawal. Mining generalized association rules. In *Proceedings of the 21st Conference on Very Large Databases (VLDB '95)*, Zürich, Switzerland, September 1995.
10. R. Srikant and R. Agrawal. Mining quantitative association rules in large relational tables. In *Proceedings of the 1996 ACM SIGMOD Conference on Management of Data*, Montreal, Canada, June 1996.
11. L. Wall, T. Christiansen, and R. L. Schwartz. *Programming Perl*. O'Reilly & Associates, California, 2 edition, September 1996.
12. R. Wirth and J. Hipp. The CRISP-DM data mining process in practice. submitted, 1999.

An Adaptive Method of Numerical Attribute Merging for Quantitative Association Rule Mining

Jiuyong Li, Hong Shen, and Rodney Topor

School of Computing and Information Technology
Griffith University
Nathan Qld 4111 Australia
Email: {jiuyong,hong,rwt}@cit.gu.edu.au

Abstract. Mining quantitative association rules is an important topic of data mining since most real world databases have both numerical and categorical attributes. Typical solutions involve partitioning each numerical attribute into a set of disjoint intervals, interpreting each interval as an item, and applying standard boolean association rule mining. Commonly used partitioning methods construct set of intervals that either have equal width or equal cardinality. We introduce an adaptive partitioning method based on repeatedly merging smaller intervals into larger ones. This method provides an effective compromise between the equal width and equal cardinality criteria. Experimental results show that the proposed method is an effective method and improves on both equal-width partitioning and equal-cardinality partitioning.

keywords: Data mining, association rule, continuous attribute discretization.

1 Introduction

1.1 Association rule mining

Association rule mining was first studied by Agrawal et al. [1], and can be formally stated as follows. Let $I = \{i_1, i_2, \cdots, i_m\}$ be a set of symbols that are called *items*. The items may be goods, attributes, or events. A *transaction* T is a set of items, $T \subset I$, and a collection of transactions form a database $\mathcal{D}$. A set of items is called an *itemset*, and an itemset with k items is called a k-*itemset*. The support of itemset X, denoted as $\sigma(X)$, is the percentage of $\mathcal{D}$ in which every transaction contains X. An itemset is called a *frequent itemset* if its support is not less than a user specified *minimum support* ζ, or $\sigma(X) \geq \zeta$. An implication in the form of $X \to Y$ is an association rule, where $X, Y \subset I$ and $X \cap Y = \emptyset$. The *confidence* of rule $X \to Y$ is the ratio of $\sigma(X \cup Y)$ to $\sigma(X)$, denoted by $\kappa(X \to Y)$. If $\kappa(X \to Y) \geq \eta$, where η is a user specified *minimum confidence*, the rule is called a *strong rule*. For example, suppose 30% of students have taken both Computer Programming and Word Processing, and 80% of the students who have taken Computer Programming also have taken Word Processing. Then the rule "(Computer Programming) $\to$ (Word Processing)" has support of 30% and confidence of 80%. The goal of association rule mining is to find strong rules in databases, which is normally achieved by first finding frequent itemsets and then forming association rules.

1.2 Quantitative association rule mining

Mining association rules in databases of numerical and categorical attributes rather than boolean attributes is called mining quantitative association rules [13]. An example of a quantitative association rule is Age $\in [40, 50] \wedge$ Married $\rightarrow$ Cars $= 2$.

There are several possible methods for quantitative association rules mining. One is to consider individual categorical states and separate numerical values as items, and then use a boolean association rule mining algorithm. After all rules are obtained, the rules with adjacent numerical values are grouped [9, 14]. For example rule $Age = 50 \wedge Married \rightarrow house$ and rule $Age = 55 \wedge Married \rightarrow house$ are combined as $Age \in [50, 55] \wedge Married \rightarrow house$. This method suffers from difficulties of mining on certain numerical values such as insufficient support from the database to some individual numerical values and too many numerical values on a particular attribute.

A second method of quantitative association rule mining is to map quantitative attributes into boolean attributes, then use algorithms of boolean association rule mining. Mapping a categorical attribute to a boolean attribute is straightforward: it can be realized by enumerating categorical states to a set of positive integers (items). As to numerical attributes, the common way is to cut a continuous attribute to some intervals then map all values in an interval to an item. Converting a continuous attribute to a set of discrete values is called *discretization*.

There are several methods to do this [2, 6, 5, 3]. Many methods are supervised discretization methods in which optimal classes are known beforehand. However, in many data mining problems, the optimal classes are not known, so unsupervised discretization is more suitable. There are few unsupervised discretization methods. The two most frequently used methods are the following.

1. Equal-width discretization divides the continuous attribute range into N intervals of equal width. For example, ages from 20 to 60 can be divided into four intervals of width 10 years. This method can be easily implemented, but has the clear drawback that there may be too few instances in some intervals and too many in other intervals, and both cases hinder mining high quality association rules.

2. Equal-depth (or equal-cardinality) discretization divides the continuous attribute range into N intervals so that there are $1/N$ of the total instances in each interval. This method avoids the possible imbalance inherent in the equal-width discretization method, but it may separate similar attribute values into different intervals and group dissimilar attributes into the same interval.

Equal-depth discretization method is preferred in general [7, 11, 13]. A key problem in using this method is choosing the number of intervals. Small interval size tends to result in the loss of interesting rules, and large interval size tends to reduce the accuracy of rules. To deal with this problem, a measure of K-partial completeness is defined to decide how many intervals should be cut in a continuous attribute [13]. However, even with this measure, this method may not work very well on highly skewed data as stated by Srikant and Agrawal [13]. A main cause of these problems is that equal-width discretization method and equal-depth discretization method do not consider both value densities and value distances at the same time.

In addition to the above, methods based on clustering have also been proposed for unsupervised discretization [4, 11]. In [11], a method for clustering numeric attributes to mine distance based association rule was proposed, where an association rule is represented by $C_y \rightarrow C_x$, where C_x and C_y are density clusters.

Our work is motivated by the concept of clustering, but does not form association rules directly from clusters like [11]. We discretize numerical attributes and then convert quantitative association rule mining to boolean association rule mining. Our proposed discretization method is an unsupervised discretization method. It initially places each numerical attribute value in a separate interval, and then selectively merges similar adjacent intervals. It uses a merging criterion that considers both value densities and value distances of numerical attributes, and produces proper value density and suitable interval width so that association rules can be easily found from them. After numerical attributes are discretized as a set of disjoint intervals, each interval can be interpreted as a boolean attribute, thus transforming quantitative association rule mining into boolean association rule mining.

In this paper, we first define a criterion for merging adjacent intervals and develop a numerical attribute merging algorithm. Next we present a quantitative association rule mining algorithm. Finally, we implement both algorithms and compare our proposed discretization method with equal-width and equal-depth discretization methods.

2   Numerical attribute merging algorithm

The goal of our work is to partition a numerical attribute into a set of disjoint intervals by minimizing differences within intervals and maximizing differences between intervals in light of clustering[10]. Intervals with too few attribute value occurrences in the database would prevent itemsets from having sufficient support and intervals with too many attribute values would fail to discriminate between attribute value occurrences and would hence fail to lead to useful association rules. Hence, we present a merging algorithm to produce a set of intervals with suitable attribute value occurrences.

Initially, suppose that a numerical attribute has m distinct values, $I = \{x_1, x_2, \ldots, x_m\}$, where attribute value x_i has n_i occurrences in the database (weight). Let $N = \sum_{i=1}^{m} n_i$ be the total number of attribute value occurrences. Without loss of generality we further assume that $x_i < x_{i+1}$ for all $1 \leq x \leq m-1$ (we can simply sort these values otherwise). Define $I_1, \ldots, I_m$ to be a set of m maximal disjoint intervals on I, where each I_i originally contains x_i, $1 < i \leq m$. Let each interval I_i have a *representative centre* c_i initially defined to be x_i, $1 \leq i \leq m$.

In general, suppose that an interval I_k contains attribute values $\{x_1, x_2, \ldots x_k\}$ and $N_k = \sum_{i=1}^{k} n_i$ attribute value occurrences, and has representative center c_k. Define the average intra-interval distance of I with respect to c to be

$$\text{Dist}(I_k, c_k) = \frac{1}{N_k} \sum_{i=1}^{k} n_i \mid x_i - c_k \mid. \tag{1}$$

Assume that two adjacent intervals $I_i = \{x_1, \ldots, x_i\}$ and $I_{i+1} = \{x_{i+1}, \ldots, x_{i+j}\}$ contain attribute value occurrences $N_i = \sum_{p=1}^{i} n_p$ and $N_{i+1} = \sum_{p=i+1}^{i+j} n_p$, and have representative centres $c_i = \sum_{p=1}^{i} x_p n_p / N_i$ and $c_{i+1} = \sum_{p=i+1}^{i+j} x_p n_p / N_{i+1}$ respectively, $1 \leq i+j \leq m$. The union, $I' = I_i \cup I_{i+1}$, of the two intervals containing $i + j$ attribute values and $N_i + N_{i+1} = \sum_{p=1}^{i+j} n_p$ attribute value occurrences in total thus has its representative centre given by the average weighted value of (c_i, n_i) and (c_{i+1}, n_{i+1}):

$$c = \frac{c_i \sum_{p=1}^{i} n_p + c_{i+1} \sum_{p=i+1}^{i+j} n_p}{\sum_{p=1}^{i+j} n_p} = \frac{c_i N_i + c_{i+1} N_{i+1}}{N_i + N_{i+1}}. \tag{2}$$

The intra-interval distance of I with respect to c calculated by Equation (1) is then uniquely defined by c_i and c_{i+1} as follows. When $x_i \leq c \leq x_{i+1}$ which holds in our algorithm, noting that $\sum_{p=1}^{i} x_p n_p = c_i N_i$ and $\sum_{p=i+1}^{i+j} x_p n_p = c_{i+1} N_{i+1}$ we can derive this distance as follows:

$$
\begin{aligned}
\mathrm{Dist}(I', c) &= (N_i + N_{i+1})^{-1} \Sigma_{p=1}^{i+j} n_p \mid x_p - c \mid \\
&= (N_i + N_{i+1})^{-1} (\Sigma_{p=1}^{i} n_p (c - x_p) + \Sigma_{p=i+1}^{i+j} n_p (x_p - c)) \\
&= (N_i + N_{i+1})^{-1} (\Sigma_{p=i+1}^{i+j} n_p x_p - \Sigma_{p=1}^{i} n_p x_p + (\Sigma_{p=1}^{i} n_p - \Sigma_{p=i+1}^{i+j} n_p)c) \\
&= (N_i + N_{i+1})^{-1} (c_{i+1} N_{i+1} - c_i N_i + (N_i - N_{i+1}) \frac{c_i N_i + c_{i+1} N_{i+1}}{N_i + N_{i+1}}) \\
&= \frac{2 N_i N_{i+1}}{(N_i + N_{i+1})^2} (c_{i+1} - c_i).
\end{aligned}
\tag{3}
$$

Based on the above equation, we may now define the difference between I_i and I_{i+1}, denoted by $\mathrm{Diff}(c_i, c_{i+1})$, to be $(N_i + N_{i+1}) \mathrm{Dist}(I', c)/2$ so that intervals will be merged according to the increasing order of their differences.

We can see from the above definition that the difference between two intervals is determined first by the distance between their representative centers and then by the number of attribute value occurrences in each interval. That is, if two pairs of intervals are the same distance apart, the pair with fewer attribute value occurrences in each interval has a smaller difference.

Next we consider how to choose a pair of adjacent intervals to merge. Given m consecutive intervals $I_1, \ldots, I_m$, whose representative centers are $c_1, \ldots, c_m$, there are $m-1$ pairs of adjacent intervals. We test every pair of adjacent intervals, and then merge the two with the smallest Diff, say I_t and I_{t+1}. The merged interval $I_t = I_t \cup I_{t+1}$ has representative centre c_t and number of value instances N_t updated as follows.

$$
\begin{aligned}
c_t &= (N_t c_t + N_{t+1} c_{t+1})/(N_t + N_{t+1}); \\
N_t &= N_t + N_{t+1};
\end{aligned}
$$

We repeatedly merge the pair of adjacent intervals with minimum difference in this way.

We now propose a criterion for terminating this merging process before we have reduced the data to a single large interval. If the density of each interval is large enough to form a rule, namely $N_i/N > \zeta$, or the representative centers of each pair of adjacent intervals are so far apart that they are unlikely to be in one group, for example $(c_{i+1} - c_i) > 3\overline{d}$, where $\overline{d}$ is the average distance of adjacent values of a numerical attribute, the numerical attribute merging procedure stops.

After executing the above procedure, the whole range of numerical attribute values is partitioned into a set of adjacent intervals, where the number of values in each interval is large enough to reach the user specified minimum support or each interval is too isolated to be merged into an adjacent interval.

The above procedure may be summarised as follows.

Algorithm 1 *Numerical attribute merging algorithm*
Input: An ordered sequence of numeric attributes $\{x_1, \ldots, x_m\}$.
Output: An ordered sequence of disjoint intervals $I_1, \ldots, I_{m'}$ covering $x_1, \ldots, x_m$, $m' < m$.
For each x_i $(1 \leq i \leq m)$ do
 Let I_i contain x_i;

Let $c_i = x_i$ be the representative centre of I_i;
End
Let $m' = m$;
For each interval pair (I_i, I_{i+1}) $(1 \leq i < m')$ do
    Let $Diff(c_i, c_{i+1}) = \frac{N_i N_{i+1}}{N_i + N_{i+1}}(c_{i+1} - c_i)$;
End
While (termination condition is not satisfied) do
    Let t be such that $Diff(c_t, c_{t+1})$ is minimal;
    Let $c_t = (N_t c_t + N_{t+1} c_{t+1})/(N_t + N_{t+1})$;
    Let $N_t = N_t + N_{t+1}$;
    Merge I_t and I_{t+1} into a new interval I_t;
    Let $m' = m' - 1$;
    Recompute $Diff(c_{t-1}, c_t)$ and $Diff(c_t, c_{t+1})$;
End;
Output intervals $I_1, \ldots, I_{m'}$;

3 Quantitative association rule mining

Quantitative association rule mining is the process of mining association rules for databases with both categorical attributes and numerical attributes. In a quantitative association rule $X \to Y$, X and Y may be the combination of boolean values, categorical states and numerical intervals. In the previous section, we have discussed how to find suitable intervals of numerical attributes. In this section we give a brief description of our algorithm for quantitative association rule mining. It consists of the following four steps.

3.1 Pre-processing

In this stage, the goal is to convert categorical and numerical attributes to boolean attributes on which boolean association rule mining algorithms can be applied. This is achieved by enumerating the values of categorical attributes and mapping interval sets of numerical attributes to a set of items. The core of this stage is to find suitable intervals for each numerical attribute, which affects the mining performance greatly. In our algorithm, interval finding is realized by Algorithm 1. After sets of cut-points of numerical attributes are found, all values in one interval are interpreted as an item. For example, different temperature ranges represent different items in Table 1. After that we can use boolean association rule mining on these items.

sex	code	cough	code	temperature	code	$\cdots$
male	1	bad	3	$35.0 - 36.9$	6	$\cdots$
female	2	slight	4	$36.9 - 37.1$	7	$\cdots$
—	—	no	5	$37.1 - 42.0$	8	$\cdots$

Table 1. An example of converting quantitative attributes to a set of items

3.2 Frequent itemset finding

The following efficient algorithm for frequent itemset finding was developed in [12]. The data structure *set trie* is important in the algorithm, since it allows efficient generation of candidates and verification and storage of frequent itemsets. Some similar data structures have also been used for association rule mining.

The set trie we use is an ordered and labeled root tree that can store a set and all its subsets conveniently. Its main characters are listed below.

Given a sorted set of positive integers $L = \{l_1, l_2, \ldots, l_n\}$, where $l_i < l_{i+1}$ if $i < j$.

1. Each node in set trie is labeled by an element in L, and more than one node (or leaf) in a set trie can have the same labels.
2. Labels of son nodes are ranked higher than their parents by the order in set L.
3. Each node stores all nodes on the path from the root to it.

An example of a set trie that stores set $\{1, 3, 5, 6\}$ and all its subsets is depicted in Figure 1. Frequent itemset finding involves four steps:

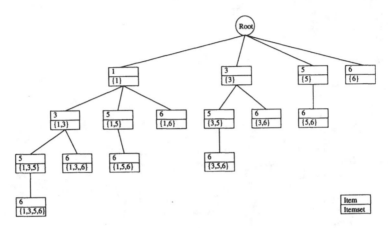

Fig. 1. An example of set trie

1. Initiating a set trie.
   We first find all frequent 1-itemsets and frequent 2-itemsets, and then initiate a set trie. Nodes in the first layer of set trie are added directly from all frequent items. Nodes in the second layer are those items having *frequent links* (two items that form a frequent 2-itemset are called having frequent link between them) with nodes in the first layer.
2. Generating candidates for frequent itemsets
   Our candidate generation is based on the following observation: If an itemset is frequent, all its subsets are frequent itemsets and links among all items contained in it are frequent links. Candidates are generated as follows. Suppose that a node has m frequent itemsets, $\{i_1, i_2, \ldots, i_{k_1}\}, \{i_1, i_2, \ldots, i_{k_2}\}, \ldots,$ $\{i_1, i_2, \ldots, i_{k_m}\}$, as its sons in the k-th layer of a set trie. Candidates in the $(k+1)$-th layer under the node i_{k_1} of k-th layer are $\{i_1, i_2, \ldots, i_{k_1}, i_{k_q}\}$, where $\sigma(i_{k_1}, i_{k_q}) \geq \zeta$ and $k_1 < k_q \leq k_m$. We can generate all candidates in the $(k+1)$-layer of the set trie by this way. The candidate generator based on set trie is very efficient since candidates only relate to siblings under a same parent rather than all k-itemsets so that much searching time is saved. A newly generated candidate is added in the tree as a new leaf.
3. Counting support of candidates
   A tree structure can be easily searched in breadth-first or depth-first. However in a set trie, we do not search the whole trie but *trace* it by a transaction. We illustrate tracing procedure by the following example. Suppose that a transaction has k frequent items, $\{i_1, i_2, \ldots, i_k\}$. In the first layer we only go to nodes $i_1, i_2, \ldots, i_k$, and mark them. Then we go into subtrees rooted by the marked nodes, and mark nodes $i_2, \ldots, i_k$ in the second layer of the subtrees. And so on. Support of each itemset under marked nodes is

incremented by 1. As the length of a transaction is far smaller than the size of set I, tracing set trie only searches a small part of the whole and set trie hence is very fast.

4. Deleting infrequent itemsets
If an itemset is proved to be infrequent, then all its supersets can not be frequent itemsets. In a set trie, supersets are stored in subtrees rooted by nodes storing the prefix subsets of them, as illustrated in Figure 1. If a node stores an infrequent itemset, the whole subtree including itself can be removed from the set trie. When there is no infrequent itemset to be removed, all frequent itemsets are stored in the set trie and are easily located since themselves are paths.

3.3 Rule forming

After all frequent itemsets are obtained, the task here is to test whether two disjoint subsets of an frequent itemset can form a rule. If there are the user specified targets, this step will be very simple. Otherwise we have to test all subsets as consequences in turn. For a consequence Y, which is an item or an itemset, we first search set trie for frequent itemsets $\mathcal{Z} = \{S_i | Y \subset S_i\}$. Then we obtain a set of rule $\{X_i \rightarrow Y, i = 1, 2, \ldots, m\}$, where $\kappa(X_i \rightarrow Y) > \eta$. For the convenience of rule pruning, rules with a same consequence are stored together and storage structure is also the set trie, since it is convenient for searching and counting in the post processing procedure.

The rule forming by the criterion of the minimum support and the minimum confidence may produce many uninteresting redundant rules. Rule pruning in the following section can resolve the problem of redundancy. Measures of interestingness are very application oriented.

3.4 Post-processing

There may be some redundant rules in the result of mining, if some of them account for some similar facts, such as $A \rightarrow C$ and $A \wedge B \rightarrow C$. The goal of rule pruning is to select a set of minimally overlapping rules from a raw rule set without losing information. Given support and confidence, an interesting rule is the one with the highest confidence, hence the pruning method we propose is to choose the rule with the highest confidence and delete other similar rules.

For a rule $X \rightarrow Y$, if $(X \cup Y) \subset T$, then we say that rule $X \rightarrow Y$ covers transaction T. On the other hand, if $(X \cup \neg Y) \subset T$, then we say that rule $X \rightarrow Y$ uncovers transaction T.

For a set of rules $\mathcal{R} = \{ X_i \rightarrow Y \mid 1 \leq i \leq m \}$ and a database $\mathcal{D} = \{T_1, \ldots, T_n\}$, the total covered transactions of rule set $\mathcal{R}$ over $\mathcal{D}$ is

$$Cov(\mathcal{R}) = \bigcup_{i=1}^{n} T_i, \quad \text{where } (X_k \cup Y) \subset T_i \text{ for any } (X_k \rightarrow Y) \subset \mathcal{R}.$$

The *coverage* of rule set $\mathcal{R}$ is the ratio of the size of $Cov(\mathcal{R})$ to the number of all transactions.

Consider two rules $X_1 \rightarrow Y$ and $X_2 \rightarrow Y$ where $\kappa(X_1 \rightarrow Y) > \kappa(X_2 \rightarrow Y)$. If both of them cover the same data set, rule $X_2 \rightarrow Y$ loses support when transactions covered by rule $X_1 \rightarrow Y$ are removed from database. As a result, the confidence of rule $X_1 \rightarrow Y$ is reduced as well.

If we choose a rule, and then remove all transactions covered by the rule from database, supports and confidences of the rest rules will change. For rule $X \rightarrow Y$, there are $\sigma(X) = \sigma(X \cup Y) + \sigma(X \cup \neg Y)$ and $\kappa(X \rightarrow Y) = \sigma(X \cup Y)/(\sigma(X \cup Y) + \sigma(X \cup \neg Y))$. Once we store a rule covering transactions in cov_i and uncovering transactions in $uncov_i$, and update them after each rule is selected, supports and confidences of rest rules can be updated easily. The ultimate goal is to simplify the raw rule set while maintaining total coverage unchanged.

A pruning algorithm selecting high confidence rules and keeping the same total coverage as the raw rule set is given below.

Algorithm 2 *Pruning the rule set*
Input: *Database* $\mathcal{D} = \{T_1, \ldots, T_n\}$, *itemset* Y, *and rule set* $\mathcal{R} = \{X_i \rightarrow Y \mid 1 \leq i \leq m\}$.
Output: *Pruned rule set* $\mathcal{R}' \subseteq \mathcal{R}$.
   Let $\mathcal{R}' = \emptyset$;
   For each rule $(X_i \rightarrow Y) \subset \mathcal{R}$ do
      Let $cov_i = \bigcup_{j=1}^{n} T_j$, where $(X_i \cup Y) \subset T_j$;
      Let $uncov_i = \bigcup_{j=1}^{n} T_j$, where $(X_i \cup \neg Y) \subset T_j$;
   End
   Let $Cov = \bigcup_{i=1}^{m} cov_i$;
   Let $m' = m$;
   While $(Cov \neq \emptyset)$ do
      Let d be such that $\kappa(X_d \rightarrow Y)$ is minimal;
      Let $\mathcal{R} = \mathcal{R} \setminus (X_d \rightarrow Y)$;
      Let $\mathcal{R}' = \mathcal{R}' \bigcup (X_d \rightarrow Y)$;
      Let $m' = m' - 1$;
      Let $Cov = Cov \setminus \{T_k \mid (X_d \cup Y) \subset T_k\}$;
      For each $(X_i \rightarrow Y) \subset \mathcal{R}$ do
         Let $cov_i = cov_i \setminus \{T_k | (X_d \cup Y) \subset T_k\}$;
         Let $\kappa(X_i \rightarrow Y) = |cov_i|/(|cov_i| + |uncov_i|)$;
      End;
   End;
   Output rule set $\mathcal{R}'$.

4 Performance results

Quantitative association rule mining algorithm depends critically on the discretization of continuous attributes. If discretization produces a set of suitable intervals, the computed association rules will have a large total coverage. The method proposed in this paper has been evaluated by comparing its performance with equal-width and equal-depth discretization methods.

We implemented our quantitative association rule mining algorithm and tested it on some databases from the Machine Learning Database Repository at the University of California at Irvine. A brief description of the database is given in Table 2.

Database name	Records	Attributes	Classes
Glass Identification	214	9 Numerical	3
Heart Disease	270	7 Numerical + 6 Categorical	2
Iris Plant	150	4 Numerical	3
Wisconsin Breast Cancer	699	10 Numerical	2

Table 2. Brief description of databases

The experiment was conducted by comparing the proposed algorithm methods with equal-width and equal-depth discretization methods, in which numerical attributes are partitioned into 5 or 10 equal value intervals or equal density intervals respectively. They are denoted as equal-width 5, equal-width 10, equal-depth 5 and equal depth 10.

In the experiment, we do not find all possible rules but some interesting rules with consequences as the labeled classes. To avoid finding too few rules from the small distributed items and too many rules from the large distributed items at a fixed minimum support, we use local support instead of support. The local support of a rule $X \to Y$ is the support of $X \cup Y$ in the sub-database of transactions that include Y.

The experiment results are displayed in Figure 2. From Figure 2, we can see

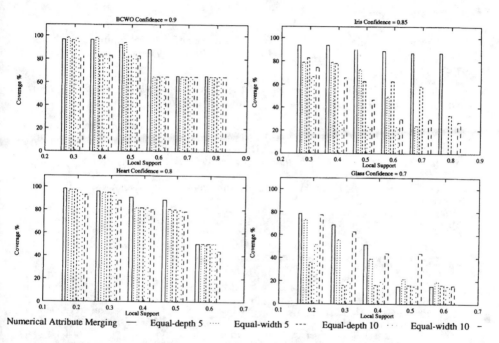

Fig. 2. Comparison of mining result of three class blind methods

that the overall results of our numerical attribute merging method is better than others. In 24 trials, only 1 trial is worse, 4 trials are marginally lower, and the other 19 trials are better than or equal to equal-width and equal-depth methods. We observed that no other method in the experiment achieves this performance.

It is reported [5, 8] that performances of all discretization methods have little difference except that supervised discretization methods are better than unsupervised discretization methods. In the case that labelled classes are known, the supervised discretization methods are good choices. When the class information is unknown, the method proposed in this paper is a good one. Since it considers both instance densities and value distances, it has the merits of both equal-depth and equal-width methods. Let us consider two extreme cases. If the termination condition of Algorithm 1 does not include the restriction of the density in an interval, the merging result will become equal-width partition. On the other hand, if the termination criterion has no distance restriction, then the merging result will be equal-depth partition. Therefore our proposed method is an adaptive method that generalizes the equal-depth and equal-width methods.

5 Conclusion

In this paper, we have introduced an unsupervised discretization method that uses a clustering based criterion to merge adjacent intervals until some termination criterion is reached. The numerical attribute merging algorithm is evaluated in comparison with equal-width and equal-depth discretization methods. Experiment results show that the proposed method gains certain improvement in quantitative association rule mining over these existing methods. This improvement comes from the fact that our method is an adaptive method that generalises both equal-width and equal-depth methods.

References

1. R. Agrawal, T. Imielinski, and A. Swami. Fast algorithms for mining association rules in large database s. In *20th Int'l Conf. on Very Large Databases (VLDA)*, june 1994.
2. J. Catlett. On changing continuous attributes into ordered discrete attributes. In Y. Kodratoff, editor, *Proceedings of the European Working Session on Learning : Machine Learning (EWSL-91)*, volume 482 of *LNAI*, pages 164–178, Porto, Portugal, March 1991. Springer Verlag.
3. Jesús Cerquides and Ramon López de Màntaras. Proposal and empirical comparison of a parallelizable distance-based discretization method. In David Heckerman, Heikki Mannila, Daryl Pregibon, and Ramasamy Uthurusamy, editors, *Proceedings of the Third International Conference on Knowledge Discovery and Data Mining (KDD-97)*, page 139. AAAI Press, 1997.
4. Thierry Van de Merckt. Decision trees in numerical attributes spaces. In *IJCAI-93*, 1993.
5. James Dougherty, Ron Kohavi, and Mehran Sahami. Supervised and unsupervised discretization of continuous features. In *Proc. 12th International Conference on Machine Learning*, pages 194–202. Morgan Kaufmann, 1995.
6. Usama M. Fayyad and Keki B. Irani. Multi-interval discretization of continuous-valued attributes for classification learning. In *IJCAI-93*, 1993.
7. T. Fukuda, Y. Morimoto, S. Morishita, and T. Tokuyama. Mining optimized association rules for numeric attributes. In ACM, editor, *Proceedings of the Fifteenth ACM SIGACT-SIGMOD-SIGART Symposium on Principles of Database Systems, PODS 1996*, volume 15, pages 182–191. ACM Press, 1996.
8. Ron Kohavi and Mehran Sahami. Error-based and entropy-based discretization of continuous features. In Evangelos Simoudis, Jia Wei Han, and Usama Fayyad, editors, *Proceedings of the Second International Conference on Knowledge Discovery and Data Mining*, pages 114–119. AAAI Press.
9. B. Lent, A. Swami, and J. Widom. Clustering association rules. In *Proceedings of the 13th International Conference on Data Engineering (ICDE'97)*, pages 220–231, Washington - Brussels - Tokyo, April 1997. IEEE.
10. Kaufman Leonard and Rousseeuw Peter. *Finding Groups in Data: An Introduction to Cluster Analysis*. Wiley-Interscience Publication, 1990.
11. R. J. Miller and Y. Yang. Association rules over interval data. *SIGMOD Record (ACM Special Interest Group on Management of Data)*, 26(2):452–??, ???? 1997.
12. Jiuyong Li Hong Shen and Paul Pritchard. Knowledge network based association discovery. In *Proc. of 1999 International Conference on Parallel and Distributed Processing Techniques and Applications, (PDPTA'99)*, 1999.
13. Ramakrishnan Srikant and Rakesh Agrawal. Mining quantitative association rules in large relational tables. *SIGMOD Record (ACM Special Interest Group on Management of Data)*, 25(2), 1996.
14. Ke Wang, Soon Hock William Tay, and Bing Liu. Interestingness-based interval merger for numeric association rules. In Rakesh Agrawal, Paul E. Stolorz, and Gregory Piatetsky-Shapiro, editors, *Proc. 4th Int. Conf. Knowledge Discovery and Data Mining, KDD*, pages 121–128. AAAI Press, 1998.

Discovering Tendency Association between Objects with Relaxed Periodicity and its Application in Seismology [1]

Changjie TANG [1]   Rynson W. H. LAU [2]   Huabei YIN [1]   Qing LI [2]
Lu YANG [1]   Zhonghua YU [1]   Limin XIANG [1]   Tianqing ZHANG [1]

[1] Computer Department, Sichuan University, Chengdu, China 610064
chjtang@scu.edu.cn
[2] Department of Computer Science, City University of Hong Kong, Hong Kong
{rynson,csqli}@cityu.edu.hk

Abstract: Relaxed periodicity is proposed to describe loose-`cyclic behavior of objects while allowing uneven stretch or shrink on time axis, limited noises, and inflation / deflation of attribute values. The techniques to mine the relaxed periodicity and the association between objects with relaxed periodicity are studied. The proposed algorithms are tested by the data in the *Seismic database of Annin River area*, and its results are interesting to seismology.

1   Introduction

Recently, the investigations on prediction of natural disaster pay more attention to the periodic phenomena and correlation between objects with periodicity, such as the earthquake and its premonitions (for instance, the earthquake magnitude and the Radon concentration in the groundwater). Usually, the repetitive phenomena in the real world are not strictly periodic in the mathematical sense because of blending with noises and inflation /deflation, or stretching unevenly on the time axis. This kind of phenomena is referred as *Relaxed Periodicity* [1].

Previous researchers have considered periodic phenomena. J. Han et al. [2,3] studied the technique for mining segment-wise periodicity in regard to a fixed length period. It is shown that data cube provides an efficient structure and convenient way for interactive mining of multiple-level periodicity [2]; some good results on the partial periodic patterns are presented in [3]. Ozden et al. investigated the mining of cyclic association rules in [4]. Agrawal et al. proposed fast Similarity search Method in the presence of Noise, Scaling, and Translation in [5]. Sakoe and Chiba proposed dynamic programming algorithm in [6] to solve the stretch and shrink in the time axis, but only considering the full matching in voice recognition. Few attentions were paid to mining the association between objects with relaxed periodicity.

This paper investigates techniques for mining association between objects with relaxed-periodicity.,the main contributions of this article include the following:

- Different from [1], the concept of *tendency* is improved and refined. The tendency itself is now with anti-noise capacity (in old method, anti-noise is coded in

[1]   This project is in part supported by The National Science Foundation of China grant, #69773051 and the Hong Kong CERG grant, #9040339.

algorithm). The definition of tendency can ignore limited noise and determine the tendency of object. The idea is based on the observation that a moving object with inertia can overcome resistance and keep its moving status.

- The *candidate periodicity* with n peaks is introduced, and the *relaxed confidence* is introduced to evaluate the correctness of relaxed periodicity. The relaxed match confidence is introduced to describe similarity of two giving time series. These new concepts make the processing of periodicity simple and easy to understand.
- The method for mining tendency association between objects with relaxed periodicity is proposed. The *Relaxed match confidence* is introduced to describe the association between two objects with relaxed periodicity.
- The proposed algorithms are tested by the *Seismic Database of Annin River Area*. The result shows that there exist some associations between the *earth deforms* and *seismic magnitude* in the sense of relaxed periodicity.

The remainder of the paper is organized as follows. Section 2 surveys related work. Section 3 defines the model for relaxed periodicity. Section 4 describes our algorithms for mining relaxed periodicity from temporal databases. Section 5 discusses the application of relaxed periodicity in seismic study. Section 6 discusses the performance of our algorithms. Finally, a conclusion is given in Section 7.

2   Related works

Finding periodic patterns in time series data (or temporal databases) is a hot topic of KDD [1,2,3,4,5,6]. Some methods have been developed for searching periodicity pattern in large databases. Most of them can be classified into two categories:

(1) Full Periodic Pattern (FPP). This kind of investigation emphasizes the contribution of every time point to the cyclic behavior. For example, FFT (Fast Fourier Transformation) treats the time series as inseparable flows of values. Some researchers considered numerical curve patterns for time series, but only concentrated on symbolic patterns while ignoring other characteristics such as the global tendency. FPP method is scarcely applicable because the strict full periodic phenomena are rare in the real world. The mixture of periodic events and non-periodic events of the real objects makes this method expensive in time and space.

(2) Partial Periodic Pattern (PPP). It specifies the behavior of the time series at some but not all points in time. For example, Mr. Smith reads evening paper from 7:00 p.m to 7:30 p.m every weekday, but his activities at other time do not have such regularity. A series of algorithms based on such patterns have been proposed in [2,3], whose investigations are quite fruitful. But these methods encounter following problems in practice:

- **Intrinsic noises.** Most repetitive behaviors of real objects are not the periodicity in the strict mathematical sense. Usually they are accompanied with intrinsic noises that cannot be eliminated by data cleaning process. For instance, Mr. Smith's shopping list shows that the purchase pinnacle of beverage almost always appears in holidays. But due to the celebration of the birthday of a friend on a weekday, there is an abrupt increase in Mr. Smith's purchase list. The data is correct, but looks like disturbance to the global tendency.
- **The time series are stretching unevenly on the time axis.** The distance of peak to peak (or valley to valley) is unevenly. It looks like stretched or compressed unevenly. This kind of phenomena widely exists in seismic databases.

- **Pre-experiential periodicity.** Previous studies are based on the pre-experiential values of periodicity. But periodicity of many objects in the real world is unknown until our mining processes succeed in, for example, the seism research, weather study, etc..

To solve these problems, we propose the *Anti-Noise Algorithm for Relaxed Periodicity* mining (ANRP Algorithm) in this paper.

3 Preliminary Concepts

To formally describe the mining techniques of tendency association of objects with relaxed periodicity, we need some preliminary concepts.

3.1 Logical chronon, Interval and Time Series

In our model, the *logical chronon* (or time granularity) is the smallest time interval configured by the user(s). The logical chronon can be configured as Second, Minute, Hour, Day, Ten-days、Month、Quarter and Year etc.. The start time point of our system is denoted as 0, the k-th chronon is denoted as k. The system time domain is denoted as $Sys\_T=\{0,1,2,...,k,...Now,...,MaxSysTime\}$. The subset $\{t,t+1,t+2,..., t+n=t'\}$ of Sys_T, is denoted as $[t, t']$, and is called time interval. The number of chronons in that interval, i.e. n, is called the length of time interval. It is easy to see that the chronon t_k is the same as interval $[t_k, t_{K+1})$. The others temporal concepts can be found in [7].

The event domain, denoted as EventDom, is the domain of the measurement of the events we considered. An event related to object obj, occurred at chronon t and with the measurement value e, is denoted as $e_t(obj)$,or simply e_t if obj is understood. The time-ordered set of events related to obj is denoted as $E(obj)=\{e_{i+1},e_{i+2},...,e_{i+n}\}$. $E(obj)=\{e_{i+1},e_{i+2},...,e_{i+n}\}$ is called the time series. The interval $[i+1,i+n]$ is called the life span of the time series E(obj). Time series can be retrieved from temporal database, text, historical database, log file, or HTML files. These concepts are generally compatible with the concepts in [2,3].

3.2 Tendency and its Inertia in Time Series

Tendency reflects the trend of a computable object varying with time. There are five kinds of tendency: Up, Peak, Down, Valley, and Unknown. To overcome the noise, we introduce the inertia of tendency. In fact, inertia of tendency reflects the essential property of object. For example, in the stock market, a small shakeout can not disturb the up tendency of the stock of a big company, but may turn the stock of the small company weakened. The idea is borrowed from the intuition from kinetics and kinematics. Notice that although the concept of tendency shares some similarity with the Trend in [1], the concept here is essentially different. Here the inertia of object is considered as constant and measured as capacity to overcome noise.

The idea to define tendency of an object at specific time point is as follows. In addition to checking values at specific points, we check the object status at previous and next time point, then define tendency according to the intuition and the semantic meaning with anti-noise capabilities. If the noise is smaller than the threshold, then it keeps the previous tendency by inertia.

To formalize above observations, we now define the *Tendency*.

Definition 1. (Tendency) Let E(obj)={$e_{i+1}, e_{i+2}, ..., e_{i+n}$} be a time series, [t, t'] be the life span of E(obj), g be the current logical chronon (i.e. time granularity), TendencyType be the enumerate set {Up, Peak, Down, Valley, Unknown}.

(1) The tendency map of object obj is the map from the Tendency of Attribute to TendencyType:

ObjTendency: [t, t'] →TendencyType

Its value ObjTendency(t,obj) is called the tendency of obj at time t.

(2) L= Length ([t, t'])/g is called the number of checkpoints for object obj. The Set TimeArray = {t_k| t_k=t+gk, 0<=k<=L} is called the Time array for object obj. The set TendencyArray = {V_k | V_k = ObjTendency(t_k,obj), 0<=k<L} is called the Tendency Array of obj, whose k-th member is denoted as ObjTendency [k].

Definition 2. Let EventDom be the event domain, E(obj)={$e_{i+1}, e_{i+2}, ..., e_{i+n}$} be a time series, *Left, Middle, Right* be three adjoining time point in the life span of the time series E(obj). Let InertiaV in EventDom be the inertia value of obj.

The tendency of obj at *middle* is defined by checking the tendency at *Left*, and the values at *middle, left* and *Right*, and determined as Table-1.

Note that, InertiaV is in Event Domain. It is measured as the anti-noise capacity of object. For simplicity, here we consider the Inertia of obj to be a constant. It is easy to extend this definition for variable inertia.

	If		Then define
Tendency of *Left*	The relation between *Left* and *Middle*	the relation between *Middle* and *Right*	Tendency of *Middle*
up	*Left <= Middle* + InertiaV	*Middle* + InertiaV < *Right*	Up
	Left <= Middle + InertiaV	*Middle* + InertiaV >= *Right*	Peak
Peak	*Left >= Middle* − InertiaV	*Middle* − InertiaV > *Right*	Down
	Left >= Middle − InertiaV	*Middle* − InertiaV <= *Right*	Peak
Down	*Left > Middle* + InertiaV	*Middle* − InertiaV > *Right*	Down
	Left > Middle + InertiaV	*Middle* − InertiaV <= *Right*	Valley
Valley	*Left < Middle* − InertiaV	*Middle* + InertiaV < *Right*	Up
	Left < Middle − InertiaV	*Middle* + InertiaV >= *Right*	Valley

Table1. The definition of the tendency at *Middle* in Definition 2.

3.3 Peak-Valley Series and Relaxed Periodicity

Definition 3 (Peak-Valley Series). Let E(obj)={a_1, a_2, ...,a_m} be the time series.

(1) a_k is said to be a *peak* value if $a_{i-1}< a_i= a_{i+1}=...=a_j>a_{j+1}$; k = Round ((j + i)/2), 1<=k<=m.

(2) a_k is said to be a *valley* value if $a_{i-1}> a_i= a_{i+1}=...=a_j<a_{j+1}$; k = Round ((j + i)/2), 1<=k<=m.

(3) The sub series of E(obj) consisting of all peak values of E(obj) is called the *peak series* of object obj. The sub series of E(obj) consisting of all peak and valley values of E(obj) is called the *peak-valley Series* of object obj.

(4) A peak-valley series containing n peaks is referred as *n-Span*.

Definition 4 (Candidate periodicity with n peaks). Let E(obj)=$\{a_1, a_2, ...,a_n\}$ be the time series, Peaks = $\{P_1,P_2,...,P_i,...,P_j,...,P_r\}$ be r adjoining peaks of the object obj, and symbol Time(P_j) denote the time of the peak P_j, n=j-i,where r>=j>i, i,j$\in$[1..m], then CP(n)=Time(P_j)–Time(P_i) is said to be a *candidate periodicity* with n peaks.

Note that, candidate periodicity with n peaks, i.e. CP(n), in fact , is a span of n peaks. Different from the periodicity in the usual sense, the confidence of CP(n) is unknown until our mining process successfully stops. Furthermore, CP(n) is not a constant in the peak-valley series, and hence it does not reflect the global repetitive behavior of the object.

Because the indeterminacy of candidate periodicity with n peaks, we use confidence to measure its correctness, which tells us that how often CP(n) repeats in the time series. Formally we have:

Definition 5 (Relaxed confidence of candidate periodicity). Let the context be as that in the above definitions, gap>=0 be a predefined number. The *relaxed confidence* of candidate periodicity with n peaks and with length of TimeLength is defined as: Relaxed_Confidence_CP(n,TimeLength,gap)=Numerator/Denominator, where Numerator is the number of candidate periodicity satisfying |CP(n)-TimeLength|<=gap, and Denominator is the total number of candidate periodicity with n peaks.

It is easy to see that when gap=0, the relaxed confidence degenerates as traditional confidence. To calculate the Denominator in above definition, we have following:

Lemma 1. Let Peaks=$\{P_1,P_2,...,P_r\}$ be the peak series of object obj and n<=r. The number of candidate periodicity with n peaks is r-n+1.
Proof. It is easy to see that for each i, 1<=i<=r-n+1 , the set $\{P_i,P_{i+1},...,P_{i+n-1}\}$ contains adjoining n peaks, and P_{i+n-1} - P_i is a candidate periodicity. Thus the total number of candidate periodicity is r-n+1.

Definition 6 (Relaxed periodicity). Let the context be as that of the above defini-tions. Let MinConfidence be the minimal confidence (configured by the user). Let CP(n) be a candidate periodicity of n peaks, C be the relaxed confidence of CP(n). If C>=MinConfidence, then CP(n) is called a relaxed periodicity with confidence not less than MinConfidence, or simply, relaxed periodicity when MinConfidence is understood.

From the definition it is clear that the idea to find a relaxed periodicity is:
(1) Take any n adjoining peaks $P_i,P_{i+1},...,P_{i+n-1}$, CP(n)=$P_{i+n-1}$ - P_i is a candidate periodicity.
(2) Scanning the time series, calculate the confidence of CP(n).
(3) If its confidence is big enough (i.e., greater than a pre-defined threshold MinConfidence), then the candidate periodicity CP(n) is promoted to be a relaxed periodicity.

Example 1 Figure1 illustrates the concepts defined in this section.. f(t) is the time considered. It reaches its Peak at t_i (i = 1, 2, 3, ... , 9). Spans (2-Peaks, 3-Peaks, ...) and Relaxed candidate Periodicity (RP-2, RP-3, ...) are also shown in Figure 1. Here we assume gap=0 for the simplicity.

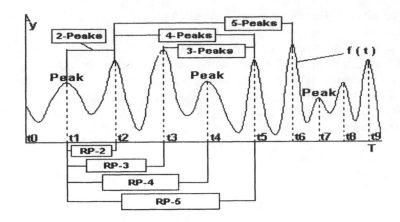

Figure1. Example 1

4 The tendency association of objects with relaxed periodicity

4.1 Get time series

According to the concepts in Section 3, it is easy to retrieve the time series from a temporal database, a text, or a log file. To mine the association between objects with relaxed periodicity, we need time series of two objects, denoted as Time_Serial_1 and Time_Serial_2. The attribute values concerned and time stamp must be kept in the time series. The result can be stored in the following format:

Time_Serial_X(time-stamp,attribute1,attribute2,....,attributeT),

where X=1,2; T=1,2,...

4.2 Get the Tendency Series

The Algorithm 1 in the following can *mine* the tendency series from time series. Different from the original time series, the tendency series ignore the exact attribute values, but concentrate on tendency of the object.

Algorithm 1. (The anti-noise tendency algorithm with inertia)
Input: Database including concerned attributes, inertia of the object.
Output: Tendency Series.
Steps:
(1) Retrieve the time series from database, stored in $\{a_1, a_2, ...,a_m\}$.
(2) Decide the tendency of a_1 by comparing a_1 and a_2. The value falls in {Peak, Valley}.
(3) For (i=2; i<m; i++)
$\quad$ {Left=a_i; Middle=a_{i+1}; Right=a_{i+2};
$\quad\quad$ Determine the tendency of middle according to the Table-1.}
(4) Decide the tendency of a_m by comparing a_{m-1} and a_m. The values falls in {Peak, Valley}.
$\quad$ Note that in this algorithm, if two adjacent records have the same values on the

concerned attribute, then they will have the same tendency. Thus it is possible that more than one peak (or valley) can appear in an adjacent position, such as the following tendency series shows: Peak--down--down--valley--valley--up--peak--peak--down.

4.3 Get Peak-valley Series

The Algorithm 2 can mine the Peak_Valley Series from Tendency Series.

Algorithm 2 Get Peak-Valley Series
Input: Tendency Series.
Output: Peak _Valley series.
Steps:
(1) Result = Input;
(2) Scan Result for adjoining peak (valley). If there are k adjacent peaks (valleys), keep the middle peak (valley), i.e. the [k/2]-th peak(valley), and delete rest (k-1) peaks(valleys).
(3) Delete all Up and Down from Result.

4.4 Mine the relaxed periodicity

Giving a predefined minimal confidence MinConfidence, the Algorithm 3 can mine the relaxed periodicity with relaxed confidence not less than MinConfidence.

Algorithm 3. Mine the relaxed periodicity.
Input: Peak_Valley_Series;
       MaxSpan, //the maximum span for candidate periodicity - a positive integer
       MinSpan , //the minimum span for candidate periodicity - a positive integer
       MaxTimeLength,   // It is a multiple of logical Chronon
       Min_Confidence, Gap, // two predefined numbers
Output: Relaxed Periodicity P and its confidence C.
Procedure GetRelaxedPeriods( )
for (i= 2;MinSpan<=i<MaxSpan; i ++)
  for (TimeLength=1; TimeLength <= MaxTimeLenth; TimeLength++)
    scan Peak_Valley_Series calculate total_Peaks;
    Total_i_span = total_Peaks – i + 1; // number of i-span; see Definition 3 and
                                // Lemma 1.
    Valid_i_Span = number of i-Span that satisfying |RP(i)- TimeLength| <= Gap;
    confid = Valid_i_Span /Total_i_Span;
  }
if (confid >= Min_Confidence) {
  C = confid; P = TimeLength; // output
  Output "P as relaxed periodicity of i peaks, confidence = C";
}.

Example 2. Applying Algorithm 3 to the time series of seismic magnitude retrieved from the data warehouse for *Annin River Area*, the result is shown in Table 2. Here, TLen means Time Length. k-Span means a span contains k peaks, and the logical Chronon is Ten_days. We can explain the result of Table 2 by examining specfic cells. For instance, the first cell (with Span = 2-span, TLen=2, and the relaxed confidence = 0.7194) has the following meaning: in the seismic history segment of that area, there are many seismic magnitude peaks. Among them, about 0.71% spans with two peaks satisfying |length -20 days|<=gap, where gap is a small number (say, 1 day). Note that when TLen=11, the confidences for 3-span,4-span,5-span and 6-span are relatively high. This tells us that 11 chronon (i.e. 110 days) has a special seismic meaning to that area, which implies that there may be some interesting rules to be revealed.

Span / TLen	2-Span	3-Span	4-Span	5-Span	6-Span
2	0.71				
3	0.3597				
4	8.9928				
5	0.3597	0.361			
6	18.705	0.361	2.8986		
7	0.3597	0.631	0.3623		
8	26.6187	8.3032	0.3623	27.6364	
•9	43.8848	0.361	0.3623	9.8182	
10		0.361	0.3623	2.1818	
•11		48.0144	0.7246	0.3636	27.7372
12			0.3623	0.3636	11.3139
13		31.7689	0.3623	3.6364	0.3649
14		31.7689	4.3478	0.3636	1.4599
15			14.4927	0.3636	0.7299
16			26.4492	1.0909	0.3649
17			0.3623	2.5455	0.3649
•18			48.1884	5.4545	0.3649
•19			0.3623	41.4545	0.3649
20					4.3796
21				4.3636	5.1095
•22				0.3636	41.6058
23					
24					4.7445

Table2. The result of Algorithm3 for seismic magnitude (C=m %)

4.4 Mine the association between two peak-valley series

In the mathematical sense, it is easy to understand that the associations of two peak-valley series can be classified into the following types:

- Synchronization. Two series get the peak and valley at the same time.
- Fixed time delay. One series is behind another series with fixed time delay. Like sin(x) and cos(x).
- Reversal phase. Like sin(x) and -sin(x),

Seismologists observe that when the Radon concentration in the groundwater reaches a specific level, the seismic magnitude will also reach to a specific level. Scanning the time series of seismic magnitude and time series for *Radon concentration in the groundwater*, seismologists have found synchronization in the sense of relaxed periodicity. The attributes synchronizing with earthquake are called seismic premonitions. It is very useful in prediction of earthquake.

In many cases, two peak-valley series are running with fixed phase difference. When first object gets the i-th peak, delaying for a phase time, the second object gets its i-th peak. Usually, the peak of the first object is regarded as a prediction for the corresponding peak of the second object, which is very useful in event predication. To formalize this observation we introduce the following:

Definition 7 (Relaxed match confidence) Let S1 and S2 be two peak-valley series.

(1) The peak-valley series check condition is the condition expression of relational algebra (such as (Age>10 and Age<25 or salary<1000)).

(2) Let Cond1 and Cond2 be peak-valley series check conditions for S1 and S2, respectively, and both do not involve time attributes. Let Correlation be one of the values in {Synchronization, Fixed time-delay, Reversal-phase}, Gap be a non-negative number.
Then *Relaxed match confidence* is defined as

Relaxed_ Match _Confidence(S1,S2,Correlation,Cond1,Cond2,Gap)
=Numerator/ Denominator

Where Numerator is the number of records satisfying Correlation with error less than gap, and Denominator is the number of records in series S1 satisfying Cond1.

Note that in the above definition, S1 and S2 are not symmetry; also, when gap = 0, relaxed match confidence gets degenerated to traditional mach confidence.

Algorithm 4 (Naive evaluation algorithm for relaxed match confidence)
Input: Two peak-valley series S1 and S2, Correlation
Cond1, Cond2, Logical Chronon, Gap, which is a non-negative number.
Output: Relaxed match confidence.
Steps: (SQL-like)
(1)   Select TimeStamp, attribute concerned into TempR1
(2)   From peak-valley Series S1
(3)   Where Cond1 is true.
(4)   Select TimeStamp, Attribute concerned into TempR2
(5)   From peak-valley Series S2
(6)   Where Cond2 is true.
(7)   Select TimeStamp, Attribute concerned
(8)   From R1, R2
(9)   Where Correlation match error is not greater than gap.

Theorem 1 Let the context be as that of Algorithm 4. Suppose the sizes of two time series are m and n, respectively. Then the complexity of Algorithm 4 is $O(m*n+m+n)$. *Proof.* In Algorithm 4, the sentences 1-3 just scan the first time series of size m. The computation complexity can be evaluated by $O(m)$. Similarly, the computation involved in sentences 4-6 can be evaluated by $O(n)$, Sentences 7-9 are doing a join operation, and complexity is $O(m*n)$. Thus the total complexity is $O(m*n+m+n)$.

Theorem 1 shows that Algorithm 4 is a naive algorithm whose idea is simple, yet efficiency needs to be improved. (The improving work will be discussed elsewhere.)

5 Application and Testing in seismic database

Annin River Area (or referred as Anninhe) is a geometric area with geometric fault structure located in Sichuan province. It covers about 150 KM^2 in the intensely active status. The seismic database for Sichuan Province is a large database. The data we concerned in this paper are the "Earthquake catalog from 1970 to 1995 at Anninhe", and "Earth deform database from 1986 to 1996 at Anninhe". We prepare the data by traditional methods, i.e., to reorganize a small data warehouse for our testing purpose. After data cleaning, the total number of records is about 12000.

5.1 Mining the relaxed periodicity for earthquake magnitude

(1) By Algorithm 1, mine out the Tendency series for each time point related to the seismic catalog.
(2) By Algorithm 2, mine out the peak-valley Series from Tendency series.
(3) By Algorithm 3, mine out the relaxed periodicity of earthquake and their complete support ratio from peak-valley series. The results are as shown in Fig.2.

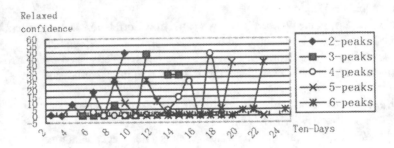

Figure 2. The relaxed periodicity of earthquake and relaxed confidence.

5.2 Mining the relaxed periodicity for Earth deform

The procedure is similar to above. Figure 3 shows the earth deform in two directions.

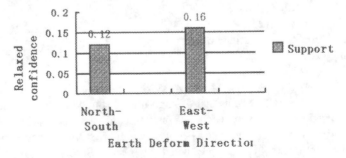

Figure 3. The earth Deform in two directions.

5.3 Mine the association of Earthquake and Earth deform

(1) Set Min_confidence=25%, the relaxed periodicity for the peak-valley series of

earthquake is shown in Table 3, where the logical chronon (i.e., the Time granularity) is ten-days,

(2) Set Min_confidence=40%, the relaxed periodicity for the peak-valley series of earthquake is shown in Table 4, where the logical chronon is ten-days,

From Tables 3 and 4, we can see that there are 11 relaxed priorities with confidence>25% and 5 relaxed priorities with confidence>40. The confidence is big enough. Furthermore, the same periodicity with different span has different confidence. Among them, the relaxed periodicity of 11 Chronons (that is, 110 days) has no less than one higher confidence. Thus we conclude that 11 chronons is a relative stable relaxed periodicity.

(3) Set configures as follows: Condition1="The_Earth_Deform=Peak", Condition2 ="Earth_Quake=Peak and Magnitude>3" and Correlation="TimeDelay=30 days". By Algorithm 4, we mine the association between the relaxed periodicity of the earthquake magnitude and the relaxed periodicity of the deform of earth. The result and explanation are shown in Table 5.

The above results are interesting to seismologists. As the seismic behavior is very complicated, it is not easy for people to get the intuition by reviewing the picture or curves. The results may be surprising to some people and worth further seismic study.

Span	Relaxed Periodicity (confidence)
2-Peaks	8 (26.6187%); 9 (43.8848%)
3-Peaks	11(48.0144%);13(31.7689%); 14(31.7189%)
4-Peaks	15 (26.4492%); 18 (48.1884%)
5-Peaks	8 (27.6364%); 19 (41.4545%)
6-Peaks	11 (27.7372%); 22 (41.6058%)

Table 3. Mining Peak_valley Series for Earthquake magnitude (Min_Support=25%).

Span	Relaxed Periodicity (confidence)
2-peaks	9 (43.8848%)
3-peaks	11 (48.0144%)
4-peaks	18 (48.1884%)
5-peaks	19 (41.4545%)
6-peaks	22 (41.6058%)

Table 4. Mining peak-valley Series for Earthquake magnitude (Min_Support=40%).

Earth Deform Direction	Support Ratio	Explanation
North-South	5/49	A month later than the peak of Earth Deform in this direction, there are 5 earthquake with magnitude>3,
East-West	8/50	A month later than the peak of Earth Deform in this direction, there are 8 earthquake with magnitude > 3,

Table 5. The association between the time series of Earthquake and earth deform.

6 The performance of algorithms

We have presented four algorithms to mine the association between two time series with relaxed periodicity. The performance of these algorithms and the testing environment are as follows: CPU: Pentium II 200 with 32MB RAM.Test data: "earthquake catalog from 1970 to 1995", 6000 records., " earth deform database from 1986 to 1996", 6000 records.

Algorithms:	1	2	3	4
Execution time:	60s	70s	10s	10s

Hence, the main costs in time are used for data cleaning and pre-processing. The performance of the algorithms is not very fast, but acceptable.

7 Summary

Mining association between objects with relaxed periodicity is useful in prediction of natural disasters, especially in seismic premonition's study. The method to mine the association between two time series with relaxed periodicity is proposed, and four algorithms are implemented with acceptable performance. Theorem 1 shows that Algorithm 4 is still naive, and its efficiency remains to be improved. Thus the current investigation is still preliminary and much further research needs to be done.

References

1. C. Tang, Z. Yu, and T. Zhang, "Discover Relaxed Periodicity In Temporal Databases," *Proc. of the Int. Conference on Database System for Advanced Application*, April 1999.

2. J. Han, W. Gong, and Y. Yin, "Mining Segment-wise Periodic Pattern in Time Related Databases," *Proc. of the International Conference on Knowledge Discovery and Data Mining*, Aug. 1998, 177-181.

3. J. Han, G. Dong, and Y. Yin, "Efficient Mining of Partial Periodic Patterns in Time Series Database", 15th International Conference on Data Engineering (ICDE99), Sydney, Australia, March 23-26, 1999.

4. B. Ozden, S. Ramaswamy, and A. Silberschatz, "Cyclic Association Rules," *Proc. of IEEE International Conference Data Engineering*, pp. 412-421, 1998.

5. R. Agrawal, K. Ling, H. Sawhney, and K. Shim, "Fast Similarity Search in the Presence of Inertia, Scaling, and Translation in Time-Series Databases," *Proc. of VLDB*, 1995.

6. H. Sakoe, and S. Chiba, "Dynamic Programming Algorithm Optimization for Spoken Word Recognition," *Readings In speech Recognition*, Eds. Waibel and Lee, pp. 159-165, Morgan Kaufman, 1990.

7. A. Tansel et al, *Temporal Databases - Theory, Design and Implementation*, The Benjamin/Cummings Publishing Company, pp. 418-455, 1997.

8. U. Fayyad and G. Piatetsky-Shapiro, *Advanced in Knowledge Discover and Data Mining*, AAAI Press and The MIT Press, 1996.

9. X. Wang, C. Zhang, and X. Pen, "Basic Segmentation Characteristics on Late Quaternary Anninghe Active Faults," In *Earthquake Research in Sichuan*, pp. 51-61, 1998.

10. W. Cheng, "The Association Between Active Statistics Seismic Data," *The Research of Medium-term and Short-term Seismic Prediction in Sichuan*, Chengdu Map Publishing House, pp. 49-55, 1994.

Algebraic Operations on Bags in a Web Warehouse*

S. S. Bhowmick[1]   S. K. Madria[2]   W. -K. Ng[1]   E.P. Lim[1]
{p517026,wkn,aseplim}@ntu.edu.sg, skm@cs.purdue.edu

[1] Center for Advanced Information Systems, School of Applied Science,
Nanyang Technological University, Singapore 639798, SINGAPORE

[2] Department of Computer Science,
Purdue University, West Lafayette, IN 47907

Abstract

In this paper, we discuss various algebraic operations on *web bags* in the context of our *web warehousing project* called WHOWEDA (WareHouse Of WEb DAta). Informally, a web bag is a *web table* which allows multiple occurrences of *identical web tuples*. We examine how some of the web operations such as *web union*, *web intersection*, *web join* and *local web coupling* behave in the context of web bags. Our study reveals that the presence of identical web tuples accentuate the computational efficiency of some of the web algebraic operators.

1 Introduction

Sets and *bags* are closely related structures. When a set is allowed to have multiple occurrences of an element, it is called a bag or multi-set. While sets have been studied intensively by the database community, relational bags have recently received attention for various reasons [9]. Recently, there has been increased research interest in data models and query languages for Web data [8]. However, we are not aware of any work that addresses the concept of bags in the context of a web warehouse.

We have introduced *web bag* in a web warehouse as a part of our *Web Information Coupling Systems* (WICS) in [3]. WICS is one of the components of our web warehousing system, called WHOWEDA (*Warehouse Of Web Data*) [1, 5] which we are currently building. It is a system for managing and manipulating coupled information extracted from the Web. WICS is based on a collection of methods for organizing Web data centered on the notion of *web table*. For more details about WICS, the reader is referred to [6].

We are interested in the three components of web bag in the context of Web data: (1) resolving the limitations of search-engines and existing web query systems. Specifically, how web bag can help us to discover knowledge related to

* This work was supported in part by the Nanyang Technological University, Ministry of Education (Singapore) under Academic Research Fund #4-12034-5060, #4-12034-3012, #4-12034-6022. Any opinions, findings, and recommendations in this paper are those of the authors and do not reflect the views of the funding agencies.

(a) Query graph (web schema) of 'Diseases'. (b) Query graph (web schema) of 'Drugs'.

Fig. 1. Query graphs (web schema).

query traversed path, visible documents or web sites, luminous documents or web sites [2, 3]; (2) analyzing different web algebraic operations with respect to web bags; and (3) performing a cost benefit analysis with respect to storage, transmission and operational cost of web bags and analyzing issues and implication of materializing web bags as opposed to web tables containing distinct web tuples. We have studied (1) and (3) in [3] and [4] respectively. We therefore do not discuss components (1) and (3) further in this paper. This paper addresses the component (2). We examine how web algebraic operations are affected when they are applied over web bags instead of web tables containing distinct web tuples. In particular, we show how the web operations such as *web select*, *local web coupling*, *web join*, *web union* and *web intersect* are affected due to the presence of duplicate web tuples in a web bag.

2   Background

Informally, a web bag is a web table containing multiple occurrences of *identical web tuples*. A web tuple is a set of inter-linked documents retrieved from the WWW which satisfies a *query graph* or *web schema* [5]. In WICS, a user specifies a query using a query graph. A query graph is a directed, connected graph consisting of *node* and *link variables* and *constraints* over some or all of these variables in the form of predicates and connectivities. Figure 1(a) is an example of a query graph specified by an user. When a query graph is evaluated using global web coupling operator [5], it may return a set of inter-linked documents (called web tuples) by retrieving those portions of Web that match the structure and constraints specified in the query graph. We materialize the set of web tuples retrieved from the Web satisfying the query graph in the form of a *web table*. Then we assign the query graph as the web schema of the materialized web table. We have defined a set of web algebraic operators such as *web select*, *web project*, *web join*, *web union*, *local web coupling*, etc. with web semantics to manipulate web tables [5].

A web bag may only be created by eliminating some of the nodes from web tuples of a web table using the *web project* operator [3]. A web project operator is used to isolate data of interest, allowing subsequent queries to run over a smaller, perhaps more structured web data. Unlike its relational counterpart, a web project operator does not eliminate *identical* web tuples autonomously.

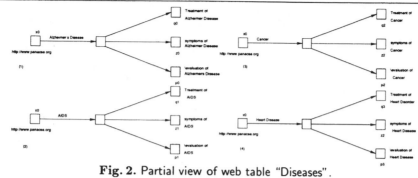

Fig. 2. Partial view of web table "Diseases".

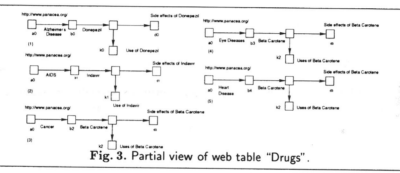

Fig. 3. Partial view of web table "Drugs".

Thus, the projected web table may contain identical web tuples (web bag). The duplicate elimination process is initiated explicitly by a user. The justification for not eliminating duplicate web tuples autonomously is three fold. First, existence of identical web tuples (web bag) enables us to discover useful knowledge (visible documents, luminous documents and luminous paths) from a web table [3]. Second, existence of duplicate web tuples in a web table eliminates the cost of duplicate removal from that web table [4]. Third, the computational efficiency of some of the web operation may increase if a web table contains identical tuples. The following example briefly illustrates the notion of web project and web bag.

Example 1. Assume that there is a web site at http://www.panacea.org/ which stores disease and drug related information. Suppose a user, Bill wishes to find the following information at two instants of time t_1 and t_2: (1) A list of diseases and their symptoms, treatment and evaluation strategies and (2) a list of drugs for various diseases, their side effects and uses. These queries are specified as two query graphs as shown in Figures 1(a) and 1(b) respectively. The query graph are evaluated using global web coupling [5] operator and a set of results in the form of web tuples satisfying each query graph is stored in web tables **Diseases** and **Drugs** respectively (Figures 2 and 3).

Suppose Bill now wants to extract information related to side effects of drugs used for various diseases using WICS. Clearly, this information is already stored in table **Drugs**. Moreover, Bill may wish to eliminate the instances of node variables b and k since these nodes are irrelevant to his needs. The elimination of

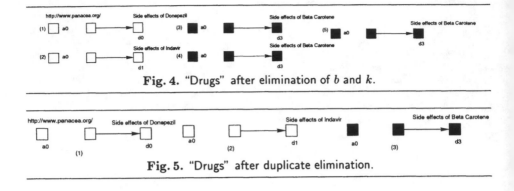

Fig. 4. "Drugs" after elimination of b and k.

Fig. 5. "Drugs" after duplicate elimination.

these node variables can be performed by the web project operator and the resultant collection of web tuples is shown in Figure 4. The third, fourth and fifth web tuples (each web tuple depicted as a set of black nodes) in the figure are identical (URL of instances of node variables and the *connectivities* of each web tuple are identical to other) and thus, the collection of web tuples form a web bag. A user may explicitly initiate the elimination of duplicate tuples (fourth and the fifth tuples in this case). The web table created after the removal of identical web tuples is shown in Figure 5. ∎

3   Web Algebraic Operations

We have introduced a set of web algebraic operators to manipulate information residing in web tables in [6, 5]. In this section, we discuss how some of the web operations such as *web select*, *web union*, *web intersection*, *web join* and *local web coupling* behave when they are operated on web bags instead of web tables with distinct web tuples.

3.1   Web Select on Bag

The **select** operation on a web bag is similar to that of on a web table [5]. It extract web tuples from a web bag satisfying certain conditions. The selection conditions are expressed as predicates on node and link variables, as well as connectivities of web tuples. We apply the selection condition to each web tuple independently. As always with web bags, we do not eliminate duplicate web tuples in the result. The **web select** operation augments the schema of a web bag by incorporating additional conditions into the schema. Note that the creation of a web bag after web select operation depends on the selection conditions. It is not necessary that a select operation on a web bag will always result in a web bag. It may also create a web table with distinct web tuples if the identical web tuples in the input web bag does not satisfy the selection conditions. Furthermore, we can augment the structure of a web bag by keeping a pointer to link all the identical web tuples in each multiplets. In this case, web select operation is applied only on one of the web tuple in the multiplet and all other identical web tuples are returned automatically. Thus, the computational cost can be reduced by the

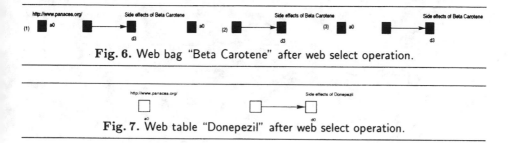

Fig. 6. Web bag "Beta Carotene" after web select operation.

Fig. 7. Web table "Donepezil" after web select operation.

application of web select on web bags. We illustrate web select operation on a web bag with an example given below:

Example 2. Consider the web bag in Figure 4. Suppose we wish to select all the web tuples containing the side effects of **Beta Carotene**. The selection condition is expressed as predicate on the node variable d, i.e., instances of d must contain the keyword "Beta Carotene". The last three web tuples in Figure 4 meets the selection condition. The resultant collection of web tuples is stored in **Beta Carotene** and are shown in Figure 6. Note that Figure 6 is a web bag since all the web tuples are identical. Thus, a web select on a web bag may result in a web bag. However, if we wish to store only distinct web tuples then we eliminate the identical web tuples from the selected collection of web tuples.

Now, suppose we wish to select all the web tuples containing the side effects of **Donepezil**. The first web tuple in Figure 5 meets the selection condition. Hence the result is a web table with one web tuple (Figure 7). Thus, the creation of web bag after web select operation depends on the selection condition. ∎

3.2 Web Join and Local Web Coupling on Bags

We have introduced the concept of web join and local web coupling in [7] and [6] respectively. Local web coupling and web join may be used to gather useful, composite information from two web tables. Local web coupling provides a means to manipulate information residing in a web warehouse to derive additional useful information. Given two web tables or web bags, local coupling is initiated explicitly by specifying a pair(s) of web documents and a set of keyword(s) to relate them. The result of local web coupling is a web table consisting of a set of collections of inter-related Web documents from the two input tables. The web join operator, on the other hand, combines two web tables or web bags by *concatenating* a web tuple of one table or web bag with a web tuple of other table whenever there exists *joinable nodes* (documents with identical URL and last modification date).

Although it is advantageous to couple related information from two web tables using local web coupling and web join operators, these operators may also combine irrelevant information. The existence of irrelevant information in the result of web join or local web coupling operation increases the size of the resultant web table. This adversely affects the storage cost of coupled or joined

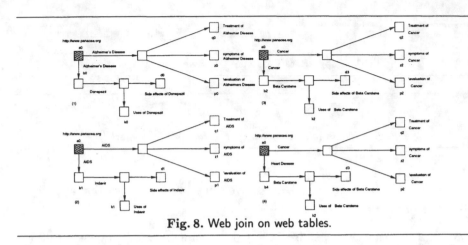

Fig. 8. Web join on web tables.

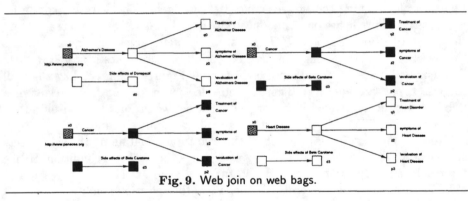

Fig. 9. Web join on web bags.

web table and increases the cost of subsequent web operations. Thus, a web project operation preceding web join or local web coupling enables us to filter out these irrelevant information from the input web tables and thus, reduces the cost of subsequent web operation.

A web project operation on the input web tables may create web bags. Thus, local web coupling or web join may be performed over web bags in lieu of web tables. If we allow web bags then the total number of nodes in the resultant web bag created by web join or web coupling operation will be lesser than that in the web table created by directly performing web join or web coupling on the input web tables (web join or local web coupling operation not preceded by web project operation). However, the total number of web tuples in the resultant web bag or web table in both these cases will be identical. If we do not allow web bag then there is an overhead of removing duplicate web tuples from the input web tables. However, the joined or coupled web table will not only contain lesser number of nodes, but also fewer web tuples (due to the elimination of some web tuples in the input web tables) compared to the web table created by direct application of web join or local web coupling on the input web tables. Thus, removal of duplicate web tuples from input web tables will result in a joined

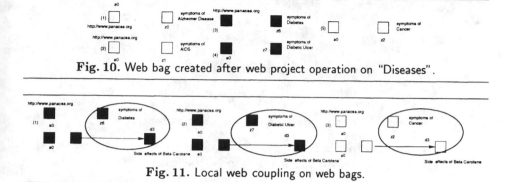

Fig. 10. Web bag created after web project operation on "Diseases".

Fig. 11. Local web coupling on web bags.

or coupled web tables with optimum storage cost, compared to that of allowing web bag as the result of web join or web coupling operation. However, if the cost of duplicate elimination is greater than the saving in storage cost (compared to that of the web bag) then it is beneficial to store the result of web join or local web coupling as a web bag. We illustrate web join operation on bags in the following example:

Example 3. Suppose Bill wishes to find the symptoms, evaluation strategies and treatment of various diseases along with drugs for these diseases and their side effects. Clearly, these information are already stored in tables **Diseases** (Figure 2) and **Drugs** (Figure 3). The web join operator enables us to compute these related information from the two web tables. In particular, web join concatenates web tuples in the web tables based on the joinable nodes (a and x in Figures 1(a) and 1(b) since they have identical URL). A portion of the joined web table is shown in Figure 8. The patterned boxes in Figures 8 and 9 refers to the joinable nodes over which concatenation of the web tuples is performed respectively. Each web tuple in the joined web table contains information related to the symptoms, treatment and evaluation procedures of a particular disease, and a drug with their uses and side effects.

However, the above web join operation may also couple irrelevant information. The node variables related to list of drugs and their uses (node variables b and k) are irrelevant for Bill in the above example. But these irrelevant information are present in the joined web table (Figure 8) as web join operation does not provide a mechanism to the user to eliminate these irrelevant node variables. Thus, Bill may wish to eliminate the node variables b and k using web project operation before performing a web join. If we allow web bags then the web project operation creates a web bag as shown in Figure 4. Performing a web join between the web table **Diseases** (Figure 2) and the web bag in Figure 4, the partial view of resultant collection of joined web tuples is shown in Figure 9. Note that the collection of joined web tuples contains identical web tuples (second and third web tuples in Figure 9) and forms a web bag. The size of each web tuple in Figure 9 is smaller than the corresponding joined web tuple in Figure 8. Moreover, each tuple in Figure 9 does not contain irrelevant information. ∎

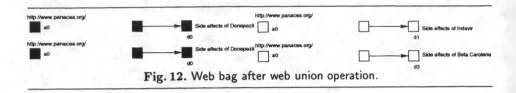

Fig. 12. Web bag after web union operation.

We now depict local web coupling operation on web bags.

Example 4. Suppose Bill wishes to extract those web tuples in Diseases and Drugs in which the symptoms of various diseases and side effects of drugs contains "liver problem". Suppose Bill removes irrelevant nodes from Diseases by eliminating all nodes excluding those containing list of diseases (x) and symptoms of diseases (z) using web project operation. The resultant collection of web tuples is shown in Figure 10. Assume that the symptoms of diabetes and diabetic ulcer are identical and they represent the same web document. Thus the third and fourth web tuples (tuples with black nodes) in Figure 10 are identical and they form a web bag.

Suppose we perform local web coupling operation on the web bags in Figure 10 and Figure 4 on the node variables z and d based on the keyword "liver problem". We assume that one of the side effects of the drug Beta Carotene is "liver problem" and the symptoms of diabetes, diabetic ulcer and cancer includes "liver problem". The partial view of the collection of web tuples created after local web coupling operation is depicted in Figure 11. Each coupled web tuple is constructed by integrating relevant web tuples from Diseases and Drugs. In each coupled web tuple, the nodes participating in the coupling operation are encircled. Furthermore, note that the resultant collection of web tuples is a web bag since the first two web tuples are identical (tuples with black nodes). Thus, a local web coupling between web bags may result in a web bag. However, eliminating irrelevant nodes from the input web tables reduces the size of the coupled web table or web bag. ∎

3.3 Web Union on Bags

The union of two web bags result in web tuples from two web bags satisfying either one or both web schemas. Note that the definition of web union of two bags is similar to that of union of web tables [5]. However, when we take the union of two web bags, we add the number of occurrence of each web tuple. That is, if W_{b_i} is a web bag in which the tuple t appears n times, and W_{b_j} is a web bag in which the tuple t appears m times then in the web bag $W_{b_i} \cup W_{b_j}$, web tuple t appears $n+m$ times. Note that web union behaves differently, depending on whether we think of W_{b_i} and W_{b_j} as web tables or web bags. If we consider the concept of web bag to compute $W_{b_i} \cup W_{b_j}$ then the result may not be a collection of distinct web tuples even if we consider W_{b_i} and W_{b_j} as web tables. In particular, if web tuple t appears in both W_{b_i} and W_{b_j} then t appears twice in $W_{b_i} \cup W_{b_j}$ if we consider the concept of web bag for web union. But if we consider the result to be a web table with distinct web tuples then t appears only

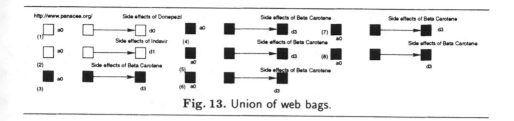

Fig. 13. Union of web bags.

once in $W_{b_i} \cup W_{b_j}$. Allowing the collection of web tuples created by web union of W_{b_i} and W_{b_j} to be a web bag minimize the computational time of web union operation. This is because if we compute the web union $W_{b_i} \cup W_{b_j}$ and insist on a set as the result then each web tuple in W_{b_j} must be checked for membership in W_{b_i}. If found to be in W_{b_i} then this web tuple of W_{b_j} is not added to the web union result; otherwise it is added to the result. However, if we accept a web bag as the result then we just copy all the web tuples of W_{b_i} and W_{b_j} as the result of web union, regardless of whether or not they appear in both web tables. We illustrate union operation on web bags with the following example:

Example 5. Consider the web tables in Figure 5 and Figure 7. If we allow bag as union result then the web union between these two web tables will result in a web bag as shown in Figure 12. This is because the first web tuple in Figure 5 and Figure 7 are identical. Thus, these tuples appear twice in the result (the first two web tuples in Figure 12). However, if we do not allow web bags then the result of web union is the set of tuples in Figure 12 except the second web tuple. Note that, in this case there is an additional overhead of removing one of the shaded web tuple in Figure 12. Furthermore, if we apply web union on two web bags (Figure 4 and Figure 6) then the resultant collection of web tuples is shown in Figure 13. The darkened web tuples in the figure are identical to one another. ∎

3.4 Web Intersection on Bags

The intersection of two web bags result in web tuples from two web bags satisfying both web schemas [5]. When we intersect two web bags W_{b_i} and W_{b_j}, in which web tuple t appears n and m times respectively, in $W_{b_i} \cap W_{b_j}$ tuple t appears $min(n, m)$ times. However, web intersection for bags does not decrease computational time compared to intersection over web tables. For example, consider the web bags in Figure 4 and Figure 6. Suppose, we apply web intersection operation over these two web bags. The last three web tuples in Figure 6 satisfies both the web schemas of the web bags Figure 4 and Figure 6. Thus, the resultant collection of web tuples will consist of $min(3, 3) = 3$ web tuples and is shown in Figure 14. However, if we apply web intersection on two web tables (say Figure 5 and Figure 7) in lieu of web bags then the resultant collection of web tuples are all distinct (Figure 14). That is, even if we allow web bags, the result of a web intersection over two web tables is always a web table. Note that in the case of web union the result will be a web bag.

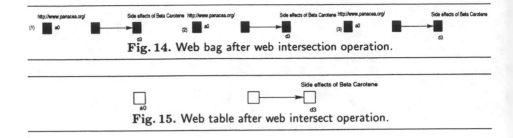

Fig. 14. Web bag after web intersection operation.

Fig. 15. Web table after web intersect operation.

4 Conclusions

In this paper, we have discussed the concept of web bag in a web warehouse. In particular, we have explained how some of the web operations i.e., web select, web union, web intersection, web join and local web coupling behave when we operate them on web bags in lieu of web tables. We find that some of the algebraic operations on web bags increase computational efficiency. As part of future work, we intend to study the performance of these algebraic operations on web bags.

References

1. http://www.cais.ntu.edu.sg:8000/~whoweda/.
2. T. BRAY. Measuring the Web. *Proceedings of the 5th International World Wide Web Conference (WWW)*, Paris, France, 1996.
3. S. BHOWMICK, S. K. MADRIA, W.-K. NG, E.-P. LIM. Web Bags: Are They Useful in A Web Warehouse? *Proceedings of 5th International Conference of Foundation of Data Organization (FODO'98)*, Kobe, Japan, November 1998.
4. S. BHOWMICK, S. K. MADRIA, W.-K. NG, E.-P. LIM. Cost-Benefit Analysis of Web Bag in a Web Warehouse: An Analytical Approach. *Proceedings of 3rd International Symposium of Database Engineering and Applications*, Montreal, Canada, August 1999.
5. S. BHOWMICK, S. K. MADRIA, W.-K. NG, E.-P. LIM. Web Warehousing: Design and Issues. *Proceedings of International Workshop on Data Warehousing and Data Mining (DWDM'98) (in conjunction with ER'98)*, Singapore, 1998.
6. S. BHOWMICK, W.-K. NG, E.-P. LIM. Information Coupling in Web Databases. *Proceedings of the 17th International Conference on Conceptual Modeling (ER'98)*, Singapore, 1998.
7. S. S. BHOWMICK, W.-K. NG, E.-P. LIM, S. K. MADRIA. Join Processing in Web Databases. *Proceedings of the 9th International Conference on Database and Expert Systems Application (DEXA)*, Vienna, Austria, 1998.
8. D. FLORESCU, A. LEVY, A. MENDELZON. Database Techniques for the World-Wide Web: A Survey. *SIGMOD Records*, Vol 27, No. 3, Sept 1998.
9. J. ULLMAN, J. WIDOM. *A First Course in Database Systems*, Prentice-Hall, 1997.

A Distributed Search System Based on Markov Decision Processes

Yipeng Shen, Dik Lun Lee, and Lian Wen Zhang

Department of Computer Science
The Hong Kong University of Science and Technology
{yipeng, dlee, lzhang}@cs.ust.hk

Abstract. This paper discusses a flat distributed search system in which selecting the relevant servers to a given query becomes difficult due to the lack of global knowledge at each server. To ensure the quality of the query results, Markov Decision Processes (MDPs) are set up for the query terms among all the autonomous search servers in the system. A new server ranking method is also designed for this MDP based system. The simulation reveals that query results with satisfactory quality can be achieved since the global optimal servers are obtained by the precomputed MDP policies.

1 Introduction

The ever increasing amount of information available on the World Wide Web (WWW) has made searching and indexing information a difficult task on the Internet. Various search engines such as AltaVista, InfoSeek, Yahoo, etc., have been developed and used nowadays.

Normally, a query submitted to the Internet search engine is composed of terms or keywords. The relevance of a document to a given query is calculated according to some formulae such as **TFxIDF** [4]. In comparison to the queries used in traditional information retrieval systems, the queries posed to the search engines on the Internet consist of only about 2 query terms on average [5].

The Web is believed to contain several hundred million pages, but the coverage of a single search engine is only a small part of the Web. Distributed search systems containing a large number of search engines can address this problem. The search engines in a distributed search system are connected as a graph, each search engine is autonomous and maintains its own index and document collection. Queries are answered via the cooperation among search engines so that the most relevant documents in the system are retrieved.

The problem of distributed searching has been investigated by many people. *Whois* + + [10] and *Discover* [8] are two typical systems with hierarchical architectures containing multiple layers. A probabilistic model for the hierarchical architecture is described in [1]. However, the autonomy of each server is weakened in the hierarchical architecture since each search engine is managed by its parent in the upper layer. The hierarchical architecture is not likely to scale up for the Internet.

An inference network model is proposed in [2]. In this model, a special global server is used to store the inference network for selecting the relevant servers when a query is posed to the distributed system. Similarly, a server containing the global knowledge which is able to select the most relevant servers from the system is assumed in [3], [6], [11] despite the different server ranking algorithms used by them. Moreover, each server in [9] should store part of the information of every other server in the system in order to pick up the relevant servers. Of course, this is not feasible on the WWW.

The motivation of this paper is to set up a system with a fully distributed architecture. The servers form a flat server architecture (network) in which every server only knows the knowledge about its neighbours. Given a query at a server in the flat distributed system, it is difficult to identify the relevant servers since the server receiving this query only has local knowledge. In order to address this problem, Markov Decision Processes (MDPs) are constructed among the server network so that the relevant servers can be identified efficiently.

Section 2 describes the distributed search system based on MDP. Section 3 discusses the server ranking method adopted by the MDP model. Section 4 presents the experimental results. In Section 5, we draw our conclusion.

2 Distributed Search System Based on MDP Model

In this section, we show how search in a distributed system can be modelled as an MDP. The main issues in our MDP model are discussed.

2.1 MDP and Distributed Searching

The MDP deals with the sequential decision process in a dynamic system. At any decision time, the decision maker chooses a decision or action from a number of alternatives based on the current state of the system. After the chosen action is executed, the decision maker receives an immediate reward returned by this action and the system may transfer to another state. The objective is to obtain the greatest reward after a series of actions. Formally, an MDP consists of four components: a set of all possible states, each state's set of possible actions, transition probability and immediate rewards obtained by the decision maker.

Given a set of servers $S = \{s_1, s_2, ..., s_N\}$, let these servers form a flat system architecture (network). If we pose a query q at server s, $s \in S$, the task is to locate the most relevant servers in S. We start at server s and determine whether to answer the query at this server or to pass the query to a neighbour in the server network. If the latter is chosen, the decision will be further processed at the neighbour who receives the query. Thus, the server where query q currently resides can be regarded as the present state of the query and S is the set of all possible states. The present state of the query changes when the query is passed to a neighbour. This is a sequential decision process and it can be naturally modelled as an MDP.

Let $A_s = \{a_1, a_2, ...\}$ be the set of all possible actions at server s. According to these actions, query q may be answered at s or passed to a neighbour of s. If the action a at s is to return itself, we obtain an *immediate reward* $r_q(s, a = s)$, which represents the relevance or the goodness score of server s with respect to q. On the other hand, if the action a is to pass the query to one of its neighbour s', the immediate reward $r_q(s, a = s')$ is 0 and the action takes us to server s'.

The optimal value function $V_q(s)$ is the expected total reward we can obtain by acting optimally from server s. Bellman's optimality principle tells us that

$$V_q(s) = max_{a \in A_s} [r_q(s, a) + \lambda V_q(T(s, a))] \qquad (1)$$

$T(s, a)$ stands for the next state (server) if action a is chosen. The transition $T(s, a)$ caused by action a is deterministic in our model. That is, the state of the query execution switches to another server with probability 1 if action a is chosen. The first term in the equation is the local reward received right away, which is zero when the action a is to proceed to another server. The second term is the reward that can be received in the future, which is zero if the action is to return the current server.

Parameter λ is a discount factor which is between 0 and 1. It captures the communication cost between adjacent servers. Due to parameter λ, the local immediate reward $r_q(s, s)$ of server s is discounted step by step in the server network when it is propagated to the other servers. The discounted reward, which is propagated to a remote server s', might be much smaller than its original value. Despite the greater initial local immediate reward of server s, the nearby servers of the remote server s' might propagate greater rewards to s' since their rewards are less discounted. Thus, the influence of server s on server s' is reduced by the parameter λ. The less the λ, the greater the reduction. We can confine the influence of a single server to an appropriate range by the parameter λ. The communication and computation cost is then reduced without losing much result precision.

The optimal policy (i.e., the optimal action $d_q(s)$ with respect to q at every server s) can be obtained as follows.

$$d_q(s) = arg\ max_{a \in A_s} [r_q(s, a) + \lambda V_q(T(s, a))] \qquad (2)$$

This optimal policy may be computed by means of *value iteration* [7]. Given a query q, value iteration starts with 0-value functions $V_{q,0}(s)$ at iteration step 0 and iteratively computes a series of value functions $V_{q,i}(s)$ ($i = 1, 2, ...$). In our MDP model, the value iteration can be simplified according to its specific Bellman equation where the transition is deterministic. That is, we iteratively compute $V_{q,i}(s)$ ($i = 1, 2, ...$) with respect to the following formula at every server s until the sequence of value functions $V_{q,i}(s)$ ($i = 1, 2, ...$) converges to the optimal value function $V_q(s)$.

$$V_{q,i}(s) = max_{a \in A_s} [r_q(s, a) + \lambda V_{q,i-1}(T(s, a))] \qquad (3)$$

2.2 Multiple Access Policy

Suppose the communication between servers is strictly confined to the server network. For a query q posted at s_{i1}, according to the optimal action a_{i1} obtained by the value iteration, q may be passed to another server s_{i2} and the delivery of q changes the current state to s_{i2} and so on. Once the query reaches a server s_{im} where the action is to stick to s_{im}, the delivery of query q stops and the query is answered at s_{im} (i.e., s_{im} is the optimal server). Later on, s_{im} is also called the *origin* of the optimal reward $V_q(s_{i1})$ at server s_{i1}.

The above discussion only copes with single cast, namely, selecting a single server from the system. For multicasting where a query may have several relevant servers, the value iteration algorithm must be revised.

The value iteration can be extended by not only keeping the greatest expected reward $V_q(s)$ and the corresponding optimal action but also memorizing the top k best expected rewards, the corresponding optimal actions and their corresponding origins. Every origin should be distinct since k different optimal servers are to be selected. In other words, a top k list is reserved in the value iteration at every server for query q. The *multiple access policy*, which provides k optimal servers with respect to a query posed at any server in the system, consists of the top k lists at all servers.

2.3 Queries with Multiple Terms

Obviously, it is not possible to set up the MDP value iteration for every possible query because of the high computation cost. However, the number of distinct single query terms is limited, especially when we focus on the frequently used terms. Thus, it is feasible to set up MDPs for all single query terms. A query with multiple terms can then be answered according to the MDP policies of the query terms contained in the query.

Suppose query $q = < t_1, t_2 >$, which has two query terms, is submitted to server s. $L_{t1}(s)$, $L_{t2}(s)$ are the two lists of top k optimal policies at server s with respect to query term t_1 and t_2 respectively. The total relevance of server s' to query q is the sum of the relevance scores of all query terms in query q.

If k is appropriately large, query q can be answered in the following manner. List $L_{t1}(s)$ and $L_{t2}(s)$ are merged into a new list $L_q(s)$ sorted by the adjusted server scores. That is, if s' appears in both $L_{t1}(s)$ and $L_{t2}(s)$, the adjusted relevance score of s' in $L_q(s)$ is the sum of its two expected rewards in $L_{t1}(s)$ and $L_{t2}(s)$. Finally, the new top k servers are picked up. Similarly, queries with more than two query terms can be processed in the same manner.

From now on, the MDP with top k access policy is constructed according to a single term t instead of a query q.

2.4 MDP Server

Value iteration assumes knowledge about the topology of the entire server network. This assumption is not true in a flat distributed system where every server is fully autonomous and only has the knowledge about its neighbours. Fortunately, there is a variation of value iteration that does not require this assumption. The variant is called *asynchronous value iteration* [7], which is adopted in our simulation experiments.

In terms of asynchronous value iteration, every server carries out its own value iteration steps whenever it is free. Not concerning about the value iteration steps of its neighbours, each server only renews its expected total reward based on the current expected rewards of its neighbours during every value iteration step. Compared to the synchronous value iteration, each server may carry out different number of iteration steps in the asynchronous value iteration.

Since every server in our system has to fulfill both the query processing task and the asynchronous MDP value iteration task, a search engine (server) is extended with some components related to the MDP policy computation and the query processing based on the calculated MDP policies. These servers are referred to as MDP servers.

3   Server Weight

In this section, we concentrate on how the relevance of servers with respect to the given query is evaluated. In the MDP, the server weight standing for the relevance of a server to a query is intended as the immediate reward obtained at that server (i.e., $r_q(s, s)$ in Formula 1).

All traditional server ranking methods depend on some global information about the other servers [12]. In a flat distributed environment, the goodness score of a server should be evaluated only upon that server's local information according to the MDP model set up so far. That is, all the servers ought to be ranked by a uniform ranking criterion with respect to their own information. The comparison or interaction between servers is accomplished during the value iteration of the MDP. The advent of the following server ranking method satisfies this requirement in the MDP model and is referred to as the *Uniform Ranking Criterion (URC)*.

The idea of *URC* comes from the term ranking method used in the query refinement of *Discover* [8] where the moderately correlated terms are given the highest ranking values. In the following formula, suppose $\bar{p}$ is a moderate value between 0 and 1, the greatest value of $\mathcal{M}_{\bar{p}}$ is obtained if $p_i = \bar{p}$.

$$\mathcal{M}_{\bar{p}} = 1 - |p_i - \bar{p}|$$

Now let's derive the *URC* server ranking method from the previous term ranking method used in *Discover*. Given a term t, despite the variation of server ranking methods, the relevance is basically calculated based on the *term frequency (TF)* and the *document frequency (DF)* of term t. In particular, TF is the crucial parameter for determining relevance. Typically, TF is normalized to a value between 0.5 and 1, which is referred to as the *normalized term frequency (tf)*. Given a document i in a collection and term t, $tf_{i,t}$ is:

$$tf_{i,t} = 0.5 + 0.5 \times TF_{i,t} / \max_{k \in i} (TF_{i,k})$$

Given term t, server s_i and its own local document collection, $stf_{i,t}$, which is the sum of the tf of all the documents containing t in s_i, is defined as follows.

Definition 1 *Total normalized term frequency for term t at server s_i is:*

$$stf_{i,t} = \sum_{doc_k \in s_i} tf_{k,t}.$$

Furthermore, $stf_{i,t}$ is obtained from $DF_{i,t}$ documents ($DF_{i,t} > 0$ if $stf_{i,t} > 0$) at server s_i. Since $tf_{k,t}$ is between 0.5 and 1 for all $DF_{i,t}$ documents, $stf_{i,t}$ is a number between $0.5 \times DF_{i,t}$ and $DF_{i,t}$. Let $atf_{i,t}$ be the *average tf* at s_i.

Definition 2 *Average normalized term frequency for term t at server s_i is:*

$$atf_{i,t} = stf_{i,t}/DF_{i,t}$$

$atf_{i,t}$ is also in $[0.5, 1]$. It stands for the average relevance of all the documents containing t. Suppose we have $stf_{i,t} = stf_{j,t}$, $i \neq j$, their corresponding atf are $atf_{i,t}$ and $atf_{j,t}$ respectively. Normally the greater atf results in better retrieval precision, while on the contrary, the recall is ensured if the server with lower atf is picked up.

According to the above discussion, the relevance of a server is generally determined by its stf value. But the user might opt for different servers depending on their different recall/precision requirements. The URC server weight is then elicited.

$$G_{i,t} = stf_{i,t} \cdot [\alpha + \beta \cdot (1 - |atf_{i,t} - \bar{p}|)] \qquad (4)$$
$$\alpha + \beta = 1, \quad 0 < \alpha < 1.$$

α in Formula 4 is called the importance weight of stf. The greater the α, the more important the stf in calculating the server weight. The latter term $\beta \cdot (1 - |atf_{i,t} - \bar{p}|)$ is adjustable so that the user can decide which atf is the most preferable (i.e., $\bar{p}$ in Formula 4). Besides, according to Formula 4, the importance of atf is further scaled up by stf so that it is proportional to the total term frequency at the server.

If the user needs to choose documents with higher relevance scores, a larger value is assigned to $\bar{p}$, whereas $\bar{p}$ is smaller if the user tends to retrieve more relevant documents regardless of their relevance scores. Nonetheless, α is generally larger than β since stf is the dominant factor in evaluating the relevance of a server to a term. The value of server weight $G_{i,t}$ is in $[0, stf]$.

The discrimination between different α parameters is demonstrated in Fig. 1. With a greater α parameter($\alpha = 0.8$), the stf takes an important role in the server weight. As long as the server has large stf, high server weight is always obtained. Whereas, a smaller α parameter causes the server weight to decrease sharply if the atf deviates from the peak point $\bar{p}$.

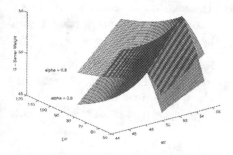

Fig. 1. URC Server Weight ($\bar{p}$ = 0.8)

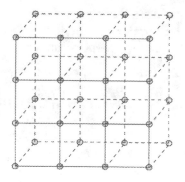

Fig. 2. Folding Mesh

4 Experimental Results and Analyses

To verify the performance of adopting the MDP model in the distributed search system, a simulator is constructed and experiments have been conducted based on some standard information retrieval document collections.

4.1 Environment Construction

Our simulator is running upon a pseudo distributed search environment. To set up this environment, the document collections, the server connections and the test queries should be constructed in advance.

Our experiments include 32 pseudo servers which form a regular flat architecture (Fig. 2). It is referred to as the *Folding Mesh*. The average node degree in the network is 4, the minimum and maximum node degrees are 3 and 5 respectively.

Four standard document collections used in performance analyses of many information retrieval systems are selected as the test data in our experiments (i.e., CACM, CISI, CRAN and MED). These document collections are available from the Smart System at Cornell University ($ftp : //ftp.cs.cornell.edu/pub/smart/$). These four original sample collections are divided and distributed to 32 servers.

Although the four sample document collections provide their collateral sample queries, these queries are descriptions or excerpts rather than queries with few terms. In accordance with the queries posed on the WWW, we extract the short queries with few terms from these sample queries. Then these extracted queries are imposed on the distributed search system and the returned query results are evaluated.

4.2 Performance Criterion

In terms of the quality of query results, a criterion called the *Effectiveness Ratio* is adopted. Suppose we combine all the local document collections together and treat the combination as one huge global document collection, then the classic text retrieval method **TFxIDF** can be applied to this combined collection. Given a query q, the performance is measured by the *Effectiveness Ratio*.

Definition 3 *The Effectiveness Ratio is the ratio between v_d and v_h (i.e., v_d/v_h), where v_h is the sum of the* **TFxIDF** *scores in the global document collection of all the documents retrieved directly from the global document collection; v_d is the sum of the* **TFxIDF** *scores in the global document collection of all the documents obtained by the selected MDP servers.*

4.3 Results

Cast Number Given a query, more than one of the 32 servers may be relevant. The more servers the query accesses, the higher result quality we achieve; on the other hand, visiting more servers increases the system's overload. Ideally we hope that a higher quality can be obtained by covering only a small portion of the distributed system.

In the following experiments, the server ranking method is the URC defined in Section 3, $\alpha = 0.7$ and $\bar{p} = 0.9$. The ranking method with these α, $\bar{p}$ values tends to select servers with great stf and atf.

The experimental result is depicted in Fig. 3. Observing the gradient of the curves, we know that the Average Effectiveness Ratio increases at a high rate at the beginning. As the number of visited servers becomes larger, the curves tend to be flat. This means the servers containing most of the relevant documents with high relevance are selected at first, the servers with less relevance are unlikely to be visited initially. Besides, the smallest Average Effectiveness Ratio is near 0.6 when eight servers among thirty two are accessed.

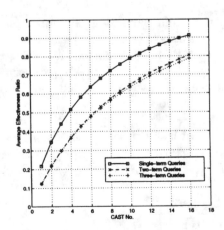

Fig. 3. Average Effectiveness Ratio and Cast Number

Reward Discount In the MDP model, the λ parameter is the discount factor of the reward that can be obtained in the future. It represents the communication delay between MDP servers.

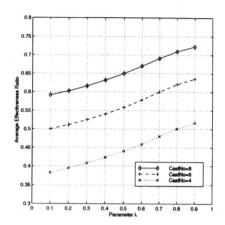

Fig. 4. Average Effectiveness Ratio and Parameter λ (Single Term Queries)

Fig. 4 is the experimental result of single term queries. Generally, the quality of the query result is proportional to the λ parameter. As λ varies from zero to one, the quality of the query result increases slowly when λ is near the two ends of the $[0, 1]$ interval. Namely, if λ is an extreme value, the variation in the result quality is small. While λ has a moderate value in $[0, 1]$, the result quality almost increases linearly. Meanwhile, it seems that visiting six servers can cover most of the relevant contents in our case.

5   Conclusion

The simulation results present the general prospect of the MDP model applied to the distributed information retrieval system on the WWW. Although each server in a flat architecture only has local knowledge at the beginning, the global optimal servers are obtained after the MDP policies are computed. As a result, adopting MDP model helps the distributed search system to improve the quality of the query result since the precomputed MDP policies can efficiently locate the most relevant servers.

Because every server in our model takes a same role, flat distributed systems are more flexible and extensible than hierarchical systems. This conforms to the need of the dynamic WWW environment.

Since the sample document collections adopted in our experiments are not large enough, our future task is to adopt larger test collections in the experiments and further refine our MDP model.

References

1. BAUMGARTEN, C. A probabilistic model for distributed information retrieval. In *Proceedings of the 20th Annual International ACM SIGIR Conference on Research and Development in Information Retrieval* (Philadelphia PA, USA, 1997), pp. 258–266.

2. CALLAN, J., LU, Z., AND CROFT, W. Searching distributed collections with inference networks. In *Proceedings of the 18th Annual International ACM SIGIR Conference on Research and Development in Information Retrieval* (1995), pp. 21–28.

3. FRENCH, J. C., POWELL, A. L., VILES, C. L., EMMITT, T., AND PREY, K. J. Evaluating database selection techniques: A testbed and experiment. In *Proceedings of the 21th Annual International ACM SIGIR Conference on Research and Development in Information Retrieval* (Melbourne, Australia, 1998), pp. 121–129.

4. HARMAN, D. Ranking algorithms. In *Information Retrieval: Data Structures and Algorithms* (Englewood Cliffs, NJ, 1992), Prentice-Hall, pp. 293–362.

5. JANSEN, B. J., SPINK, A., BATEMAN, J., AND SARACEVIC, T. Real life information retrieval: A study of user queries on the Web. *SIGIR Forum 32*, 1 (1998), 5–17.

6. MENG, W., LIU, K.-L., YU, C., WANG, X., CHANG, Y., AND RISHE, N. Determing text databases to search in the internet. In *Proceedings of the 24th VLDB Conference* (New York, USA, 1998), pp. 14–25.

7. PUTERMAN, M. L. *Markov decision processes : discrete stochastic dynamic programming.* John Wiley & Sons, New York, 1994.

8. SHELDON, M. A., DUDA, A., AND GIFFORD, D. K. Discover: A resource discovery system based on content routing. *Computer Networks and ISDN Systems 27*, 6 (1995), 953–972.

9. VILES, C., AND FRENCH, J. Dissemination of collection wide information in a distributed information retrieval system. In *Proceedings of the 18th Annual International ACM SIGIR Conference on Research and Development in Information Retrieval* (1995), pp. 12–20.

10. WEIDER, C., AND SPERO, S. Architecture for the WHOIS++ index service. Internet Working Draft, 1993.

11. XU, J., AND CALLAN, J. Effective retrieval with distributed collections. In *Proceedings of the 21th Annual International ACM SIGIR Conference on Research and Development in Information Retrieval* (Melbourne, Australia, 1998), pp. 112–120.

12. YUWONO, B., AND LEE, D. L. Server ranking for distributed text retrieval systems on the Internet. In *Proceedings of the Fifth International Conference on Database Systems for Advanced Applications* (Melbourne, Australia, April, 1997).

A Framework for Warehousing the Web Contents

Yan Zhu

DVS1, Department of Computer Science, Darmstadt University of Technology
D-64283 Darmstadt, Germany
Zhu@dvs1.informatik.tu-darmstadt.de

Abstract. This paper presents a framework for warehousing selected Web contents. In this framework, a hybrid (partially materialized) approach and extended ontologies are used to achieve Web data integration. This hybrid approach makes it possible to integrate DW data with Web-based information resources as they are needed. The Ontologies are used to represent domain knowledge related to Web sources and the logic model of data warehouses. Moreover, we define the mapping rules between Web data and attributes of data warehouses in the ontologies to facilitate the construction and maintenance requirements of data warehouses.

1 Introduction

Building data warehouses (DW) and efficiently implementing decision support or OLAP on them have become important tools for knowledge management and business intelligence. External data, such as, new product announcements from competitors, weather conditions at business activity location, and currency exchange rates may be needed to carry out meaningful OLAP. Ignoring this influence may cause the results to be incomplete, inexact or even totally incorrect [12, 15]. As Web technology develops, a vast amount of external data is already offered on the Web. If OLAP can take advantage of them, the resulting functions will be more powerful.

But warehousing Web data is a huge challenge. Some reasons are:

In a data warehousing environment, data is materialized in a DW and all queries are applied to the warehouse data to achieve a good query performance. Data in the DW is historical and nonvolatile. But most Web data is updated frequently, and the maintenance of a data warehouse that depends on Web data is more difficult compared with conventional data warehouses based on company-internal data. In contrast to the data warehousing approach, some Web data integration systems [1, 5, 6, 8, 10, 11, 19] adopt a virtual approach. In this approach, data remains at Web sources. When a query is posed, related data is integrated on the fly to give a reply. One of advantages is that data is not replicated, thereby guaranteeing to be consistent at query time. On the down side, the quality of Web data may not be as tightly controlled as that of the DW data. Moreover, since Web sources are autonomous, more sophisticated query optimization and execution methods are needed.

In order to reduce query response time, an appropriate set of Web data must be selected for materialization. On the other hand, some queries might not be answered only with materialized data in the DW. In order to support wider analyses on the DW, a virtual approach can be adopted to integrate needed Web data for producing a reply.

To integrate dynamically Web data with DW data, additional challenges must be overcome:

- The paradigm of the Web is radically different from the paradigm of the data warehouse. Data on the Web is mostly unstructured or semistructured, while a data warehouse is in most cases based on structured data in the relational or multidimensional data models.
- The process of integrating external (e.g. Web) data and internal warehouse data exacerbates a number of problems, such as, data format inconsistency, and semantic inconsistency.

In order to tackle these difficult problems, we have made the following efforts in our framework:

- Adoption of a hybrid approach. We select a set of nonvolatile or frequently queried Web data to materialize in the DW. With the aid of the virtual approach, some queries can be answered using Web data that is not materialized in the DW, or using a combination of warehouse data and Web data.
- Selection of the MIX model (Metadata based Integration model for data X-change) [3,4] as an internal data representation. This model represents data together with a description of their underlying interpretation context, and uses domain-specific ontologies to enable a semantically correct interpretation of the available data and metadata. Ontologies as a common interpretation basis can help to resolve the semantic inconsistency problem.
- Definition of mapping rules in a system-specific ontology to generate transformation codes semiautomatically. If Web data changes, e.g. because of the introduction of the Euro among the currencies, the ontology can be extended, the transformation rules can be modified, and mapping codes can be generated again, which relieves the maintenance task of data warehouses.

2 Related Efforts

In the Squirrel project [16] and the Lore system [20], the hybrid approach has already been discussed. The Squirrel project concentrates only on relational or object-oriented data sources. Its goal of using a hybrid approach is to develop a general and flexible mediator framework. Lore is a DBMS for managing semistructured information. Lore's external data manager provides a mechanism for dynamically fetching and caching external data, and integrating them with data resident in the Lore system to answer a user's query. The integrated external data is up-to-date. There are some important differences between our work and theirs. First, we integrate Web data in a DW, rather than an object repository. Compared with an object repository, a data warehouse based on a relational data model will introduce many different issues on the Web data transformation, the query performance requirement, or the warehouse maintenance. Second, in our framework, the partially materialized approach helps to answer queries that could not be answered based on DW data alone, and the dynamically integrated Web data is still historical and nonvolatile.

Among the systems for information integration that use an ontology, the DataFoundry project [9, 10] is similar to our research. It is based on a mediated data warehouse architecture with an ontology infrastructure, which is used to reduce the maintenance requirements of a warehouse. But some remarkable differences exist between our work and theirs. First, we focus on the Web data. Compared with data in scientific databases, Web data is unstructured or semistructured and has no explicit schema. Second, DataFoundry caches the most frequently accessed data to reduce query response time. In our framework, nonvolatile and frequently queried Web data is materialized in a DW.

The DWQ project [7, 8] also integrates information sources in the data warehousing environment. They consider two critical factors for the design and maintenance of particular data warehouse applications, which are conceptual modeling of the domain and reasoning support over the conceptual representation. This approach provides a system independent specification of the relationships between sources and between a source and an enterprise model at the conceptual level. By using an explicit conceptual model, the design phase and the maintenance phase of the information system can be facilitated. However the DWQ project focuses only on those sources that possess a schema. In our framework an extended ontology is used at the conceptual level, and also a metadata based object-oriented data model is used for the logical level. This makes it possible to integrate the Web data correctly and to generate transformation processes semiautomatically.

The rest of the paper is organized as follows. Section 3 gives a motivating example. The framework of the system is introduced briefly in Section 4. The ontology and a mediated data model are discussed in Section 5. Section 6 analyzes mapping mechanisms from the Web data to a star schema. The process of using an ontology to deduce transformation processes is discussed in Section 7. Section 8 will give the conclusion and discuss our future work.

3   A Tour Offer Data Warehouse Example

We define our example in a tour offer application. To simplify the problem description, we consider only tour packets for international city visits when the travel medium is aircraft. Using a tour offer data warehouse, the following inquiries are often analyzed, such as: Which city is the favorite choice in which month? What kind of hotel is booked most? What kind of influence does the local weather or currency exchange rates have on tour offers? Among inquired data, the weather data and the currency exchange rates probably lie outside the business data of a travel agency, but can be easily acquired from the Web.

In our framework, we select the past average weather data and the most common currency exchange rates for materialization in a DW. Fig.1 is the example of average weather data of Paris in 1998.

Sometimes, we also need to analyze, for example, why the monthly sold amounts of a tour offer to Spain dropped from September 1998 to January 1999. Perhaps the Spanish Peseta during that time became expensive. If we have no Peseta exchange rates in the DW, we could not answer such a query. Fortunately, the Federal Reserve Bank of St. Louis already offers historic monthly average exchange rates on the Web. We can use a virtual approach to integrate them, and then to recompose them with aggregation tour offer data from the DW to give the user a reply. Fig. 2 shows monthly currency exchange rate of Spanish Pesetas to one US$ on the Web.

A star schema of the tour offer data warehouse and a weather dimension table are defined in Fig.3.

01/06/99-Updated 06:19 PM ET

Paris, France, 1998						Temps °F
Month	Average H igh	Averag Low	Warmest Temp	Coldest Temp	Average dew point	Wet days
Jan	42	34	57	1	33	20
Feb	44	34	59	14	32	17
Mar	51	38	75	21	37	19
April	57	41	79	26	39	16
...						

Note: *Dew point is a humidity measure in Fahrenheit degrees;*
              Wet days are days with rain or melted snow or ice totaling 0.01 inches

Fig. 1. Paris' average weather data in 1998

Date	EXSPUS
...	...
1998.08	151.72
1998.09	144.33
1998.10	139.23
1998.11	143.05
1998.12	142.08
1999.01	143.55
1999.02	148.52
...	

Average of daily figures, Noon buying rates in New York.
Source: Federal Reserve Bank of St. Louis and Federal Reserve Board of Governors

Fig. 2. The exchange rates of Spanish Pesetas to one US$

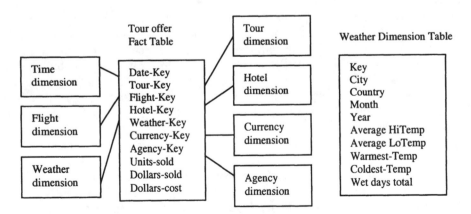

Fig. 3. The tour offer data warehouse

4   The Framework for Warehousing Web Data

Our framework showed in Fig.4 is based on a federation manager and a set of wrappers, which are introduced in [5]. In the framework, the federation manager (FM) uses a global mediated data model (MIX model) to represent data from Web sources.

The transformation processor (TP) transforms the data in the MIX model to the data in the DW, and loads the data into the DW. The task of the Incremental Maintenance Processor (IMP) is to calculate the incremental parts when Web data is updated. At first, the FM will integrate the updated Web data, the IMP will compare new MIX objects with the old copies and calculate the incremental parts. The incremental parts will also be transformed and loaded in the DW. The Query Processor (QP) provides the interface for querying the data warehouse. Upon receiving a query, the QP first determines the query on materialized data in the DW or on virtual data from the Web. If the query needs virtual data, the QP will decompose original queries, rewrite queries related to virtual data, and send them to the FM. After the replies are obtained from the Web and the DW, the QP recomposes them and sends the final answer to the user. The above process will be transparent to the user. The ontology repository consists of a domain-specific ontology, which conceptualizes domain knowledge related to the selected Web sources, and system-specific ontologies, which describe the data warehouse logical schema and define the relationship between the mediated model and the star schema of the DW. The Ontology Engine (OE) is an ontology processor, whereat concepts in the ontology can be implemented as classes, and relationships or functions in the ontology can be implemented as methods.

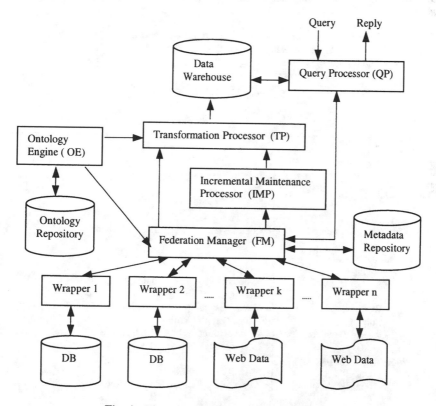

Fig. 4. The structure of warehousing Web data

```
Weather Ontology

(define-class CityName ( ?cityname)
        " A cityname is the name of a city."
        :def ( and (format ?cityname FullCityName)
                    (String  ?cityname)))
 (define-class YearString ( ?yearstring)
        "Yearstring is a kind of date notation, and is expressed as String."
        :def ( and (format ?yearstring "YYYY")
                    (string ?yearstring)))
(define-class YearNumber ( ?yearnumber)
        "Yearnumber is a kind of date notation according to ISO 8601specific year format, and is
        expressed as the number of years A. D."
        :def ( and (format ?yearnumber  YYYY)
                    (integer-range  ?yearnumber)
                        (= (i-lower-bound ?yearnumber) 0)
                        (= (i-upper-bound ?yearnumber) ∞)))
(define-class  AverageHighTemperature ( ?averagehigh)
        "An averagehigh is monthly average high temperature related to a city in a country. "
        :def (and (subclass-of AverageHighTemperature Weather-Temperature)
                (or(unit ?averagehigh Fahrenheit)
                (unit ?averagehigh Celsius ))
                (float ?averagehigh )))
(define-function Fahrenheit-to-Celsius (?T_F) : -> ?T_C
        " A fahrenheit-to-celsius convert a temperature value in fahrenheit unit to the temperature
value in celsius unit, according to equivalence T_C =( T_F -32)*5/9. "
                :def (and (member ?T_F Weather-Temperature )
                        (unit ?T_F Fahrenheit)
                        (member ?T_C Weather-Temperature)
                        (unit ?T_C Celsius)
                        (= (/ (* (- T_F 32) 5) 9) T_C )))

...
```

Fig. 5. The weather ontology

```
CompSemObj=
 <Weather, {
      <CityName, "Paris",              {< CityNameCode, "FullCityName">}>,
      <CountryName, "France",          {< CountryNameCode, "FullCountryName">}>,
      <Year, 1998,                     {< YearFormat, "YYYY">}>,
      <MonthlyAverageData,{
          <Month, 01,                  {< MonthFormat, MM>}>,
          <AverageHigh, 42,            {< AverageHighTempByMonth, "Fahrenheit">,<Scale, 1>}>,
          <AverageLow, 34,             {< AverageLowTempByMonth, "Fahrenheit">,<Scale, 1>}>,
          <Warmest, 57,                {<WarmestTempInMonth, "Fahrenheit">,<Scale, 1>}>,
          <Coldest, 1,                 {<ColdestTempInMonth, "Fahrenheit">,<Scale, 1>}>,
          <AverageDewPoint, 33,        {<AverageHumidityByMonth, "Fahrenheit">,<Scale, 1>}>,
          <WetDay, 20                  {<TotalWetDayInMonth, "Day">,<Scale, 1>}>}>
      <MonthlyAverageData,{
          <Month, 02,                  {< MonthFormat, MM>}>,
          <AverageHigh, 44,            {< AverageHighTempByMonth, "Fahrenheit">,<Scale, 1>}>,
          ... }>
  ... }>
```

Fig. 6. The integrated weather data represented based on MIX

5 The Ontology and the Mediated Data Model

Web data comes from various knowledge domains. These Web sources are developed independently and work autonomously. When we integrate Web data into a data warehouse, the inconsistencies exist not only between internal business data and external data on the Web, but also among Web data. Among these inconsistencies, semantically correct understanding and interpretation of related metadata is a key issue. A common ontology [13] serving as an agreement to use the shared knowledge in a coherent and consistent manner can help to tackle this problem. Fig. 5 is an example of the weather domain ontology, which is represented using Ontolingua [13], a knowledge representation language. Ontolingua definitions are Lisp-like forms that consist of a symbol, an argument list associated with the symbol, a documentation string, and a set of KIF [14] sentences labeled by keywords.

The MIX model is a self-describing object-oriented data model and based on the concept of a semantic object, which represents a data item together with its underlying semantic context. In MIX, in order to support the interpretation of the available data and metadata, each semantic object has a concept label associated with it that specifies the relationship between the object and the real world aspects it describes. These concept labels must be taken from a domain ontology. The MIX model may represent structured and semistructured data in a uniform way and on a common interpretation basis. In MIX, simple semantic objects (SemObj) represent atomic data items. Complex semantic objects (CompSemObj) represent objects consisting of multiple, possibly heterogeneous data elements, each of which describes exactly one attribute of the represented phenomenon.

An example of SemObj is:
< CityName, "Paris", {<CityNameCode,"FullCityName">}>
An example of CompSemObj is:
<MonthlyAverageData, {<Month, 01, {<Month Format, MM>}>, <...>,...}>

Fig.6 shows an example of the MIX model. More detailed definitions and explanations can be found in [3,4].

6 Mapping MIX Objects to the Attributes in the Star Schema

The MIX Model is an object-oriented data model, while the DW in our framework is based on the relational data model. Therefore, mapping MIX semantic objects to the data warehouse tables is roughly similar to mapping objects into relational tables [2, 17, 18, 21]. But a remarkable difference is that data in the DW is divided into facts in fact tables and descriptive attributes in dimension tables. Since business transaction data, which typically form the basis of the fact tables, will not be taken from the Web, we concentrate on mapping Web data to dimension tables. Between data values in MIX objects and attribute values in dimension tables, there could be one-to-one, one-to-many, many-to-many relationships. In the example of Section 3, the relationship between Web data values and attribute values in the dimension table is one-to-one. In some more complex cases, data values must at first be calculated, and then mapped to attribute values.

A MIX model consists of attributes and methods (conversion functions). Its attributes are either simple or complex objects. Therefore there exists a one-to-many composite aggregation relationship among parent object and children objects. In basic object-relational model mapping, we can map each complex object to a table, and implement composite aggregation in the parent table using foreign keys, which point to each child table. But in our example, weather dimensional table is redundant with city, country and year. Therefore, each complex object to a table can not be adopted in data warehousing. We map the root CompSemObj to one table in a way similar to One-Inheritance-Tree-One-Table approach. All equal ontology concepts are mapped to one column name, and all different concepts are mapped to separate column names. The physical representation of a value is mapped to an attribute value based on related column names. Semantic context associated with a semantic object can be separated from the database and stored to a metadata repository. These mapping processes can be done recursively.

The MIX model can also support inheritance, which is reflected in the inheritance of concepts in the domain ontology. Each MIX object only represents concrete integrated data values. Therefore, in the mapping we need not consider the inheritance relationship.

In the MIX model each object is identified through single or multipart key attributes, which is similar to the relational model. When an object is implemented in Java, a unique OID can be automatically assigned by the system. In a data warehousing environment, the primary key in a dimensional table can be an intelligent or non-intelligent key. In practice, unless we are absolutely certain that the identifiers will not be changed or reassigned in the future, it is safer to use non-intelligent keys. These non-intelligent keys can be automatically generated by the system. Therefore, when we map MIX objects to a dimensional table, we design an additional column in this table as primary key, one unique key value for each row can be generated by the system.

To map a nested complex semantic object structure to a table structure, we can first replace each CompSemObj with all its subobjects. This replacement will be processed recursively until there is no CompSemObj in the structure except the root CompSemObj. After the preprocessing, the mapping rules described as above are applied to this enlarged root complex semantic object.

When a semantic object occurs more than one time, a multiple attribute problem arises. For example, a book can have more than one author. But most relational databases do not support multi-valued attributes. To cope with this problem, we use separate rows to store each value of multi-valued attributes in dimensional tables.

7 Using Ontologies to Perform Transformations

In our framework, the ontology repository consists of the domain ontology and the specific ontologies about the description of the logical schema of the DW and mapping rules. The OE is an ontology processor, whereat concepts in the ontologies are implemented as classes, and relationships or functions in the ontologies are implemented as methods. The TP works under the guide of the schema of the DW and the mapping rules. Using ontologies, the transformation codes can be generated semi-automatically. As additional Web data is integrated, or when selected Web data is updated, the things we need to do are adding new concepts into the domain ontology, modifying mapping rules, then regenerating transformation codes.

Between data from Web sources and attributes in data warehouses, there are one-to-one, one-to-many, many-to-many relationships. These relationships also exist between the values in the MIX objects and the attributes in the data warehouse. In the mapping rules ontology, the correspondences are explicitly described, and the conversion functions are defined respectively. Fig. 7 is an example of the mapping rules ontology.

After the ontology has been defined, the OE can implement classes, relations and functions as Java classes and methods. By using mapping rules ontology, transformation methods can be deduced. The TP reads data represented in MIX objects and uses transformation methods to construct tables, generate column names and attribute values in the data warehouse. The process includes essential conversion of data type, data format, unit, etc.

```
Mapping Rules Definition Ontology

(define-relation CityMapping (?city ?cityname)
"Mapping cityname to city. The cityname is a member of the CityName class in the Weather Ontology, the
city is an attribute name of the WeatherSchema in the Weather Dimension Table Descriptions Ontology."
          :def ( and  (member ?city Weather-Dimension-Table-Descriptions-Ontology)
                      (member ?cityname Weather-Ontology)
                      (= (?city ?cityname))))

(define-relation YearMapping (?year ?yearstring)
"Mapping yearstring to year. The yearstring is a member of the YearString class in the Weather Ontology,
the year is an attribute name of the WeatherSchema in Weather Dimension Table Descriptions Ontology. "
          :def ( and  (member ?year Weather-Dimension-Table-Descriptions-Ontology)
                      (member ?yearstring Weather-Ontology)
                      (member ?yearnumber Weather-Ontology)
                      ((Year-Number-of ?yearstring) ?yearnumber ))
                      (= (?year ?yearnumber))))

(define-relation AverageHighMapping (?average-ht ?averagehigh)
"Mapping averagehigh to average-ht. The averagehigh is a member of the AverageHigh-Temperature class
in the Weather Ontology, the average-ht is an attribute name of the WeatherSchema in the Weather
Dimension Table Descriptions Ontology."
          :def ( and (member ?average-ht Weather-Dimension-Table-Descriptions-Ontology)
                      (member ?averagehigh Weather-Ontology)
                      (= (?average-ht ?Averagehigh))))
...
```

Fig. 7. Mapping rules definition ontology

8   Conclusions

In this paper we present a novel framework of integrating information contents from the Web for DSS and OLAP. Moreover, we also discuss how to use extended ontologies to transform the Web data for integration into data warehouses and to facilitate the maintenance requirements of the data warehouse.

At present, we are improving our framework and doing further research on the hybrid approach in a *Web Warehousing* environment. Some interesting issues we are currently looking into include how to select an appropriate set of Web data for materialization, the optimization problem of the Query Processor in the hybrid approach, the influence of Web data quality on a DW, and the further use of ontology and KR techniques in the design and maintenance of the data warehouses.

Acknowledgements

The author would like to thank Alejandro P. Buchmann for his detailed comments that helped improve this paper. The author would also like to thank Christof Bornhövd and Ronald Bourret for their productive discussions with regard to some parts of this paper.

References

1. Arens, Y., Knoblock, C. A., Shen, W-M.: *Query Reformulation for Dynamic Information Integration*, In Journal of Intelligent Information Systems, 6 (2/3) : 99-130, 1996
2. Blaha, M., Premerlani, W., Shen H.: *Converting OO Models into RDBMS Schema*, IEEE Software, 11(3) : 28-39, 1994
3. Bornhövd, C.: *MIX - A Representation Model for the Integration of Web-based Data*, Technical Report DVS98-1, Department of Computer Science, Darmstadt University of Technology, Nov., 1998
4. Bornhövd, C.: *Semantic Metadata for the Integration of Web-based Data for Electronic Commerce*, WECWIS'99, Santa Clara, USA,1999
5. Bornhövd, C., Buchmann, A. P.: *A Prototype for Metadata-based Integration of Internet Sources*, In Proc. of CAiSE'99, Heidelberg, Germany, June, 1999
6. Bayardo, R., Bohrer, W., Brice, R., et al: *InfoSleuth: Semantic Integration of Information in Open and Dynamic Environments*, In SIGMOD' 97, Tucson, Arizona, 1997
7. Calvanese, D., Giacomo, G. D., Lenzerini, M., and et al: *Description Logic Framework for Information Integration*, In Proc. of KR' 98, 1998
8. Calvanese, D., Giacomo, G. D., Lenzerini, M., et al: *Information Integration: Conceptual Modeling and Reasoning Support*, In Proc. of CoopIS'98, New York, 1998
9. Critchlow, T., Ganesh, M., Musick, R.: *Automatic Generation of Warehouse Mediators Using an Ontology Engine*, In Proc. of the 5th KRDB Workshop, Seattle, WA, 1998
10. Critchlow, T., Ganesh, M., Musick, R.: *Meta-Data based Mediator Generation*, In Proc. of CoopIS'98, New York, 1998
11. Chawathe, S., Garcia-Molina, H., Hammer, J., et al: *The TSIMMIS project: Integration of heterogeneous information sources*. In Proc. of IPSI'94, Japan, March, 1994
12. Damato, G. M.: *Strategic Information from External Sources*, White Paper, http://www.datawarehouse.com/, April, 1999,
13. Gruber, T. R.: *A Translation Approach to Portable Ontology Specifications*, Knowledge Acquisition, 5 (2): 199-220, 1993.
14. Genesereth, M.R., Fikes, R. E.: *Knowledge Interchange Format*, Version 3.0 Reference Manual. Technical Report Logic-92-1, Computer Science Department, Stanford University
15. Hackathorn, R. D.: *Web Farming for the Data Warehouse*, Morgan Kaufmann Publishers, 1999
16. Hull, R., Zhou, G.: *A Framework for Supporting Data Integration Using the Materialized and Virtual Approaches*, In Proc. of ACM SIGMOD'96, Montreal, Canada, 1996
17. Keller, W.: *Mapping Objects to Tables*, In EuroPLoP' 97, 1997
18. Keller, W.: *Object/Relational Access Layers*, In EuroPLoP'98, 1998
19. Levy, A. Y., Rajaraman, A., Ordille, J. J.: *Querying Heterogeneous Information Sources Using Source Descriptions*, In Proc. of the 22nd VLDB Conference, Bombay, India, 1996
20. McHugh, J., Widom, J.: *Integrating Dynamically-Fetched External Information into a DBMS for Semistructured Data*, SIGMOD Record, 26 (4), 1997
21. Yoder, J.W., Johnson, R. E., Wilson, Q. D.: *Connecting Business Objects to Relational Databases*, In PLoP'98, 1998

Dynamic Generation and Browsing of Virtual WWW Space Based on User Profiles

Norihide Shinagawa[1] and Hiroyuki Kitagawa[2]

[1] Doctoral Program in Engineering, University of Tsukuba,
Tennohdai 1-1-1, Tsukuba, Ibaraki 305-8573, Japan
siena@dblab.is.tsukuba.ac.jp
[2] Institute of Information Sciences and Electronics, University of Tsukuba,
Tennohdai 1-1-1, Tsukuba, Ibaraki 305-8573, Japan
kitagawa@is.tsukuba.ac.jp

Abstract. Due to the recent and rapid advance of the WWW technology, a huge amount of information is available via the Internet. However, it is difficult for users to find and utilize relevant information. Generally, querying and browsing are both indispensable to access to the required information. In this paper, we propose a scheme to support the browsing phase of the information search based on specification of the user's interest. In our scheme, each user is given virtual WWW pages reflecting his/her interest. Each virtual WWW page is dynamically generated based on the logical document structure extracted from the original page. Our approach makes it possible to browse the WWW space from his/her viewpoint and to identify required information more easily. We also show how such a scheme can be realized in a non-intrusive way in the current WWW browsing environment.

1 Introduction

Due to the recent and rapid advance of the WWW technology, a huge amount of information is available via the Internet. The number of available WWW pages is increasing incessantly, and it is difficult to find and utilize relevant information. A variety of schemes and tools have been investigated up to the present to address this issue [1] [2] [3].

Generally, both querying and browsing are required to access to and identify relevant WWW pages. In a typical scenario, first, the user gives queries to search engines and gets the set of candidate WWW pages. Then, he/she selects some from the candidate set and browses them. If necessary, he/she browses other linked pages and goes back to previous pages. In this manner, querying and browsing are used by turns to reach WWW pages which are relevant to the user's interest.

In the browsing process, the user's interest is usually implicit, while it is explicitly expressed as queries in the querying process. Therefore, it is usually the case that existing WWW pages are presented exactly in the same format and layout to all users, even if they have different interests. Thus, it is the user's responsibility to understand the structure and semantics of WWW pages and to identify relevant substructures and regions. However, it is not an easy task. In particular, in the WWW environment, the user has to manipulate a large amount of documents, most of which are unfamiliar to him/her. In addition, sometimes each WWW page contains a large amount of information. Of course, most of the WWW browsers provide the string search facility to help the user. However, simple string match is not enough to help him/her understand the page contents. Moreover, the string search facility does not change the situation that every user is given the same page presentations.

In this paper, we propose a new scheme to support the browsing process based on specification of the user's interest. In our scheme, the user's interest is explicitly expressed as a user profile. Then, virtual WWW pages named *view-pages* tailored to the user's interest are dynamically generated and presented when browsing the WWW. View-pages essentially show summaries of existing HTML pages complying with the user's interest and level of details specified in the user profile. Therefore, users of different interests are given different views of the WWW. In the view-page generation, a document model named a *logical tree* is used to model the logical structure of an HTML page and plays an important role. In this paper, we also show how view-pages can be realized in a non-intrusive way in the current WWW browsing environment. Therefore, the user can enjoy the proposed feature on the ordinary WWW browsers rather than being compelled to use special browsers tailored to this purpose.

The remaining part of this paper is organized as follows. In Section 2, we give an overview of our approach. In Section 3, we introduce a logical tree to cast logical hierarchies on HTML pages. In Section 4, we present a scheme to generate view-pages based on a user profile. The logical tree in Section 3 is used in the view-page generation. In Section 5, we show the system architecture to implement the proposed scheme non-intrusively in the ordinary WWW browsing environment. In Section 6, we mention related works. Finally, we summarize and conclude this paper in Section 7.

2　Overview

Here, we present an overview of the scheme proposed in the paper. Figure 1 illustrates our approach.

In our environment, the user's viewpoint is explicitly specified as a user profile. A user profile consists of keywords to represent the user's interest and a threshold value which controls the detail level of the presentation. Whenever the user accesses to WWW pages, view-pages are generated dynamically based on the user profile and presented to him/her. They may contain some hyperlinks referring to other WWW pages. In this sense, the user can navigate through the virtual WWW space. Each view-page is essentially a summary of the original WWW page from the viewpoint of the user's interest, and is generated as follows.

(1) We assume that WWW pages are written in HTML. In the first phase, a logical document structure embedded in the target HTML page is extracted, and

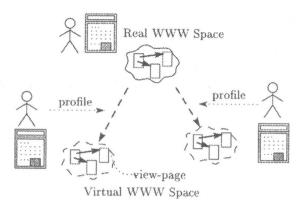

Fig. 1. Overview of the Proposed Scheme

is modeled in a document model named a logical tree. HTML pages contain tags, and some of them are used to construct the logical trees. However, as pointed in [2], the logical document hierarchy usually does not always coincide with the tag hierarchy.

(2) Similarity between each node in the logical tree and the user profile is calculated.

(3) We mark all nodes whose similarities are less than the threshold value in the user profile. A view-page is constructed by pruning away subtrees whose nodes and ancestors are all marked. This phase has to ensure that view-pages are also valid HTML documents.

The phase (1) is further explained in Section 3, and the phases (2) and (3) are elaborated in Section 4.

3 Logical Tree

In this section, we explain derivation of logical trees from HTML pages. For this purpose, first, we classify HTML tags in Subsection 3.1. Then, we show how tags in some group are used to derive logical trees in Subsection 3.2.

3.1 Classification of HTML Tags

We classify tags into the following four groups.

a) Structure-oriented tags: Tags in this group are primarily used to indicate document structures such as headings, paragraphs and lists of items. This group includes the following tags: H1, H2, H3, H4, H5, H6, P, BLOCKQUOTE, DIV, UL, OL, DL, TABLE. Generally, it is not easy to extract logical document structures from HTML documents, but tags in this group give clues to extract them. As a matter of fact, they are used to construct the logical tree as explained in Subsection 3.2.

b) Style-oriented tags: Tags in this group are mainly used to give special presentation effects. The tags STRONG, EM, TT, I, U, B, BIG, SMALL, STRIKE, S, FONT, DL are included in this group. Note that some of them are deprecated in HTML 4.0 [15], which recommends us to use style sheets instead. Elements enclosed by tags in this group are given predetermined weights when deriving feature vectors of document substructures as explained in Subsection 4.1.

c) Media-oriented tags: Tags in this group are used to embed media objects such as images and applets. They include the following tags: IMAGE, FORM, SCRIPT, APPLET, OBJECT, EMBED, MAP. They are ignored in the construction of logical trees. The contents of embedded media objects are also ignored in the derivation of feature vectors.

d) Miscellaneous tags: The other tags are ignored in the construction of logical trees. Existence of tags in this group does not have an effect on the derivation of feature vectors, and elements enclosed in those tags are treated as if they are ordinary character strings.

3.2   Derivation of Logical Trees

In this subsection, we describe derivation of a logical tree from an HTML document. Structure-oriented tags are used as important clues in the derivation. In some context, similar schemes to derive logical structures inherent in HTML documents are suggested (e.g. [2]).

A logical tree consists of the eight types of nodes: ≪*doc*≫, ≪*desc*≫, ≪*leading*≫, ≪*trailing*≫, ≪*packed*≫, ≪*block*≫, ≪*heading*≫, ≪*paragraph*≫. Given an HTML document, it is parsed according to rules in Figure 2, and the logical tree is obtained.

Each node of a logical tree has an attribute L, which indicates the hierarchy level of the node. The L-value of heading nodes associated with H1, H2, ..., H6 tags are 1, 2, ..., 6, respectvely. Each rule in Figure 2 has an annotation "*attr*", which specifies the L-value of the node on the left-hand side. Some rules also have an annotation "*cond*" and the derived logical tree has to satisfy these conditions. Therefore, nodes closer to the root have smaller L-values in the logical tree, and, in this sense, L indicates the hierarchy level. **

In the case of ≪ *desc* ≫, the "*cond*" says that the L-value of each non-≪*leading*≫ child node must be equal to each other, and the "*attr*" says that the L-value gives the attribute L of the ≪*desc*≫ node.

Given the sample HTML document in Figure 3, the derived logical tree shown in Figure 4 is derived by the rules. The dotted lines indicate node groups having the same L-value.

The ≪*leading*≫ nodes, which appear as the left-most child of ≪*desc*≫ nodes, tend to give introduction or summary of the following ≪*trailing*≫ nodes. This observation is used in the next section.

** Precisely speaking, exceptions may occur at nodes associated with BLOCKQUOTE tags.

$$\ll doc \gg \; \rightarrow \; \texttt{<BODY>} \; \ll desc \gg \; \texttt{</BODY>}$$

       $attr$: $L := 0$

$$\ll desc \gg \; \rightarrow \; \ll leading \gg \ll trailing \gg \; +| \; \ll trailing \gg \; +| \; \ll paragraph \gg \; +$$

       $cond$: $\forall c_1, c_2$ which are not $\ll leading \gg \{ c_1.L = c_2.L \}$

       $attr$: $L := c.L$ where c is not $\ll leading \gg$

$$\ll leading \gg \; \rightarrow \; \ll block \gg$$

       $cond$: $L < child.L$

       $attr$: $L := parent.L$

$$\ll trailing \gg \; \rightarrow \; \texttt{<DIV>} \; \ll trailing \gg \; \texttt{</DIV>} | \; \ll packed \gg$$

       $attr$: $L := child.L$

$$\ll packed \gg \; \rightarrow \; \ll heading \gg \ll block \gg$$

       $cond$: $L < \ll block \gg.L$

       $attr$: $L := \ll heading \gg.L$

$$\ll block \gg \; \rightarrow \; \texttt{<DIV>} \; \ll block \gg \; \texttt{</DIV>}$$
$$| \; \ll desc \gg$$

       $attr$: $L := child.L$

$$\ll heading \gg \; \rightarrow \; \texttt{<H1>}text\texttt{</H1>}|\texttt{<H2>}text\texttt{</H2>}|\texttt{<H3>}text\texttt{</H3>}$$
$$| \; \texttt{<H4>}text\texttt{</H4>}|\texttt{<H5>}text\texttt{</H5>}|\texttt{<H6>}text\texttt{</H6>}$$

       $attr$: $L := the \; level \; of \; the \; tag$

$$\ll paragraph \gg \; \rightarrow \; \texttt{<BLOCKQUOTE>} \; \ll block \gg \; \texttt{</BLOCKQUOTE>}|\texttt{<DIV>} \; \ll block \gg \; \texttt{</DIV>}$$
$$| \; \texttt{<P>}text\texttt{</P>}|\texttt{<UL>}text\texttt{</UL>}|\texttt{<OL>}text\texttt{</OL>}|\texttt{<DL>}text\texttt{</DL>}$$
$$| \; \texttt{<TABLE>}text\texttt{</TABLE>}|text-without-structure$$

       $attr$: $L := $ if tag is $\texttt{DIV}$ then $\ll block \gg.L$ else 7

Note 1: "*text*" is any character string, while "*text−without−structure*" accepts one that is not decomposable by any rule. Thus, "*text−without−structure*" accepts a string which appears immediately inside a BODY, DIV or BLOCKQUOTE element and does not contain any structure-oriented tags.

Note 2: "*node.L*" means the L-value of the *node*.

Fig. 2. Derivation Rules

4 Generation of View-pages

In this section, we explain how to construct view-pages based on the logical tree. We use the vector space model [4] [5] [6], but structure-oriented and style-oriented tags introduced in Subsection 3.1 are taken into consideration.

First, we derive a feature vector for each node in the logical tree. Second, we calculate the similarity between each node and the user profile using the feature vector. Next, we mark all nodes whose similarities are less than the threshold

```
<BODY>
    <H1> 1. heading of chapter </H1>
    <P> introduction of chapter </P>
    <H2> 1.1. heading of section </H2>
    <P> body 1.1.1 </P>
    <P> body 1.1.2 <B> IMPORTANT </B> </P>
    <H2> 1.2. heading of section </H2>
    <P> body 2 </P>
    <H1> 2. heading of chapter </H1>
    <H2> 2.0.1 heading of subsection </H2>
    <TABLE> table </TABLE>
    <P> explanation about table </P>
</BODY>
```

Fig. 3. Sample HTML Document

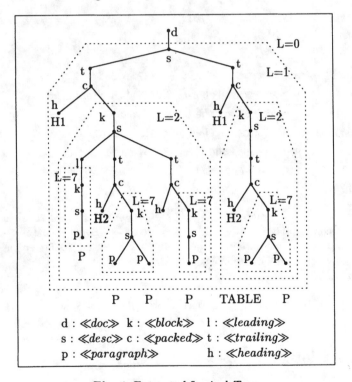

Fig. 4. Extracted Logical Tree

value given in the user profile. Finally, we construct view-pages by pruning away the subtrees whose nodes and ancestors are all marked.

4.1 Derivation of Feature Vectors

Leaf Nodes Initially, feature vectors of leaf nodes in the logical tree are derived based on the traditional tf·idf (term frequency × inverse document frequency) weighting scheme [5]. In the calculation of the idf factor, the target document set has to be fixed. We regard the set of leaf nodes as the target document set in deriving the idf. Namely, we calculate the initial tf·idf weights according to distribution of terms within the document.

Then, style-oriented tags are processed. They are usually used to emphasize some terms. Therefore, when terms occur within elements enclosed by style-oriented tags, we multiply their weights in the feature vectors depending on the types of tags. The bias factors associated with style-oriented tags are shown in Table 1.

For each leaf node n, its feature vector is formulated as follows. When a term t occurs in multiple elements enclosed by different style-oriented tags, their maximum bias factor is used:

$$v_n = (tf_t \cdot idf_{n,t} \cdot \beta_n)_{t \in \mathcal{T}}, \tag{1}$$

where β_n is the maximum bias factor associated with the style-oriented tags enclosing the term t in node n.

Non-Leaf Nodes The feature vector of each non-leaf node is given as an aggregation of feature vectors of its child nodes.

Generally, titles, headings, abstracts and introductions give good summaries of their bodies and contain many important terms [6] [7]. In the logical tree, headings appear as ≪ *heading* ≫ nodes. Moreover, ≪ *leading* ≫ nodes which appear as the first child node of the ≪ *desc* ≫ nodes tend to play a role of abstract and introduction, as mentioned in Subsection 3.2.

To reflect this property, we calculate the feature vector of each non-leaf node n as weighted sums of those of its child nodes:

$$v_n = \sharp C \cdot \frac{\Sigma_c \alpha_c \cdot v_c}{\Sigma_c \alpha_c}, \tag{2}$$

where c is a child node of n and $\sharp C$ is the total number of the child nodes. The coefficient α_c is given in Table 2.

4.2 Generation of View-pages

To generate view-pages, we must decide substructures which are likely to be relevant to the user profile. Similarity of each node in the logical tree is calculated from its feature vector and the profile vector derived from the keyword set in the user profile. In the calculation, we have to note that the length of text (namely, the numbers of terms) associated with each node differs depending on nodes. To take this into acount, we use the C-pivot measure (see Appendix) rather than the traditional cosine measure.

We generate view-pages by pruning away subtrees whose all nodes and ancestors have similarity scores lower than the threshold value in the user profile.

tag	β_n	semantics
STRONG	5	strong emphasis
EM	3	emphasis
BIG	3	big letters
U	2	underline
B	2	bold
I	2	italic
DT	2	defined term in DL

Table 1. Bias Factors β_n Associated with Style-oriented Tags

node	α_c	node	α_c
$\ll$heading$\gg$ (H1)	15	$\ll$desc$\gg$	1
$\ll$heading$\gg$ (H2)	11	$\ll$leading$\gg$	5
$\ll$heading$\gg$ (H3)	8	$\ll$trailing$\gg$	1
$\ll$heading$\gg$ (H4)	6	$\ll$packed$\gg$	1
$\ll$heading$\gg$ (H5)	4	$\ll$block$\gg$	1
$\ll$heading$\gg$ (H6)	3	$\ll$paragraph$\gg$	1

Table 2. Coefficients α_c for Child Nodes

In this process, we have to ensure that view-pages are valid HTML documents, which the user can browse on the ordinary WWW browsers. Note that careless pruning procedure may bring about document structures which do not form valid HTML documents. For instance, an HTML document must have a BODY element and it must not be empty. Therefore, we cannot delete the BODY or its subtree even if scores of all its member nodes are less than the threshold value.

Another concern is to help the user understand the document structures through view-pages. Since the headings are important clues in understanding the whole document structures, we have decided to maintain all headings in the original documents in view-pages. In addition, some appropriate indications should be given as notes when some parts or substructures have been pruned. Moreover, simple pruning may bring about unexpected rendering of the view-page. For instance, pruning the P element away from "text <P> paragraph </P> text" brings about "text text". In this case, two "text" segments are accidentally concatenated to form a single text segment.

Based on the above consideration, in the view-page generation, we substitute a "(snip)" enclosed by a pair DIV tags for each sequence of elements which are to be pruned away. The complete procedure to generate view-pages is given as followings:

1. Calculate the similarity score of every node in the logical tree.
2. Mark the nodes whose scores are less than the threshold value. Here, $\ll$doc$\gg$ and $\ll$heading$\gg$ nodes are always excluded even if their scores are low, since the BODY element is mandatory and H1, ..., H6 elements are important.
3. Identify the maximal subtrees whose nodes and ancestors are all marked.
4. Replace each sequence of HTML elements associated with the subtrees with "<DIV> (snip) </DIV>".
5. Generate the output as a view-page.

Theorem *Given an arbitrary valid HTML document, the above procedure generates a valid HTML document.*

(Proof)

It is obvious from the derivation rules in Figure 2 that each sequence corresponds to the BODY element or a sequence of child elements in a BODY, DIV or

BLOCKQUOTE element. According to the HTML syntax, the BODY element cannot be replaced by a DIV element, but this case is avoided in Step 2. BODY, DIV and BLOCKQUOTE elements can contain DIV elements. Therefore, the replacement in Step 4 preserves the conformity to HTML. Thus, the above procedure derives a valid HTML document. Q.E.D.

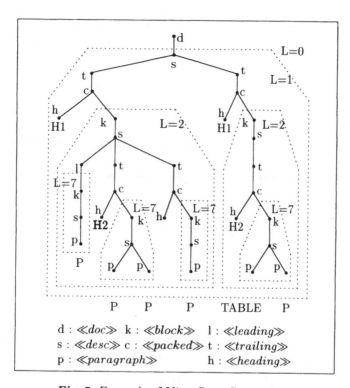

d : ≪doc≫ k : ≪block≫ l : ≪leading≫
s : ≪desc≫ c : ≪packed≫ t : ≪trailing≫
p : ≪paragraph≫   h : ≪heading≫

Fig. 5. Example of View-Page Generation

```
<BODY>
    <H1> 1. heading of chapter </H1>
    <DIV> (snip) </DIV>
    <H2> 1.1. heading of section </H2>
    <DIV> (snip) </DIV>
    <H2> 1.2. heading of section </H2>
    <P> body 2 </P>
    <H1> 2. heading of chapter </H1>
    <H2> 2.0.1 heading of subsection </H2>
    <TABLE> table </TABLE>
    <P> explanation about table </P>
</BODY>
```

Fig. 6. HTML Document for a View-page

Figure 5 illustrates the generation of a view-page. The circles are nodes whose scores are greater than or equal to the threshold value. The subtrees indicated by dotted lines are replaced by "<DIV> (snip) </DIV>" elements. Figure 6 shows the HTML document corresponding to the derived view-page.

5 Prototype System Architecture

In this section, we present the system architecture to implement the proposed scheme. We also show a sample session in the prototype system.

5.1 System Architecture

Overview One of criteria for our prototype system design has been to respect user-friendliness provided in the current WWW browsing environment. The prototype system architecture is shown in Figure 7. It consists of three modules.

- Browser
- Controller
- Browsing Assistance Engine

Solid arcs indicate requests and method invocations, and dotted arcs indicate responses and value returns.

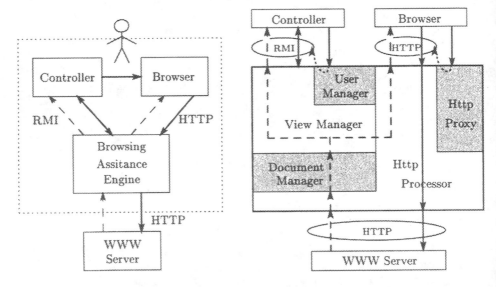

Fig. 7. Prototype System Architecture   **Fig. 8.** Architecture of BAE

The user can use an ordinary WWW browser, such as Netscape Communicator and Internet Explorer, without any modification. The Controller and the

Browsing Assistance Engine (BAE) are original to our browsing environment. For each user, a pair of the Browser and Controller instances works as a front-end module and the BAE works as a back-end module.

The BAE is the central module in our environment, and provides the view-page for each WWW page. It works as an HTTP proxy server for the Browser, and can serve multiple pairs of the Browser and Controller instances. The BAE gets the user profile from the Controller and maintains it. It generates view-pages and their logical trees using the user profile for each user. The user can disable the view-page generation feature, when he/she wants to browse WWW pages in an ordinary manner.

The Browser displays the view-page generated by the BAE. When view-pages include hyperlinks, the user can visit other pages. Then, view pages for the next pages will be generated and presented.

The Controller interacts with the user to get his/her user profile. When the user modifies the profile, it notifies the BAE of the modification. The Controller visually displays the logical tree of the current view-page, as described in Subsection 5.2. It helps the user to identify relevant substructures in each page.

In the prototype system, the Controller is implemented as a java applet and the BAE runs as a Java application program. The presentation on the screen given by the Browser and Controller is synchronized. The applet context is used for the synchronization.

Browsing Assistance Engine (BAE)   We show the internal architecture of the BAE in Figure 8. It consists of the following five modules.

- Http Proxy
- User Manager
- Document Manager
- Http Processor
- View Manager

The first three modules are created when the BAE starts its execution. The Http Processor and View Manager are instantiated and destroyed based on demands from other modules. All the modules except the Document Manager run as threads.

The Http Proxy listens to a TCP port. When the Browser requests an HTTP resource, it instantiates an Http Processor and delegates the request to it.

The Http Processor fetches the requested HTTP resource. When the requested HTTP resource is an HTML document, the Http Processor parses it, creates the DOM object, and generates the logical tree and the view-page, by calling the Document Manager and the View Manager. When the Http Processor finishes processing the request, it is destroyed automatically.

The Document Manager is responsible for parsing documents and creating the DOM objects and logical trees. It also caches them on the memory resident hash table. URI is the hash key.

The User Manager waits for the RMI connection from a Controller instance and creates a View Manager for each connection (see below).

The View Manager communicates with the Controller to maintain the user profile and generates view-pages. View-pages are generated from the DOM objects and logical trees managed in the Document Manager. The View Manager also provides the Controller with information about the current view-page such as its URI, logical tree structure and node scores.

Typical Processing Flow

Starting-up Before invoking the Browser, we have to start the BAE, and a WWW page containing the Controller applet has to reside on the host. The user has to use the BAE as an HTTP proxy server on the WWW browser.

First, the user accesses to the WWW page containing the Controller applet. Then, the Controller is downloaded and executed in the window of the original WWW browser. It creates a new window and launches another instance of the WWW browser as the Browser. The Controller can control the Browser through the applet context. Next, the Controller interacts with the User Manager in the BAE, and its View Manager is instantiated by the User Manager.

Processing an HTTP Request After the above step, the user can browse WWW pages in an ordinary manner. When a new WWW page is requested, The Http Proxy instantiates an Http Processor to process it. If the requested resource is an HTML document, the URI is registered in the View Manager as the current URI of the Browser. Otherwise, it fetches the resource and simply returns it to the Browser.

When processing a request to an HTML document, the Http Processor checks whether it is in the cache maintained by the Document Manager. If not, it fetches and parses the the HTML document. Next, the Http Processor generates a view-page by calling the View Manager and returns it to the Browser. If the requested URI is different from the last URI, the View Manager notifies the Controller to make the presentation of the logical tree up-to-date.

Change of User Profile The user can change keywords and the threshold value in his/her user profile. In this case, the Controller notifies the View Manager. When the keywords are changed, the View Manager computes the score of each node in the logical tree again.

Next, the Controller gets the current URI from the View Manager, and makes the Browser reload the current page through the applet context. The reload request is caught by the BAE, and the View Manager generates the view-page based on the updated user profile.

Changes to the threshold value in the user profile are processed in a similar manner.

5.2 Session Example

In this subsection, we show sample usage of our browsing environment. Suppose that we want documents which are related to this paper under the W3C home page (http://www.w3.org/). Here, we select {*browsing, user, profile, interest, view, paper*} as a keywords set.

First, we turn off the view-page generation feature of the BAE, and we search candidate WWW pages querying the index server existing at the W3C site. To check highly ranked WWW pages, we turn on the view-page generation feature. Figures 9 and 10 show the Controller window and the Browser window, respectively, when we browse the first document in the list.

At the top of the Controller window, there are components to input and modify the user profile. The Controller window displays the logical tree of the current page. The color of each node is determined by its score. Nodes with the highest score are displayed in red and nodes with score 0 are in blue. Nodes with scores between the extremes are displayed in orange, yellow, green and cyan.

Nodes whose scores are greater than or equal to the threshold value are tagged with large red icons. Nodes whose scores are less than the threshold value are tagged with small cyan icons. The view-page consists of the contents corresponding to the nodes tagged with the large red icons. The user can control the threshold value interactively with the aid of the colored logical tree.

The view-page displayed in the Browser window helps our understanding the contexts. Especially, we can easily identify descriptions related to the keywords. When we want to browse the next document, we go back to the document list in the query result and select it. Then, the Browser displays its view-page. We can browse other pages similarly. When view-pages include hyperlinks, we can visit the linked pages as usual. In this way, our environment supports browsing view-pages tailored to the user's viewpoint as if they were existing WWW pages.

6 Related Works

In the proposed scheme, view-pages are generated as summaries of existing HTML documents biased by the user profile. There are several works addressing automatic summarization of documents [4] [8]. However, most of them do not take the user's interest into consideration, which is important, in particular, in the browsing process. Tombros and Sanderson proposed a method to generate summaries biased by queries [9]. However, their viewpoint focuses on the querying process, and query-biased summaries are generated to help the user select appropriate documents. Our scheme focuses on the support of the browsing process. Moreover, they do not consider the case that the targets are HTML documents. To browse summaries on ubiquitous WWW browsers, the summaries must be valid HTML documents.

When summaries are used in the browsing process, it is also important that they should be generated dynamically and automatically whenever new pages are fetched. Miike et al. developed an information retrieval system which automatically generates the abstract of each document in the query result [10]. The detailness of the abstracts can be changed interactively. However, they do not consider generation of abstracts biased by queries or user profiles.

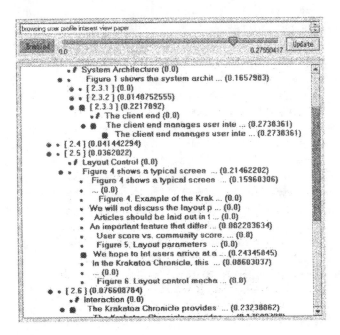

Fig. 9. Controller Window

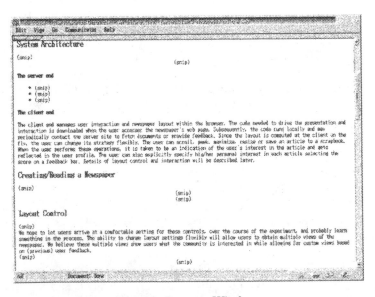

Fig. 10. Browser Window

There are a number of works to support the hyperlink navigation in the hypertext browsing. WebWatcher [3] has a feature to suggest hyperlinks which are likely to lead to the proper destinations. The system automatically acquires the user's interest from the navigation patterns. Such features may work well with our scheme.

In our scheme, scores of substructures in a document are measured. In this sense, our approach has some similarity with the passage retrieval [6] [11] [12]. However, works on the passage retrieval do not explicitly consider the browsing process. Moreover, they usually consider only simpler substructures such as sentences, paragraphs and blocks of fixed length. In our scheme, more complicated substructures are dynamically extracted in our document model.

7 Conclusion and Future Works

In this paper, we have presented a new scheme to support the WWW browsing process by dynamically providing HTML pages tailored to the user profile. This scheme makes it easy for the user to identify the interesting parts and to understand the contents of WWW pages. For this purpose, we have introduced a document model named a logical tree. In our scheme, logical document structures embedded in HTML documents are extracted in the logical tree, and summaries biased by the user profile are generated for the browsing purpose. We have also shown that the proposed scheme can be implemented non-intrusively in the current WWW browsing environment.

The remaining research issues include experimental evaluation of the proposed scheme, detailed performance analysis, and improvement of the prototype system. We are also planning to extend our scheme to make the best of hyperlinks and the referenced page contents in view-page generation. Applications of the scheme to XML documents is another interesting research issue.

References

1. P. Atzeni, A. Mendelzon and G. Mecca (eds.). *The World Wide Web and Databases*, Lecture Notes in Computer Science 1590, Springer-Verlag, 1998.
2. N. Ashish and C. A. Knoblock. Wrapper Generation for Semi-Structured Internet Sources, *ACM SIGMOD Records*, Vol.26, No.4, pp.8-15, December 1997.
3. R. Armstrong, D. Freitag, T. Joachims and T. Mitchell. WebWatcher: A Learning Apprentice for the World Wide Web, *AAAI Spring Symposium on Information Gathering from Heterogeneous, Distributed Environments*, Stanford, 1995.
4. G. Salton. *Automatic Text Processing: The Transformation, Analysis, and Retrieval of Information by Computer*, Addison-Wesley, Reading, MA, 1989.
5. G. Salton, A. Wong and C. S. Yang. A Vector Space Model for Information Retrieval, *Journal of the American Society for Information Science*, Vol.18, No.11, pp.613-620, Novemver 1975.
6. G. Salton, J. Allan and C. Buckley, Approaches to Passage Retrieval in Full Text Information Systems, *Proceedings of the 16th Annual International ACM-SIGIR Conference on Research and Development in Information Retrieval*, pp.49-58, Pittsburgh, 1993.

7. R. Willkinson. Effective Retrieval of Structured Documents. *Proceedings of the 17th Annual International ACM-SIGIR Conference on Research and Development in Information Retrieval*, pp.311-317, Dublin, 1994.

8. C. D. Paris. Constructing Literature Abstracts by Computer: Techniques and Prospects, *Information Processing and Management*, Vol.26, No.1, pp.171-186.

9. A. Tombros and M. Sanderson. Advantage of Query Biased Summarization in Information Retrieval, *Proceedings of the 21th Annual International ACM-SIGIR Conference on Research and Development in Information Retrieval*, pp.2-10, Melbourne, 1998.

10. S. Miike, E. Itoh, K. Ono and K. Sumita. A Full-Text Retrieval System with a Dynamic Abstract Generation Function, *Proceedings of the 17th Annual International ACM-SIGIR Conference on Research and Development Information Retrieval*, pp.152-161, Dublin, 1994.

11. M. Kaszkiel and J. Zobel. Passage Retrieval Revisited, *Proceedings of the 20th Annual International ACM-SIGIR Conference on Research and Development in Information Retrieval*, pp.21-29, Philadelphia, 1997.

12. J. Zobel, A. Moffat, R. Wilkinson and R. Sacks-Davis. Efficient Retrieval of Partial Documents, *Information Processing and Management*, Vol.31, No.3, pp.361-377, 1995.

13. D. K. Harman. Overview of the first TREC Text Retrieval Conference, *Proceedings of TREC Text Retrieval Conference*, pp.1-20, Washington, November 1992. National Institute of Standards Social Publication 500-207.

14. A. Singhal, C. Buckley and M. Mitra. Pivoted Document Length Normalization, *Proceedings of the 19th Annual International ACM-SIGIR Conference on Research and Development in Information Retrieval*, pp.21-29, Zurich, August 1996.

15. D. Raggett, A. Le Hors and I. Jacobs. *HTML 4.0 Reference Specification*, 24 April 1998. http://www.w3.org/TR/REC-html40/.

Appendix: C-Pivot Measure

In the vector space model with the traditional tf·idf weighting scheme, document similarities are scored by some normalized cosine measure. In the classical cosine measure, the size of each document is not explicitly considered. Therefore, when the database contains documents of different length, smaller documents tend to have higher similarity values [13].

Singhal and others proposed the *C-pivot* measure to alleviate this problem [14]. According to the C-pivotmeasure, given a collection $\mathcal{D}$ of N documents and the vocabulary set $\mathcal{T}$, the similarity $sim(v_d, v_q)$ between the document vector v_d and the query vector v_q is calculated as follows:

$$sim(v_d, v_q) = V_d \circ V_q \qquad (3)$$

$$V_d = \frac{v_d}{(1-S)\cdot U_d + S \cdot U_d} \qquad v_x = (tf_{x,t} \cdot idf_t)_{t \in \mathcal{T}} \quad (x = d, q)$$
$$V_q = \frac{v_q}{\|v_q\|} \qquad idf_t = \log(N/n_t + 1),$$

where $d \in \mathcal{D}$, U_d is the number of distinct terms in d, S is a slope constant in $[0, 1]$, $tf_{x,t}$ is the term frequency, and n_t is the number of documents including t. The slope constant is to be empirically decided.

SemiLog: A Logic-Based Query Language for Hierarchical Data in Web Documents

Seung-Jin Lim and Yiu-Kai Ng

Computer Science Department, Brigham Young University
Provo, Utah 84602, U.S.A.
{ng,sjlim}@cs.byu.edu

Abstract. Most of the textual information posted on the Web are in documents which conform to the HTML [12] or recently emerging XML [4] specification. In the past, a number of query languages have been proposed for querying data in Web documents. We notice that these query languages are incapable of inferring hierarchically structured data from linked Web documents as well as within a Web document itself. In this paper, we propose a logic-based query language, called *SemiLog*, for retrieving data in Web documents that are hierarchically structured. SemiLog is capable of handling recursive queries, which infer data that are not explicitly presented in hierarchically structured Web documents, and processing partial knowledge of data in Web documents with irregular structure to answer a given query.

1 Introduction

Data presented in HTML/XML documents (Web documents in short) are *hierarchically structured* in nature (hierarchical data in short). We recognize two types of data hierarchies: i) inter-page data hierarchy which is determined by hyperlinks among the Web documents involved, and ii) intra-page data hierarchy which is determined by the container-content relationships among the data components within a Web document. We are interested in extracting the inter- or intra-page data hierarchies of character data in Web documents.

We notice that even though some hierarchical data are not explicit, they can be inferred from the source HTML documents. Consider the three HTML documents on airline flights as shown in Figure 1. We are interested in processing queries such as "How many routes are there from SEL to LAX that are (jointly) served by the three airlines?" This query requires inferencing information that are not explicitly presented in any of the three HTML documents.

Several query languages, such as WebSQL [10], WebLog [6], Strudel [5] and Florid [5], have been designed for retrieving data from the Web. We observe that i) most of the designers of these languages perceive Web documents as (virtual) tables. Since no direct mapping between a Web document D to a table exists, these designers selectively choose a portion of D which is common to most Web documents to process; ii) Web data handled by these languages are limited to the selected portion of the source documents, and the intra-page data hierarchies of these pages are not well-exploited or their intra-page data hierarchies are often

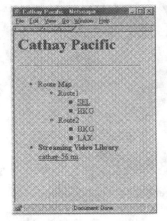  

Fig. 1. HTML documents rendered in Netscape browser adopted from the Web sites of the *Cathay Pacific Airways, Delta Airlines*, and *Singapore Airlines*

intermingled with HTML markups as in WebOQL [3]; and iii) existing Web query languages lack of inferencing capability on hierarchical data.

The capability of WebSQL in exploiting the intra-page data hierarchy of a Web document D is limited since only a few components in D, such as URL and title, are processed by the language. As in WebSQL, only chosen components of Web documents, called *rel-infon*, are considered in WebLog queries. WebOQL relies heavily on the use of markups in HTML documents for querying data, and hence the user of the language must know the internal structure of the source document beforehand. MSL [11] is a simplified object-oriented logic language which cannot handle sets, whereas OQL-doc [2] relies heavily on generalized path expressions and pattern matching, and the intra-page hierarchy of an HTML document perceived by OQL-doc is intermingled with HTML markups and character data. Lorel [1] is the query language of its semistructured data model of which its data are not directly extracted from Web documents.

We propose a logic-based query language, called *SemiLog*, for querying hierarchical data in Web documents without requiring the internal structure of the documents to be known beforehand. SemiLog deals exclusively with data (such as Routes) rather than markups and data (such as [LI]Routes[/LI]). The main contributions of this paper include the following: (i) (*a new logic-based language*) SemiLog, a logic-based, declarative query language is defined, which is capable of processing (recursive) queries on hierarchically structured Web data and infers data that is not explicitly presented; (ii) (*capability of handling partial knowledge*) SemiLog utilizes the *partial knowledge* of data structure, data type, and string patterns of Web data in answering queries; and (iii) (*extension of logic programming*) employing SemiLog on Web documents expands the application domain of deductive databases to include hierarchical/semistructured data.

This paper is organized as follows. In Section 2, the data model for representing Web documents to be queried is defined. In Section 3, the syntax and semantics of SemiLog are given, and different issues in querying data on the Web are discussed in Section 4. In Section 5, we give the concluding remark.

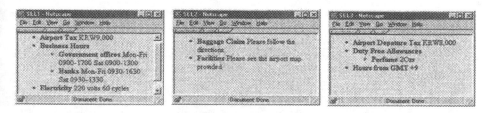

Fig. 2. HTML documents *SEL*1, *SEL*2, and *SEL*3 linked from anchor *SEL* of Cathay Pacific, Delta, and Singapore Airlines, respectively

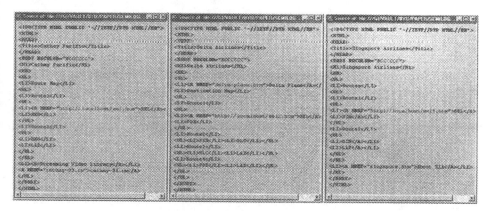

Fig. 3. Source code of the HTML documents in Figure 1, given in the same order

2   The Data Model: SDG

We develop a data model, called *semistructured data graph* (SDG), which is a graphical representation of the underlying semistructured data. We use the HTML documents rendered in the browser (as shown in Figure 1), and the HTML documents *SEL*1, *SEL*2, and *SEL*3 that are linked from the anchor *SEL* of Cathay Pacific, Delta, and Singapore Airlines, respectively[1] (as shown in Figure 2) as a running example in this paper. (The source code of the HTML documents in Figure 1 are as shown in Figure 3.)

A core construct of SDG is *objects* which are defined over the set of all possible **strings**, denoted by Σ^*, i.e., a **string** is a finite sequence of symbols in an alphabet Σ. A string in SemiLog denotes the character data that is delimited by any two HTML or XML tags, or the name of an XML element. A string in SemiLog is surrounded by a pair of single quotes. When two strings appear together in a SemiLog expression, we add a period ('.'), a string delimiter, between them. Each member of Σ^* is closed under the distributive law over ',', i.e., $A.(B,C)$ is the ordered pair $(A.B, A.C)$, where A, B, and C are strings.

Definition 1 The *label* of an object o, which is the *name* of o, is a string in a semistructured data D. An object o_1 *directly depends* on another object o_2,

---

[1] The HTML documents are based on the actual airline HTML documents; however, only portions of these documents are included in this paper.

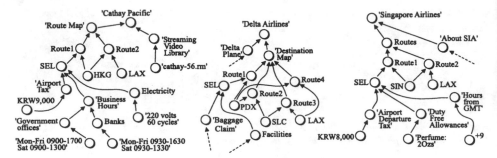

Fig. 4. An SDG for the semistructured data *Airlines*

denoted $o_1 \leftarrow o_2$, if o_1 is the immediate container of o_2 (i.e., o_2 is an immediate content of o_1) in a Web document. If $o_1 \leftarrow o_2$ and $o_2 \leftarrow o_3$, then o_1 *indirectly depends on* o_3, denoted $o_1 \leftarrow o_2 \leftarrow o_3$. When o_1 directly (indirectly, respectively) depends on o_2, o_2 is directly (indirectly, respectively) *relevant* to o_1.

Example 1 Consider the *Cathay Pacific Airways* HTML document presented in Figures 1 and 2. *'Cathay Pacific'* is one of the objects in the document. Since *'KRW9,000'* is the content of *'Airport Tax'* (as shown in Figure 2), *'Airport Tax'* $\leftarrow$ *'KRW9,000'*. Also, since *'SEL'* is the container of *'Airport Tax'* across the hyperlink as shown in Figure 3, we obtain *'SEL'* $\leftarrow$ *'Airport Tax'* $\leftarrow$ *'KRW9,000.'*

In conjunction with objects, we assume the existence of the functions *o.label*() and *con*. *o.label*() returns the label of object *o*, whereas *con* is a binary function $\Sigma^* \times \Sigma^* \to \Sigma^*$ such that $con(arg_1, arg_2) = arg_1.arg_2$, where "." is a string delimiter. The SDG of a semistructured data D is constructed according to the *dependency* constraints among the objects in D.

Definition 2 Given a semistructured data D, a *semistructured data graph* SDG $= (V, E, g)$ of D is a graphical representation of D, where (i) $v \in V$ is a node representing an object o in D and is labeled by *o.label*(); (ii) E is a finite set of directed edges; and (iii) $g: E \to V \times V$ such that $g(e) = (v_1, v_2)$ if the object denoted by v_2 directly depends on the object denoted by v_1, i.e., $v_2 \leftarrow v_1$.

Example 2 Consider the HTML documents shown in Figures 1 and 2 again, and assume that the collection of data captured in these documents is the semistructured data *Airlines*. Further assume that the dependency constraints among the data objects in these documents exist across the hyperlinks as well as within each document. The resulting SDG of *Airlines* is as shown in Figure 4.

The notation SDG_D is used to denote an SDG of semistructured data D. For instance, $SDG_{Airlines}$ in Figure 4 denotes the SDG of *Airlines*, and $SDG_{'Cathay\ Pacific'}$ is a subgraph of $SDG_{Airlines}$. We call a subgraph in an SDG G a *subSDG* of G. We now introduce a few properties of SDGs.

Definition 3 Given a sequence of dependency relationships among objects o_1, o_2, ..., o_N in a (sub)SDG as $o_1 \leftarrow \cdots \leftarrow o_N$, a *long label* of o_i, denoted $o_i.Label()$, $1 \leq i \leq N$, is defined as $o_1.Label() = o_1.label()$, and $o_i.Label() = con(o_{i-1}.Label(), o_i.label())$, $2 \leq i \leq N$.

Observe that if there are two or more paths between an object o and one of the ancestor objects of o in an SDG, then $o.Label()$ is not unique. One of the long labels of the object 'HKG' in $SDG._{CathayPacific'}$, as shown in Figure 4, is '$Cathay$ $Pacific$'.'$Route\ Map$'.'$Route1$'.'HKG', and another one is '$Cathay\ Pacific$'.'$Route$ Map'.'$Route2$'.'HKG'. Path expressions (defined below) generalize the concept of long labels and capture the hierarchy of objects in a given SDG.

Definition 4 Given a long label of an object o_N in a (sub)SDG G in the form $(o_1.label()).(\ldots).(o_N.label())$, the *path expression* (*pe*) is a binary function, *pe*: $\Sigma^* \times \Sigma^* \rightarrow \Sigma^*$, such that $pe(o_i, o_i) = o_i.label()$ $(1 \leq i \leq N)$, and $pe(o_i, o_j) = con(pe(o_i, o_{j-1}), o_j.label())$ $(1 \leq i < j \leq N)$, where o_1 denotes a root node in G. Also, $pe(V_R, o) = o.Label()$, where V_R is a root node and o is a node in SDG_{V_R}.

Given the first long label of 'HKG', $pe($'$Route\ Map$', 'HKG'$) = $ '$Route\ Map$'. '$Route1$'.'HKG'. The lexical representation of SDG_D (defined below) is useful in some applications of D, e.g., finding objects in D using textual path expressions.

Definition 5 Given an $SDG = (V, E, g)$, the *lexical representation* or *lexical SDG* of $o \in V$, denoted by L_o, is a textual representation of the subgraph S of the SDG rooted at o such that $L_o = (\biguplus_{\forall i} pe(o, o_i))$, where $\biguplus$ is the order-sensitive union operation and o_i is a leaf node in S.

Given an SDG G with subSDGs G_1, ..., G_n, the lexical representation of G is the ordered list of all the path expressions $pe(V_j, o)$ for each leaf node o in G_j $(1 \leq j \leq n)$, where V_j is the root node of G_j. For instance, if $n = 2$ and $G_1 = $ 'Cathay Pacific'.'Route Map'.'Route1'.'HKG' and $G_2 = $ 'Cathay Pacific'.'Route Map'.'Route2'.'LAX', then $G_1 \biguplus G_2 = $ 'Cathay Pacific'.'Route Map'. ('Route1'.'HKG', 'Route2'.'LAX').

3 SemiLog: A Declarative Query Language

In this section, we present the syntax and semantics of SemiLog, a language for querying hierarchical data in Web documents. The architecture of the SemiLog query processor consists of two layers: (1) the *SDG engine* [7] that fetches the source Web document D and constructs SDG_D, and (2) the *query processor* that evaluates a given query posted against SDG_D. (Observe that a graphical SDG and its corresponding lexical SDG are equivalent. Hence, whenever we refer to an SDG, it can be either the graphical or lexical version of the SDG.) In this paper, we discuss the SemiLog processor only.

3.1 Syntax of SemiLog

SemiLog is based on the notions of term, formula, rule, fact, program, and query, which in turn are defined on alphabets.

Definition 6 Four sets of alphabets are defined in SemiLog as follows:

(a) `Constants`: any string is a constant. A constant is a *term*.

(b) **Variables**: strings that begin with an uppercase letter (possibly subscripted). The special variable "_", called *anonymous variable*, is the "don't-care" variable. A variable is a *term*.

(c) **Functions**: if f is an n-ary $(n > 0)$ function symbol and $t_1, \ldots, t_n$ are terms, then $f(t_1, \ldots, t_n)$ is a *term*.

(d) **Predicates**: a predicate name is a string that starts with a lower-case letter and its corresponding predicate is of arity ≥ 0. Each argument $t_1, \ldots, t_n$ of a predicate is a term, and each predicate is called an *atom*.

Example 3 Consider Figure 1 again. The terms '*Route1*' and '*SEL*' are *constant* terms, and X is a *variable* term. Furthermore, '*Route1*'.'*SEL*'.X is a term since it can be obtained from $con('Route1', con('SEL', X))$. _._._ is also a term. A term is *ground* if it contains no variable.

Definition 7 A *literal* is an atom $p(t_1, \ldots, t_n)$ or a negated atom $\neg p(t_1, \ldots, t_n)$. A *clause* is a formula of the form $\forall X_1 \ldots \forall X_n (L_1 \vee \ldots \vee L_m)$, where $L_1, \ldots, L_m$ are literals and $X_1 \ldots X_n$ are variables occurring in $L_1 \vee \ldots \vee L_m$. A clause containing at most one positive literal is called a *Horn clause*. A Horn clause, which is a clause of the form $L_0 :- L_1 \wedge \ldots \wedge L_n$, is a *rule*, where L_0 is the *head* and $L_1 \wedge \ldots \wedge L_n$ is the *body* of the rule such that if $L_1, \ldots, L_n$ are all true, then L_0 is true. A rule is a *fact* if it is a positive unit clause (i.e., $n = 0$). A *program* in SemiLog is a collection of rules and facts. A *goal* is a rule without a head, denoted ?– *body*, and a *SemiLog query* consists of a program and a goal.

In addition to the usual predicates such as ==, $\neq$, >, <, >=, and <=, the following are built-in predicates in SemiLog (and the corresponding examples refer to the SDG in Figure 4):

- $subsdg\_of(SDG, Obj, SDG_{Obj})$: SDG_{Obj} is a subSDG of SDG G rooted at object Obj if Obj exists in G. For instance, $subsdg\_of('Airlines', 'Route2', 'Route2'.('HKG','LAX'))$ is true.

- $long\_labels\_of(SDG, Obj, LongLabels)$: $LongLabels$ is the set of long labels of object Obj if Obj exists in SDG. For instance, $long\_labels\_of('Airlines', 'HKG', \{$'*Cathay Pacific*'.'*Route* Map' . 'Route1' . '*HKG*', '*Cathay Pacific*'. '*Route Map*'.'*Route2*'.'*HKG*'$\})$ is true.

- $path\_expr\_of(LongLabel, Obj_1, Obj_2, PathExpr)$: $PathExpr$ is the path expression of object Obj_2 from object Obj_1 if both objects appear in $LongLabel$. For instance, $path\_expr\_of('Cathay Pacific'.'Route Map'.'Route2'.'HKG', 'Route2', 'HKG', 'Route2'.'HKG')$ is true.

- $in(A, B)$: $A \in B$, where B is a set and A is an element of a set. For instance, $in(\_.\_.'HKG', \{$ '*Cathay Pacific*'.'*Route Map*'.'*Route1*'.'*HKG*', '*Cathay Pacific*'.'*Route Map*'.'*Route2*'.'*HKG*'$\})$ is true.

- $contain(arg_1, arg_2)$: (i) String arg_2 is a substring of string arg_1, or (ii) arg_2, which is either a long label or a path expression, is a subpart of arg_1, which is either a subSDG, a long label, or a path expression. For instance, $contain('Route Map', 'Route')$ is evaluated to be true, where 'Route Map' and 'Route' are strings.

– $set\_of(X,\ Goal,\ Instances)$: *Instances* is the set of instances of X for which *Goal* is evaluated to be true with respect to X. For instance, $set\_of(City,\ contain(SDG_{Airlines},\ 'Cathay\ Pacific'.'Route\ Map'.'Route1'.City),\ \{'SEL',\ 'HKG'\})$ is true.

3.2 Semantics of SemiLog

The semantics of a SemiLog program (query) $\mathcal{P}$ states what the meaning of $\mathcal{P}$ is and subsequently asserts how an answer to $\mathcal{P}$ (if $\mathcal{P}$ is a query), i.e., a fact, can be obtained. The semantics of $\mathcal{P}$ can be defined by the proof-theoretical model of $\mathcal{P}$. An *SLD-refutation*, which is based on the *resolution method*, is a proof-theoretical model and is used to ascertain the semantics of $\mathcal{P}$.

Definition 8 [9] A *resolution* resolves a clause using modus tollens, instantiation, and conjunction along with a number of given facts. A *linear resolution* is a resolution where a goal is the first clause to be resolved. An *SLD-resolution* is a refinement of the linear resolution method with a selection function. A *selection function* chooses a subgoal (i.e., a literal) from a goal to be evaluated next. An *SLD-refutation* is an SLD-resolution which has the *empty clause* as the last goal in the derivation and denotes that the goal is evaluated to be true.

Using the proof-theoretical model, an answer to a query Q in SemiLog is obtained by an SLD-refutation with substitutions for the variables in Q.

Definition 9 A *substitution* θ is a finite set of *bindings* $\{V_1/t_1,\ \ldots,\ V_n/t_n\}$, where each V_i is a distinct variable and each t_i is a term such that $V_i \neq t_i$, $1 \leq i \leq n$. Given two terms s_1 and s_2, a substitution θ is called a *unifier* of s_1 and s_2 if $s_1 \circ \theta = s_2 \circ \theta$, i.e., if replacing each occurrence of V_i in either s_1 or s_2 by t_i $(1 \leq i \leq n)$ causes s_1 and s_2 to become identical.

In the process of obtaining substitutions for the variables in a SemiLog query, facts and other variables are used. A *path*, i.e., the (long) label of a node, in an SDG is considered to be a *fact* in a SemiLog program. Other facts can be inferenced by recursive rules in a program such that these facts are not associated with any explicit paths in the SDG (as will be demonstrated in the recursive query example given in Section 4.3).

Example 4 Given the $SDG_{Airlines}$ in Example 2, the following rules

$reachableCityByCathayPacific(Cities)$:− $set\_of(City,\ contain(SDG_{Airlines},$
  $'Cathay\ Pacific'.'Route\ Map'.'Route1'.City),\ Cities)$.
$reachableCityByCathayPacific(Cities)$:− $set\_of(City,\ contain(SDG_{Airlines},$
  $'Cathay\ Pacific'.'Route\ Map'.'Route2'.City),\ Cities)$.

determines the cities that can be reached by *Cathay Pacific*, and the goal ?− $reachableCityByCathayPacific(X)$ retrieves all such cities. There exist three bindings for the variable *City*, i.e., $City/$'SEL,' $City/$'HKG,' and $City/$'LAX.' Each of these bindings is a unifier of the variable *City* in the term '*Cathay Pacific*'.'*Route Map*'.'*Route1*'.*City* or '*Cathay Pacific*'.'*Route Map*'.'*Route2*'.*City*.

By the unification process of the SLD-refutation, the formal meaning of a fact as an answer to a query is formulated in SemiLog.

4 Querying SDGs Using SemiLog

When querying data presented in an SDG using SemiLog, we deal with a problem which does not occur in querying relations in the relational database model as well as in the deductive database model. The problem is that the structure of the semistructured data D represented in its SDG is often irregular and the schema of D is often not well-defined.

Suppose that we want to know what type of electricity is available in Seoul (*'SEL'*), an object in $SDG_{Airlines}$. One assumption can be made is that the data hierarchy as represented in $SDG_{Airlines}$ of the semistructured data *Airlines* is fully known to the user. Another assumption is that the user has partial knowledge or no knowledge at all of the underneath hierarchy of $SDG_{Airlines}$. If the user knows the entire data hierarchy of $SDG_{Airlines}$, then the following goal and rule are sufficient to answer the query:

> *Goal*: ?– *electricityInSEL*(X).
> *Rule* 1: *electricityInSEL*(X) :– *contain*($SDG_{Airlines}$,
>   *'Cathay Pacific'.'Route Map'.'Route1'.'SEL'.'Electricity'.X*).

However, expressing a rule using a complete, long label or path expression of an object is not always possible if the data hierarchy of an SDG to be queried is not fully known to the user. Incorrect long label of an object leads to failure of a query, a typical, potential challenge when we deal with hierarchical data.

In addition to structural irregularity, type relaxation in hierarchical data may also cause potential difficulty in expressing and evaluating a query. For instance, suppose that we want to confirm if *'Last Updated'* is not later than 'April 5, 1997.' Without further information about the data type, it is not easy to postulate whether date is of the form 'April 5, 1997' as used in U.S.A., '5 April 1997' in U.K., or '1997-4-5' in some Asian countries.

We also notice that incomplete knowledge of the labels is another potential problem in expressing and evaluating a query on hierarchical data, although it is not a unique problem with hierarchical data. For instance, we may not know whether the label of the object which denotes the airport tax is *'Airport Tax,'* *'Airport Departure Tax,'* or something else.

4.1 Partial Knowledge and Search Boundary Reduction

We consider the following partial knowledge of an SDG and make use of them in querying information from the SDG. These partial knowledge are considered for deriving an efficient query evaluation strategy for processing semistructured data presented in an SDG. Three types of partial knowledge are of particular interest:

- *Partial knowledge of the data hierarchy (ds-knowledge)* of an SDG is caused by the fact that the data hierarchy of the corresponding semistructured data D is irregular and the schema of D is often not well-defined. Ds-knowledge in an SDG is useful in query processing when generalized path expressions with wildcards can be used, or a smart query processor [6] is employed. We adopt the top-down, breadth-first search approach in evaluating an SDG query, i.e., an object is searched by using the breadth-first approach from the root node of a (sub)SDG and the *search space* is reduced as the (sub)SDG is traversed downward. This approach refrains from using wildcards as much as possible and reduces the cost of processing wildcards on a query processor.

- *Partial knowledge of data types* (*dt-knowledge*) used in an SDG is caused by type relaxation in hierarchical data. In order to handle *dt*-knowledge, we adopt the concept of *synonym* [6] and extend it to a *customizable synonym vocabulary* (CSV) of commonly used strings, such as date and time. CSV can be customized by the system designer or an end-user. A query language which is supported by CSV is more flexible in expressing queries. For instance, 'April 5, 1997', '5 April 1997', or '1997/4/5' can be used to express a date.

- *Partial knowledge of strings* (*as-knowledge*) used in an SDG is caused by the fact that the vocabulary of strings in hierarchical data is infinite. Expressing a query using the label of an object is not trivially succinct. *As*-knowledge could be useful when we perform a keyword search. In order to deal with *as*-knowledge, SemiLog uses the built-in predicate $contain(S_1, S_2)$ as defined in Section 3.1. For instance, if we look for information about '*Airport Tax*' at the '*SEL*' airport. We may not know whether the associated object label is '*Airport Tax*,' '*Airport Departure Tax*,' or '*Airport Fee*.' In this case, either $contain(X, 'Airport Tax')$, $contain(X, 'Airport Departure Tax')$, or $contain(X, 'Airport Fee')$ can be included in a SemiLog query to retrieve the desired information, where X is the variable denoting the target object.

In conjunction with using various types of partial knowledge, we are interested in expressing a query using partial knowledge and yet to obtain a favorable performance in query evaluation. This goal can be accomplished with a little effort in an SDG using the data hierarchy embedded in it. The top-down, breadth-first search approach applied to an SDG minimizes the search space during query processing, which enhances the efficiency in query processing.

4.2   Expressive Power of SemiLog and Complexity of Its Queries

SemiLog is capable of simulating various operations in relational algebra, including *selection, projection, set union, set difference*, and *set intersection*. Note that in the relational model, *projection* applies to attributes, whereas *selection* applies to tuples; however, these mappings do not apply to an SDG since there is no distinctive notion of *tuples* generated by selection or *attributes* generated by projection applied to an SDG. In either case, the retrieved data are subSDG(s) of an SDG S, i.e., an aggregation of objects in S. In addition, SemiLog is capable of expressing recursive rules and the *group* and *ungroup* operations based on the *nest* and *unnest* operations in nested relational algebra.

A SemiLog query can be expressed as $\pi_L \sigma_P S$, where S is a list of (sub)SDGs, $L = \mathcal{L}_1, \mathcal{L}_2, \ldots, \mathcal{L}_n$ ($n \geq 1$) is a list of long labels of objects in S, P is a predicate defined over objects in S, π is the projection operation, and σ is the selection operation. Given a SemiLog query q, the cost of processing q includes the cost of (i) finding the set of candidate nodes R in S that are reachable from the root

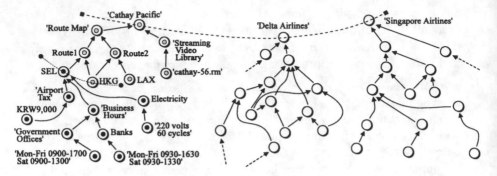

Fig. 5. Search space reduction for the query Q in Section 4.3

node of the corresponding SDG by using the long labels in L, and (ii) determining which nodes in R satisfy P by evaluating P against R. It has been analyzed (see [8]) that the cost of processing a non-recursive (recursive, respectively) query is $\mathcal{O}(n)$ ($\mathcal{O}(n^2)$, respectively), where n is the number of nodes in S.

4.3 Sample SemiLog Queries

We demonstrate three different types of SemiLog queries using the (partial) knowledge of data hierarchy and labels of objects in $SDG_{Airlines}$. These queries include (1) a query such that the data hierarchy and the labels of objects are fully known, (2) a query such that the data hierarchy and the labels of objects are partially known, and (3) a recursive query.

Fully known data hierarchy and object labels. Consider the query Q *"What are the business hours of banks in the city where the airport SEL is located?"* Suppose the data hierarchy and the object labels of $SDG_{Airlines}$ in Figure 4 are fully known. Q can be written as follows:

$$\text{Goal 1: } ?-\ businessHoursOfBanksInSEL(X). \tag{1}$$
$$\text{Rule 1: } businessHoursOfBanksInSEL(X)\ :- \tag{2}$$
$$subsdg\_of(SDG_{Airlines},\ 'Cathay\ Pacific',\ A)\ \wedge \tag{3}$$
$$subsdg\_of(A,\ 'Route\ Map',\ B)\ \wedge \tag{4}$$
$$subsdg\_of(B,\ 'Route1',\ C)\ \wedge\ subsdg\_of(C,\ 'SEL',\ D)\ \wedge \tag{5}$$
$$subsdg\_of(D,\ 'Business\ Hours',\ E)\ \wedge\ subsdg\_of(E,\ 'Banks',\ F)\ \wedge \tag{6}$$
$$set\_of(G,\ contain(F,\ 'Banks'.G),\ X). \tag{7}$$

SemiLog reduces the search space for processing a query by using an SDG. If an SDG spans further in width than in height, i.e., there are more direct relevant objects, it becomes more beneficial in using the SDG in a top-down, breadth-first search manner as an exhaustive searching throughout the entire SDG can be avoided. Figures 5 illustrates the reduced search space as lines (3) and (5) of Q are evaluated. The subgraphs beneath the first (second, respectively) dashed line with dots at the ends represent the search space when line (3) (line (5), respectively) is evaluated. In order for the constant *'Cathay Pacific'* to be found at line (3), the objects at or above the dashed-line with square dots at the ends are examined. Similarly, objects at the dashed-line with round dots at the ends and one level above are examined when line (5) is evaluated till *'SEL'* is found.

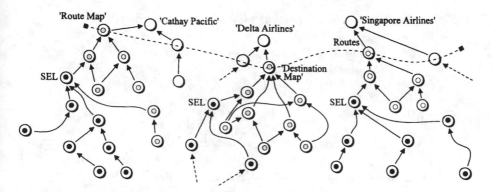

Fig. 6. Search space reduction for the query Q in Section 4.3

Partially known data hierarchy and object labels. Assume that we want to post the same query Q but the data hierarchy of $SDG_{Airlines}$ is not fully known. Further assume that it is partially known that: (i) 'SEL' is described as a route city of an airline, if the airline has a route to 'SEL,' and (ii) '$Business$ $Hours$' (if exists) is directly relevant to 'SEL,' and '$Banks$' is directly relevant to '$Business Hours$.' With this assumption, query Q can be expressed as follows:

$$Goal\ 2:\ ?-\ hoursOfBanksInSEL(X). \tag{8}$$
$$Rule\ 2:\ hoursOfBanksInSEL\ (X)\ :- \tag{9}$$
$$in(A,\ csv(\text{'Route Map'}))\ \wedge\ subsdg\_of(SDG_{Airlines},\ A,\ B)\ \wedge \tag{10}$$
$$subsdg\_of(B,\ \text{'SEL'},\ C)\ \wedge\ subsdg\_of(C,\ \text{'Business Hours'},\ D)\ \wedge \tag{11}$$
$$subsdg\_of(D,\ \text{'Banks'},\ E)\ \wedge\ set\_of(F,\ contain(E,\ \text{'Banks'}.F),\ X). \tag{12}$$

where $csv(\text{'Route Map'})$ is a CSV for '$Route Map$.' This CSV is needed in this query, assuming as-knowledge is used, i.e., we do not know whether the object we are looking for is labeled as '$Route Map$,' '$Destination Map$,' or others.

At line (10), $SDG_{\text{'Route Map'}}$ is first bound to variable B and the objects at and above the dashed-line with squares at the end (as shown in Figure 6) are examined. Note that more objects are examined for this query than the first one specified in this section due to ds- and as-knowledge. This query is less efficient than the first one due to incomplete knowledge of $SDG_{Airlines}$. However, we have shown in this query that ds- and as-knowledge are useful in reducing the overall search space when compared with the exhaustive searching approach.

Recursive query. Consider the query P "*Which airports are reachable from SEL either directly or indirectly?*" In this query, we need to take into consideration the following cases: airport X is reachable (i) directly from SEL by an airline, (ii) by transferring to the same airline at intermediate airports, and (iii) by transferring to different airlines at intermediate airports. This query can be expressed as follows, where $connected(X, Y)$ indicates that there is a non-stop flight from City X to City Y:

$$Goal\ 3:\quad ?-\ reachable\ (\text{'SEL'},\ X).$$
$$Rule\ 3.1:\ reachable(X, Y)\ :-\ connected(X, Y).$$

Rule 3.2: $reachable(X, Y) :- reachable(X, Z) \land connected\ (Z, Y)$.

Rule 3.3 : $connected\ (X, Y) :-$
$$subsdg\_of(SDG_{Airlines}, in(A, csv(\text{'Route Map'})), B) \land$$
$$long\_labels\_of(B, \_\_\_\_, L) \land in(L_1, L) \land$$
$$(L_1 == \_.C.X) \land in(L_2, L) \land (L_2 == \_.C.Y) \land (X \neq Y).$$

5 Conclusions

In this paper, a logic-based query language, SemiLog, is proposed for querying hierarchical data in Web documents. We present a data model, semistructured data graph (SDG), which is a graphical representation of the hierarchical data in a Web document and its linked documents, on which SemiLog queries can be posted. Formal syntax and semantics of SemiLog are presented. As defined, SemiLog is capable of handling (recursive) queries which make use of partial knowledge of the given semistructured data in Web documents. A number of SemiLog queries are included in this paper to demonstrate the usefulness of SemiLog. As examined, SemiLog has rich expressive power, and the cost of evaluating a non-recursive (recursive, respectively) SemiLog query is $\mathcal{O}(n)$, ($\mathcal{O}(n^2)$, respectively), where n is the number of nodes in the given SDG.

References

1. Abiteboul S., Quass, D., McHugh J., Widom J., Wiener J,: The Lorel Query Language for Semistructured Data. Journal on Digital Libraries **1:1** (1997) 68–88
2. Abiteboul, S., Cluet, S., Christophides, V., Milo, T., Moerkotte, G., Simeon, J.: Querying Documents in Object Databases. Int. J. on Digital Libraries (1997) 5–19
3. Arocena, G.O., Mendelzon, A.O.: WebOQL: Restructuring Documents, Databases and Webs. Proceedings of the 14th Intl. Conf. on Data Engineering (1998) 24–33
4. Bray, T., Paoli, J., Sperberg-McQueen, C.: Extensible Markup Language (XML) 1.0 W3C Recommendation 10-February-1998. http://www.w3.org/TR/1998/REC-xml-19980210 (February 1998)
5. Florescu, D., Levy, A., Mendelzon, A.O.: Database Techniques for the World-Wide Web: A Survey. SIGMOD Record, **27:3** (September 1998) 59–74
6. Lakshmanan, L.V.S., Sadri, F., Subramanian, I.N.: A Declarative Language for Querying and Restructuring the Web. Post-ICDE IEEE Workshop on Research Issues in Data Engineering (February 1996)
7. Lim, S.-J., Ng, Y.-K.: WebView: A Tool for Retrieving Internal Structures and Extracting Information from HTML Documents. Proceedings of the 6th International Conference on Database Systems for Advanced Applications (April 1999) 71–80
8. Lim, S.-J., Ng, Y.-K.: SemiLog: A Logic-Based Query Language for Hierarchical Data in Web Documents. http://lunar.cs.byu.edu/papers.html/semi.ps
9. Lloyd, J.W.: Foundations of Logic Programming, 2nd, extended edition. Springer-Verlag, New York (1993)
10. Mendelzon, A.O., Mihaila, G., Milo, T.: Querying the World Wide Web. Proceedings of the Conf. on Parallel and Distributed Information Systems (1996) 80–91
11. Papakonstantinou, Y., Abiteboul, S., Garcia-Molina, H.: Object Fusion in Mediator Systems. Proceedings of the 22nd Intl. Conf. on VLDB (1996) 413–424
12. Raggett, D., Hors, A.L., Jacobs, I.: HTML 4.0 Specification - W3C Recommendation. http://www.w3.org/TR/REC-html40 (April 1998)

Reduction of Object Overlap in Three-Dimensional Browsing Space for Internet Data

TOSHIHIRO KAKIMOTO[1] and YAHIKO KAMBAYASHI[2]

[1] Fujitsu Lab., Akashi, Japan
[2] Department of Social Informatics, Kyoto University, Kyoto, Japan

Abstract. One of the important problems for handling information retrieval in Internet is to create efficient and powerful visualization mechanisms for the browsing process. One promising way to solve the visualization problem is to map each candidate data object into a location in three-dimensional (3D) space using a proper distance definition. In this paper, we will introduce the functions and organization of a system to achieve an efficient browsing process in 3D information search space. It has the following major functions:
(1) Calculation of the location of the data objects in 2D space using the given distance definition.
(2) Construction of 3D browsing space by combining 2D spaces, in order to find the required data objects easily.
(3) Generation of the oblique views of 3D browsing space and data objects by reducing the overlap of data objects in order to make navigation easy for the user in 3D space.
Examples of this system applied to book, web and slide data are shown.

1   Introduction

Due to the recent rapid development of computer and network technologies it is important to develop a new information retrieval process to efficiently search a variety of multimedia data from various distributed data sources in Internet. Since it is impossible to know properties of such data in advance, visualization methods play a central role to find required data. In this paper we will develop a method for efficient and effective visualization using 3D browsing space, since it is easy to understand and more data objects can be displayed than in the 2D space commonly used. One problem with the visualization of 3D space is that some data objects will be hidden behind other data objects. We introduce a method to generate oblique views to increase the number of data objects that can be displayed. In the following sections, in order to achieve efficient browsing in 3D browsing space we will discuss related work, the method of transforming the structure of 3D browsing space, and oblique views for 3D browsing space.

2 Related Work

In this section we will show related work on methods for constructing an overview structure for data objects, and the method of constructing 3D space for visualization.

(1) Constructing an information structure for the overview of data objects

In the studies on methods of constructing the structure for the overview of data objects, there is the study on creating of the overview of clusters generated by the clustering algorithm (Scatter/Gather [1][2]), the study on overviewing the category hierarchy generated by semantic relations extracted from data objects (Galaxy of News [3]), the study on overviewing the classes generated by the URL links between WWW home pages, and so on.

The Scatter/Gather system uses fast document clustering to produce an outline, similar to a table of contents, of large document collections. With Scatter/Gather, rather than being forced to provide keywords, the user is presented with a set of clusters, an outline of the corpus. The user needs only to select those clusters which seem potentially relevant to the topic of interest. The methods of clustering are classified into hierarchical clustering, nonhierarchical clustering and hierarchical mode clustering [4][5]. These methods pose difficult problems on how to determine the number of clusters and how to find the meaning of each cluster.

The Galaxy of News system has a relationship construction engine that constructs an associative relation network to automatically build implicit links between related articles. Since it is very difficult to extract semantics automatically, further research is required to use the system practically.

As the model does not assume links among data objects, we can not use the method applied to URL links among Web pages.

A method that does not have the problems mentioned above is Kohonen's self-organizing map (SOM) [6][7] that creates a mapping from multidimension feature space to 2D space and generates a distribution according to the similarity between features. Therefore, we will use SOM.

Research on SOM's application to document or video classification is reported in [8][9]. This research uses 2D maps, which are clustering results using SOM. Though we also use a similar 2D map, our system employs a special feature selection to achieve a user required distribution. In other methods of the dimensional reduction like SOM there is Multidimensional Scaling(MDS). As MDS needs complex calculation, we didn't use it.

(2) Visualization of the information structure in 3D space

Information Visualizer [12][13] is a well known method for visualizing the information structure for surveying in 3D space. It has several kinds of representations. These are Perspective Wall for information that has linear structure, Cone Tree for a hierarchical relation, Document Lens for focusing on one page in a document, and The Hyperbolic Tree Browser for a hierarchical structure such as an organization chart.

The Galaxy of News system [3] has the functions to display a hierarchical structure, which consists of the semantic relations of keywords, titles, articles in 3D space, and to zoom up on these objects along this structure. There are also many tools for the visualization of links among Web home pages [14][15], for example Apple's HotSaucer. These tools have the functions to display a tree structure or a link structure in 3D space, to zoom up on these displayed objects and to show the relations between the displayed objects dynamically by the zoom ratio.

These methods can not be applied to construct 3D space from 2D space. The 3D view of SOM's results is reported in [10][11]. One of these studies employs a method of viewing the document landscape by using VRML [10]. SOM is also used for the classification of video cuts[11]. In this paper, we introduce other techniques for scattering the data objects in 3D space.

3 Method for Constructing 2D Information Distribution Space

We will show a method of constructing the information distribution space, which is one of the core methods of the browsing process [16]. This method has the following objectives:
1) The data objects are distributed uniformly in a 2D-display screen with limited size for a user to observe the characteristics of these data objects more clearly.
2) A user can select the features and see these features in 2D information distribution space. By changing features for constructing the 2D space, the user can see the set of data objects in a different way.

This method consists of two processes. One is the selection of the features for distributing the data objects in a space. The other is the mapping from the feature vector space to 2D space using Kohonen's Self-Organizing Map [7,8]. We assume that a set of keywords is specified for each object. For text data, an automatic keyword extraction procedure (consisting of morphological analysis and selection of nouns) may be applied.

The methods of the selection of the features are the following methods and the combinations of their methods.
1) A user specifies the features.
2) A system selects the features to divide the data objects into two pieces evenly for distributing them uniformly in a space.(see [16])
3) A system selects the features to highly cooccur with the user specified features.
4) A system selects the features to have the high variance and less correlation with the selected features. We use these methods to select the features, the number of which is capable of looking at and recognizing them at a time.
In this section in order to easily understand the explanation it is assumed that the data objects are home page text and the features are keywords.

3.1 Mapping from multidimensional space to 2D space

A multidimensional space consists of the coordinates of the selected keywords and has the data objects located in it. The value of the coordinate of a data object is the value of the frequency of the keyword in the data object. We define the similarity between the data objects as a cosine function and map the multidimensional space into 2D space utilizing Kohonen's Self-Organizing Map (SOM) [6][7]. This map is an $L \times L$ square mesh where L is a minimum integer exceeding the square root of m, which is the number of the data objects. The following is a simple explanation of the algorithm of SOM, which is used in this paper.

The set of 295 data objects is one of the retrieved home page texts from the 1,095 home page texts of science and technology. We assume that the set of home page texts is retrieved with the keyword "biology" and the selected keywords are "energy", "protein", "gene", "research", cell", "plant", "evolution", "mutation", "variation". Each document has a feature vector, which has the frequency of each keyword as an element, as in the following vectors. These values are extracted from the table of contents.

Document A:(1,0,0,2,0,0,2,0,0),
Document B:(0,0,3,0,5,1,2,0,0).

The dimension of these feature vectors is so high enough as not to be able to understand the similarity between them. The method of Kohonen's self-organizing map orders these feature vectors according to the similarity defined between them in a lower dimensional space. In general, this lower dimension space is a 2D space in which it is easy to perceive the distribution of these feature vectors. In the following, we explain the method of ordering the feature vectors on the map vectors assigned to each lattice of the 2 dimensional square lattice.

The ordering consists of 2 steps. 1) Select the map vector which is the most similar to the feature vector. 2) Modify the map vector within the range centered around the selected map vector so as to be more similar to the feature vector than before. The rate of this variation decreases according to the increase in the learning steps and the increase in the distance between this map vector and the selected map vector. The range also decreases according to the increase in the learning steps. Thus the variation of the value of the map vectors is decreasing while the amount and range of the adjustment is decreasing. This learning process converges at the stable state of the value of the map vectors. In practice we iterate this process until the variations in the value of these map vectors are less than a threshold value. These processes distribute the feature vectors on the 2 dimensional mesh.

After the map is calculated using SOM, the data objects are allocated to the location of the map vector with the nearest distance. This is the information distribution space.

3.2 Evaluation of the method

(1) precision and recall rate for browsing process

If the similarity is proportional to the degree of user's requirements and the retrieved set consists of data objects distributed in the limited area, the concept of precision and recall rate which are used in the hunting process are applied to the browsing process. Hatano[11] proposed the following definition.

If the retrieved set is the set of data objects existing in the neighborhood ($= N(r)$,r is the radius of the neighbourhood.) and the set required by a user is the set of data objects ($= S(s)Cs$ is the threshold), the similarity of which is more than the threshold, the precision and recall rate are formulated as follows.

precision rate$= \#(N(r)) \cap S(s))/\#(N(r))$

recall rate$= \#(N(r)) \cap S(s))/\#(S(s))$

:$\#()$ is the number of elements in the set.

These definitions include two parameters(r, s). As s is varied dependent on the degree of the user's needs, the value is not determined before a user uses it. r is able to be determined using the same way of hunting process (keyword search), because in the case of the fixed s it is possible dependent on the distribution of the data objects that the values of the similarity of the data objects are reversed dependent on the value of r. Furthermore if the definitions of the precision and recall rate are the functions of the similarity, these values are more precise. In the following we show introducing the similarity and determining r in the framework of the browsing process.

If the set of retrieved result is the set of data objects in the neighbourhood which is within the circle of radius r and the center data object i and the set required by user is the set of data objects which has the similarity with data object i which is larger than s, the following formulas are defined.

extended precision rate$= 1/n \sum_i (\sum_{j \in S_i(s)} s_{ij} \times d_{ij} / \sum_{j \in S_i(0)} f(s_{ij}) \times d_{ij})$

$s_{ij} = \sum_l a_{il} \times a_{jl}$Fthe similarity of data objects i and j

$d_{ij} = 1(d_{ij} \leq r), = 0(d_{ij} > r)$

$f(s_{ij}) = s_{ij}(s_{ij} > s), = s_{ij} + 1 - s_{ij}/s(s_{ij} \leq s)$

$f(s_{ij})$ is the penalty function which is proportional to the similarity while the similarity is more than the threshold s and increases in the proportion of the difference between the similarity and the threshold while the similarity is less than and equal the threshold.

Next we determine the parameter r as follows. In the browsing process, the neighborhood of one data object is divided into the area to be able to look at a time and the area to explore the data objects fit for user's needs. In this information distribution space, the area to look at a time is the area of 9 data objects which corresponds to the 9 meshes in Kohonen's map. the number 9 is the maximum number of chunks in the model of memory[17]. This number is corresponding to $\sqrt{2}$ of r. In the case of r which is more than $\sqrt{2}$, in the recall rate we introduced the discovery coefficient$= \alpha/g(r_{ij})$ which represents the easiness of discovering and the similarity. We defined the following discovery rate.

discovery rate$= 1/n \sum_i (\sum_{j \in S_i(s)} s_{ij} \times (\alpha/g(r_{ij}))/ \sum_{j \in S_i(s)} s_{ij})$

Table 1. the calculated results for 3 data sets

item	S&T	Iwanami	homepage	note
no. of data	1,095	1,211	60,929	
ave. byte	4,024B	2,282B	1,295B	/1 data
ave. no. of KW	139KW	83KW	29KW	/1 data
ave. max. KW freq.	14	7	3	/1data
precision	0.589905	0.671519	0.783553	r=1.42
ext. precision	0.542621	0.590230	0.713687	r=1.42
recall	0.551551	0.486946	0.413098	r=1.42
discovery	0.644421	0.572295	0.530771	

notejthe above results are calculated in case of 9 keywords
and the threshold value of the similarity is 0.7.

The example of the discovery coefficient is $\alpha/g(r_{ij}) = 1(r_{ij} \leq \sqrt{2}), = 2/r_{ij}^2$ $(r_{ij} > \sqrt{2})$ and is used in the following evaluation. This formula explains that the labour of browsing in the 2D space is proportional to the square of the distance. As the extended precision rate is not fit for the concept of the discovery coefficient, the discovery coefficient is not used in the extended precision rate. Using these rates, we can evaluate browsing process like hunting process. In order to use the fixed value of r, the discovery rate decrease dependent on the number of the data objects. This point is treated in the next section.

(2) results of calculation

We applied this method to the three kinds of data sets. They are 1,095 science and technical book (S&T)[18] as the data of one limited field, 1,211 book (Iwanami Shinsyo) as the data of overall fields and 60,930 home page documents (home page)as the data of manifold documents. We evaluated it with the 35 sets, 12 sets and 35 sets each of which is a retrieved result set including data for more than 100 book in the case of the former two data sets or 1,000 book in the case of the last home page data set. The profiles of these data sets are shown in table1 and the values in the table are the average values of the sets. The method of keyword extraction from japanese sentence is to delimit a japanese sentence using kinds of japanese character, select the kanji or katakana characters, where the number of the characters is more than and equal 2 characters and discard the needless words. The result of the evaluation for three kinds of datas is summarized as follows.

1) As the discovery rate is the one to add the degree of discovering the data objects to the denominator of extended recall rate, the discovery rate is 0.1 higher than the extended recall rate. This indicates that it is better to look around the neighborhood.

2) The extended precision rate is the one to introduce the coefficient of penalty in the similarity under the threshold and the similarity instead of 1. The extended precision rate is less than the precision rate, because the data objects of the higher precision rate is small. The decreasing rate of the extended

precision rate is 0.047 in S&T book, 0.081 in Iwanami book and 0.070 in home page. This rate of decreasing similarity is lower in small field than in large field.

Thus the discovery rate and the extended precision rate which we introduced reflects the distribution through similarity and are fitter as the evaluation indicator of browsing process than the precision rate and the recall rate.

4 3D browsing space

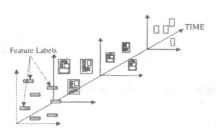

Fig. 1. The image of time coordinate space

Fig. 2. Example of time coordinate

For Internet we will use the first pages of Web home pages to represent the the Web home pages. One example is shown in Fig.9. Most other examples use cover pages of books in this paper. A 3D space is organized by several 2D spaces arranged in parallel. The order of these 2D spaces is determined by the selection of a feature used for the z coordinate, which is called a navigation coordinate. Fig.1 shows the case when "time" is used as the navigation coordinate. For example, objects are first classified by years and for each set, a 2D space is generated. One example is shown in Fig.2. Objects with similar features are located at similar places at the same or different 2D plane. For "time", we can use century or other kinds of proper time-period. For the navigation coordinate we can use other values such as number of sales, number of some specific keywords, etc. As the xy-plane has not coordinates, we introduced feature label's plane in the front of the top plane. This plane has the labels indicating the selected feature. Each label is allocated at the position of the most similar data object in xy-plane. Another method to organize 3D space is to use hierarchy index structure. If there are too many objects in one 2D space, we will find clusters for objects. We put one representative object for each cluster in the next 2D plane. By repeating this method, we can get the space structure shown in Fig.4.

In walking through 3D space, oblique views are introduced in the following section to provide a better user interface.

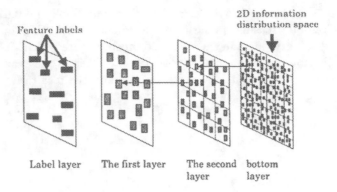

Fig. 3. Hierarchy of spaces

5 Oblique Views for 3D Space

A typical example of views for 3D space is shown in Fig.4. Although a user can see data objects in front of him/her, it is rather difficult to know information in the back, since data objects in the back will be hidden. If a user is interested in a particular cluster of data objects, the hidden data objects in the back also have similar features. In order to overcome this difficulty, we have introduced oblique views of 3D space. An example of such a view is shown in Fig.5, where the data objects in the front will not cover the objects in the back. The following problems exist for realizing such a view.

(1) To develop an algorithm to convert conventional 3D space into an oblique view.

(2) To realize a natural walk through view in such an oblique space like the former space.

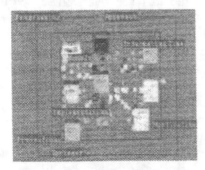 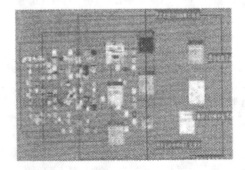

Fig. 4. Front View of 3D Space   **Fig. 5.** Oblique View of 3D Space

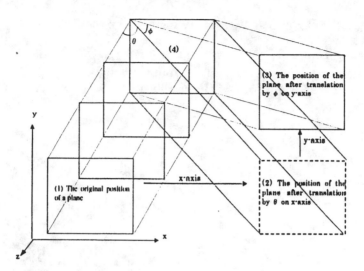

Fig. 6. The conversion of 3D space

Conversion process is shown in Fig.6. Let θ and ϕ be angles for x-axis and y-axis to generate oblique view respectively. $\theta = 0°$ and $\phi = 0°$ correspond to the case when no conversion of the space is made.

1) A user can specify θ and ϕ. Default values used to generate the view in Fig.6 are $\theta = 22°$ and $\phi = 0°$.

2) Assume that the location of a data object is given by (a, b, c). The new location of the same object is (a', b', c). As the movement of the objects is parallel to the xy plane, the value for z-axis is not influenced by the conversion. If the value for z-axis of the bottom plane is , a' and b' are shown as follows.

$$a' = a + (c - z_0)\tan\theta \qquad b' = b + (c - z_0)\tan\phi$$

In Fig.6, the original top plane is shown by (1). The result of the conversion of x-axis only θ is shown in (2). The top plane after the conversion by both θ and ϕ is shown in (3). Here we select one of the data objects in the bottom plane and its location is assumed to be (d, e, f). By this conversion the location of this particular data object will not change.

In Fig.6, the planes of the top and bottom are shown. The bottom plane (shown by (4)) is not influenced by the conversion.

[Walk through in the oblique space]

We assume that the position of a user moves from (a, b, c) to (a', b', c') and (e, f, g) is the position for (a, b, c) in the oblique view. The new position of the user's view point (e', f', g') in the oblique view corresponding to $(a', b'.c')$ is as follows. Position of x-axis and y-axis are modified by the distance of movement of z-axis.

$$e' = a' + (c' - c)\tan\theta \qquad f' = b' + (c' - c)\tan\phi \qquad g' = c'$$

This function prevents a user departing from the oblique space.

The amount of the translation can be specified by a user. Otherwise it is auto-

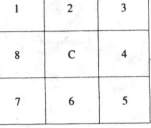

Fig. 7. Divisions of xy-plane

Fig. 8. Spiral arrangement of data objects

matically calculated by a system as follows. In order to realize this function, the direction and the displacement are determined at first. We divide 2D space into 9 same divisions as Fig.7. It is assumed that the division which a user browses is the division where the eye point exists. If the division is not the center division, the direction of inclining z axis is the reverse of the position of the division. If the displacement is in x direction, the displacement is $l_x/3 = l_z \times \sin\theta$, where l_x is the x-length of the space, l_z is z distance between layers and θ is angle of x-axis. If the division is the center division, the direction and the displacement are determined as follows. The divisions around the center division are numbered as Fig.7. The number of division is the one where has the minimum value of the covering area of the data objects in the division. The displacement is twice the one of the around division.

Other methods of the reduction of overlays are as follows. 1) If the more than two data objects are located at the same position, they are located at the spiral positions along the z-axis (see Fig.8). 2) A user may move the data objects overlapping the data object which he/she looks at.

If the data objects which are of interested to the user are located in the center of each plane, overlap of such objects in different planes can be avoided.

6 Conclusion Remarks

In this paper we discussed the functions of a browsing navigator to improve the efficiency of retrieving data objects from distributed sources and we showed user interfaces for information search in 3D space. For distributed digital libraries,

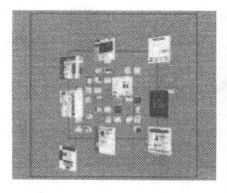

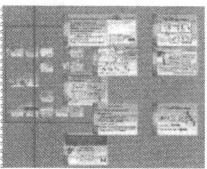

Fig. 9. 3D space of home pages   **Fig. 10.** 3D space of slides

since it is hard to know the features of data in advance, it is desirable to use browsing process accessing human vision capabilities. A variety of views of the search space will help users find candidate data.

The same program can be used to see properties of the given set of data. For example, Fig.9 shows a set of home pages whose distances are determined by the words contained in each home page. Another example is Fig.10, which shows clustering of slides used for one lecture.

References

1. D.R. Cutting, D.R. Karger, J.O. Pederson and J.W. Turkey : Scatter/Gather : A Cluster-Based Approach to Browsing Large Document Collections, ACM SIG-IR'92, pp318-329, 1992.
2. D.R. Cutting, D.R. Karger and J.O. Pederson : Constant Interaction-Time Scatter / Gather Browsing of Very Large Document Collections, ACM SIG-IR'93, pp126-134, 1993.
3. Earl Rennison : Galaxy of News, An Approach to Visualizing and Understanding Expansive News Landscape, UIST'94, pp.3-12, 1994.
4. G. Salton : The SMART Retrieval System. Prentice Hall, Englewood Cliffs, N.J., 1971.
5. A.K. Jain and R.C. Dubes : Algorithms for Clustering Data. Prentice Hall, 1988.
6. T. Kohonen : The Self-Organizing Map, Proc. of the IEEE, Vol.78, No.9, 1990.
7. T. Kohonen, J. Hynninen, J. Kangas and J. Laaksonen : SOM_PAK : The Self-Organizing Map Program Package. In Technical Report A31, Helsinki University of Technology, Laboratory of Computer and Information Science, Espco, 1996.
8. Q. Qian, X. Shi and K. Tanaka : Document Browsing and Retrieving Based on 3D Self-Organizing Map. In Proc. Of Workshop on New Paradigms in Information Visualization and Manipulation in Conjunction with CIKM'95, 1995.
9. S. Tsukada : Clustering of Texts Using Self-Organizing Map. In National Convention Record of IPSJ, pp.187-188, 1993.
10. K. Lagus, T. Honkela, S. Kaski and T. Kohonen : Self-Organizing Maps of Document Collections: A New Approach to Interactive Exploration. In Proc. of the

2nd Int. Conf. On Knowledge Discovery and Data Mining (KDD-96), pp.238-243, 1996.

11. K. Hatano, T. Kamei and K. Tanaka : Clustering and Authoring of Video Shots Using Hybrid-type Self-Organizing Maps. In Proc. of International Symposium on Digital Media Information Base, Nara, Japan, pp.150-158, 1997

12. George G. Robertson, Stuart K. Card, and Jock D. Mackinley: Information Visualization Using 3D Interactive Animation. CACM, Vol.36, No.4, 1993.

13. R. Rao, J.O. Pedersen, M.A. Hearst, J.D. Mackinlay, S.K. Card, L. Masinter, P. Halvorsen and G.G. Robertson : Rich Interaction in the Digital Library.@CACM, Vol.38, No.4, pp29-39, 1995.

14. Z. Mountaz : Interactive Dynamic Maps for Visualization and Retrieval from Hypertext Systems. Information Retrieval and Hypertext, edited by M.Agosti and A.Smeaton, Kluwer Academic Publishers, 1996.

15. J. Assa, D. Cohen-Or and T. Milo : Displaying Data in Multidimensional Relevance Space with 2D Visualization Maps. IEEE Visualization '97, 1997.

16. T. Kakimoto and Y. Kambayashi : Method of Selecting Optimal Characteristic Value for Browsing Space. The Transactions of the Institute of Electronics, Information and Communication Engineers D-I, Vol.J82-D-I, No.1, pp.130-139, January, 1999(in Japanese).

17. R.C. Atkinson and R.M. Shiftn : The Control of Short-Term Memory. Mind and Behavior, Scientific American, pp.153-161, 1980.

18. T. Taniguchi, Y. Sawada, T. Yoshida, T. Kakimoto, M. Nagao, M. Harada, T. Ishikawa: Development of Digital Library "Ariadne"(2), Information Management, Vol.38, No.4, pp.324-337 ,1995(in Japanese).

ScoopCast: Dynamic Video Production and Delivery from Indexed Live Video Stream

Kazutoshi SUMIYA[1], Tomoaki KAWAGUCHI[2], Akihiro DOI[2],
Katsumi TANAKA[1] and Kuniaki UEHARA[1]

[1] Kobe University, Rokkodai, Nada, Kobe 657-8501, Japan
{sumiya,tanaka,uehara}@kobe-u.ac.jp
[2] Nippon Telegraph and Telephone West Corporation, Japan
t.kawaguchi@bch.west.ntt.co.jp, a-doi@kobe01.ksi.ntt.co.jp

Abstract. In this paper, we propose a new framework for indexing, delivering, and filtering live video streams in the Internet broadcasting environment for grass root users. We discuss the scheduled program skeleton to describe fixed scenario of broadcast programs. In addition, we propose the dynamic program producing mechanism based on a degree of broadcast priority to avoid conflicts from unspecific number of providers. To verify the validity of the mechanism, we implemented a prototype called ScoopCast which can deliver video stream using multicast networks.

1 Introduction

Recently, the Internet has become popular, and digital-broadcasting technology has been developed. Services for providing video streams and text information for more than one user at the same time on a network have been drawing much attention. Editing and transmitting video streams have become easier, even in mobile computing environments. In network computing environments, the Internet connection services with 10Mbps lines by CATVs have started. And also, network connection services, such as ADSL and VDSL are to follow in the near future. On the other hand, in the wireless network-computing environment, experiments of high-speed network, beyond 1Mbps by portable cellular phone, show that they are ready for practical use.

For reasons mentioned above, users would not be only receiving video stream but also sending stream and various kinds of data. If anyone could transmit his video streams taken by himself, there would be very large amounts of raw video streams (live video streams) everywhere in the world. Furthermore, if anyone could edit raw video streams easily, his original program would be transmitted to public networks. Synthesizing the raw video streams dynamically from somewhere may lead to a new paradigm of video broadcasting.

In our research, a broadcasting program is not limited to current TV programs. An usual TV program is to be produced by professional directors based on a fixed scenario at a television station. On the other hand, the program we propose is a dynamically synthesized video stream made of some raw video streams by *amateurs*. Generally, gathering many kinds of user's raw video streams would express the user's intentions to attend the program. For example, in a marathon live broadcasting, scoop video streams from the roadside spectators could be collected abundantly. The video streams would contain events that occur unexpectedly.

In this paper, we propose a new framework for indexing, delivering, and filtering live video streams in the Internet broadcasting environment. The basic idea is providing a system to manipulate video streams for grass root users. The requirements for the system are as follows:

- real-time indexing and transmitting mechanism for raw video streams
- dynamic program producing mechanism with raw video streams and their indexes
- autonomous filtering method for multiple video streams

Raw video streams should be analyzed and indexed according to their contents for authoring. Next, the video streams should be transmitted to a network as indexed video streams. And then, programs are dynamically combined with multiple raw video streams. Finally, viewers would select a video stream as a program for filtering. We have been developing a prototype system called ScoopCast for experimentation [1, 2].

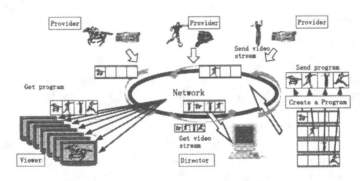

Fig. 1. The outline of ScoopCast on a network

The rest of this paper is organized as follows: Section 2 describes our motivation and approach. Section 3 discusses video indexing for live video stream. Section 4 discusses real-time video description model. Section 5 describes a dynamic program producing mechanism based on a degree of broadcast priority. Section 6 discusses implementation issues on ScoopCast. Finally, Section 7 gives a conclusion and discusses our future work.

2 Motivation and Our Approach

Because of innovation of high-speed networks and digital video equipment, raw video streams taken by users in general should be distributed and processed in widespread use. The video streams contain very important contents, especially

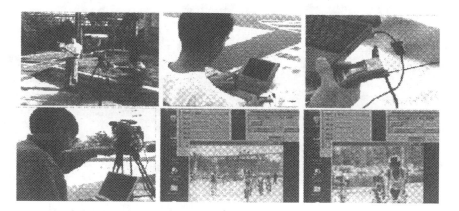

Fig. 2. An experimental environment

live video streams. A valuable live video stream can be a scoop. On the other hand, in a case of news programs, current TV broadcast stations make programs from video materials which reporters have gathered in advance. Therefore, current TV programs can not handle the real-time video streams which are sent from users, located somewhere. The basic concept of our approach is as follows:

- When a user takes a scoop video, the user immediately indexes the raw video streams using a keyword description. At the same time, the user transmits the video streams and their indexes to networks.
- A user prepares a program condition which describes the contents as keywords. The program is ready for receiving raw video streams which match the keywords. If an index of raw video stream matches the keyword, the video stream is adapted as a portion of the program.
- When a user watches programs, the user selects a program by the means of a keyword filter. The user can choose his favorite programs.

There are three kinds of users in our approach. We call the users *providers*, *directors*, and *viewers*, respectively. Of course, by provider and director, we do not mean professional ones but anyone playing those roles. In a case, a user can be playing more than one role concurrently. In our approach, raw video streams are classified into two types:

1. scheduled program video - component of a fixed scenario produced in advance
2. scoop video - unexpected events and happenings

A scoop video stream can be inserted to scheduled program video streams because the scoop should be transmitted immediately.

Figure 1 shows the outline of ScoopCast on a network. Providers, directors, and viewers join the network. Providers transmit video streams to the network with their indexes; directors receive and edit the video stream for their aim, and send authored programs; viewers receive the programs and select them. Figure 2 shows an experimental environment of ScoopCast.

ScoopCast can be applied to various kinds of programs; for example sport broadcasts, festivals, and so on. The contents of the program would be dynamically changed according to the situation. In a marathon race, it is impossible to predict when an unexpected event would occur. The broadcast staff can not cover the whole race, but roadside spectators can cover many of the events. If the spectators can capture an event with a video camera and transmit it to the network, the video stream can be used as a scoop.

Various methods have been proposed for automatic editing of programs by script languages[3, 4]. In other methods, scenario languages are used for editing programs[5, 6, 7]. These methods are useful for editing stored material data. However, they are not effective to edit the raw video streams on the spot.

ActionSnaps system in PRAJA Presence environment is designed for semi-automatic production and multi-perspective viewing of live event summaries from multimedia inputs[8]. However, the system can not annotate raw video stream lively, and handle multiple video stream currently.

We propose a real-time delivering function for raw video streams. And also, we propose a dynamic program editing function.

When providers transmit their raw video streams, necessary functions are the following: 1) real-time raw video stream transmitting function, 2) real-time contents description function. On the other hand, when directors edit their programs, program editing function described as a script is necessary. In the following sections, we explain the details of these functions.

3 Video Indexing for Live Video Stream

3.1 Video Indexing

It is very difficult for directors to edit raw video streams delivered from unspecific number of providers manually. Because raw video streams may arrive suddenly, they must decide immediately to adapt the video stream as a scoop. To judge whether a video stream is valuable, description methods of the contents are needed.

Although it is possible to describe contents with natural languages one by one, it is not practical. Various methods have been proposed for giving descriptions to news and video streams. One method proposes closed caption as text description[9]. In another method, the telops inserted in the news video stream are extracted by an image recognition technique to be used for description[10]. However, these methods are not useful for real-time description of video streams.

We have developed two real-time description methods: (1) real-time description method by event tools, (2) real-time description method by speech recognition. Users can put these tools to their proper use. Using these tools, sets of keywords and time stamps can be attached on the video stream as the ancillary data.

Fig. 3. (a)Indexing by event tool and (b)Indexing by speech recognition

Indexing by Event Tool We developed a real-time event description tool based on rules[11]. Figure 3(a) shows the screen image of the tool for baseball games. Events of the game are described as the game proceeds. The tool can be operated by a user interface (such as a mouse) and can describe the events using keywords. Also, related information such as player's records and URLs of the teams are displayed.

Indexing by Speech Recognition To create indexes for live video stream in real-time, *speech recognition techniques* are useful. We have developed a real-time description system using a speech recognition tool[12]. Users tell the situation through a microphone and the tool extracts keywords from their sentences. That is, video streams are described by keywords. This tool is implemented in Java language and designed by ViaVoice98 as speech recognition engine. Figure 3(b) shows the experimental environment of the tool. Users tell the situation like an *announcer* at on-the spot broadcasting, watching the video image on the display.

3.2 Temporal Indexes for Live Video Stream

In section 3.1, we detect the time that a keyword is attached as time stamps. The value is called *transaction time*. The transaction time denotes the time(s) when the fact is (logically) current in the system.

On the other hand, we should calculate the *valid time* of each keyword to extract reasonable period of video streams. In other words, the valid time is the period when the keyword expresses the situation.

In section 4, we propose an automatic description method based on a finite automaton model.

4 Real-time Video Description Model

4.1 Index for Video Stream

We define a description model for live video streams. An index is the description unit of a video stream. Index I_V for video stream V is as follows:

$$I_V = \{r | r = (d, dt, tt, v), v \subseteq V\} \tag{1}$$

where r is the index record. d is the description (keyword), dt is the description type, tt is the transaction time, and v is the valid time.

The description is classified into two types: 1) event type and 2) situation type. The event type is used for phenomenon in the video stream. For example, phenomenon of a baseball game are "strike", "hit", "home run", "fine play", and so on. The situation type is used for conditions in the video stream. For example, conditions of a baseball bame are "strike count", "ball count", "score", and so on.

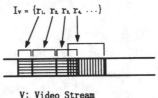

V: Video Stream

Fig. 4. Index I_V for video stream V

Furthermore, event type description is classified into two types: 1a) atomic event type and 1b) complex event type. The atomic event type is used for simple events. On the other hand, the complex event type is used for a combination of simple events. For example, "three strike" is a result of several action.

The transaction time is the moment the index record is stored in the system. The valid time is the period the index record is reasonable.

$$v = [t_s, t_e] \tag{2}$$

where v is the interval which the index record is valid. t_s is start time and t_e is end time.

4.2 Description Type

There are two kinds of description type as we mentioned. The event type description d_e is as follows:

$$d_e = (object, role, event) \tag{3}$$

where $object$ is substance, $role$ is a part, and $event$ is phenomenon. For example, in a baseball game, ("$McGwire$", "$batter$", "$home\ run$") is a event type description.

The situation type description d_s is as follows:

$$d_s = (situation, value) \tag{4}$$

where $situation$ is the condition of the target, and $value$ is its numeric value. For example, in a baseball game, ("$strike\ count$", "2").

4.3 Estimating Valid Time

To attach indexes to video streams, we calculate the valid time of the index. The estimation is to be separated according to description type.

Atomic Event Type Valid time $r_{e_i}.v$ of index record r_{e_i} is as follows:

$$r_{e_i}.v = [r_{e_{i-k}}.tt + l, r_{e_i}.tt + l] \qquad (5)$$

where $r_{e_i}.tt$ is the transaction time of the index record, $r_{e_{i-k}}.tt$ is the transaction time of the latest index record, and l is the time lag[3] (Figure 5(a)).

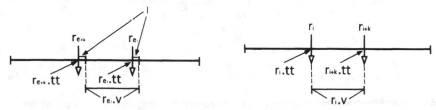

Fig. 5. (a)Valid time of atomic event type (b)Valid time of situation

Complex Event Type An index record of complex event type is a combination of several atomic events. We propose an automatic description method based on a finite automaton model which express the characteristics of the description target. The input is a list of index records and the output is a valid interval. We have started analyzing the description capability of the method but will not discuss in detail because the issue is not within the scope of this paper.

Situation Type Valid time $r_{s_i}.v$ of index record r_{e_i} is as follows:

$$r_{s_i}^{\cdot}.v = [r_{s_i}.tt + l, r_{s_{i+k}}.tt + l] \qquad (6)$$

where $r_{s_{i+k}}.tt$ is the transaction time of the index record, $r_{s_i}.tt$ is the transaction time of the latest index record which *situation* is same and *value* is different (Figure 5(b)). For example, if the description of target index record is ("strike count", "2"), the matched latest index record is ("strike count", "1").

5 Dynamic Video Production

5.1 Degree of Broadcast Priority

All directors produce a video program based on their intentions by combining raw video streams. There are two kinds of raw video streams as we mentioned:

---

[3] The time lag is caused by estimation process, and so on. This value is generally constant.

a scheduled program video and a scoop video. Directors generally prepare a timetable for live broadcasting which contains pairs of material and period for broadcasting. In other words, directors combine scheduled program video streams in advance. However, because a scoop video arrives unexpectedly, the broadcast time of the video can not be scheduled beforehand.

Generally, the priority of scoop video is greater than scheduled program video, because the contents are fresh and valuable enough for immediate transmission. Of course, value of scoop videos may be changed as time passes. That is, scoop videos which contain the same contents, do not always have same order of priority. We propose a computation mechanism for broadcast priority of live video streams. The priority $P(t)$ at time t is decided by the production of priority evaluation function $P_i(t)$ and priority evaluation function $P_f(n)$:

$$P(d,t) = w_1 P_i(d,t) * w_2 P_f(d,n) \tag{7}$$

where t is the current time and n is the iteration of the scoop. P is the priority evaluation function, P_i is the priority evaluation function of *importance*, and P_f is the priority evaluation function of *freshness*.

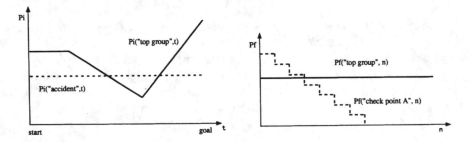

Fig. 6. (a)Priority of importance (b)Priority of freshness

Priority of Importance The priority of importance in a scenario may be changed. For example, in a marathon race, the priority of the video capturing the "top group" in the start scene and the finish scene is higher than those of other scenes. On the other hand, the priority of a certain player's "retire" and "accident" event video is always higher.

The priority function of importance is as follows:

$$P_i(d,t) = D \times T \rightarrow [0,1] \tag{8}$$

where D is a set of all the possible description and T is a set of all the time. Figure 6(a) shows an example of priority of importance for "top group" and "accident".

Priority of Freshness The priority of freshness may be decreased generally. That is, the degree of attention of an event which occurs repeatedly decreases generally[4] . For example, in a marathon race, the priority of the video capturing "check point A" is decreased as the description is created repeatedly.

The priority function of freshness is as follows:

$$P_i(d, n) = D \times N \rightarrow [0, 1] \tag{9}$$

where D is a set of all the possible description and D is a set of all the description frequency number. Figure 6(b) shows an example of priority of freshness for "top group" and "check point A".

5.2 Calculation of Broadcast Priority

In some cases, a combination of several descriptions occurs simultaneously. For example, when description "player A" and "retire" occur, the union of the description only make sense. Union of multiple description is as follows.

$$P(a \ b, t) = \alpha * P(a, t) + \beta * P(b, t) \tag{10}$$

where $\alpha + \beta = 1$. We know that this formula is heuristic, however, this is likely to be domain specific.

5.3 Scheduled Program Video

A scheduled program video is the combination of planned scenarios produced in advance. It is defined as a set of the description:

$$S = \{s_1, s_2, \ldots, s_n\} \tag{11}$$
$$s_i = (D_i, [t_s, t_e)) \tag{12}$$

where D_i is an event description, s_i is a planned scenario , t_s is start time of the scenario, and t_e is end time of the scenario.

Directors define the video program based on scheduled program videos. If a scoop does not happen, the scheduled program videos itself would be transmitted. However, if scoops happen, the scoops would be inserted into the scheduled program video.

---

[4] In some cases, the priority of freshness may not be decreased.

6 ScoopCast: A Prototype System

6.1 Scheduled Program Skeleton

The scheduled program video is described by a scheduled program skeleton(SPS). The SPS is a timetable for live broadcasting which contains pairs of material and period for broadcasting. Because directors do not know the providers, the time they send a scoop, and the nature of the scoop, they can prepare only the scheduled program video as event descriptions and periods for broadcasting. A SPS consists of two parts:

- Semantic contents description: keyword, position, and so on.
- Control condition for transmission: possible period in which a scoop can be inserted and the quality of the video stream (size, f/s).

6.2 Multicast based Video/Index Delivery

The multicast network provides a very useful way to deliver video streams to an unspecific number of users. Think about the case in which two video streams are broadcast at same time. Generally, providers must broadcast each viewer in uni-cast networks, causing the network traffic to increase excessively. However, in a multicast network, providers transmit a video stream only once. Recently, multicast networks have been drawing much attention and have been used for videoconference systems, such as Vic (a videoconference tool)[13].

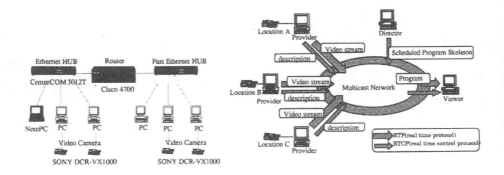

Fig. 7. (a)Machine environment (b)System outline

We have designed a video stream delivering mechanism using multicast networks. In the mechanism, providers, directors, and viewers join the network, and they can transmit and receive video streams. Delivering data involves not only video streams but also their indexes as keywords. The indexes are described in RTCP packets (Real-time Control Protocol packets) [14] on the network.

In multicast networks, RTP (Real-time Transport Protocol) is generally adapted to sending video and audio data, and RTCP packets are transmitted at all times. If indexes are embedded in the packets, the indexes can be observed at all points in the networks. SDES (source description) is a type of RTCP packet, and the source description element is reserved for user extension. In our research, indexes are described by keywords in the source description element to describe the video stream.

6.3 System Outline

In this research, we developed a prototype system which dynamically edits the raw video data stream transmitted from more than one providers. Dynamic editing is based on the SPS in which the program progression is described by script and the video stream selection method based on priority. The functions of the system are as follows:

- Automatic switching of the scoop video stream by using SPS determined by the priority evaluation
- Handling of real-time scoop video streams
- Handling of an unspecified number of distributed scoop video streams

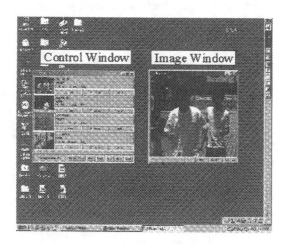

Fig. 8. Screen image of viewer's window

ScoopCast is composed of the director and the provider. The director transmits SPS, and the provider transmits the scoop video stream in accordance with SPS which it received. ScoopCast is implemented by using the multicast network. By using multicast transmission, it becomes possible to transmit an SPS produced by the director to unspecified number of providers at the same time. The director transmits an SPS by using RTCP like the description information. The provider transmits a scoop video stream by using RTP. The system outline is shown in the Figure 7(b).

We developed ScoopCast by expanding the function of Vic which is used widely as a video conference system in Mbone (the abbreviation of IP Multicast

Backbone)[15]. Vic stands for the videoconference tool, and it was develop by
Network Research Group [16] of Lawrence Berkeley National Laboratory. In
ScoopCast, SPS was implemented on SDES. There are three functions added to
Vic:

- SPS transmission function by the director Transmission of SPS as a SDES
  packet in the network.
- SPS reception function by the provider Reception of a SPS as a SDES packet,
  and execution in accordance with the scenario described in the SPS.
- Event transmission function by the provider

Transmission of user's event information as a SDES packet in the network.
As director's SPS transmission function, we implemented the UI for making SPS
using Tk widget. The information on the UI for SPS production is transformed
to SPS format, and transmitted as SDES packet on the network. On the other
hand , the provider's SPS reception function was expanded so it interprets SPS
as a control signal and behaves according to control conditions. The provider
transmits a scoop video corresponding to the contents of a SPS requirement. As
for the time condition of the SPS, we used the timer of the Win32 system. We
used the machines shown in Figure 7(a) for development.

The viewer receives the image which was edited by the director and transmitted by the multicast. Figure 8 shows the viewer's image window.

7 Conclusion and Future Work

In this paper, we proposed a new framework for authoring, delivering, and filtering live video streams in the Internet broadcasting environment for grass root
users. We designed the scheduled program skeleton to describe fixed scenario
of broadcast programs. In addition, we proposed the dynamic program producing mechanism based on a degree of broadcast priority to avoid conflicts from
unspecific number of providers. To verify the validity of the mechanism, we implemented a prototype called ScoopCast which can deliver video stream using
multicast networks. The multicast network provides a very useful way to deliver
video streams to unspecific number of users. We expect that high-speed networks
will become popular even at home in the near future. And also the digital video
equipments such as digital video cameras and mobile terminals are expected to
be in widespread use. We hope that the network-based communication of video
streams would constitute a new broadcasting system in the future.

Acknowledgements

The authors would like to extend their deep appreciation to Dr. Yutaka Ki-
dawara, Kobe Steel, Ltd., Mr. Toru Iijima, NEC Coporation, and Mr. Takyuki
Akasako, NTT Communicationware Corporation. This Research is partly supported by the Japanese Ministry of Education Grant-in-Aid for Scientific Research on Priority Area(A):"Advanced databases", area no. 275 (08244103). This

research is also supported in part by "Research for the Future" Program of Japan Society for the Promotion of Science under the Project "Advanced Multimedia Contents Processing" (Project No. JSPS-RFTF97P00501).

References

1. Kawaguchi, T., Doi, A., Tanaka, A.: A synchronized transmission mechanism for image and indexed information in multicast. In *Proc. of National Convention of IEICE (in Japanese)* (1997) B7–146
2. Kawaguchi, T., Doi, A.: A synchronized display mechanism for image and indexed information in multicast. In *Proc. of National Convention of IEICE (in Japanese)* (1997) B7–76
3. Harada, K., Tanaka, E., Ogawa, R., Hara, Y.: Anecdote: A multimedia storyboarding system with seamless authoring support. In *Proc. of ACM Multimedia'96* (1996) 341–351
4. Baecher, R., Rosenthal, A., Friedlander, N., Smith, E., Cohen, A.: A multimedia system for authoring motion pictures. In *Proc. of ACM Multimedia'96* (1996) 31–42
5. Kamahara, J., Kaneda, T., Ikezawa, M., Shimojo, S., Nishio, S., Miyahara, H.: A new scenario language for analysis and synthesis of the TV news program. In *Proc. of the 4th International Conference on Multimedia Modeling'97* (1997) 85–88
6. Ueda, H., Hayashi, M., Kurihara, T.: Desktop TV program creation - TVML (TV program Making Language) editor -. In *ACM Multimedia'98 State of the Art Demos* (1998)
7. Hayashi, M., Ueda, H., Kurihara, T.: TVML (TV program Making Language) - automatic TV program generation from text-based script -. In *Proc. of Imagina'99* (1999) 31–42
8. Jain, R., Gupta, A.: PRAJA presence technology. In *PRAJA white paper* (1998)
9. Shahraray, B., Gibbon, D.: Automated authoring of hypermedia documents of video programs. In *Proc. of ACM Multimedia'95* (1995) 401–409
10. Ariki, Y. Teranishi, T.: Indexing and classification of TV news articles based on telop recognition. In *Proc. of 4th Int'l Conference on Document Analysis and Recognition '97* (1997) 422–427
11. Kawaguchi, T., Doi, A., Iijima, T., Sumiya, K., Tanaka, K.: Broadcasting and filtering mechanism for indexed video stream. In *Proc. of Data Engineering Workshop (DEWS'98) (in Japanese)* (1998)
12. Akasako, T., Iijima, T., Sumiya, K., Tanaka, K.: A real-time indexing method for live video stream. In *Proc. of Data Engineering Workshop (DEWS'99) (in Japanese)* (1999)
13. MacCanne, S., Jacobson, V.: Vic: A flexible framework for packet video. In *Proc. of ACM Multimedia'95* (1995) 511–522
14. RTP/RTCP:RFC1889.
15. *Online document available at URL http://www. mbone.com/mbone/waht-is-mbone.html.*
16. *Online document available at URL http://www-nrg.ee.lbl.gov/.*

About Tours in the OTHY Hypermedia Design

Franck Barbeau[1] and José Martinez[2]

[1] MAIF – Service Bureautique, 200, Av. Salvador Allende
79038 Niort Cedex 9 – France
Franck.Barbeau@irin.univ-nantes.fr
[2] IRIN/CID – Université de Nantes, IRESTE – La Chantrerie – BP 60601
44306 Nantes Cedex 3 – France
Jose.Martinez@irin.univ-nantes.fr

Abstract. Hypermedia design has received considerable attention and methodologies appeared to conceive hypertexts, especially to alleviate the well-known disorientation problem. The Object To Hypermedia (OTHY) approach that we proposed takes into account object-orientation to balance page customisability —with respect to different types of objects— with uniformity —within a single class. In this paper, we again take advantage of this trade-off to introduce a generalisation of the tour concept that is able to fit several needs, mostly directed to traditional and new database requirements, but also demanded by end-users to better visualise data. Moreover, we benefited from the reflexivity of our framework in order to implement quite easily some of the envisioned new tours. This proves convenient and opens perspectives for an even more general approach.

1   Introduction and motivations

In many organisations, a single desktop computer has to access to a lot of independent sub-systems (different databases stored into different kinds of database management systems, files), located on different servers, sometimes physically distant. A study of the users' needs conducted in such a large organisation, namely MAIF (*Mutuelle Assurance des Instituteurs de France*), a French insurance company with 4,500 employees and as many computers, highlighted three main requirements. Among them, the most important need was the possibility to navigate easily among this mass of information, with the ease offered by the Web technology. This *navigation* must be possible not only for one database, but also between databases with common or related elements. In other words, users demand a single interface to the whole information system. Of course, several other requirements are important, e. g., querying, accessing heterogeneous databases, etc., which have been introduced in the design of our prototype [1]. Nevertheless, users want to be given different and powerful ways to browse the data in order not to rely on querying, which is badly considered for casual uses. In a way, they want to be able to browse data much like a set of queries had already been issued on the database and they just have to visit the results. Consequently, we shall concentrate only on navigational issues hereafter, and show that our extensions can effectively address the **group by** clause of a query language, and more, when simpler tours can only simulate the **order by** clause.

Our proposition offers a customisable hypertextual view of relational and object-oriented databases, and an extensible set of hypermedia tools and concepts. The basic aim of the work is to allow conventional database accesses with an hypermedia interface. [19] recommends the use of an OODBMS as the more rational solution to store hypertext data, e. g., Hyperwave is an Internet hypermedia system based on an object-oriented database engine [13]. An underlying structure to the hypertext exists and it is usually clearly translated by the interface [16]. This decreases considerably the user concentration, and increases the freedom to move around the objects of the database, as with PESTO [3] for instance.

This paper is organised as follows: First, in Section 2, we give a very short background on the tour concept. Then, we generalise and open the notion of guided and indexed tour in order to fit new needs, e. g., accessing multidimensional data sets. Next, in Section 3, we provide the guidelines for implementing these extensions. In particular, we take advantage of the reflexivity of our OTHY framework. This is illustrated by a somewhat complex example. Finally, in the conclusion, we shall point out how this property can be generalised even more.

2   Generalising guided and indexed tours

Of special interest is the notion of tour in hypermedia design [16]. More precisely, literature generally differentiates guided tours from indexed tours. We based our first implementation of these concepts on RMM (*Relationship Management Methodology*) [2] [10]. *Guided tours* look like linked lists of pages that can be accessed sequentially through a next button (and optionally a previous one too.) *Indexed tours* allow to access more rapidly to a set of pages through an intermediate page, the so-called index. Both kind of tours can be sorted. For instance, if an author is very prolix, it is wise to order his or her books according to some classifying criterion (dates of publication, alphabetical order of titles...). Therefore, we can admit that the following definition is sufficient to characterise these tours.

Definition 1. A tour is a way of browsing a (sorted) set of objects.

Providing more general alternatives is the goal of the following subsection.

2.1   Generalised tours

Guided and indexed tours can be seen has two alternatives to access to a (sorted) set of data. RMM, which is based on entity-relationship modelling, introduces guided tours, indexed tours, but also index guided tours [10]. However, the latter appears as a basic combination of the former ones.

OOHDM (*Object-Oriented Hypermedia Design Model*) [17] [18], the second methodology that most influenced OTHY, is based on OMT (*Object Modeling Technique*) [15]. It adds some constructs to ease the development of hypermedia databases. However, it does not address adequately the qualification notation. The common semantics of this construct is a set restriction. Therefore, this construct introduces the potential for a set of related objects with possibly intersecting subsets of such objects. For instance, each researcher has written several papers. He or she may share the authorship with some co-authors. For any given co-author, say A, there exists a set of co-authored papers and we may be interested in browsing through the papers that A and B wrote together. If there are more than two writers for a given paper, then the corresponding sets will intersect, i. e., some papers written by A and B can also appear in the set of papers written by A and C. (Mathematically, the generalisation of this example would be a kind of trellis traversal, the trellis being ordered by set inclusion of the occurring co-authorships.) Therefore, from the navigational point of view, the simple index guided tour extension of RMM is not sufficient to deal with that situation.

We are now ready to generalise the definition of a tour, in order to deal with the previous example as well as new requirements in the database field such as semi-structured and/or multi-dimensional data.

Definition 2. A tour is a way of browsing elements of a structure and possibly the structure itself.

The reader may point out that this definition applies to a whole hypertext. That is mainly true, but we can argue that the common definition looks more like the following one.

Definition 3. A browser is a tool to navigate an hypertext, i. e., a graph of nodes [5] [7] [8] [9] [14].

As far as they are comparable, Definition 1 and Definition 3 can be seen as subcases of Definition 2, where the structures are respectively a set and a graph. Of course, with structured data, in particular the database schemas that we manipulate, the graph of instances obeys to the typed database schema. So, OTHY and other tools already work with something that is more than just a graph of nodes.

However, there is a major difference between Definition 3 and the previous ones. Definition 3 is applicable to a set of existing instances, mostly connected through "hard-coded" links (foreign keys in relational databases, references with OIDs —Object IDentifiers— in object-oriented databases, but also methods that compute a set of related items [1]) whereas Definition 1 and Definition 2 provide a way to browse a collection of objects that do not have necessarily pre-defined references between themselves. Technically, the next and previous buttons of guided tours do not exist in the original data. They have been introduced by the browsing tool. Neither is the index materialised in the database, for indexed tours.

2.2 Some generalised tours: guided indexed tours and indexed guided tours

For the sake of the demonstration, we shall mix guided and indexed tours in two different ways: guided indexed tours, and indexed guided tours. First, our *indexed guided tours* are an extension of guided tours with some kind of index for allowing fast accesses to parts of an ordered collection. For instance, if a researcher has written a considerable number of papers, and that they are presented in lexicographic order, then it would be appreciated by the user to reach a given paper through a hierarchical index consisting of, say, two levels rather than scanning the tenths of preceding papers. In Fig. 1, one can access to the papers written by Daniel Schwabe through a chronological index consisting of a year level and an additional month level, if necessary.

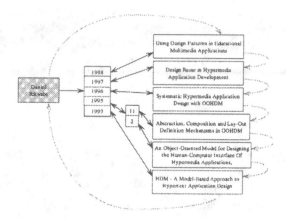

Fig. 1. An Indexed Guided Tour.

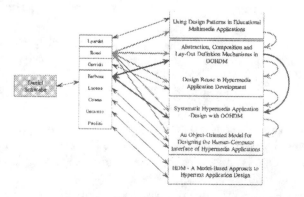

Fig. 2. A Guided Indexed Tour.

Secondly, our *guided indexed tours* are an extension of indexed tours (See Fig. 2) that allow guided tours on a subset of a more important collection. This subset can be a partition, corresponding to a **group by** in a query language like OQL (*Object Query Language*) [4], or to the qualification in an OMT schema, as discussed previously. In the latter case, objects have to be *shared* by the various guided tours, not duplicated, as shown in Fig. 2 where the light grey tour includes the bold one.

Both extensions are more general than the index guided tours of RMM. Moreover, we can envisage an extensible and customisable set of tours thanks to our broad definition of what is a tour, and of its subsequent implementation in our OTHY framework, to be detailed in the forthcoming section.

3 Tour implementation through OTHY reflexivity

The possibility for desktop computers in one organisation to access to different conceptual and physical sources of information requires the use of a "universal client." Therefore, we use a Java applet to obtain this uniqueness. This applet allows users to navigate in a well-known environment and possibly to be integrated more easily with XML documents in the near future. Therefore, we developed OTHY V1, the core of our proposal, in Java. However, note that the translation could be envisaged with any output format, including HTML/XML.

3.1 OTHY overview

OTHY is a framework [6] [11] [12] for translating objects into hyper-linked components. Basically, OTHY works as follows (See Fig. 3): The main OTHY function accepts an instance of any class and a (partial) mapping, so called a *directory*, from class names to specific transducers. A *transducer* is a functional object that is an instance of a class belonging to the `Transducer` hierarchy, part of the OTHY framework. Each transducer is responsible for creating a "page" that presents the data associated to the given instance.

Definition 4. A transducer is a function instance of a set of transducers that implements a translation from an instance to a page, i. e., the main purpose of OTHY (*Object To Hypermedia*):

$$Transducer = \{\ t_i : Instance \rightarrow Page\ \}$$

Transducers help to give a standard presentation to all instances belonging to the same class. This is important to limit user's disorientation. Nevertheless, the presentations can be customised at the class level by testing the instance state.

Using a directory of transducers turns out to be very important to allow different kinds of users (i. e., roles from the database viewpoint) to browse the databases with customised views, i. e., the same instance can appear with a different visual presentation, including colour, title, number of displayed attributes, etc. In the Internet context, various directories can be designed and implemented for employees, foreigners, partners, etc., depending on their identification.

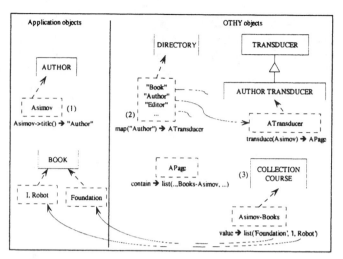

Fig. 3. OTHY at work.

Definition 5. A manager associates each user, at "login-time", to a corresponding directory, to allow different users to call different transducers for the very same instance:

$m : User \rightarrow Directory$

where a **directory** is also a functional object:

$Directory = \{ d_i : Class \rightarrow Transducer \}$

Thanks to a *meta-schema* of the (federated) database, which is also managed by OTHY, the class to which the instance pertains is first retrieved, then its properties (i. e., attributes, methods, and possibly associations.) Through the directory, the class name leads to the corresponding transducer. Either a generic transducer, possibly parameterised when created, generates a standard presentation, or it is a specific one that is in charge of producing the "page" for a particular class or hierarchy of the application domain. (In the latter case, this specific transducer must have been provided by an application programmer, thereby extending and customising OTHY by inheritance. A specific transducer can also take advantage of its knowledge of the application schema to retrieve connected instances, particularly those that are related to the current instance by an aggregation, and to present them within a single page, e. g., the lines of an invoice.)

Each page should incorporate *anchors* in addition to the own properties of the instance to be displayed. There is a hierarchy of anchors in OTHY to deal with various uses: back, next, and previous buttons for guided tours, etc. These anchors reference related instances of the current object.

Definition 6. A page contains anchors that reference either *one instance*, or *a collection of instances*.

Clicking on an anchor generates either a new call to the main OTHY function, with the related instance as a parameter (e. g., back button or next buttons, or a link from a car to his or her owner), or *a tour if the anchor references a collection of instances*. We extended the tour concept extension in order to further customise the way data can be browsed.

3.2 Generalised tours design and implementation guidelines

Similarly to the `Directory` and the `Transducer` hierarchies that provide basic functionalities and allow extensibility and customisability through inheritance and/or subtyping, we introduced interrelated `Tour/Anchor` hierarchies to cope with already implemented versions and possibly *unforeseen* variations. In order to achieve this difficult goal, we simply *cannot* provide any pattern at the root of the hierarchy level.

Definition 7. A **tour** is one possible way to navigate into a collection of instances. To a set of instances is associated a new set of inter-linked instances, derived from the former, and an entry point in the generated structure:

$$Tour = \left\{ \quad \tau_j: \begin{array}{ccc} 2^{Instance} & \to & Instance \times 2^{Instance} \\ \{ i \} & \to & (i'_0, \{ i' \}) \end{array} \right\}$$

In Section 2, we dwell upon the similarity and difference between Definition 2 and Definition 3. Similarly to Definition 3, the `Tour` abstract class cannot implement something more specific than an hypergraph traversal. In contrast, such an hypergraph does not exist and has to be constructed on-the-fly. Therefore, the generic sketch algorithm is as follows: First, when a tour object is created, its corresponding constructor method, i. e., τ_j, is responsible for building a particular structure based on properties of the objects of the set to be navigated. This structure certainly consists of interconnected objects such as the nodes of a tree, etc.

Then, this structure has to be navigated. To avoid the tedious task of providing an *ad hoc* traversal algorithm for each kind of tour, we give the following rule of implementation: "*Let rely on the OTHY framework itself, i. e., take advantage of reflexivity.*" Effectively, some objects from the generated traversal structure have to be displayed, e. g., the index for an indexed tour. Therefore, let simply provide a transducer for each such generated object, and record the tour class name and the corresponding transducer in the directory.

Of course, this is just a guideline and simple tours can be implemented without requiring the explicit construction of the traversal structure. This is the case for guided and single-level indexed tours, as already implemented in OTHY. For instance, guided tours do maintain only an index variable and linked pages are actually created only when they are to be displayed.

3.3 An example: the guided multi-level indexed tour

Guided indexed tours are mostly guided tours for which it is possible to use the index first in order to avoid a lengthy scan of the first objects in the collection. It is also possible to go up and down the index to move rapidly to distant parts of a large collection. When the index consists of a single node, our notion of guided indexed tour is identical to the RMM definition.

In contrast, *indexed guided tours* are mostly indexed tours with the possibility to browse the neighbourhood of a located member of the collection. This kind of tour is not defined in the RMM method. It is of interest for grouping sub-sequences rather than just ordering the collection. As an example, let us imagine that a map is divided recursively into quadrants. Such a tour allows the user to locate rapidly a particular region and then to browse only the objects pertaining to the last quadrant. With a guided indexed tour, browsing would have crossed the limits of the region.

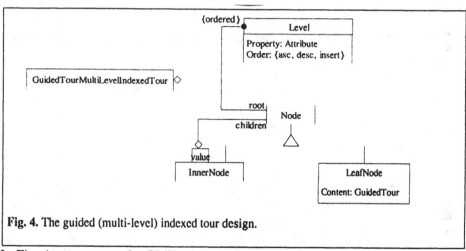

Fig. 4. The guided (multi-level) indexed tour design.

In Fig. 4, we propose the OMT schema of an extension named a *guided multi-level indexed tour*. It is a kind of tour that can discriminate hierarchically on an ordered set of properties of the set instances, e. g., State, then City, and finally Street to access to customers' records. Then, customers can be presented with a standard guided tour, possibly sorted on the Name property. At run-time, the constructor will require the set of instances along with the list of properties, one per level. It is the task of the constructor to construct the tree, and to call, for each leaf, the guided tour constructor with the corresponding subset of instances. At compile-time, it is the duty of the programmer to provide *ad hoc* transducers for the Node hierarchy classes, and possibly to add Anchor classes to deal with the tree traversal.

Some other kinds of tours that we thought of are: an indexed guided tour variation, the index of which being a B-tree; an R-tree like guided indexed tour for accessing multi-dimensional data (MAIF owns a geographical database); a 2D matrix can answer simpler needs ; a trellis tour has been mentioned in Section 2.1. In point of fact, a designer can provide any kind of traversal of a set of objects by taking advantage of various properties that these objects can exhibit.

4   Conclusion and future works

Offering several ways to browse sets of data is extremely important for end-users that are navigating into a large and complex database (or a set of loosely coupled hetero-geneous databases.) Effectively, in addition to limiting the disorientation problem, this also diminishes the cognitive overhead of having to remember several paths that lead to parts of the final result. Also, this postpones the moment when the user will have to start querying the database rather than browsing it, something that is unfriendly for casual and/or naive end-users.

In this paper, we introduced our OTHY framework and detailed the design and im-plementation of one of its sub-hierarchies in order to deal with an extensible collection of tours. This has been illustrated through two combinations of the well-known guided and indexed tours. This proved relatively easy to develop thanks to the genericity and the reflexivity of our framework (transient objects can be managed like database ob-jects from the point of view of the translation into a "page.")

In Section 2, we discussed whether Definition 2 can apply to a whole hypertext. Ef-fectively, what has been reached here is a way to create any kind of object in memory, based on underlying stored objects, and to browse the former and the latter either with generic techniques, or by providing *ad hoc* browsing methods. This has been exempli-fied in this paper with the tour concept. In our opinion, it is possible to apply it to any other kind of data, in particular views, as of the database meaning. But, at MAIF, people are also interested in the automatic gathering and organisation of documents relevant to a given issue, e. g., retrieving all the information related to a given accident (policyholder, contract ...) Therefore, a wider perspective is to combine this feature with meta-interpretation in order to fully customise the accesses to the underlying databases, even at run-time.

References

[1] Barbeau, F., Martinez, J.; *OTHY: Object To HYpermedia*; Proc. of the 11th Conference on Advanced Information Systems Engineering (CAiSE*99), Heidelberg, Germany, June 1999, pp. 349-363

[2] Bieber, M., Isakowitz, T.; *Designing Hypermedia Applications*; Communications of the ACM, August 1995, Vol. 38, No. 8, pp. 26-29

[3] Carey, M., Haas, L., Maganty, V., Williams, J.; *PESTO: An Integrated Query/Browser for Object Databases*; Proc. of the 22nd Int'l Conf. On Very Large Data Bases (VLDB'96), Mumbai (Bombay), India, 1996, pp. 203-214

[4] Cattel, R. G. G., Barry, D., Bartels, D., Berler, M., Eastman, J., Gamerman, S., Jordan, D., Springer, A., Strickland, H., Wade, D.; *The Object Database Standard: ODMG 2.0*; Morgan Kaufmann Publishers, Inc., San Francisco, California, 1997, 270 p.

[5] Conklin, J.; *Hypertext: An Introduction and Survey*; IEEE Computer, September 1987, pp. 17-41

[6] Fayad, M. E.; Schmidt, D. C.; *Object-Oriented Application Frameworks*; Communications of the ACM, October 1997, Vol. 40, No. 10, pp. 32-38

[7] Halasz, F., Schwartz, M.; *The Dexter Hypertext Reference Model*; Communications of the ACM, February 1994, Vol. 37, No. 2, pp. 30-39

[8] Hardman, L., Bulterman, D.C.A., Van Rossum, G.; *Links in Hypermedia: the Requirement for Context*; Hypertex'93 Proceedings, November 1993, pp. 183-191

[9] Hardman, L., Bulterman, D.C.A., Van Rossum, G.; *The Amsterdam Hypermedia Model: Adding Time and Context to the Dexter Model*; Communications of the ACM, February 1994, Vol. 37, No. 2, pp. 50-62

[10] Isakowitz, T., Stohr, E. ; Balasubramanian, P. ; *RMM: A Methodology for Structured Hypermedia Design*; Communications of the ACM, August 1995, Vol. 38, No. 8, pp. 34-44

[11] Johnson, R.E., Foote, B.; *Designing Reusable Classes*; JOOP, Vol. 1, n° 2, June/July 1998, pp. 22-35

[12] Johnson, R.E.; *Frameworks = (Components + Patterns)*; Communications of the ACM, October 1997, Vol. 40, No. 10, pp. 39-42

[13] Maurer, H. (Ed.); *HyperG is now HyperWave: The Next Generation Web Solution*; Addison-Wesley Publishing Company, 1996

[14] Nielsen, J.; *HyperText and HyperMedia*; Academic Press, Inc., San Diego, California, USA, 268 p.

[15] Rumbaugh, J., Blaha, M., Premerlani, W., Eddy, F., Lorensen, W.; *Object-Oriented Modeling and Design*; Prentice Hall, 1991

[16] Rutledge, L., Hardman, L., van Ossenbruggen, J., Bulterman, D.C.A.; *Structural Distinctions Between Hypermedia Storage and Presentation*; Proc. of the 6th ACM Int'l Multimedia Conf. (MM'98), Bristol (UK), 14-16 September 1998

[17] Schwabe, D., Rossi, G., Barbosa, S.D.J.; *Abstraction, Composition and Lay-Out Definition Mechanisms in OOHDM*; Proc. of the ACM Workshop on Effective Abstractions in Multimedia, San Francisco, California, November 4, 1995

[18] Schwabe, D., Rossi, G., Barbosa, S.D.J.; *Systematic Hypermedia Application Design with OOHDM*; Proc. of The 7th ACM Conf. on Hypertext, Washington D.C., March 16-20, 1996, pp. 116-128.

[19] Smith, K.E., Zdonik, S.B.; *InterMedia: A Case Study of the Differences between Relational and Object-Oriented Database Systems*; Proc. of the Int'l Conf. on Object-Oriented Programming Systems, Languages, and Applications (OOPSLA'87), Orlando, Florida, October 1987

Aspect-Oriented Design (AOD) Technique for Developing Distributed Object-Oriented Systems over the Internet

Joon-Sang Lee, Sang-Yoon Min, and Doo-Hwan Bae

Department of Computer Science
Korea Advanced Institute of Science and Technology
E-mail: {joon, bae, sang}@se.kaist.ac.kr

Abstract. While software development techniques for identifying specifying, and analyzing functional requirements of software systems are quite mature, existing traditional design methods are not mature enough to capture non-functional requirements such as concurrency, performance, fault tolerance, distribution, and persistence of a software application. Very recently, Aspect-Oriented Programming (AOP) approach has been introduced to provide an implementation-level programming framework for separately developing basic functionalities and non-functionalities of a software application. However, this is just an implementation-level approach. There are still needs for supporting AOP concepts at the design level, and for providing the traceability between the design model and the implementation model. In this paper, we propose an approach called Aspect-Oriented Design (AOD), which supports the concept of AOP at design level, for developing distributed object systems over the Internet. We also demonstrate the usability of the proposed approach with Multi-media Video Conference Systems (MVCS) example.

1 Introduction

The Internet makes it possible for users or applications to access the variety of resources and other applications distributed over the world. Accordingly, a lot of Internet applications have been developed in the form of distributed systems over the Internet. As object technology is quite mature for developing software systems, there have been many researches on the object-oriented development methodology and the object-oriented programming platform for developing the distributed systems. However, most of them do not provide the sufficient systematic means for the traceability between design level and implementation level. Moreover, existing object-oriented design methods lack in dynamic support for the properties of physical distributions of objects.

At present, both design methods and programming techniques are quite mature for developing basic functionalities identified through the requirement analysis. Object-oriented technology well supports a lot of software engineering's principles such as modularity, understandability, and extensibility. It systematically helps software developers to design and implement the basic functionality of an application. However, with respect to the non-functionality of an application, there are little systematic means supporting existing software development techniques, especially at design level. Aspect-Oriented Programming (AOP) was proposed to separately implement non-functional behaviors and basic functional behaviors. It also effectively coordinates the two different types of behaviors in an integrated way [9]. Since AOP is just a programming framework to separately implement the basic functionality and the non-functionality of an application, it can be adapted to any existing programming languages. Object-oriented programming can be extended with AOP by the help of meta-object protocols [4], [1].

In order to model Internet applications with the *de facto* standard object-oriented modeling language UML [12], we propose an Aspect-Oriented Design (AOD) method. AOD is the counterpart of aspect-oriented programming in the design phase, so that it supports separation of concerns that software designer can specify basic functional behaviors and non-functional behaviors in the different layers such as meta-level architecture [2], and integrate those aspectual behaviors into the whole behavior of an application as well. We use a high-level meta-object protocol for distributed object systems called *di*MOP [13], as the infra-structure for aspect-oriented design specification. *di*MOP plays a role of domain-specific meta-object protocol, where all specifications could be implemented by means of existing meta-object protocol facilities. In addition, as object-oriented specification languages we adopt an extended class diagram CDSM [13] and a new state diagram DCOS [13], in order to incorporate *di*MOP. Those specification languages can well support the aspect-oriented design specifications in terms of distributed object-oriented model. Furthermore, the design specifications modeled by means of our aspect-oriented design method can be implemented by means of an appropriate aspect-oriented programming in a straightforward way. In other words, our design approach supports the traceability. In order to demonstrate that our aspect-oriented design method is both practical and useful, we present Multi-media Video Conference Systems (MVCS) as an exemplary design specification model.

The rest of this paper is organized as follows. Section 2 explains the high-level meta-object protocol for distributed systems called *di*MOP. Section 3 briefly explains about the properties of DCOS and CDSM as specification languages. Section 4 presents MVCS as an application of our Aspect-Oriented Design (AOD), and in Section 5 we show the example of functional and non-functional decompositions of MVCS. In section 6, we conclude.

2 *di*MOP: A High-Level Meta-Object Protocol

Meta-Object Protocol (MOP) is an object-oriented mechanism to realize the behavior of meta classes. As can be indicated by the word *Protocol*, MOP provides software developers with constructs to reflect the strategy on message dispatching mainly in terms of run-time protocols. However, MOP can be realized by means of static modeling language features such as meta class and meta relation (i.e. instantiation relation between classes). By inheriting from the primary meta class such as *Class*[1] in Open C++ [1] and Open Java [11], the meta class redefines the interpretation strategies on all classes instantiated from it. This section introduces a high-level MOP for distributed object systems, called *di*MOP, that can be incorporated into UML so that the behavior of meta classes can be defined with UML.

2.1 Overview of *di*MOP

*di*MOP extends the ordinary object-oriented model with the properties of distributed environments, and provides an abstraction mechanism to specify the behavioral characteristics of distributed object systems. Such extension and provision make it possible to incorporate the concept of MOP into the object-oriented design model considering several non-functional requirements related to distributed object systems such as distribution, synchronization, and method scheduling policy of each constituent object at design level. As a result, the design method incorporating *di*MOP could systematically specify the behavioral properties such as object migrations in distributed object systems.

2.2 Abstraction of Reflective Aspects for Distributed Object Systems

In MOP, the base object does not need to know any information about its meta object. Thus, its behavior can be specified independently of its meta-class specification. In contrast, since the meta object is a meta program to manipulate the behavior of its base object, it must view the reflective information about its base object as its external problem domain in order to act upon that reflective information. Indeed, even though the meta object can hold various information about internal structures and interpretation strategies of its base object, the actual reflective information may be restricted to the behavioral characteristics of the target application domain. In *di*MOP, reflective information about the base objects consists of the synchronization, method-scheduling, and distribution policy of each object, in the form of high-level constructs. This information is represented by the means of *meta attributes*, and initialized, modified, and manipulated by each corresponding *meta methods*[2] in an abstract way. Each of the meta attributes can be defined as an abstract data type which has the specific semantics for its interpretation strategies on its own reflective aspect. Besides the built-in meta attributes defined in *di*MOP, additional meta attributes for other reflective aspects can be defined, offering extensibility to *di*MOP.

---

[1] It defines the basic interpretation strategies on ordinary classes primarily provided by the programming language.

[2] This function plays a role of reification/deification in metaprogramming [4], [2].

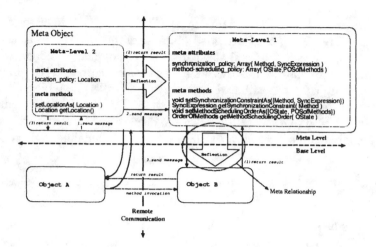

Fig. 1. Architecture of *di*MOP

2.3 Architecture of *di*MOP

The basic mechanism of *di*MOP is similar to those of conventional MOPs provided by CLOS, Open C++ [1], and Open Java [11]. However, *di*MOP can be distinguished from other MOPs with respect to abstraction and distribution. In the architecture of *di*MOP, each meta object is internally constructed as a two-level meta tower to distinguish remote communications from local communications as shown in Figure 1. The meta object at the meta-level 1 defines the synchronization and method-scheduling policy of its base object. The other meta object at the meta-level 2 defines the distribution policy of its base object, transitively.

*di*MOP deals with reflective aspects mainly relevant to the message dispatching for method invocations. When a method in the object B at the base level is invoked by the object A, the method invocation will be processed as follows: First, the message sent by the base object A is intercepted by its meta object at the meta-level 2. Second, the method invocation is interpreted according to the distribution policy defined in the meta object at the meta-level 2. Third, it is interpreted according to the synchronization and method-scheduling policy defined in the meta object at the meta-level 1. When the result of the method invocation returns, it will be delivered in the reverse order; 1→ 2→ 3→ (1)→ (2)→(3) as shown in Figure 1.

3 Design Specification Languages

We use the collaboration diagram of UML and our extensions[3] to the existing class diagram and state diagram of UML, in order to decompose the basic

---

[3] Class Diagram Supporting *di*MOP (CDSM) and Dynamically Configurable Object Statemachine (DCOS) [13]

functionality and the non-functionality of MVCS. The object-oriented specification model written in both an extended class diagram CDSM and a new state diagram DCOS is executable, and also can represent dynamic configuration behaviors [13]. Additionally, since those specifications incorporate the high-level meta-object protocol for distributed object systems called *di*MOP, they fundamentally can support aspect-oriented design of distributed object systems. The built-in aspects of *di*MOP covers the message dispatching strategies on physical distributions, method synchronizations, and method scheduling of each object.

3.1 Class Diagram Supporting *di*MOP

Class Diagram Supporting diMOP (CDSM) is an extension to the conventional class diagram of UML. Unlike the existing class diagram of UML, CDSM includes additional syntax and semantics for incorporating *di*MOP and specifying dynamic configuration behaviors. CDSM extends the semantics of *Composite Aggregation* of UML for dynamic configuration behaviors. It adopts active objects and multi-threaded concurrency as its inter-object concurrency model. In addition, it provides a way to explicitly specify meta classes and meta relationships with a newly defined relation.

3.2 Dynamically Configurable Object Statemachine

Dynamically Configurable Object Statemachine (DCOS) is proposed as a new state diagram to to specify dynamic configuration behaviors and to incorporate *di*MOP systematically. It satisfies *synchrony hypothesis* that all transitions does not consume any time to complete, and thus adopts quasi-concurrent model[5] as its own inner-object concurrency, in other words, at a time only one thread of control can be executed within an object.

DCOS adopts *Extended OCL* (EOCL) that is an extension to conventional *Object Constraint Language* (OCL) of UML to represent the changes of system structure and object state systematically. It incorporates *di*MOP by providing separate specifications for base classes and meta classes, so that can provide syntax and semantics for base class and meta class, in an integrated way with CDSM.

4 Multi-media Video Conference System

In order to demonstrate the usability of DCOS and CDSM in the development of distributed object systems, we apply them to Multimedia Video Conference Systems (MVCS). We identify four major types of actors: chair-in-chief, chairmen, speakers, and observers and list up the normal scenarios as follows:

- A chair-in-chief manages the global procedure of the conference events. The chair-in-chief decides whether the conference will be closed immediately or after when all underlying sessions are finished.

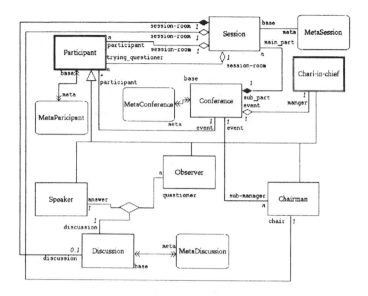

Fig. 2. The CDSM specification of MVCS

- A participant registers for a conference, then browses currently progressing sessions, and joins one of them. After the session is over, all of the participants will leave it.
- A chairman initiates a session, and then allows the speakers to make their presentation in order. After each presentation is over, the chairman chooses a participant having comments or questions, and allows only the speaker and the chosen participant to discuss together. When other participants want to join in that discussion, they can join under the chairman's permission. When the chairman is acknowledged the signal of the discussion end by the participating discussants, the chairman decides whether to continue further discussion. Once the discussion is over, the chairman initiates the next speaker's presentation.

5 Specifying Functional and Non-functional Behaviors of MVCS

The system structure of MVCS and the possible collaborations are specified in CDSM and in the collaboration diagram as shown in Figure 2 and Figure 3, respectively. The partial class model of MVCS shown in Figure 2 describes the relationship among the classes: Conference, Session, Participant, and Discussion. A class Participant is categorized into three types: Speaker, Objserver, and Chairman. In a conference there is only one Chair-in-chief who schedules a series of sessions and manages the conference registration. A conference contains

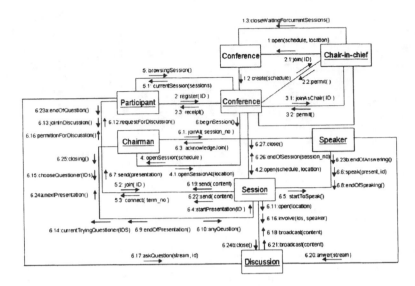

Fig. 3. Collaboration model of MVCS

multiple sessions at a point of time, and in each session there is a chairman to manage the speaker's presentation and to mediate the discussion between observers and speakers. Before the first session begins, it is necessary that all of expected chairmen have already registered for the conference. Accordingly, all of expected speakers should register for that conference and join in his own session, before the session begins. The partial collaborations described above are shown in Figure 3.

A class Session plays a role of partitioning the speaker's presentations into several groups, and becomes the unit of concurrent execution. The DCOS specification of the class Session is shown in Figure 4. Class Session is associated with a meta class MetaSession, which lets the instances of the class Session be the remote object and tunes the basic strategies on method synchronization and scheduling. The non-functional decomposition of the class Session is done by means of the meta class provided by *di*MOP. The DCOS specification of the meta class MetaSession is shown in Figure 5. It describes the non-functionality such as explicit object migration by methods *open* or *moveTo* and state-based synchronization constraints that the number of participants joining in a session should be less than 60 for the efficient progress of a session. These non-functional aspects can be modeled by means of meta classes.

A class Discussion plays a role of broad-casting the session discussion between questioners and a speaker to the participants. The number of questioners simultaneously joining in a discussion is decided by the chair, and even while discussing, new questioners can be added in the discussion under the permission of the chair. If the participants in a discussion speak at the same time, the scheduling priority of delivering each speaking to all of the session participants

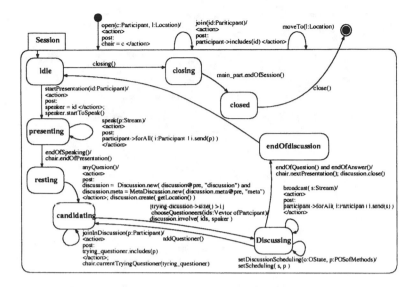

Fig. 4. DCOS specification of a class Session

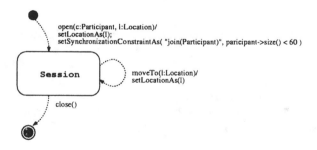

Fig. 5. DCOS specification of a meta class MetaSession

can be dynamically modified by the chairman, which is specified in the meta class MetaDiscussion. In other words, the chairman decides the priority to speak among the participants, The DCOS specifications of the class Discussion and the meta class MetaDiscussion are shown in Figure 6 and in Figure 7, respectively.

6 Conclusion

We have proposed Aspect-Oriented Design (AOD) method, which supports to model non-functionality: the issues of physical distributions as well as the basic functionality of distributed object-oriented systems. AOD makes it possible to separately specify the basic functional behavior and non-functional behavior of an application, and also to coordinate them based on a well defined meta-level architecture *di*MOP. As the object-oriented modeling language supporting

164

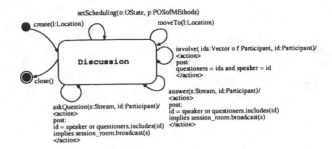

Fig. 6. DCOSspecification of a class Discussion

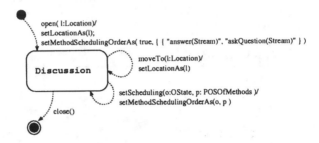

Fig. 7. DCOS specification of a meta class MetaDiscussion

AOD, we use UML-based diagrams such as the collaboration diagram of UML, and Class Diagram Supporting *di*MOP (CDSM) and Dynamically Configurable Object Statemachine (DCOS).

References

1. S. Chiba, "A metaobject Protocol for C++", *In Proceedings of OOPSLA*, pp. 285-299, 1995.
2. P. Maes and D. Nardi, *Meta-Level Architectures and Reflection*, ELSEVIER SCIENCE PUBLISHERS, 1988.
3. G. Helm, I. Holland, and D. Gangopadhyay, "Contracts: Specifying Behavioral Compositions in Object-Oriented systems", *In Proceedings of OOPSLA '90*, ACM SIGPLAN Notices, vol. 25, no. 10, pp. 303-311, 1990.
4. G. Kiczales, J. ds Rivieres, and D.G. Bobrow, *The Art of the Metaobject protocol*, MIT Press, 1991.
5. P. Wegner, "Demensions of Object-Oriented Modeling", *IEEE Computer*, pp. 12-20, 1992.
6. W. Harrison and H. Ossher, "Subject-Oriented Programming (A Critique of Pure Objects)", *In Proceedings of OOPSLA '93*, ACM SIGPLAN Notices, vol. 28, no. 10, pp. 411-428, Oct. 1993.
7. C. Szyperski, "Component-Oriented Programming A Refined Variation on Object-Oriented Programming", The Oberon Tribune, vol 1, no 2, December, 1995.

165

8. G. Kiczales, "Beyond the Black Box Abstraction: Open Implementation", *IEEE Software*, vol. 13, no. 1, January, 1996.

9. Kiczales G., Lamping J., Mendhekar A, Maeda C., Lopes C. V., Loingtier J.M., Irwin J, "Aspect-Oriented Programming", Invited Talk, *In Proceedings of ECOOP '97*, LNCS 1241, pp. 220-243, 1997.

10. C. Szyperski, *Component Software: Beyond Object-Oriented Programming*, ACM Press, 1997.

11. M. Tatsubori and S. Chiba, "OpenJava: Yet another reflection support for java", *In 14th Proceedings of JSSST*, pp. 201-204, 1997.

12. H.E. Eriksson and M. Penker, *UML Toolkit*, Wiley Computer Publishing, 1998.

13. J.S. Lee and et al., "Developing Distributed Software Systems by incoporating meta-Object Protocol (*di*MOP) with Unified Modeling Language (UML)", *In Proceedings of 4th International Symposium on Autonomous Decentralized Systems*, pp. 65-72, March 1999.

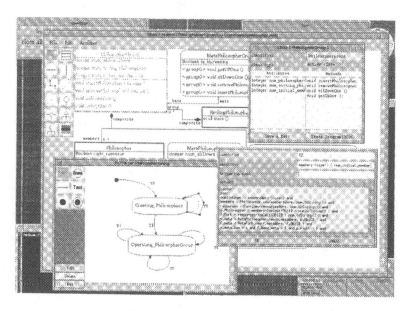

Fig. 8. A prototype development environment for CDSM and DCOS: *di*MOPer

Modeling Enterprise Objects in a Virtual Enterprise Integrating System: ViaScope

Xiaochun Yang[1], Guoren Wang[1], Ge Yu[1], and Dik Lun Lee[2]

[1] Dept. of Computer Science & Engineering, Northeastern University,
Shenyang, China 110006
{wanggr,yuge}@ramm.neu.edu.cn
[2] Dept. of Computer Science, Hong Kong University of Sci. and Tech.
Hong Kong, China
dlee@cs.ust.hk

Abstract. The construction of information integrating systems for virtual enterprises raises a set of issues concerned with coupling the systems of independent enterprises in a controlled, flexible and easily-understood manner. In particular, these independent enterprises are typically large-scale, scattered on the Internet, and they involve in different kinds of heterogeneous data or information. Basically, the information architectures rely on wide ranges of data sources that are not completely federated. Moreover, making those architectures fatally ends up in a new system. In order to solve these problems, we review the research work related to this paper as well as the needs to study on the constraints between distributed objects. According to distributed object paradigm, we present the enterprise object modeling techniques in a CORBA/IIOP based enterprise integrating system, ViaScope, which provides an infrastructure to support a uniform access to distributed enterprise resources, and describes the scheduler model supporting constraints of enterprise-wide information processing.

1 Introduction

Information integrating systems have become a mature technology gradually during 20 years' development, by which it is possible to exchange, transform, share and integrate different distributed, heterogeneous, and autonomous data sources. However, following the booming Internet and virtual enterprises (VE), traditional information integration techniques are not suitable for the challenge of the new requirements.

Traditional integrating methods can be classified into two approaches: point-to-point translation[1, 2] and common data model translation[3, 4].

- Point-to-point translation, as shown in Fig.1.a, translates the schema defined by one model to another model directly by applying some precise translation algorithms or rules. The disadvantage of this approach is that the translation algorithms are pair-wise specific and can not be used for all pairs of source and target models. There is no uniform approach to support algorithm development for different data models. As a result, the existing algorithms are rather complex, and entirely based on the system developers' understanding of the source and target models.

- Common data model translation, as shown in Fig.1.b, on the other hand, it avoids the development of a large number of unsharable translation algorithms by using a common data model (CDM). Instead of translating a source model to a target model directly, it divides the translation process into two steps: The source model is first converted into the CDM which is in turn translated into the target model.

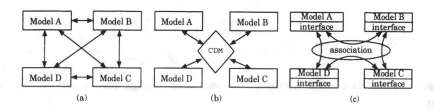

(a)   (b)   (c)

Fig. 1. Three approaches to solving heterogeneity of models

All the above methods are not suitable for large scale resources sharing in a VE environments where people, information, and material were associated together through Internet. As applications become more and more complex and distributed, the limitations of the two approaches float on the surface gradually. They are expensive for sharing information through Internet, and unusable for large scale distributed environment. It is not practice to translate each model to a common data model, furthermore, it is difficult to find out a suitable uniform model to support all kinds of heterogeneous models. So, a new method has been presented to solve this problem.

- Interface translation, as showed in Fig.1.c, requires each component system adopting different data models should provide its interface conforms to uniform interface protocol. The kernel of the object is invisible for the outside. Thus, they communicate with each other through their interfaces.

Compared with the former two approaches, the last one has following advantages: 1) Low complexity. For N data models, the point-to-point translation approach requires N*(N-1) dedicated translation algorithms, the common data model translation approach needs 2*N algorithms, while interface translation approach needs only N interfaces. 2) High extensibility. If a new model is added into the integrating system which handles N models, only 1 new algorithm need to be developed instead of the 2*N algorithms in the point-to-point translation approach and 2 algorithms in the common data model translation approach.

CORBA/IIOP[5] is one of the example of the interface translation approach. Relying on the software bus–a middleware called ORB, it solves the distributivity and heterogeneity of platforms. Thus, we introduce CORBA to support the information integration for virtual enterprise.

So far, there are some successful projects, such as WONDA[6], VENICE[7], PRODNET[8]. The representative system WONDA has made a relatively successful experiment to construct a virtual enterprise based on CORBA. It adopts the Business Object model[9] identified by OMG Business Object Domain Task Force (BODTF) to describe distributed objects. However, the sort of Business Objects is too precise to suit for the existing defect in some legacy applications. For member enterprises, they enter into a VE with a set of resources, including some applications. Some of these applications were designed long time ago, in which information can't be distinguished clearly, that is, we can't determine exactly what kind of Business Object a legacy application should belong to. Since these applications might be very important to those member enterprises, we have to pay more attention to them. In order to incorporate legacy applications in a VE, we should customize them to fit the needs of the VE, and integrate them effectively to fully joint projects.

The rest of this paper is organized as follows. In Section 2, an Enterprise Object Model (EO) is proposed. In Section 3, the definition of the constraints between enterprise objects is described. In Section 4, the implementation issues including the enterprise event object and scheduling model for enterprise objects are discussed. Finally, in Section 5, the conclusion and future work are presented to support the integrity constraints.

2   Enterprise objects

Different from the modeling domain of business objects, ViaScope pays more attention to the pre-existing applications and enterprise resources, such as database supporting different models and architectures which have been inherited over the past years and reflect the internal changes that occurred in the enterprise. Thus, distributed objects in VE should have ability to represent the local enterprise resources, and provide access interface conforming to common protocols.

Definition 1. Enterprise Information Source (EIS). Suppose s is a data source containing some information for enterprise, it has its own service system (SS), such as DBMS, file system, and so on. An EIS can be expressed as a 3-tuple:

$$EIS = < S\_data, SS, S\_MetaData > \qquad (1)$$

S_data is the shared data belonging to data source, $S\_MetaData$ is metadata of the data source. If the data source has schema, $S\_MetaData$ contains its schema information. In the extreme case, an EIS is just an application or a service, it has no its own data or schema, and the S_data and $S\_MetaData$ might be nil.

In CORBA, objects can be defined in different granularity. When registering a Database Management System (e.g. RDBMS) to CORBA, an object can be used to represent a row in a relation or a database itself. When fine granularity objects are registered, due to insertion and deletion of objects, it may be necessary to recompile the IDL code. Furthermore IDL codes will be voluminous. Therefore, we defined the whole EIS as a distributed object.

Definition 2. Enterprise Object (EO). In ViaScope, an EIS can be wrapped and represented as an EO. An EO can be defined as a 2-tuple:

$$EO =< eid, \Phi > \tag{2}$$

Here, *eid* denotes EO's object identifier, it expresses an object uniquely. Φ is used to describe EO's interface including states and operations of the EO. An EIS can be encapsulated and extracted to an EO. The structure information can be mapped into EO's properties represented with $STATE(\Phi(EO))$, and the implementations of correspondent SS can be mapped into EO's operations represented with $OP(\Phi(EO))$. Note, $\Phi(EO)$ defines the external characteristics of the EO. However, in order to access some public information easily, CORBA provides some local interface embedded in $\Phi(EO)$. So we can called $\Phi(EO)$ main interface to distinguish it from the other local interfaces. In order to give a clearly description, we introduce $\varphi(EO)$ to represent the set of EO's local interfaces. Clearly, $\varphi(EO) \subseteq STATE(\Phi(EO))$.

An example is given through the following codes, interface *CAD_Designing* is the main interface, and *Drawing* is a local interface. If a user wants to create a drawing, she or he only needs to access the *CAD_Designing*'s operation *new-Drawing*.

```
    interface Drawing {

        string          designer;
        sequence<string>  part_no;
    };
    interface CAD_Designing {
        Drawing          newDrawing ( in string drawing_name);
        sequence<string>  deleteDrawing ( in string drawing_name);
    };
```

3 Constraints between EOs

From global viewpoints, an information integrating system is similar to a database system, and each distributed object joining integration manages its internal information autonomously. On the other hand, these objects depend on each other to finish information integrating tasks together. Thus, integrating system should guarantee data's correctness and consistency. The integrity constraints of an information integrating system can be defined as Theta Constraint, Reference Constraint, and Cover Constraint. Theta Constraint requires two EO's partial attributes are analogous, Reference Constraint describes the potential association between two EOs, and Inclusion Constraint defines the affiliation between two EOs.

Definition 3. Theta Constraint. Suppose an integrating system has two EOs O_i, O_j, $i \neq j$, $\exists\ x, y \in STATE(\Phi(O_i)) \cap STATE(\Phi(O_j))$, if $O_i.x\ \theta\ O_j.x$, then $O_i.y\ \theta'\ O_j.y$ (θ and θ' are comparison operators). Then we say, there is a theta constraint between O_i and O_j. A theta constraint is expressed as follows.

$$C_{theta} < O_i, O_j >= x : \theta \rightarrow y : \theta' \tag{3}$$

If θ and θ' are equivalence operators, then the theta constraint is also simply called an equivalence constraint. An equivalence constraint between states x and y of enterprise objects O_i, O_j is described as follows.

$$C_{eql} < O_i, O_j >= x \rightarrow y \tag{4}$$

Definition 4. Reference Constraint (RC). Suppose an integrating system has two EOs O_i, O_j, $i \neq j$, if $\exists\ m \in \varphi(O_i)$, x is an attribute of m, and $\exists\ n \in \varphi(O_j)$, y is an attribute of n. If either of the following two conditions comes into existence, we say there is a reference constraint between O_i and O_j.

1) x and y represent the same semantics, for $\forall\ m_i \in m$, $\exists\ n_j \in n$, $m_i.x = n_j.y$, then we say the constraint is a Single Reference Constraint (S-RC). A S-RC is expressed as follows.

$$C_{ref} < O_i, O_j >= x \xrightarrow{r} y \tag{5}$$

2) x is a set type, the element of x and y represent the same semantics, assume $ext(n.y)$ is a set representing values of attribute y of interface n, for $\forall\ m_i \in m$, $m_i.x \subseteq ext(n.y)$. we say the constraint is Multiple Reference Constraint (M-RC). A M-RC is expressed as follows.

$$C_{ref} < O_i, O_j >= x \overset{r}{\Rightarrow} y \tag{6}$$

RC is a very popular restriction in VE environment. For example, assume the following three systems are independent in a VE: *Manufacturing system*, *CAD_Designing system* and *Management system*. There are two potential constraints among them. One constraint is between *Manufacturing system* and *CAD_Designing system* that specifies each product in *Manufacturing system* must be offered by a drawing in the *CAD_Designing system*. Another is between *CAD_Designing system* and *Management system* that specifies each part referred to in one drawing must exist in the *Management system* (show as Fig.2). If a part is deleted, then any future drawings will not be allowed to reference this part, and those existing drawings which referenced the part are no longer valid.

Definition 5. Inclusion Constraint. Suppose an integrating system has two EOs O_i, O_j, $i \neq j$, if $\exists\ m \in \varphi(O_i)$, x is an attribute of m, and $\exists\ n \in \varphi(O_j)$, y is an attribute of n, $ext(m.x) \subseteq ext(n.y)$, we say there is an Inclusion Constraint between O_i and O_j. An Inclusion Constraint is expressed as follows.

$$C_{inclusion} < O_i, O_j >= x \xrightarrow{i} y \tag{7}$$

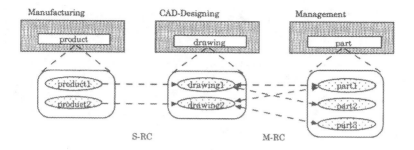

Fig. 2. Example of RC

4 Managing EOs in ViaScope

4.1 Incorporating EOs

Each member company as an EO enters into a VE with a set of resources, including software systems and data. Some of these EOs were originally designed to perform specific functions for that member company. In general, in order to incorporate the EOs in the VE, these EOs may need to be encapsulated to fit the needs of the VE. There are three kinds of approaches to encapsulate an EO to support the incorporation among EOs:

- *Code Rewrite.* In the worst case, we can simply rewrite the original code to encapsulate the behavior of the component to fit the needs of the VE. Certainly, this is the least desirable method of component customization.
- *Code Mapping.* If the existing component system's codes are invisible, we can provide a mechanism to add codes or to replace codes of a method without having to access to the source codes. Code mapping includes properties mapping and methods mapping.
  - *Properties Mapping.* This is done by some systems[3]. For example, in order to support schema based integration, we can write an interface for it, and provide some public properties in the interface to map the methods provided by a legacy system. The attributes in the interface can be accessed directly. Then at integrating-time, we can configure the component to behave in a certain way by setting the properties to the appropriate values. Thus, the behavior of a component is encapsulated indirectly through the values of properties.
  - *Behaviors Mapping.* Mapping each method to the corresponding API as well as providing a single method to map multiple APIs. Here, some context was added in the implementation of the interface so as to notify the other component systems to behave at a certain time.
- *Methods Scheduling.* It is the most flexible approach. We can introduce the ECA[10] rules to encapsulate the codes and, in effect, encapsulate the behavior of the EO. Here, the events of ECA rules act as "hooks" and rules are essentially "codes".

By using Methods Scheduling, the example of constraints between *CAD_Designing* system and *Management* system can be translated into following ECA rules:

```
E1: CAD_Designing.drawing.contain.insert_object(obj_key)
C1: Management.part.exist(obj_key)
A1: commit (E1)                                              (R1)
E2: CAD_Designing.drawing.contain.modify_object
          (old_obj_key,new_obj_key)
C2: Management.part.exist(new_obj_key)
A2: commit (E2)                                              (R2)
E3: Management.part.delete_object(obj_key)
A3: CAD_Designing.drawing.delete_object
          (designing.drawing.contain.lookup(obj_key))       (R3)
```

4.2 Enterprise event object

Apparently, events in a rule play an active role, that is, an event triggers a rule in a pre-defined way. When events have been defined to be associated with a certain method, the actual codes for posting the events can be generated automatically and inserted into the proper places. For example, the new class to deal with the events can be generated to inherit from the old one. By using this way, we can enhance the behavior of the old method or to replace the behavior of it. In order to manage this kind of active objects in VE, we give the definition of enterprise event object.

Definition 6. Enterprise Event Object (EEO). An Enterprise Event Object is an active EO which is interesting to the other members in VE. It can be a "real world" external event(e.g. time event, failure machine crash), or an internal event(e.g. data updating). Clearly, EEO is a sub-class of EO, and some EEOs are typically service objects or applications.

In CORBA, each distributed object uses IDL to describe its interface to the rest of the world. The only way to achieve specification is through inheritance. In order to give a definite description of EO and EEO, ViaScope provides Enterprise Object Definition Language (EODL) which extends IDL syntax to produce EOs specifications. The exact description is showed in Fig.3.

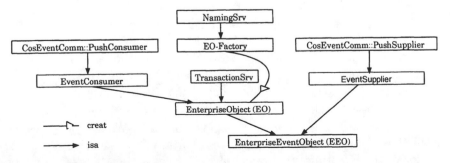

Fig. 3. Description of EO and EEO in ViaScope

In ViaScope, EOs are typically distributed objects that represent matters in a specific domain handled by the VE. Clearly, an EO is a transactional distributed object that its interface inherits from the *TransactionSrv* object's interface which defined by ViaScope. And each EO is also an event consumer whose interface inherits from the *EventConsumer* object's interface, and then inherits form CORBA's *CosEventComm::PushConsumer*.

An EEO is a sub-type of EO and has the ability to push high level semantic events to users indicating that significant changes have occurred. The posted event is received by a consumer of the EEO. Thus, the supplier of the EEO is in charge of detecting the occurring of a "real world" event and posting the event. However, it is not in charge of finding who the consumers are and how the event is handled. Therefore an EEO's interface inherits from the *EventSupplier* interface that allows its registration within the Event Service as an event pusher. ViaScope provides three kinds of approaches to post events as follows:

- *Semi-active Posting.* EEO pushes messages to a proxy node to wait for others to access it. An EEO with semi-active approach has a name and an argument list for the proxy node. The message is constructed by an EEO (setting the values of the arguments) and posted in synchronous or asynchronous manner. It is useful for recruit new members (allies) when constructing a VE.
- *Active Posting.* EEO sends events as soon as some corresponding operations is invoked. It is the major form which mostly suitable for the following two situations: 1) When an EO registers in ViaScope, it sends its registration to the system. 2) An EEO may be interest of to other EOs. When an method is called, it produce an event to trigger a corresponding rule and schedule other EOs. The rules can be used to define the behavior of an EEO to satisfy the enterprise integrity constraint or business logic.
- *Timer Posting.* In ViaScope, one kind of EEO, timers can be set to produce asynchronous event based on a time specification. A timer event can be fixed (posted at specific time) or periodic (repeatedly posted in some time interval). Once the timer event has been created and initialized, it will be posted asynchronously at a specified time or time intervals. It is suitable for monitoring all members in VE. Once an anticipant event didn't give any response during a prescriptive period of time, timer will broadcasting this exception message.

4.3 Scheduler for EOs

In order to support EOs' incorporations, we design a scheduler model for ViaScope. The model, showed in Fig.4, mainly based on CORBA/IIOP includes five major parts: Distributed-Event-Monitor, Rules-Producer, Event-Scheduler, Rules-Repository, and Log&Exception-Processor.

1) When an EEO is invoked, local Distributed-Event-Monitor filters the message produced by the EEO, and checks weather it came from a local registered EEO. If not, the Distributed-Event-Monitor ignores it.

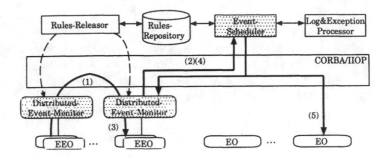

Fig. 4. Scheduler Model for EEOs in ViaScope

2) If the checked message is a synchronous message, the Distributed-Event-Monitor suspends this invoke operation, copys the message and posts it to the Event-Scheduler. If the checked message is an asynchronous message, the Distributed-Event-Monitor notifies the message to the Event-Scheduler and lets it pass under the same time.

3) According to the received message, the Event-Scheduler matches rules in Rules-Repository, and schedules the other EOs, including some EEOs and other ordinary EOs, non-EEOs. In order to managing and rehabilitating effectively, the scheduling information should be kept in Log&Exception-Processor.

4) As to the synchronous message, the Event-Scheduler returns scheduler information to the corresponding local Distributed-Event-Monitor to inform it do some processing for the EEO, such as terminating it or letting it continue.

The scheduler model provide a high flexible management for a virtual enterprise because:

- It is easy to combine two or more applications to obtain a new application that is the true sum of the functionality expressed in those applications.
- It is easy to maintain applications without the source code. Moreover, when this code is available, modifications can be done at a high level.
- Component systems can be easily integrated to support the needs of the virtual enterprise. Ideally, each component should perform only its designated functions, that is, a component should not contain any code that implements integration logic or any enterprise-level constraints and rules.

5 Conclusions and future work

This paper gave an overall introduction for the modeling EOs in a VE information integrating system– Viascope. We have developed a complete environment and set of tools for integrated access to diverse and dynamic heterogeneous enterprise information sources. We focus on studying modeling the EO, as well as the constraints between EOs. In order to support integration between EOs, we present the active EO, named EEO to ensure the integrity constraints in a

VE integrating system. The scheduler model for EOs is also described. Our EO model is suitable for encapsulating the legacy applications, combining two or more applications to obtain a new logical application, and suitable for separating enterprise logic from application logic. We now partially implemented the VE information integrating system based on IONA's Orbix, and experimented with information integration techniques to several quite different CIMS information sources. Our implementation so far has helped us to refine our integration technique. We have used object-oriented integration techniques including EO wrapper, EO scheduler, enterprise rules processing, repository management and maintenance, etc. We plan to continue to study the problem of information integration between enterprises, and increase the types of information sources.

6 Acknowledgement

This work was partially supported by the Huo Yingdong Youth Foundation and by the 863/CIMS Research Grant: 863-511-946-003.

References

1. C.M.R.Leung, and G.M.Nijssan: Relational database design using the NIAM conceptual schema, Information Systems, 13(2), (1988)
2. E.Ozkarahan: Database management concepts, design and practice, Chapter 10, Prentice Hall (1990)
3. X.Yang, G.Yu, B.Zhang: Study on a CORBA-based Plug and Play Mechanism for Distributed Information Sharing Environments, *SCOPE Technical report, Dept.CS, Northeastern University* (1998)
4. D.K.Hsiao, M.N.Karnel: Heterogeneous databases: proliferations, issues, and solutions, IEEE transaction on Knowledge and Engineering, 1(1), (1989)
5. Object Management Group : The Common Object Request Broker Architecture and Specification, revision 2.0 (1995).
6. O.Richard, A.Zarli. WONDA: An architecture for Business Objects in the Virtual Enterprise. OOPSLA'98 Workshop on Objects, Components & VE (1998)
7. J.Severwright and R. Singh: VE Technological Requirements: the VENICE project. OOPSLA'98 Workshop on Objects, Components and the Virtual Enterprise (1998)
8. L.M.Camarinha-Matos: A platform to support production planning and management in a virtual enterprise, Proceedings of CAPE's 97, IFIP International Conference on Computer Applications in Production and Engineering (Chapman & Hall), Detroit, USA (1997).
9. BODTF: The Business Object Component Architecture- Revision 1.1, OMG Document: bom/98-01-07
10. A.Aiken, J.M.Hellerstein, and J.Widom: Static analysis techniques for prediction the behavior of active database rules, ACM Transactions on Database Systems, 20(1):3-41, (1995)

Object-Oriented Design of an E-Commerce System for Retailing Business

Simon Fong[1], and Chan Se-Leng[2]

[1] School of Applied Science, Nanyang Technological University
Singapore
`asccfong@ntu.edu.sg`
[2] Electronic Commerce and Call Center, Digiland Shopping Mall, GES Group
Singapore
`slchan@ges.com.sg`

Abstract. Business issues for E-commerce cross the entire range of business activities from attracting customers to fulfilling their orders, and from sales to customer service. Architectures for commerce systems may look different, but they all have to address the same issues and provide answers for a common set of questions. In particular, there are four core business issues namely *Attract*, *Interact*, *Act* and *React* that are identified to be common across a range of E-Commerce systems. In this paper, we present an object-oriented architectural design for an Internet-based retail business. The design is layout according to the four core business activities. It captures the fundamental functions that make a successful online retail. The technique used is Unified Modeling Language (UML) [1] which is acclaimed to be appropriate for modeling complex software systems. Our model can serve as a high-level system design framework for online retail, and it can be modified to suit other E-commerce domains such as Business-to-Business commerce.

1 Introduction

The invention and subsequent spread of the World Wide Web, provided the technical foundation for many different applications, including those for business in particular. Since its introduction, the Web has changed the ways that companies do business. It offers new markets, new ways to get close to customers, and new ways to work with business partners.

With this new development, there are currently three main categories of commerce sites operating on Internet. They are Consumer retail (that sell physical goods direct to an individual end user), Business-to-Business commerce (those with online catalogs selling products to other businesses, e.g. supply-chain), and Information commerce (which distribute digital goods such as information products and services online with fulfillment right over the network). The three main types of business sites that operate on Internet have similarities in the requirements. All of them need to attract customers, present products, assemble orders, do transactions, accomplish fulfillment, and deliver customer service.

Recently, we observe that there are many retail stores have already been set up on the Internet, but only a few of them are successful in making profit. There are many factors that contribute to the success (or failure) of an online retail store. Instead of proposing an invincible solution that will guarantee to make profit, we present an architectural design of E-commerce retail in this paper, that is based on the four core business activities that would be discussed in the next section. This design should meet the requirement of having most if not all the important elements of a successful E-commerce retail system. Approaching the design of a system with a high-level architecture can enable a system that evolves and adapts over the long term as technologies and business requirements change. Retail business is chosen as a case study here. Our design can however be extended to apply on the other business types and models.

1.1 Different sizes of retail business

Retail business occurs at many scales, from small shop to large multinational. The larger enterprise will naturally have more complex requirements for electronic commerce than the smaller.

Small shop - A small ongoing business may have a relatively static catalog, and simple requirements for record keeping and order entry. Orders would be collected by a commerce service provider, and sent to the shop by fax. Online payment would be by credit card or not required at all. Customer service would be most easily handled by telephone. Typical merchandising techniques would be occasional sales.

Medium sized direct marketing - Depending on the number of items in the catalog, the online catalog would be produced either by a product database together with display templates to generate catalog pages on the fly, or by a desktop catalog authoring system generating product pages. Online orders would require shopping cart features, tax and shipping charge calculation, and credit card payment, and would be delivered to the store electronically. Given sufficient size, a customer registration database and online customer service would be included. Merchandising techniques would include promotions, sales, and perhaps membership discounts.

Large retailer - The most demanding retailer would require a highly dynamic Web site with the capability to handle frequent product and pricing changes. Product display would be linked to inventory on hand. Order taking could include traditional credit cards, as well as on-account purchasing. Orders would be routed electronically to the retailer's enterprise resource planning system. Merchandising techniques could be highly complex, including one-to-one marketing and cross-selling. For international sales, support of multiple languages and currencies would be needed.

1.2 Core business activities

For all the E-commerce businesses mentioned above, four core business activities are identified at a high level though the details will certainly be different for different businesses. The four core activities that are also known as the generic commerce value chain by [2] are shown in Figure 1.

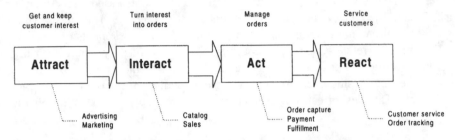

Figure 1. The four core business activities.

This value chain is somewhat analogous to the well-known 4-phase model which consists of information, agreement, settling and support phases. However the value chain we use here is more relevant to the activities or dynamics of the E-commerce business, and these are the interactions between the functional units within the retail organization we want to model. Furthermore, the value chain is more 'strategic' in business sense.

Attract customers - The first of the four core business activities is *attract*. This means whatever steps the company takes to pull customers into the Web site, whether by paid advertising on other Web sites, email, television, print, or other forms of advertising and marketing. The idea is to make an impression on customers and draw them into the detailed catalog or other information about products and services for sale.

Interact with customers - The second core activity is *interact*. This means turning customer interest into orders. This one is generally content oriented and includes the catalog, publication, or other information available to the customers over the Internet. Technically, content may be static or dynamic, that means it may change infrequently or frequently, editorially. Static content typically consist of prepared pages that must be recreated whenever the information on them changes. Dynamic content is generated at the time of the request, drawing upon one or more information sources to produce an appropriate page of information for the client. Dynamic content is often used when the editorial content changes frequently, or when the natural storage medium is a database.

Act on instructions - The next activity is *act*. Once a buyer has searched through a catalog and wants to make a purchase, there must be a way to capture the order, process payment, handle fulfillment, and other aspects of order management.

React to customer inquiries - Finally, after a sale is complete, the customer may have some questions or difficulties that require service. Usually companies who are in E-commerce provide the facilities of help desk or call center to handle customer inquiries.

2 System design for an E-Commerce retail

Different companies will, of course, have different business issues and goals. In this paper, we have set out to explore many that are common across retail businesses. Even when the issues are not directly on target for a particular retail store, we hope that they will inspire others that are, leading to a successful plan for E-commerce. In our design, we assume that an online retail store would have the following fundamental components: a Web server, a transaction server, a content management server, a marketing server, a call center (or help desk) and Web customers. These important components have the typical interaction such that the Web customers interact with the Web server for all the online services, and they communicate with the call center for customer service if any. Behind the Web server, there are business logistics and functions supported by the other servers. We are modeling a medium to large scale of online retail system. A simplified model of such a typical online retail store is shown in Figure 2.

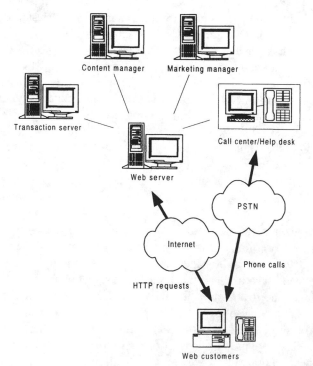

Figure 2. A simplified model of an E-Commerce retail.

The significance of our design is on how these fundamental components to be modeled as 'objects' and how these objects work together to facilitate the four core business activities: *Attract*, *Interact*, *Act* and *React*. The technique we used for the architectural design is Unified Modeling Language (UML) [1]. UML is an industrial standard language for specifying, constructing, visualizing and documenting the artifacts of a software-intensive system. It is shown in [3] that UML is an appropriate technique to design systems for electronic commerce.

3 Architectural design with UML

The UML model of the online retail consists of three parts: The object model that covers the *Attract* and *Interact* activities, the object model that covers the *Interact* and *Act*, and the object model for *React*. Together, they can join and form the whole architectural design of the online retail.

3.1 Attract and Interact

Attracting customers includes such diverse activities as advertising, promotions, sales, loyalty points and similar mechanisms. All these activities need advertising. Advertising puts the product in front of consumer eyes. On the Internet, advertising takes many forms, including banners on popular sites, e-mail newsletters, or simply listings on widely used search engines [4]. The object model of Figure 3 consists of a class Marketing Manager that deals with the advertising issues in the retail. A superclass called Marketing Message is a generic form of message that is sent by the Marketing Manager to all the customers. They can be emails, physical mails, or messages that appear in some other media such as TV or banner in an eye-catching place. For *Attract* and *Interact*, the Marketing Manager and the Content Manager play an important role in the Web Store (that serves as a physical Web server well as the implication of the whole retail store). While the Marketing Manager takes all the initiatives in actively broadcasting the advertising messages, the Content Manager must provide the content that support the corresponding marketing events.

The Content Manager is a superclass from which two subclasses, Regular Content Manager and Strategic Content Manager are inherited. As their names suggest, the Regular Content Manager is responsible for organizing and displaying normal Web content, such as the storefront, the usual buttons and graphics, and the usual catalog. Whereas the Strategic Content Manager specializes in setting up special Web pages for promotion events, such as Christmas, Valentine's Day and school holidays, etc. For those events, the normal Web pages and/or the catalog may need to be customized according to the theme of sales and promotions. A sale means special prices for products for a limited period, perhaps with limits on the number of units available to a buyer. Sales are used as general promotions to build a customer base and increase awareness, and also as a way to clear built-up inventory, such as after a major holiday. A promotion can be quite complex as it might include a special price on a bundle of products. All the above-mentioned mechanisms would be supported by the following classes: Inventory Manager, Pricing Control Manager and Marketing Manager in our model as shown in Figure 3.

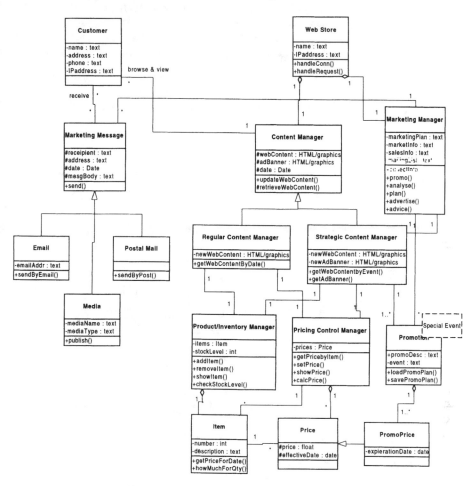

Figure 3. The *Attract* aspect of the E-commerce system object model.

3.2 Attract and Interact

Interaction between the customers and the Web retail store is usually in the form of content browsing, information searching and placing orders. For stores with up to a few hundred items, the catalog no longer be easily created or modified manually with some desktop publishing tools. Orders and payments can still be easily accepted by email or by submit form using CGI. However, farther upscale of the retail size, frequent price changes and product changes make a simple desktop publishing model untenable. In this case, a desktop database, coupled to an authoring tool up to an online database creating Web content on the fly, would be used. At the most complex end of the market, dynamic catalogs, perhaps driven by real-time inventory information, would be used. The complexity of the technology would require on-going information systems support. The class Content Manager and the other classes are designed to handle the content update in our model. A suggestion from [5] is to use a standard CGI program to translate commands sent from the Web server into standard ODBC format, and send them to the database. Intermediate programs perform additional logic with database information to dynamically construct Web pages. To speed up the process of running CGI programs, some Web servers implement custom APIs that allow direct communication with the database.

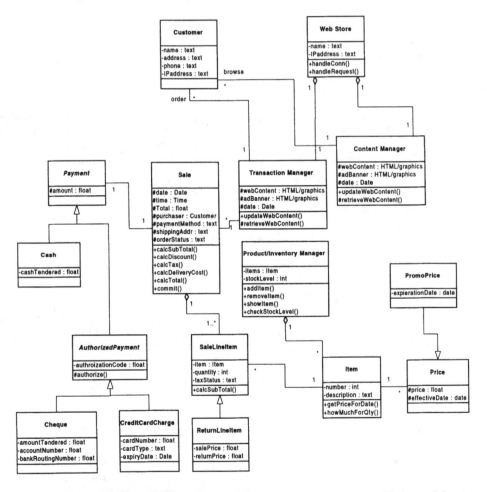

Figure 4. The *Interact* aspect of the E-commerce system object model.

For medium to large scale of retails, the order processing functions can become complex. They usually include the following kinds of activities: shopping cart (for order aggregation), order validation, order tracking, calculation of sales and taxes, calculation of shipping and delivery charges and presentation of the rolled-up order to the customers. In Figure 4, our model has a class called Transaction Manager that acts as a transaction server and handles all the order transactions from the customers. There is a class called Sale that captures each order placed by the customers. The class Sale is analogous to a shopping cart, such that it contains the aggregated items the customer buys, with the total price, tax and delivery charges worked out.

3.3 React

The aspect *React* refers mainly to customer service. For example, a customer who has inquiries, may call the help desk, email the Webmaster or submit a query through the Web site. In Figure 5, our model has a class called Web Feedback Manager that routes all the emails or query submission from customers to the appropriate attendant such as the Marketing manager or executives. On the other hand, a call center that is represented by the class Call Center Manager in our model is responsible for handling incoming calls from the customers. These calls are usually phone orders, feedback, complaints or just customers' inquiries about the products and the service. The calls are recorded and stored in a database as log files for latter use. A good online retail shop would usually have a hotline phone number and a call center for providing the best possible customer services.

The facilities mentioned above are of short-term "*react*". The customers are often responded and replied at the earliest convenience for their inquires. To improve on the customer service and how better the products can be marketed to the customers, it is necessary to know about the customers. This is a long-term "*react*". In our model in Figure 5, we proposed that the activities within the online retail to be logged. For example, as the customers navigate the Web site, they left "traces" as Web logs. These Web logs contain information about their IP addresses, time and date of the visit and which pages they have visited. This information is valuable as it gives insights about how well the retail shop is running online [6]. In our design, there is a specialized role or class called Market Intelligence Manager, from which two types of monitors are derived. Their main function is to monitor the internal operation of the retail business, as well as the external market. The Internal Market Monitor and the External Market Monitor have a data miner that converts the log data into business intelligence, and a Web information agent that collects valuable information from the Web respectively [7]. The information gathered from the external market includes those about the competitors and the market trends. When both external and internal business intelligence are obtained and updated regularly, the online retail may learn how to further improve the operations of the business, and be better guided on future strategies [8].

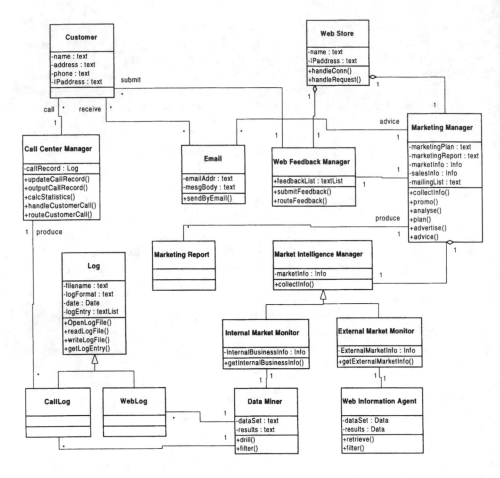

Figure 5. The *React* aspect of the E-commerce system object model.

4 Conclusion

In this paper, we discussed the components and architectural design for a Web-based online retail, and introduced the object models in the notions of Unified Modeling Language. The design is grounded on the four core business activities that nearly all E-commerce retails would have. The advantages of following the four core business activities are as follow. (1) the design is generic, it can fit well into any retail business, (2) the design gives a good insight of how these four core activities could be implemented, (3) the design can be easily extended to other business domains than retail because they have similar requirements. Furthermore, approaching the design of a system with a high-level architecture can enable a system that evolves and adapts over the long term as technologies and business requirement change.

From a software engineering point of view, many design methodologies have been put forward. Such techniques as object-oriented design, rapid prototyping, formal methods, and so on can all be used in the design of E-commerce systems. We do not advocate here any particular method or set of such methods. However, we do recommend a hybrid approach that combines object-oriented design together with rapid prototyping. Our design presented in this paper could be used as a blue print for building a medium to large scale of retail store. The design by no means is exhaustive in details. System architect or analyst turns the design into creation that includes management of content, the transaction processing, fulfillment, and technical aspects of customer service. In short, the architect fills in the next level of detail for the complete system, and the software engineers implement the detail.

5 Future Directions

The potential of applying the UML modeling technique to designing E-commerce systems is large. The online retail shop we have presented in this paper is our first step in modeling a complete set of E-commerce models for different business domains. There are many other forms of E-commerce businesses and models to be studied by using UML. Moreover, the full features and capacity of UML are yet to be exploited. The model so far concerns mainly on the data and actions. We are pursuing the following challenges as future directions. How could the information flow within the E-commerce be defined and verified by UML? How could the processes be modeled by UML? Modeling an E-commerce system as a soft real-time system in UML. Extending our current model to other E-commerce domains.

References

1. Y. Yang, et. al., "A UML-based Object-Oriented Framework Development Methodology", IEEE Software Engineering Conference 1998, Asia Pacific, pp.211-219, 1998.
2. W. Treese, L. Stewart, "Designing Systems for Internet Commerce", Addison Wesley, ISBN 0-201-57167-6, 1998.
3. S. Ambler, "Building Object Applications that Work", Cambridge University Press/SIGS Books, ISBN 0521-64826-2, 1998.
4. J. Palmer, D. Griffith, "An Emerging Model of Web Site Design for Marketing", Communications of the ACM, Vol.41, No.3, pp.45-53, March 1998.
5. J. Novak, P. Markiewicz, "Internet World: Guide to Maintaining and Updating Dynamic Web Sites", Wily Computer Publishing, ISBN 0-471-24273-X, 1998.
6. M. Drott, "Using Web Server Logs to Improve Site Design", ACM Communications, pp.43-50, 1998.
7. H. Wang, T. Vickers, "The Design of an Intelligent Agent for Retrieving and Compiling Information over the WWW", Asia Pacific Web 1998, pp.319-324, 1998.
8. R. Buchanan, C. Lukaszewski, "Measuring the Impact of Your Web Site", Wiley Computer Publishing, 1997.

Extended Awareness Support for Cooperative Work in Non-WYSIWIS Condition

Yusuke Yokota, Hiroyuki Tarumi, and Yahiko Kambayashi

Kyoto University, Sakyo Kyoto 606-8501, Japan,
{yyokota,tarumi,yahiko}@i.kyoto-u.ac.jp

Abstract. Most conventional groupware systems only support cooperative work in WYSIWIS (What You See Is What I See) or relaxed-WYSIWIS condition. Although the WYSIWIS principle enables users to receive awareness information easily, it also limits flexibility of a system. VIEW Media supports cooperative work in both WYSIWIS and non-WYSIWIS conditions with the aim of providing more general framework for groupware systems. Non-WYSIWIS condition needs more rich awareness information than WYSIWIS condition for smooth interaction among users. Thus VIEW Media provides extended awareness support functions that can summarize, abstract, and customize awareness information. This paper describes customization functions of VIEW Media realizing cooperative work in non-WYSIWIS condition and functions supporting extended awareness information, then some examples for the extended awareness information, such as shared pointers, virtual seats, and channel checker are shown.

1 Introduction

The evolution of personal computing environment and network technology enables us to collaborate on computer networks. Various researches on CSCW (Computer-Supported Cooperative Work) area study possibility of forms of cooperative work. The WYSIWIS (What You See Is What I See) principle is one of the important notion of synchronous cooperative work. The principle assumes that users see the same view of the documents or applications. It can avoid the confusion of perception of the situation among users, however, limits the flexibility of collaboration. The relaxed-WYSIWIS principle enables users to see different parts of the same documents. It increases the flexibility of cooperative work to some extent. VIEW Media, developed in our laboratory, provides general framework for groupware systems and supports cooperative work in non-WYSIWIS condition, in addition to above two principles. To support more advanced or complex cooperative work than conventional groupware systems, non-WYSIWIS is required. Typically, when each user has different position or responsibility for given work, it is not desirable that all users share the same view of the documents regardless of the contents of them. In such case, each part of documents may have different access rights to users, therefore each user sees slightly different view of documents.

Awareness is an understanding of the activities of others, which provides a context for your own activity[1]. To support non-WYSIWIS condition, conventional approaches to providing awareness information is not sufficient. When each user sees different view of documents, inconsistency of awareness among users will often happen. A precise model of awareness information and a mechanism of processing the information are required to mediate the inconsistency. VIEW Media has a generalized model of awareness. It can provide awareness information ensuring security and privacy of users. When a large number of users exist, a quantity of awareness information also becomes too large to display all the information. Our model can treat such case by processing, summarizing, and abstracting the information.

The remainder of the paper is organized as follows. In Section 2, a simple example is presented to show requirements of non-WYSIWIS condition and extended awareness. Section 3 describes a model and mechanisms realizing non-WYSIWIS view. In Section 4, we discuss extended awareness information of VIEW Media and show some examples. Section 5 concludes the paper.

2 An Application Example

In this section, an application that requires non-WYSIWIS condition is illustrated. This application supports conference among users who have different access rights to documents.

In this application, documents of rating report in a company are assumed to be used. The rating reports are made to each employee of a company. Some evaluators write the comments about evaluation of employees in it. The first phase evaluator can create a report and write comments for the first phase. The second phase evaluator can read comments for the first phase and write comments for the second phase. The last phase evaluator can read comments for the first and second phases and write comments for the last phase. The first phase evaluator cannot read comments for the second and last phases, and the second phase evaluator cannot read comments for the last phase. Evaluators can discuss evaluation each other through a voice conversation tool.

The situation described above will be illustrated in Figure 1. It shows the inheritance of access rights for the situation. In this figure, there are three environments illustrated as boxes. The outermost environment (A) represents the access rights of the first phase evaluators. The inside environment of the outermost (B) and the inner most environment (C) represent the access rights of the second phase evaluators and the last phase evaluators respectively. Users in A can read the first phase document. Users in B inherit the access rights of the users in A. Thus users in B also can read the first phase document. In addition to this, they can read the second phase document. Users in C inherit the access rights of the users in B and can read the last phase document. This structure of environments controls access rights of documents during conferences.

In this situation, users see slightly different contents of a document according to environments where they belong to when they see the identical document,

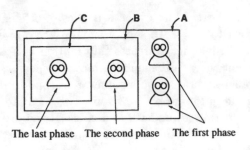

The last phase   The second phase   The first phase

Fig. 1. Access rights and environments

because of annotations or hiding part of documents. To realize such a situation, flexible customization mechanisms of documents, namely, functions for cooperative work in non-WYSIWIS condition are required. When the non-WYSIWIS condition is realized, a system has to pay attention to discussion channels of users. For example, if a user in C refers to the comments that cannot be seen by users in A, a discussion channel should be established only between users in B and C.

This application also needs an awareness support mechanism for smooth conversation in a conference when specific parts of documents are hidden from some participants. The mechanism should give a participant the information about other participants and visualize statuses of users and workspaces.

It appears that participants should be able to freely obtain information about documents for a conference from following two viewpoints as well as information about other participants: (1) How much each hidden part of documents is open to other participants. (2) How much some part of documents is open to each participant. In some cases, the information of (1) or (2) themselves needs to be hidden.

3   Supporting Non-WYSIWIS Condition

Most groupware systems introduce WYSIWIS or relaxed-WYSIWIS principles so that all users can see the same display contents. It enables users to share the same perception in contents of cooperative work and helps users to promote work smoothly. However, the principle does not suit all condition of cooperative work. For example, when a user wants to show only a part of his/her own document, because of security reason to others, or when a teacher wants to use a textbook with annotations while students use a textbook without them, the principle is too restrictive. In these cases, it is required that users can modify part of documents for flexible cooperative work. VIEW Media provides this flexibility and realizes cooperative work under the non-WYSIWIS condition.

3.1 The Fundamental Objects of VIEW Media

VIEW Media defines four types of fundamental objects constructing workspace of the system:

- *User surrogate objects* represent users participating in workspace. A user surrogate object contains profile and state information of a corresponding user.
- *Hypermedia component objects* organize shared hypermedia documents. Hypermedia is used as a basic data format for cooperative work on VIEW Media. Results of collaboration are stored as hypermedia component objects in an object repository of VIEW Media. The hypermedia model of VIEW Media was designed for flexible customization, which is based on the Dexter Hypertext Reference Model[4].
- *Equipment objects* provide various communication methods for interaction among users such as chat tools, shared pointers and so forth.
- *Environment objects* are containers of other fundamental objects. A user has access to objects in the same environment where his/her user surrogate object resides. An environment object can have child environments with inheritance relationship. Basically, definitions of a parent environment and objects contained in it are inherited by child environments. Therefore, users in an environment have access to objects contained not only in the environment but also in ancestor environments of it. Environment objects provide an environment model that plays the most important role in VIEW Media.

Figure 2 represents main attributes of and relationships among these four fundamental objects.

3.2 The Customization Mechanism of VIEW Media

VIEW Media provides the customization mechanism for hypermedia component objects. The mechanism is based on the Object Deputy Model[9].

Environment objects have the most important role in the mechanism. An environment object has an attribute called *viewDefinition* as shown in Figure 2. The *viewDefinition* is an ordered set of customization operations to hypermedia component objects. When a user intend to refer to some hypermedia components, the environment object to which the user belongs behaves as follows:

1. fetching the required hypermedia components.
2. making the copies of them.
3. applying the set of customization operations stored in the *viewDefinition* to the copies.
4. providing the customized copies of hypermedia components for the user.

Thus, the customization does not affect the source hypermedia components and users always receive the customized copies of hypermedia components (Figure 3). It guarantees the independence of customizations in each environment. For example, if a user modifies some hypermedia component by customization operations, the modification only affects the users who belong to the same environment or its child environments.

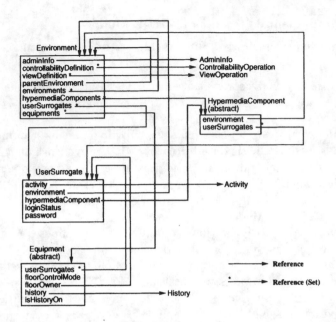

Fig. 2. Main attributes of and relationships among the four fundamental objects

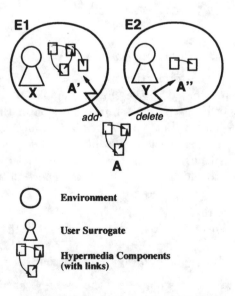

Fig. 3. Customization mechanism

4   Extended Awareness Functions

Providing awareness information becomes more important when users collaborate under non-WYSIWIS condition than WYSIWIS or relaxed-WYSIWIS condition. The degree of WYSIWIS, flexibility of collaboration, and needs of explicit awareness information are mutually related. The strict WYSIWIS view of a system enables users to assume that all other users have the same recognition and needs less explicit awareness information than relaxed-WYSIWIS or non-WYSIWIS, though flexibility of it is limited. The relaxed-WYSIWIS view permits users to see the different part of the same documents and relieves the limitation of the strict WYSIWIS view and provides flexibility of collaboration to some extent. It requires more awareness information than strict WYSIWIS. For example, an awareness support tool providing information that shows what part of documents each user browses, like shared pointers, will be required. The non-WYSIWIS view, having much potential of flexible collaboration, does not guarantee the recognition of users to be the same at any time, so that more explicit awareness information is needed than other two conditions.

4.1   Handling Awareness Information

A system supporting non-WYSIWIS view should have an explicit model to manage awareness information. VIEW Media introduces the notions of *controllability* and *observability* as generalization of awareness[15]. There are several reasons of modeling awareness information.

Controlling awareness information. Awareness information should be controlled by a system to provide precise awareness information in some cases. The "control" mainly means selecting or reducing the information for some reasons: (1) In general, users have different positions or responsibilities under non-WYSIWIS condition because of the flexibility of it, as opposed to users under WYSIWIS or relaxed-WYSIWIS condition who tend to have the same position or responsibility because of limitation of flexibility. It is required controlling awareness information for ensuring security or privacy of users in such a situation. An example of such a situation is described in Section 2. (2) The number of users also will be a reason of controlling awareness information. When the number of users becomes large, providing awareness information of all users is not realistic, because the information may occupy the greater part of the screen. It is required filtering the information not much related with a user who receives the information.

To control awareness information, a system must handle the contents or semantics of the awareness information and the information about relationship among users. Thus, awareness information model that enables handling contents or semantics of the information and represents relationship among users is required.

Processing awareness information. Not only controlling but processing awareness information will be required by a system supporting the non-WYSIWIS principle. We propose grouping, taking statistics, and abstraction as typical processing methods. To realize such processing, the representation of awareness information should be easy to deal with. *Grouping* is used as a method of generating awareness information of groups. For example, when some groups work concurrently, users may want awareness information that indicates a status of each group roughly estimated instead of the information about each user. The system summarizes each attribute of awareness information about each user and shows the summarized information in a precise manner. Ordinarily, awareness information provides *current* statuses of users. In contrast to this, *statistical awareness information* summarizes a sequence of awareness information of objects (users or groups) from the past to now. The system needs to have a kind of history buffer for storing awareness information. *Abstraction* is also a method of ensuring security or privacy of users. This method extracts only necessary information from source awareness information and shows the extracted information in an abstract way. For example, a system extracts an activity of a user from video and audio data and shows the activity as a kind of symbolic characters representing the user. It controls the degree of exposure of awareness information so that undesirable information will be suppressed.

The principal usage of awareness information will be classified into two types: identifying characteristics of individual users and comparing characteristics among users. To support the latter usage, it is required to normalize awareness information for comparison. It will be achieved by applying methods described above.

4.2 Examples

We developed several tools providing awareness information based on the notion discussed above. Selected example tools are presented here.

Shared Pointer. Figure 4 shows the screen of a prototype system of VIEW Classroom, a distance learning system which have been developed in our laboratory[5]. Shared pointers are used in the window on the upper left side of the screen. The shared pointer can indicate explicit awareness information, such as a role or a name of a user with a text string, his/her activity with a color of the pointer. Each user has different pointer sharing status. Figure 4 represents a screen of a student (Iwamoto). The status of pointer sharing is shown in *Pointer Sharing Graph* window, located in the lower right side of the screen. It represents that "Students" can share pointers of "Teacher" and "Questioner", however, pointers of "Students" are not shared with any other users. The status of pointer sharing is dynamically changed according to a situation of collaboration, indicated in *Environment Transition Graph* window located in the next side of the *Pointer Sharing Graph* window.

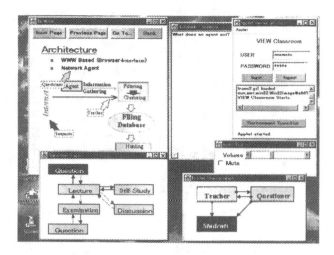

Fig. 4. Shared pointers with explicit awareness information

Virtual Seats. Virtual seats are also the feature of VIEW Classroom providing awareness information used by teachers. When the number of students attending a distant classroom session becomes large, a teacher will be unable to grasp statuses of all students and hesitate whom s/he should choose for questions. A teacher can issue a query that selects students to a system. The condition of the query includes a record of a student, the number of times a student speaks, and so forth. The system generates a window of virtual seats composed of selected students by the query. The teacher can use the virtual seats as representatives of students. For example, when 500 students exist in a lecture, a teacher can select 50 students satisfying some conditions. Each seat of virtual seats indicates a status of a student. Virtual seats also provide *abstract audio awareness information.* They transmit activity of students. For example, when many students are annotating a textbook, the sound of writing with a pencil will be generated. When many chat channels exist among students, the prepared sound of a chat will be played. These are examples of abstract awareness functions: they convert medium of awareness and abstract necessary information from source information. The teacher can reconstruct virtual seats by issuing a new query according to the change of a situation during a lecture.

Channel Checker. Figure 5 shows a conference support system with *Channel Checker*[8], which provides awareness information. This system is a prototype implementation of the system described in Section 2, thus each user has different access rights to documents. Figure 5 is a screen of a user in the second phase evaluation group. In the document browser, the contents written in the first phase evaluation are always seen by the user. The contents written in the second phase evaluation are masked with gray rectangles. When the user want to see the contents, s/he has to move his/her pointer into the rectangles, then the contents

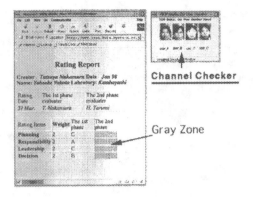

Fig. 5. Information of access rights to shared documents

will be appear. This function is closely related with the functions of *Channel Checker*. The contents written in the last phase evaluation are not shown. Thus, the user does not know the existence of the contents.

When the user moves his/her pointer into the gray rectangles, *Channel Checker* shows who can see the contents of the part and the channel for voice conversation will be changed so that the user can speak only users who can see the contents. Therefore, when the user speaks about the contents masked with the rectangles, the contents of the conversation are not transmitted to users who cannot see the part and security or privacy will be ensured.

Environment and Awareness. Use of VIEW Media to realize a debate system is discussed in [16], where environment information is displayed for awareness purpose.

5 Conclusions

We discussed requirements and mechanisms of non-WYSIWIS view for cooperative work and generalization and extension of awareness information. Awareness information should have a precise model for controlling and processing the information. Extended awareness information mechanism supports ensuring security and privacy and the large number of participants on the systems. Proposed methods of processing the information are used for not only identification of users but also comparison among users. Several examples for providing awareness information are shown as explanation in the real usage.

Acknowledgments

We wish to thank Hajime Iwamoto and Tatsuya Nakamura for the design and implementation of the shared pointer mechanism and the prototype conference system with Channel Checker, respectively.

References

1. Dourish, P. and Bellotti, V.: Awareness and coordination in shared workspaces. Proc. 4th Int. Conf. on Computer-Supported Cooperative Work (1992) 107–114
2. Edwards, W. K.: Policies and roles in collaborative applications. Proc. the ACM 1996 Conf. on Computer-Supported Cooperative Work (1996) 11–20
3. Greenberg, S. and Roseman, M.: Using a room metaphor to ease transitions in groupware. Technical Report 98/611/02, Department of Computer Science, University of Calgary (1998)
4. Halasz, F. and Schwartz, M.: The dexter hypertext reference model. *CACM*, 37(2) (1994) 30–39
5. Iwamoto, H. and Kambayashi, Y.: Dynamic control mechanisms for pointer share. Proc. the 13th Int. Conf. on Information Networking (1998) 10A-2.1–6
6. Lee, J. H. et al.: Supporting multi-user, multi-applet workspace in cbe. Proc. the ACM 1996 Conf. on Computer Supported Cooperative Work (1996) 344–353
7. Mansfield, T., Kaplan, S., Fitzpatrick, G., Phelps, T., Fitzpatrick, M. and Taylor, R.: Evolving orbit: A progress report on building locales. Proc. the Int. ACM SIG-GROUP Conf. on Supporting Group Work : The Integration Challenge (Group97) (1997) 241–250
8. Nakamura, T., Yokota, Y., Konomi, S., Tarumi, H. and Kambayashi, Y.: A conference user interface supporting different access rights to shared hypermedia. Proc. of the Asia Pacific Conf. on Computer Human Interaction (APCHI'98) (1998) 38–43
9. Peng, Z. and Kambayashi, Y.: Deputy mechanisms for object-oriented databases. Proc. IEEE 11th Int. Conf. Data Engineering (1995)
10. Prakash, A., Shim, H. S., and Lee, J. H.: Data management issues and tradeoffs in cscw systems. IEEE Transactions on Knowledge and Data Engineering, 11(1) (1999) 213–227
11. Roseman, M. and Greenberg, S.: Teamrooms: Network places for collaboration. Proc. the ACM 1996 Conf. on Computer Supported Cooperative Work (1996) 325–333
12. Shen, H.-H. and Dewan, P.: Access control for collaborative environments. Proc. of ACM 1992 Conf. on Computer-Supported Cooperative Work (1992) 51–58
13. Smith, R. B., Hixon, R. and Horan, B.: Supporting flexible roles in a shared space. Proc. the ACM 1998 Conf. on Computer-Supported Cooperative Work (1998) 197–206
14. Spellman, P. J., Mosier, J. N., Deus, L. M., and Carlson, J. A.: Collaborative virtual workspace. Proc. the Int. ACM SIGGROUP Conf. on Supporting Group Work : The Integration Challenge (Group97) (1997) 197–203
15. Yokota, Y. and Kambayashi, Y.: Customization support environments of active hypermedia systems for cooperative work. Advanced Database Systems for Integration of Media and User Environments '98, World Scientific (1998) 21–26
16. Yokota, Y., Sugiyama, K., Tarumi, H. and Kambayashi, Y.: Evaluation of Non-WYSIWIS Functions of VIEW Media, Proc. 2nd Int. Symposium on Cooperative Database Systems for Advanced Applications (CODAS'99), Springer (1999) 88–99

Query Length, Number of Classes and Routes through Clusters: Experiments with a Clustering Method for Information Retrieval

Patrice Bellot, Marc El-Bèze

Laboratoire d'Informatique d'Avignon (LIA)
339 ch. des Meinajaries, BP 1228
FR-84911 Avignon Cedex 9 (France)

{patrice.bellot,marc.elbeze}@lia.univ-avignon.fr

Abstract. A classical information retrieval system ranks documents according to distances between texts and a user query. The answer list is often so long that users cannot examine all the documents retrieved whereas some relevant ones are badly ranked and thus never retrieved. To solve this problem, retrieved documents are automatically clustered. We describe an algorithm based on hierarchical and clustering methods. It classifies the set of documents retrieved by any IR-system. This method is evaluated over the TREC-7 corpora and queries. We show that it improves the results of the retrieval by providing users at least one high precision cluster. The impact of the number of clusters and the way to browse them to build a reordered list are examined. Over TREC corpora and queries, we show that the choice of the number of clusters according to the length of queries improves results compared with a prefixed number.

1 Introduction

A classical information retrieval system retrieves and ranks documents extracted from a corpus according to a similarity function based on word co-occurrences in the texts and in a query. Generally, users cannot examine all the documents retrieved whereas some relevant items are badly ranked and thus never recovered. We have chosen to automatically cluster retrieved documents in order to assist the user in locating relevant items. According to the so-called "Cluster Hypothesis" [12], relevant documents are more likely to be similar one to another than to irrelevant ones. This hypothesis has received some experimental validations: [2], [6], [10], [4] or [11].

For a query, there are roughly two kinds of documents, those that are relevant and those that are not. In this way, we may decide to cluster retrieved documents in two classes. But this can be done only if the retrieved documents are distributed according to two main topics: relevant and irrelevant. The queries provided by a user are generally short. Given the ambiguity of natural language, they are often related to different topics.

For example, the title of the TREC-7 query 351 is "Falkland petroleum exploration"[1]. Retrieved documents may be about 'exploration', 'petroleum exploration' or 'Falkland exploration'. They are not necessarily completely relevant and may not be relevant at all. The irrelevant documents discuss a lot of very different topics and cannot be grouped in a thematically homogeneous cluster. Furthermore, pertinent documents can deal with some completely or slightly different topics according to the number of distinct meanings the query words have, or according to the subjects they are related to. Hence, the retrieved documents may be clustered in several classes, each one possibly containing some relevant documents. The restriction of the classification to the retrieved documents and not to the collection as a whole allows a quick clustering. It can be used efficiently on WWW documents and with any classical Internet IR-system.

The clustering effect for the set of documents retrieved has been described numerous times in the literature, including [1] and [9]. In this article, the impact of the number of clusters and different ways to browse them to provide a new ranked list of documents will be examined. It will be shown that this algorithm allows to create at least one high precision cluster, improving the precision levels at 5 or 10 documents and recall values for low precision rates[2]. We will show that choosing the number of clusters according to query sizes improves results compared to those obtained with a prefixed number. We tried successfully this method over TREC-6 corpora and queries with the parameters learned during TREC-7.

2   A Clustering Algorithm

An important criterion for an IR system is the time the user has to wait for an answer. We have used a K-means like method [3] to cluster the retrieved documents, in particular because the time it requires is lower than the one that is needed by hierarchical algorithms. This list of documents is obtained by using the IR-system developed at the LIA. It is described in [8]. To improve the computation of distances, the Part Of Speech (POS) tagger and the lemmatizer developed at the LIA are used.

The main classification step is performed as follows:

Find an initial partition (see 2.3)

- Repeat:
  - compute the centroids *i.e.*, for each cluster, the set of documents which are the closest to the cluster's geometric centre (see 2.2);
  - allocate each document to the cluster that has the lowest distance;
- until there is little or no change in cluster membership.

Since the cluster's centroids are computed only at the beginning of an iteration, cluster memberships are order-independent. A document cannot be assigned to multiple clusters and it can be placed in a cluster only if it is sufficiently close. Hence, clusters are not confused by distant items but not all documents may be

---

[1] For a description of the seventh Text Retrieval Conference, see [13].
[2] Nevertheless, the global recall level is not modified.

assigned to a class at the end of the process. The maximal number of classes is fixed at the start of the procedure. In the clusters, documents are ranked as they were before classification.

Since this process may be seen as post-processing, it can be used with any IR-system that returns a list of documents to a user query.

2.1 Distance between Documents

Let R and D be two documents, u a term (a lemma) with a rough syntactical tag appended, and $N(u)$ the number of documents containing u in the corpus as a whole.

Given S, the number of documents in the corpus, the *information quantity* of a term in a document is based on its occurrences in the corpus —IDF(u)— (and not in the set of documents to cluster) and on its frequency in the document —TF(u)—.

The information quantity of a document is the sum of the weights of its terms:

$$I(D) = \sum_{u \in D} \text{TF}(u).\text{IDF}(u) = \sum_{u \in D} -\text{TF}(u).\log_2 \frac{N(u)}{S} \tag{1}$$

We assume that the greater the information quantity of the intersection of the term sets from two documents, the closer they are.

In order to allow convergence of classification process and to measure the quality of the partition, we must have a true distance (verifying the triangular inequality). That is the case[3] of the so-called *MinMax* distance between two documents D and D':

$$d(D, D') = 1 - \frac{I(D \cap D')}{\text{Max}\big(I(D), I(D')\big)} \tag{2}$$

In order to provide the users with a ranked list of documents from the partition or an arranged view of the clusters, we have to compute distances between a cluster and a query ("which cluster is the closest to the query ?"). This may be accomplished using the indices given by the IR system as it will be explained in the next section.

2.2 Cluster Centroids

The distance between a cluster and an item (a document or a query) is equal to the lowest distance between the query and one of the cluster centroids. We have chosen to represent a cluster C by the k documents that are closest to its geometric centre. For each document, we compute the sum of distances that separate it from other texts in the same cluster and choose the k documents corresponding to the k smallest distances as centroids.

Let N_i $(1 \le i \le k)$ be a centroid of C and let d be the distance between a document and a cluster:

$$d(D, C) = \min_{1 \le i \le k}\big(d(D, N_i)\big) \tag{3}$$

---

[3] On average, over the 50 queries of TREC-7, 6 iterations are made before convergence.

Because the centroids are documents, the indices given by the IR system can be used to rank the clusters according to the query.

2.3 Initial Partition

The result of this cluster-based method depends on the initial set. We have used a partial hierarchical method to obtain the initial partition:

1. for each couple of documents i and j such that $d(i,j) < threshold^4$:
- if i and j are not yet in a class, create a new one;
- if i and/or j are already allocated, merge all the documents of the class containing i (resp. j) with those of the class containing j (resp. i);

2. *partial hierarchical classification*: after this first step, the number of classes created may be greater than the number of clusters wanted. So, as long as the number of classes is greater than the predefined one: a) compute class representatives; b) compute distances between every pair of classes; c) merge the two closest classes (this can be done by using distances between centroids [7]).

3 Experiments over TREC-7 Corpora

3.1 Routes through the Clusters

To evaluate the quality of the classification, we can explore clusters in different ways. We can first consider the best ranked cluster which should contain most relevant documents. We can look at the best ranked documents of each cluster, *i.e.* at the documents for each theme which are the closest to the query. Finally, we can present each cluster to the user so that he could choose those which contain the largest number of relevant documents [4].

Let L_{C_n} be the list of documents constructed from the succession of the clusters ranked according to their distances with the query: $L_{C_n} = C_1 \cdot C_2 \cdot C_3 \cdots$

Let L_n be the list of documents constructed from the succession of the n first ranked items in each ranked cluster ($C_{i,j}$ is the j-th document of the i-th cluster):

$$L_n = \left(C_{1,1} \cdot C_{1,2} \cdot C_{1,3} \cdots C_{1,n}\right) \cdot \left(C_{2,1} \cdots C_{2,n}\right) \cdots \left(C_{1,n+1} \cdot C_{1,n+2} \cdots C_{1,2n}\right) \cdot \left(C_{2,n+1} \cdots C_{2,2n}\right) \cdots$$

Let $L_{n_1,n_2,\ldots}$ be the list of documents constructed from the succession of the n_i first ranked items[5] in each ranked cluster C_i:

$$L_{n_1,n_2,\ldots} = \left(C_{1,1} \cdot C_{1,2} \cdot C_{1,3} \cdots C_{1,n_1}\right) \cdot \left(C_{2,1} \cdots C_{2,n_2}\right) \cdots \left(C_{1,n_1+1} \cdots C_{1,2n_1}\right) \cdot \left(C_{2,n_2+1} \cdots C_{2,2n_2}\right) \cdots$$

To help to measure how much the classification groups relevant documents, we use the list of relevant documents supplied by NIST for TREC-7. For each query, we

---

[4] The threshold value is chosen so that the number of documents assigned at the end of step 1 is greater than half the total number of documents.

[5] We choose $n_i > n_{i+1}$ to favor the first ranked classes.

select the best clusters according to the number of relevant documents they contain. [6] and [11] used this method of evaluation.

L_{qrels} is defined as the list of documents constructed from the succession of the clusters ranked according to the number of relevant items they contain. L_{qrels} can be seen as the *best route* through the clusters.

The evaluations presented below have been obtained by means of the `trec_eval` application over the 50 queries (351 to 400) of TREC-7. The corpus was the one used for TREC-7 (528.155 documents) [13]. We have used the IR system developed by LIA and Bertin & Cie [8] to obtain the lists of documents to cluster. Whenever possible, the first 1000 documents retrieved for each query have been kept to cluster them.

3.2   The same Number of Classes for each Query

Usually, the number of classes is defined at the start of the process. It cannot grow but it can be reduced when a class empties. In next figures, the indicated numbers of clusters correspond to the values initially chosen. The documents that are not assigned to a class at the end of the classification are allocated to a new one (at the last position in the ranked list of clusters).

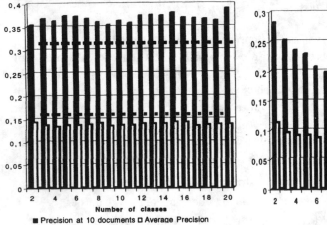

■ Precision at 10 documents □ Average Precision

Fig. 1. L_{qrels} with different numbers of classes (precision at 10 and average precision without classification are respectively indicated by the top and the bottom dashed lines)

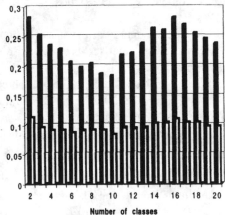

Number of classes

■ Precision at 10 documents □ Average Precision

Fig. 2. L_{Ci} with different numbers of classes

By choosing the same number of classes –from 2 to 13– for all queries, the levels of the average precision over all relevant documents are lower than those without classification with lists L_{qrels} and L_{C_n} (Fig. 1 and Fig. 2). The decrease rate varies from 1.2% to 2% (see the bottom dashed line in Fig. 1). Fig. 1 and Fig. 2 show that those lists do not allow to globally improve results of the retrieval: the average precision decreases since the relevant documents that are not in the first cluster are ranked after all items of that one.

The differences between results indicated in Fig.1 and in Fig. 2 measure how much the above-defined distance ranks the clusters. The average precision decrease is about 5% when clusters are ranked according to the computed distances and not according to the number of relevant documents they contain.

However, the first ranked cluster –according to the distances to the queries– is very often better than the next ones as shown in Fig. 3 where we have compared lists $C_1.C_2$ and $C_2.C_1$. With this second list, the relative decrease of the average precision over the 50 queries equals 18% (from 0.11 to 0.09).

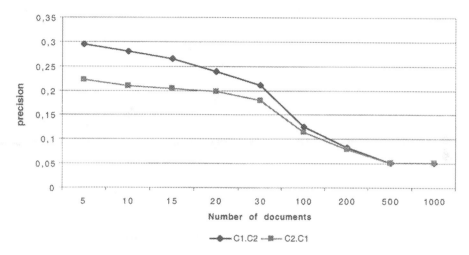

Fig. 3. Precision of lists $C_1.C_2$ and $C_2.C_1$

On the other hand, with list L_{qrels}, the precision at 10 documents is greater than the one obtained without classification. With 5 clusters the relative increase of precision at 10 documents is equal to 12.8% (from 0.33 to 0.374). At 5 documents, the relative increase equals 10.5%. These values confirm –see Fig. 1 where the top dashed line shows the precision value without classification– that the classification helps to group relevant documents together by creating a class containing a large rate of relevant items well ranked: precision is increased at a low number of documents.

For each query, one class with a high level of precision exists. Those classes often have a low population rate[6]. In fact, they are the ones that should be proposed at first. Indeed, a high precision short list makes a better impression than a long one with a great number of scattered relevant documents. In the first one, users can browse all documents and what they are looking for is likely to be quickly accessed.

3.3 Experiments with Different Routes

Table 1 and Fig. 4 show some results obtained with 3 clusters. One can see that precision at low level of recall with lists L_n is better than those of list L_C

---

[6] The population rate is the number of documents in the class divided by the total number of documents retrieved for the query.

(succession of each cluster's contents). However, only list L_{qrels} allows to obtain better results than without classification. At recall 0.1, the relative increase of precision of list L_5 over list L_C equals 18.5% (from 0.27 to 0.32).

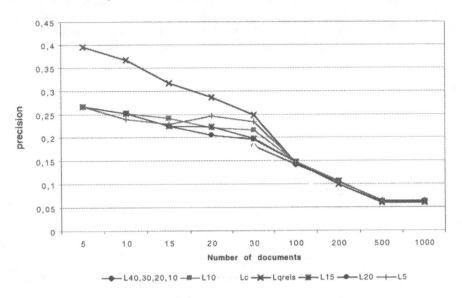

Fig. 4. Precision for different ways to browse the clusters

(3 clusters)	Precision at recall 0.00	Precision at recall 0.10	Precision at 5 docs	Precision at 10 docs	Precision at 15 docs	Precision at 20 docs
without classification	0,58	0,38	0,36	0,33	0,32	0,30
L_{qrels}	0,63	0,37	0,40	0,37	0,32	0,29
L_C	0,48	0,27		0,25	0,23	0,21
L_5	0,51	0,32		0,24		0,25
L_{10}	0,50	0,31	0,27		0,24	0,22
L_{15}				0,25		
L_{20}	0,49	0,30			0,23	0,21
$L_{40,30,20,10}$		0,29				

Table 1. Different ways to browse automatically the clusters

4 Choice of Number of Clusters according to Query Length

4.1 Linear Correlation Deduced from TREC-7

In section 3.2, we have shown that the number of classes –the same for all queries– does not strongly influence the global results. However, that is not the case if we examine each query independently. It has been found that the shorter the query, the higher the number of clusters must be. This can be explained by the fact that the topics of the retrieved documents are more varied when the query is short and, therefore, more ambiguous. Over the 50 TREC-7 queries, the correlation coefficient between the best numbers of classes and the query sizes equals -0.56. The linear correlation is verified at a 5% risk according to a Fisher test. The equation deduced from the correlation coefficient, the query sizes and the best numbers of classes, is:

$$\text{Class number} = -0.525 \cdot (\text{query size}) + 10.65 \qquad (4)$$

4.2 Experiments over TREC-7

By choosing the number of clusters according to equation (4), we improve clearly the best results obtained previously[7]. Compared with the rate without classification (see Table 2 and Fig. 5), the relative increase of the precision at 5 documents is equal to 22% (from 0.36 to 0.44) and equals 10% when compared with the value obtained with constant number of clusters.

	Precision at recall 0.00	Precision at recall 0.10	Precision at 5 docs	Precision at 10 docs	Precision at 15 docs
without classification	0,58	**0,38**	0,36	0,33	**0,32**
L_{qrels} (2 clusters)	0,65 +12%	0,33 -13%	0,42 +17%	0,37 +12%	**0,32** =
L_{qrels} (5 clusters)	0,67 +16%	0,32 -16%	0,39 +8%	0,32 -3%	0,27 -15%
L_{qrels} with linear regression	**0,75** +29%	0,33 -13%	**0,44** +22%	**0,37** +12%	0,31 -3%

Table 2. Improvements by choosing the number of clusters according to query sizes (TREC-7)

---

[7] In Table 2 and in Table 3, the lists L_{qrels} are obtained by ranking clusters according to their precision values and not according to the number of relevant documents they contain.

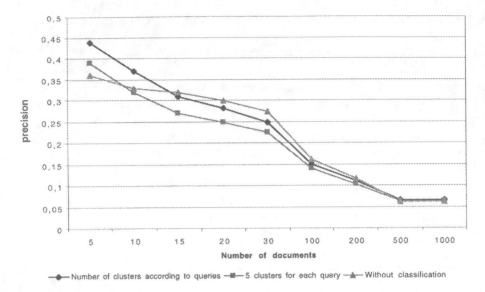

Fig. 5. Precision by choosing the number of clusters according to query sizes (TREC-7)

4.3 Test over TREC-6 Corpora and Queries

The results shown in Table 2 have been obtained with the same corpus that the one used to compute equation (4). Thus, we have chosen to test equation (4) parameters on TREC-6 corpora and queries. The results in Table 4 confirm the improvements shown in 4.2 by using the same method over TREC-6 *with the equation computed during TREC-7*. The absolute improvements (see Table 3) of the precision levels at 5, 10 and 15 documents are equal to 7%, 3% and 1% compared with the results obtained with 5 clusters for each query. The mean number of clusters used by means of this method is equal to 5.

	Precision at recall 0.00	Precision at recall 0.10	Precision at 5 docs	Precision at 10 docs	Precision at 15 docs
Without classification	0,62	0,41	0,41	0,33	0,30
L_{qrels} (3 clusters)	0,63	0,46	0,39	0,35	0,32
L_{qrels} (5 clusters)	0,61	0,45	0,41	0,34	0,32
L_{qrels} with linear regression	**0,68**	**0,47**	**0,46**	**0,37**	**0,33**

Table 3 - Results by choosing the number of clusters according to query sizes (TREC-6)

5 Conclusion

We have shown how classifying retrieved documents helps to regroup the relevant ones. It increases the effectiveness of retrieval by providing users at least one cluster with a precision higher than the one obtained without classification. The process of classification is quick and can be used with any IR-system used on the WWW. We have examined with TREC corpora and queries how the cluster numbers and how the way to browse them automatically by means of different routes impact on the classification. The quality of the results obtained can be compared with those reported in [6] and [11] since, when the best cluster is selected, the *absolute* increase in precision is equal to 8% at 5 documents and to 4% at 10 documents. Moreover, we have shown that a variation of the number of clusters according to the query length improves the results over TREC-7 and over TREC-6. Organizing the set of documents retrieved according to the sizes of the user's queries is an important new result especially if they are written in natural language.

6 References

1. Allen, R.B., Obry, P., Littman, M.: An interface for navigating clustered document sets returned by queries, Proceedings of COCS (1993), pp.166
2. Cutting, D.R., Karger, D.R., Pedersen, J.O., Tukey, J.W.: Sactter/Gather: a Cluster-based Approach to Browsing Large Document Collections, in ACM/SIGIR (1992), 318-329
3. Diday, E., Lemaire, J., Pouget, J., Testu, F.: Eléments d'Analyse des Données, Dunod Informatique (1982)
4. Evans, D.A., Huettner, A., Tong, X., Jansen, P., Subasic, P.: Notes on the Effectiveness of Clustering in Ad-Hoc Retrieval, in TREC-7, NIST special publication (1998)
5. Frakes, W.B., Baeza-Yates R. (Editors): Information Retrieval, Data Structures & Algorithms, Prentice-Hall Inc.(1992), ISBN-0-13-463837-9
6. Hearst, M.A., Pedersen, J.O.: Reexamining the Cluster Hypothesis: Scatter/Gather on Retrieval Results, in ACM/SIGIR (1996), 76-84
7. Kowalski, G.: Information Retrieval Systems, Theory and Implementation, Kluwer Academic Publishers (1997) ISBN-0-7923-9926-9
8. de Loupy, C., Bellot, P., El-Bèze, M., Marteau, P.F.: Query Expansion and Automatic Classification, in TREC-7, NIST special publication #500-242 (1999), 443-450
9. Sahami, M., Yusufali, S., Baldonaldo, M.Q.W.: SONIA a service for organizing networked information autonomously, in ACM/DL (1998), 200-209
10. Schütze, H., Silverstein, C.: Projections for Efficient Document Clustering, in ACM/SIGIR (1997), 74-81
11. Silverstein, C., Pedersen, J.O.: Almost-Constant-Time Clustering of Arbitrary Corpus Subsets, in ACM/SIGIR (1997), 60-66
12. Van Rijsbergen, C. J.: Information Retrieval, Buttherwords, London (1979)
13. Voorhees, E.M., Harman, D.: Overview of the Seventh Text REtrieval Conference (TREC-7), NIST special publication (1999)

Self-Organizing Neural Networks for Data Projection

Mu-Chun Su and Hisao-Te Chang

Department of Electrical Engineering, Tamkang University, Taiwan, R.O.C.
muchun@ee.tku.edu.tw

Abstract. In this paper we present a nonlinear projection method for visualizing high-dimensional data as a two-dimensional scatter plot. The method is based on a new model of self-organizing neural networks. An algorithm called "double self-organizing feature map" (DSOM) algorithm is developed to train the novel model. By the DSOM algorithm the network will adaptively adjust its architecture during the learning phase so as to make neurons responding to similar stimulus be clustered together. Then the architecture of the network is graphically displayed to show the underlying structure of the data. Two data sets are used to test the effectiveness of the proposed neural network.

1 Introduction

In recent years various artificial neural networks have been proposed for clustering data. Among them, one is the ART models [1]-[3] and the other is the self-organizing feature map [4]. Both of them can organize input data into clusters using an unsupervised learning paradigm. There are a number of ways to design an unsupervised learning network that self-organizes into a feature map. Basically, there are two different models of self-organizing neural networks originally proposed by Kohonen [4] and Willshaw and Von Der Malsburg [5], respectively. The self-organizing feature map (SOM) algorithm developed by Kohonen has received much more attention in the literature than other approaches. Recently, numerous technical reports have been written about successful applications of the self-organizing feature map algorithm developed by Kohonen. These applications widely range from simulations used for the purpose of understanding and modeling of computational maps in the brain [6] to subsystems for engineering applications such as motor control [7], speech recognition [8], vector quantization [9], and adaptive equalization [10]. Kohonen *et al* [11] provided partial reviews.

The development of the self-organizing feature maps is originally motivated by a distinct feature of the human brain. The brain is organized in such a way that different sensory inputs are represented by topologically ordered computational maps. The feature-mapping model introduced by Kohonen is not meant to explain neurobiological details. Rather, the model tries to capture the essential features of computational maps in the brain and yet remain computationally tractable. The ordinary SOM algorithm took a computational shortcut by fixing the architecture of the network through the whole learning procedure. However, a biological neural network will become bigger as it develops. In other words, the architecture of a biological neural network varies during the growing process. Fritzke proposed a special neural network that can determine its shape and size during the simulation in an incremental fashion [12]. Alahakoon *et al* also proposed another neural network whose shape and size can be adapted during the self-organizing process [13]. However we can not find any evidence that these two models were built to explain the neurobiological phenomenon. In this paper a new model of self-organizing neural networks is proposed. An algorithm called "double self-organizing feature map (DSOM) algorithm is developed to train the novel model. By the DSOM algorithm the network operates according to the same self-organization principles as the SOM algorithm but adapts its architecture according to the structure of the input data. One possible application of the model is data projection.

Generally speaking, data mining or knowledge discovery has been defined as the non-trivial process of extracting implicit, previously unknown, and potentially useful information from data [14]. The data mining process involves preprocessing, mining, and analysis. Although data projection by itself can hardly be called a complete mining tool, appropriate display of data points is very helpful at the very beginning of a data mining process. Data projection algorithms project high-dimensional data onto a low-dimensional space to facilitate visual inspection on the data. This can provide better insight into the data since clustering tendencies in the data may become apparent from the projection. Usually analysts choose a projection algorithm to project data and then explore the intrinsic dimensionality and analyze the clustering tendency of high-dimensional data by viewing the final scatter plot of the projected data. The problem associated with this approach is that there are many local minima on the object function to be minimized by the projection algorithm and it is usually unavoidable for the algorithm to get stuck in some local minimum. Of course a simple way to overcome the problem is to rerun the algorithm using a different set of corresponding parameters. The next question is which set of parameters is more appropriate. Here we propose a different solution to the problem. In our opinion, it will be more useful if we display a sequence of intermediate scatter plots during the projection process. By viewing these scatter plots analysts can discover more information about the data and even know how to adjust the corresponding parameters to rerun the algorithm. Therefore we propose a nonlinear projection algorithm based on the novel self-organizing neural networks incorporated with the DSOM algorithm. The display of the architecture of the network allows us to visualize high-dimensional data as a two-dimensional scatter plot and explore the underlying structure of the data set.

The paper is organized as follows. Section 2 will briefly present the Kohonen's SOM algorithm. The new model of the self-organizing neural networks and the DSOM algorithm are discussed in Section 3. In Section 4 two computer simulations are given. Finally the conclusions of this study are presented in section 5.

2 Review of the SOM Algorithm

The principal goal of self-organizing feature maps is to transform patterns of arbitrary dimensionality into the responses of one- or two-dimensional arrays of neurons, and to perform this transform adaptively in a topological ordered fashion. A typical architecture of the network is shown in Figure 1. The essential constituents of feature maps are as follows [2] :

• an array of neurons that compute simple output functions of incoming inputs of arbitrary dimensionality,
• a mechanism for selecting the neuron with the largest output,
• an adaptive mechanism that updates the weights of the selected neuron and its neighbors.

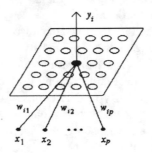

Fig. 1. The ordinary network architecture in the conventional SOM algorithm.

The training algorithm proposed by Kohonen for forming a feature map is summarized as follow:

Step 1: Initialization: Choose random values for the initial weights $\underline{w}_j(0)$.

Step 2: Winner Finding: Find the winning neuron j^* at time k, using the minimum-distance Euclidean criterion:

$$j^* = \arg \ \min_j \left\| \underline{x}(k) - \underline{w}_j \right\| \ , j = 1, \cdots, N^2 . \tag{1}$$

where $\underline{x}(k) = [x_1(k), \cdots, x_p(k)]^T$ represents the kth input pattern, N^2 is the total number of neurons, and $\left\| \cdot \right\|$ indicates the Euclidean norm.

Step 3: Weights Updating: Adjust the weights of the winner and its neighbors, using the following rule

$$\underline{w}_j(k+1) = \underline{w}_j(k) + \eta(k)\Lambda_{j^*}(k)[\underline{x}(k) - \underline{w}_j(k)] \tag{2}$$

where $\eta(k)$ is a positive constant and $\Lambda_{j^*}(k)$ is the topological neighborhood function of the winner neuron j^* at time k. A typical choice of $\Lambda_{j^*}(k)$ is the Gaussian-type function

$$\Lambda_{j^*}(k) = \exp(-\frac{d^2_{j^*,j}}{2\sigma^2}) \tag{3}$$

where the parameter σ is the "effect width" of the topological neighborhood and $d_{j^*,j}$ is the lateral distance between neurons j^* and j in the discrete output space. It should be emphasized that the success of the map formation is critically dependent on how the values of the main parameters (*i.e.* $\eta(k)$ and $\Lambda_{j^*}(k)$), initial values of weight vectors, and the number of iterations are predetermined.

The transformation makes topological neighborhood relationship geometrically explicit in low-dimensional feature maps. In this sense, it can be regarded as a neural-network-based projection method. However, if the trained map is not calibrated by the labeled data, the inherent structure of the data can not be visualized. From the viewpoint of the cluster analysis, it is very difficult to observe the cluster tendency based on an unlabeled SOM. To make SOMs be able to cluster data, several different approaches have been proposed. An interpretation using contiguity-constrained clustering method was proposed by Murtagh to complement usage of the SOMs [15]. A nonlinear projection method based on Kohonen's SOM was proposed to facilitate visualization of data [16]-[17]. In this method, a special display technique is proposed to display the inherent structure of the data on a two-dimensional image. Su *et al* proposed another display method based on the accumulated responses of each neuron on the network [18]. The number of clusters can be estimated from the digital image transformed from the accumulated responses. Basically, these aforementioned methods involve two phases. In the first phase, the Kohonen's SOM algorithm is used to project data onto a two-dimensional neural array. Then the trained map is further processed to analyze the structure of the data set.

3 The New Model of Self-Organizing Neural Networks

An important property of the Kohonen SOM algorithm is the ability to project high-dimensional input data onto a two-dimensional crisp rigid grid. By using labeled data to calibrate trained maps, this makes a visualization of complex data possible. The question is what if no information about the pattern class labels is available *a priori*. Understandably, we then can not find any information about the underlying structure of the data set from the rigid grid. That is, the predetermined rigid structure of neural networks implies limitations on the data visualization and projections. A solution to encounter the limitation is to adjust the architecture of the network during a self-organization process. The neurons should "search" a suitable position in the two-dimensional continuous output space such that the inherent structure of the data can be preserved as well as possible. This idea was also motivated by the biological phenomenon. The sizes of neurons will change as the subject grows. This means the relative positions of neurons will vary as the process of self-organization of the biological neural network progresses.

3.1 Network Architecture

The initial topology of the network is a rectangular grid. Each neuron j has an n-dimensional synaptic weight vector $\underline{w}_j$ attached. In addition to the vector $\underline{w}_j$, another two-dimensional position vector $\underline{p}_j$ is also attached to neuron j. The vector $\underline{p}_j$ can be regarded as the location of neuron j in the continuous output space.

3.2 Network Dynamics

During the self-organization process, not only the synaptic weight vectors but also the position vectors are adapted. The adaptation of the synaptic weight vectors $\underline{w}_j$'s is given as follows:

$$\underline{w}_j(k+1) = \underline{w}_j(k) + \eta(k)\Lambda_{j^*}(k)[\underline{x}(k) - \underline{w}_j(k)] \tag{4}$$

where

$$\eta(k) = \eta_0 \frac{1}{k+1} \tag{5}$$

and

$$\Lambda_{j^*}(k) = \exp[-s_w(1+\frac{k}{k_{\max}})\left\|\underline{p}_j(k) - \underline{p}_{j^*}(k)\right\|^2] \tag{6}$$

Here $\|\cdot\|$ denotes the Euclidean norm , η_0 is the learning rate , s_w is the scalar parameter which regulates how fast the function $\Lambda_{j^*}(k)$ decreases , and $k_{\max}$ is the maximum number of iterations .

The synaptic vectors $\underline{w}_j$'s are expected to become prototypes of the input vectors $\underline{x}$. The next goal is how to project the prototypes into the 2-dimensional output space so as to preserve the inherent structure of the data as well as possible. Most projection methods, such as Sammon's nonlinear mapping [19], attempt to optimize a cost function. If a gradient-based algorithm is asked to optimize such a cost function, it is unavoidable for the algorithm to get stuck in a local minimum since there may exist many local minima on the error function. In order to overcome the local minimum problem, genetic algorithms or the simulated algorithm are an alternative choice.

Here we propose a heuristic method to find a nonlinear mapping via adjusting the position vectors $\underline{p}_j$'s. The basic idea is very simple and straightforward. Similar to the Sammon's nonlinear mapping, we try to create a two-dimensional configuration of points in which interpattern distances are preserved. Instead of optimizing a cost function based on interpattern distance, we adopt the Kohonen SOM algorithm to adjust the position vectors $\underline{p}_j$'s. By using the topology-preserving property of the SOM algorithm, we can make similar position vectors move near to each other. The updating formula is given as follows:

$$\underline{p}_j(k+1) = \underline{p}_j(k) + \eta(k)h_{j^*}(k)[\underline{p}(k) - \underline{p}_{j^*}(k)] \tag{7}$$

where

$$\eta(k) = \eta_0 \frac{1}{1+k} \tag{8}$$

and

$$h_{j^*}(k) = \exp[-s_w(1 + \frac{k}{k_{max}})\|\underline{p}_j(k) - \underline{p}_{j^*}(k)\|] \tag{9}$$
$$\times \exp\{-s_x[\|\underline{w}_j(k) - \underline{x}(k)\| - \|\underline{w}_{j^*}(k) - \underline{x}(k)\|]^2\}$$

Here s_w and s_x are two predetermined scalar parameters. This formula tells us that

(1) If neurons have similar responses as the winner neuron j^* (i.e. $\|\underline{w}_j(k) - \underline{x}(k)\| \approx \|\underline{w}_{j^*}(k) - \underline{x}(k)\|$) then their position vectors $\underline{p}_j(k)$'s should be adjusted to move near to the winner's position vector $\underline{p}_{j^*}(k)$.

(2) If neurons that are closer to the winner (i.e. $\underline{p}_j(k) \approx \underline{p}_{j^*}(k)$) then the updating step should be larger.

(3) In addition, the weighting function is chosen as a decreasing function of iterations.

The whole adaptation procedure referred to as the " Double Self-Organizing Feature Map " (DSOM) algorithm is summarized as follows:

Step 1: Present an input pattern $\underline{x}$ into the network.

Step 2: Locate the best matching neuron j^* using the minimum-distance Euclidean criterion given in Eq. (1).

Step 3: Update the synaptic vectors $\underline{w}_j$'s by Eqs. (4)-(6).

Step 4: Update the position vectors $\underline{p}_j$'s by Eqs. (7)-(9).

Step 5: Go to step 1 until it converges or some terminating criteria is satisfied.

By visualizing the scatter plots of position vectors $\underline{p}_j$'s, we can explore various properties, such us the clustering tendency and underlying structure of the data.

4 Simulation Results

To test the performance of the new self-organizing neural networks, two data sets were used. Among these are one artificial data set and one real data set. During the simulations, the values of $\eta(k)$, $\Lambda_{j^*}(k)$, and $h_{j^*}(k)$ were updated after one epoch instead of one iteration. The maximum number of epochs in all the computer simulations is 50 and the network sizes to be trained are all 9×9.

Example 1: 2-D data set

The first data set contains 579 2-dimensical data points, shown in Fig. 2. The data set consists of 3 normally distributed clusters. There is no clear border between clusters. Figs. 3(a)-3(d) illustrate the sequences of updating the position vectors $\underline{p}_j$'s. Initially the plane vectors were set up to form a square grid shown in Fig. 3(a). As the adaptation procedure progressed, these 81 plane vectors were merged to 3 clusters. Obviously, there are three clusters in Fig. 3(d), therefore, we estimate the number of clusters in the data set is three. This estimate is consistent with the actual number of clusters in the artificial data set.

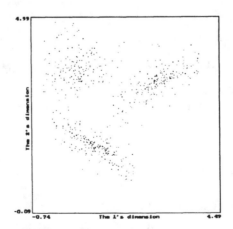

Fig. 2. The 579 patterns in the 2D data set.

213

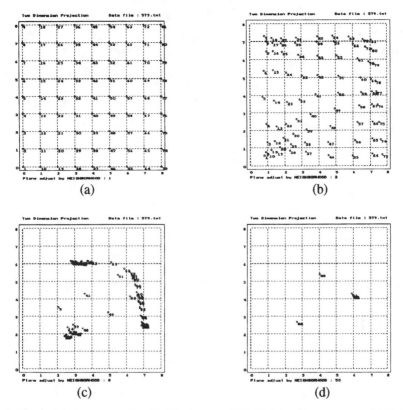

(a)

(b)

(c)

(d)

Fig. 3. The training sequence for the 2D data set: (a) Initial position vectores. (b) Position vectors after 2 epochs. (c) Position vectors after 8 epochs. (d) Position vectors after 50 epochs.

Example 2: Iris data set

The iris data set has three subsets (*i.e.* iris setosa, iris versicolor, and iris virginica), two of which are overlapping. The Iris data are in a four-dimensional space and there are total 150 patters in the set. There are 50 patterns from each of the three species. Figs. 4(a)-4(d) illustrate the updating procedure. Obviously, there are two major clusters in Fig. 4(d). By further examining the largest cluster it can be divided into two subclusters based on the principal components of the two subclusters. This observation is consistent with our *a priori* knowledge about the iris data set.

214

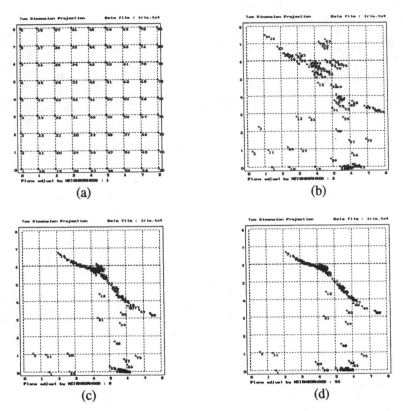

Fig. 4. The training sequence for the iris data set: (a) Initial position vectores. (b) Position vectors after 2 epochs. (c) Position vectors after 8 epochs. (d) Position vectors after 50 epochs.

5 Conclusion

In this paper, a new model of self-organizing neural networks is proposed. The development of this new model of neural networks was not only motivated by the analysis about projection but also by a distinct feature of the human brain. The DSOM algorithm is proposed to train the proposed neural networks. From a sequence of scatter plots of plane vectors the number of clusters in a data set can be roughly estimated by counting the number of major clusters.

Acknowledgements:

This project was partly supported by the National Science Council (NSC) of Taiwan, R.O.C., under the Grant NSC-87-2213-E032-006.

References

[1] G. Carpenter and S. Grossberg, "Adaptive resonance theory: Stable self-organization of neural recognition codes in response to arbitrary lists of input patterns," Proc. 8th Annual Conf. Cognitive Sci. Soc., pp. 45-62, 1986.

[2] G. Carpenter and S. Grossberg, "ART2: Self-organization of stable category recognition codes for analog input patterns," Appl. Optics, Vol. 26, No. 23, pp. 4919-4930, 1987.

[3] G. Carpenter and S. Grossberg, "ART3: Hierarchical search using chemical transmitter in self-organizing pattern recognition architectures," Neural Networks, Vol. 3, pp. 129,-152, 1990.

[4] T. Kohonen, *Self-Organization and Associative Memory*, 3rd ed. New York, Berlin: Springer-Verlag, 1989.

[5] D. J. Willshaw and C. von der Malsburg, "How patterned neural connections can be set up by self-organization," Proceedings of the Royal Society of London, Series B, vol. 194, pp. 431-445, 1976.

[6] H. J. Ritter, T. Martinetz, and K. J. Schulten, Neural Computation and Self-Organizing Maps: An Introduction, Reading, MA: Addison-Wesley, 1992.

[7] T. M. Martinetz, H. J. Ritter, and K. J. Schulten, "Three-dimensional neural net for learning visuomotor coordination of a robot arm," IEEE Trans. Neural Networks, vol. 1, pp. 131-136, 1990.

[8] T. Kohonen, "The 'neural' phonetic typewritter," Comput., Vol. 21, pp. 11-22, March, 1988.

[9] S. P. Luttrell, "Hierarchical vector quantization," IEE Proceedings, vol. 136, Part I, pp. 405,413, 1989.

[10] T. K. Kohonen, J. Kangas, J. Laaksonen, and K. Tokkola, "LVQ-PAK: the learning vector quantization program package," Helsinki University of Technology Finland, 1992.

[11] T. Kohonen, E. Oja, O. Simula, A. Visa, and J. Kangas," Engineering application of the self-organizing map," Proceedings of the IEEE, vol. 84, no. 10, pp. 1358-1383, 1996.

[12] B. Fritzke, "Growing cell structures-a self-organizing network for unsupervised and supervised learning," Neural Networks, vol. 7, no. 9, pp. 1441-1460, 1994.

[13] D. Alahakoon, S. K. Halgamuge, and B. Srinivasan, "A self growing cluster development approach to data mining," IEEE Int. Conf. on Systems, Man, and Cybernetics, pp. 2901-2906, Orlando, 1998.

[14] W. Frawley, G. Piatetsky-Shapiro, and C. Matheus, "Knowledge Discovery in Database: An overview," AI Magazine, Vol. 14, No. 3, pp. 57-70, 1992.

[15] F. Murtagh, "Interpreting the Kohonen self-organizing feature map using contiguity-constrained clustering," Pattern Recognition Letters, vol. 16, PP. 399-408, 1995.

[16] M. A. Kraaijveld, J. Mao, and A. K. Jain, "A nonlinear projection method based an Kohonen's topology preserving maps," IEEE Trans. on Neural Networks, vol.6, No. 3, PP.548-559, 1995.

[17] J. Mao and A. K. Jain, "Artificial neural networks for feature extraction and multivariate data projection," IEEE Trans. on Neural Networks, vol.6, No. 2, PP. 296-317, 1995.

[18] M. C. Su, N. DeClaris, and T. K. Liu, "Application of neural networks in cluster analysis," in IEEE International Conference on Systems, Man, and Cybernetics, PP. 1-6, Orlando, 1997.

[19] J. W. Shammon Jr., "A nonlinear mapping for data structure analysis," IEEE Trans. on Computers, vol. 18, pp. 491-509, 1969.

ROC Performance Evaluation of Web-Based Bibliographic Navigator Using Extended Association Rules

Minoru Kawahara[1] and Hiroyuki Kawano[2]

[1] Data Processing Center, Kyoto University, Kyoto 6068501, JAPAN,
kawahara@kudpc.kyoto-u.ac.jp,
WWW home page: http://www.kudpc.kyoto-u.ac.jp/~kawahara/index.html
[2] Department of Systems Science, Kyoto University, Kyoto 6068501, JAPAN,
kawano@i.kyoto-u.ac.jp,
WWW home page: http://www.kuamp.kyoto-u.ac.jp/~kawano/index.html

Abstract. It is very effective for search users to provide meaningful keywords which are derived by text mining algorithm. We are developing our search engine "Mondou" using weighted association rules, as the web-based intelligent database navigation system. In this paper, we focus on the computing cost to derive appropriate keywords, we carefully determine system parameters, such as $Minsup$ and $Minconf$ threshold values. In order to evaluate the performance and characteristics of derived rules, we use the techniques of ROC graph. We propose the ROC analytical model of our search system, and we evaluate the performance of weighted association rules by the ROC convex hull method. Especially, we try to specify the optimal threshold values to derive effective rules from INSPEC database, which is one of the huge bibliographic databases.

1   Introduction

In the research fields of data mining[2] and text mining [1], various algorithms have been proposed to discover interesting patterns, rules, trends and representations in databases. Most of discovered patterns or rules are very simple as knowledge for experts, but they are sometimes helpful for beginners, who don't have background or domain knowledge.

Therefore, we focused on the advantage of association rules [6], we extended it and implemented our proposed algorithm in our web search engine "Mondou" (http://www.kuamp.kyoto-u.ac.jp/labs/infocom/mondou/). Our Mondou provides associative keywords to search users. Moreover, by extending the basic algorithm of Mondou, we constructed the web-based bibliographic navigation interface[3], using the "Open Text" database. In Figure 1 and 2, we show the present images of Mondou .

However, when we implemented our algorithm, we had very hard problem to determine system parameters, such as minimum support threshold $Minsup$ and minimum confidence threshold $Minconf$. Then, in our previous works[3], we tried to adjust the $Minsup$ value dynamically.

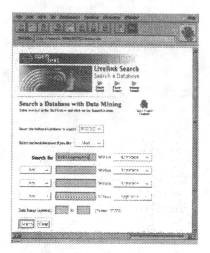

Fig. 1. The query window of **Mondou**.

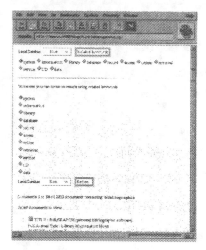

Fig. 2. The search results by **Mondou**.

Then, in this paper, we propose a method which specifies the optimal thresholds based on the ROC (Receiver Operating Characteristic) analysis[5]. We evaluate the performance of our algorithm using the characteristics of **Mondou**.

In Section 3, we define several parameters for the ROC analysis and propose a model in order to evaluate the performance of our **Mondou** system. In Section 4, we evaluate the performance of **Mondou** system based on the experimental results using INSPEC database. Finally, we make concluding remarks and discuss the future works in Section 5.

2 ROC Analysis

ROC graphs have been used in the signal detection theory to depict tradeoffs between the hit rate and the false alarm rate. ROC graphs illustrate the behavior of a classifier without regard to class distribution or error cost, they decouple classification performance from these factors. Moreover, the ROC convex hull method is an effective way to compare multiple classifiers, it specifies the optimal classifier with the highest performance[5].

2.1 ROC Graph

An instance can be classified into two classes: the positive class P or the negative class N, and positive y (yes) or negative n (no) are assigned by a classifier. We define that $p(c \mid I)$ is the posterior probability that instance I is positive c. The true positive rate TP of a classifier is the following equation:

$$TP = p(y \mid P) \simeq \frac{\text{positive correctly classified}}{\text{total positives}}. \tag{1}$$

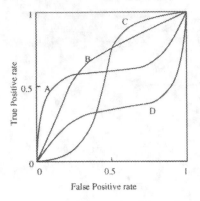
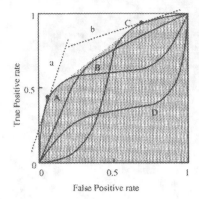

Fig. 3. An ROC graph of four classifiers.

Fig. 4. Lines a and b show the optimal classifier.

The false positive rate FP of a classifier is as follows:

$$FP = p(y \mid N) \simeq \frac{\text{negative incorrectly classified}}{\text{total negatives}} \qquad (2)$$

When we consider the concepts of ROC curves in the graph, FP is plotted on the X axis and TP is plotted on the Y axis on the graph for several instances. Thus we can draw monotone curves which are shown in Figure 3.

Moreover, TP is higher and the point is located in the upper area, it represents that an instance is classified correctly by the classifier. The right point (FP is higher) represents that an instance is classified incorrectly. Therefore the ROC curve near the area of higher TP and lower FP, that is the most-northwest line, shows better performance. Thus, the curve A is better than curve D, because it dominates in all points.

2.2 ROC Convex Hull Method

In this subsection, we try to consider the evaluation of the different classifiers. We define that $c(classification, class)$ is an error cost function, and that $c(n, P)$ is the cost of a false negative error and $c(y, N)$ is the cost of a false positive error. It is also defined that $p(P)$ is the prior probability of a positive instance, so the prior probability of a negative instance is $p(N) = 1 - p(P)$.

Then the expected cost represented by a point (FP, TP) on the ROC graph is as follows:

$$p(P) \cdot (1 - TP) \cdot c(n, P) + p(N) \cdot FP \cdot c(y, N).$$

If both of two points, (FP_1, TP_1) and (FP_2, TP_2), have the same performance, we can represent the following equation:

$$\frac{TP_2 - TP_1}{FP_2 - FP_1} = \frac{p(N) \cdot c(y, N)}{p(P) \cdot c(n, P)}.$$

This equation means the slope of an iso-performance line through two points, (FP_1, TP_1) and (FP_2, TP_2), which have the same performance. Hence, the slope of an iso-performance line is specified by $p(N)/p(P)$ and the ratio of error $c(y, N)/c(n, P)$. Therefore, a classifier is potentially optimal if it lies on the north-west boundary of the convex hull drawn as the border between the shaded and unshaded areas in Figure 4.

3   ROC Analytical Model of Bibliographic Navigation System

In this section, we apply the ROC analysis to **Mondou** style bibliographic navigation system. Let's assume that $\bigcup$ is the set operator of union, $\bigcap$ is the set operator of intersection, and $||$ is the set operator to count the number of items. Moreover, we define following parameters:

Definition G: A set of keywords including in a query
$\quad n$: The number of keywords in **G**
$\quad k_i$: The i'th keyword in **G** $(1 \leq i \leq n)$
$\quad \mathbf{K}_i$: The set of bibliographies covered by k_i
$\quad \mathbf{B}$: The set of bibliographies covered by **G**
$\quad m$: The number of keywords derived from **G**
$\quad r_j$: The j'th keyword derived from **G** $(1 \leq j \leq m)$
$\quad \mathbf{R}_j$: The set of bibliographies covered by r_j

Figure 5 shows a status of coverage by **B** and $\mathbf{R}_j$ in the universal set **U**, which means all bibliographic data in the system. The bibliographic data covered by all keywords in **G** is $\mathbf{B} = \bigcap_{i=1}^{n} \mathbf{K}_i$. Then, in a retrieved set, the positive instance is those **B** that decreases the number of bibliographies and the negative instance is those $\overline{\mathbf{B}}$ that increases the number of them. Thus the true positive instance is $\mathbf{B} \cap \bigcup_{j=1}^{m} \mathbf{R}_j$, and the false positive instance is $\overline{\mathbf{B}} \cap \bigcup_{j=1}^{m} \mathbf{R}_j$. TP and FP are represented by the following equations.

$$TP = \frac{|\, \mathbf{B} \cap \bigcup_{j=1}^{m} \mathbf{R}_j\, |}{|\, \mathbf{B}\, |}, \; FP = \frac{|\, \overline{\mathbf{B}} \cap \bigcup_{j=1}^{m} \mathbf{R}_j\, |}{|\, \overline{\mathbf{B}}\, |}$$

For instance, in Figure 5, the true positive instance is $\mathbf{B} \cap \mathbf{R}_2$ and the false positive instance is $\overline{\mathbf{B}} \cap \mathbf{R}_2$.

Using the definitions of TP and FP, we illustrate ROC graphs by plot of points (FP, TP) using different $Minsup$ values as different classifiers. We can choose the best classifier based on the value of $Minsup$.

4   Performance Evaluation of Mondou for INSPEC

Our **Mondou** system can handle full INSPEC database, it includes 3,012,864 titles from January 1987 to December 1997. In this section, we only use 330,562

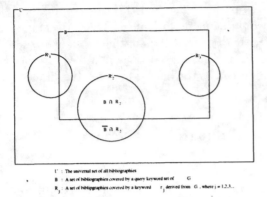

Fig. 5. Status of bibliographies covered by keywords in a bibliographic database.

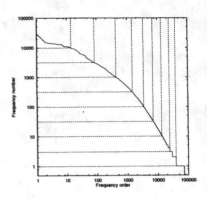

Fig. 6. The frequency of keywords.

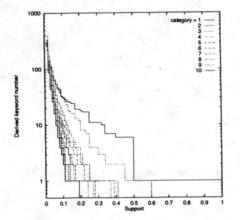

Fig. 7. Average number of derived keywords for each category.

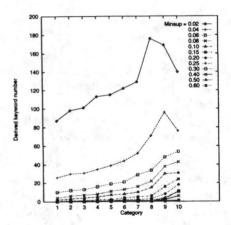

Fig. 8. Average number of derived keywords by *Minsup*.

titles in 1997, $| U |$, to evaluate the performance of our algorithm. In Figure 6, we present the frequency of keywords in `Title` attribute. Moreover, using the log scale graph for frequency of keywords, we can divide into several classes in order to draw curves on an ROC graph, which is shown in Figure 6. We also plot averages of (FP, TP) derived from specific keywords, considering the categories in an ROC graph.

In order to avoid the unstability of an interaction between *Minconf* and *Minsup*, we try to fix $Minconf = 0.01$, and we change *Minsup* gradually. The average numbers of keywords derived from the sampled keywords are shown in Figure 7 for each category. It is clear that the lower *Minsup* becomes, the more rapidly the number of derived keywords becomes. It is also shown that higher frequency of keywords are, the lower *support* of the keywords is. The numbers of derived keywords are different for each category, when *Minsup* is fixed.

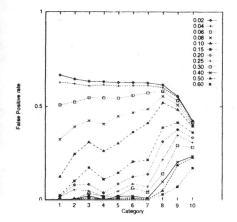

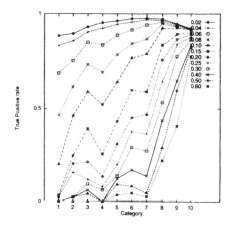

Fig. 9. Value of FP for each category.

Fig. 10. Value of TP for each category.

Table 1. The optimal $Minsup$ derived from the ROC convex hull.

Slope	Classifier ($Minsup$)
$0.0000 \sim 0.0638$	AllPos
$0.0638 \sim 0.2597$	0.02
$0.2597 \sim 0.2746$	0.08
$0.2746 \sim 0.4126$	0.10
$0.4126 \sim 0.4535$	0.20
$0.4535 \sim 0.5478$	0.25
$0.5478 \sim 0.5751$	0.30
$0.5751 \sim 0.9644$	0.40
$0.9644 \sim 3.6601$	0.60
$3.6601 \sim 4.4116$	0.60
$4.4116 \sim 12.906$	0.40
$12.906 \sim 227.06$	0.60
$227.06 \sim$	AllNeg

Table 2. The most optimal $Minsup$ derived from the ROC convex hull except categories from 8 to 10.

Slope	Classifier ($Minsup$)
$0.0000 \sim 0.0638$	AllPos
$0.0638 \sim 0.4791$	0.02
$0.4791 \sim 0.7195$	0.04
$0.7195 \sim 0.8103$	0.06
$0.8103 \sim 1.0589$	0.10
$1.0589 \sim 1.7351$	0.15
$1.7351 \sim 3.2032$	0.25
$3.2032 \sim 4.3497$	0.30
$4.3497 \sim 12.906$	0.40
$12.906 \sim 227.06$	0.60
$227.06 \sim$	AllNeg

Based ont the following values of $Minsup$ { 0.02, 0.04, 0.06, 0.08, 0.1, 0.15, 0.2, 0.25, 0.30, 0.4, 0.5, 0.6 }, we show the numbers of derived keywords in Figure 8. It is able to conjecture that TP will be higher derived from a lower frequent keywords, because derived keywords are increased to cover more the bibliographic items. Moreover Figure 9 and Figure 10 show that TP is rather than bigger than FP according to the $Minsup$–FP and $Minsup$–TP curves. So it is required to control the value of $Minsup$ according to the frequency of the keywords appeared in the query.

Figure 11 shows the ROC graph plotted by the averages of (FP, TP) for each category and each $Minsup$ with the boundary of the convex hull. Table 1 shows the best classifiers for each slope of iso-performance line, that is the best $Minsup$, in Figure 11. In Table 1, "AllPos" represents to derive all related keywords and "AllNeg" represents to derive no related keywords.

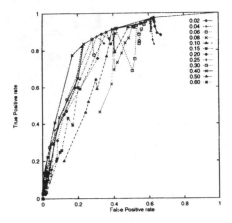
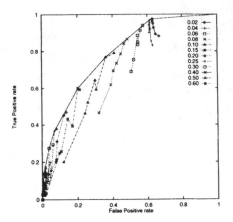

Fig. 11. The ROC graph of *Minsup* with the iso-performance line.

Fig. 12. The ROC graph of *Minsup* with the iso-performance line without categories from 8 to 10.

As shown in Figure 11, the ROC convex hull was pulled by a part of plots near the upper area and warped. It is also found that there is a jumping point where *Minsup* takes the value from 0.02 to 0.08 in Table 1 . It is also clear that lines in 8, 9, 10 categories converge, which are shown in Figure 9 and Figure 10.

This is the reason that such keywords in those categories only appear less than 10 times in the target INSPEC database, and that it is impossible to derived effective keywords from so few tuples. Therefore, in Figure 12, we present the ROC graph without such categories and show Table 2 having the optimal *Minsup* values.

By the way, $p(N)/p(P)$ of a keyword can be represented by $\frac{p(N)}{p(P)} = \frac{|\mathbf{U}| - |\mathbf{B}|}{|\mathbf{B}|}$, where $\mathbf{B}$ represents a set of bibliographic items covered by the keyword. | $\mathbf{B}$ | is given as the hit counts retrieved by the keyword, and | $\mathbf{U}$ | is $330,562$.

The ratio of error cost $c(y, N)/c(n, P)$ may be given by the system administrator. In this experience, we determine values of the cost not to derive any keywords for the meaningless categories from 8 to 10. From Table 2, when we have the value of slope (3) is not less than 227.06, it makes classifier to be All-Neg. Hence $\frac{|\mathbf{U}| - |\mathbf{B}|}{|\mathbf{B}|} \cdot \frac{c(y,N)}{c(n,P)} = 227.06$ leads $R_{error} = \frac{c(n,P)}{c(y,N)} = \frac{330562 - |\mathbf{B}|}{227.06 \times |\mathbf{B}|}$, where R_{error} is the error cost ratio of the false positive and true negative, so that the more expensive R_{error} is, the fewer retrieval omission is.

If R_{error} is substituted | $\mathbf{B}$ |$= \{10, 1\}$ for, then R_{error} becomes $\{145, 1455\}$. From these R_{error} values, *Minsup* are specified as shown in Table 3 and Table 4. Based on the values, the number of derived keywords, the ratio of no derived keyword and the sampled keywords (NDK) and the average value of *Minsup* are shown in Table 5.

The result by using our algorithm[3] is also shown in Table 5, where our algorithm reduces the number of derived keywords, if keywords are derived more than the maximum threshold *Maxkey* as described in Section 1.

Table 3. $Minsup$ at $R_{error} = 145$.

Category	$p(N)/p(P) \cdot 1/R_{error}$	Optimal $Minsup$
1	$0.0000 \sim 0.2211$	AllPos ~ 0.02
2	$0.2211 \sim 0.7139$	$0.02 \sim 0.04$
3	$0.7141 \sim 2.2706$	$0.04 \sim 0.25$
4	$2.2728 \sim 7.1847$	$0.25 \sim 0.40$
5	$7.2075 \sim 22.565$	$0.40 \sim 0.60$
6	$22.790 \sim 69.076$	0.60
7	$71.235 \sim 207.24$	0.60
8	$227.97 \sim 569.93$	AllNeg
9	$759.91 \sim 1139.9$	AllNeg
10	2279.7	AllNeg

Table 4. $Minsup$ at $R_{error} = 1455$.

Category	$p(N)/p(P) \cdot 1/R_{error}$	Optimal $Minsup$
1	$0.0000 \sim 0.0220$	AllPos
2	$0.0220 \sim 0.0711$	AllPos ~ 0.02
3	$0.0712 \sim 0.2263$	0.02
4	$0.2265 \sim 0.7160$	$0.02 \sim 0.04$
5	$0.7183 \sim 2.2487$	$0.04 \sim 0.25$
6	$2.2712 \sim 6.8839$	$0.25 \sim 0.40$
7	$7.0990 \sim 20.653$	$0.40 \sim 0.60$
8	$22.718 \sim 56.797$	0.60
9	$75.729 \sim 113.59$	0.60
10	227.19	AllNeg

Comparing the number of keywords in Table 5, it is found that the more frequent keywords in a query are, the fewer keywords are derived by the basic proposed algorithm, but the result is opposite to it by the ROC algorithm. We have the following reason:

By the mining association algorithm, if association rules are derived from a highly frequent keywords, then there are many retrieved bibliographies and the *support* is fewer relatively. By the basic algorithm, $Minsup$ is fixed so that only keywords which are frequent cooccurrent of the query keywords can exceed the threshold. As a result, a few keywords are derived from such frequent keywords.

By using the proposed ROC algorithm, if the frequency of query keywords is lower, then the value of $p(N)/p(P)$ becomes less so that the threshold is lower such value of $Minsup$ as shown in Table 3 and more keywords can exceed it to be derived.

It is also that the basic algorithm derives highly frequent keywords from very popular keywords, but the ROC algorithm can also derives low frequent keywords.

For example, by the basic algorithm with $Minsup = 0.08$, the keywords derived from "performance", which belongs to category 2 and appears 5,536 times, and to which the 8 keywords, { system(1), high(1), simulation(2),

Table 5. The derived result by our basic algorithm and ROC algorithms.

Category	Basic Algorithm $Support = 0.08$			ROC Algorithm $R_{error} = 145$			ROC Algorithm $R_{error} = 1455$		
	keyword number	NDK [%]	$Minsup$ average	keyword number	NDK [%]	$Minsup$ average	keyword number	NDK [%]	$Minsup$ average
1	5	0	0.08	89	0	0.02	265	0	AllPos
2	6	0	0.08	58	0	0.03	227	0	AllPos
3	8	0	0.08	4	35	0.17	103	0	0.02
4	9	0	0.08	2	80	0.34	82	0	0.03
5	10	0	0.08	2	95	0.50	5	15	0.16
6	12	0	0.09	2	94	0.60	2	56	0.34
7	12	0	0.10	1	94	0.60	1	88	0.49
8	8	4	0.18	0	100	AllNeg	2	64	0.60
9	8	13	0.31	0	100	AllNeg	3	36	0.60
10	10	3	0.27	0	100	AllNeg	0	100	AllNeg

Table 6. The average distances from the point $(1,0)$ on the ROC graph.

Category	Basic Algorithm ($Support = 0.08$)	ROC Algorithm ($R_{error} = 145$)		ROC Algorithm ($R_{error} = 1455$)	
	distance	distance	remainder	distance	remainder
1	0.8211	0.9477	0.1266	0.9510	0.1299
2	0.8940	0.9725	0.0785	0.9791	0.0851
3	0.9119	0.9008	-0.0111	1.0056	0.0937
4	0.9322	0.9857	0.0535	1.0156	0.0834
5	0.9926	0.9976	0.0050	0.9541	-0.0385
6	0.9929	0.9968	0.0039	0.9852	-0.0077
7	1.0262	1.0001	-0.0261	1.0013	-0.0249
8	1.0159	1.0000	-0.0159	0.9940	-0.0219
9	1.0351	1.0000	-0.0351	1.0229	-0.0122
10	1.1413	1.0000	-0.1413	1.0000	-0.1413

model(1), control(1), evaluation(2), analysis(1), network(1) }, are highly related, where the number in braces represents the category to which the keywords belong, and all of derived keywords belong to category 1 or 2, which hold high frequency of keywords. In the other case, when we have $Minsup = 0.02$, we derive additional keywords except of the above mentioned keywords and 71 keywords are derived totally. There are 10 keywords in category 1, 24 keywords in category 2, 29 keywords in category 3, and 8 keywords in category 4. It is clear that there are various keywords which have relatively low frequency in the category 3 and 4.

Next, we show the table 5 which presents the average distance between points (FP, TP) and the point $(1,0)$. On ROC graphs, when the distance is longer from the point $(1,0)$, the performance becomes higher. We conclude that the ROC algorithm shows higher performance than the basic algorithm on any R_{error} values. Therefore the ROC algorithm can derive low frequent keywords even though the basic algorithm derives only highly frequent keywords which are little significant as knowledge[3].

Moreover, when we focus on the gap of 0% and non 0% in Table 5, we have to pay an attention that the numbers of derived keywords is quite different. It seems that the frequencies of keywords, which effect on $p(N)/p(P)$, have a weak boundary. Thus, when we specifies R_{error} dynamically according to the frequencies of query keywords, it is very effective to apply our proposed method to determine the threshold values even in any situations.

5 Conclusion

The technique of data mining becomes to be used widely in various fields. However it is too hard to specify the effective thresholds. In this paper, we evaluate the performance of rules based on the characters of ROC graphs. Moreover, considering the ROC convex hull method, we try to determine the threshold values of our proposed algorithm. In the future, to derive more meaningful rules, we need to extend ROC evaluation much more.

Acknowledgment

A part of this work is supported by the grant of Scientific Research (10780259, 08244103) from the Ministry of Education, Science, Sports and Culture of Japan. We thank Nissho Iwai Infocom Co., Ltd. for the support of "OpenText" Database.

References

1. Feldman, R.: *Practical Text Mining*, Second Symposium on Principles of Data Mining and Knowledge Discovery (PKDD-98), Nantes, France (1998).
2. Han, J., Nishio, S., Kawano, H. and Wei, W.: *Generalization-based Data Mining in Object-oriented Databases Using an Object Cube Model*, Data and Knowledge Engineering, No.25, pp.55-97 (1998).
3. Kawahara, M., Kawano, H. and Hasegawa, T.: *Implementation of Bibliographic Navigation System with Text Data Mining*, Systems Science Vol.24, No.3, pp.101-118 (1998).
4. Kawahara, M. and Kawano, H.: *Performance Evaluation of Bibliographic Navigation System with Association Rules from ROC Convex Hull Method*, Transactions of the IPSJ:Database, Vol.40, No.SIG3(TOD1), pp.105-113 (1999).
5. Provost, F. and Fawcett, T.: Analysis and Visualization of Classifier Performance: Comparison under Imprecise Class and Cost Distributions, *Proc. of 3rd Int'l Conf. on Knowledge Discovery and Data Mining (KDD-97)*, pp. 43-48 (1997).
6. Srikant, R. and Agrawal, R.: Mining Generalized Association Rules, Dayal, U., Gray, P. M. D. and Nishio, S. (Eds.), *Proc.21st VLDB*, pp. 407-419, Zurich, Switzerland (1995).

Specifying and Reasoning about Workflows with Path Constraints

Wenfei Fan[1] and Scott Weinstein[2]

[1] Temple University, Philadelphia, PA 19122, U.S.A.
fan@joda.cis.temple.edu
[2] University of Pennsylvania, Philadelphia, PA 19104, U.S.A.
weinstein@linc.cis.upenn.edu

Abstract. One of the most common frameworks for specifying workflows is *control flow graph* [2, 10, 12, 18]. Although a control flow graph can depict local execution dependencies of the tasks in a workflow, it is not capable of expressing global dependencies and is not helpful in reasoning about workflow properties. Recently, a path constraint theory has been developed for semistructured data [1, 6–9]. It has proven useful for semantic specification and query optimization in the database context. To overcome the limitations of flow control graphs, this paper generalizes the path constraint theory to specify and analyze workflows. More specifically, it proposes a path constraint language and shows that both local and global dependencies, as well as sub-workflows, can be naturally expressed in the language. This allows one to reason about workflows in the traditional logic framework. The paper also establishes the decidability of several verification problems associated with workflows.

1 Introduction

A workflow is loosely defined as a collection of cooperating, coordinated tasks (activities) designed to achieve a goal. Workflow management requires process modeling, i.e., specifying the flow of control among the tasks that make up a workflow. One of the most common frameworks for process modeling is *control flow graph* [2, 10, 12, 18]. A typical control flow graph represents the tasks in a workflow as vertices, and the successor relation on the tasks as edges. It has two distinguished nodes, called the *initial task* and the *final task*, respectively. It also specifies local execution dependencies of the tasks: whether all the successors of a task must be executed concurrently ("AND" relation), or it suffices to execute only one of them non-deterministically ("OR" relation). An example of control flow graphs is shown in Figure 1, which depicts a simplified workflow of the review process for conference papers. It specifies the following local dependencies:

- *AND:* when the initial task "distribute papers" is finished, all its successors, i.e., "review 1", "review 2" and "review 3", must be executed.
- *OR:* when the task "joint review" is finished, one of its successors, i.e., either "accept" or "reject", should be executed.

Flow control graphs are commonly used in commercial workflow management systems (see [12] for a survey of commercial workflow products).

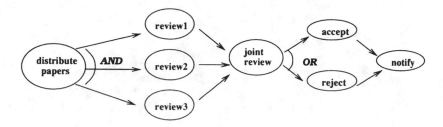

Fig. 1. A control flow graph

As observed by [10], control flow graphs, however, are not capable of expressing global execution dependencies. For example, the following global dependencies cannot be depicted in a flow control graph:

- if "accept" is executed, then none of the reviews votes for "reject";
- if "reject" is executed, then one of the reviews votes for "reject".

Worse still, control flow graphs are not very helpful when it comes to reasoning about workflow properties. There are a number of verification problems associated with workflows (see, e.g., [13]). Among them are:

- *Consistency problem:* given a finite set Σ of (local and global) dependencies, whether there is a workflow execution satisfying all the dependencies in Σ.
- *Implication problem:* given a finite set $\Sigma \cup \{\varphi\}$ of (local and global) dependencies, whether all the workflows satisfying Σ also satisfy φ.

As it stands, a control flow graph does not help in answering these questions.

To overcome the limitations of control flow graphs, a number of models and languages have been proposed. Among them are triggers (see, e.g., [12]), temporal constraints [16, 17] and Concurrent Transaction Logic (CTR) [4, 10]. As pointed by [10], triggers are not expressive enough to specify global dependencies. While temporal constraints are capable of expressing both local and global dependencies, many important questions in connection with reasoning about these constraints are still open. CTR is a well established formalism and is powerful enough to specify both local and global dependencies. It also allows reasoning about workflow properties. However, CTR is not designed for workflow specifications and is somewhat complicated. It is not clear whether its full expressive power is needed for studying workflows.

Recently, a path constraint theory [1, 6–9] has been developed for semistructured data as found for instance on the Web. It has proven useful for semantic specification and query optimization in the database context. In addition, path constraints are definable in first-order logic and as a result, reasoning about path constraints can be carried out in the traditional logic framework.

This paper generalizes the path constraint theory to specify and analyze workflow properties. To do this, we propose a path constraint language and show that, despite the simple syntax of the language, it is capable of expressing both local and global dependencies, as well as sub-workflows, i.e., workflows contained in a task. In addition, the consistency and implication problems associated with workflows become the decision problems studied in first-order logic (see, e.g., [5]). In this setting, we establish the decidability of these problems.

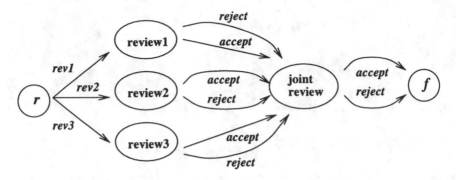

Fig. 2. A deterministic edge-labeled graph

An example. To demonstrate the use of path constraints in studying workflows, let us consider again the workflow of paper reviews with slight modification. We represent the workflow as a rooted, edge-labeled, directed, deterministic graph, as shown in Figure 2. In this graph, the root r denotes the initial task "distribute papers", f is the final task "notify", the vertices represent the tasks, and the edges represent the successor relation on the tasks. These are the same as in Figure 1. However, Figure 2 differs from Figure 1 in the following aspects:

- Its edges are labeled with actions. More specifically, an edge labeled K from node o to o' stands for that o' is activated by action K after task o is executed.
- The "AND" and "OR" relations are not depicted in Figure 2. We use path constraints to describe these relations.

Observe that Figure 2 is deterministic, i.e., the edges emanating from any node in the graph have distinct labels. The rational behind this is that for each task, any action leads to just one of its successor tasks.

Local and global dependencies given above can be captured by the following, which are typical path constraints studied in this paper.

- *Local dependencies:*
  - *AND:* all the actions following the initial task must be executed.
    $$\forall x\,(\epsilon(r,\,x) \rightarrow \exists y\,(rev1(x,\,y)) \wedge \exists y\,(rev2(x,\,y)) \wedge \exists y\,(rev3(x,\,y)))$$
  - *OR:* one of the actions following the task "joint review", i.e., either "accept" or "reject", is executed. Moreover, OR is exclusive.
    $$\forall x\,(\_\cdot\_(r,\,x) \rightarrow \exists y\,(accept(x,\,y) \vee reject(x,\,y)))$$
    $$\forall x\,(\_\cdot\_(r,\,x) \rightarrow \forall y\,\neg(accept(x,\,y) \wedge reject(x,\,y)))$$
    Similarly, we can specify these for "review 1", "review 2" and "review 3".
- *Global dependencies:* if "joint review" takes action *accept*, then none of the reviews takes action *reject*. In contrast, if "joint review" takes action *reject*, then one of the reviews must take action *reject*.
  $$\forall x\,(\_\cdot\_\cdot accept(r,\,x) \rightarrow \forall y\,\neg(\_\cdot reject(r,\,y)))$$
  $$\forall x\,(\_\cdot\_\cdot reject(r,\,x) \rightarrow \exists y\,(\_\cdot reject(r,\,y)))$$

Here r is a constant denoting the root node (the initial task), variables range over vertices (tasks), edge labels are treated as binary relations, the symbol "." stands for concatenation, and a path is a sequence of edge labels separated by

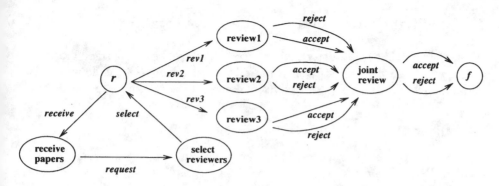

Fig. 3. A graph representing sub-workflows

"·". We treat a path α as a logic formula $\alpha(x, y)$, which is true in a graph if α is a sequence of edge labels from x to y. In particular, ϵ denotes the empty path, i.e., the path of length zero, and "_" is the wildcard symbol, which matches any edge label. For example, $rev1 \cdot accept(r, x)$ and $\_ \cdot \_(r, x)$ are path formulas and both lead to the task "joint review" in Figure 2. A path constraint is a first-order logic sentence of a certain form defined in terms of paths.

We can also specify sub-workflows by means of path constraints. For example, suppose that the initial task is composed of sub-tasks "receive papers" and "select reviewers", as depicted in Figure 3. This can be expressed by:

$$\forall x\, (\epsilon(r, x) \rightarrow receive \cdot request \cdot select(r, x))$$

When costs are attached to the actions, i.e., edge labels, this form of path constraints can also be used to study workflow optimization, along the same lines of query optimization investigated in the database context [1, 6–9].

In summary, we model a workflow as a deterministic edge-labeled graph with a set of path constraints. The graph depicts the basic structure of the workflow, and the path constraints specify its dependencies. In this way, we can clearly separate the basic structure of a workflow from its dependencies. This allows us to focus on the essential properties of the workflow, and to interpret the consistency and implication problems for workflows as the satisfiability and implication problems for path constraints, respectively. For example, let Σ be the set of path constraints given above, and a workflow execution be represented as a path expression θ from the initial task r to the final task f:

$$rev1 \cdot accept \cdot reject(r, f) \wedge rev2 \cdot accept \cdot reject(r, f) \wedge rev3 \cdot accept \cdot reject(r, f)$$

Then the question whether the execution is legal (i.e., whether $\bigwedge \Sigma \wedge \theta$ is satisfiable) is an instance of the satisfiability problem for path constraints. Moreover, let φ be a path constraint: $\forall x\, (\_ \cdot \_ \cdot accept(r, x) \rightarrow \forall y\, \_ \cdot accept(r, y))$. Then the question whether any workflow satisfying Σ must also satisfy φ (i.e., whether Σ implies φ) is an instances of the implication problem for path constraints.

Organization. The rest of the paper is organized as follows. Section 2 presents our model for workflows and define our path constraint language. Section 3 establishes the decidability of the consistency and implication problems for workflows. Section 4 extends our model and constraint language to capture temporal specifications. Finally, Section 5 identifies directions for further research.

2 Specifying workflows with path constraints

We model a workflow as a deterministic, rooted, edge-labeled, directed graph together with a set of path constraints. In this section, we present the deterministic graph model and define a path constraint language for workflow specifications.

2.1 Deterministic structures

We represent the basic structure of a workflow as a rooted, edge-labeled, directed graph with deterministic edge relations. In the graph, the root node denotes the initial task, another distinguished node denotes the final task, the vertices represent tasks, the edges represent the successor relation on the tasks, and the edge labels denote the actions that activate the tasks. In addition, the edges emanating from any node in the graph have distinct labels. Formally, such graphs can be described as logic structures of a signature

$$\sigma = (r,\ f,\ E),$$

where r is a constant denoting the root (the initial task), f is another constant denoting the final task, and E is a finite set of binary relation symbols denoting the edge labels (actions). We require that these structures are deterministic, i.e., for any edge label $K \in E$ and node a in the structure, there exists at most one edge labeled K going out of a. Such structures are called *deterministic structures*. A deterministic structure G is specified by giving $(|G|,\ r^G,\ f^G,\ E^G)$, where $|G|$ is the set of nodes in G, r^G is the root node, f^G is another distinguished node in $|G|$, and E^G is the set of binary relations on $|G|$.

2.2 A path constraint language

We first present the notions of paths and path expressions.

A path is a sequence of edge labels. Formally, paths are defined by the syntax:

$$\rho ::= \ \epsilon \mid K \mid K \cdot \rho$$

Here ϵ is the empty path, $K \in E$, and $\cdot$ denotes path concatenation. We have seen many examples of paths in Section 1, e.g., $rev1 \cdot accept$.

A path ρ is said to be a *prefix* of ϱ, denoted by $\rho \preceq \varrho$, if there is γ such that $\varrho = \rho \cdot \gamma$. For example, $rev1 \cdot accept \preceq rev1 \cdot accept \cdot reject$.

The *length* of path ρ, denoted by $|\rho|$, is defined by:

$$|\rho| \ = \ \begin{cases} 0 & \text{if } \rho = \epsilon \\ 1 & \text{if } \rho = K \\ 1 + |\varrho| & \text{if } \rho = K \cdot \varrho \end{cases}$$

For example, $|\epsilon| = 0$ and $|rev1 \cdot accept| = 2$.

A path can be expressed as a first-order logic formula $\rho(x, y)$ with two free variables x and y, which denote the tail and head nodes of the path, respectively. For example, $rev1 \cdot accept$ can be described as $\exists z\,(rev1(x, z) \cdot accept(z, y))$. We write $\rho(x, y)$ as ρ when the parameters x and y are clear from the context.

By treating paths as logic formulas, we are able to borrow the standard notion of models from first-order logic (see, e.g., [11]). Let G be a deterministic structure, $\rho(x, y)$ be a path formula and a, b be nodes in $|G|$. We use $G \models \rho(a, b)$ to denote that $\rho(a, b)$ holds in G, i.e., there is a path ρ from a to b in G.

By a straightforward induction on the lengths of paths, it can be verified that deterministic structures have the following property.

Lemma 1. *Let G be a deterministic structure. Then for any path ρ and node $a \in |G|$, there is at most one node b such that $G \models \rho(a, b)$.*

This shows that any task of a workflow can be uniquely identified by a path.

Next, we define path expressions. Let x and y be variables or constants r, f. *The set of path expressions from x to y*, denoted by $PE(x, y)$ and ranged over by $p(x, y)$, is the smallest set having the following properties:

- For any path $\rho(x, y)$ from x to y, $\rho(x, y) \in PE(x, y)$;
- If $p_1(x, y)$ and $p_2(x, y)$ are in $PE(x, y)$, then so are $p_1(x, y) \wedge p_2(x, y)$, $p_1(x, y) \vee p_2(x, y)$ and $\neg p_1(x, y)$.

We further define *the set of path expressions from x*, denoted by $PE(x, \_)$ and ranged over by $q(x, \_)$, to be the smallest set such that

- if $p(x, y) \in PE(x, y)$, then $\exists y\, p(x, y)$, $\forall y\, p(x, y)$ and $p(x, f)$ are in $PE(x, \_)$, where f is the constant denoting the final task;
- if $q_1(x, \_), q_2(x, \_) \in PE(x, \_)$, then so are $q_1(x, \_) \wedge q_2(x, \_)$, $q_1(x, \_) \vee q_2(x, \_)$ and $\neg q_1(x, \_)$.

Intuitively, a path expression $p(x, y)$ in $PE(x, y)$ is a logic formula about paths from x to y, and it has at most free variables x and y. Similarly, $q(x, \_)$ in $PE(x, \_)$ is a logic formula about paths from x, and it has at most free variable x. It is easy to see that $p(x, y)$ (resp. $q(x, \_)$) has the following properties:

- There are only finitely many paths occurring in $p(x, y)$ (resp. $q(x, \_)$).
- The wildcard symbol "$\_$" is definable in $p(x, y)$ (resp. $q(x, \_)$) by using disjunction "$\vee$" when E, the set of binary relations in signature σ, is finite.

Using path expressions, we define our path constraint language P^w as follows.

Definition 1. *A path constraint of P^w is an expression of one of the following forms:*

- *The* local form: $\forall x\, (p(r, x) \rightarrow q(x, \_))$;
- *The* global form: $\forall x\, (p(r, x) \rightarrow s(r, \_))$;
- *The* inclusion form: $\forall x\, (p(r, x) \rightarrow t(r, x))$;

where $p(r, x), t(r, x) \in PE(r, x)$, i.e., path expressions from the root node r to x, $q(x, \_) \in PE(x, \_)$, i.e., a path expression from x, and $s(r, \_) \in PE(r, \_)$, i.e., a path expression from root r.

For example, all the path constraints given in Section 1 are expressible in P^w by rewriting the paths containing wildcard "$\_$". More specifically, the constraints specifying AND and OR relations can be expressed as P^w constraints of the local form, those specifying global dependencies can be expressed in the global form, and those specifying sub-workflows can be expressed in the inclusion form.

Let G be a deterministic structure and φ be a P^w constraint. The notion of G *satisfying* φ, denoted by $G \models \varphi$, can be interpreted using the standard definition of models from first-order logic [11].

3 The consistency and implication problems

In this section, we first describe the consistency and implication problems for workflows, and then establish the decidability of these problems.

The *consistency problem* for workflows is to determine, given any finite set of (local and global) dependencies, whether there exists a workflow execution that satisfies all the dependencies.

The *implication problem* for workflows is the problem of determining, given any finite set $\Sigma \cup \{\varphi\}$ of (local and global) dependencies, whether all the workflows that satisfy Σ also satisfy φ.

These problems are important because, among others, we want to detect and correct errors in workflow specifications and executions as early as possible.

As demonstrated earlier, we can express local and global dependencies as path constraints of P^w. In addition, we can represent a workflow execution as a path expression θ from the initial task r to the final task f, i.e., $\theta \in PE(r, f)$. Therefore, the consistency and implication problems for workflows can be interpreted as the (finite) satisfiability and (finite) implication problems for P^w, respectively.

The *(finite) satisfiability problem for P^w* is the problem to determine, given any finite subset Σ of P^w and $\theta \in PE(r, f)$, whether there is a (finite) deterministic structure G such that $G \models \Sigma$ and $G \models \theta$.

Let $\Sigma \cup \{\varphi\}$ be a finite subset of P^w. We use $\Sigma \models \varphi$ ($\Sigma \models_f \varphi$) to denote that Σ *(finitely) implies* φ. That is, for every (finite) deterministic structure G, if $G \models \Sigma$, then $G \models \varphi$. The *(finite) implication problem for P^w* is the problem to determine, given any finite subset $\Sigma \cup \{\varphi\}$ of P^w, whether $\Sigma \models \varphi$ ($\Sigma \models_f \varphi$).

See Section 1 for instances of these decision problems for P^w.

Proposition 1. *The satisfiability and finite satisfiability problems for P^w are decidable in linear-space, and so is the consistency problem for workflows.*

Proposition 2. *The implication and finite implication problems for P^w are decidable in linear-space, and so is the implication problem for workflows.*

Proof sketch of Proposition 1: We prove Proposition 1 by giving a small model argument (see [5] for in-depth presentations of small model arguments): *Claim:* Let Σ be a finite subset of P^w and $\theta \in PE(r, f)$. If there is a deterministic structure G such that $G \models \Sigma$ and $G \models \theta$, then there is a finite deterministic structure H such that $H \models \Sigma$, $H \models \theta$ and in addition, the size of H is linear in the length of Σ and θ.

This claim suffices. For if it holds, then the satisfiability and the finite satisfiability problems for P^w coincide and thus are decidable. To show the claim, assume that there is a deterministic structure G satisfying Σ and θ. To construct H, let $Pts(\Sigma, \theta) = \{\varrho \mid \varrho \text{ is a path, } \varrho \text{ occurs in } \theta \text{ or in some } \phi \in \Sigma\}$, and $CloPts(\Sigma, \theta) = \{\rho \mid \varrho \in Pts(\Sigma), \rho \preceq \varrho\}$. Here $\rho \preceq \varrho$ means that path ρ is a prefix of ϱ, as defined in Section 2. Let $E_{\Sigma, \theta}$ be the set of edge labels appearing in some path in $Pts(\Sigma, \theta)$. Then we define H to be $(|H|, r^H, f^H, E^H)$ such that

- $|H| = \{f^G\} \cup \{a \mid a \in |G|, \rho \in CloPts(\Sigma, \theta), G \models \rho(r^G, a)\}$; note that $r^G \in |H|$ since $\epsilon \in CloPts(\Sigma, \theta)$;

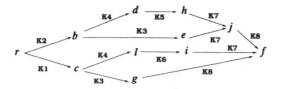

Fig. 4. An example workflow

- $r^H = r^G$, $f^H = f^G$;
- for all $a, b \in |H|$ and $K \in E$, $H \models K(a, b)$ iff $K \in E_{\Sigma,\theta}$ and $G \models K(a, b)$.

It is easy to verify that $H \models \Sigma$ and H is deterministic, since G has these properties. By Lemma 1, the size of $|H|$ is at most the cardinality of $CloPts(\Sigma, \theta)$, which is no larger than the length of Σ and θ. ∎

Proposition 2 can be verified along the same lines.

4   Incorporating temporal specifications

In [15], Klein proposed two forms of constraints, which are commonly used in workflow specifications. Below are two typical Klein constraints on the workflow depicted in Figure 4.

Form 1: if task l is executed, then e must also be executed (before or after l).
Form 2: if d and g are both executed, then d is executed earlier than g.

Klein constraints of the first form can be expressed as P^w constraints of the global form: $\forall x\, (K1 \cdot K4(r, x) \rightarrow \exists y\, (K2 \cdot K3(r, y)))$. Note that here we use the property described in Lemma 1: we identify the tasks l and e with paths $K1 \cdot K4$ and $K2 \cdot K3$, respectively. However, Klein constraints of the second form specify a temporal ordering, which is not expressible in P^w.

To capture this, we introduce a temporal relation *no_later*. Let G be a graph representing a workflow and a, b be two vertices in G. The relation *no_later* is interpreted as follows: *if $G \models no\_later(a, b)$ then a is executed no later than b*. In graph representation, this relation is depicted as edges labeled with *no_later*. The relation *no_later* is a pre-order, i.e., reflexive and transitive.

Formally, we extend the signature σ defined in Section 2 to be

$$\sigma^t = (r,\ f,\ E,\ no\_later).$$

Here r, f and E are the same as presented in Section 2, and *no_later* $\notin E$. We model a workflow as a deterministic structure G of σ^t satisfying the following.
(1) The relation *no_later* is a pre-order, i.e., G must satisfy the following:

reflexive condition: $\forall x\, no\_later(x, x)$
transitive condition: $\forall x\, y\, z\, (no\_later(x, y) \wedge no\_later(y, z) \rightarrow no\_later(x, z))$.

(2) The temporal semantics of the successor relation is explicitly captured by *no_later*. That is, for any edge label $K \in E$ and nodes a, b in the structure G, if $G \models K(a, b)$ then $G \models no\_later(a, b)$.

Now we extend P^w by including constraints of the *Klein's form*:

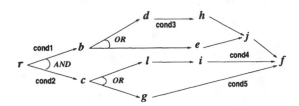

Fig. 5. A control flow graph with transition conditions

$$\forall x\, y\ (p(r, x) \wedge q(r, y) \rightarrow no\_later(x, y)).$$

Here $p(r, x)$ and $q(r, y)$ are path expressions from root r to x and y, respectively. It asserts that if tasks x and y are both executed, then x is executed no later than y. For example, $\forall x\, y\ (K2 \cdot K4(r, x) \wedge K1 \cdot K3(r, y) \rightarrow no\_later(x, y))$ asserts that if tasks d and g are both executed, then d is executed no later than g, referring to Figure 4. Here again we use the property described in Lemma 1: we identify the tasks d and g with paths $K2 \cdot K4$ and $K1 \cdot K3$, respectively.

It should be mentioned that by treating the relation no_later as a pre-order, we do not require the graphs to be acyclic.

It is not hard to show that Propositions 1 and 2 still hold in this new setting, by using a slight modification of the proof of Proposition 1 given in Section 3. In other words, the consistency and implication problems for workflows remain decidable when the temporal relation no_later is incorporated.

We should remark that there are many other ways to treat temporal (modal) operators in first-order logic. See, e.g., [3] for detailed discussions.

5 Conclusion

To overcome the limitations of control flow graphs, we have proposed an approach based on path constraints [1, 6–9] to specifying and analyzing workflows. We have defined a path constraint language, P^w, and demonstrated how to model a workflow as a deterministic, rooted, edge-labeled, directed graph with a set of P^w constraints. We have shown that P^w is capable of expressing both local and global dependencies, as well as sub-workflows. In addition, we have established the decidability of the consistency and implication problems for workflows.

Several questions are open. First, in general flow control graphs, some transition conditions may be attached to edges, as shown in Figure 5. In other words, some actions are executed only if certain transition conditions are met. A question here is: do the decidability results established here still hold in the presence of transition conditions? The answer to this question varies depending on how the transition conditions are defined. It should be mentioned that this question is also open for CTR when it is used to specify workflows [10].

Second, complex workflows may involve iteration, synchronization and failure recovery [2, 14]. We need to extend our model and path constraint language to capture such complex semantics.

Finally, can path constraints help in reasoning about the equivalence of workflows, and therefore, help in optimizing workflows?

Acknowledgements. We thank Ming-Chien Shan for suggestions.

References

1. S. Abiteboul and V. Vianu. "Regular path queries with constraints". In *Proc. 16th ACM Symp. on Principles of Database Systems (PODS'97)*, 1997.
2. G. Alonso, D. Agrawal, A. El Abbadi, M. Kamath, R. Günthör, and C. Mohan. "Advanced transaction models in workflow contexts". In *Proc. 12th Intl. Conf. on Data Engineering (ICDE'96)*, 1996.
3. H. Andréka, J. van Benthem, and I. Németi. "Back and forth between modal logic and classical logic". In *Bulletin of the IGPL*, Vol. 3(5): 685-720, 1995.
4. A. J. Bonner. "Workflow, transactions and datalog". In *Proc. 18th ACM Symp. on Principles of Database Systems (PODS'99)*, 1999.
5. E. Börger, E. Grädel, and Y. Gurevich. *The classical decision problem*. Springer, 1997.
6. P. Buneman, W. Fan, and S. Weinstein. "Path constraints on semistructured and structured data". In *Proc. 17th ACM Symp. on Principles of Database Systems (PODS'98)*, 1998.
7. P. Buneman, W. Fan, and S. Weinstein. "Interaction between path and type constraints". In *Proc. 18th ACM Symp. on Principles of Database Systems (PODS'99)*, 1999.
8. P. Buneman, W. Fan and S. Weinstein. "Query optimization for semistructured data using path constraints in a deterministic data model". In *Proc. 7th Intl. Workshop on Database Programming Languages (DBPL'99)*, 1999.
9. P. Buneman, W. Fan, and S. Weinstein. "Path constraints in semistructured databases". To appear in *J. Comput. System Sci. (JCSS)*.
10. H. Davulcu, M. Kifer, C. R. Ramakrishnan, and I. V. Ramakrishnan. "Logic based modeling and analysis of workflows". In *Proc. 17th ACM Symp. on Principles of Database Systems (PODS'98)*, 1998.
11. H. B. Enderton. *A mathematical introduction to logic*. Academic Press, 1972.
12. D. Georgakopoulos, M. Hornick, and A. Sheth. "An overview of workflow management: From process modeling to workflow automation infrastructure". In *Distributed and Parallel Databases*, 3(2): 119 - 153, April 1995.
13. A. H. M. ter Hofstede, M. E. Orlowska, and J. Rajapakse. "Verification problems in conceptual workflow specifications". In *Data & Knowledge Engineering (DKE)*, 24(3): 239-256, 1998.
14. D. Hollingsworth. "The workflow reference model". WfMC standard TC00-1003, 1995. Available from http://www.aiim.org/wfmc/mainframe.htm.
15. J. Klein. "Advanced rule-driven transaction management". In *IEEE COMPCON.*, 1991.
16. M. P. Singh. "Semantical considerations on workflows: An algebra for intertask dependencies". In *Proc. 5th Intl. Workshop on Database Programming Languages (DBPL'95)*, 1995.
17. M. P. Singh. "Synthesizing distributed constrained events from transactional workflow specifications". In *Proc. 12th IEEE Intl. Conf. on Data Engineering (ICDE'96)*, 1996.
18. D. Wodtke and G. Weikum. "A formal foundation for distributed workflow execution based on state charts". In *Proc. 6th Intl. Conf. on Database Theory (ICDT'97)*, 1997.

Prototyping Web-Based SmartFlow Multi-application System Using Smart Card Technology

Patrick C. K. Hung   Kamalakar Karlapalem

Department of Computer Science
University of Science and Technology
Clear Water Bay, Kowloon, Hong Kong.
e-mail: {cshck,kamal}@cs.ust.hk

Abstract. These days smart cards are replacing traditional magnetic cards for payment transactions. One of the main reasons is the enhanced security capabilities built into a smart card. Most of the related works in smart card only concentrates on the single application such as network access control, prepaid phone card or debit card. With popularity in web technologies, there is a trend towards smart cards being used for different electronic commerce applications such as electronic purse for payment transaction over Internet. But the payment protocols proposed so far do not support negotiation, bargaining or privacy issues between the parties. Based on the framework of CapBasED-AMS (a web based secure workflow management system), we developed a prototype system called SmartFlow to demonstrate multi-applications on the Internet using a smart card. The main focus of this paper is to present the framework of SmartFlow and demonstrate a negotiation and bargaining protocol for electronic commerce activities in both static and dynamic environment. We have already implemented the prototype system with these functionalities.

1   Introduction

Internet is a new media for conducting business activities and facilitating electronic commerce [1]. The Internet is largely insecure because of its open access to the public even though several security protocols are in place. Most of the related works of smart card concentrates only on payment applications like Mondex [3, 5, 18] and CyberCash [19]. They do not support untraceable secure digital money and are not applicable for on-line Internet payment environment [17]. Moreover, some of the related work concentrates only on the single application or even the security aspects of hardware/firmware, the encryption method and the key management, or they propose the on-line shopping protocol for exact payments (no change given). Further, the shopping protocols proposed so far do not support negotiations, bargaining or privacy among the parties. Even though some related works [6, 7] discuss about negotiation, they only consider the static approach in negotiation and bargaining for business activities.

We developed a web-based workflow system called "CapBasED-AMS" (Capability-based and Event-driven Activity Management System) [11, 12, 13, 14, 15, 16] that will be used to support electronic commerce activities. The CapBasED-AMS deals with the management and execution of activities. Based on the framework of CapBasED-AMS, we model the business activities with the technology of smart card to develop another multi-application system called SmartFlow [9]. The security and privacy issues of SmartFlow are described in [10]. The main focus of this paper is to present the framework of SmartFlow (see figure 1) to demonstrate multi-applications on the Internet using a smart card. It includes a secure token-based payment model, a protocol for negotiation and bargaining during business activity for both static and dynamic environments. In the figure 1, *SmartFlow Multi-Application System* is based on the framework of *CapBasED-AMS* with the database to support the electronic commerce activities using smart card. There is a set of *Application Servers* for supporting different applications that interact with the *SmartFlow*. For example, one *Application Server* is for payment transaction, and another is for software dissemination, etc. On the client side, the user accesses the *SmartFlow* system from a *Trusted Client* through a *Browser* using HTTP and TCP/IP protocol. Each *Trusted Client* is attached with a *Smart Card Reader* to interact with the use *Smart Card*. Finally, we implemented the prototype system SmartFlow to demonstrate the concepts developed in this paper.

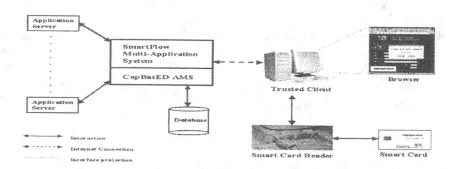

Fig. 1. Architecture of SmartFlow Multi-Application System

The rest of the paper is organized as follows, section 2 presents the overview of features and functionalities supported by SmartFlow Multi-Application System, section 3 describes the negotiation and bargaining approach, and section 4 presents the conclusion and future research.

2   Web-based SmartFlow Multi-Application System

Fig. 2. Denominations in SmartFlow

In SmartFlow system, the digital money is called SmartCash that has a particular denomination scheme. In our prototype system, we use the value of Hong Kong dollar bills 1000, 500, 100, 50, 20 and 10 as shown in figure 2. The system will generate SmartCash including unique identifiers (sequence numbers) such as the serial number on dollar bills. The advantage of applying denomination scheme is to have the ability to protect the digital money because each SmartCash denomination bill is individually protected by a security mechanism. Therefore, each SmartCash denomination bill can be monitored, verified and validated individually. That is, when the SmartCash is stolen (by hacking in Internet) by a third party, the loss is only limited to the SmartCash stolen but it does not reveal SmartCash left in the smart card. Also decrypting SmartCash denominations does not help decrypt other SmartCash denomination bills. That is, each SmartCash denomination bill is individually encrypted. As shown in figure 3, there are four types of parties involved in SmartFlow.

The *Bank* assigns SmartCash of different denominations as *Customer*'s request, and generates identifiers for different denominations based on the card issuer code of smart card. The *Bank* will only insert the unique identifier of denomination into the relevant slot in the smart card when the issuer code is matched. It means that only the card with the correct card issuer code can hold it, and no other card can hold it. Therefore, the value of denomination can only be redeemed by the *Bank* which holds the key to declare the value of the denomination note. This hidden note value scheme is able to hide the SmartCash value because the third party can only view the SmartCash identifier and not the value of each SmartCash bill even after decrypting the SmartCash. The *Customer* can only know how much value is in the smart card without knowing the card issuer code and the identifier of each denomination. This concept is called blind SmartCash in order to prevent the other parties except *Bank* to know the content of SmartCash, and this scheme can prevent the hacker from capturing

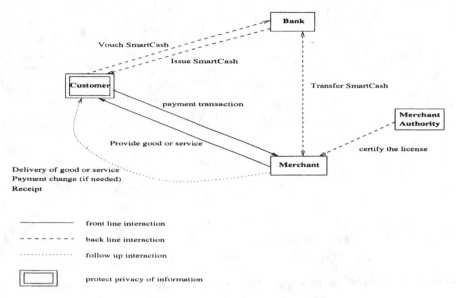

Fig. 3. Parties Involved in SmartFlow

the SmartCash and produce the counterfeit money.

The *Bank* verifies the SmartCash identifier, if the identifier is verified then the *Merchant* receives the money. All these interactions between *Bank* and *Customer* or *Bank* and *Merchant* are called back line interactions because they only involve *Bank* to *Customer* or *Bank* to *Merchant* at the back of *Customer* to *Merchant* business activity. In the front line interaction, the privacy of *Customer* information must be protected. It means that the *Merchant* does not know the personal information of the *Customer*, especially the private information. The *Customer* trusts and knows certain information about the *Merchant* to provide goods or services. Also the payment module of *Merchant* is provided and certified by the trusted *Bank* with some security features, e.g., prevention of duplicate, or counterfeit SmartCash to be inserted or retrieved from smart card.

3 Negotiation and Bargaining between Customer and Merchant

There are different ontologies on the concepts of negotiation and bargaining in different business environments. In the retail business environment, a customer may negotiate with the retailer about the terms of goods or service to purchase (e.g., payment method, value-added services such as extended warranties, special gift wrapping, discount, etc). The customer may also bargain about the price with the retailer. But for some other retail business environment, there is no bargaining or negotiation like supermarket or video shop. But in an auction environment, a customer is actually bargaining with other customers for the auctioned goods or service. In SmartFlow, the protocol and mechanism for negotiation and bargaining can be supported in static and dynamic environments by smart card. First of all, smart card is used for the identity of participants in order to authenticate the trusted parties. Secondly, smart card is acted as a mobile agent to collect and retrieve the information during negotiation and bargaining activities. Lastly smart card can be used to distinguish the affinity for neighours' recommendations.

3.1 Static Negotiation and Bargaining

Before the execution of business activity, the *Customer* can store information and constraints for negotiation and bargaining on the smart card. For example, the *Customer* can define the *Good or Service Identifier* that is to be purchased, the *Expected Price* that is the maximum price the *Customer* would like to pay, the *Event List* represents the list of events related to this business activity, and the *Condition Expression* is used to define the logical expression of the events. For example:

Static Negotiation and Bargaining Specification

Good or Service Identifier	: Microsoft Windows 98
Expected Price	: Hong Kong Dollar 650
Event List	: I. Shipping_Service(Mail)
	II. Refund_Policy(14 days)
Condition Expression	: I AND II

In this example, the customer is looking for the product *Microsoft Windows 98* and the expected price is *Hong Kong Dollar 650*. Further, the event list contains two events *I. Shipping_Service(Mail)* and *II. Refund_Policy(14 days)* . The condition expression is *I AND II* so it means that the customer requires both events to be satisfied. Based on the events raised, an Event-Condition-Action Rule [2] (ECA Rule) is triggered within SmartFlow system. When events are raised, conditions in the corresponding ECA rules are evaluated, and corresponding actions are triggered if the conditions are satisfied. In this example, the business activity can be successfully executed if there is a merchant who can provide the *Microsoft Windows 98* at the price of *Hong Kong Dollar 650* and can satisfy both *Event I AND II*.

In figure 4, the *Customer* inserts the smart card into the trusted terminal which may be the personal computer of *Customer* at home or even though a terminal at the *Bank*. SmartFlow will assign a trusted *Negotiation and Bargaining Agent* for searching the appropriate *Merchant* that can satisfy the given specifications and conditions. First of all, the agent will try to find a set of potential merchants. Then it will select the most appropriate *Merchant* based on the *Locator* and *Recommendor*. The *Locator* is an agent that will find the merchant that is geographically close to the *Customer*. In this example, the agent will only search those *Merchant* candidates which are located in the same area as the *Customer*. The *Recommendor* is also an agent that based on the *Past Record* and *Rating* from other *similar Customers* called *Neighbour*'s recommends a merchant to the customer. The *Neighbour* has high affinity to the customer in terms of goods and services ordered in the past. The *Customer* can rate the goods or service from a specific *Merchant* and the agent can adapt the *Collaborative Filtering Technology* [4, 8] to identify the neighbours. In this example, the agent will find neighbours who have also purchased Windows 98 for the customer and then evaluates merchants on their rating. Note that the agent does not release any information about the *Customer* to *Merchant* and also the information of *Merchant* to the *Customer* before binding. This blind scheme can also protect the privacy of *Customer* from the third parties and also ensure that the secure business information of *Customer* will not be released to parties who do not need to know. In this way, by using set of static conditions a merchant is selected and to process the business activity. There is no more searching after the merchant is selected. This is suitable for finding the best fixed price shop to buy certain type of goods, such as books.

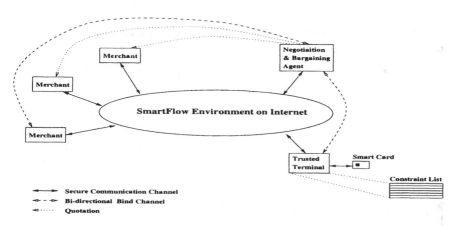

Fig. 4. Static Negotiation and Bargaining in SmartFlow

3.2 Dynamic Negotiation and Bargaining

In addition to the static negotiation and bargaining approach, the smart card can also be used to interact with the *Merchant* in dynamic negotiation and bargaining approach. The *Customer* needs to generate a set of ECA rules just like the static approach, but the *Customer* may need to interact with the *Merchant* dynamically at run time for negotiation and bargaining. In SmartFlow, there is a standard *Negotiation and Bargaining Template* (application domain specific) to generate the ECA rules for both *Customer* and *Merchant* as shown below:

Customer : Negotiation and Bargaining Template

Product ID	:	Windows 98
Type	Condition	Comment
Expected Price	HKD 650	Maximum price
Warranty	1 Year	Minimum period
Refund Policy	2 Week	Minimum period
Shipping	Mail	Method of shipping required
Others	...	

In the *Customer* side, it specifies the *Product ID* to purchase. The *Expected Price* of product that is the maximum price to be paid, and the *Warranty* of product that is the minimum period of time for warranty service required by *Customer*. The *Refund Policy* is the minimum period of time for *forgiving refund policy*. The *Shipping* is the method of product shipping required. Furthermore, there may be *Other* requirements specified in the template by *Customer*. Similarly, the *Merchant* may also define a set of constraints for the *Product ID* in the template as shown below.

Merchant : Negotiation and Bargaining Template

Product ID	:	Windows 98
Type	Condition	Comment
Expected Price	HKD 600	Minimum price
Warranty	1 Year	Maximum period
Refund Policy	3 Week	Maximum period
Shipping	Mail, Self Pick-up	Method of shipping offered
Discount	5 percentage off if amount $\geq$ HKD 2000	Conditional offer
Others	...	

Based on the information stored in the template, the SmartFlow generates a set of ECA rules to define runtime database schema that is stored in the smart card for the *Customer* and in the trusted server for the *Merchant*. On the *Customer* side, the ECA rules are generated and stored in the smart card as shown below.

Customer : ECA Rules in Customer Smart Card

Product ID :		Microsoft Windows 98	
ECA ID	Event	Condition	Action
ECA1	start	found(merchant)	request1(Price $\leq$ HKD 650)
ECA2	replied(request1)	approved(request1)	request2(Warranty $\geq$ 1 Year)
ECA3	replied(request2)	approved(request2)	request3(Refund Policy $\geq$ 2 Weeks)
ECA4	replied(request3)	approved(request3)	request4(Shipping $\approx$ Mail)
ECA5	replied(request4)	approved(request4)	proceed(payment)

On the other hand, the *Merchant* also has a set of ECA rules to handle the negotiation and bargaining of a good or service which is stored in the server as shown below.

Merchant : ECA Rules in Trusted Merchant Server

Product ID :		Microsoft Windows 98	
ECA ID	Event	Condition	Action
ECA11	received(Price)	Price $\geq$ HKD 600	approved(request)
ECA12	received(Warranty)	Warranty $\leq$ 1 Year	approved(request)
ECA13	received(Refund Policy)	Refund Policy $\leq$ 3 Weeks	approved(request)
ECA14	received(Shipping)	Shipping $\approx$ Mail or Self Pick-up	approved(request)
ECA15	received(Any)	Amount $\geq$ HKD 2000	discount(10 percentage off)

The *Customer* inserts the smart card into the trusted terminal (shown in figure 5), the SmartFlow system will assign a trusted *Negotiation and Bargaining Agent* for searching the appropriate *Merchant* that can provide the specific product or specific service sought. Similar to the static environment, the agent will try to find a set of potential *Merchants* which are able to provide the goods or service. Then, it will select the most appropriate *Merchant* based on the criteria as in static approach and bind it to the *Customer* by using blind scheme. After that, the agent will initiate a negotiation and bargaining activity as shown in figure 6 that involves the ECA rules stored in the smart card and merchant's server, and with human intervention (if required). This is a kind of negotiation and bargaining activity because both parties do not know each others ECA rules and intention. Moreover, no third party can participate except the SmartFlow agent.

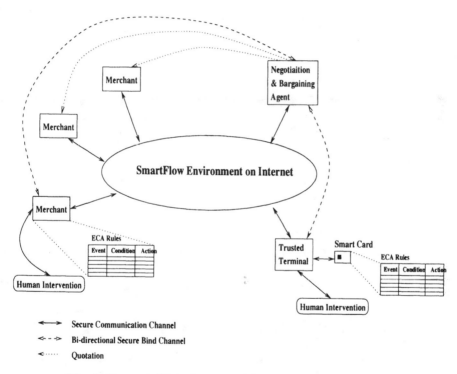

Fig. 5. Dynamic Negotiation and Bargaining in SmartFlow

During the execution of negotiation and bargaining activity as shown in figure 6, the ECA rules will be retrieved from the smart card of *Customer* when the *Merchant* is waiting for reply from *Customer*. The agent acts as a mediator to determine the results of negotiation and bargaining based on the balance of benefits of both parties. In this example, the *Customer* initially requests *Price* ≤ *650* by rule ECA1 in smart card. The *Merchant* can accept the condition of *Price* ≥ *HKD 600* from the *Customer*. The *Matcher* is pro-active in helping the *Customer* in bargaining. It can start from the *Customer* side with the lowest bid, and from the *Merchant* with the highest bid, and after multiple interactions they may decide on a mutually beneficial *Price* as HKD 625. Otherwise, the

Customer may try a different merchant. Also, this does not limit a *Customer* or *Merchant* from bargaining and negotiating with multiple merchants or customers sequentially or concurrently. This depends on the functionality of the *Matcher* module. Similarly, all other requests of *Warranty* $\geq$ *1 Year, Refund Policy* $\geq$ *2 Weeks* and *Shipping* $\approx$ *Mail* can be handled either concurrently or sequentially by the *Matcher* module. If there is no ECA rule to handle the event from either *Customer* or *Merchant*, human intervention will be involved. The negotiation and bargaining agent will activate *Customer* or *Merchant* for taking decisions. For example, after the rule ECA1 from the smart card of *Customer* is triggered, the *Merchant* will approve the first request and so on. The *Merchant* can also act as an activator to initiate the negotiation and bargaining with the *Customer*. For example, using rule ECA15 the *Merchant* can offer discount if the amount purchased by the *Customer* exceeds Hong Kong Dollar 2000 at anytime.

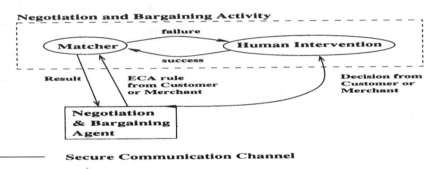

Fig. 6. Negotiation and Bargaining Activity

4 Conclusion and Future Research

As electronic commerce gets successful in a big way, there is a need to support payment transactions in Internet. We use the concept of smart card to emulate the purse and support micro-payment transactions across Internet. We have implemented a prototype SmartFlow Electronic Commerce System wherein we can store SmartCash, use SmartCash for executing micro-payment transactions with change, and provide high security and privacy. We also present a static and dynamic approach for negotiation and bargaining in business activities. We are currently working on the multi-applications by using Java Card on Internet, workflow on smart card, payment risk management and evaluation. Further, we are also developing the protocol for supporting bargaining and negotiation of payment types, receipts and different currencies. We are now integrating the prototype system with the Java card and XML on Internet.

References

1. N. R. Adam and Y. Yesha. Electronic Commerce: Current Research Issues and Applications. *Springer-Verlag Berlin Heidelberg*, 1996.
2. S. Chakravarthy and D. Mishra. Snoop: An Expressive Event Specification Language For Active Database. *Data and Knowledge Engineering*, November 1994.
3. A. M. Froomkin. Flood Control on the information Ocean: Living with Anonymity, Digital Cash, and Distributed Database. *http://www.law.miami.edu/ froomkin/articles/oceanno.htm*.
4. N. Good, J. B. Schafer, J. Konstan, A. Borchers, B. Sarwar, J. Herlocker, and J. Riedl. Combining Collaborative Filtering with Personal Agents for Better Recommendations. *Proceedings of the 1999 Conference of the American Association of Artifical Intelligence (AAAI-99)*, July 1999.
5. J. Graves. Electronic Payment Protocols: Mondex. *http://www.ini.cmu.edu/ jg4o/90-742/mondex.html*.
6. R. Guttman and P. Maes. Agent-mediated Integrative Negotiation for Retail Electronic Commerce. In *the Workshop on Agent Mediated Electronic Trading (AMET'98)*, 1998.
7. R. Guttman and P. Maes. Cooperative vs. Competitive Multi-Agent Negotiations in Retail Electronic Commerce. In *the Second International Workshop on Cooperative Information Agents (CIS'98)*, 1998.
8. J. Herlocker, J. Konstan, A. Borchers, and J. Riedl. An Algorithmic Framework for Performing Collaborative Filtering. *Proceedings of the 1999 Conference on Research and Development in Information Retrieval*, August 1999.
9. P. C. K. Hung and R. S. C. Ieong. A Framework for Smart Card Payment on Internet. In *the Hong Kong International Computer Conference'98*, 1998.
10. P. C. K. Hung and R. S. C. Ieong. Security and Privacy Issues in Smart Card Payment on Web. In *the CSCWID'98, 15 - 18 July, 1998, Tokyo, Japan*, 1998.
11. P. C. K. Hung and K. Karlapalem. A Framework for Modeling Security and Integrity in CapBasED-AMS. In *the Hong Kong International Computer Conference'97*, 1997.
12. P. C. K. Hung and K. Karlapalem. Task Oriented Modeling of Document Security in CapBasED-AMS. In *IPIC'96, Rethinking Documents*, Boston, November, 1996.
13. P. C. K. Hung and K. Karlapalem. A Paradigm for Security Enforcement in CapBasED-AMS. In *Second IFCIS Conference on Cooperative Information Systems*, CHARLESTON, June, 1997.
14. P. C. K. Hung and K. Karlapalem. A Logical Framework for Security Enforcement in CapBasED-AMS. In *to appear in International Journal on Cooperative Information Systems*, December, 1997.
15. P. C. K. Hung, H. P. Yeung, and K. Karlapalem. CapBasED-AMS: A Capability-based and Event-driven Activity Management System (Demonstrations). *Proceedings of the ACM SIGMOD Conference on Management of Data*, June 1996.
16. K. Karlapalem and P. C. K. Hung. Security Enforcement in Activity Management System. In *NATO-ASI on Workflow Management Systems and Interoperability*, Turkey, August, 1997.
17. Mondex. Mondex for the Internet. *http://www.mondex.com/mondex/*.
18. P. I. M. C. P. Release. PRIVACY INTERNATIONALS MONDEX COMPLAINT IS UPHELD: Electronic Cash is anything. *http://www.privacy.org/pi/activities/mondex/*, 1996.
19. A. H. Stephen Crocker, Brian Boesch and J. Lum. CyberCash: Payments Systems for the Internet. *http://info.isoc.org/HMP/PAPER/181/*.

Temporally Constrained Workflows*

Eleana Kafeza   Kamalakar Karlapalem
Department of Computer Science
Hong Kong University of Science and Technology
Clear Water Bay, Kowloon, HONG KONG
e-mail: `{kafeza, kamal}@cs.ust.hk`

Abstract

Although temporal aspects during a workflow execution are of major importance, it is only recently that the problem of temporal coordination of workflow activities is being addressed. As the demand for time management in workflow applications increases, temporal coordination can no longer be limited to being a result of value dependencies between activities. It must be conceptualized, modeled and supported as a part of the WFMS. In this work, we propose a temporal process specification model and develop formalism to determine the consistency of the specification. In the execution level, we show that finer control on activities execution can be achieved by exploiting their temporal constraints. Furthermore, we discuss different scheduling policies to illustrate the trade-off between temporal-constraint violation and missed deadline.

1 Introduction

Workflow management systems emerged as a technology for the automation of business processes. Typical workflow applications include healthcare, education, telecommunications, manufacturing, finance, banking, and office automation. Workflow applications cater to highly competitive business environments and need to take full advantage of the existing technology. Web-based WFMS are being developed in order to support the demands of applications based on the web infrastructure. Most of web-based real time applications (such as, tele-medicine or video conferencing) need to access and display multimedia objects. Thus, the workflow systems supporting these applications/business processes need to access, display and manipulate multimedia objects that often reside in different sites. As a result, the workflow management system must be able to provide the tools for advanced temporal specification of presentation of multimedia objects modeled as workflow activities and at the same time schedule and monitor their execution. This requires checking the consistency of the specification and scheduling workflow

* This work has been partially funded by RGC CERG Grant HKUST 742/96E.

activities. Note that for complicated applications the workflow specification might be done at run-time, that is, dynamically.

A tele- medicine example: Assume that a doctor is treating a patient resident at a remote location. While the doctor is reviewing the patient history, the patient's previous X-rays have to be displayed on his monitor (maybe retrieved by the database of another hospital). Upon completion of the activity "show X-rays", the graphical results recent medical tests must be displayed at the same time, and while a query is executed on a database regarding similar cases is being executed. The whole file with the diagnosis is then shipped to the administration office for administrative work.

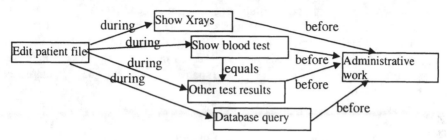

Figure 1 : Time constrained process specification

The fundamental issues that WMS must deal with, both theoretically and as a technology, are the coordination and control of multiple, possibly parallel or otherwise synchronized activities performed by different "processing entities" (agents). Temporal coordination can no longer be limited to being a result of value dependencies between activities: it must be conceptualized, modeled and implemented as a part of the WFMS.

During the workflow specification phase, users need to represent time-related information such as temporal relationships among multimedia activities, duration of activities, and deadlines that is checked for consistency. At run time, scheduling algorithms must execute activities according to the specification, detect temporal inconsistencies and adjust inconsistent execution to a consistent one whenever possible while trying to meet the deadlines.

In this paper, we present a formal model for incorporating time-related information in the workflow specification. Based on the existing WfMC model where a workflow is represented as a graph with nodes representing activities and edges parallel/serial execution, we augment the semantics of the edges by adding labels. Labels specify the temporal relationships between the associated activities. In this manner, temporal constraints are naturally incorporated in the existing model. We show how different kinds of consistency checking can be done at pre-processing time in order to verify the validity of the specification. In particular, we are concerned with specification, duration and deadline consistency. Furthermore, we present scheduling algorithms and actions that can be taken at run time in order to correct the possible inconsistencies during workflow execution.

The main objectives of this paper are:

- to incorporate in workflow specification phase temporal constraints. We translate different types of dependencies such as data, duration and temporal dependencies as binary temporal constraints among activities. In this way, we provide a unified model for specifying and handling time related dependencies.
- to support the proposed model with consistency checking functionality. Since in a workflow specification there are numerous dependencies, it is often possible that these dependencies contradict each other.
- to provide templates of algorithms for both global activities scheduling and agent scheduling.

Existing workflow commercial systems provide primitive support for time management, focusing on process simulations, assigning deadlines to activities and initiate exception handling upon missing a deadline at run time [1,3,5,11]. It is only recently that the need for time-management in workflow management system has been identified. Furthermore, there is limited research in the literature regarding time management in workflow systems [7,8] and none of these adequately addresses relative synchronization.

The paper is organized as follows. In section 2, we present the time-constrained process specification. In section 3, we describe the consistency checking algorithms. The workflow system architecture is described in section 4 and in the last section, we discuss scheduling policies.

2 Temporal constraints in Workflow Model

We first develop the framework for modeling temporal constrains in a workflow. We assume a function $time(e)$ that returns the time of occurrence of event e.[1] The order of occurrence of activity start and completion events are used to define the temporal constraints in a workflow. Note that occurrence of events depict activity start and complete.

In a workflow instance an activity is an interval $[a_i(t_{start}), a_i(t_{complete})]$ where $a_i(t_{start})$ is the time t_{start} when the event $a_i(start)$ occurred and $a_i(t_{complete})$ is the time $t_{complete}$ when the event $a_i(complete)$ occurred.

We denote as $(a_i(t_{complete})$ ° $a_j(t_{start}))$ an instantaneous event where $a_i(t_{complete})$ = $a_j(t_{start})$. Instantaneous events represent rendezvous points where two activities meet and synchronize which each other. Note that in the implementation level equality can be interpreted according to the needs of the application.

Definition 1: A set of event occurrences Cv = { $a_1(t_x)$, $a_2(t_y)$, ...,$a_n(t_y)$: x,y are *start* or *complete*} constitute an *instantaneous event occurrence*, denoted as $(a_1(t_x)°a_2(t_y)°...°a_n(t_y))$, iff $a_1(t_x)=a_2(t_y)=...=a_n(t_y)$. ∎

We denote the deadline for activity instance a_i as *deadline*(a_i) (i.e., $time(a_i(complete))$; $a_i(t_{complete}) \leq deadline (a_i)$).

Given two activity intervals $[a_i(t_{start}), a_i(t_{complete})]$ and $[a_j(t_{start}), a_j(t_{complete})]$, there are thirteen time relations that can be associated [6]. In this work, for simplicity of presentation we concentrate on seven, namely, *before, meets, overlaps, starts, covers,*

---

[1] We assume that all the organizations adhere to a global clock whose variance does not affect the synchronization and scheduling of the workflows.

finishes, *equal* -we exclude their inverses (i.e., before is inverse of after, and so on). We denote temporal relations as TC = {**b, m, o, s, c, f, e**}, respectively. The relations with their meaning and the corresponding time constraints are depicted in Table 1. The first and second columns are the name and the symbol of the relation while the last column specifies the constraints imposed on the occurrences of the corresponding *start* and *complete* events by a temporal relation. ∎

Definition 2: Given two activities a_i and a_j, we say that they are constrained by relation $\rho_i \in$ TC denoted as $\rho_i(a_i,a_j)$, iff their intervals $[a_i(t_{start}), a_i(t_{complete})]$ and $[a_j(t_{start}), a_j(t_{complete})]$ satisfy the constraints of relation ρ_i of table 1.

Table 1: Temporal relations and their corresponding constraints

Relation	Symbol	Meaning	Constraint
a_i before a_j	**b**		$a_i(t_{start}) < a_i(t_{complete}) < a_j(t_{start}) < a_j(t_{complete})$
a_i meets a_j	**m**		$a_i(t_{start}) < a_i(t_{complete})^\circ a_j(t_{start}) < a_j(t_{complete})$
a_i overlaps a_j	**o**		$a_i(t_{start}) < a_j(t_{start}) < a_i(t_{complete}) < a_j(t_{complete})$
a_i starts a_j	**s**		$a_i(t_{start})^\circ a_j(t_{start}) < a_i(t_{complete}) < a_j(t_{complete})$
a_i covers a_j	**c**		$a_j(t_{start}) < a_i(t_{start}) < a_i(t_{complete}) < a_j(t_{complete})$
a_i finishes a_j	**f**		$a_j(t_{start}) < a_i(t_{start}) < a_i(t_{complete})^\circ a_j(t_{complete})$
a_i equal a_j	**e**		$a_i(t_{start})^\circ a_j(t_{start}) < a_i(t_{complete})^\circ a_j(t_{complete})$

Definition 3: Let $A = \{a_1,a_2,...,a_n\}$ be a set of activities and ρ a set of constraints on them. A *time-constrained process* P is a relation on A such that $P=\{(a_i,a_j) \mid a_i,a_j \in A$ and $\exists \rho_i(a_i,a_j) \in \rho\}$. ∎

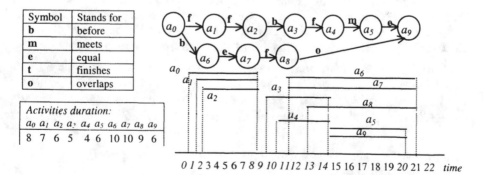

Symbol	Stands for
b	before
m	meets
e	equal
t	finishes
o	overlaps

Activities duration:

a_0	a_1	a_2	a_3	a_4	a_5	a_6	a_7	a_8	a_9
8	7	6	5	4	6	10	10	9	6

0 1 2 3 4 5 6 7 8 9 10 11 12 13 14 15 16 17 18 19 20 21 22 *time*

Figure 2 : Time constrained process specification

A time-constrained workflow process is an extension over existing workflow model represented a graph[2] $P_G(A,E)$ where A is the set of nodes, and E the set of labeled

---

[2]In existing workflow specification there exist two kinds of structural control information AND and OR. For simplicity of this presentation we do not include OR paths in our specification since their functionality in our model is similar to the one described in the WFMC specification.

edges. The nodes of the graph represent the activities and an edge is labeled ρ_i iff the activitiés linked by the edge are constrained by temporal relation ρ_i. The resulting graph is an *Interval Graph* [9,10].

Example 2: In Figure 2, we depict the time-constrained process specification graph and one possible execution of its activities. Constraints on activities express restrictions on the execution of the activities. For example, the label o between a_8 and a_9 denotes that activity a_9 can start executing after activity a_8 started and it should complete execution after a_8 completes. ∎

3   Consistency Checking

Workflow management systems exhibit three functional areas: *build-time, run time control* and *run time interactions*[4]. The workflow process and its constituent activities are defined in *built-time*. At *run-time,* the workflow definition is interpreted and the workflow engine creates instances and schedules the activities as specified to the appropriate agents.

As workflow definitions tend to get larger and workflow execution correctness requirements tend to be more complicated, the one way of facilitating correct scheduling is to guarantee the consistency of the definition. In the general case, this is infeasible because correctness requirements are application specific and no reasoning mechanism can be adopted to guarantee their consistency. In existing approaches, semantic constraints associated with initiation and completion time of activities are modeled as expressions which when evaluated determine the time of the next activity to be started.

One of the advantages of explicitly modeling time-related information is that we can use well-founded techniques to verify the consistency of the time-related specification. By using temporal reasoning in *built time* we can decide whether or not there can exist at least one execution that satisfies the temporal requirements.

Definition 3: A *time-constrained process execution specification* is a tuple $P_e(A, Ev, \rho, <)$ where $A = \{a_1,...a_n\}$ is a set of activities, $Ev = \{a_1(t_{start})\ a_1(t_{complete}), ...,(a_i(t_x)^{\circ}\ a_j(t_y)), ..., a_n(t_{start}), a_n(t_{complete})\}$ is the set of event occurrences of A and $<$ is a relation on Ev such that for every two activities related with temporal relation $\rho_i \in \rho$, the corresponding ordering of table 1 holds. ∎

Lemma: *An execution specification $P_e(A, Ev, \rho, <)$ is consistent iff $<$ is a partial order.* ∎

The above lemma is a specialization of the path consistency algorithm [9]. At the representation level, we model event information by an *event graph* where a node represent event occurrences, and edges their corresponding order of execution. This graph is derived by the Interval graph and is called Pointgraph [9]. From the above lemma we can conclude that *a time-constrained process specification is, consistent iff the corresponding event graph is acyclic.* The *event graph* is used for consistency verification and for dynamic scheduling (section 5). In the following figure, we present the event graph for the example 2 specification. Note that *instantaneous* events are represented as one node. The variable *time* denotes the time of actual event execution.

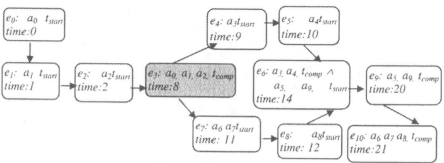

Figure 3 The event graph

4 System Architecture

The user specifies the time-constrained process using the *process definition tool* Figure 4. A separate tool the *verification tool* is responsible for checking the consistency of the specification by implementing the algorithms described in section 3. When an inconsistency is detected, the user is presented with the constraint that was violated and the specification is modified. Both of them communicate with the workflow database in order to acquire the necessary information about activities.

The workflow engine is responsible for the runtime control environment within the enactment service. In the workflow engine we incorporate a specific tool for scheduling, the *global scheduling tool*. This tool is a set of global scheduling algorithms, responsible for interacting with the agents, submitting activities and monitoring the execution. The global scheduler is responsible for identifying inconsistencies and initiation of the exception handling mechanism if required. Different instances might have different global schedulers depending on the workflow application requirements.

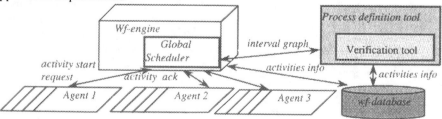

Figure 4 Temporal Workflow Management System architecture

5 Scheduling policies

5.1 Overview

In this section, we describe the functionality and the responsibilities of the global activity scheduler and the agents' schedulers. Since there are many scheduling policies with respect to the order and the time of event occurrence requests, we present *templates* of algorithms. *Global scheduler:* we present two different templates: *pseudo-static* and *dynamic* global scheduler template. In environments where workflow execution is expected to behave as specified a pseudo-static template is developed because it avoids the added complexity of the *dynamic* case. In the next section, we present example algorithms from both templates.

♦ *Agent scheduler:* we can choose among the well known policies:
- FIFO: schedule the start requests in the order they appear in the local queue
- EDF: from the start requests schedule the one with the earliest deadline first.
- SJB: schedule the start request that corresponds to the activity with the shortest expected duration.

The agent selection policy depends on the global scheduler specific algorithm. The FIFO policy results in a simplified implementation. There are cases where existing agents cannot incorporate additional logic for scheduling. EDF can result in achieving more deadlines but missing more temporal constrains [2].

5.2 Pseudo-static Global Scheduler Template

Static scheduling is not applicable in workflow applications since due to OR-constructs the complete execution path is not known a-priori. A pseudo-static scheduling is based on the idea of scheduling statically event requests until the next OR construct. After that, wait until the necessary information about which OR path is taken is available and schedule again until the next OR construct.

Within the limits of two OR constructs, the scheduler extends the partial order to a total order. Example policies for producing the total order are:

- breadth-first traversal of the event graph,
- a predefined order based on the event occurrence,
- assigning same priority to each level traversed.

The scheduler submits activities to the agents according to the total order. Each event when requested has a timestamp that denotes its order of execution. We assume a global counter that denotes the timestamp of the current event. Each agent upon the occurrence of an event (e.g. the initiation or completion of an activity) it updates the global counter with the event's timestamp. In the post-processing phase, the scheduler examines the completion time of events and checks whether occurred before their deadlines or based on the agents' acknowledgement checks whether an inconsistency occurred.

```
pseudo-static global scheduler template
    while not end of event graph do
    traverse the graph according to a policy until the next OR-construct
      for every visited node
          assign timestamp the order of traversal
          request the corresponding event occurrence by the responsible agent
          upon receiving acknowledgement post-processing

end
```

Figure 5 The pseudo-static scheduler template

An example of pseudo-static scheduler: suppose that we apply the pseudo-static approach to the event graph of Figure 3 using the vital-activities policy where e_4 and e_5 are vital. The pseudo-static scheduler would produce the following execution order: $(e_0,1)$, $(e_1, 2)$ $(e_2,3)$, $(e_3,4)$, $(e_4,5)$, $(e_5,6)$, $(e_7,7)$, $(e_8,8)$, $(e_6,9)$, $(e_9,10)$, $(e_{10},11)$. The agents adopt FIFO policy. Figure 6 presents the agent's FIFO scheduling policy.

Agent's FIFO for pseudo-scheduler template

repeat check counter
    if front(queue).timestamp equals counter+1   //agent has next event
    update the counter
    if   start event initiate activity else
    if completion event
        if activity already completed :inconsistency   // out of order
        else wait until the completion of corresponding activity //delay
        check instantaneous properties
        if actual completion time >deadline :inconsistency   //missed the deadline
until end-of-wf execution

Figure 6 : Agent's FIFO for pseudo-scheduler template

Suppose that Agent A is responsible for events $(e_0,1)$ and $(e_1, 2)$ and agent B is responsible for $(e_2,3)$ and $(e_3,4)$. At first Agent A initiates activity a_0 and sets the global clock to 1. It then starts a_1 and sets the global clock to 2. In the sequel agent B, initiates a_2 since it has a timestamp event with the number 3 that is the current clock plus one. It then checks event with timestamp 4 i.e. whether one of the activities $a0$, $a1$, *and* $a2$ have already been finished. If yes it signals inconsistency if not it waits until all of them complete. Based on the agent's capabilities, it can delay the completion of some such that all of them complete in the same time. Nevertheless, if they do not complete "instantaneously" (as specified by the application) the agent still reports an inconsistency.

5.3 Dynamic Global Scheduler Template

The dynamic algorithm based on the current state of the event graph, computes the set of enabled but not yet scheduled activities and dispatches them to the corresponding agents. Upon receiving a reply from an agent checks whether constraints and deadlines where satisfied and computes the next available set. This is the backbone for the dynamic scheduler. There can be several variations and extensions to this template for inconsistency privation or correction. Events are submitted based on the partial order as specified by the event graph and the total order actually depends on the agents' execution.

```
while not end-of-graph
    for all enabled events
        if start event submit activities to agents
        else if completion event request activities completion
    upon receiving ack post-processing
    compute new enabled set of events

end-while
```

Figure 7: the dynamic scheduler template

5.4 Example dynamic schedulers

A dynamic Global scheduler and FIFO agent: according to this policy, the main priority upon execution is to maintain the consistency of the temporal relationships. The scheduler delays specific events in order to achieve a consistent execution. When an out of order completion event is acknowledged, the global scheduler does not update its completion until the appropriate time. In this way, it delays subsequent events from being requested but does not cause a consistency violation. The drawback is that delays introduced by the scheduler may cause activities to miss their deadlines. This functionality is part of the post-processing phase. We delay activities completion in cases where meeting the constraints is more important that missing some deadlines.

Example 3: Suppose that $overlaps(a_0, a_1)$, then the consistent order of execution is $a_0 t_{start}$ $a_1 t_{start}$, and $a_0 t_{complet}$ and $a_1 t_{complete}$. Suppose that a_1 was finished earlier than expected and a_0 lasted more, then the *covers* constraint was actually executed. By delaying the actual completion of a_1 we can maintain the constraint but we might miss the deadline due to the completion delay. ∎

$$a_0 \quad \vdash\!\!-\!\!-\!\!-\!\!-\!\!\dashv \qquad d_1$$
$$a_1 \vdash\!\!-\!\!-\!\!-\!\!-\!\!-\!\!-\!\!\dashv\!-\bullet$$

Specified execution

$$a_0 \vdash\!\!-\!\!-\!\!-\!\!-\!\!-\!\!-\!\!\dashv \qquad d_1$$
$$a_1 \quad \vdash\!\!-\!\!-\!\!\dashv\!-\!-\!-\!-\!-\bullet$$

Actual execution

A dynamic global scheduler with EDF agent: when we are concerned more about *deadlines*, we incorporate agents that schedule using EDF policy. The global scheduler submits enabled activities to the agent. The agent then schedules first the activity with the earliest deadline.

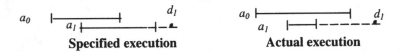

Specified execution   **Actual execution**

Example 4: Activities a_1, a_2 and a_3 are all after activity a_0. Activities, a_1 and a_2 are constrained by *finish* while activities a_2 and a_3 are constrained by *overlaps*. Agent *B* has to execute a_1 and a_3 and according to the EDF chooses a_3 first. In the resulting execution, a_2 meet the deadline but the *finish* constraint might be violated. ∎

In this section, we illustrated algorithms combining different scheduling policies for the global scheduler and the agent scheduling policy. These examples illustrate the trade-off between choosing an algorithm and the consistency violations that arise. Thus, by above set of examples we not only showed that traditional real-time scheduling algorithms can be applied, but also that the dependency between the global and agent scheduler needs to be taken into consideration for maintaining temporal constrain consistency and deadline compliance during workflow execution. We are currently developing a simulation test bed to evaluate and study these dependencies.

6   Conclusions

In this work, we proposed a framework for incorporating time-management information in workflow execution and specification. We argue that the current approach for handling time-related issues in workflow contexts is inadequate to support sophisticated time control, as needed by complex workflow applications.

We provided tools for consistency checking and templates of algorithms for scheduling. We demonstrated the functionality of the templates through example algorithms. Moreover, we exploited both aspects global activity scheduler and agent scheduling policies to illustrate how they can be combined depending on the application requirements and specification. In particular, we showed that the interdependencies between the global scheduler and agent schedulers in meeting the temporal constraints consistency and deadline compliance. Therefore, we advocated a comprehensive treatment for specifying temporal constraints and showed its utility in scheduling activities at run time. We have also brought out the limitations of standard scheduling algorithms in meeting the requirements of temporal workflow execution.

References

1.   A.Dogac, L.Kalinichenko, M.T. Ozsu, A.Sheth. Advances in Workflow Management Systems and Interoperability.*NATO Advanced Study Institute*. 1997.
2.   C.M. Krishna, K.G. Shin, Real time systems, McGraw-Hill Companies,Inc, 1997.
3.   F.Leymann and D.Roller. Business process management with flowmark. *Proceedings of the 39th IEEE Computer Society International Conference*, San Francisco, , February 1994.
4.   Glossary- A Workflow Management System Coalition Specification. Technical report, The Workflow Management System Coalition, Brussels, Belgium
5.   InConcert. Technical product overview. Xsoft. a division of xerox. 3400 Hillview Avenue, Palo Alto, CA 94304.
6.   J.F.Allen.Maintaining knowledge about temporal intervals.*Comm.ACM*, 26:832-843,1983.
7.   Johann Eder, E. Panagos, M. Rabinovich, Time Constraints in Workflow Systems, *(CAiSE 99), Heidelberg, Germany, 1999*.
8.   P. Dadam, M.Reichert, The ADEPT WfMS project at the university of Ulm, *1st European workshop on Workflow and Process Management (WPM'98)*, Zuerich, Switzarland, 1998.
9.   P.Van Beek. Reasoning about qualitative temporal information. *Artificial Intelligence*, 58:297-326,1992.
10. R. Dechter, I. Meiri and J. Pearl, Temporal Constraints Networks, *Artificial Intelligence*, 49, pp 61-95, Elsevier, 1991.
11. TeamWare Flow. Collaborate workflow system for the way people work. P.O.Box 780, FIN-00101, Helsinki, Filand.

A Simple MDCT-Based Speech Coder for Internet Applications

Cheuk Fai Kwong, Wing Man Pang, Hon Cheung Wu, and Keang-Po Ho

Department of Information Engineering,
The Chinese University of Hong Kong
Shatin, N.T., Hong Kong

E-mail: kpho@ie.cuhk.edu.hk

Abstract. A very simple speech coder is investigated based on modified discrete-cosine transform (MDCT), run-length coding, and entropy code. The speech signal is first passed through a MDCT, quantized by a uniform quantizer, and run-length coded to achieve good compression ratio. Not suitable for wireless communication systems, the speech coder is perfect for Internet and speech storage applications. With a performance far better than most speech coders for wireless applications, low data-rate speech of 3 kbit/s can be achieved with a signal-to-noise ratio (S/N) of about 12 dB.

1 Introduction

Currently, most of the speech-coding schemes are based on synthesis by analysis. Those schemes largely base on the speech generation model of human being by modeling the vocal tract as a time-varying linear filter. Code-excited linear prediction (CELP) [1]-[2] and its variations are the most popular scheme and used in G.723.1 [3], MPEG-4 [4], G.729 for PCS [5], US federal standard 1016 [6], G.728 [7], and all major digital cellular phone systems, including GSM, NA-TDMA (IS-54), and CDMA (IS-136).

G.723.1 [3] is a very popular speech coder for Internet phone and audiovisual teleconference applications. Variable data rate is provided by silence detection such that no data packet is transmitted during the silence period. However, most of the speech-coding schemes [1]-[7] are designed for wireless communications and even G.723.1 [3] is also intended for mobile communication. Internet and data storage is a total different environment and better speech coding can be designed accordingly. The fast expansion of Internet for various applications, including those for voice, is well known. Special speech coder for Internet applications is required to fully exploit the special characteristics of Internet and the TCP/IP protocol.

In wireless communication, the bit-error-rate (BER) is usually very high due to the noisy channel and entropy coding is not suitable to be applied. If entropy coding such as Huffman code or arithmetic code is used, a single bit error will

Fig. 1. Schematic diagram of the MDCT-based speech encoder.

induce the loss of synchronization till the next re-synchronization point (usually an end-of-block, EOB), resulting in a long burst of erroneous samples at the speech decoder output. In Internet applications, bit error is very unlikely but packet loss happens routinely. The EOB may also be eliminated if a packet contains a block and the packet boundary can be served as the block boundary. In data storage, bit error is also unlikely due to strong error protection. Therefore, may not applicable to speech coding for wireless applications, entropy coding can be used in Internet applications without any significant drawback.

Usually, a constant data-rate channel is provided in most wireless communication system for each subscriber. Most speech coding schemes generate a constant data rate. Even G.723.1 [3] has two fixed data-rates when voice activities are detected and its application over Internet uses an additional algorithm to detect speech activities. For Internet with variable data rate and packet length, there must exist a better speech coding method suitable for Internet applications.

With fixed data-rate and insensitive to single-bit error, though very suitable for wireless applications, CELP and its variations may not good for adaptation to Internet applications. For example, linear prediction generates a fixed number of coefficients regardless of the nature of the speech. All linear prediction coefficients are coded and generate a fixed number of bits per frame to be sent though a constant data-rate channel. Although an additional silence-detection algorithm partially solves the problem, a new speech coder with intrinsic silence elimination can solve the problem in a better way.

In this paper, transform coding is applied to speech coding. Although transform coding is widely used in image, video, and audio coding, for example, JPEG, MPEG video, and MPEG audio [8-12], its application in speech coding is far from successful. If speech coding is used for wireless communication, transform coding in its elementary form may not be suitable. Without entropy coding, transform cannot be used for speech coder having a data rate less than 8 kbit/s (for 8 kHz sampling rate) because each transformed coefficient requires at least one bit to be represented. Focusing on Internet applications, with run-length coding, the transform based speech coder here can achieve a data rate as low as 3 kbit/s with a signal-to-noise ratio (S/N) performance 1 dB better than the 8 kbit/s VSELP and CS-ACELP for IS-54 and G.729, respectively. For the Internet without bit error but with packet loss, the data packet can also serve as a natural boundary of a data block to eliminate the need of EOB re-synchronization point.

2 MDCT-Based Speech Coding

The optimal transform for transform coding is Karhunen-Loeve transform (KLT) for its optimal energy packing and orthogonal signal separation. However, fast transform algorithm is not available for KLT. Modified Discrete-cosine transform (MDCT) with fast transform algorithm [12] is found to be a good approximation of KLT for a wide range of signal, and DCT is used widely in JPEG and MPEG. The schematic diagram of the speech encoder is shown in Fig. 1. The decoder is

just the inverse function of the encoder with Huffman code decoder, de-quantizer, and inverse-MDCT.

MDCT is used instead of DCT to eliminate aliasing or blocking effect. In MDCT, 2N samples are transformed to N transform coefficients. To recover the signal, 2N transform coefficients are used to get back the original N samples. The aliasing or blocking effect can be removed due to overlapping of the samples. The definitions of forward and inverse MDCT is given below.

Forward MDCT:

$$y(j) = \sum_{i=0}^{2N-1} x(i) \cdot \sqrt{\frac{1}{N}} \cdot \cos \frac{(2i+1+N)(2j+1)\pi}{4N} \tag{1}$$

Inverse MDCT:

$$z(j) = \sum_{i=0}^{N-1} y(i) \cdot \sqrt{\frac{1}{N}} \cdot \cos \frac{(2j+1+N)(2i+1)\pi}{4N} \tag{2}$$

where $x(i)$ and $y(j)$ are the original samples and transform coefficients, respectively. MDCT can be calculated by fast transform algorithm using fast Fourier transform [12]. After MDCT, the transformed coefficients are quantized by

$$\tilde{y}_k = \left\lfloor \frac{y_k}{\Delta_k} - \frac{1}{2} \right\rfloor \tag{3}$$

where Δ_k is quantization level of the kth MDCT coefficient, and $\lfloor a \rfloor$ is the large integer smaller than a. The quantization level Δ_k depends on the required qualify factor of the encoded speech. By varying Δ_k, speech coded bit stream of different data rate can be generated for different qualify factor. The quantization level Δ_k of different MDCT coefficient may be designed according to the spectral response of human hearing mechanism. In this paper, for simplicity, quantization levels Δ_k are the same for all MDCT coefficients.

Table 1. Partial list of MDCT coefficient category

Category	Values included in category	Additional bits
1	-1, 1	0, 1
2	-3, -2, 2, 3	00, 01, 10, 11
3	-7, ..., -4, 4, ..., 7	000, ..., 011, 100, ..., 111
4	-15, ..., -8, 8, ..., 15	0000, ..., 0111, 1000, ..., 1111
... and more		

Table 2. Partial list of Huffman code

Run /Category	1	2	3	4	5	6
0	11	00	010	10001	10000110	101110110111001
1	011	10011	100000	101111100	1001000001011	101110110111000111000100
2	10110	10111111	1011101110	10000100100000	101110110111000111000101	101110110111000111000110
3	100101	1001000100	101110010100	101110110111000111000111	101110110111000111001000	101110110111000111001001

and more

Similar to JPEG, after the MDCT process, the large-value coefficients are usually concentrated in the beginning of the block, corresponding to low frequency components. There are many consecutive zeroes within the same MDCT block. Run-length coding gives a large compression ratio of the quantized MDCT coefficients. The quantized MDCT coefficients are separated into run length pairs (r, c), where r is the number of zeroes before the MDCT coefficients and c is the category of the MDCT coefficients.

Usually, the MDCT coefficients at the end of the block are all zeroes. To further save a large number of bits, after the last non-zero coefficient of the block, an EOB is inserted for the case of data storage, and a packet is sent for the case of Internet applications. If the last coefficient of the block is not zero, an EOB is also inserted or a packet is sent.

The non-zero quantized coefficients are divided into categories based their code length in binary representation as shown in Table I.

For each category, additional bits with length the same as the category number are required to define which member in the category is being coded. The negative value is coded to one's complement. These bits are appended to the Huffman codeword specified for the run length/category pair.

The run-length sequence is then encoded into bits using Huffman coding. Huffman coding is a simple entropy code suitable for lossless compression. The basic principle of Huffman coding is to code more frequent samples by fewer bits and vice versa.

Huffman code is found to be close to the entropy limit of the code. In Huffman code, no codeword is the prefix of the other codewords. For example, the run-length sequence can be coded as Table II.

The speech signal can thus be encoded by using MDCT followed by run-length code. The operation is very simple and fast MDCT algorithm is well studied. The complexity of the algorithm should be smaller than that for CELP and its variations.

3 Performance

Combined MDCT and entropy coding, the performance of the speech coding is improved and a high S/N can be achieved for low data rate. As indicated previously, the quantization levels Δ_k can be used to control the quality factor and data rate of the compressed speech. The compressed speech is a three male and three female speech downloaded from the Internet [13]. The log-spectral distance is used to calculated the S/N as

$$S/N = -10\log_{10}\left\{\frac{\int_0^\infty [10\log_{10} A(j\omega) - 10\log_{10} B(j\omega)]^2 d\omega}{\int_0^\infty [10\log_{10} A(j\omega)]^2 d\omega}\right\} \tag{4}$$

where $A(j\omega)$ and $B(j\omega)$ are the power spectrum of the input and output speech of the speech coder, respectively. This distortion measurement is phase invariant in which the phase shift of the speech is not considered as distortion. Table III is the compression ratio, data rate, and S/N of the MDCT based speech coder. The number of samples per MDCT frame is 64, corresponding to a processing delay of 8 ms. The compression scheme generates variable number of compressed data bits per frame and the data rate is the average data rate. When the compressed speech is transported though Internet, the packet length is varied packet to packet. Silence period is automatically detected because all MDCT coefficients are zeroes and the block just contains an EOB. An empty packet can be transmitted. No packet is required to transmit if a packet sequence number is used for synchronization purposes.

The simple MDCT speech coder is compared with other speech coders for wireless communication purpose [14]. Table IV is a list of other speech coding schemes, the corresponding data rate and S/N.

Fig. 2 shows the S/N as a function of data rate for the MDCT scheme in Table III and other speech coding for wireless applications in Table IV. From Fig. 2, the MDCT-based simple speech coder performs far better than other speech coding schemes. With the same data rate, the MDCT coder is performed at least 2 dB better than other standards. For the same S/N, 20 to 50% the data rate reduction can be achieved. For a data rate of only 3 kbit/s, the DCT coder can achieve the same S/N as the 8 kbit/s VSELP and CS-ACELP speech coder.

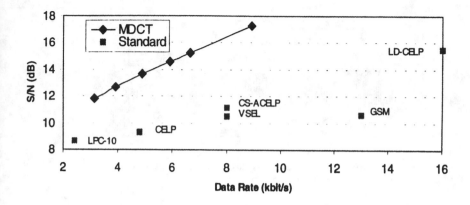

Fig. 2. S/N as a function of data rate of our MDCT scheme and other speech coding standards in Table IV.

Fig. 3 shows the speech waveform before (upper trace) and after (lower trace) the MDCT-based speech coder/decoder with a data rate of 4 kbit/s. From Fig. 3, the distortion with respect to the original speech waveform is relatively small. The major distortion is the smooth out of small amplitude waveform produced by MDCT. With MDCT coding, the major tones and pitches of the speech waveform are still retained.

4 Conclusions

A very simple MDCT-based speech coder is investigated. With run-length coding of the MDCT coefficients, very good quality speech coding can be achieved in low data rates. Because of the usage of entropy coding, appropriate for Internet applications, the speech coder is not suitable for wireless communication systems.

The S/N performance of the simple MDCT speech coder is found to be far better than most speech-coding schemes for wireless communication applications. The S/N of the MDCT speech coder is at least 3 dB better than that of other speech coders with the same data rate. A 4 kbit/s MDCT-based speech coder can achieve a S/N 1 dB better than VSELP and CS-ACELP, both having 8 kbit/s.

The speech coder is designed specially for Internet and data storage applications without bit errors. A compressed MDCT block may be transmitted within a data packet to avoid error propagation due to packet loss.

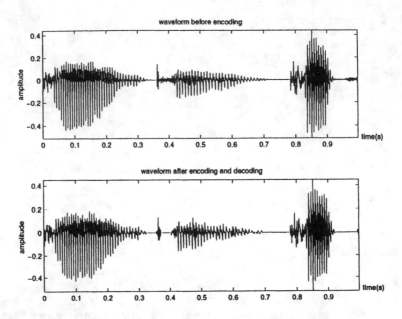

Fig. 3. The speech waveform before (upper) and after (lower) speech coding for a data rate of 4 kbit/s. The *x*-axis is the sample number.

Table 3. Compression ratio and bit rate at different quantization constant

Δ_t	Content size (bit)	Compression ratio	data rate (kbit/s)	S/N (dB)
0.15	66272	41.40	3.16	11.84
0.11	82666	33.19	3.94	12.65
0.08	103140	26.60	4.91	13.65
0.06	124197	22.09	5.91	14.60
0.05	139471	19.67	6.64	15.23
0.03	186791	14.69	8.89	17.30

Table 4. Other speech coding schemes and the corresponding S/N

Speech Coding	Standard	Data Rate (kbit/s)	S/N (dB)
LD-CELP	G.728	16	15.48
RPE-LPT	GSM	13	10.61
VSELP	IS-54	8	10.51
CS-ACELP	G.729, PCS	8	11.14
CELP	US FS 1016	4.8	9.31
LPC-10	US Gov.	2.4	8.66

References

[1]   M. R. Schroeder and B. S. Atal, "Stochastic coding of speech signals at very low bit rates," *ICC '84*, pp. 1610-1613.

[2]   B. S. Atal, V. Cuperman, and A. Gresho, editors: *Advances in Speech Coding*, Kluwer Academic Publishers, July 1991.

[3]   ITU Recommendation G.723.1 - Dual rate speech coder for multimedia communications transmitting at 5.3 and 6.3 kbit/s, 1996.

[4]   ISO/IEC CD 1449-3 (draft), Coding of audiovisual objects, Part 3: Audio, 1997.

[5]   ITU Recommendation G.729 - Coding of speech at 8 kbit/s using conjugate-structure algebraic-code-excited linear-prediction (CS-ACELP), 1996.

[6]   D. P. Kemp, R. A. Sueda, and T. E. Tremain, "An evaluation of 4800 bps voice coders," *Proc. ICASSP '89*, pp. 200-203.

[7]   ITU Recommendation G.728 - Coding of speech at 16 kbit/s using low delay code excited linear prediction, 1992.

[8]   Y. F. Dehery, M. Lever, and P. Urcum, "A MUSICAM source codec for digital audio broadcasting and storage," *ICASSP '91*, pp. 3605-3608.

[9]   K. Brandenburg, G. Stoll, F. Dehery, and J. D. Johnston, "The ISO-MPEG-1 audio: A generic standard for coding of high-quality digital audio," *J. Audio Engr. Soc.*, vol. 42, pp. 780-792, 1994.

[10]   ISO/IEC 11172-3, "Information technology- coding of moving pictures and associated audio for digital storage media at up to about 1,5 Mbit/s - Part 3 Audio," 1993.

[11]   ISO/IEC 11172-3, "Information technology- coding of moving pictures and associated audio for digital storage media at up to about 1,5 Mbit/s - Part 2 Video," 1993.

[12]   Wang Jianxin, Dong Zaiwang "A fast algorithm for modified discrete Cosine transform" *1996 Int'l Conf. on Communication Technology, Beijing, China*, pp. 445-448, May 1996

[13]   http://www.lincom-asg.com/ssadto/quiet/3m3f_pcm128000.au

[14]   http://www.lincom-asg.com/ssadto

Supporting Real-Time Faxing over the Internet

K. Jin, S.C. Hui and C.K. Yeo

School of Applied Science, Nanyang Technological University
Nanyang Avenue, Singapore 639798
{p7179293e, asschui, asckyeo}@ntu.edu.sg

Abstract. Most existing Internet faxing systems, which use Simple Mail Transfer Protocol and Transmission Control Protocol as the underlying transportation layer for fax delivery, are unable to support real-time fax delivery as traditional faxing. In this paper, an Internet real-time faxing system that supports real-time transmission of fax messages is described. The system is known as RTFaxing which consists of two gateways: Fax-In Gateway (FIG) and Fax-Out Gateway (FOG). FIG is responsible for the reception, processing, compression and transmission of fax-image data to FOG through the Internet. FOG then decompresses and reconstructs the fax-images for dispatching to the destination fax machines. Buffering mechanism, and adaptive control and recovery mechanism have been incorporated into the RTFaxing system to minimise the impact of delay jitters and packet loss.

1 Introduction

Internet fax communication allows users worldwide to exchange fax messages without incurring the high costs associated with international toll charges. Using the Internet, transcontinental faxing is achieved at the mere costs of local telephone calls and nominal Internet connectivity charges. Most of the existing Internet faxing systems offer the basic Mail-to-Fax capability [1, 2], which allow users to send email to a fax machine. Some other systems [3, 4] offer Web-to-Fax capability allowing users to send a fax from the World Wide Web (WWW). As fax machines are still widely in use, Fax-to-Fax systems [5, 6] allow a fax to be sent directly from a conventional fax machine to another through the Internet. However, most of these systems utilise Simple Mail Transfer Protocol (SMTP) [7] or Transmission Control Protocol (TCP) [8] as the underlying transportation layer for fax delivery. This causes time delay in delivering the fax messages to the receiving fax machine due to the nature of these communication protocols. As traditional faxing supports real-time delivery of fax messages over the Packet Switch Telephone Network (PSTN), the transmission of fax messages based on SMTP and TCP is unable to emulate traditional faxing.

A number of Internet real-time faxing systems such as Brouktrout's Real-Time IP Fax [9] and Telogy's Golden Gateway [10] has recently been developed based on User Datagram Protocol (UDP) [11] for real-time fax transmission over the Internet. As UDP is a connectionless-oriented protocol with no guarantee of arrival of data, there is no guarantee on the quality of communication due to the high transmission delay and packet loss of the Internet environment. The on-time delivery of data is dependent on network performance. Under varying network load conditions, the data packets will suffer varying degrees of delay. The variance in delay produces jitters in the received data that are undesirable for real-time fax services. In addition, the unreliability of the network can give rise to packet loss and data duplication that will further deteriorate the data quality.

Different mechanisms have been developed in order to tackle these problems. Buffering mechanism [12] is used to adjust the play-out time of arriving voice/video packets at the destination to minimise the impact of delay. Various voice/video recovery mechanisms [13,14,15] such as embedded coding [13], Xor mechanism [14] and combined rate and control mechanism [15] have also been proposed to eliminate or minimise the impact of packet loss. In this research, we have developed an Adaptive Control and Recovery (ACR) mechanism which integrates the adaptive transmission control [16] with dynamic recovery [13,15] for fax packet data recovery. Together with a buffering mechanism, the ACR mechanism has been implemented into RTFaxing, an Internet real-time faxing system to support real-time fax delivery over the Internet.

The rest of this paper is organised as follows. Section 2 gives an overview on Internet faxing environment. Section 3 briefly describes the ACR mechanism. The architecture of the RTFaxing system is then presented in Section 4. Finally, the conclusion is given in Section 5.

2 Internet Faxing Environment

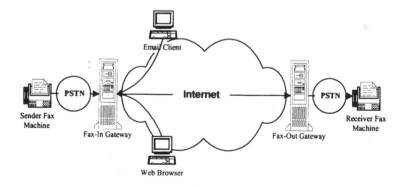

Fig. 1. Internet faxing environment.

Fig. 1 shows an Internet faxing environment. Users can send faxes to a destination fax machine using a Web browser (Web-to-Fax), an electronic mail program (Mail-to-Fax) or a fax machine (Fax-to-Fax) through the Fax-In Gateway. Once a fax message is created, it will be transferred as a fax-image file to the receiving fax gateway server (or Fax-Out Gateway) through the Internet. Upon receipt of the fax-image file, the Fax-Out Gateway will transmit the received fax-image file to the destination fax machine through the Public Switched Telephone Network (PSTN) using the standard

ITU (International Telecommunication Union) Group 3 and Group 4 protocols [17,18].

Two methods are commonly used for transporting fax-image files across the Internet: electronic mail and direct file transfer via Internet sockets. The electronic mail system can be viewed as a transparent, reliable and robust means for fax delivery. The use of Simple Mail Transfer Protocol (SMTP) [7] to route fax messages to their intended fax gateway servers is advantageous as no extra routing mechanisms are needed. However, mail messages might get lost or significantly delayed (i.e. for a few hours to days) occasionally due to faulty or heavily overloaded SMTP servers.

If all gateway servers are directly connected on to the Internet, then one gateway can directly access all other gateways using their unique IP addresses. Transmission Control Protocol (TCP) [8], the connection-oriented protocol of the Transmission Control Protocol/Internet Protocol (TCP/IP) [19] suite, can be used to transfer the fax-image files directly between the Fax-In Gateway and the Fax-Out Gateway. As TCP ensures reliable and error-free data transmission and reception, no extra error-detection and correction procedures need to be incorporated. However, fax transmission using TCP is unable to achieve real-time as retransmission is required when a packet is lost during transmission.

Real Time Protocol (RTP) [20] is very suitable for use in supporting real-time fax delivery. It provides end-to-end delivery services for data with real-time characteristics. These services include payload type identification, sequence numbering, time-stamping and delivery monitoring. Applications typically run RTP on top of User Datagram Protocol (UDP) [11] to make use of its multiplexing and checksum services. RTP itself does not provide any mechanism to ensure timely delivery nor other quality of service (QoS) guarantees, but relies on lower-layer services to do so. It does not guarantee delivery or prevent out-of-order delivery, nor does it assume that the underlying network is reliable and delivers packets in sequence. The sequence numbers included in RTP allow the receiver to reconstruct the sender's packet sequence.

3 Adaptive Control and Recovery Mechanism

As data packets can be lost during the transmission of fax messages over the Internet, an Adaptive Control and Recovery (ACR) mechanism is developed for fax packet data recovery based on the approach proposed by Busse et al. [16]. The ACR mechanism minimises packet loss by controlling the transmission rate dynamically from the source based on the network congestion condition with fax packet data recovery at the destination. Multiple redundancies are used to enable better reception and recovery of fax data during congested network condition. Fig. 2 shows the ACR mechanism that consists of four phases as follows:

- *Packet Loss Analysis.* This phase analyses the packet loss received from incoming receiver reports and uses a low-pass filter to smooth the packet loss rate statistics.
- *Network State Classification.* In this phase, the smooth loss rate generated from the first phase is used for the classification of the network state. Three network states, namely, *Unloaded, Loaded* and *Congested,* have been defined according to some predefined thresholds.

- *Dynamic Bandwidth Adjustment.* The bandwidth requirement of the Fax-In Gateway is dynamically adjusted to increase, hold or decrease according to the Unloaded, Loaded or Congested network state respectively.
- *Transmission Control.* The ACR mechanism is based on multiple redundancy transmission to achieve packet loss recovery, it determines the number of data streams to be transmitted based on the packet loss rate. Once decided, the data streams are compressed using Joint Bi-level Image experts Group (JBIG) [21] compression technique for Internet transmission.

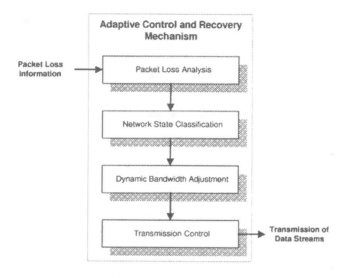

Fig. 2. Adaptive Control and Recovery Mechanism.

The performance of the ACR mechanism for fax-image transmission has been carried out. The main objective of the performance measurement is to illustrate the effects of network packet loss on the quality of fax-images when it is transmitted over the Internet with and without the use of the ACR mechanism. It measures the visual quality of the transmitted fax-images subjectively by a group of evaluators.

It is difficult to quantify "acceptable" or "good" quality fax-images as it is subjected to individual interpretation. In this experiment, we have defined "acceptable" quality as the contents and meaning conveyed by the fax-images can be interpreted by the user. To carry out the experiment, a group of ten evaluators participated in the experiment. A total of 100 fax-images were transmitted from the Fax-In Gateway to Fax-Out Gateway under different network load conditions with and without ACR mechanism. The test fax-images are classified into four types based on their basic characteristics as follows: text/line art, table, photo/graphics and drawing/layout. They are common document types used for fax communication within an office environment. In this experiment, 25 different fax-images belonging to each type are used for transmission. Text/line art is the most common type with mainly textual information. Table usually contains information listed as items within it for quotation purposes. Photo/graphics refers to the type of documents that usually consist of a lot of black pixels in electronics term. For drawing/layout, it contains important information on dimensions and lines.

Table 1. Evaluation results of transmission without ACR mechanism.

Transmission Period	Fax-image Type	Acceptable Quality (%)	Average (%)
Loss Rate at Constant 15.6 kbps	Text/Line Art	69.3	67.4
	Table	63.2	
	Photo/Graphics	74.4	
	Drawing/Layout	62.6	
Loss Rate at Constant 128 kbps	Text/Line Art	30.3	28.7
	Table	26.4	
	Photo/Graphics	35.3	
	Drawing/Layout	22.7	

Table 2. Evaluation results of transmission with ACR mechanism.

Transmission	Fax-image Type	Acceptable Quality (%)	Average (%)
Low Network Load Condition	Text/Line Art	90.5	89.5
	Table	88.2	
	Photo/Graphics	94.3	
	Drawing/Layout	84.8	
Heavy Network Load Condition	Text/Line Art	86.8	84.7
	Table	83.5	
	Photo/Graphics	89.3	
	Drawing/Layout	79.0	

The measurement results of the transmission without using ACR mechanism are given in Table 1. As shown, the average percentage for "acceptable quality" by the evaluators at constant transmission rates of 15.6 kbps and 128 kbps are 67.4% and 28.7% respectively. Therefore, the perceived quality of the received fax-images is unacceptable. On the other hand, the evaluation results of the transmission using ACR mechanism are given in Table 2. It can be seen that the average percentage of "acceptable quality" by the evaluators for heavy network load condition is 84.7% which is lower than that of 89.5% for low network load condition due to its higher packet loss rate. Therefore, the transmission of fax-images with ACR mechanism is able to produce acceptable quality during both heavy and low network conditions.

In addition, among the four types of fax-images, the photo/graphics fax-image is the least affected by packet loss as one can simply predict the loss information from the rest of the information received. In contrast, the drawing/layout fax-image is most affected as some important dimensions and lines are lost during transmission.

4 System Architecture of the RTFaxing System

Fig. 3 shows the architecture of the RTFaxing system. As shown, it consists of two major server gateways: Fax-In Gateway (FIG) and Fax-Out Gateway (FOG). FIG is responsible for the reception, processing, compression and transmission of fax-image data to FOG through the Internet. FOG then decompresses and reconstructs the fax-images for dispatching to the destination fax machines. Buffering mechanism, and adaptive control and recovery mechanism have been incorporated into the RTFaxing system to minimise the impact of delay jitters and packet loss.

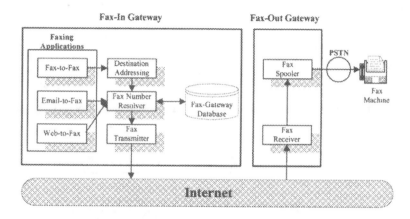

Fig. 3. System architecture.

4.1 Fax-In Gateway

Fax-In Gateway comprises four components, namely, Faxing Applications, Destination Addressing, Fax Number Resolver and Fax Transmitter.

Faxing Applications aim to provide a convenient and simple interface to the Fax Transmitter. Three fax applications have been developed. The Web-to-Fax and Email-to-Fax applications entail the popular World Wide Web and email respectively. The Fax-to-Fax application allows fax users to send and receive fax messages over the Internet using traditional fax machines. The Faxing Applications act as the user interface to receive the fax messages from fax senders through the Web, email or fax machines. As the interface is designed as the upper layer of the RTFaxing system, it hides the complexity of the lower layer from the fax users who can simply compose their fax messages for dispatch. Once the fax-image data and the necessary destination fax number are captured by the FIG, it is queued at the Fax Transmitter for delivery to the appropriate FOG over the Internet.

Fax-to-Fax application requires an address method to capture destination information from fax sender in order to deliver the fax-images to the specified fax machine. A number of destination addressing methods including Dual Tone Multi-Frequency (DTMF), Optical Character Recognition (OCR) and Web-Assisted Addressing (WAA) [22] are supported. DTMF can be used for the input of destination fax numbers using a conventional touch tone keypad on the fax machine. Different frequencies corresponding to different key presses are captured and readily distinguished using this method. OCR recognizes the destination fax number by scanning the fax for written or typed characters. The WAA employs the easy-to-use interface of the Web to capture the destination fax number.

The Fax Number Resolver identifies a FOG capable of handling a particular IDD fax number from the Fax-Gateway Database that is used to store the information of all the available FOGs. It returns a FOG's IP address by looking up the Fax-Gateway Database. The retrieved information is then passed to the Fax Transmitter for further processing.

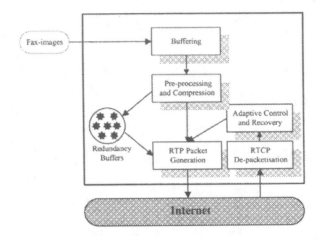

Fig. 4. Fax Transmitter.

An overview of the Fax Transmitter is given in Fig. 4. The Fax Transmitter is responsible for buffering, pre-processing and compression, as well as packetisation and transmission of fax-image data. It consists of the following components: *Buffering, Pre-processing and Compression, Redundancy Buffers, RTP Packet Generation, RTCP De-packetisation* and *Adaptive Control and Recovery* mechanism.

In *Buffering*, the fax-image data received from traditional fax machine, email client or Web browser are placed in a queue for further processing. The *Pre-processing and Compression* component checks the queue regularly and processes the received fax-image data on a first-come-first-serve basis.

The fax-images queued for processing are in Group 3 compressed format. Although these fax-images are compressed, the fax-image is still too big to be sent to the FOG as a single packet. Therefore, each fax-image is further divided into a number of smaller fax-images. In order to reduce the bandwidth needed under the current network condition, the JBIG compression algorithm is used to further compress the smaller Group 3 fax-image data before packetisation. JBIG can reduce the fax-image data size by about 2.23 times. Since it is a lossless technique, the data can be compressed without any information loss. The compressed data can subsequently be used for both the primary and redundant streams.

Redundancy Buffers are used to store fax-image data for redundancy data transmission. Data redundancy enhances the recovery capability for lost fax-image data. In order to implement it without hogging excessive bandwidth, the compressed primary data are stored in the redundancy buffers for subsequent transmission.

RTP Packet Generation stamps the compressed primary and redundant data based on the RTP format. It computes all the required information necessary to complete the RTP headers. In particular, it generates a sequence number in the header of each packet. The sequence number serves two purposes. First, it can be used to order the incoming packets at FOG, which may have arrived out of sequence due to different network paths and delivery delays. Secondly, it allows the receiver to monitor the packet loss rate and delay experienced by the packets.

The function of *RTCP De-packetisation* is to de-packetise all incoming RTCP packets from the FOG and extract the packet lost information such as fraction lost and cumulative number of packets lost. After de-packetisation, the packet loss information will be passed to the *Adaptive Control and Recovery (ACR)* component for analysis. The ACR mechanism has been discussed in Section 3.

4.2   Fax-Out Gateway

The Fax-Out Gateway consists of two components, namely, Fax Receiver and Fax Spooler. When fax-image data packets arrive at FOG through the Internet, it is processed by the Fax Receiver to decompress and reconstruct the fax-images. As shown in Fig. 5, Fax Receiver comprises the following components: RTP De-packetisation, Packets Data Buffering and Ordering, Fax-image Data Decompression, Packet Loss Reporting, Fax-image File Reconstruction and RTCP Packetisation.

RTP De-packetisation performs the reverse process of *RTP Packet Generation* of Fax Transmitter. When the RTP packets are received, the *RTP De-packetisation* component depacketises the incoming packets to retrieve the RTP header, and the primary and redundant streams.

The *Packets Data Buffering and Ordering* mechanism then places the data into the correct slot of the buffer. It also recovers the lost primary data using redundant data during data placement. It is done as follows. The sequence number of the data stream is compared to that of the last data in the buffer that has been decompressed by the *Fax-image Data Decompression*. The decompression process occurs when the buffer is half full. If it is smaller, this indicates that a late loss has happened. The late data stream has to be discarded. If not, the primary data in the packet is processed. If the buffer slot in which the primary data should be placed has been occupied, then duplication has occurred. In this case, the duplicated data will be dropped. In most cases, the compressed data of primary stream can be successfully placed into the buffer in the correct sequence. The mechanism then carries on checking which slot the redundant stream should be located. If the slot is empty, the redundant stream is used to recover the lost primary data.

Since both primary stream and redundant streams are compressed using JBIG, the *Fax-image Data Decompression* decompresses the JBIG data into Group 3 format. The Group 3 fax-image data are then passed to the *Fax-image File Reconstruction* for fax-image reconstruction.

As there are more than one data packet for each fax-image transmitted and received, it is necessary to reconstruct the original Group 3 fax-image from the data received from the different packets. According to the standard fax protocol [20], the last stream of Group 3 fax-image should contain the control information, Return-to-control (RTC). Therefore, in the event that the RTC control information is lost, the file reconstruction process will add this control information, which is equivalent to 6 times the end-of-line (EOL) (i.e. 000000000001) information, to the end of the fax-image reconstructed. Once completed, the reconstructed fax-image is then dispatched to the Fax Spooler.

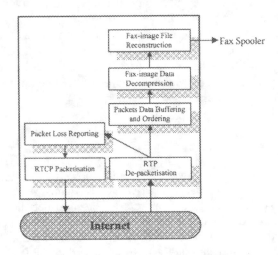

Fig. 5. Fax Receiver.

Packet Loss Reporting computes the packet loss rate and other information into a sender report periodically. This can be used by FIG for adaptive control and recovery purposes. The sender reports are then passed to *RTCP Packetisation* for transmission.

Fax Spooler is responsible for spooling the reconstructed fax images to the destination fax machines through the local PSTN using the necessary interface of both hardware and software. The software is a background process for sending commands to the fax hardware via the drivers. It checks the reconstruction time of the fax-image waiting at the output queue to ensure first-in-first-out processing. The recipients will then be able to receive their faxes from their fax machines.

5 Conclusion

In this paper, the architecture of the Internet real-time faxing system, RTFaxing, which has incorporated the Adaptive Control and Recovery mechanism to support real-time transmission of fax communication over the Internet is described. The Adaptive Control and Recovery mechanism improves the quality and reliability of real-time fax-image transmission. Experimental results have shown that the use of ACR mechanism for transmission has enhanced the quality of fax data transmission and achieve "acceptable" quality of fax-images with good real-time performance. The RTFaxing system consists of two gateway servers: Fax-In Gateway and Fax-Out Gateway. The Fax-In Gateway supports faxing through a Web browser, email client or fax machine, while the Fax-Out Gateway is responsible for receiving the fax image over the Internet and transmitting it to a receiver fax machine over PSTN.

References

1. Gulfnet Kuwait: Mail-to-Fax Help Page. URL: http://www.kuwait.net/fax.help
2. The Phone Company: The Phone Company's Remote Printing Service. URL: http://www-usa.tpc.int/tpc_home.html
3. FaxMail Ltd.: Send a Free-Fax. URL: http://www.faxmail.co.nz/freefax.htm
4. Interpage Network Services Inc.: Interpage WWW Free Fax Demonstration. URL: http://www.interpage.net/sub-wwwfax.html
5. FaxSav Inc.: FaxSav for Fax-to-Fax Overview - Internet Faxing. URL: http://www.faxsav.com/prodandserv/html/fs_overview.html
6. FaxMate Inc.: Service@fax to fax. URL: http://www.faxmate.com/html_en/2_ser/f2f.html
7. Postel, J.B.: Simple Mail Transfer Protocol. University of Southern California, Information Sciences Institute, RFC821, URL: http://www.isi.edu/in-notes/rfc821.txt (1992)
8. Postel, J.B.: Transmission Control Protocol, DARPA Internet Program Protocol Specification. University of Southern California, Information Sciences Institute, RFC 793, URL: http://www.isi.edu/in-notes/rfc793.txt (1981)
9. Brooktrout Technology Inc.: Welcome to Brooktrout. URL: http://www.brooktrout.com/.
10. Telogy Networks Inc.: Telogy.com Homepage. URL:http://www.telogy.com/
11. Postel, J.B.: User Datagram Protocol. University of Southern California, Information Sciences Institute, RFC 768, URL: http://www.isi.edu/in-notes/rfc768.txt (1980)
12. Schulzrinne, H.: Voice Communication Across the Internet: A Network Voice Terminal. Department of Electrical and Computer Engineering & Computer Science, University of Massachusetts. URL :ftp://gaia.cs.umass.edu/pub/hgschulz/nevot/ (1992)
13. Hardman, V., Sasse, M.A., Handley, M., Watson, A.: Reliable Audio for Use over the Internet. Proceedings INET95 (Ohahu, Hawaii) (1995)
14. Shacham, N., McKenney, P.: Packet Recovery in High Speed Networks Using Coding and Buffer Management. Proceedings of IEEE Infocom (1990) 124-131
15. Bolot, J.C., Vega-Garcia, A.: A Control Mechanisms for Packet Audio in the Internet. Proceedings of the Conference on Computer Communications (IEEE Infocom). San Francisco, California (1996) 232-239
16. Busse, J., Deffner, B., Schulzrinne, H.: Dynamic QoS control of multimedia applications based on RTP. Computer Communications, 19 (1996) 49-58
17. International Telecommunications Union: ITU Telecommunication T.4. Standardisation of Group 3 Facsimile Terminals for Document Transmission (1996)
18. International Telecommunications Union: ITU Telecommunication T.6. Facsimile Coding Schemes and Coding Control Functions for Group 4 Facsimile Apparatus (1988)
19. Comer, D. E.: Internetworking with TCP/IP. Vol 1. New Jersey: Prentice-Hall (1995)
20. Schulzrinne, H., Casner, S., Frederick, R., Jacobson, V.: RTP: A Transport Protocol for Real-Time Applications. Network Working Group, Audio-Video Transport Working Group, RFC 1889. URL: http://www/isi.edu/in-notes/rfc1889.txt (1996)
21. International Telecommunication Union: ITU Recommendation T.82. Telecommunication Standardisation Sector of - Information Technology - Coded Representation of Picture and Audio Information - progressive Bi-Level Image Compression (1993)
22. Chong, L.S.K., Hui, S.C., Yeo, C.K., Foo, S.: A WWW-assisted Fax System for Internet Fax-to-Fax Communications. World Wide Web, 1 (1998) 209-219

Developing Quality of Service Capabilities for Distributed Imagery Dissemination Services

Andrew K Lui, Mark W Grigg and Michael J Owen

DSTO C3 Research Centre, Information Technology Division,
Defence Science and Technology Organisation,
Fernhill Park, Bruce, Canberra ACT 2617, Australia
{Andrew.Lui, Mark.Grigg, Michael.Owen}@dsto.defence.gov.au

Abstract. This paper describes a distributed imagery dissemination service with quality of service support. A novel dissemination framework has been designed to allow the graceful handling of performance bottlenecks when a required resource type is exhausted. Instead of rejecting or down scaling QoS proposals, the framework attempts to relieve the bottleneck by altering the resource requirements. Based on a notion called resource requirement management, techniques such as user interaction and image compression can be applied in the framework to reduce the requirement on the exhausted resource type at the expense of other resource types. This notion is particularly applicable in imagery dissemination services. In this paper we illustrate the effect of a number of processes in relieving the network bottleneck. Finally, we present a prototype implementation of the framework, based on the design of an imagery dissemination pipeline for heterogeneous environments.

1. Introduction

Disseminating digital imagery in a distributed environment such as the Internet can consume substantial network and system resources. A typical imagery server may be required to handle over thousands of orders each day. At peak times, the inadequacy of resources can quickly lead to performance degradation. One strategy is to allocate sufficient resource to some selected orders, while rejecting other orders for which the requirements cannot be met at the time. Quality of service (QoS) [1] enhances this strategy by allowing servers and users to negotiate an agreed level of performance. The users have the opportunity to specify the desired quality of an imagery dissemination service. By applying appropriate resource management, the server can then set out to satisfy the agreed level of quality.

The aim of this paper is to introduce QoS capability for distributed imagery dissemination services that relies on the notion of resource requirement management. QoS is realised by the reservation of required resource types for the dissemination of imagery. If a required resource type becomes exhausted (e.g. the network), the server usually refuses to accept further orders until the resource type is available again. Resource requirement management provides an approach that the bottleneck caused by the exhausted resource type can be relieved. This approach is supported by providing the server options in executing the order. The key is to design a number of techniques that can execute the order with the same service quality, but with different requirements in terms of resources. Because changing from one option to another will alter the resource requirement, the server can manage the resource requirements of its service. Potentially, the server has more leverage in evading the bottleneck by choosing the most appropriate option at its disposal. Through our work in image dissemination in heterogeneous environments, we have discovered and applied a number of image dissemination techniques that possess the property needed for resource requirement management.

Existing work on providing QoS for distributed multimedia services is often inflexible in its resource management. Most rely on the underlying system and network QoS guarantees for transmitting multimedia data [2-4]. One drawback is that the current TCP/IP network used throughout the Internet provides only a best effort and not a guaranteed service [5]. Only emerging network technologies such as ATM [6] and RSVP [7, 8] will to a certain degree deliver network QoS guarantees. In a best-effort network, techniques like the Transmission Availability Forecaster (TAF) [18] can be used to predict the likely bandwidth.

This work is a part of a research effort into the management and dissemination of imagery in the Australian Defence Force (ADF). A primary contributor to this research is a project called Imagery Management and Dissemination (IMAD) being undertaken at the Defence Science and Technology Organisation (DSTO). The objective of the project is to research and develop advanced techniques in distributed imagery management and dissemination. Its major research areas include distributed systems and architecture [9], image coding [10, 11], geo-referenced querying [12], content-based image retrieval and storage management [13].

The remainder of this paper is structured as follows. Section 2 begins with a description of the IMAD project. We introduce the concept of QoS in the context of performance management and discuss the role of QoS in the management of system and network resources. The approach of using resource requirement management in the design of servers is then discussed. Section 4 discusses in greater detail the use of resource requirement management in the context of distributed imagery dissemination servers, followed by a description of an imagery dissemination framework based on this notion. Finally we discuss our experience and indicate directions for further research.

2. Background

The IMAD project is pursuing the design of an advanced information system for imagery data management in the ADF. The ADF, like many other large organisations, faces the problem of owning an ever-increasing amount of imagery data. The problem is further complicated by the trend that large organisations are often geographically dispersed. Imagery data gathered at a local repository is not readily accessible from other parts of the organisation. The IMAD approach is to federate the local repositories into a distributed imagery library. Using the communication infrastructure, imagery data is then accessible across the whole organisation.

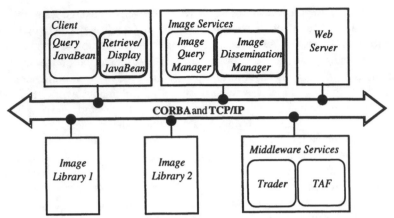

Fig. 1. Components of the IMAD system. The highlighted Image Dissemination Manager and Retrieval JavaBean are the main components involved in this work.

2.1 The IMAD Architecture

The IMAD architecture is a component-based design that emphasises system flexibility and function extensibility. A schematic diagram of the IMAD architecture is illustrated in Fig. 1. A middleware layer, such as CORBA [16], provides an object-level connection between all components in the systems. The components in the IMAD architecture can be categorised into *image libraries*, *imagery services* and *middleware services*. A library not only stores imagery but also provides services for access to the imagery. The Geospatial Imagery Access Specification (GIAS) [14] standard has been adopted as the application programming interface (API) to the IMAD library. An imagery service provides advanced functionality for access to the imagery, such as querying and dissemination of images. Middleware services include generic distributed system services such as location services (traders) and Transmission Availability Forecaster (TAF) [18]. The client applications are connected via the middleware allowing access to the IMAD components. Potentially many libraries and imagery services and hundreds of users could be connected in an IMAD distributed imagery system.

Prior to the dissemination, the desired imagery can be located via the query service. The imagery dissemination service is then called upon to deliver the actual imagery data. The capability to efficiently disseminate imagery data relies heavily upon the available network and system resources.

2.2 Performance Management and Quality of Service

Resource availability is an important factor affecting system performance. To ensure resource availability, using resources economically is an important constraint for a server to continue offering stable services. However, the user's perspective of performance is more concerned with the quality of services. In most cases, the higher the desired quality the more resources are demanded of the server.

Quality of service is a key component in performance management. In simple terms, the QoS is a contract between the server and the user regarding the agreed level of quality of the service. The server will strive to satisfy the user by reserving and allocating resources towards fulfilling the contract. On the other hand, the user will expect the server to deliver the agreed QoS. Such a mutual understanding is achieved through a negotiation process. More economic use of resources is often entailed because the server can make informed management decisions. Because the server can refuse highly demanding contract proposals, the user is more likely to specify the exact requirement rather than the best service available.

2.3 QoS Processes

A QoS is established by several processes including negotiation, mapping and realisation. Negotiation sets up a QoS contract through proposals and counter-proposals. Mapping is the mechanism of projecting a QoS requirement onto resource reservation. Realisation delivers the QoS by allocating the resources for distributed applications.

Admission control is a part of the QoS negotiation process that a decision is made on a QoS proposal. A positive decision is backed up by the reservation of required resources. If any of the required resources is not available, then the proposal cannot be accepted. A more intelligent admission control can work with a scheduler to predict future resource consumption. In the event of urgency, it can cause the suspension of an existing order to free up required resources immediately. The effectiveness of admission control generally improves with smarter negotiation that allows counter-proposals to be made rather than an inflexible rejection.

A recent advance in distributed multimedia systems is the adoption of QoS. Traditional QoS parameters in networking (e.g. throughput, latency, ordered delivery, etc) are joined by new definitions of QoS parameters relevant to media quality (e.g. frame rate, sample rate, etc of a video service). Distributed multimedia QoS is often considered in a layered structure: *user-application-system-network*. This approach is found in a number of significant contributors of QoS architectures such as the Internet Engineering Task Force (IETF) [7] and the ISO [15]. The QoS in the upper layer is satisfied by reserving the lower layer system and network resources.

3. Resource Management in Image Dissemination

In real servers, all resources including network, cpu and secondary storage access are limited in their capacity. There are times when any one of the required resources is exhausted and cannot be reserved for QoS proposals. In such cases QoS negotiation can follow one of the two paths: rejecting the QoS proposals; or scaling back the QoS proposals to fit the resource availability. Both of these measures ensure that already allocated resource continues to deliver the agreed QoS to the already admitted orders. However, the former path is likely to frustrate users. The latter path will result in a degradation of service quality that may be unacceptable to the user. The exhausted resource type thus becomes the performance bottleneck of the server. We suggest that improving the performance of the server rest on the removal of the bottleneck.

The performance bottleneck is usually caused by the exhaustion of the most required resource type. For example, disseminating a large image in pixels is typically network-bound or disk access-bound, because of the large transmission rate required. One approach to avoid the bottleneck is to increase the capacity of the most required resource type. This approach is not always a feasible or preferred option because of cost. Another approach is to reduce the requirements on that resource type.

Resource requirement management describes the notion of managing the resource requirements of the services provided by a server. Resource requirement management is supported by designing the server in the following way. A service provided by the server is supported by multiple options of techniques. An essential characteristic of these options of techniques is that they impose different resource requirements on the server. The server can therefore manage the resource requirement by switching the options at its disposal. For example a data dissemination service may be normally network bound if the data is transmitted uncompressed. An alternative option of transmitting compressed data can be provided so that a reduction in the transit data size will reduce network resource requirements. On the other hand, the compression and decompression processes increase the system resource requirements. The flexibility provides the server leverage in managing the resource requirements of its services.

In the following section, we will investigate an application of resource requirement management. In the event that the required resource cannot be reserved because of exhaustion, the server attempts to alter the resource requirement by considering different options of available processes. This approach is more attractive than simply rejecting the QoS proposal or scaling back the service quality. The work will focus on distributed imagery dissemination services in which resource requirement management is particularly flexible and powerful.

3.1 Resource Requirement Management

The notion of resource requirement management is particularly applicable to QoS management in imagery dissemination services. An image server is required to serve imagery data in a variety of formats, communication protocols, and with various degree of interactivity. These options have a range of different resource requirements, resource requirement management can occur by switching between the options.

In the following we investigate in more detail the notion of resource requirement management in QoS management. Three cases about managing network resources are presented to illustrate how the application of a process can alter the resource requirements and consequently relieve the bottleneck. The first case involves the switching of requirements on network resources and system resources. The second case demonstrates that timeliness is another resource type that can be harnessed. The third case shows how the user's expertise can be leveraged to reduce the requirements on other resource types. Lastly, an example case about managing server system resource is presented. A summary of the example cases is shown in Table 1.

Table 1. Examples of processes used in resource requirement management.

Process	Reduced Requirement	Increased Requirement
Data Compression	Network	Server and Client CPU
Scheduling	Network	Time
Interactivity	Network	User Time and Expertise
Client Side Processing	Server CPU	Client CPU

Using System Resource to Relieve Network Bottleneck. In imagery dissemination services, the network resource is the most likely bottleneck because of the volume of imagery data and the current bandwidth of the Internet. Image compression provides an option of reducing the requirement on the network at the expense of system resources on both the server side (encoding) and the client side (decoding). IMAD employs a wavelet based image-compression technique with embedded coding of the wavelet coefficients allowing variable perceptual quality control. One useful characteristic of this technique is that the perceptual quality of the resulting imagery data can therefore be controlled precisely. The specified QoS can be guaranteed.

Sacrificing Timeliness. Similarly, network resource requirements can be reduced by allowing more time for dissemination. In the context of the timely dissemination of imagery data, time is considered an important resource type. Two techniques may be applied: reducing network bandwidth and hence the transmission time increased; or delaying dissemination until the server is less busy. Both can be realised using a scheduler.

Exploiting User Expertise with Interactivity. Network resource requirements can also be reduced if only the essential imagery data is transmitted as it is required. Here the expertise of the user can be exploited in indicating interactively the essential imagery data and the time when it is required. A process providing such interactivity can first transmit just enough imagery data for a quick inspection at a lower perceptual quality. The user can then indicate to the server to send more data associated with an interesting area in the imagery. In the resulting imagery, only the important areas are rendered with the specified perceptual quality. Network resource is therefore saved at the expense of the user's time and expertise.

Client Side Processing Relieving Server System Resource. Processes like image processing and format conversion consume significant server cpu resource. By adding an image processing module on the client side, system resource consumption on the server can be reduced.

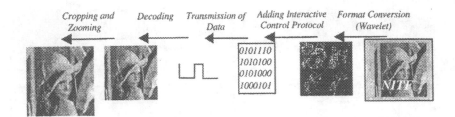

Fig. 2. An example IMAD's imagery dissemination pipeline. The image compression and user interaction processes used in this pipeline reduce the requirement on network resources. Also, carrying out cropping and zooming on the client side reduces the resource requirement on the server's cpu.

4. Imagery Dissemination Framework with QoS Support

In this section we present a framework of image dissemination that exploits the property of resource requirement management for QoS management. The framework is an extension of an original dissemination system built that can adapt to the various resource requirements in heterogeneous environments. The framework encapsulates the requirement for a flexible dissemination system in an imagery dissemination pipeline. A CORBA communication channel connects the client and the server side. This channel is used mainly for transmitting control. The transmission of imagery uses a separate communication channel to avoid the overheads associated with transferring large amounts of data using CORBA.

4.1 Imagery Dissemination Pipeline

The server side pipeline prepares the ordered imagery product in a form suitable for network transmission. Three processes can be applied to the imagery product on the server side, including format conversion (e.g. image compression), arranging the data stream (e.g. image tiling), and transmission (e.g. FTP or socket). Major components on the server side include a scheduler, an image store and a transmission manager. The scheduling coordinates the preparation processes, such as the migration of imagery from tertiary storage and acquiring the necessary resource reservation. The image store contains a JAI [17] based image processing module and a cache manager for storing copies of images after various processing. The transmission manager handles the actual transmission of imagery. In the absence of underlying network QoS supports, it also provides a certain degree of bandwidth management. The server side components can be distributed in a local cluster of commodity computers, resulting in a highly scalable multiserver.

The client side pipeline is then responsible for transforming the received imagery data to satisfy the requirement of the users and their applications. The client side has a decoding module and a JAI based imagery processing module.

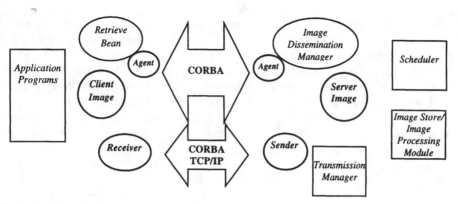

Fig. 3. A schematic diagram illustrating the major components of the imagery dissemination pipeline.

The server and the client coordinates via matched pairs of objects (see Fig. 3). First the client `RetrieveBean` negotiates with the `ImageDisseminationManager` object for a QoS contract. Then a `ClientImage` object and a `ServerImage` object are spawned respectively on the client and the server side. They are responsible for the coordination of complex operations including queuing for resources, managing interactivity, and transmitting metadata of imagery products. Within the pair of objects, a `Receiver` and a `Sender` are created to handle the actual transmission of imagery data. IMAD has developed a variety of subclasses of these objects to encapsulate the various techniques used in resource requirement management. An illustration of the operations of an instance of the pipeline is shown in Fig. 2.

The scheduler controls the activity of the server side pipeline. The scheduler controls the timeliness of the dissemination services, such as the starting time of a session, the duration of the session.

4.2 IMAD QoS Parameters and QoS Negotiation

QoS parameters allow the users to specify the desired quality of service. The QoS parameters provided by IMAD QoS can be grouped into three categories: session, imagery quality and imagery processing. Using QoS parameters, users can specify the desired quality of service. Then negotiation takes place between the server and the client to settle on a QoS contract. The success of the negotiation is helped by the flexibility provided by resource requirement management. Session parameters specify how clients interact with the server. Imagery Quality parameters specify the requirement on the quality of image. Image Processing parameters allow the specification of desired imagery formats and the application of image processing operations.

IMAD QoS provides helper objects to hide the complexity of QoS negotiation from the user. Negotiation takes place between a client agent and a server agent. The client agent has the flexibility to represent the best interest of the users in the negotiation process. Each client agent can be implemented with different characteristic behaviour in the negotiation process. At times it is not possible to get an image dissemination order accepted and the desired QoS obtained. The user can select the agent that behaves in a similar way to the user. For example, one agent may opt for a short waiting time and perceptual quality may be sacrificed; another may be accepting a longer waiting time in order to obtain the imagery product in a certain format. On the other hand, the server agent first generates a prioritised set of feasible pipeline configurations based on the image dissemination order. From the scheduler the agent predicts the different resource consumption of the order with each configuration. Once the prioritised set is established, QoS proposals from the client side can be evaluated that admission or counter-proposals can then occur.

Once the negotiation has agreed on a QoS, pairs of server and client side objects will be spawned in the manner described in the previous section. Table 2 shows examples of IMAD QoS parameters.

Table 2. Examples of IMAD QoS Parameters.

QoS Categories	Example QoS Parameters
Session	SessionLength, MaxWaitingTime, AsynchronizedSession
Image Quality	PerceptualQaulity, ErrorResilence
Image Processing	FormatConversion, Scaling, Filtering

5. Conclusions and Future Work

This work began with an observation that high performance imagery dissemination services require the support of good resource management. We have suggested the development of QoS capabilities to improve the economy of resource usage.

The major contribution of this work is a novel framework of resource management in high performance distributed imagery dissemination services. The image dissemination framework is based on the notion of resource requirement management. The framework ties together various techniques of imagery dissemination in the areas of image compression, transmission protocol and client-server interaction. These techniques offer different resource requirements to give the server more leverage to cope with resource inadequacy. The framework, consisting of an imagery dissemination pipeline, allows IMAD QoS to exploit the benefits of such flexible resource management easily. An agent approach is suggested to encapsulate the complexity of QoS negotiation.

Through this work many research issues have been raised. Some of them are described in the following paragraphs.

As the IMAD prototype system is evaluated in situations similar to those in the defence environment, the types of possible requirements and applications can be understood in more detail. The set of QoS parameters will be refined to satisfy these requirements. The issues of perceptual quality of imagery will be investigated in greater depth.

Accurate prediction of resource requirements is important to provide information for QoS negotiation and reservation. High accuracy is difficult to achieve because the resource requirements may vary greatly from one order to another due to difference in image attributes such as size and format. Experiments will be conducted to test various methods in obtaining accurate predictions.

Currently, our approach has been developed to operate effectively over an Internet like system, which ensures only a best-effort approach in data transmission. The advances in new network technologies such as the ATM and IPv6 will provide the much-sought network QoS guarantees. More work will be required to harness the network QoS appropriately to improve the existing approach.

References

1. Campbell, A. et. al..: A Review of QoS Architecture. Multimedia Systems **3** (1995)
2. Hong, J. et al: A Corba-Based Quality of Service Management Framework for Distributed Multimedia Services and Applications. In: Proceedings IFIP/IEEE International Workshop on Distributed Systems Operations and Management (1998)
3. Steinmetz, R., and Nahrstedt, K.: Multimedia: Computing, Communications and Applications. Prentice Hall (1995)
4. Nahrstedt, K., and Steinmetz, R.: Resource Management in Networked Multimedia Systems. IEEE Computer **28** (1995) 52-63
5. Kaufman, D.H.: Delivering Quality of Service on the Internet. Telecommunications Feb (1999)
6. Campbell, A. et. al.: A Quality of Service Architecture, Computer Communication Review **1** (1994) 6-27
7. Barzilai, T.P. et. al.: Design and Implementation of an RSVP-based Quality of Service Architecture for an Integrated Services Internet. IEEE Journal on Selected Areas in Communications **16** (1998) 397-413
8. Zhang, L. et. al.: RSVP: A New Resource Reservation Protocol. IEEE Network **7** (1993) 8-19
9. Grigg, M. et. al.: Component Based Architecture for a Distributed Imagery Library System. In: Proceedings of 6th International Conference on Distributed Multimedia Systems (DMS 99), Japan (1999)
10. Grigg, M.: Error Resilient Coding Techniques Applied to Transmission of Imagery over HF Radio. In: Proceedings of International Pictorial Coding Symposium (PCS 96), Melbourne (1996)
11. Prandolini, R.: On EZW Encoding of Surveillence Imagery Matched for Spatial Scale on Viewer Resolution. In: Proceedings of International Symposium on Signal Processing and its Applications (ISSPA 99), Brisbane (1999)
12. Coddington, P.D. et. al.: Interfacing to OnLine GeoSpatial Imagery Archives. In: Proceedings of Australasian and Regional Information Systems Association Conference, Leura (1999)
13. Whitbread, P., and Vincent, A.: Modelling Hierarchical Imagery Asset Management Architectures. In: Proceedings (SIMTEC 98)
14. NIMA: GeoSpatial and Imagery Access Services (GIAS) Specification, version 3.3, N0101-D. (1998)
15. ISO: Quality of Service Framework. ISO/IEC JTC1/SC21/WG1 N9680 (1995)
16. OMG: The Common Object Request Broker: Architecture and Specification, revision 2.2 (1998)
17. Sun Microsystems Inc.: Java Advanced Imaging API (1999)
18. Blair, W.D., and Jana, R.: A Transmission Availability Forecast Service for Internet Protocol Networks. DSTO Research Report DSTO-RR-0146 (1999)

A Unified Model of Internet Scale Alerting Services

Annika Hinze, Daniel Faensen

Institute of Computer Science
Freie Universität Berlin,Germany
faensen,hinze@inf.fu-berlin.de

Abstract In the last years, alerting systems have gained strengthened attention. Several systems have been implemented. For the evaluation and cooperation of these systems, the following problems arise: The systems and their models are not compatible, and existing models are only appropriate for a subset of conceivable application domains. Due to modeling differences, a simple integration of different alerting systems is impossible. What is needed, is a unified model that covers the whole variety of alerting service applications. This paper provides a unified model for alerting services that captures the special constraints of most application areas. The model can serve as a basis for an evaluation of alerting service implementations. In addition to the unified model, we define a general profile structure by which clients can specify their interest. This structure is independent of underlying profile definition languages. To eliminate drawbacks of the existing non-cooperating solitary services we introduce a new technique, the Mediating Alerting Service (MediAS). It establishes the cooperation of alerting services in an hierarchical and parallel way.

1 Introduction

Electronic publication becomes more and more popular. Since the readers do not want to be forced to regularly search for information about new documents, there is strong need for alerting services. An alerting service keeps its clients informed about new documents and events they are interested in. Currently, several implementations of alerting services exist for different applicational domains, such as Salamander [12], Siena [2], or Keryx [1]. The underlying models of these services do not meet all requirements found in applications suitable for wide area networks, such as digital libraries. Additionally, the models for existing alerting services mainly cover the applications the services are designed for. In this paper, we provide a *unified model for alerting services* that considers the special constraints of different application domains. The interests of clients are defined as so-called profiles. Since several profile definition languages are used in the different services, we give a *general structure of profiles* for alerting services, independent of the profile definition language. The large number of existing alerting services for a certain application domain has several drawbacks. The users have to define their interest at different services in different ways. The available notifications are mostly bound to the supply of individual services, information from different suppliers is not combined. We therefore introduce and propose the use of a *Mediating Alerting Service (MediAS)*, that connects several suppliers and clients.

The remainder of this paper is structured as follows: In Section 2, we provide an overview of the structure and tasks of an alerting service. We introduce scenarios for the conceivable application domains of alerting services and name the problems with existing alerting services in detail. Section 3 introduces our architectural model for alerting services and Section 4 outlines our event-based model. In Section 5, we propose the use of a mediating alerting service. Section 6 provides an overview of some related systems and models. Section 7 gives some directions for our future work.

2   Event Notification Service

In this section, we introduce the general structure and tasks of an alerting service. We present a collection of possible scenarios in which Internet-scale event services are applicable. The main purpose of this collection is the motivation and validation of an event model that covers all applications. Based on the scenarios and the derived common requirements for alerting services, we will point out the problems with existing alerting services and their models.

Tasks of an Alerting Service   Alerting services connect suppliers of information and interested clients. In our example of scientific papers the suppliers are publishing houses and the clients are the interested scientists. Alerting services inform the clients about the occurrences of events on objects of interest. Objects of interest are located at the supplier's side. Events can be changes on existing objects or the creation of new objects, e. g., the publication of a journal article. Clients define their interest by personal profiles. The information about the occurring events is filtered according to these profiles and notifications are sent to the interested users (clients). Fig. 1 depicts the data-flow in a high-level architecture of an alerting service. Keep in mind that the data-flow is independent from the delivery mode, such as push or pull. The tasks of an alerting service can be subdivided into the following steps: First, the observable event classes are to be determined and offered to the clients. Then, the client's profiles have to be defined and stored. The occurring events have to be observed and filtered. Before creating notifications, the events are integrated in order to detect combinations of events (e. g., two conferences happen to be at the same time). After duplicate recognition the messages can be buffered in order to enable efficient notification (e. g., by merging several messages into one notification). According to a given schedule, the clients have to be notified.

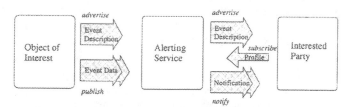

Figure1. Data-flow in an Alerting Service

Scenarios   We present a selection of application domains of alerting services to demonstrate the need for a unified and extended event model and a Mediating Alerting Service.

Stock ticker   Selected stock values are pushed to registered clients. Delivery can be immediate (to paying customers) or deferred. Clients can be off-line. In that case, notifications are lost without consequences. A client can be a PC with an analysis software that reacts on events like threshold crossing of a share value by notifying its user or by reacting autonomously. Cardinality of the relation between supplier and client is usually $1 : n$, size of notification messages is small (a few bytes) but they are sent with high frequency. Encryption can be required. Objects of interest are identifiable in advance, the clients subscribe to objects by selecting from a given list of objects (n out of m).

Digital Library   In a digital library, users want to be notified on new publications they are interested in. They define their interest by specifying certain bibliographical metadata (e. g., a journal or an author) or by Information Retrieval-like queries. Information suppliers can be publishing houses or universities' technical report servers. The offered documents reside on publisher's side within a database, file systems, or other repositories. Within the profiles, the clients have to specify the source. Notifications can include the full document or a pointer to it (DOI, URL). To avoid an unnecessary high frequency of notification deliveries, users can specify a time interval (e. g., weekly) within which notifications are collected and then delivered altogether. Since users do not know each supplier and do not want to register at different suppliers' interfaces, a service covering many suppliers and giving unified access to their repositories operates between clients and information sources. Departments or working groups may have overlapping user profiles. Cardinality between suppliers and clients can be $n : m$, notifications can be large (several MB). Frequency of notifications is low, delivery has to be guaranteed. Objects of interest are unknown at the time of profile definition and usually come into existence later. Clients can be interested in only parts of objects, e. g., in a mathematical proof that is part of an article, which is part of a journal issue.

Software Update Registered users of software (programs, data) automatically get updates pushed from their vendors via the Internet. To avoid too frequent delivery, users can specify that only every second update is really of interest. While notification frequency is low, their size can become huge. It depends on previous events whether an update event is to be forwarded to the client. We call dependence of events on other events *event patterns*.

Remote monitoring and control A power station is equipped with a variety of probes and sensors. Multiple devices of the same type ensure reliability by redundant measurement. Measured values are pushed in real-time to the monitors. Monitoring is done at different places, several control rooms and by replicated software agents. A client can request information from certain probes or probe classes. Additionally, it can require to be notified only if two or more probes deliver the same value or if a probe did not deliver new measurements for a certain time interval. Cardinality of supplier to client can be $1 : (1$ out of $m)$, that means 1 of m redundant clients has to handle an event. Reliable connections and real-time delivery is required. Notification delivery in the case of at least two related event occurrences is another example of an *event pattern*. Events that indicate that nothing happened in a time interval are called *passive events*.

Other conceivable example scenarios are mobile computing, traveller information systems and replication services.

Dimensions for Model Evaluation From the scenarios in the previous section, the following dimensions to classify and evaluate event models and alerting services emerge:

Cardinality Associations between suppliers and clients cover the range from $1 : 1$ to $m : n$. The Remote Monitoring and Control scenario shows that the notion of a $1 : (n$ out of $m)$ cardinality is useful.

Notification size Depending on application type, the size of a notification can range from a few bytes to several megabytes. By delivering pointers to objects instead of the objects themselves, the size can be reduced significantly.

Notification frequency Can vary from high frequent (in the range of seconds) to, say, once a year or only once at all.

Guaranteed delivery In a digital library, for instance, it is necessary to guarantee delivery of notifications even if clients are offline.

Real time Remote monitoring and control can require real time delivery of notifications.

Passive events In some cases, it is useful to be notified if during a specified interval *nothing* happened, e. g., if a server does not handle requests anymore.

Event pattern Clients register for events that depend on other events.

Composed objects Objects do not need to be atomic, but can consist of other objects.

Object repositories Clients can subscribe to repositories to get informed about the changes within that repository. To subscribe to information objects that do not exist at the time of the profile definition, clients refer to the repository the object will appear in.

Profile definition Clients can subscribe to concrete objects (e. g., by referring to their identifier), by specifying meta-data that describe the objects of interests or (in the case of digital libraries) using an IR-like query.

Scalability Can be achieved by redundant alerting services, duplicated parts of services or a hierarchy of services if profiles of different clients are overlapping.

Encryption Scenarios that cover delivery of privacy data or data that are liable for costs can require encrypted delivery. Encryption is handled on protocol level.

Reliability and Acknowledgment Acknowledgments can be used to implement reliable delivery. These characteristics will not be considered in our model, since they have no influence within the modeling level used here.

Drawbacks of Existing Models In the following part, we show the drawbacks of the existing models for alerting services regarding the requirements described above.

Terminology: The term alerting service itself bears the problem that on the one hand there exist several names for this kind of service (Alerting Service , Notification Service, Profile Service, etc.), while on the other hand several different concepts are called notification service (see Section 6). Additionally, the different models for alerting systems use identical terms to describe different concepts. For example consider the term *Channel*: In the CORBA model, an event channel is an intervening object that allows multiple suppliers to communicate with multiple consumers asynchronously [14]. CDF [7] or Netcaster Channel [13] are similar to television broadcast channels. In contrast to CORBA, CDF Channel has an observer function for the channel objects. Further evaluation of the implementation of alerting services with channels can be found in [8].

States of non-existing objects: In most event-based models, an event is defined as *a state transition of an object of interest at a particular time*, where the state of an object is the current value of all its attributes (e. g., [14, 11]). The binding of events to the object of interest cannot be weakened in general as the events are strongly related to the objects (opposite to clock-time events). Consider the case of a scientific paper or article that is published. This object appears at a specific time, the state of the object is then the content of the paper and its meta-data such as author and title. But what is the state of the object before it exists? So the term of an event as a state transition of the object is not appropriate here. Rosenblum and Wolf [15] define an event as an *instantaneous effect of the termination of an invocation of an operation on an object*. This definition associates the event with the invoker of the operation instead of with the object of interest. As a consequence, the invoker has to communicate with the observer in order to announce the event. But it cannot be generally presupposed that invokers actively announce events to observers, due to several reasons.

Composed Objects: The notifications sent to the clients are the messages that are seen as the physical representation of the events [2] that the clients are subscribed to. Since the events relate to identifiable objects of interest, the notifications contain or refer to these objects. However, clients are often not interested in whole documents or sites (they are interested in an article instead of the whole journal, or even in a single mathematical proof instead of the article), therefore, substructures need to be identifiable as objects.

How to register that nothing happened: "Send message if the value of share S does not change for a period of days." Existing models of alerting services cannot handle this kind of profile, as neither an operation is performed on the object of interest, nor does the object of interest change its state. We are aware of the fact that this construct is contradictory to the intuitive notion of an event as *something that happens*.

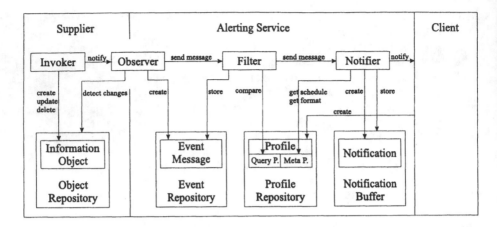

Figure2. Architectural Model of an Alerting Service

3 Architecture

In this section we introduce a general architectural model for alerting services that is used for the identification of components involved in the event model presented in Section 4. The involved components and their relations are shown in Fig. 2. Objects of interest are so-called *information objects* that are located at the supplier's side, optionally in an *object repository*. Information objects can be persistent (e. g., documents) or transient (e. g., measured values). The objects can be organized hierarchically. Changes of theses objects (creation, update, deletion) are induced by an *invoker*. Responsibility of the *observer* is the detection of changes of single objects or in the *object repositories*. For the observer change detection can be an active task or it is passively informed by the invoker. Any change is an event. A detailed definition of the term event will be given in Section 4.1. Events are reported as materialized *event messages* to the *filter*. The filter has knowledge of the client's profiles and compares the event with the query part of the profiles. If a profile and event match, the filter delivers the event message to the *notifier*. For the detection of *event patterns*, events are stored in the *event repository*. The *notifier* in turn checks the schedule part of the *profile*. The event messages are buffered until the notifications become due, they are then edited according to the format specified by the client and delivered. The buffering is also needed for the notification of offline clients to guarantee delivery. The client's profiles contain information about the events the client is interested in, a *schedule*, a notification *protocol*, and a notification *format*. A detailed description of the profile structure is given in Section 4.1. For scalability and reliability the components of the alerting service can be duplicated. While invoker and object repository usually reside at the supplier's side, not all information suppliers implement an observer. An alerting service that covers this type of suppliers could implement an observer as a wrapper for each supplier. The observer is enforced to keep various information on the repository if it is not notified by the invoker and the supplier's interface does not offer a search for changes since a specified date. Alternatively, the observer can be moved to the supplier's side and perform its tasks as an agent of the alerting service there.

4 Unified Event Model

In this section, we introduce our event-based model for alerting services. First, we define the terms used within the model. Then, we formally describe the tasks of an alerting service. Due to space limitations the event model is presented in a shortened version. An extended version with all details can be found in [10].

4.1 Terms and Definitions

Object In correspondence to other models, we use objects to encapsulate the functionality of model participants. In our model, an *object* can be any logical entity residing on a hardware component within a network. Hardware and human beings can also participate but are represented by the software-based proxies. Each object is uniquely identifiable; for simplicity reasons, we refer to the identifier as a handle (e. g., a URL). Considerations of a naming model for alerting services can be found in [15]. The objects, that are offered by *suppliers*, such as journals or news-pages, we call *objects of interest*. Objects have a *state*. The state of an object is the value of its attributes. A set of objects offered by a supplier is referred to as *repository*. A supplier can offer one or more repositories. Since repositories can also be seen as objects of interest, we consider a hierarchy of objects, whereas the items within the repositories are called information objects. Information objects can also be composed of other objects, e. g., journals consist of articles. Therefore, objects need to carry information about their position within the hierarchy.

Event Based on the scenarios, we get a set of possible events regarding information objects: A new information object appears; existing information objects are changed; existing information objects are deleted; for a certain interval of time the information object remains unchanged. Similar to the model used for Event Action Systems [11] we divide events into two classes: *time events* and *object events*. Time events involve clock times, dates, and time intervals. Object events involve changes of non-temporal objects. We additionally distinguish *active* and *passive events*. Active events are state transitions of the repository at a particular time; they are observer-independent. State transitions can be actions such as insertion, deletion, or change of a data-object. In the context of databases, as in digital libraries, the notion of state transition is in close relation to integrity constraints. Each transaction on the database underlies several constraints (e. g., the key of a tuple has to be unique) and the operations are accepted only if the constraints are fulfilled. Allowed operations transfer the database from a valid state to another valid state. This process is called a *state transition*. As final consequence, both constraints and given set of values ensure an invariant state space. A state transition of a particular information object occurs if its attribute values are changed. Passive events involve counters and object properties at a specified time. They have to be observed. Passive events model the fact that for a given time interval an object did not change. Examples are also given in Section 2.

Profile A profile is the formally defined information need of a client. Each profile consists of two parts, a description of events the client is interested in (*query-profile*) and the conditions for the notification (*meta-profile*).

Query-profile: In addition to primitive events (time and object events), they can specify event patterns. Event patterns are Boolean combinations of events. For time events, we distinguish between points (t_e), intervals ($[t_{start}, \infty)$, $(\infty, t_{end}]$, or $[t_{start}, t_{end}]$) and frequencies (e. g., weekly) in time (absolute). Time events can also be given in relation to another event, e. g., "X weeks after the conference" (relative) or by using combinations. For time events, client and server need to define a reference (e. g., a common time zone). Passive events need to specify the objects and their attributes (see active events), and constraints as time or counters. For active events, clients have to define the objects and the type of state transition to be observed on the object and possibly further attribute values they are interested in. Additionally, the repository of the objects has to be defined. Identification of objects can be done by giving (1) the object handles, (2) metadata about the objects, or (3) values of attributes of the objects. For example, the subscription to subject-based Internet-channels is covered by (2). For composed objects, the level of the concerned attribute within the hierarchy should also be given. Possible state transitions are the occurrence of a new object, the change of an object, or the removal of an object. The change of an object can concern the structure (changing set of attributes, changing range of attributes), or the values of the attributes. Additionally, clients can be interested in the changing number of values, or in different changes of the value itself.

The following items have to be defined within a *meta-profile*:

1. content of notification (e. g., object-handle, object itself, information about the object/event and/or their numbers),
2. structure of notification (number of events reported in the message, instructions for the merging of notifications, ranking mechanism),
3. notification protocol (e. g., e-mail, desktop-icon, download),
4. time-policy for event detection (frequency of observations),
5. time-policy for notification such as scheduled (e. g., daily) or event-dependent (e. g., on n events) or depending on event-attributes ("X weeks before the conference").

Notification A notification is a message reporting about events. Clients are notified according to the time-policy given in their profiles. Notifications created by observers have to be evaluated to discover patterns or duplicates. Before sending notifications, depending on the profile, they have to be edited (e. g., duplicate removal, merging, formating) in order to ensure that clients get only one notification at the time.

4.2 Model

The clients of an alerting service get information about the possible profile types from the service. Suppliers inform the service (and so the clients) about possible events by means of advertisements. An alert relation describes a connection between repositories of information objects, clients, and events the client wants to get notified about. The *alert relation A* is therefore a relation of a set of *repositories R*, a set of *clients C*, and a set of *profiles P*: $A \subseteq R \times C \times P$. Clients may *register* or *unregister* for certain events happening on certain repositories, for instance by subscribing to an event channel, such as CDF channels. The corresponding tuples $\{[r, c, p]\}$, where r denotes the repository, c the client, and p the profile regarding an event on r, are inserted into, or deleted from, the relation. An event channel E is a projection of the alert relation onto the repositories and the profiles: $E = \Pi_{R,P}(A)$. Here, we employ the notion of the relational algebra. Within a projection duplicate tuples are deleted. According to this model, a CORBA channel is only a communication medium and not covered by the definition of a channel given above. Another conclusion is, that clients that are interested in the same events at the same repository are subscribed for the same event channel, as in CDF channels or mailing lists. *Events* can happen at any time, they are caused by invokers that perform actions on the repository. Let t_e be the time a state transition e in repository r has been caused by an invoker. An observer can learn of events in two ways. Either an observer is notified by the invoker at time $t^{obs} \geq t_e$. Or the observer proceeds according to a time schedule $T^{obs} = \{t_i | t_i = t_0 + i\delta_{obs}, i \in \mathbb{N}\}$ The observer registers all state changes on r in the interval $(t_{i-1}, t_i]$ at time $t^{obs} = t_i$. The observer creates a message reporting the occurrence of the event and forwards it to the filter. The profile filter compares the reported events to the profiles. With Carzaniga [2], $p \sqsubset e$ denotes that an event e matches a profile p. Notifications to the following clients must be produced: $C_{i-1,i}(r, e) = \Pi_C(A_{i-1,i}(r, e))$, where $A_{i-1,i}(r, e) = \sigma_{(A.R=r) \wedge (A.P \sqsubset e)}(A)$ is the set of alert relations affected by events

e in r at $t_e \in (t_{i-1}, t_i]$. A similar sequence is conceivable for passive events, as well as for the subsequent handling of event patterns and notifications. For the complete formalism, again, we have to refer to the extended paper version [10].

Several conclusions can be drawn from the model: The observers either have to be informed by the invokers or they have to be aware of the state of the repository (and the objects contained in the repository). In the latter case, observers, therefore, need to be initialized with the states of all existing objects in the repository. They can only detect changes with frequencies less or equal to the observation frequency. Otherwise, observers can miss events within their observation interval. If two events regarding the same object happen within the same observation interval, these events can weaken or intensify each other. For example, if the events that a value of an attribute increases and decreases happen shortly one after another, these two events neutralize each other. For passive events, filters initially have to know about the existence of objects, and, therefore, they have to be initialized with all existing objects. For the recognition of changed objects, different update strategies have to be considered (versions, in-place-update and shadow-update, see [5]).

5 Mediating Alerting Service

In this section, we motivate and propose the use of a mediating alerting service. Consider the application domain of a digital library. For full coverage of scientific publications, users have to register at a variety of suppliers ($n : m$ cardinality), some even unknown to the user, with different interfaces for profile definition. Notification format and protocol are heterogeneous, and many suppliers do not offer an alerting service. In addition, the notifications of different providers cannot be combined. As solution to the problems mentioned above and pointed out in previous sections, and as an implementation of both the architectural and the event model, we propose a *Mediating Alerting Service (MediAS)*.

In MediAS, multiple alerting services cooperate in a hierarchical and parallel manner. That means that alerting services are clients (or suppliers) for other alerting services. An alerting service can also cover multiple suppliers employing multiple observers. In turn, one observer can deliver event messages to multiple filters. MediAS integrates the view to the information suppliers. Its *observers* serve as wrappers for the suppliers' interfaces. For suppliers that implement their own alerting services the observer acts as a *client* and is notified of all changes in the suppliers' repositories. Other suppliers are queried regularly by the observer that wraps the suppliers' interfaces. Profiles are stored in MediAS' repository. If profiles of different clients are overlapping (as it is expected in a digital library environment, e. g., profiles owned by library users of a working group or university department), several instances of MediAS can cooperate hierarchically, which improves scalability. A MediAS which is the client of a different MediAS submits an integration of its profiles to its supplier. That ensures that the client MediAS will be notified of all information objects its clients are interested in.

Problems arise when an alerting service is notified by other alerting services whose coverages are overlapping. It can happen that notifications of the same event are delivered more than once. The MediAS must take this into account and filter out duplicate events. A similar problem can be caused by observers covering the same repository or suppliers providing similar objects (e. g., two digital libraries that offer the same journals). In addition to the problems that are well examined in the area of non-sequential processing when having parallel tasks, the duplication of the event repository forces replication to ensure reliable detection of event patterns.

6 Related Work

Event services and *event action systems* are related systems to be considered for the definition of model and architecture. *Event services* support the asynchronous message exchange between objects. They depend on an event-based infrastructure (such as JEDI [6]). Examples are event notification services (such as SIENA [3, 2], SIFT [17], or the CORBA Event Service [14]). Alerting aervices can be built upon event services. This is especially useful in the handling of asynchronous events. There is a class of infrastructures that we do not consider here. These infrastructures do not realize a notification service, though they are published as such, e. g., the Java Distributed Event Specification. An investigation of these frameworks can be found, e. g., in [2]. Also, we do not consider local event-based procedures in operating systems, such as IPCs and interrupt handling.

Event Action Systems are software systems in which events occurring within the system trigger actions. The reaction is performed according to action specifications defined by the users. The triggered actions may generate other events, which trigger other actions, and so on. The actions are, in contrast to common event-based infrastructures, relevant to human beings rather than notifications to other software components [2]. The alerting services considered here are closer related to event-action systems than to common event-based infrastructures. An example of an event-action system is Yeast [11].

Active databases [9, 4] can serve as triggers for alerting services. The underlying model is based on ECA-rules (Event-Condition-Action), that can also be applied to alerting services, where the conditions are defined in the profiles and the action is sending the notification. They cover the repository, the observer, and the filter facility, but the complex handling of scheduled notification profiles are beyond the means of active databases. A system-independent design framework for scalable event notification services has been proposed by Rosenblum and Wolf [15]. We have shown the restrictions of this model in Section 2. Due to its independence of specialized applications, it serves as a basis for our model for alerting services.

The Simple Digital Library Interoperability Protocol (SDLIP) from Stanford University [16] is designed for distributed information retrieval in a digital library environment. Alerting on new or changed objects is not focus of SDLIP. However, when starting an asynchronous search, a client can specify the address of an object that implements an interface which will receive the delivery. The server would submit new documents to that "receiver". One only needs to make the query long-lasting. In our terminology a query is a *query-profile*.

7 Conclusion and Outlook

In this paper, a general structure and architecture for an integrative and scalable alerting service has been defined. We proposed a general event-based model for alerting services. Moreover the paper introduced a general structure for profile definitions for notification services and motivated the use of a Mediating Alerting Service (MediAS).

Expanded event-based model: Based on the requirements of scenarios for alerting services, we introduced an expanded model for Internet-scale alerting services. The models covers various scenarios, whereas existing models for notification services apply only for a restricted range of scenarios (as shown in Section 2). The model offers a general terminology for the description of alerting service components. It extends the notion of events to cover states of non-existing objects. In addition, it introduces the notion of composed objects and the notion of passive events. It can be used as a basis for the comparison of different systems.

General profile structure: In this paper, we defined the general structure of profiles independently from the profile definition language. Several languages and protocols have been proposed [1, 16]. One of our next steps will be the definition of a general profile definition language for bibliographic alerting services.

MediAS: We proposed the use of a mediating alerting service to overcome the drawbacks of the various existing implementations. Disadvantages of existing alerting services are, among others, the need for the clients to define their profile many times in many different ways, duplicate notifications cannot be avoided, and event patterns can be recognized only in a very restricted manner. In a MediAS, parts of the service can work distributed in hierarchical or parallel order. Further research will support the decision which part of the service should be duplicated and in which order the cooperating services are to be arranged. MediAS is under development at the Freie Universität Berlin.

References

1. S. Brandt and A. Kristensen. Web push as an Internet notification service. held at W3C Workshop on Push Technology, Boston, Massachusetts, September 1997.
2. A. Carzaniga. *Architectures for an Event Notification Service Scalable to Wide-area Networks.* PhD thesis, Politecnico di Milano, Milano, Italy, December 1998.
3. A. Carzaniga, E. Di Nitto, D. S. Rosenblum, and A. L. Wolf. Issues in supporting event-based architectural styles. In *3. Internat. Software Architecture Workshop*, Orlando, USA, November 1998.
4. S. Chakravarthy and D. Mishra. Snoop: An expressive event specification language for active databases. *Knowledge and Data Engineering Journal*, 14:1–26, 1994.
5. A. Crespo and H. García-Molina. Awareness services for digital libraries. In *Research and Advanced Technology for Digital Libraries. ECDL '97, Pisa, Italy*, volume 1324 of *LNCS*, pages 147–171. Springer, September 1997.
6. G. Cugola, E. Di Nitto, and A. Fuggetta. Exploiting an event-based infrastructure to develop complex distributed systems. In *Proceedings of the 20th International Conference On Software Engineering (ICSE98)*, Kyoto, Japan, April 1998.
7. C. Ellermann. Channel Definition Format (CDF). Technical report, W3C, Microsoft, 1997.
8. D. Faensen, A. Hinze, and H. Schweppe. Alerting in a digital library environment – do channels meet the requirements? In *Research and Advanced Technology for Digital Libraries. ECDL '98, Heraklion, Greek*, number 1513 in LNCS, pages 643–644. Springer Verlag, 1998.
9. N. Gehani, H. V. Jagadish, and O. Shmueli. Composite event specification in active databases. In *Proceedings of the 18th Conference on Very Large Databases, Morgan Kaufman pubs. (Los Altos CA)*, Vancouver, August 1992.
10. A. Hinze and D. Faensen. A unified model of internet scale alerting services. Technical Report Number tr-b-99-15, Freie Universität Berlin, 1999. available at http://www.inf.fu-berlin/inst/pubs/tr-b-99-15.abstract.html.
11. B. Krishnamurthy and D. S. Rosenblum. Yeast: A general purpose event-action system. *Transactions on Software Engineering*, 21(10), Oct.1995.
12. G. R. Malan, F. Jahanian, and S. Subramanian. Salamander: A push-based distribution substrate for internet applications. In *USENIX Symposium on Internet Technologies and Systems, Monterey, California, December 8-11, 1997*, volume 32, 1997.
13. Netscape Netcaster. http://developer.netscape.com/software/netcast.html.
14. OMG. *CORBAservices: Common Object Services Specification.* Object Management Group, November 1997. available at http://www.omg.org/corba/sectran1.htm.
15. D. S. Rosenblum and A. L. Wolf. A design framework for internet-scale event observation and notification. In *Proceedings of the 6th European Software Engineering Conference*, volume 1301 of *LNCS*, pages 344–360, Berlin, 1997.
16. The Simple Digital Library Interoperability Protocol (SDLIP). available at http://www-diglib.stanford.edu:8080/ testbed/doc/SDLIP/sdlip.htm.
17. T. W. Yan and H. García-Molina. SIFT - a tool for wide-area information dissemination. In *USENIX 1995 Technical Conference on UNIX and Advanced Computing Systems, Conference Proceedings*, pages 177–186, January 1995.

Supporting Internet Applications Beyond Browsing: Trigger Processing and Change Notification

(Extended Abstract)

Ling Liu, Calton Pu and Wei Tang

Georgia Institute of Technology
College of Computing
Atlanta, GA 30332-0280 USA
{lingliu, calton, wtang}@cc.gatech.edu

Abstract. This paper presents the design and implementation methodology of the JCQ system, a Java-based Continual Query system for update monitoring over Web information sources. A continual query is a standing query that monitors updates of interest using distributed triggers and notifies users whenever the updates reach specified thresholds. In this paper we focus on the strategies and techniques developed in JCQ for scalable and efficient trigger firing and the execution model for flexible and robust change notification. We evaluate our approach through a performance study of the most recent release of the JCQ system and a comparison with related work.

1 Introduction

The World Wide Web (the Web) publishes a vast amount of information that changes continuously. These rapid and often unpredictable changes to the information sources create a new problem: how to detect and represent the changes, and then notify users of the changes. Many application systems today have the need for tracking changes in multiple information sources on the web and notifying users of changes if some condition over the information sources is met. Example applications include military and civilian situation assessment, network management, business process control, program trading, to name a few.

We have developed a continual query system, which offers a system-supported update monitoring facility. A goal of the continual query system is to provide timely response (and alert) to critical situations, while reducing the effort and time users spend hunting for the updated information and avoiding unnecessary traffic on the net. The most recent version of the continual query system software is developed in pure Java. We refer to this version of the continual query system JCQ. One of the salient features of our JCQ system is its ability to provide scalable continual query services for active delivery of the desired information at the right time to the right user.

The main focus of this paper is to describe the strategies and mechanisms developed in JCQ to address the problem of scalable distributed trigger processing in the presence of large numbers of continual queries. It is well known that built-in trigger facilities in most of commercial RDBMS products are quite popular with application developers because it is a convenient mechanism for integrity constraint checking and update alerting across all applications of a database. Unfortunately, current trigger systems in commercial database products have very limited scalability. Numerous commercial systems allow only one trigger per table to be defined for each of the three basic types of update events (Insert, Delete, and Modify). Our experience with the initial prototype of the continual query system [7] shows that many web applications could effectively use large numbers of triggers in individual information sources (for instance by installing large numbers of continual queries). Thus a new challenge for an Internet-scale update monitoring system (e.g., JCQ) is to provide mechanisms for *responsive* and *scalable* trigger processing in the presence of thousands or even millions of continual queries over the online information sources.

The approach we propose for implementing a highly scalable continual query system achieves scalability by exploring a number of types of parallelism at query-level, event-level, condition-level, and data-level and a sophisticated continual query index based on various trigger patterns. This approach gives good response time for continual queries, while supporting a large number of distributed triggers that would be expensive if processed naively. A key idea behind the JCQ approach is to classify all installed continual queries into a number of groups, according to the trigger structures (called primitive trigger patterns) they use. This idea is motivated by our observation that many of the installed continual queries use the same primitive trigger patterns, except for the appearance of different constant values in the trigger specification. An example of such coincidence is when a very large number of continual queries are installed over a single web (such as online retail bookstores, the stockmaster.com web source, or the national weather service web site nws.noaa.org). By grouping continual queries that have the same (or similar) trigger patterns together, the overall trigger processing cost can be dramatically reduced. This approach also scales well to the large numbers of concurrently running continual queries.

2 JCQ Overview

JCQ is built on a three-tier architecture: client, server, and wrapper/adapter. This architecture was motivated by the need for providing scalable and reliable continual query processing, and the need for sharing information among structured, semi-structured, and unstructured remote data sources. The first tier is the client tier. The client manager coordinates client requests and the communication with the JCQ server. The second tier is the JCQ server. It is responsible for coordinating with the trigger condition evaluator and event detection manager to monitor updates of interest, and coordinate with JCQ wrappers and adapters to track the new updates to the source data. The third tier is the JCQ wrappers/adapters tier. A wrapper is a source-specific program that translates a server-tier query into a source-specific data fetch request. Once the source data is fetched and filtered, the wrapper returns the result or the location where the result is stored to the CQ manager. In addition to the common data wrapping capability, a JCQ wrapper installs a source-specific event detector that, on behalf of the JCQ server, continually watches the update events at the corresponding data source site(s), and signals the CQ manager whenever an update event of interest occurs. The implementation platform includes a Sun Ultra-sparc system running Solaris 2 operating system (the host environment), Java as the programming language (although there are still some Perl and native languages for downward compatibility considerations), and Java servlets (replacing CGI scripts) as the networking gateway programs for better performance and maintenance. All the client-side GUI interfaces are Web-accessible, which means using a standard Web browser, such as Netscape 3.0 or Internet Explorer

4.0 above, a user can interact with the JCQ system. We plan to develop two sets of GUI interfaces: simple interface is CGI-Javascript-HTML based; advanced interface is pure Java Applet+Servlet based. For people who only have slow network connections, simple interface is appropriate. The pure Java interface would respond better with faster Internet connections.

3 Scalable Trigger Processing

In JCQ there is no restriction on how many continual queries a user can create and how many users can register with the system. Quite often, the system faces the situation where thousands or even millions of continual queries are running concurrently (50 users with the average of 20 continual queries per user will reach a thousand). Thus, one of the main challenges that the JCQ system needs to address is the *scalability* of the continual query processing strategy, namely how to guarantee the responsiveness of a continual query system in the presence of large numbers of concurrently running continual queries.

Motivation. General speaking, a continual query (Q, T_{cq}, Stop) can be seen as a "long-running query" in the sense that it, once started, runs continually until its Stop condition becomes true. Typically, after the first run of the query component Q, the subsequent run of Q will be fired only if the trigger condition T_{cq} is evaluated to be true. Thus, most of the cost in running a continual query is spent on the continuous testing of its trigger condition T_{cq}. The bottleneck in a single test of the trigger condition T_{cq} is the time spent on the network connection to the remote site(s), the network bandwidth consumption in fetching the relevant page, and the server processing cost in detecting the newly updated information.

In addition, we have observed that, quite often among a large number of continual queries being installed, many of them are either against a single web information source or have a similar trigger structure (such as all monitor Intel stock price changes with different update thresholds). An obvious solution is to find smart indexing structure and indexing algorithms that can index all installed continual queries based on their trigger structure. As a result, the number of triggers that must be tested continuously against remote site(s) (web data sources) can be dramatically reduced.

Based on this observation, an obvious guideline in designing optimization strategies for continual queries is to look for opportunities throughout the process of a continual query, and design mechanisms that can reduce the server processing and network bandwidth consumption, while enhancing the scalability of distributed trigger processing. There are several alternative ways in which continual queries (CQs) can be processed. For example, a continual query can be processed independently, or be grouped with some other continual queries according to the data source(s) they monitor over or the trigger structures they share.

CQ Indexing Techniques. There are two motivations behind the indexing strategies for large number of continual queries. The first motivation is based on the general premise that a large number of triggers often share some of the predicate variables but often take different constant values in their trigger conditions. Thus by some canonical transformation, trigger patterns can be derived, and each pattern groups a set of change monitors sharing the same trigger expression template. The second motivation is to use the indexing techniques as both a facilitator for deriving polling queries that can serve for a group of continual queries, and a mechanism for speeding up the testing and execution of the CQ triggers (i.e., the filter query portions of the CQ triggers).

The first indexing technique is called *indexing by source*. It forms groups of CQs by indexing CQs on the data sources identified in the trigger expressions. For each group of CQs, a polling query is derived from the set of trigger expressions of the CQs. Since different data sources may offer different search capability, this indexing approach may not produce the most efficient polling plan, especially when more than one network connection is required for each group of CQs. For example, the weather.noaa.gov web site offers only search capability based on a single location. Therefore, to carry out a CQ that requests to monitor the weather condition at more than one location, say Portland and Seattle, two parallel polling requests to the weather.noaa.gov will be generated. Here is the basic idea: Given an indexing strategy, we first utilize the groups partitioned by index to construct one polling query per partition. Then we refine (optimize) the polling query expression by taking into account the query capability descriptions of the corresponding information sources and the parallelization capability at the JCQ server.

The second indexing technique is called *indexing by trigger pattern*. It forms groups of CQs by indexing CQs on both the source names listed in their trigger expressions and the trigger patterns derived from their trigger expressions. See [13] for more detail.

As many factors may affect the choice of each indexing strategy for distributed triggers, in the JCQ system we expect to produce guidance to update monitor implementors as to which strategies will be most effective for optimizing continual queries in which situations. This guidance will consist, for each application area, and for each access pattern of the Web data sources, of a description of the optimization process, the expected performance gains, and the performance metrics used for each of the alternative strategies. A key issue here is to investigate each potential alternative from a set of related and possibly conflicting factors that affect the optimization time, the complexity of coding, the quality of resulting plan, and the scalability of the method, and to understand the tradeoffs between the choices.

Implementation Strategy. The main components of the JCQ trigger manager are shown in Figure 1. The CQ trigger index manager coordinates the work among

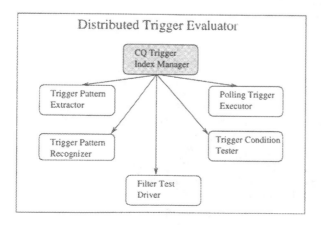

Fig. 1. Distributed trigger manager architecture

trigger extractor, trigger pattern recognizer, polling trigger executor, and trigger condition tester. Trigger pattern extractor transforms the trigger condition into a canonical representation that can be recognized by the trigger pattern recognizer. If the trigger pattern is new, a new trigger pattern will be created. Otherwise, the CQ is indexed into one of the existing pools of CQs according to its trigger structure. The polling trigger executor is responsible for multi-threaded execution of polling trigger queries. Each polling trigger corresponds to a trigger pattern. The triggers of the similar pattern is grouped together though the continual query index on trigger pattern. Once the polling trigger returns the result of a polling trigger query, the multithreaded trigger condition tester is invoked to evaluate the rest of the CQ triggers of the same pattern concurrently. Each thread evaluates the filter portion of a trigger expression T_{cq}.

Due to the space limitation, readers may refer to [13] for further details.

4 Event Notification in JCQ

Event notification is a software facility that provides mechanisms for notification of event occurrences. Generally speaking, an *Event Notification Service* (ENS) protocol has minimum and maximum latency bounds on both event observation and update notification. The notification can be provided by either a server-initiated push or a client initiated pull delivery. The notification service may enforce application-specific delivery constraints, such as delivery based on user priority, access control and security constraints.

In the JCQ system, events may be defined in terms of time dimension (e.g., every 10 minutes or 10am everyday) or in terms of physical or information space (e.g., a hand clap, a light being switched on, or IBM stock price dropped by 10%). Events are either primitive or composite. The JCQ event notification facility is utilized in at least three ways: first, we use the event notification facility to notify users of their continual query service subscription, including both the subscription for JCQ system service, the expiration of their installed continual queries, and the expiration of their JCQ subscription. Second, we use the event notification facility to send the users the update alert and the differential results of the data items being monitored. Third, the JCQ event notification facility is designed to allow an external event observer to be loosely coupled with the change notification. Such coupling enhances both the tracking capabilities as well as the update monitoring functionality of JCQ. It also offers JCQ users with services for alerting and notifying users of the information changes of interest, and the capability of taking appropriate actions to react to the changes.

Consider a complex update monitoring request "*start monitoring the stock price updates of IBM, Intel, Microsoft, and Dell for three days when NASDAQ reaches 2000, and report to me whenever the stock price of any of these companies drops by 5%*". This monitoring request can be easily modeled by two continual queries:

```
create CQ_A as
  Query:   none
  Trigger: When NSASAQ reaches 2000
  Notify:  Install CQ_B
  Stop:    a month (by default)

Create CQ_B as
  Query:   stock price changes on IBM, Intel, Microsoft, Dell
```

```
Trigger: when stock price of IBM or Intel or MSFT or Dell drops by 5%
Notify:  wtang@cse.ogi.edu
Stop:    after 3 days
```

In the current implementation of JCQ, we require the users to explicitly register the event observation function to be called and the method of remote invocation when a notification service is subscribed. In the rest of this section, we discuss the research and engineering issues involved in the design and implementation of the JCQ event notification service. For example, what types of events should be considered at the notification phase, when to notify users of the changes, how to guarantee in-time delivery of the notification, and what mechanism to use to deliver the notification.

Notification Service Architecture. The design goal of the notification service is to make it reusable and configurable, so it can easily be incorporated into other system architectures. The first design choice is to decide whether to build the notification service as a standalone one or as a component of JCQ.

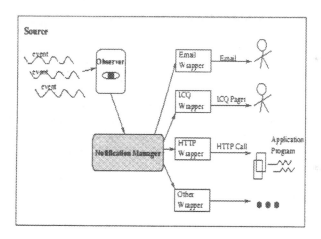

Fig. 2. Standalone notification service

In the standalone architecture (Figure 2), the main components are: source, observer, notification manager, and wrapper set. The wrapper set is bundled with the notification service. This architecture is considered "loosely coupled" with the source event observer. And the observer could be provided by or combined with the source and connect to the notification manager through HTTP connection.

The notification service can also be designed as a component of a system. In this case, the notification service may cooperate with other system components in a tightly coupled fashion. The source observer is usually provided by the software system using a set of source wrappers. For example, in JCQ we choose to implement the notification service as a component of JCQ so that the trigger facility can be reused to implement richer set of notification conditions such as "notify Todd whenever CQ trigger condition becomes true twice consecutively". The JCQ notification service can reside on the same server as the JCQ engine or reside on a machine connected to the JCQ server within a local area network. Compared with the "loosely coupled" notification service, a "tightly coupled" one has the advantage of less network communication overhead, but it loses some flexibility and harder to be implemented generically. Due to the space limitation, readers may refer to [13] for further details.

Discussion. Latency is an important factor in the JCQ notification service. The *source observer* (whether it is source-initiated or polling-based) sets the sampling latency, bounding the delay from source event occurrence until observation. We refer to such delay as the *observation interval* or the *sampling latency*. This "observation interval" determines the minimum resolution of event frequency. The notification manager controls the latency from observation until notification. We refer to such latency as the *delivery latency* or *delivery interval*, which determines the maximum resolution of notification frequency.

Achieving low sampling latency (less than delivery latency) may require source-initiated observation. Hard-to-decide polling intervals often make polling-based event observation inefficient. But in case of unavailability of source-initiation, the polling approach is the way to go.

In determining which side (source or notification server) should initiate notification delivery, one needs to know which party has enough information on its counterparts. If an event source knows its listeners, the source can initiate notification delivery upon event observation. For example, a printer can send a message to the owner of the print job upon print completion (in Unix, this is achieved by simply using "-m" option for *lpr*). However, if an unknown set of users want to monitor a single source (e.g., the current job queue of some printer), a client-polling policy is more appropriate. For example, Unix users can use "lpq" to list a printer job queue.

Event notifications can be exchanged directly between sources and end-receivers, or through an intermediate party (server) using "end-to-end" delivery or "store-and-forward". In a very large scaled environment (such as the Internet), the use of intermediation parties (or proxies) is common.

In terms of delivery constraints, the *Event Notification Service* (ENS) is responsible for ensuring certain guarantees before delivering a notification to the recipients. For example, whether it supports real time delivery or not, whether to retry in case of message lost. Currently, we use "no retry" policy in the JCQ system for simplicity. The JCQ system can support up-to-minute delivery currently. Performance improvements on reducing both the sampling and the delivery latency are under way. In addition, security constraint is also an important responsibility of the ENS. For example, in case of a firewall, the ENS need to have the knowledge of proxies to be used to pass the firewall. To ensure correct notification, the notification manager maintains a subscription list, which could be an editable and audible "first-class" object. An initial verification is performed at the time of a notification service subscription. For example, in JCQ system, the email addresses should be checked upon user registration in order to guarantee that the correct email addresses are used for the users to receive notification. We are interested in incorporating more advanced quality of service (QoS) properties into the event notification service of the continual query system.

5   Performance Measurement and Evaluation

We have reported our strategies for scalable trigger processing and change notification facilities in JCQ. An immediate question one would ask is what is the performance characteristics of the CQ system and and how well does it scale? In this section, we report our initial experiments conducted on OpenCQ, an earlier version of the Continual Query system, developed using Perl CGI and Java. This is partly because the JCQ system has not fully completed the testing phase at the time of the writing and partly because we believe these initial measurements are interesting and useful for understanding the Continual Query system in general and the implementation strategies adopted by JCQ. It is important to note that we expect JCQ to perform much better than OpenCQ in all aspects. This is primarily because JCQ is a multithreaded system with in-depth exploration of parallel processing.

The parameters and factors we use in the performance study are shown below.

Parameters & Factors	Values
Network bandwidth (Kbps)	100Mbps/sec (local), 2Mbps/sec (remote)
Source update frequency (times/minute)	1 for stock source
Server average CPU load	dynamic factor
Query size	from 8KB to 200KB
Trigger size	from a few bytes to less than 10KB
Max number of active CQs	25
Retry interval	there is no retry after a failure
Minimum time interval for time-based CQ	10 minutes
Polling interval for content-based CQ	5 minutes

The following measures are selected for the initial performance evaluation.

1. *Execution time*: including trigger time, query time, notification time and total execution time.
2. *Average CPU load (in # of jobs)*: on Unix, using "uptime".
3. *I/O cost*: including database access and file operations (reads and writes).
4. *Workload characterization*: including trigger size distribution, query size distribution, and locality of interests.

A CQ status history log (March 9 - April 30, 1999) is shown in Figure 3. Figure 4 shows the trigger evaluation time, the query processing time, the notification time in comparison with the total roundtrip execution time for a continual query. The trigger time and the query time both include cache creation or refresh time and differential result generation time. From the set of CQs we run for this performance study, we observe that the curve of CQ execution time matches the curve of the CPU load of the server machine. The CPU load was measured using the CPU uptime at the beginning of a CQ evaluation and the CPU uptime at the end of the evaluation.

There are many factors that affect the system performance and CQ execution time. For example, *database access time* is a known performance factor. By grouping database accesses into batch jobs, we can efficiently reduce the CQ evaluation time. It also helps if we keep the database connection open (persistent) until the end of CQ evaluation. Another factor is *CGI vs. Java servlets*. CGI is process-based, while Java servlets are thread-based. By replacing the CGI calls to servlet calls, we can save valuable system resources. Furthermore, *cache management* is also a critical factor during a normal CQ evaluation. We are working on implementing more efficient cache structure to speedup CQ evaluation. A promising solution is to employ the *Differential Evaluation Algorithm* [5] for version control and cache management. In addition, strategies for handling *server failures due to timeout* are important. Timeout may be caused by either slow network connections or host failure. In either case, we may consider the host is unavailable. To find out as early as possible the host unavailability can certainly improve system performance by reducing idle waiting time. Our performance

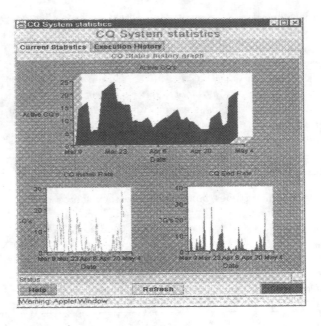

Fig. 3. CQ system status history screenshot

evaluation also considers the *logging overhead*. To provide higher availability and re-liability of the JCQ system, we adopt the "write-ahead-logging" protocol in the CQ system. Before any changes are written to stable storage, a log is written to stable storage first. However, logging overhead is not negligible. One possible workaround is to use separate resource manager as the logging manager and/or divide the application into groups of small "transactions" and exploit maximum parallelism. Finally, explor-ing asynchronous execution as much as possible will also help reducing the overall idle waiting time of the system.

6 Related Work and Concluding Remarks

The paper describes the design and implementation of a prototype system for *data update monitoring* in a distributed open environment (such as the Internet). It uses the *continual query* concept as a powerful means for supporting continual monitoring of information updates. The work presented here is built on top of previous work in *Continual Queries* [5] as well as in DIOM [6]. One of the main design goals of JCQ is the scalability of distributed trigger processing for a large number of continual queries. We explore a number of parallel processing opportunities at the query level, the event level, the condition level, and the data level. The main idea is to group continual queries according to their trigger structures (commonality in the predicates specifying the triggers). Since the variants of the same structure can be processed together at low cost, successful grouping leads to highly scalable trigger and query processing.

There has been considerable research done on data update monitoring in databases. Powerful database techniques such as active databases and materialized views have

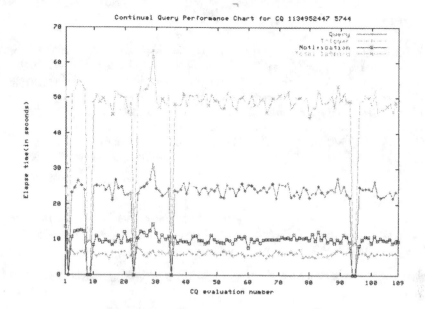

Fig. 4. CQ execution times

been studied extensively. These techniques have been proposed primarily for "data-centric" environments with a close-world assumption, where data is well organized and centrally controlled in a database. When applied to an open information universe as the Internet, these assumptions no longer hold, and some of the techniques do not easily extend to scale up to the distributed interoperable environment. Comparing with the state-of-art of research in active databases [12, 9, 10, 4, 11, 3], the JCQ system differs primarily in the following three ways: First, the JCQ system targets at update monitoring on the Web, handling both structured database sources and semi-structured sources such as HTML files. Second, the continual query concept can be seen as a practical and useful simplification of the ECA rules. In continual queries, user-defined actions are queries only and actions defined by the systems are side-effect free operations such as email notification and differential result display. This simplification made an efficient implementation practically feasible. Third, the JCQ system provides efficient and scalable trigger processing to handle large numbers of concurrently running continual queries on a variety of data sources. There are several systems developed towards monitoring Web source data changes. A main problem with these systems is that they are tailored to a particular domain of data source or application such as news in SIFT [14] or pre-wrapped sources such as [2], lacking of the generality and extensibility of the JCQ system.

References

1. E. Anwar, L. Maugis, and S. Chakravarthy. A new perspective on rule support for object-oriented databases. In *Proceedings of ACM SIGMOD Conference*, 1993.

2. S. Chawathe, S. Abiteboul, and J. Widom. Managing and querying changes in semistructured data. In *Proceedings of the ACM SIGMOD International Conference on Management of Data*, Tucson, Arizona, May 1997.

3. L. Haas, W. Chang, G. Lohman, J. McPherson, P.Wilms, G. Lapis, B. Lindsay, H. Pirahesh, M. Carey, and E. Shekita. Starburst mid-flight: As the dust clears. *IEEE Transactions on Knowledge and Data Engineering*, pages 377–388, March 1990.

4. E. Hanson. Rule condition testing and action execution in ariel. In *Proceedings of ACM SIGMOD Conference*, 1992.

5. L. Liu, C. Pu, R. Barga, and T. Zhou. Differential evaluation of continual queries. In *IEEE Proceedings of the 16th International Conference on Distributed Computing Systems*, Hong Kong, May 27-30 1996.

6. L. Liu, C. Pu, and Y. Lee. Adaptive approach to query mediation across heterogeneous information sources. In *International Conference on Cooperative Information Systems(CoopIS)*, Brussels, Belgium, June 1996.

7. L. Liu, C. Pu, and W. Tang. Continual queries for internet-scale event-driven information delivery. *IEEE Knowledge and Data Engineering*, 1999. Special Issue on Web Technology.

8. L. Liu, C. Pu, W. Tang, and W. Han. CONQUER: A Continual Query System for Update Monitoring in the WWW. *International Journal of Computer Systems, Science and Engineering*, 1999. Special Issue on WWW Semantics, edited by Dan Suciu and Letizia Tanca.

9. D. McCarthy and U. Dayal. The architecture of an active database management system. In *Proceedings of the ACM-SIGMOD International Conference on Management of Data*, pages 215–224, May 1989.

10. U. Schreier, H. Pirahesh, R. Agrawal, and C. Mohan. Alert: An architecture for transforming a passive dbms into an active dbms. In *Proceedings of the International Conference on Very Large Data Bases*, pages 469–478, Barcelona, Spain, September 1991.

11. M. Stonebraker and L. Rowe. The design of POSTGRES. In *Proceedings of 1985 SIGMOD International Conference on Management of Data*, pages 374–387. ACM/SIGMOD, 1985.

12. J. Widom and S. Ceri. *Active Database Systems*. Morgan Kaufmann, 1996.

13. Ling Liu, Calton Pu and W. Tang. Supporting Internet Applications Beyond Browsing: Trigger Processing and Change Notification *Manuscript*, Oregon Graduate Institute, Department of CSE, April 1999.

14. T. W. Yan and H. Garcia-Molina. SIFT - a tool for wide area information dissemination. In *Proceedings of the 1995 USENIX Technical Conference*, pages 177-186, 1995.

Improving Computer Support for Cooperative Applications over Internet

J.C. Burguillo, M.J. Fernández, M. Llamas, and L. Anido

Universidade de Vigo, Vigo 36200, Spain,
jrial@ait.uvigo.es,
WWW home page: http://www-gist.ait.uvigo.es/~jrial

Abstract. The development of environments for telecooperation over Internet is an increasing necessity for speeding up learning, development and cooperation. In this paper, we introduce an architecture model and a protocol, designed to allow multiple on-line communication among several collaborating tools. An abstract event model, which supports remote operation, is also presented. In the practical field we discuss the features of TeleMeeting, a system developed in Java, that supports the previous concepts and incorporates several tools to improve the "virtual meetings" over Internet.

1 Introduction

During the last years, several concepts have become popular with Internet and WWW apparition: Teleworking, Telemedicine, Teleteaching, Telecooperation, etc. New technologies have contributed definitively to this process. In the present day networked scenario, computer support for cooperative work (CSCW) enables new possibilities for sharing information and tasks.

However, although clearly powerful and useful, the approach followed by the WWW does not directly support additional collaborative forms of information sharing. Electronic mail, HTTP and FTP still remain the basic tools used for supporting collaboration in widely dispersed working groups. Several researchers have suggested that for changing this situation new tools should be developed to assist the complex task of building cooperative systems, together with common platforms to facilitate system deployment [1, 2].

Furthermore, decentralisation seems to be the trend in business and academia due to the problems that arise in the design of multiuser systems based on centralised and replicated architectures [3]. This only can be achieved if new, effective methods for information sharing are made available.

The aim of this paper is to discuss a new architectural solution, to support on-line collaborative work, together with the protocols needed to communicate different agents over the network. At the same time, we explore the possibilities of Java [4] to foster user-interaction and decentralised tool support.

In the next sections, we present our proposed cooperative architecture, the TCOP protocol, and an abstract event model developed to support remote operations. In section 5 we discuss the TeleMeeting environment, which is an implementation of the previously described model. In section 6, we present an alternative to this architecture model and finally, we outline our present and future working lines.

2 Cooperative Architecture

The proposed architecture is based on a typical client-server model. Three main elements interact:

- *Client interface*: it is a gateway module, running on the client machine that connects client tools with the server. This is not a compulsory module. It was designed to simplify the communication with the server and to speed up tool deployment.
- *Client tool*: it is the collaborating application running on the local machine. If the *client interface* is not present, then this tool should implement the server communication protocol.
- *Server*: it creates, maintains and manages all connections and information transfers among concurrent cooperative tools on remote clients.

We took from IRC (Internet Relay Chat)[5] the concept of room. In our model, a room is "a virtual channel where tools interchange any kind of information". In a given room, participants should connect using the same kind of application, for instance; in a chat room every user should connect with the same kind of chat tool.

Client tools behaviours depend on their role and state. We distinguish three roles (*root, room operator* and *room client*) and four states (*standard, listening, lecturer* and *local*).

For the listening state, the client tool only receives information (passive); for the lecturer state, it can send information but can not receive it; the standard state is the aggregation of the two previous ones; and, for the local state, clients can not send nor receive information.

Three kinds of room access were defined: *free, password restricted* and *granted*. For granted rooms, the room operator allows or denies access to individual client tools.

This model helps programmers in two ways. First, it simplifies the development and implementation of new on-line collaborative tools. Second, it makes information exchange among collaborative applications simpler. Furthermore, connecting a new kind of tool to the environment is a dynamic process without server reconfiguration.

3 Tele-cooperation Protocol (TCOP)

TCOP (Tele-Cooperation Protocol) has been designed to support the dialog among server and client tools. The protocol has several commands to handle client requests: connect to a tool, send private messages, get unfinished work initiated by other tools, change state, exit environment, etc. It also has several server-originated commands: return a port connection, allow connection for a new tool, send private messages, return participant IDs, etc.

4   Abstract Event Protocol (AEP)

An interesting feature that should be offered by collaborative systems is teleoperation. For instance, whenever the user performs any action (mouse dragging, key pressed, menu access, etc.) on the local tool; it should be possible to sent it over the network to other clients, which will execute the action as it was generated locally. This feature offers support for remote presentations, remote tutoring and remote operations in a master/slave mode from one to many or many to many.

In a platform independent system, it may be desirable to code and sent events generated by particular programming languages following an abstract model. Then, tools written in different programming languages can use this scheme to map them to the corresponding local context.

To get this feature we need to code events into an abstract representation. If the tool needs to broadcast a particular kind of event, it only needs to map it to the common representation and send it over the network. At the same time, they must be aware of events coming from other tools, to unmap and execute them as if they were local.

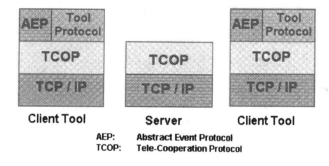

Fig. 1. Architecture layers

In figure 1 we present the architecture model and related protocols. Any application may use its own protocol over TCOP. Optionally, tools may use the service offered by AEP. This service is transparent for the server.

5   TeleMeeting Environment

In this section, we discuss an implementation of the previous architecture and protocols. The TeleMeeting environment is composed by a server and several clients configured following the guidelines commented in previous sections. Client selection was based on the following criteria: they should be adequate to analyse system's performance and they should offer common, useful functionalities that are typically required in collaborative systems.

We chose Java as the implementation language. Java is platform independent and browsers can load dynamically Java applets in a safe manner. With Java, we only need a commercial browser with a Java Virtual Machine for accessing the system. Java also offers more user interaction and less delay than Common Gateway Interface (CGI) based applications [6].

5.1 Connection Procedures

The clients request the server to create new rooms, join to existing ones, manage the room or leave the system.

The participants can access to the system in two ways:

- Using a commercial Internet browser.
- Via a custom-developed application which connects directly to the server.

The connection phase follows these steps:

1. The client interface sends a connection request with a description of the client tool.
2. The server checks the request. If the request is accepted, it returns a port for connection,
3. The tool connects to the server in that port and receives information about other clients and room state.

5.2 The Server Side

The server checks every room connection, accepting orders sent by tools. When the server receives information from a client, it checks the destination: the message could be related to room management, it can be a private message for another client tool, or it should be sent to every tool in the room. At the same time, several rooms can be active for different kinds of tools. The server can log client actions for a specific room.

5.3 TeleMeeting Clients

In the next paragraphs we present different client tools developed as Java applets. These applications are offered as basic functionalities in the system and can be accessed with a standard browser.

These tools have been selected to test the general approach outlined in previous sections. They cover different communication scenarios. We developed a chat client, a file transfer client, a shared whiteboard client and a telebrowsing client.

All of them connect to the server following TCOP. The management tasks, done at the server side, are independent from the tools connected. Every client implements its own application protocol over TCOP. The shared whiteboard and the telebrowsing client are the most specific. We will comment them briefly.

The whiteboard offers a shared graphical editor to every participant in a meeting room. Every picture drawn locally will be seen by every client connected to the same room. This is done thanks to the abstract event model (AEP) that allows whiteboards to recognise remote events.

With the telebrowsing tool, users can show presentations remotely. When a lecturer selects a new HTML page with this tool, every other users' browser fetch that HTML page automatically and present it to the user. This tool is very useful to complement other collaborative systems, for instance, multi-point presentations using videoconference.

6   Client-Subserver Architecture Model

In this section we present an alternative architecture to take advantage of the proposed environment. Combining Java applets and applications we could develop a new model transparent to TeleMeeting. We will call *subservers* to native applications, which run as independent servers and use TeleMeeting to connect to their clients. The reader can view the model as a *multiple* CGI (Common Gateway Interface). It could be interesting to implement simulation environments, where several clients access to a central subserver.

In this model, every client can query the subserver. Other clients are informed about the request and subserver's replies, so every tool can update its state. The model, presented in figure 2, has several advantages that we comment briefly:

1. Local libraries in the remote machine can be accessed.
2. We obtain a distributed environment without overloading the TeleMeeting server.
3. It is an ideal model for one to many simulation environments.
4. Already developed software can be reused.

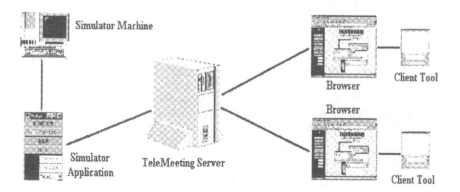

Fig. 2. Subserver architecture

7 Conclusions and Further Work

In this paper we have presented an architecture model and the corresponding protocols designed to improve communication-related features in collaborative on-line applications. The model presented here and the underlying TCOP protocol, allow programmers to add new types of applications dynamically, without recompiling the system.

As a practical implementation of the proposed model, we have introduced the TeleMeeting environment, which offers a rich variety of cooperation possibilities. The environment was designed using Java. Several client tools have also been developed, demonstrating the possibilities of this language to implement environments as complex as the discussed before.

At the same time, we tried to improve system features. One of our present working lines, almost finished, is aimed to enrich this model incorporating memory managers for rooms. The key idea is to share memory between client tools and improve the possibilities for communication in this distributed environment.

The system described in this paper is part of a bigger one that also provides operating system capabilities. This new design incorporates security and encryption features and off-line communication among users that do not comply with the model described in this work.

8 Acknowledgements

We would like to thank Alejandro García González for his work during the implementation phase. We are also grateful to anonymous referees for their judicious comments. Finally, we appreciate the European Community Socrates ODL Project *WeMeet* 56420-CP-1-98-1-BE-ODL-ODL from which we extracted helpful ideas.

References

1. Patterson, J.: Comparing the programming demands of single-user and multi-user applications. Proceedings of UIST'91. ACM Press, November (1991) 87–94.
2. Dewan, P. and Choudhary, R.: A high-level and flexible framework for implementing multi-user interfaces. ACM Transactions on Information Systems, **10(4)** (1992) 345–380.
3. Greenberg, S., Roseman, M., Webster, D. and Bohnet, R.: Human and technical factors of distributed group drawing tools. Interacting with Computers, **4(3)** (1992) 364–392.
4. Gosling, J., Joy, B. and Steele, G.: The Java Language Specification. Addison-Wesley ISBN 0-201-63451-1
5. RFC 1459: Internet Relay Chat. Available by anonymous ftp from ftp.rx.internic.net/rfc
6. Trevor, J., Bentley, R. and Wildgruber, G.: Exorcising daemons: A modular and lightweight approach to deploying applications on the Web. Computer Networks and ISDN Systems: Proceedings of the 5th International W3 Conference, North Holland, **28 (7-11)** (1996) 1053–1062.

A Data Registry-Based Approach for Semantic Representation and Exchange of XML Documents

Hong-Seok Na, Jin-Seok Chae and Doo-Kwon Baik

Software System Lab., Dept. of Computer Science & Engineering, Korea University, 1, 5-ka, Anam-dong, Sungbuk-gu, SEOUL, 136-701, KOREA
{nhs, jin92, baik}@swsys2.korea.ac.kr
http://swsys2.korea.ac.kr/index.html

Abstract. XML users can make their own document structure and tagsets by freely defining the DTD with their intention. This freedom of defining tagsets and the structures, however, prevents the interchange of an XML document between two applications without knowing the other's DTD. In this paper, we proposed a method to represent meaning of tags in XML documents using data registries as a semantic sharing environment. The key idea of the method is to attach a data element identifier in data registries to the corresponding tags in XML documents. Based on the method, we designed a converting process for XML documents, which make it possible to exchange XML documents between applications automatically even if they use different DTDs.

1 Introduction

Today's web gives people unprecedented access to online information and services. But this information is delivered in format-oriented, handcrafted hypertext markup language (HTML), making it understandable only through human eyes[1]. Software applications and search engines have difficulty using the information because it is not semantically encoded.

A solution to this problem may be XML(Extensible Markup Language). Developed by the World Wide Web Consortium(W3C), XML is a simplified(but strict) subset of the ISO's SGML(Standard Generalized Markup Language) that maintains SGML's features of extensibility, structure, and validation[2]. With XML, application designers can create sets of data element tags and structures that define and describe the information contained in a document, database, object, catalog or general application, all in the name of facilitating data interchange[3].

XML documents, the unit of data exchange, are based on DTDs(Document Type Definition). DTD is a document which defines the structure of tagsets, used in XML documents. XML standard specification defines the syntax of DTDs. Therefore, it is possible to share data in XML documents between applications if they use a standardized DTD. Such standardized DTDs include CML DTD[4] used in chemistry domain, Math DTD[5] in mathematics. Using standardized

DTD makes it possible to share tags and attributes defined in the DTD, and to understand semantics of the XML documents.

However, XML is not a cure-all for system interoperability, but a widely accepted foundation layer on which to build[1]. Current and proposed practice in the XML community do not address the administration, maintenance, integration, and standardization of data element definitions, nomenclature, value encodings, etc. If a system cannot understand tags and attributes in a DTD, it cannot understand the XML document based on the DTD, either. Therefore, web environment in which many different applications interact with each other like e-commerce, requires human intervention to communicate using XML documents. For example, suppose that DTD A defines a tag <Product_Number> that represents the meaning of "the number of a specific product", and DTD B defines tag <Product#> representing the same meaning. Then, applications based on DTD A cannot understand the meaning of the tag <Product#> on reading a XML document based on DTD B.

It seems that every firm and every industry are creating their own DTDs. The result of this is a number of DTDs like MathML and CML. This situations are inadequate for applications such as electronic commerce and systems integration. To share the semantics of DTDs in different domains, it is need to develop some kinds of mechanisms for representation and understanding of XML tags.

In this paper, we propose a method that makes it possible for applications of different DTDs to represent and exchange the semantics of XML documents using ISO/IEC 11179-based data registries. The main idea of the method is to attach semantic meaning defined in data registries to the corresponding tags in DTD and XML documents. By representing the exact meaning of tags using the data element identifier, applications can understand the meaning of tagsets in XML documents even if the documents are made on the basis of different DTDs.

2 Semantic Representation of XML Documents using Data Registries

2.1 Data Registry

A data registry is basically a database for metadata including data elements, definitions, value domains, tags, etc. It also encompasses the associated administrative processes for managing the proposing, specification, recording, evolution, continuing stewardship and standardization of the metadata.

The describing unit of data in a data registry is data element[6]. A data element is a unit of data for which the definition, identification, and permissible values are specified by means of a set of attributes. It is composed of three parts - object class, property, and representation. The *object class* is a set of ideas, abstractions, or things in the real world that can be identified with explicit boundaries and meaning, and whose properties and behavior follow the same rules. The *property* is a peculiarity common to all members of an object class. And the *representation* describes how the data are represented, i.e. Combination

313

of a value domain, datatype, and, if necessary, a unit of measure or a character set.

Each data element has an unique identifier, all users and programs using the data registry can identify a data element by the identifier. A data element also contains its definition, name, context, representation format, and so on.

A data registry plays a role of unique identification, registration and service about data. There are several attempts to standardize data registries, notably ISO/IEC 11179(Data Element Definition), and ANSI X3.285(A Metamodel for ISO 11179)[6].

2.2 Representing Semantics of XML Tags using Data Element Identifier

As mentioned above, XML documents using same DTD can be semantically and syntactically exchanged between applications (because they use same document structure and tagsets), but documents using different DTDs cannot understand the meaning of the documents even if they have similar structures or contents. For example, DTD A used tag <Title> and DTD B used <TTL> for a book's title, they could not communicate each other.

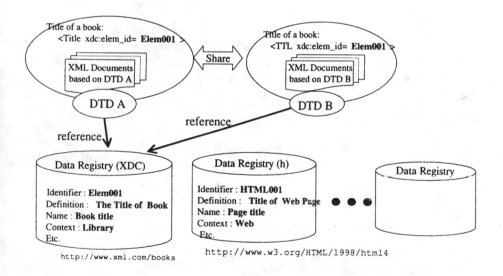

Fig. 1. The Overall Structure of the Registry-based Semantic Representation

We use the data element identifier as a semantic representation unit of XML tags. Figure 1 shows the approach for semantic representation of XML tags based on data registries. The XDC data registry located in the URL of "http://www.xml.com/books" contains data elements describing metadata about book. The tag <Title> of DTD A and <TTL> of DTD B have an attribute "elem_id" indicating a concept defined as a data element in the XDC data registry. By just adding an attribute pointing a data element, we can represent the exact meaning of tag in XML documents.

Figure 2 shows a part of DTD A which defines tags and attributes referencing data elements in the data registry, named XDC. The first line in figure 2 defines the structure of tagsets that the tag <Book> must have five tags - <Title>, <Author>, <Price>, <Pages>, and <Date>. The second line means that users of the DTD will use tag <Title> and that the tag will contain some text value in XML documents. The fifth line means the tag <Title> has an attribute "elem_id" and this attribute has the fixed value "Elem001". The prefix 'XDC' is an XML namespace[7] indicating the location of the referenced data registry.

```
<!ELEMEMT  Book  (Title, Author, Price, Pages, Date)>
<!ELEMENT  Title  (#PCDATA) >

<!ATTRIBUTE Book xmlns:xdc CDATA #Fixed "http://www.xml.com/books">
<!ATTRIBUTE Book xdc:oc_id CDATA  #Fixed  "Oc001">
<!ATTRIBUTE Title xdc:elem_id CDATA  #Fixed  "Elem001">
```

Fig. 2. A Part of the DTD A in figure 1

XML namespaces provide a simple method for qualifying tag and attribute names used in XML documents by associating them with namespaces identified by URI references. XML namespaces also provide a coarse granularity mechanism to facilitate sharing of schemas(DTDs) or fragments thereof. In particular XML namespaces permit one to partition the namespace of XML tags sets into several pieces - indicated by prefixes, e.g., "xdc:elem_id", which are expanded into URLs. That is, Namespaces are a simple and straightforward way to distinguish names used in XML documents, no matter where they come from. We use the XML namespace mechanism to distinguish data elements of different data registries.

```
<Book xdc:oc_id="oc001" xmlns:xdc="http://www.xml.com/books">
      <Title  xdc:elem_id = "elem001"> XML: A Primer</Title>
      <Author  xdc:elem_id = "elem002">Simon St. Laurent</Author>
      <Price  xdc:elem_id = "elem003">31.98</Price>
      <Pages  xdc:elem_id = "elem004">352</ Pages>
      <Date  xdc:elem_id = "elem005">1998/01</Date>
</Book>
```

Fig. 3. An XML Document based on the DTD in Figure 2

Figure 3 is an XML document generated with the DTD in figure 2. All XML documents based on the DTD use tag <Title>, and the attribute "xdc:elem_id" of the tag contains the fixed value "Elem001". This means that the semantic and structural information of the tag <Title> is in the data registry of location "http://www.xml.com/books" with the form of data element having identifier "Elem001". These attribute-value pairs can be inserted automatically with general XML editors.

3 XML Documents Exchange

Let's suppose a situation that company A uses DTD A for personnel management and company B uses DTD B for the same object. If an application of company A would sent a person's personnel records to company B using XML document, it is necessary to make the document understood by the receiving application of the company B.

In our approach that attaches a data element identifier representing the concept of tags in XML document, the converting process can be done automatically if XML documents are made by the DTDs referencing common data registries.

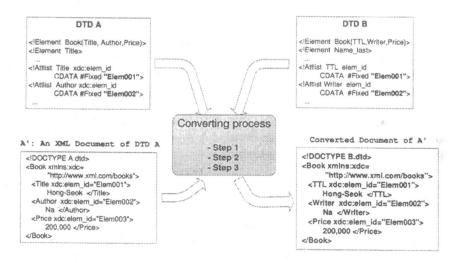

Fig. 4. Input and Output of the Converting Process

The converting process consists of three steps

- *Step 1.* Reads two different DTDs, and one XML document
- *Step 2.* Constructs a mapping table
- *Step 3.* Replaces the tags in the XML document with the corresponding tags in mapping table

Figure 4 shows the input and output of the converting process. In the first step, the process takes two DTDs, the document sender's DTD and the receiver's

DTD, and one XML document to be converted. After parsing the two DTDs, it constructs a mapping table in the second step.

The table consists of three columns - "Elem_ID", "DTD A" and "DTD B". The column "Elem_ID" contains the data element identifier in the data registry as the unique concept. The column "DTD A" has the tag names defined in the DTD of sender's corresponding to the identifier, and the column "DTD B" has the tag names defined in DTD of receiver's.

Then, the process replaces the tags in the XML document with the corresponding tags in mapping table, generating a document that the receiver can understand. In figure 4, the tag <Title> in document A' is replaced with the tag <TTL>, since they have the same data element identifier "Elem001". Like this, the tag <Author> is replaced with the tag <Writer> and so on. As a result, the receivers can get XML documents converted as their DTDs, understand and use the documents directly.

4 Conclusion

In spite of XML's main advantages enabling users to define tags and structures of their documents freely, the lack of semantic representation scheme for XML tags prevents automatic exchange of XML documents in internet environment.

In this paper, we proposed a method that make it possible for applications using different DTDs to represent, exchange and search the semantics of XML documents without human intervention. We believe that the proposed method and environment will increase the interoperability of XML documents.

Our future research will include XML document search engine based on data registries and constructing an environment supporting semantic exchange of XML documents.

References

1. Robert J. Glushko, Jay M. Tenenbaum, Bart Meltzer: An XML Framework for Agent-based E-commerce, Communications of ACM, Vol. 42, No.3 (1999) 106-114
2. Rohit Khare, Adam Rifkin: XML: A Door to Automated Web Applications, IEEE Internet Computing, July & August (1997) 78-87
3. Rik Drummond, Kay Spearman: XML Set to Change the Face of E-Commerce, Network Computing, Vol.9, No.8 (1997) 140-144
4. P.Murray-Rust: Chemical Markup Language, Version 1.0, January (1997) available at http://www.venus.co.uk/omf/cml/
5. Mathematical Markup Language (MathML) 1.0 Specification, W3C, July (1998) available at http://www.w3c.org/TR/1998/REC-MathML-19980407
6. Information technology - Specification and standardization of data element, ISO/IEC 11179-1 Final Committee Draft, June (1998)
7. Namespaces in XML, W3C, January (1999) available at http://www.w3.org/TR/1999/REC-xml-names-19990114

Organization of Mobile Networks
Under Privacy Constraints

Toshihiko Hamano[1], Hiroki Takakura[2] and Yahiko Kambayashi[1]

[1] Department of Social Informatics, Kyoto University
[2] Department of Electrical Engineering, Kyoto University
Yoshida-Honmachi Sakyo Kyoto, 606-8501, Japan
{thamano, takakura, yahiko}@kuis.kyoto-u.ac.jp

Abstract. In order to process requests for mobile computing environment, locations and requests from users have to be stored in the system. If these data are stored in one centralized system, it may be rather easy to get history of locations/requests of a specific user. Since it is not desirable to obtain such information by other users, we will introduce a system which will store such information in distributed way. User related information is stored in Information Kiosks. Users' requests are sent to the central network by adding request ID without disclosing user ID. The central network is also allowed to broadcast information to be used by users. For practical reason we select hierarchical form for the network. How to process requests from users in such mobile systems is discussed. In order to get information not stored in the Kiosk nearby, we propose a system to form adhoc LAN among neighboring mobile terminals. The function can be used to realize applications using the real and virtual world together.

1 Introduction

Due to the recent development of portable computers, Internet technology, GPS systems and wireless communication technology, mobile systems are becoming very popular. In order to realize powerful mobile systems, there are still problems to be solved, which are not considered in conventional fixed structured distributed systems. Broadcast scheduling, location dependent query processing, energy consumption problems of batteries are examples of such problems. Some of typical papers on mobile databases are [2, 5, 7].

In this paper we will discuss system architecture in order to realize efficient processing of location dependent queries and the privacy problems of users. Location data of users and the history of data usage of each user are distributed in various systems and without special rights it is impossible to merge them together. We believe that the privacy problem of mobile systems is very important but not discussed in previous literature.

We will mainly discuss the problem of keeping privacy of users in a system shown in [6] as NaviArea in this paper, which uses hierarchical communication structure. Since in the mobile system locations of the all users and requests from the users have to be used for query processing, the history of users' location together with request(contents, time of request) can be recovered using such data. Disclosure of such information will violate the privacy of users. In order to avoid the concentration of such privacy related data, the central system located in the top of the hierarchy is designed not accept users' requests directly. The central system can (1)communicate (bi-directional) with the systems located at one-level down in the hierarchy and (2)broadcast information to all subsystems in the hierarchy and all the user terminals (uni-directional). Users can get information (1)through the broadcast by the central system, and (2)by direct communication with the system located at the lowest level of the hierarchy (we call such systems as Information Kiosks). The central system is assumed to store most required data and it is connected to outside network in order to get information not stored in the system. The system which are not the central nor the Information Kiosks store (1)various location dependent data which are obtained by the network in the subarea such as traffic information in the area and (2)cache of data sent from the system located at one level above in the network hierarchy. The Information Kiosks store (1)cache of data, (2)location dependent data such as shopping information of its covering area and (3)user related information such as IDs of users and requests. Note that user data related to privacy are only distributedly stored in Kiosks.

Due to the above restricted structure we have a new problem on realizing efficient query processing. The request of a user is transmitted to the nearest Kiosk. If the request cannot be found in the data stored at the Kiosks, the request together with the request ID is sent to the system located in one-level above in the hierarchy. The user ID is hidden to the subsystem. If the corresponding data are not stored in the subsystems in the hierarchy, the request is processed by the central system. The request for location dependent data is sent to the corresponding subsystem. If the request is not location dependent and the corresponding data are not stored in the subsystems on the path from the Kiosk to the central system, the request is sent to the central system, which is connected to a wide-area network.

Although the Kiosk located at each subarea may store data related to the area, the user may need information of neighboring subareas in order to make schedules, for example. Such data are not usually stored in the Kiosk for that area. As there may be mobile users which moved from the neighboring areas, they may have required information. In order to get such information quickly we propose to utilize adhoc LAN among users located in small area as shown in [3, 8]. Such LAN also help users to know each other and exchange information on their hobbies. Such a function can be also used in order to realize new applications(see [4], for example) by combining the real world and the network (virtual) world.

Rest of the paper is organized as follows. Section 2 shows outline of network structures of NaviArea. Section 3 discusses a method of mobile information sharing. Mechanisms for keeping privacy is discussed in Section 4.

2   The System Organization

2.1   Outline of NaviArea

NaviArea is designed to be used for navigation of shopping and sight-seeing[6] using mobile systems. The mobile network consists of Kiosks and several kinds of Stations. Their covering areas form a hierarchy. We assume that they are actually communication lines as shown in Figure 1.

2.2 Distribution of location information

In order to avoid centralization of location/activity history of users, we will store most of these information in Information Kiosk in distributed way. Mobile terminals can only communicate bi-directionally with Information Kiosks and other user terminals nearby. All other Stations will transmit information by broadcast mode without identifying the receivers. Information can transmit through communication lines.

In order to hide user information, one Kiosk is assigned to each user, which is called the home Kiosk for the user. It stores the correspondence between the real name of the user and the coded name of the user. The first part of the code corresponds to the home Kiosk, so that information required for some user dependent process is obtained from the Kiosk (security levels, etc.). If a user buys something from a shop, with a credit card with coded name, the shop have to ask the correctness to the home Kiosk. We assume that cards do not require signature but some secret password. Whenever the user come back to the home Kiosk, the coded name can be changed if required. The user history of activities are stored in the user terminal and Kiosks in a distributed way.

If the location history is required for computing the charge for communication cost, the home Kiosk will collect necessary information for changing purpose. The user terminal, of course, stores its location history, which will not be used, since mobile terminal is rather easy to crush and the owner can change the contents.

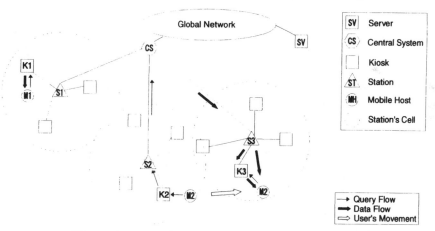

Fig. 1. An example of network structure of NaviArea

3 Adhoc LAN among Users' Mobile Terminals

We introduce adhoc LAN among users' mobile terminals. It help users to get necessary information rapidly.

There is time interval between a Station's broadcast of a program and the next broadcast of the same program. Even if a user knows the program, s/he may not be able to get required information because mobile connections is not so reliable. If users fail to obtain the information from Stations, generally, they must wait for the next broadcast. In such a case it will be desirable if we permit users to be able to get information from other users nearby.

It is also useful that users may get other areas' information which they cannot get directly from the Kiosk. It can be attained from other users come from neighboring areas. Adhoc LAN is also important to realize shopping between the user's terminal and the shop's terminal which is also regarded as a mobile host although it cannot move in general.

There are two way of data distribution shown as follows.

- PULL method

When a mobile terminal requires information, if other mobile terminals have the required information in adhoc LAN, the mobile terminal try to acquire the information from one of them as well as the Kiosk. This realizes a function of cache at accessing to the low-speed upper level network. If the request is given to the Kiosk and the information is not stored, the time to process will be very long(because the request will be transmitted to other Stations) and it is much more efficient if the information is attained by another mobile host.

- PUSH method

Some users may wish to disseminate its own information. For example, they bought something at very low price in shop A or they look at some accidents somewhere. If the information is useful for other users, they can share the information through adhoc LAN.

Here, we discuss a mechanism of data providing and acquiring in those two methods mentioned above. Mobile terminals which are on the side of providing data is referred as a transient server(TS). Mobile terminals which are on the other side, the side of acquiring data is referred as a transient client(TC). Figure 2 shows the time flow chart of the processes of data provision and acquisition.

In the PULL method, a TC requests for necessary data to adhoc LAN by utilizing the known addresses such as uniform resource locator (URL). As shown in Figure 2, first requirement for data transfer occurs in the side of TC. A TS is determined in adhoc LAN after that. Data are provided and acquired as follows. First, a TC sends requests for necessary data by broadcast to adhoc LAN. Then, surrounding hosts receive the signal. Among them, mobile terminals which have and can provide the requested data are able to reply to the requests. The host which responds to the requests first become a TS. The host broadcasts to adhoc LAN that a TS is already determined, and sends entities of the data to the TC.

In the Push method, on the other hand, first requirement for data transfer occurs in the side of TS. A TC can be determined after that. Data are provided and acquired as follows. At first, a TS which wishes to disseminate its own data broadcasts indexes of the data capable of providing in adhoc LAN. After that, a TC sends requests for necessary data to the TS. Then the server sends entities of the data to the clients.

For shopping there is another type of communication to be supported by the system, secret communication between two mobile hosts. It is especially useful for negotiations of price, sending information of credit cards, etc. The one-to-one secret communication can be used between two mobile hosts in order to communicate like telephone.

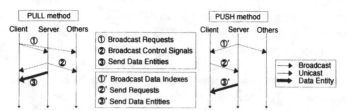

Fig. 2. Time flow of data provision and acquisition

4 Mechanisms of Information Acquisition

4.1 Kiosk: A gateway to the global network

Kiosks deal with user's requests and also have a function as cache for the global network. Kiosks provide information for users according to their requests and work as gateways to the global network for mobile terminals. When a user has requirements for acquiring some information, s/he sends the requests to the nearest Kiosk with which s/he can communicate. If the Kiosk has requested information at that time, it sends the information to the mobile terminal. In case that the Kiosk does not have the information, it publishes a query ID and sends the request to Stations or a central server with the query ID in order to hide the user's name. The mobile terminal also receives the query ID. By combining ID of the Kiosk and query number in each Kiosk, unique query ID in the whole system of NaviArea can be generated and utilized. Then, the Kiosk receives the required information from Stations. Thus, the Kiosk obtain and can provide the requested information for users. In this process, in order to keep user's privacy, the Kiosk does not disclose user's name and network address to the global network. That is, Kiosks also have a function of filtering user's personal information. Therefore location information of each user is only known to each Kiosk. Different from conventional methods of organizing mobile networks, systems on the global network cannot grasp locations of users.

4.2 Query processing under the movement of users

One of the most significant issues in mobile computing is that a data requested by a mobile terminal should be surely send to the mobile terminal even if the host moves away while a query of the request is processed. This issue is discussed based on Figure 1. For example, if M2 sends a request to K2 and both K2 and S2 do not have the requested data, S2 sends the request to SV. If M2 moves out of K2's cell to another cell(K3's) during the query processing, the requested data have to be forwarded to K3 and M2 could get it there.

This kind of issue has been solved in conventional systems that central systems manage each mobile terminal's location and movement[1]. However, since our system does not allow to know MH's location, there are some problems.

(1) K2 cannot directly forward the data to K3 because K2 cannot know where M2 goes.
(2) Though K3 knows where M2 is, K3 cannot tell it to other hosts in order to prevent SV from knowing M2's location.

There are the following strategies for the problems.

(i) If a user is waiting for the response of the request, s/he will transmit the request ID to the Kiosk s/he moved. The Kiosk will send the ID to the Stations which are located in higher positions in the hierarchy. The information will be obtained from a Station directly or the original Kiosk.

(ii) If the original Kiosk cannot identify the location of the user, broadcast functions can be used. The user have to send information whether s/he received the information to the nearest Kiosk.

5   Conclusion

This paper discussed information sharing mechanisms among mobile users in wireless hierarchical networks under privacy constraints. If location and movement of users is stored in the central system on the global network, the privacy may not be protected. In order to handle that problem, a hierarchical network organization is proposed and the central system does not store locations of users. Users' locations are stored by many subsystems called Information Kiosks each of which cover only a small area. The global network provides information for mobile systems indirectly and each subsystem accepts user requests. When the information is not cashed in the subsystem, it requests to the central system without disclosing the user's name. The broadcast plan is changed if similar requests are given. Otherwise the information will be sent to the subsystem directly. An example of such information is location dependent one. One of the problems of broadcast is that it may takes a lot of time to get information because of its sequential nature. In order to handle the problem information stored by other mobile users nearby is used. Improvement of performance using cache distributed in the hierarchy is considered. Further improvement is one of the future problems.

References

1. B. R. Badrinath and T. Imielinski, "Location Management for Networks with Mobile Users", *MOBILE COMPUTING*, pp.129-152, 1996.
2. D. L. Lee, Q. Hu and W. -C. Lee, "Indexing Techniques for Data Broadcast on Wireless Channels", *Proceedings of the 5th International Conference on Foundations of Data Organization (FODO '98)*, pp.175-182, 1998.
3. F. Bennett, D. Clarke, J.B. Evans, A. Hopper, A Jones and D. Leask, "Piconet: Embedded Mobile Networking", *IEEE Personal Communications*, pp.8-15, Vol. 4, No. 5, 1997.
4. H. Tarumi, K. Morishita, M. Nakao and Y. Kambayashi, "SpaceTag: An Overlaid Virtual System and its Application", *Proceedings of International Conference on Multimedia Computing and Systems (ICMCS'99)*, Vol.1, pp.207-212, 1999.
5. S. Acharya, M. Franklin, S. Zdonik and R. Alonso, "Broadcast Disks: Data Management for Asymmetric Communication Environments", *Proceedings of ACM SIGMOD International Conference on Management of Data*, 1995.
6. T. Hamano, H. Takakura and Y. Kambayashi, "A Dynamic Navigation System Based on User's Geographical Situation", *Lecture Notes in Computer Science 1552*, pp.368-379, 1998.
7. T. Imielinski and B. R. Badrinath, "Querying in Highly Mobile and Distributed Environments", *Proceedings of the 18th International Conference on Very Large DataBases*, 1992.
8. "BlueTooth", http://www.bluetooth.com/

Mean Time Offset Protocol for Cluster of Auction Servers over TCP/IP Network

Kok Meng Yew, Zahidur R.M., and Sai Peck Lee

Faculty of Computer Sc. & Information Technology
University Malaya
Kuala Lumpur, Malaysia

yew@fsktm.um.edu.my, zahidur@siswazah.fsktm.um.edu.my,
saipeck@fsktm.um.edu.my

Abstract

The diffusion of electronic commerce in society is already accepted. Real time application like auction, stock broker, needs a robust system. Using a single server does not guarantee, how strong the hardware and operating system are, the immunity to active or passive adversary. To minimize the single point of failure, cluster of servers are commonly replaced by a single server. In the case of auction protocol using secret sharing scheme, the time of opening and closing of session and synchronization of server message passing are very crucial. But the physically separated servers over TCP/IP network and the drift of clock for each server, make it challenging to have a single clock. TCP/IP was designed to provide the best-effort service. This puts the designer to difficulty in providing a real-time service solution over TCP/IP. In this paper we propose a protocol to calculate mean time offset of a set of servers with minimal chance of error introduced by the unpredictable time delay due to TCP/IP network.

1 Introduction

The real-life application of electronic commerce like auction, stock broker, is already accepted in society. A robust system for e-commerce is crying demand of time. A single server does not guarantee the immunity to active or passive adversary though present hardware and operating system are too strong to withstand. The commercial auction servers like eBay use a single auction server over HTTP and hence there is no problem for synchronization but the server failure is fatal [1]. To minimize the single point of failure, cluster of servers is deployed. The cluster of servers can use the protocol like secret sharing for various applications like auction. The secret sharing requires that all the servers to be synchronous. In some protocols like auction, the closing and the opening of service is crucial. If a single auction server is used, the problem is not so critical as the bidder has to know only one time offset of the auction server for real-time auction. Modern computer clock is accurate but not precise. Almost all general purpose computers suffer from the problem of having some clock offset from real clock.

Auction servers which use secret sharing protocol, are physically separated, may be in different time zone and surely have some offset from the real time clock [2, 3]. The communication delay over TCP/IP is not predictable. TCP/IP was designed to provide the best-effort service. This makes providing real-time services over TCP/IP very difficult [4]. To overcome this problem and to provide an acceptable and desirable quality of service in real time, we propose a protocol by introducing server mean time offset (MTO). Our protocol is not designed to achieve a good throughput, but to provide a predictable mean time offset of a set of servers in order to guarantee the correctness of time-critical transactions.

2 Time offset calculation

In the time offset calculation, it is assumed that the servers have no provision of changing clock setting. The cluster of servers consists of n servers connected over TCP/IP network. Because it is connection oriented protocol, it can alleviate the load on the server site. To determine the clock offset with respect to each other server, it can be carried out by sending a message at time T_1 to the other server in network. The receiving server notes the time (T_2) at which it receives the message and provides a response by sending to the server with time of origin of this message in its clock (T_3). The originating server now receives the response at time T_4 in its clock frame. This can be shown in Figure 1.

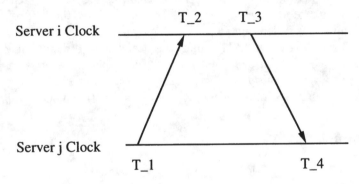

Fig. 1. Timing diagram for server i and server j.

Let we consider that the clock of $server_1$ deviates by δ_1 from the real clock. That is at any time T can be represented by

$T = T_{real} + \delta_1$

In modern computer the clock is almost accurate and no need to consider the drift of clock. Similarly the time on $server_2$ is

$T = T_{real} + \delta_2$

where δ_2 is the offset from the real clock for $server_2$.

The times recoded in the above protocol can now be written by

$$T_1 = T_{1real} + \delta_1$$
$$T_2 = T_{2real} + \delta_2$$
$$T_3 = T_{3real} + \delta_2$$
$$T_4 = T_{4real} + \delta_1$$

where $T_{n\,real}$ is the actual time in standard time frame.
The time delay of message 1 in two clocks is

$$T_2 - T_1 = T_{2real} - T_{1real} + \delta_2 - \delta_1$$
$$= T_{\Delta_{21}} + \delta_2 - \delta_1$$

And the time delay of message 2 in two clocks is

$$T_4 - T_3 = T_{4real} - T_{3real} + \delta_1 - \delta_2$$
$$= T_{\Delta_{43}} + \delta_1 - \delta_2$$

Where $T_{\Delta_{21}}$ and $T_{\Delta_{43}}$ are the time delay over network. Due to the characteristics of TCP/IP network, it is unpredictable that these values should be equal. The clock offset of the two servers can now be calculated by

$$t_{off_{12}} = \delta_1 - \delta_2$$
$$= \frac{T_4 - T_3 + T_1 - T_2}{2} + \frac{T_{\Delta_{43}} - T_{\Delta_{21}}}{2}$$

In generally, for ith server and jth server, the clock offset can be calculated by

$$t_{off_{ij}} = \frac{T_{4i} - T_{3j} + T_{1i} - T_{2j}}{2} + \frac{T_{\Delta_{43ij}} - T_{\Delta_{21ij}}}{2}$$

For ideal case, it can be safely assume that the time delay $T_{\Delta_{43}} = T_{\Delta_{21}}$. But in reality they are not the same. Instead of having a costly precise real-time server, for the purpose of general use, it is realistic to assume that the participant servers are almost near real time. With this assumption, the servers choose a mean time T_{mean} such that

$$T_{mean} = T_{real} + \delta = T_{real} + \frac{\sum_{i=1}^{n} \delta_i}{n}$$

By choosing a mean time between a set of servers like auction server, it will be a low cost provision for synchronization of servers. In the proposed protocol, after calculating offset from different server clocks, each server passes these offset values to other servers. Each server now calculates the offset from mean time

$$t_{off\,mean_i} = T_i - T_{mean} = \delta_i - \delta$$
$$= \frac{\sum_{i,j=0}^{n} t_{off_{ij}} - t_{off_{ji}}}{n}$$

where T_i is ith server time. As in this calculation, time delay in both direction are used, it is realistic to assume that the probability of unexpected delay for the TCP/IP network is reduced though it is not eliminated. Thus, this includes some unexpected error in calculation due to unpredictable delay in the TCP/IP network, but now in reduced probability.

It is worthy to note that the mean time offset is different for different servers as different server has different deviation from mean time. As it is hard to calculate real time, in our calculation we don't have to use real time but the server's own time. Then we safely consider that all the participant servers are now synchronized with mean time which is little deviated from real time. To over come the problem with different time zone, the auction server will send the time for T_1, T_2, T_3 and T_4 as UTC.

3 Mean Time Offset protocol overview

To achieve the above server mean time offset (MTO), we designed a protocol between the participant servers. This protocol is influenced by the Network Time Protocol [5]. NTP is a protocol deployed for synchronizing clocks in computer systems over the Internet. But this protocol lacks of synchronizing set of servers without the presence of a synchronized server. There is no provision for acquisition or authentication in the proposed protocol. The recipient server does not require to store any information of requesting server. After the completion of protocol, there will be no difference between requesting and recipient as all of the servers in turn take both the roles.

In what may be the most common (unsymmetric) mode a requesting server sends an MTO messages to recipient server.

Now we can informally state the protocol by the following statements:

1. Send Message1: The protocol starts by sending a message containing sender ID, the current time T_1 and recipients ID.
2. Reply Message1: In reply, the receiver sends own ID, receive time T_2, sending time T_3 and initiator ID.
   Sender now notes the time T_4 when it receives the reply of message1. Step 2 and 3 will be repeated for all the servers. After step 2, the sender calculates the time offset between all other servers.
3. Send Message2: Send sender ID, clock offset w.r.t destination server T_{off} and destination server ID.
4. Reply Message2: In reply to Message2, the destination server sends its ID, clock offset w.r.t. sender T_{off} along with an additional data ALREADY_SENT. It is set to TRUE if server did send already, else it is set to FALSE.

Repeat step 3 and 4, for all the servers in the system. The fourth step is required for very unreliable TCP/IP network. After waiting a predefined time, or if the sender receives all the responses, it calculates SMTO and the protocol terminates.

The mean time offset will be calculated well before the auction servers start the auction. The time for any auction related service then will be calculated as $T_{present_i} + t_{off_i}$ where $T_{present_i}$ is current time of ith auction server and t_{off_i} is offset from mean time. All the servers are now synchronized with clock T_{mean}. As the mean time offset is calculated for each auction service, the variations in network traffic will affect only that particular auction.

3.1 Sequence and state diagram of the protocol

The sequence diagram of the above protocol is shown in the Figure 2. The diagram is self explanatory.

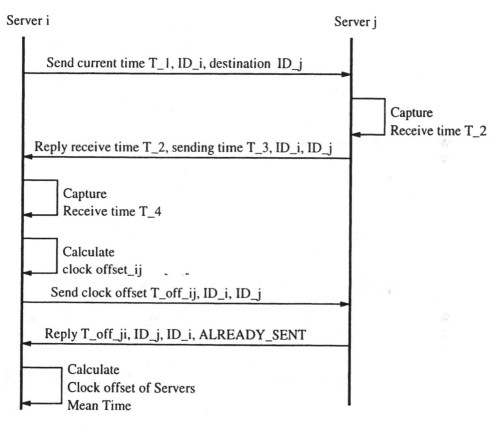

Fig. 2. Sequence diagram of Mean Time Offset protocol.

In Figure 3, the state transition is shown. As the protocol does not terminates until a predefined timeout or receiving all the response and ready to receive responses from other servers, most of the time it is in wait state. A message can not be synchronized as the sending and receiving can not take place at a time. This leads the server to change its state according to message state.

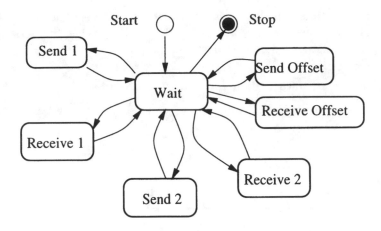

Fig. 3. State diagram for Mean Time Offset protocol

4 Conclusion

To make computational cost low, the conventional security features are not added. But if we assume some realistic assumption, our proposed protocol is a secured one till the assumption remains valid. It is safe to assume that the servers are normally well protected from adversaries, only message passing over unsafe network is vulnerable to attack. If we further assume that the modern computer clock drift are not too much from real clock and as clocks are not set by our protocol, it can be easy to detect attack on message by inspecting too much offset from real clock just after step 2. In this paper we introduce a novel protocol for calculating servers mean time . This protocol can be used against time adversary. The SMTO is low cost to implement in calculation and implementation sense.

References

1. Reuters, "e-bays web site goes down again," tech. rep., Reuters, Jul 1999.
2. M. P. Wellman and P. R. Wurman, "Real time issues for internet auctions," in *First IEEE workshop on Dependable and Real-time E-Commerce Systems (DARE-98)*, Jun 1998.
3. C.-S. Peng, J. M. Pulido, K.-J. Lin, and D. M. Blough, "The design of an internet-based real-time auction system," in *First IEEE workshop on Dependable and Real-time E-Commerce Systems (DARE-98)*, Jun 1998.
4. H. Schulzrinc and J. Rosenberg, "Timer reconsideration for enhanced rtp scalability," in *INFOCOM'98, Sanfransisco, CA*, mar-apr 1998.
5. D. Mills, "Internet time syncronization: the network time protocol," *IEEE Transactions on Communications*, vol. 30, pp. 1482–1493, oct 1991.

A Comparative Analysis of Transition Mechanisms for IPv6/IPv4 Routing Environment

Waleed Hosny

Electronics Research Institute
Cairo, Egypt

Tarek Kamel

Electronics Research Institute
Cairo, Egypt

Samir Shaheen

Faculty of Engineering
Cairo University
Cairo, Egypt

Abstract. This paper introduces an analysis for IPv6/IPv4 routed protocols on different transition mechanisms named IPv4 compatibility mechanisms that can be implemented by IPv6 hosts and routers. These mechanisms include providing complete implementations of both versions of the Internet Protocol (IPv4 and IPv6), and tunneling IPv6 packets over IPv4 routing infrastructures. They are designed to allow IPv6 nodes to maintain complete compatibility with IPv4, which should greatly simplify the deployment of IPv6 in the Internet, and facilitate the eventual transition of the entire Internet to IPv6.

1 Introduction

The key to a successful IPv6 transition is compatibility with the large installed base of IPv4 hosts and routers. Maintaining compatibility with IPv4 while deploying IPv6 will streamline the task of transitioning the Internet to IPv6. This paper defines a set of mechanisms that IPv6 hosts and routers may implement in order to be compatible with IPv4 hosts and routers.

The mechanisms in this paper are designed to be employed by IPv6 hosts and routers that need to interoperate with IPv4 hosts and utilize IPv4 routing infrastructures. We expect that most nodes in the Internet will need such compatibility for a long time to come, and perhaps even indefinitely.

However, IPv6 may be used in some environments where interoperability with IPv4 is not required. IPv6 nodes that are designed to be used in such environments need not use or even implement these mechanisms.

The mechanisms specified here include:

Dual IP layer (also known as Dual Stack): A technique for providing complete support for both Internet protocols - IPv4 and IPv6 - in hosts and routers.

Configured tunneling of IPv6 over IPv4: Unidirectional point-to-point tunnels made by encapsulating IPv6 packets within IPv4 headers to carry them over IPv4 routing infrastructures.

Automatic tunneling of IPv6 over IPv4: A mechanism for using IPv4-compatible addresses to automatically tunnels IPv6 packets over IPv4 networks. IPv4-compatible IPv6 address is IPv6 address format that employs embedded IPv4 addresses.

The mechanisms defined here are intended to be part of a transition toolbox that is a growing collection of techniques which implementations and users may employ to ease the transition. The tools may be used as needed. Implementations and sites decide which techniques are appropriate to their specific needs. In This paper the core set of transition mechanisms are considered, but these are not expected to be the only tools available. Additional transition and compatibility mechanisms are expected to be developed in the future, with new documents being written to specify them.

2 Transition Mechanisms: An Overview

2.1 Definition

The main consideration of the paper is the routing aspects of IPv4 to IPv6 transition. The approach outlined here is designed to be compatible with the existing mechanisms for IPv6 transition [8].
During an extended IPv4-to-IPv6 transition period, IPv6-based systems must coexist with the installed base of IPv4 systems. In such a dual internetworking protocol environment, both IPv4 and IPv6 routing infrastructure will be present. Initially, deployed IPv6-capable domains might not be globally interconnected via IPv6-capable internet infrastructure and therefore may need to communicate across IPv4-only routing regions. In order to achieve dynamic routing in such a mixed environment, there need to be mechanisms to globally distribute IPv6 network layer reachability information between dispersed IPv6 routing regions. The same techniques can be used in later stages of IPv4-to-IPv6 transition to route IPv4 packets between isolated IPv4-only routing region over IPv6 infrastructure.
The IPng transition provides a dual-IP-layer transition, augmented by use of encapsulation where necessary and appropriate. Routing issues related to this transition include:

(1) Routing for IPv4 packets

(2) Routing for IPv6 packets
    (2a) IPv6 packets with IPv6-native addresses
    (2b) IPv6 packets with IPv4-compatible addresses

(3) Operation of manually configured static tunnels

(4) Operation of automatic encapsulation
    (4a) Locating encapsulators
    (4b) Ensuring that routing is consist with encapsulation

Basic mechanisms required to accomplish these goals include:

Dual-IP-layer Route Computation
Manual configuration of point-to-point tunnels
Route leaking to support automatic encapsulation

2.2 Addressing in Transition Mechanisms

The transition uses two special formats of IPv6 addresses, both of which hold an embedded IPv4 address: IPv4-compatible IPv6 address format, and IPv4-mapped IPv6 address format.
IPv4-compatible addresses are assigned to IPv6/IPv4 nodes that support automatic tunneling, and have the following structure:

Fig. 1. IPv4-compatible IPv6 address format

80 bits	16 bits	32 bits
(10 octets)	(2 octets)	(4 octets)
0:0:0:0:0	0000	Ipv4 address

The addresses of IPv4-only nodes are represented as IPv4-mapped IPv6 addresses. These addresses have the following structure:

Fig. 2 - IPv4-mapped IPv6 address format

80 bits	16 bits	32 bits
(10 octets)	(2 octets)	(4 octets)
0:0:0:0:0	FFFF	Ipv4 address

The remainder of the IPv6 address space (that is, all addresses with 96-bit prefixes other than 0:0:0:0:0:0 or 0:0:0:0:0:FFFF) is termed "IPv6-only address space" because it may only be used by IPv6 nodes.

IPv4-compatible IPv6 addresses are designed to be used by IPv6 nodes that wish to interoperate with IPv4 nodes. These addresses are listed in the DNS in both IPv6 "AAAA" records and IPv4 "A" records. The AAAA record holds the entire 128-bit (16 octets) address, while the "A" record holds the IPv4 address portion (the low-order 32-bits).

Both types of address records are listed so that proper responses are made to queries from both IPv4 and IPv6 hosts.

IPv4-mapped IPv6 addresses are only used to represent the addresses of IPv4 nodes. They are never assigned to IPv6 nodes. Thus they are listed in the DNS only in "A" records. Even though the addresses of all IPv4 nodes can be represented as IPv4-mapped IPv6 addresses, they are not listed in "AAAA" records. This practice simplifies DNS administration.

IPv6-only addresses are only assigned to IPv6 nodes and can not be used for interoperation with IPv4 nodes. Thus these addresses are listed in the DNS only in "AAAA" records. They can not be listed in "A" records because they do not hold an embedded IPv4 address.

When administrators assign IPv4-compatible IPv6 addresses to IPv6 nodes, they must assign the low-order 32-bits (the IPv4 address portion) according to the IPv4 numbering plan used on the subnet to which that node is attached. The IPv4 address part must be a valid, globally unique, IPv4 address.

The entire space of IPv6-only addresses is available for use in a global IPv6 addressing plan that is not burdened with transition requirements. This allows, for example, the addressing plan for auto-configured addresses to be developed independent of the transition mechanisms.

Figure 3 below summarizes, for each of the three types of IPv6 addresses, what type of node may be assigned to what type of address, and whether the address holds an embedded IPv4 address or not.

Fig. 3 Nodes addressing assignment

Address Type	High-order 96-bit prefix	Embedded IPv4 Addr	Type of Node
IPv4-mapped	0:0:0:0:0:FFFF	Yes	Ipv4-only
IPv4-compatible	0:0:0:0:0:0	Yes	IPv6/IPv4 or Ipv6-only
IPv6-only	All others	No	IPv6/IPv4 or Ipv6-only

The ability of IPv4-only, IPv6/IPv4 and IPv6-only nodes configured with the various types of address to interoperate is depicted in Figure 4.

Fig.4 - IPv4-IPv6 interoperability capabilities

	IPv4-only node	IPv6/IPv4 node with IPv4-compatible address	IPv6/IPv4 node withIPv6-only address	IPv6-only node withIPv4-compatible address	IPv6-only node with IPv6-only address
IPv4-only node	D	D	N	T	N
IPv6/IPv4 node with IPv4-compatible address	D	D	D	D	D
IPv6/IPv4 node with IPv6-only address	N	D	D	D	D
IPv6 only node with IPv4-compatible address	T	D	D	D	D
IPv6-only node with IPv6-only address	N	D	D	D	D

D: Direct interoperability
T: Interoperability with aid of a translating router
N: Non interoperable

2.3 Types of Transition Mechanisms

This section presents types of IPv6/Ipv4 transition mechanisms. Document [5] is the main reference for this section

2.3.1 Dual IP layer (Coexistence Mechanism)
The most straightforward way for IPv6 nodes to remain compatible with IPv4-only nodes is by providing a complete IPv4 implementation. Such nodes are called IPv6/IPv4 nodes. IPv6/IPv4 nodes have the ability to send and receive both IPv4 and IPv6 packets. They can directly interoperate with IPv6 nodes using IPv6 packets. Conceptually, the protocol layering in IPv6/IPv4 dual nodes is represented in Fig. 5.

Fig. 5. Protocol layering in IPv6/IPv4 dual nodes

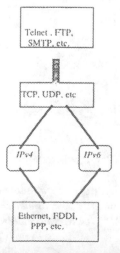

The dual IP layer technique may or may not be used in conjunction with the IPv6-over-IPv4 tunneling techniques, which are described in section 3.3. An IPv6/IPv4 node that supports tunneling can support both configured and automatic tunneling, or configured tunneling only. Thus, three configurations are possible:
- IPv6/IPv4 node that does not perform tunneling;
- IPv6/IPv4 node that performs configured tunneling and automatic tunneling;
- IPv6/IPv4 node that performs configured tunneling only.

6 packets all the way to their end
6 packets to an intermediary
IPv6/IPv4 router.

2.3.2 Configured and Automatic Tunneling

IPv6 packets can be carried across segments of an IPv4-complete topology by using the IPv6-over-IPv4 tunneling technique. An IPv6/IPv4 node that has IPv4 reachability to another IPv6/IPv4 node may send IPv6 packets to that node by encapsulating them within IPv4 packets (see Fig. 6). In order for this technique to work, both nodes must be assigned IPv4-compatible IPv6 addresses. This is necessary because the low-order 32-bits of those addresses are used as source and destination addresses of the encapsulating IPv4 packet.

Fig. 6 - Encapsulation and decapsulation of IPv6 packets

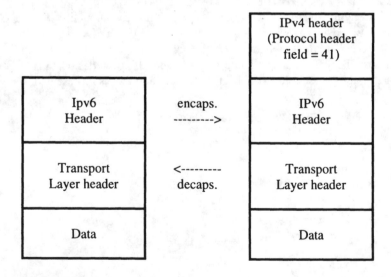

IPv6 packets to an intermediary IPv6/IPv4 router.

6

Both types of tunneling make use of the IPv4 address embedded in IPv4-compatible IPv6 addresses. In automatic tunneling, the *tunnel endpoint* address is taken from the IPv4 address embedded in the IPv6 destination address. No additional configuration information is needed because the destination address is carried in the IPv6 packet being tunneled.

In configured tunneling, the *tunnel endpoint* address is that of an intermediate IPv6/IPv4 router. That address must be configured. This configuration information could come in the form of a routing table entry on a host, or neighbor configuration information on a router.

Automatic tunneling is a basic feature of the transition. Hosts and routers will make extensive use of automatic tunneling when there is still a significant amount of IPv4 routing infrastructure. Hosts use configured tunneling less often, while routers may commonly use configured tunnels.

In both types of tunneling (automatic and configured), the source address of the IPv4 header of the tunneled packet is the low-order 32-bits of the IPv4-compatible IPv6 address of the node that performs the encapsulation. The IPv4 destination address is low-order 32-bits of the IPv4-compatible IPv6 address of the *tunnel endpoint*.

Except for the case of header translating routers, the intermediary routers on the path between the encapsulating node and the decapsulating node do not look at the IPv6 header of the packet. They route the packet based entirely on its IPv4 header. This is the case even if the routers along the path are IPv6/IPv4 routers. Figure 7 summarizes the two types of tunneling.

Fig. 7

Tunneling Type	Encapsulating Node	Decapsulating Node	Tunnel Endpoint IPv4 Address
Automatic	Source Host	Dest. Host	Low order 32-bits of dest. Host IPv6 address
Automatic	Router	Dest. Host	Low order 32-bits of dest. Host IPv6 address
Configured	Source Host	Router	Low order 32-bits of decapsul. router IPv6 address
Configured	Router	Router	Low order 32-bits of decapsul. router IPv6 address

2.3.3 Header translation

Header translation is an optional mechanism that is used when one wishes to allow IPv6-only nodes to interoperate with IPv4-only nodes. Header translation is performed by header translating routers, which interconnect IPv4-complete and IPv6-complete areas. Most of the traffic crossing the boundary between these areas must be translated. This traffic can come in a number of different forms:

i) terminating IPv4 traffic - IPv4 packets that are addressed to a node inside the IPv6-complete area;

ii) transit IPv4 traffic - IPv4 packets that are addressed to a node that is outside the IPv6-complete area, but that must pass through the IPv6-complete area;

iii) terminating IPv6 traffic - IPv6 packets that are addressed to a node inside the IPv4-complete area;

iv) transit IPv6 traffic - IPv6 packets that are addressed to a node outside the IPv4-complete area, but that must pass through the IPv4-complete area;
v) encapsulated IPv6 traffic - IPv6 packets encapsulated in IPv4 packets.

Header translators are IPv6/IPv4 routers. They operate by translating the headers of IPv4 packets into IPv6, and IPv6 headers into IPv4. They require some configuration information in order to know which packets should be translated, and which should be simply forwarded unmodified.

Figure 8 illustrates the case where header translation is being used to communicate between an IPv4-complete area and an IPv6-complete area. Header translators must translate all IPv4 packets that are addressed to nodes located within the IPv6-complete area, or that must transit the IPv6-complete area.

Fig. 8 - Interoperation by means of translation

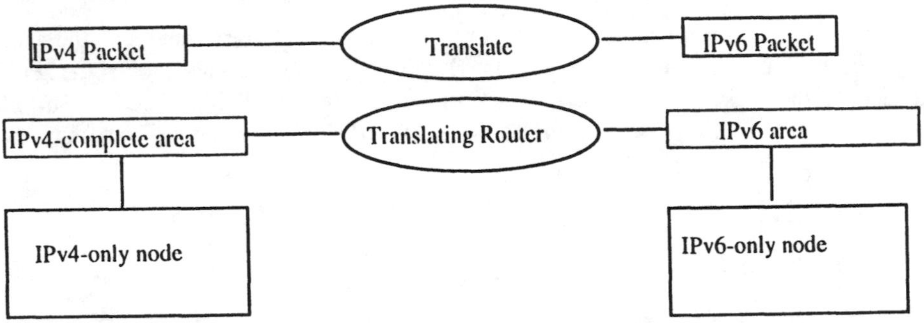

When translating IPv6 packets to IPv4, translating routers use the low-order 32-bits of the source and destination IPv6 addresses to generate the addresses for the IPv4 packet. Both the source and destination must be IPv4-compatible IPv6 addresses in order for the packet to be translated.
When translating IPv4 packets to IPv6, translating routers add the prefix 0:0:0:0:0:0 to the IPv4 source address to generate the source address for the IPv6 packet. They add either the prefix 0:0:0:0:0:FFFF or 0:0:0:0:0:0 to generate the destination address. Determining which prefix to add requires some configuration information. Translators use the 0:0:0:0:0:0 prefix if the destination is located within the attached IPv6-complete area, and the prefix 0:0:0:0:0:FFFF if the destination is located outside.

3. Problem Definition

4   4 routing.
There is at least one IPv4 router attached to every subnet in an IPv4-complete area. These areas may also have partial IPv6 routing to some subnets, but no IPv6 routing

is required. An area that provides only IPv4 routing would be considered an IPv4-complete area, as would one in which IPv6 routing was in the process of being deployed.

6   6 routing.
There is at least one IPv6 router attached to every subnet in an IPv6-complete area. These areas may also have partial IPv4 routing to some subnets, but this is not required. A topology of dual IPv6/IPv4 routing, with IPv4 routing in the process of being de-commissioned, would be considered an IPv6-complete area, as would one which provides only IPv6 routing.

IPv4-complete areas naturally impose some restrictions on what types of hosts can operate within their boundaries. Since there is no guarantee that IPv6 traffic can be handled, only hosts that can send and receive IPv4 can safely be deployed. This means that IPv4-only and IPv6/IPv4 hosts can be freely deployed within IPv4-complete areas, but that IPv6-only hosts generally cannot.

Like IPv4-complete areas, IPv6-complete areas have natural restrictions on what types of hosts they can support. Since an IPv6-complete area carries only IPv6 traffic, only hosts that can send and receive IPv6 packets can be deployed. That means that IPv6/IPv4 and IPv6-only hosts can be freely deployed within IPv6-complete areas, but that IPv4-only hosts generally cannot.
Figure 9 explains the different possible routing cases that can be used in the analysis

Fig. 9

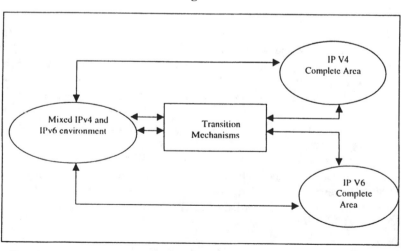

Routing Cases
Host V6 → Host V6   (No IP V4 in between)
Host V6 → Host V6   (With IP V4 in between)
Host V4 → Host V6
Host V6 → Host V4
Host V4 → Host V4   (No IP V6 in between)
Host V4 → Host V4   (With IP V6 in between)

4. Comparative Analysis of Transition Mechanisms for IPv6/IPv4 Routed Protocols

4.1 Various Solutions and Scenarios

In this section we analyze the different mechanisms to solve the different routing topologies problems

4.1.1 Basic Dual-IP-layer Operation
In the basic dual-IP-layer transition scheme, routers may independently support IPv4 and IPv6 routing. Other parts of the transition, such as DNS support, and selection by the source host of which packet format to transmit (IPv4 or IPv6) are discussed in [1]. Forwarding of IPv4 packets is based on routes learned through running IPv4-specific routing protocols. Similarly, forwarding of IPv6 packets (including IPv6-packets with IPv4-compatible addresses) is based on routes learned through running IPv6-specific routing protocols. This implies that separate instances of routing protocols are used for IPv4 and for IPv6 (although note that this could consist of two instances of OSPF and/or two instances of RIP, since both OSPF and RIP are capable of supporting both IPv4 and IPv6 routing).

A minor enhancement would be to use a single instance of an integrated routing protocol to support routing for both IPv4 and IPv6. At the time that this is written there is no protocol which has yet been enhanced to support this. This minor enhancement does not change the basic dual-IP-layer nature of the transition.

For initial testing of IPv6 with IPv4-compatible addresses, it may be useful to allow forwarding of IPv6 packets without running any IPv6-compatible routing protocol. In this case, a dual (IPv4 and IPv6) router could run routing protocols for IPv4 only. It then forwards IPv4 packets based on routes learned from IPv4 routing protocols.
Also, it forwards IPv6 packets with an IPv4-compatible destination address based on the route for the associated IPv4 address. There are a couple of drawbacks with this approach:
(i) It does not specifically allow for routing of IPv6 packets via IPv6-capable routers while avoiding and routing around IPv4-only routers;
(ii) It does not produce routes for "non-compatible" IPv6 addresses. With this method the routing protocol does not tell the router whether neighboring routers are IPv6-compatible. However, neighbor discovery may be used to determine this. Then if an IPv6 packet needs to be forwarded to an IPv4-only router it can be encapsulated to the destination host.

4.1.2 Manually Configured Static Tunnels
Tunneling techniques are already widely deployed for bridging non-IP network layer protocols (e.g. AppleTalk, CLNP, IPX) over IPv4 routed infrastructure. IPv4 tunneling is an encapsulation of arbitrary packets inside IPv4 datagrams that are forwarded over IPv4 infrastructure between tunnel endpoints. For a tunneled protocol, a tunnel appears as a single-hop link (i.e. routers that establish a tunnel over a network layer infrastructure can inter-operate over the tunnel as if it were a one-hop,

point-to-point link). Once a tunnel is established, routers at the tunnel endpoints can establish routing adjacencies and exchange routing information. Describing the protocols for performing encapsulation is outside the scope of this paper (see [1]). Static point-to-point tunnels may also be established between a host and a router, or between two hosts. Again, each manually configured point-to-point tunnel is treated as if it was a simple point-to-point link.

4.1.3 Automatic Tunnels

Automatic tunneling may be used when both the sending and destination nodes are connected by IPv4 routing. In order for automatic tunneling to work, both nodes must be assigned IPv4-compatible IPv6 addresses. Automatic tunneling can be especially useful where either source or destination hosts (or both) do not have any adjacent IPv6-capable router. Note that by "adjacent router", this includes routers which are logically adjacent by virtue of a manually configured point-to-point tunnel (which is treated as if it is a simple point-to-point link).

With automatic tunneling, the resulting IPv4 packet is forwarded by IPv4 routers as a normal IPv4 packet, using IPv4 routes learned from routing protocols. There are therefore no special issues related to IPv4 routing in this case. There are however routing issues relating to how IPv6 routing works in a manner which is compatible with automatic tunneling, and how tunnel endpoint addresses are selected during the encapsulation process. Automatic tunneling is useful from a source host to the destination host, from a source host to a router, and from a router to the destination host. Mechanisms for automatic tunneling from a router to another router are not currently defined.

4.1.3.1 Host to Host Automatic Tunneling

both source and destination hosts make use of IPv4-compatible IPv6 addresses, then it is possible for automatic tunneling to be used for the entire path from the source host to the destination host. In this case, the IPv6 packet is encapsulated in an IPv4 packet by the source host, and is forwarded by routers as an IPv4 packet all the way to the destination host. This allows initial deployment of IPv6-capable hosts to be done prior to the update of any routers.

A source host may make use of Host to Host automatic tunneling provided that the following are both true:

- the source address is an IPv4-compatible IPv6 address.
- the destination address is an IPv4-compatible IPv6 address.
- the source host does know of one or more neighboring IPv4-capable routers, or the source
  and destination are on the same subnet.

If all of these requirements are true, then the source host may encapsulate the IPv6 packet in an IPv4 packet, using a source IPv4 address which is extracted from the associated source IPv6 address, and using a destination IPv4 address which is extracted from the associated destination IPv6 address.

Where host to host automatic tunneling is used, the packet is forwarded as a normal IPv4 packet for its entire path, and is decapsulated (i.e., the IPv4 header is removed) only by the destination host.

4.1.3.2 Host to Router Configured Default Tunneling

In some cases "configured default" tunneling may be used to encapsulate the IPv6 packet for transmission from the source host to an IPv6-backbone. However, this requires that the source host be configured with an IPv4 address to use for tunneling to the backbone.

Configured default tunneling is particularly useful if the source host does not know of any local IPv6-capable router (implying that the packet cannot be forwarded as a normal IPv6 packet directly over the link layer), and when the destination host does not have an IPv4-compatible IPv6 address (implying that host to host tunneling cannot be used).

Host to router configured default tunneling may optionally also be used even when the host does know of a local IPv6 router. In this case it is a policy decision whether the host prefers to send a native IPv6 packet to the IPv6-capable router or prefers to send an encapsulated packet to the configured tunnel endpoint.

Similarly host to router default configured tunneling may be used even when the destination address is an IPv4-compatible IPv6 address. In this case for example a policy decision may be made to prefer tunneling for part of the path and native IPv6 for part of the path, or alternatively to use tunneling for the entire path from source host to destination host.

A source host may make use of host to router configured default tunneling provided that ALL of the following are true:
- the source address is an IPv4-compatible IPv6 address.
- the source host does know of one or more neighboring IPv4-capable routers
- the source host has been configured with an IPv4 address of an dual router which can serve as the tunnel endpoint.

If all of these requirements are true, then the source host may encapsulate the IPv6 packet in an IPv4 packet, using a source IPv4 address which is extracted from the associated source IPv6 address, and using a destination IPv4 address which corresponds to the configured address of the dual router which is serving as the tunnel endpoint.

When host to router configured default tunneling is used, the packet is forwarded as a normal IPv4 packet from the source host to the dual router serving as tunnel endpoint, is decapsulated by the dual router, and is then forwarded as a normal IPv6 packet by the tunnel endpoint.

The dual router which is serving as the end point of the host to router configured default tunnel must advertise reachability into IPv4 routing sufficient to cause the encapsulated packet to be forwarded to it.

The simplest approach is for a single IPv4 address to be assigned for use as a tunnel endpoint. One or more dual routers, which have connectivity to the IPv6 backbone and which are capable of serving as tunnel endpoint, advertise a host route to this address into IPv4 routing in the IPv4-only region. Each dual host in the associated IPv4-only region is configured with the address of this tunnel endpoint and selects a route to this address for forwarding encapsulated packet to a tunnel end point (for example, the nearest tunnel end point, based on whatever metric(s) the local routing protocol is using).

Finally, in some cases there may be some reason for specific hosts to prefer one of several tunnel endpoints, while allowing all potential tunnel endpoints to serve as backups in case the preferred endpoint is not reachable. In this case, each dual router with IPv6 backbone connectivity which is serving as potential tunnel endpoint is given a unique IPv4 address taken from a single IPv4 address block (where the IPv4 address block is assigned either to the organization administering the IPv4-only region, or to the organization administering the local part of the IPv6 backbone). In the likely case that there are much less than 250 such dual routers serving as tunnel endpoints, we suggest using multiple IPv4 addresses selected from a single 24-bit IPv4 address prefix for this purpose. Each dual router then advertises two routes into the IPv4 region: A host route corresponding to the tunnel endpoint address specifically assigned to it, and also a standard (prefix) route to the associated IPv4 address block. Each dual host in the IPv4-only region is configured with a tunnel endpoint address which corresponds to the preferred tunnel endpoint for it to use. If the associated dual router is operating, then the packet will be delivered to it based upon the host route that it is advertising into the IPv4-only region. However, if the associated dual router is down, but some other dual router serving as a potential tunnel endpoint is operating, then the packet will be delivered to the nearest operating tunnel endpoint.

4.1.3.3 Router to Host Automatic Tunneling

In some cases the source host may have direct connectivity to one ormore IPv6-capable routers, but the destination host might not have direct connectivity to any IPv6-capable router. In this case, provided that the destination host has an IPv4-compatible IPv6 address, normal IPv6 forwarding may be used for part of the packet's path, and router to host tunneling may be used to get the packet from an encapsulating dual router to the destination host.

In this case, the hard part is the IPv6 routing required to deliver the IPv6 packet from the source host to the encapsulating router. For this to happen, the encapsulating router has to advertise reachability for the appropriate IPv4-compatible IPv6 addresses into the IPv6 routing region. With this approach, all IPv6 packets (including those with IPv4-compatible addresses) are routed using routes calculated from native IPv6 routing. This implies that encapsulating routers need to advertise into IPv6 routing specific route entries corresponding to any IPv4-compatible IPv6 addresses that belong to dual hosts which can be reached in an neighboring IPv4-only region. This requires manual configuration of the encapsulating routers to control which routes are to be injected into IPv6 routing protocols. Nodes in the IPv6 routing region would use such a route to forward IPv6 packets along the routed path toward the router that injected (leaked) the route, at which point packets are encapsulated and forwarded to the destination host using normal IPv4 routing.

Depending upon the extent of the IPv4-only and dual routing regions, the leaking of routes may be relatively simple or may be more complex. For example, consider a dual Internet backbone, connected via one or two dual routers to an IPv4-only stub routing domain. In this case, it is likely that there is already one summary address prefix which is being advertised into the Internet backbone in order to summarize IPv4 reachability to the stub domain. In such a case, the border routers would be configured to announce the IPv4 address prefix into the IPv4 routing within the backbone, and also announce the corresponding IPv4-compatible IPv6 address prefix into IPv6 routing within the backbone.

A more difficult case involves the border between a major Internet backbone which is IPv4-only, and a major Internet backbone which supports both IPv4 and IPv6. In this case, it requires that either

the entire IPv4 routing table be fed into IPv6 routing in the dual routing domain (implying a doubling of the size of the routing tables in the dual domain); or

Manual configuration is required to determine which of the addresses contained in the Internet routing table include one or more IPv6-capable systems, and only these addresses be advertised into IPv6 routing in the dual domain.

4.2 A Comparative Summary for Various Scenarios

Clearly tunneling is useful only if communication can be achieved in both directions. However, different forms of tunneling may be used in each direction, depending upon the local environment, the form of address of the two hosts which are exchanging IPv6 packets, and the policies in use.

Figure 10 summarizes the form of tunneling that will result given each possible combination of host capabilities, and given one possible set of policy decisions. This table is derived directly from the requirements for automatic tunneling discussed above.

The example in Figure 10 uses a specific set of policy decisions: It is assumed in table 1 that the source host will transmit a native IPv6 where possible in preference over encapsulation. It is also assumed that where tunneling is needed, host to host tunneling will be preferred over host to router tunneling. Other combinations are therefore possible if other policies are used.

Note that IPv6-capable hosts, which do not have any local IPv6 router, must be given an IPv4-compatible v6 address in order to make use of their IPv6 capabilities. Thus, there are no entries for IPv6-capable hosts which have an incompatible IPv6 address and which also do not have any connectivity to any local IPv6 router. In fact, such hosts could communicate with other IPv6 hosts on the same local network without the use of a router. However, since this document focuses on routing and router implications of IPv6 transition, direct communication between two hosts on the same local network without any intervening router is outside the scope of this document.

Also, Figure 10 does not consider manually configured point-to-point tunnels. Such tunnels are treated as if they were normal point-to-point links. Thus any two IPv6-capable devices which have a manually configured tunnel between them may be considered to be directly connected.

Fig. 10 - Summary of Automatic Tunneling Combinations

Host A	Host B	Result
IP v4 compatible address with no local IP v6 router	IP v4 compatible address with no local IP v6 router	Host to Host tunneling in both directions
IP v4 compatible address with no local IP v6 router	IP v4 compatible address with local IP v6 router	A→ B host to host tunnel B→ A IP v6 forwarding plus Router to host tunnel
IP v4 compatible address with no local IP v6 router	Incompatible address with local IP v6 router	A→ B Host to router tunnel plus IP v6 forwarding B→ A IP v6 forwarding plus Router to host tunnel
IP v4 compatible address with local IP v6 router	IP v4 compatible address with local IP v6 router	End to End native IP v6 in both directions
IP v4 compatible address with local IP v6 router	Incompatible address with local IP v6 router	End to End native IP v6 in both directions
Incompatible address with local IP v6 router	Incompatible address with local IP v6 router	End to End native IP v6 in both directions

5. Conclusion

The two major protocol mechanisms used in the transition - tunneling and header translation - are based on some assumptions about the way that routing topologies will develop. The general model is that IPv4 routing infrastructures will incrementally evolve into IPv6. In most cases, IPv6 routing will initially be deployed in parallel with an already existing IPv4 routing infrastructure. The deployment of IPv6 routing will take place by upgrading existing IPv4-only routers to IPv6/IPv4. This will occur over a period of time, not all at once. The site will eventually be transformed into a complete dual IPv6/IPv4 infrastructure. At some later point, IPv4 routing will be turned off. This process will also likely be incremental. The later transition may take place by upgrading IPv6/IPv4 routers to IPv6-only, or by "turning off" the IPv4 software in IPv6/IPv4 routers. After this stage, a pure IPv6 infrastructure will be formed. The above described model is represented in the next figure.

IPv4-complete and IPv6-complete areas can be interconnected with header translating routers, as illustrated in Figure 11, below. The translating router allows IPv4-only hosts in the IPv4-complete area to interoperate with IPv6-only hosts in the IPv6-complete area.

Fig. 11 - IPv6 routing deployment

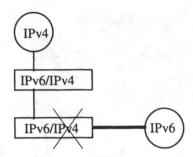

The basic mechanism for routing of IPv4 and IPv6 involves dual-IP-layer routing. This implies that routes are separately calculated for IPv4 addresses and for IPv6 addressing.

Tunnels (either IPv4 over IPv6, or IPv6 over IPv4) may be manually configured. For example, in the early stages of transition this may be used to allow two IPv6 domains to interact over an IPv4 infrastructure. Manually configured static tunnels are treated as if they were a normal data link.

Use of automatic encapsulation, where the IPv4 tunnel endpoint address is determined from the IPv4 address embedded in the IPv4-compatible destination address of IPv6 packet, requires consistency of routes between IPv4 and IPv6 routing domains for destinations using IPv4-compatible addresses.

6. References

1. S. Deering, R. Hinden, Internet Protocol, Version 6 (IPv6) Specification, *RFC 1883*, December 1995.
2. R. Hinden, S. Deering, IP Version 6 Addressing Architecture, *RFC 1884*, December 1995.
3. Conta, S. Deering, Internet Control Message Protocol (ICMPv6) for the Internet Protocol Version 6 (IPv6), *RFC 1885*, December 1995.
4. J. McCann, S. Deering, Path MTU Discovery for IP version 6, Internet Draft, *draft-ietf-ipngwg-pmtuv6-03.txt*, May 1996.
5. M. Degermark, B. Nordgren, S. Pink, Header Compression for IPv6, Internet Draft, *draft-degermark-ipv6-hc-00.txt*, February 1996.
6. ˙ Conta, S. Deering, Generic Packet Tunneling in IPv6 Specification, Internet Draft, *draft-ietf-ipngwg-ipv6-tunnel-01.txt*, February 1996.
7. S. Thomson, C. Huitema, DNS Extensions to support IP version 6, *RFC 1886*, December 1995.
8. R. Gilligan, E. Nordmark, Transition Mechanisms for IPv6 Hosts and Routers, *RFC 1933*, April 1996.
9. D. Haskin, R. Callon, Routing Aspects of IPv6 Transition, Internet Draft, *draft-ietf-ngtrans-routing-aspects-01.txt* , May 1996.

10.   G. Malkin, RIPng for IPv6, Internet Draft, *draft-ietf-rip-ripng-03.txt* , June 1996.

11.   Y. Rekhter, P. Traina, IDRP for IPv4 and v6, Internet Draft, *draft-ietf-idr-idrp-v4v6-02.txt*, January 1996.

12.   R. Coltun, J. Moy, OSPF Version 2 For IP Version 6, Internet Draft, *draft-ietf-ospf-ospfv6-02.txt*, June 1996.

13.   M. Shand, M. Thomas, Multi-homing Support in IPv6 , Internet Draft, *draft-shand-ipv6-multi-homing-01.txt*, June 1996.

14.   T. Narten, E. Nordmark, W. Simpson, Neighbor Discovery for IP Version 6 (IPv6), Internet Draft, *draft-ietf-ipngwg-discovery-06.txt* , March 1996.

15.   R. Callon, D. Haskin, Routing Aspects Of IPv6 Transition, RFC 2185, September 1997.

Scalable Protocols for the Internet to Reduce Service Time and Server Load

P. Krishna Reddy and Masaru Kitsuregawa

Institute of Industrial Science
The University of Tokyo
7-22-1, Roppongi, Minato-ku
Tokyo 106, Japan
{reddy, kitsure}@tkl.iis.u-tokyo.ac.jp

Abstract. In this paper, we have proposed scalable protocols for the Internet to reduce service time and server load. In this approach, we assume that a client cooperates by acting as a server to the cached web pages. To reduce the service time, the server forwards the incoming requests to other clients which have cached the web pages. As a result, the service time scales well as server load increases. Also, with these protocols, the traffic is evenly distributed among the network. This approach is a generalization of caching technology. However, for implementation, the proposed approach requires support from the Internet user, system development, and governing communities. If adopted, we believe that the proposed approach provides a scalable solution to the problems of server overloading and long service times in the Internet.

1 Introduction

Currently, the World Wide Web (or Web) is experiencing exponential growth. In coming ten years, billions of users will employ powerful computing and display devices and try to pull multi-media information, which will put huge demand on the corresponding servers and network links [1]. As a result, load on the popular servers could increase in an unbounded manner. Also, the increasing use of the Web results in increased network bandwidth usage, thus straining the capacity of the networks on which it runs. As a result, it leads to more and more servers becoming "hot-spot" sites where the high frequency of requests makes servicing difficult. The best example is the case of many multi-media information servers on the Internet, which are unreachable as soon as they become popular. The main reason for this is current protocols for accessing distributed information systems do not scale, partly due to the inability of servers to cope with the increasing volume of client requests. Therefore the distributed large-scale, dynamic nature of the Internet speaks to the need for open, flexible, and scalable solutions.

In this paper we propose a scalable approach to cope with the increasing server load. The basic principle derives from client-peer architecture [2], where each participating computing node is capable of both client and server roles. It can be observed that the client-peer architecture is scalable because distributed server can run on all nodes, and therefore server resources could scale with the systems as a whole. That is each computer (new) shares the load and accesses resources from other servers. In this paper we have tried to extend same idea to Internet. In case of the Internet, it can be noticed that a client (user) caches a large number of web pages and this information is not used once client scans these pages. In the proposed approach, for the sake of improved performance, a client cooperates by acting as a server to web pages cached by it. When a server serves information to a client, the necessary information (i.e., details of web pages served and client) is recorded in the cached page informer (CPI) of the corresponding server. With the help of CPI, the server redirects incoming requests to the client which has recently copied corresponding web page. In this way, the server load could be reduced by distributing it among other clients.

Since the WWW suffers with the problems of high latency, network congestion, and server overload, considerable effort has been spent investigating different methods to improve performance. The fundamental issues that have been considered include cache topology, cache replacement policy, cache consistency, whether caching is server- or client initiated, and cache-ability of different objects. There are two basic approaches to caching that have been explored: client side and server side solutions. In the server side solutions, servers shed load by duplicating their documents at caching servers spread throughout WWW [3, 6]. Client side solutions usually use some sort of caching proxy [7] that fields requests from one or more clients and caches objects on the client's behalf. However, proxy caches are not always efficient. First, caching only works with statically and infrequently changing documents. Dynamically created documents, which are becoming more popular with commercial content providers, currently can not be cached. Also, the effectiveness of client-based caching for WWW is limited. In [4] it was concluded that proxy-caching is ultimately limited by the low level of sharing of remote documents amongst clients of the same site. These findings agrees with Glassman's predictions[10] and was further confirmed for general proxy caching by Abrams et al [8].

In [5], the reasons for limited effectiveness of WWW client-based caching are given. The access patterns in a WWW exhibit three locality of reference properties: temporal, geographical and spatial. Temporal locality of reference implies that recently accessed objects are likely to be accessed again in the future. Geographical locality of reference implies that an object accessed by a client is likely to be accessed again in the future by "nearby" clients. The property is similar to the processor locality of reference exhibited in parallel applications. Spatial locality of reference implies that an object "neighboring" a recently accessed object is likely to be accessed in the future. If client-based caching is done on a per-session basis (i.e., the cache is cleared at the start of each client session), then the only locality of reference property that could be exploited is the temporal locality of reference. The results of client based caching study [3] suggest that for a single client, the temporal locality of reference is quite limited, especially for remote documents.

In [9] a protocol that allows multiple caching proxies to cooperate and share their caches, thus increasing their robustness and scalability. Our approach differs from this as in our approach the clients or proxies do not communicate with each other. Our approach is a generalization of "caching" technology to increase Internet performance. Using the proposed approach, both temporal and geographical locality of references could be exploited to reduce server load and service time.

The rest of the paper is organized as follows. In the next section we explain the architectural framework and present server and client protocols. In section 3, we discuss the design issues and advantages. In the last section we provide conclusions.

2 Architectural framework and protocols

In this paper we refer user's machines that access the Internet as clients and computers that provide information as servers. The URL (Uniform resource locator) uniquely identifies a Web page. A web page may be an HTML text file, image file, sound file or video file or combination of all these.

Figure 1 depicts the proposed architecture. In this architecture, each server maintains the CPI database. The received URL requests are stored in the server queue. These URLs are served as per the server protocols, which will be explained later. When a server serves a page, the information such as URL of the page, client address, page size is stored in the CPI database. To reduce the load, the server redirects the URL requests to the corresponding clients which cached these pages. Therefore, from the server, a page is either directly transferred to the target client or its URL request is forwarded to other client which has cached the corresponding page, which would in turn transferred to the requested client.

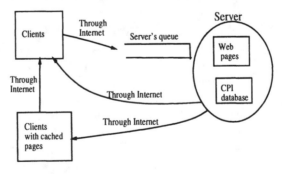

Figure 1: Depiction of architecture

2.1 Simple protocols

We first present client and server protocols under simplified assumptions. Next, we explain drawbacks of these protocols and present final protocols. We assume that each server maintains a CPI database. Also, url_i denotes the URL of the i'th page and $page\_size_i$ denotes the size of the page pointed by url_i.

We make following assumptions for simple protocols.

- All the requests sent by a server reaches to client.
- All pages received by a client are cached by the client. For this purpose we assume that unlimited memory is available at the client.
- A client is up around the clock.

Simple client protocol

1. To access a web page, a client sends url_k to the corresponding server.
2. On receiving a web page, a client caches it.
3. When a client receives a request from the corresponding server to serve the cached page, it sends the page to the client specified by the server.

Simple server protocol

All the client's requests are stored in the server's queue. Initially, CPI contains no information.

1. For each URL request url_k in the server queue, CPI database is checked. If $url_k \notin CPI$ the page is sent directly to the requested client after entering the information $< url_k, client\_id, page\_size_k, creation\_time_k >$ in CPI. (In this $client\_id$, indicates the address of the client which has requested the web page url_k. The variable $creation\_time_k$ specifies the instant when the web page url_k was created at the server. This variable is used to determine whether the cached version has become obsolete or not.)
2. Otherwise, the request is forwarded to the client which has cached the page url_k after entering the information $< url_k, client\_id, page\_size_k, creation\_time_k >$ in the CPI.

2.2 Limitations of simple protocols

We now explain the limitations of simple protocols and propose improvements to overcome them.

- **Server performance**
  In simple protocol, a server always redirects the URL requests to those clients which have cached these pages. When the performance is OK, following proposed protocols indeed deteriorates performance by increasing service time. In fact, the proposed solution is effective in situations when the server's performance is unacceptable. We define variable 'threshold service time (TST)' to separate server's mode of operation. The variable TST denotes maximum mean service time at which the server's performance is acceptable. If the service time exceeds TST, we say the server performance is slow and unacceptable.
- **Page size**
  The simple protocols do not take the page size into consideration. It is obvious that the request redirected by a server travels first to the client which has cached it and then to the target client. Therefore it travels more distance

than the distance from the server to the client. This results in an overhead if the server depends on the clients to serve even small pages. However, if page is large enough, the overhead caused by longer distance could be nullified by utilizing the server time to process other requests. Obviously it would be efficient if small pages are directly served by a server. To facilitate this, we define a variable *threshold page size* (TPS). If the page size exceeds TPS, the server tries to request the clients to serve the corresponding page.

– **Rejections**
When a server redirects request to other clients that has cached a web page, the request might not reach the client. Even though it reaches, the client might not oblige the request. Because the redirected request could not have reached the client due to transmission failures or the client's computer might be down. The simple protocol does not consider the possibility of such rejections. We incorporate the handling of rejections in the improved protocol as follows.

We assume a page could be cached either by a client or by a proxy server/ISP. This information is sent by a client machine when it sends URL request to the server. We assume that a client operates at least for some duration which is termed as a threshold operating time (TOT). Otherwise, if a client (proxy server or ISP) which operates around the clock caches pages, it has to follow cache management mechanisms to accommodate new pages by deleting old pages[11]. We term the duration of cached page as an 'age' of the page. We define the term 'threshold age (TA)', which specifies the maximum duration the client keeps in a cache. If age exceeds TA, the client deletes the page. The variables TOT and TA could be fixed in an adaptive manner.

If a redirected request could not reach the client which has cached the web page, corresponding error message is received by the server which has redirected the request. In this situation the server has to handle the rejected requests in a prioritized manner and therefore should be served by the server itself. So, in the improved protocol we maintain two queues for a server. One is 'normal queue' in which all the client's URL requests are stored. And the other is 'priority queue' where those requests which could not be served by the clients (cached) are stored.

– **CPI entry for rejected requests**
The simple protocols assume that the clients always cache web pages sent by the server with out fail. Since the client could reject the request, this assumption is invalid unless the target client confirms the receipt. So, we incorporate boolean variable *confirm* in the entry of CPI. Initially, the confirm is *no*, when the client acknowledges the receipt of the page the confirm is set to *yes*.

– **Caching by multiple clients**
It can be observed that if multiple clients request a page within a short duration, it would be cached at multiple clients. In this case when a server receives a request from a client, it has to select appropriate client among multiple clients to forward a request. We assume that given two server addresses,

distance between them can be calculated through appropriate protocol. The distance may be a function of bandwidth of the weakest link, number of hubs, transmission time between the two and so on. By knowing distance, when multiple clients cache a web page, the server forwards the incoming URL request to the client which is nearer to the target client.

2.3 Protocols

We now present final protocols by incorporating the improvements discussed in the preceding section.

Client protocol

1. When a client sends the URL request, it sends the identifier of the machine which would cache that page. (It may be either identifier of the client or proxy server/ISP.)
2. When a client receives a request from the corresponding server to serve the cached page, it sends the page to the client specified by the server. When a client receives a web page it caches that page and sends the acknowledgment to the original server.
3. When a client receives a request from the corresponding server to serve the cached page, it sends the page to the client specified by the server.
4. For a page, if the age exceeds TA (or TOT) it is deleted from the client's cache.

Server protocol It is to be noted that we maintain two queues for a server : priority queue and normal queue (see section 2.2).

1. If the request is from a priority queue, send the page to the requested client after step 6.
2. If the request is from a normal queue and *mean service time* $\leq TST$ send the page to the requested client after step 6.
3. If the request is from a normal queue and *mean service time* $> TST$ the following actions are performed.
   (a) For each url_k in the input queue if $page\_size_k \leq TPS$ send the page to the requested client.
   (b) For each url_k in the queue, if $page\_size_k > TPS$,
      i. If $url_k \in CPI$ and $confirm = yes$ and $age(url_k) \leq TA$ (or TOT) and cached page is not obsolete, the request is redirected to the corresponding client that has cached url_k after performing actions in step 6. (If multiple clients cache url_k the request is redirected to the client that is nearer to the requested client)
      ii. Otherwise, the page is directly sent to target client after step 6.
4. For any url_k, if $age(url_k) \geq TOT$ ($age(url_k) \geq TA$) the entry is deleted from CPI.
5. If a server receives acknowledgment from the requested client, it updates corresponding CPI entry field as "$confirm = yes$".

6. Suppose the request is for url_k. If $page\_size(url_k) \geq TPS$, then $< url_k, client\_id,$ $page\_size(url_k), creation\_time_k, confirm = no >$ is entered in the CPI database.

3 Design issues and advantages

3.1 Design issues

In the proposed approach, we assume that a client serves the pages it has cached. This requires inclusion of serving capability to the Internet browsers. If some other server (proxy/ service provider) provides caching facility for a client, this should be indicated in the client's request so that the Server could redirect requests to proxy server. This requires modification of browser protocols and data request format.

Also, the proposed approach requires cooperation from web community (user, system development and governing communities) for its realization. Already, proxy servers and mirrors are employed to reduce the server load. The proposed solution is a more generalized notion of a proxy server technology, providing opportunity to every client to cooperate in reducing the server load.

3.2 Advantages

- The implementation of proposed protocols is simple and modular. It is simple because implementation does not lead to major changes in the existing architecture. Also, it is modular because the server can implement the proposed protocols even if a single client cooperates in serving the cached pages. The server protocols could be extended gradually to other clients.
- It is a fully scalable solution. As the server load increases, the number of clients that cache the data increases. Therefore, increasing number of requests are forwarded to clients. With respect to server's point of view this substantially reduces its load. Also, with respect to client's point of view the load imposed on it is very very less. As a consequence, the service time and server load could be considerably reduced without burdening the clients.
- The proposed solution balances the traffic over the entire network. In this approach the clients exchange pages. As clients span over wide area, the corresponding load is also distributed among the network, which increases the link usage.
- If every client cooperates, more load could be served with less powerful architecture. So large amounts of load can be served with less expensive server architectures.

4 Conclusions

In this paper we have proposed scalable server and client protocols to reduce service time and server load in the Internet environment. In this approach, we have assumed that a client cooperates by serving pages cached by it to other clients as directed by original server. With this approach the service time can scale well with the increasing server load. Also, this approach distributes the load evenly among the network. However, the proposed approach requires modification of protocol format, inclusion of a server functionality to existing Internet browsers and support from Internet community for its implementation. Currently, caching technology is employed to reduce the service time and server load. The proposed solution is a generalization of caching technology. As a part of future work, we will evaluate the performance through simulation experiments and then conduct the experiments on the Internet.

Acknowledgments

This work is supported by "Research for the future" (in Japanese Mirai Kaitaku) under the program of Japan Society for the Promotion of Science, Japan.

References

1. Phil Bernstein et. al., The asilomar report on database research, ACM SIGMOD RECORD 27(4), 1998.
2. Thomas E.Anderson, Michael Dahlin, jaenna M.Neefe, David A Patterson, drew S.Roselli, and Randolph Wang. Server-less network file systems. ACM Transactions on Computer Systems, 14(1):41-79, February 1996.
3. Azer Bestavros, Using speculation to reduce server load and service time on the WWW, proc. of ACM Fourth International Conference On Information and Knowledge Management (CKIM'95), 1995, 403-410.
4. Azer Bestavros, Robert Carter, Mark Crovella, Abdelsalam Heddaya, and Sulaiman Mirdad. application level document caching in the internet. In IEEE SDNE'96: The second International Workshop on Services in Distributed and Networked Environments, June 1995.
5. Azer Bestavros and Carlos Cunha, Server initiated document dissemination for the WWW. IEEE Data Engineering Bulletin, 19(3):3-11, September 1996.
6. T.T.Kwan, R.E.McGrath, and D.A.Reed. NCSA's world wide web server : design and performance. IEEE Computer, 28(11):68-74, November 1995.
7. A.Luotonen and K.Altis. Worl-Wide Web proxies. Computer Networks and ISDN Systems, 27(2), 1994. ¡URL: http://www1.cern.ch/ PapersWWW94/luotonen.ps¿
8. Marc Abrams, Charles R.Atandridge, Ghaleb Abdulla, Stephen Williams, and Edward A. Fox. Caching proxies: limitations and potentials. In proceedings of the Fourth International Conference on the WWW, Boston, MA, December 1995.
9. Radhika Malpani, Jacob Lorch and David Berger, Making world wide web caching servers cooperate. In 4th International world wide web conference, pages 107-117, Boston, Dec. 1995.
10. Steven Glassman. Acaching relay for the worl wide web. In proceedings of the first International Conference on the WWW, 1994.
11. S.Williams, M.Abrams, C.R.Standridge, G.Abdulla, E.A.Fox. Removal policies in network caches for Worl-Wide Web documents. ACM SIGCOMM, 1996, pp. 293-305.

An Integrated Approach for Flexible Workflow Modeling

Yongjie Ren, K.F. Wong, and B.T. Low

Department of Systems Engineering and Engineering Management
Chinese University of Hong Kong
Shatin, N.T., Hong Kong
{ygren, kfwong, btlow}@se.cuhk.edu.hk

Abstract. This paper proposes an integrated workflow model known as the Multi-Agent Workflow Model (MAWM). MAWM was designed to offer high flexibility in business process modeling. The central idea of MAWM is based on our conventional business perspective about labor division and cooperation. This idea is reflected in the concept agent-workflow. MAWM includes three sub-models, namely organization, process and data sub-models. Activity-based and communication-based methods are integrated in the process sub-model. They are used to model different types of business activities.

1 Introduction

Today, workflow is widely used as an enabling technology in business process automation and reengineering. The business processes are modeled as workflows under this technology. Current workflow modeling methods mainly fall into two categories: activity-based (or Input-Process-Output, IPO-based) and communication-based (or Language/Action, LA-based). Although there are other kinds of classification, such as [4] which groups all workflow methods into four categories: activity-oriented, object-oriented, role-oriented and speech-act oriented. They can basically be classfied to one of the two major methods.

There are several papers discuss the limitations of these two modeling methods. The major drawback of activity-based modeling method is inflexibility. And the communication-based methos is criticized of difficult to use and with poor expressive power. These two modeling methods are based on two extreme views: the activity-based method tends to model everything as tasks, sub-tasks or atomic actions; and the communication-based method tends to model everything as a communication cycle. But in practice, business activities behave differently. Some activities are simple whose behave could be determined at definition time, but some could not. Thus, none of the two modeling methods alone are suitable for modeling all types of business activities.

This paper presents an agent-based workflow model MAWM. It borrows the concept and methodology of Multi-agent Systems (MAS) and is comprised of three sub-models: a process sub-model for business process activity modeling;

a role-based agent sub-model for organization modeling and an object-oriented data sub-model for business process data object modeling. Activity-based and communication-based methods are integrated in the process sub-model. They are used to model different types of business activities.

The rest of this paper is structured as follows: The next section introduces the basic idea of the Multi-Agent Workflow Model (MAWM). This paper mainly focuses on the description of the the process sub-model. This is given in Section 3. Section 4 discusses some special flexible properties of our model. Finally, Section 5 concludes the paper.

2 Basic Ideas

In describing a business process in an organization, The following crucial perspective is adopted in the proposed method: (1) Labor division. Each member or unit in an organization has his own responsibility (or role) in a business process. (2) Cooperation. All members or units in an organization have to cooperate with each other to reach the goal of the business process.

Based on this perspective, the new workflow model (namely, the Multi-Agent Workflow Model, MAWM) is defined. MAWM facilitates clear modeling of the above mentioned aspects. In practice, neither activity-based nor communication-based method alone is suitable for modeling both aspects. The activity-based method is more suitable for modeling individual work in a business process, i.e., the divided work; and the communcation-based method is more suitable for modeling the cooperative activities. MAWM integrates these two methods to model different kinds of activities in a business process.

Figure 1 describes the basic idea of MAWM. The business process is mapped into an overall workflow. The agent-workflow concept is introduced to represent work division. The cooperation in the business process is mapped into the cooperation among different agent-workflows. Based on this, the entire workflow is separated into work and flow streams. The former represents the divided work and the latter the cooperation between the work. The work stream includes different types of work actions, such as data accesses, workflow control operations, application calling operations or manual actions. The flow stream includes different flow actions such as requesting, promising, etc. Also dependencies may exist among the actions in both streams. The activity-based method is used to model work actions and process elements tasks, sub-tasks are introduced, they are called work activities together with work actions; the communication-based method is used to model flow actions. process elements conversations and conversation fragments are introduced, they are called flow activities. In summary, a business process described using MAWM is represented by an overall workflow, which in turn is composed of a series of agent-workflows (awf).

In addition to the basic idea to model the business process, resources involved in the business process are also modeled in MAWM. As a result, MAWM includes three sub-models: a *process sub-model* is used to model the activities and dependencies among them in the business process; an *agent sub-model* based on role theory is used to model the organization structure; and an object-oriented *data sub-model* is used to model the data object manipulated in the business process.

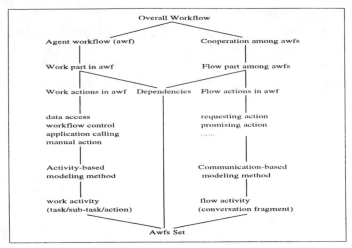

Fig. 1. Workflow model perspective in MAWM

3   Business Process Modeling - Process Sub-Model

3.1   Overall workflow and agent-workflow

A business process is represented as an overall workflow in MAWM model. The overall workflow defines the schema of the business process. The overall workflow is decomposed into agent-workflows according to the responsibilities (e.g. roles) of the organizational objects (i.e. the agents) involved in the overall workflow. Each agent-workflow represents the work to be carried out by the agent or role.

3.2   Task, sub-task and action

Depending on the complexity, an agent-workflow can be decomposed into tasks. The task can be further decomposed into smaller tasks (refer to as sub-tasks) and atomic actions. Tasks, sub-tasks and actions are grossly referred to as activities.

There are two kinds of activities, namely work and flow activity. The flow activity is represented by the process elements defined in next subsection. The work activity can be represented and decomposed into atomic actions including data access, workflow control, application calling and manual actions.

3.3   Flow activity and cooperation

Here the flow is different from the conventional data or control flow. It represents the cooperative activity among different agents. The modeling of cooperative acitvity is based on *speech-act theory* [2]. Instead of using speech-act primitives or conversation as basic process elements, we adopt a strategy similar to Dietz's essential transactions [3] to divide a conversation into some fragments, and use these conversation fragments as process elements to model the cooperative activity.

Currently, two kinds of cooperative activities are identified and modeled in MAWM: coordination and negotiation. Comparing with the cooperative classification in [5], we exclude collaboration and co-decision from our modeling although negotiation is one of the key process in collaboration and co-decision. From this point, our scope about workflow follows the definition in [1] which does not regard collaborative processes as workflow processes.

We use two kinds of conversation to model the cooperative work between agents. They are conversation for action and for possibility [7]. The former is used to model coordination; the later to model negotiation.

Conversation for Action: Coordination Modeling The basic protocol of conversation for action is described in Figure 2 using a state-transition diagram. It shows the case of a conversation for action initiated by a request.

With this diagram, we divide it into two fragments from state 3: conversation_I and conversation_II (along the dashed line). With regard to the four phases in conversation for action, fragment conversation_I corresponds to the first two phases, conversation_II corresponds to the fouth phase of the conversation. These two conversation fragments are divided further according to the participants in the conversation. Consequently, the following process elements are prided in MAWM:

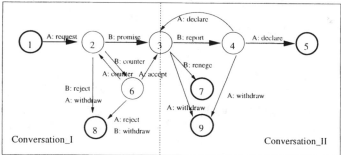

Fig. 2. Fragment in Conversation for Action (Adapted from [6])

- *Customer_I*: the behavior of the customer in conversation_I.
- *Provider_I*: the behavior of the provider in conversation_I.
- *Customer_II*: the behavior of the customer in conversation_II.
- *Provider_II*: the behavior of the provider in conversation_II.
- *Customer_I_II*: the behavior of the customer in the whole conversation.
- *Provider_I_II*: the behavior of the provider in the whole conversation.

With these process elements, we can model the coordinative activities in the agent-workflow. These process elements can also interleave with the other activities. Figure 3 shows some possible interleavings. The rectangle represents the work activity and the rounded rectangle the flow activity. Note that partial conversation is possible in practical.

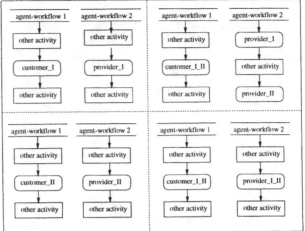

Fig. 3. Interleaving of Acting and Conversing

Conversation for Possibility: Negotiation Modeling In business process, negotiation may occur independently or as part of the other cooperative activities (coordination, collaboration or co-decision). We use *conversation for possibility* to model negotiation process. Two process elements are used to represent the negotiation process: Negotiation_I and Negotiation_II. They former represents the behavior of the negotiation initiator, the later the behavior of the negotiation parnter in the negotiation process.

4 Flexible properties of MAWM

A flexible workflow model should be able to cope with the dynamic and complexity of the business process environment. In our model, we regard personal process fragment as the key to the flexibility and the concept agent-workflow is used for this purpose. With agent-workflow, the dynamic modification can be fulfilled by the user easily and transparent to the other users or process fragments. Some other flexible properties includes:

- *Dynamic construction of workflow.* When a new workflow is initiated, the first agent associated to the workflow defines its agent-workflow. It sends a request to other agents seeking for cooperation if needed. Once the other agents received the request, it may dynamically define a new agent-workflow if it does not already exist. Further, it will send requests to the other agents according to the specification of the task.
- *Alternative support.* Alternative scenario selection is also supported at the agent-workflow granularity. When there is more than one alternative agent-workflow, the workflow engine will select either the one suggested by the

human agent at run-time or the one by the computer agent according to its built-in knowledge.

- *Dynamic linking between a task and its implementation.* This is important but complex, especially in a business environment where tasks are mostly distributed and autonomous. In MAWM, dynamic linking takes place at the agent-workflow granularity. The mechanism is similar to overridding in the object-oriented paradigm.

5 Conclusion

This article describes an agent-based workflow model, namely MAWM. It models labor division and cooperation in a typical business process clearly. An integrated approach is used in the model. In addition to using a process sub-model to model the business process activities, two other sub-models are used to model the organization and data objects used in a workflow. These three sub-models are integrated together as the overall workflow model. Activity-based method and communication-based method are integrated in the process sub-model.

Compare with the other hybrid or integrating modeling methods, activity-based and communication-based are used to model different kinds of activities in our model, and the basic process elements for communication are conversation fragments, rather than the whole conversation or speech act primitives.

Acknowledgements

This work is partially supported by the National Natural Science Foundation, project No. 69633020.

References

1. W.M.P. van der Aalst, "The Application of Petri Nets to Workflow Management", *Journal of Circuits, Systems and Computers*, 1998.
2. J.L. Austin, *How to do things with words*, Harvard University Press, 1962.
3. J.L.G. Dietz, "Business Modeling for Business Redesign", *27th Hawaiian International Conference on System Specification (HICSS-27)*, Hawaiian, 1994.
4. P. Kueng, P. Kawalek, P. Bichler, "How to Compose an Object-Oriented Business Process Model?", *IPG: Working Paper, available by http://www.cs.man.ac.uk/ipg*, 1996.
5. G. De Michelis, "Computer Support for Cooperative Work: Computers Between Users and Social Complexity", in C. Zucchermaglio et. al (eds.) *Organizational Learning and Technological Change*, 307-330, 1995.
6. T. Winograd and R. Flores, *Understanding Computers and Cognition*, Addison-Wesley, 1986.
7. T. Winograd, "A Language Perspective on the Design of Cooperative Work". In *Proceedings of the First Conference on CSCW*, ACM Austin, 203-220,1986.

Integrating Different Signature Purposes in Workflow Systems – A Case Study

Karl R.P.H. Leung[1], Lucas C.K. Hui[2], and Ricky W.M. Tang[2]

[1] Department of Computing and Mathematics,
Hong Kong Institute of Vocational Education (Tsing Yi),
Hong Kong.
kleung@computer.org,
[2] Department of Computer Science and Information Systems,
The University of Hong Kong,
Hong Kong.
{hui, wmtang2}@csis.hku.hk

Abstract. Many workflow models treat digital signatures in a most primitive way without considering their different uses in different situations. Some signature requirements in a workflow cannot be met or require a lot of extra work to archive by these primitive implementations. There is a need to develop different handling methods for different signature purposes in order to handle the requirements efficiently. In this paper, implementation and integration of the different signature purposes will be discussed through a case of the real world usage.

1 Introduction

Workflow Systems Background An electronic workflow system captures information, their transformation processes, scheduling and routing between the processes, agents conducting the processes and the presentation of information. Different modeling and classification methods of these workflow components led to different implementations of electronic workflow systems. Different implementations emphasize different aspects of workflow, and may put less weight on some workflow components. Examples of workflow implementations include Lotus Notes and Flowmark.

Most of the research on workflow such as METEOR [3] and WfMC [2], and commercial workflow engines such as Lotus Notes and Flowmark discussed above, focus on the management of workflow with different kinds of technology such as database. Few of them include signatures in their studies. Signatures, at best, are only a kind of operation in the tasks. In these research systems encrypting a form is almost the base level of abstraction. Hence the purposes of the signatures inside a form is outside their scope.

Encryption and Digital Signatures A digital signature [7] is a data item that accompanies a digitally encoded message, and can be used to ascertain the originator of the message and the fact that the message has not been modified since it left the originator. Different public key cryptographic schemes have been used to implement digital signatures and data encryption , for example the Rivest-Shamir-Adleman (RSA) scheme , Digital Signature Algorithm (DSA) scheme , the elGamal Scheme , and the elliptic curve digital signature algorithm (ECDSA) scheme . To implement digital signatures with these schemes, each user owns a key-pair containing a secret key (also called the private key) and a public key. The secret key is meant to be only known by the owner, and the public key is known to the public. The mathematical properties of the public key system guarantee the following:

- A message, the plaintext, after being encrypted with a private key, when and only when being decrypted with the corresponding public key, will become the plaintext itself; and

- Given the public key, there is no computationally feasible way to compute the corresponding private key.

Public key cryptography does provide a way to authenticate an electronic message. However, authentication is not the only function of a hand-written signature. Depending on the context of the paper-based message, hand-written signatures are also used for many other purposes, including but not limited to: authorization, generation of time stamp, providing evidences for accountability, and voting. These properties are related to the organization model and behavior, and require much more information from the organization in addition to the message and keys to operate. These consequences are usually ignored by research results in public key cryptography, which treats all types of content in a message as identical.

2 Review of Different Signature Purposes

In this section, multiple purposes of signatures in workflow systems and the extended data model to handle them are reviewed. Detailed discussion on these purposes can be found in [5] [4].

Authentication Authentication serves to maintain data integrity and non-repudiation of origin.

Authorization When a signature is used for authorization purpose, it approves the invoking of the processing of certain restricted tasks or allocation of resources such as information resources or physical resource objects.

Proxy Signature When an actor who is responsible for a particular task is not available, someone has to sign on behalf of him/her. The signer is called the proxy and the signature is the proxy signature.

Time Stamp Time stamp signatures are used to prove that at some point of time, the form has been passed by a certain agent.

Witness A witness signature is used to certify the happening of an event as a third party.

Anonymous Signature Anonymous Signature is used when the identity of the signer is not supposed to be revealed to the form reader. However, It is usually sensible for the form reader to have the knowledge that the signer belongs to a certain group context.

Multiple Signatures It is very common for a form to be processed and approved by more than one person. In this case, multi-signatures on a form are required to handle the processing. According to different needs, two methods to handle multi- signatures are proposed: sequential multi-signatures and parallel multi- signatures. Sequential multi-signatures are further refined to be dependent or indenpendent, and parallel multi-signatures classified by their fork and join modes.

3 Case study

In this section, we will discuss the employment of different signature purposes in the total order management process of Procter & Gamble Worldwide, after its redesign in 1994 (Figure 1). Details of this case can be found in [1]. The *Liaison* Workflow Engine with signature extensions [6] is used to implement the case.

Fig. 1. Total Order Management Process after Redesign (1994)

Proper implementation of different signature purposes is important in this case because this process involves a lot of different signature purposes that are crucial to the integrity, accountability and security of the system. This can be demonstrated by simply omitting signature of the *time-stamping* purpose on the invoice in billing phase. Serious arguments can arise over the date of delivery with no proof from either party. Primitive single-purpose signature scheme is also not practical here because of the complex interaction of multiple signatures and other workflow information. Thus, an integration of different signature purposes schemes is used to solve this problem.

The total order management includes the entire ordering, shipping, and billing processes. It begins with order generation, order acquisition, then goes through order processing, shipment control and billing and finally the delivery execution and the financial transactions to settle the bill. In each stage, different signature purposes requirements are identified and the appropriate solutions are applied. The prototype of Signature Manage is used to implement and demonstrate these solutions.

Order Generation In this stage, agents will provide customers with product pricing and policy data for them to make purchase decisions and thus generate orders. As these marketing data are restricted, signature should be employed to ensure proper authorization of access.

The order generation agent will first issue a request for the product pricing and policy data to his/her supervisor. The supervisor, who has the authority to grant access to the marketing data, will grant the access by signing a signature of the *authorization* purpose (Figure 2) on the request form. The request form is then kept by the requesting agent.

When the agent wants to get the data, the request form will be presented to the manager of the data, who will verify the authorization signature to ensure that the requesting agent was properly authorized. Verification will check both the validity of the signature and the eligibility of the authorizing signer to the data.

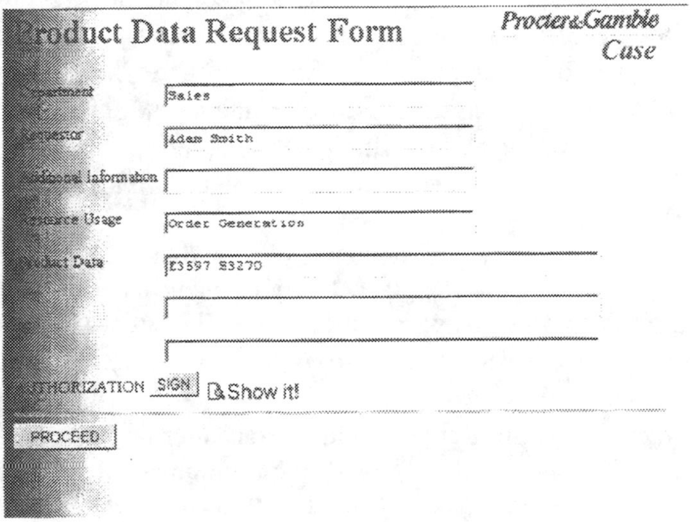

Fig. 2. Authorization–Resource Authorization

Upon successful verification, the manager will give the data to the requester, and then the requesting agent can serve the customer with the information.

Order Acquisition After customers have made their purchase decision and placed their order, an order receipt will be sent back to them. The date of issue on the receipt is important as it can serve as the evidence of the ordering date, so signature for the time-stamping purpose should be used.

The agent issuing the order receipt will sign using signature for the *time-stamping* purpose. The order receipt is kept by the customer and the signature on it can be verified to get the signing date if there is disrupt about the date of ordering in the future.

Order Processing Order processing includes the order entry, checking, maintenance and change to the order, and the final transmission of the order to the plant. It also includes the enquiries on the status of the order.

In order entry, the entrying agent will enter the ordering information and then sign on the order form for *authentication* purpose to ensure data integrity, so that no subsequent modifications can be done undetected. Then the order will go through order checking.

Order checking includes a number of checks such as credit check and order quality check that can be performed simultaneously. The result of all the checking must be collected in order for the order to proceed to the next step. To carry out this task efficiently, copies of the order form will be made and sent to different agents to do the checking at the same time, each checking result is signed by the checking agent for the *accountability–strong* purpose, because they will be held responsible if there are errors in their checking result. Before the beginning of the next step–order maintenance, all the checking results have to be collected back. This is achieved by the application of *join-all* case in the *parallel multiple signature* scheme.

In the order maintenance phase, customers can change their orders through their agent before the orders go to the plant. Every change should be signed by the agent to make sure that the change is authenticative. The signature purposes used are *authentication* and *accountability–strong* because the agent is also accountable for the change.

When the order finally arrives at the plant, all signatures on the order form starting from order entry are verified. The signatures on order entry, order checking and order maintenance are signed in a fixed sequence and are dependent. This is because if signature verification in any stage fails, the stages follow cannot continue, knowing that not all the information on the form are intact. This dependent sequential addition of signatures on the same form can be handled by the *Dep* case of *Sequential Multiple Signature* scheme.

Anytime in the order processing, customers can make order inquiry to check the status of their orders. An agent can make the appropriate query for the inquiring customers and reply them with correct information. For the reply to the queries, the integrity of the content is important but who sent them out is of little importance. This is archivable by the agent signing the reply using the *authentication* and *accountability–weak* signature purposes.

Shipment Control and Billing Shipment control is to check whether the ordered products are available now, and then assign proper carrier (trucks/ship/etc.) to transport the products to the customers. On the other hand, the main process in billing will be issuing invoice.

In the product availability check, the checking agent may send multiple requests simultaneously to different plants to check their stock level. The plant managers will report back their stock level with their signatures on it to ensure data integrity. It is not necessary for the agent to wait for the replies of all plants as the shipment can begin as soon as enough products are located, so the checking agent only wait until the replied plants have the stock level to satisfy the order. This use of simultaneously signed forms is supported by the *join-min* case of the *parallel multiple signature* scheme.

After the products are located, carrier assignment will be generated automatically by computers with load balancing information considered. This generated assignment is usually optimal for cost effectiveness but for the need of monitoring and sometimes special carrier load planning, the manager in charge of shipment should be informed of the assignment. The managers do this by signing the information using signature for the *begin-informed* purpose. Because of the large amount of carrier assignment generated everyday, the manager may not be able to read every assignment personally. He/she can assign other agents in the department to do this work instead. The assigned agent(s) will sign using their own signature but their signatures should have the same authority as the manager's signature. This is supported by the *proxy* signature purpose. The manager will first delegate the signing right by signing on a *proxy* form, then the assigned agents can sign normally using their own signature. Upon verification, the validity of the signature as well as the proxy form will be checked to ensure that the one delegating the signing right is actually eligible to sign.

The issue of invoice will follow the carrier assignment and the signature on it will serve the *time-stamping* purpose. This signing order (sign after carrier assignment) is fixed, but the two signatures are not related. This kind of sequential signing of not related signatures is supported by the *Indep* case of *Sequential Multiple Signature* scheme.

Delivery Execution This phase is the actual delivery of products and the update of shipment status. The shipment status update requests will be signed for the *authentication* purpose.

Financial Transactions Receivables are collected in this phase. The update of account information, clearance of accounts and related documents need signatures of the *accountability–strong* purpose to make the processing agent responsible for the documents they processed.

4 Conclusion

This paper summaries and integrates the different signature purposes described in previous works on signature purposes [6]. The integration appears in the form of the Signature Manager extension to the *Liaison*Workflow model. We have verified the design of this integration in Section 3, with a case study on the *Total Order Management Process* of *Procter & Gamble* [1]. This includes the employment of digital signatures of different purposes in the order generation, order acquisition, order processing, shipment control, billing, delivery execution and the financial transactions. Sucessful implementation of this case demonstrates the importance of signature purposes in workflow systems. Further studies will be carried out in the future to continue the testing and verification of this design.

References

1. Prof. Theodore H. Clark and James L. Mckenney. Procter & gamble: Improving consumer value through process design. Technical Report 195-126, Harvard College, Harvard Business School, Harvard College, 1995.
2. B. Pernici G. Pozzi F. Casati, P. Grefen and G. Sanchez. Wide workflow model and architecture. Technical Report 96-19, Center for Telematics and Information Technology (CTIT), Universiy of Twente, April 1996.
3. N. Krishnakumar and A. Sheth. Managing heterogeneous multi-system tasks to support enterprise-wide operations. *Distributed and Parallel Databases*, pages 155–186, 1995.
4. Karl R.P.H. Leung and Lucas C.K. Hui. Multiple signature handling in workflow systems. *Submitted to a forum*, 1999.
5. Karl R.P.H. Leung and Lucas C.K. Hui. The need of signatures handling in electronic workflow systems. *To appear in the Proc. of the 5th International Conference on Information Systems Analysis and Synthesis (ISAS'99)*, July–August 1999.
6. Karl R.P.H. Leung, Lucas C.K. Hui, and Ricky W.M. Tang. Extending the liaison workflow engine to support different signature purposes. *To appear in the Proc. of 1999 Asia Pacific Software Engineering Conference (APSEC 99)*, 1999.
7. B. Schneier. *Applied cryptography : protocols, algorithms, and source code in C*. Wiley: New York, 2 edition, 1995.

Management of Workflow over the Web Supporting Distributed Process Evolution

Sang-Yoon Min[1], Doo-Hwan Bae[1], Sung-Chan Cho[1], and Young-Kwang Nam[2]

[1] Korea Advanced Institute of Science and Technology, 373-1 Kusong-dong, Yusong-gu, Taejon 305-701, South Korea
[2] Yonsei University, 234 Maji, Heungup, Kwangwon, 220-710, South Korea

Abstract. With the emergence of the Internet, the Web became a widely-used collaboration environment for business process activity. Business process itself is a very evolable entity. In this paper, we introduce a workflow management system called SoftPM/W^2 for the business processes over the Web. For efficient workflow management, SoftPM/W^2 provides integrated formal representation of business process elements, generation of business data model from business process model, a view-based mechanism for distributed evolution, and unique evolution control mechanism.

1 Introduction

Workflow evolution means the dynamic changes on the instance of initial business process model. In transaction-oriented business domain such as banking process, evolutions may hardly occur. However, evolutions often occur in the domains of long term business process such as the Web-based business activity collaboration. Human involvement usually exists. Refinement on exsiting business process is often required. These evolutions are unavoidable[10].

For such distributed workflow evolution, it is more reasonable to let the evolution be made in distributed manners because business process activities are mostly carried out by distributed participants. In this sense, workflow management mechanism must provide some means to allow each participant to make changes on business process instance. Then, the changes made by each participant should be reflected into the overall business process in consistent manners. In workflow evolution management, some of the major technical issues are business process modeling, process modification, and change control techniques.

The business process modeling technique is the most fundamantal mechanism to manage the process changes. For the systematic and consistent management of process change, the overall business process must be defined in unambiguous way. SoftPM/W^2 uses a high-level Petri-net called *MAM net*[7, 8] as the process modeling formalism. MAM net supports an integrated activity-oriented modeling of business process activities, business data, and participants. SoftPM/W^2 also automatically generates business-data oriented model to observe business process in data-oriented perspective.

Each participant needs an effective means to make changes on process. Participants usually have knowledges only on the portion of the process of their own interest. They usually have vague idea on how the entire business process looks like. Participants want to see only the portions of the process of their own interest. We call this *views* of each participant. SoftPM/W^2 extracts views from the both business process model and business data model for each participant.

Simply allowing each participant to freely modify the business process possess high risks because a modification on a critical portion of the business process can raise unexpected consecutive modifications. SoftPM/W^2 supports the control of modification by analyzing the degree of the impact caused by modifications.

In architectural perspective, SoftPM/W^2 is implemented with pure Java in a thin client/server architecture. SoftPM/W^2 supports the execution of business process over the Web. Participants can evolve the business process through a Java Applet in any web browser.

In this paper, we propose a process-oriented approach to the workflow management over the Web environment. Its prototype implementation is called SoftPM/W^2. SoftPM/W^2 is a retailored version of a process management system, SoftPM[8], which we had previously developed for software process domain.

This paper is organized as follows: In Section 2, the business process modeling mechanism is described. In Section 3, we explain the view-based mechanism for workflow evolution. In Section 5, we give conclusion and future work.

2 Business Process Modeling

In our approach, business process is modeled in the activity-oriented perspective which we call business process model. Then, the corresponding data-oriented model is automatically generated. We call this business data model.

To demonstrate our approach throughout this paper, we use the ISPW-6 process example[6] which desribes the requirement change management activities during software system development. The ISPW-6 example consists of five collaborating activites: *modify design, modify code, modify test plan, modify unit test package*, and *test unit*. There are five involving participants: two design engineers, two software engineers, and one quality assurance engineers.

SoftPM/W^2 provides a easy-to-use graphical modeling layer above underlying MAM net formalism for designing business process model. The modeling mechanism is similar to drawing a PERT chart. Fig.1 shows the process model of the ISPW-6 example.

The goal of the business data model is to provide an data-oriented perspective of software process. In SoftPM/W^2, a business data model is represented as a directed graph with nodes representing the business data and arcs representing the usage dependencies among business data. The business data model is generated from corresponding business process model. Fig.2 shows the business data model generated from the business process model shown in Fig.1.

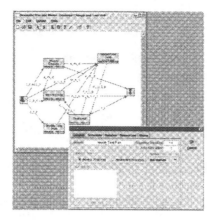

Fig. 1. Business Process Model of ISPW-6 Example

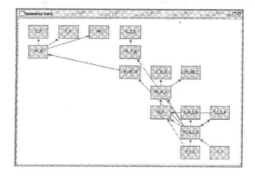

Fig. 2. Business Data Model of ISPW-6 Example

3 Workflow Evolution

In our approach, we define views for each corresponding participant, in both business process model and business data model. Each participant manipulates business process through their views. Then, such distributed modifications are reflected into the global business process model.

3.1 Views

The view of a participant in business process model is a subset of process activities, which are related to the participant. Intuitively, the activities carried out by the participant are the main constituent activities of the participant's view. In addition, other activities having data-depedency on those main constituent activites should be considered. The data dependency between two activities exists when business data is passed from one to the other, or when the activities use the same business data. Before giving the definition of a view in SoftPM/W^2 approach, we define the following attributes of business process.

- *Require*(p): the set of business activities which require the participant p for its execution
- *Dependent*(a): the set of business activities which are data-dependent on the activity a.

Then, the view of participant p can be defined as follows:

$$V_p = Require(p) \cup \{p_i \mid p_i \in Dependent(a_i) \ for \ all \ a_i \in Require(p)\}$$

The view extraction can be automated. Fig.3(a) shows the the client Web-browser showing the business process view of the quality assurance engineer in the ISPW-6 example.

The view of a participant in the business data model is a subset of the business data model. The view consists of the business data manipulateted by the activities carried out by the participants, and other business data which has usage dependency to the business data manipulated by the participant. Fig.3(b) shows the client Web-browser showing the business data view of the quality assurance engineer in the ISPW-6 example.

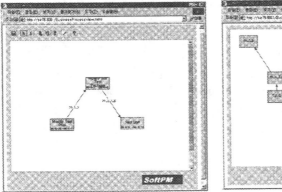 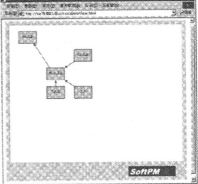

(a) Business Process View   (b) Business Data View

Fig. 3. Views of the Quality Assurance Engineer

3.2 Controlling Evolution

Controlling of evolution are achieved by limiting the permission on process modification. The permission is determined by the degree of impact caused by the modification. The degree of impact can be determined by several factors according to the specific characteristics of process and organization. In our approach, we consider usage-dependency relations between business data since workflow has very data-dependent behavior in general.

Using the dependency relationships represented in the business data model, we can perform the change impact analysis on business data. Change impact value(CIV) of an artifact node r_i is computed by counting the number of data nodes that have dependency on r_i, and dividing the number by the total number of data node in his/her view. Thus, change impact value(CIV) is defined as follows:

$$CIV(r_i) = \frac{\#\{r_j \in Data\ nodes\ in\ the\ view | \exists\ a\ path(r_j, r_i)\}}{\#(Data\ nodes\ in\ the\ view)}$$

If a participant are trying to modify an activity, each business data produced by the activity are analyzed by calculating their CIVs. If the sum of the CIVs is less than the control value specified by manager, the modification can proceed. Otherwise, it is not allowed.

4　Conclusion and Future Work

With efforts primarily from industry, workflow management has emerged as a widely-accepted techinique to integrate and automate the execution steps of business process. Various prototypes and commerical products have been introduced[2–5, 9–11].

Comparing to the existing approaches, there are several characteristics of SoftPM/W^2 which distinguishes itself from them. Those characteristics are the integrated formal representation of business process elements(i.e. business process activity, business data, participants), the generation of data-oriented model from activity-oriented model, the support of distributed workflow evolution over the Web through a view-based approach, unique evolution control, and with the change impact analysis.

Most of the existing approach from industry do not fully support the formal modeling of business process. Some approaches[1, 2, 4, 11] from research community support the formal modeling using Petri nets or Statechart. However, they do support integrated modeling of business process elements including all business process activity, business data, and participants. None of the existing approach provides a mechanism for generating business-data model from their business process model. In their approaches, they build different perspecitive models independently that may cause inconsistency between models and require extra modeling effort. In business process modeling domain, a few approaches[1, 10] address the workflow evolution. The OPSIS approach[1] emplyeed a view-based process change. However, they do not provide specific means for the distributed evolution.

We have some future works for more advanced research. We plan to port SoftPM/W^2 into CORBA environment as a distributed object system over the

Web environment. Along with the adoption of CORBA, we are trying to objectifying actual business data entities to support the migration data objects over the Internet.

References

1. Using Views to Maintain Petri-net-based Process Models, in *Proc. of Int'l Conf. on Software Maintenance*, (Oct. 1995).
2. G. Dinkhoff, V. Gruhn, A. Saalmann, and M. Zielonka, Business Process Modeling in the Workflow Management Environment LEU, in *Proc. 13th Int. conf. on the Entity-Relationship Approach* (1994) 46–63.
3. D. DeRoure, W. Hall, and S. Reich, An Open Architecture for Supporting Collaboration on the Web, in *Proc. of 7th Int'l Workshop on Enabling Technologies: Infrastructure for Collaborative Enterprises*, (June 1998).
4. V. Gruhn and S. Wolf, Software Process Improvement by Business Process Orientation, *Software Process Improvement and Practice* 1 Pilot Issue (Aug. 1995) 49–56.
5. Special Issue on Workflow Systems. *Bulletin of the Technical Committee on Data Enginering* 18(1), (1995)
6. M. Kellner, P. Feiler, A. Finkelstein, T. Katayama, L. Osterweil, M. Penedo, and H. Rombach, ISPW-6 Software Process Example, in *Proc. 6th Int. Software Process Workshop*, (Oct. 1990) 176–186.
7. S. Min, I. Han, W. Park, and D. Bae, An Approach to Process Management Based on Formal Process Modeling and Analysis, in *Proc. 4th Asia-Pacific Software Engineering Conf. and Int. Computer Science Conf.* (Dec. 1997) 292–301.
8. S. Min, H. Lee, and D. Bae, SoftPM: A Software Process Management System Reconciling Formalism with Easiness, to be published in *Information and Software Technology*, (1999).
9. C. Mohan, State of the Art in Workflow Management Systems Research and Products, Tutorial presented at ACM SIGMOD Int'l Conf. on Management of Data, (1996).
10. M. Reichert, C. Hensinger, and P. Dadam, Supporting Adaptive Workflows in Advanced Application Environment, in *Proc. EDBT Workshop on Workflow Management Systems*, (March 1998) 100–109
11. D. Wodtke, J. Weissenfels, G. Weikum, and A. Dittrich, The Mentor Project: Steps Towards Enterprise-Wide Workflow Management, in *Proc. of 12th Int'l Conf. on Data Engineering*, (March 1996).

Data Placement and Retrieval Policy for Serving Video Operations through Sequential Access in Video Server

Keun Hyung Kim , Seog Park

Dept. Of Computer Science
Sogang University
Seoul, 121-110, Korea
{khkim, spark}@dblab.sogang.ac.kr

Abstract

Because video server needs a storage system with large bandwidth in order to provide more users simultaneously with the real time retrieval requests, the storage system generally have the structure of disk array, which consists of multiple disks. For the storage system in order to serve multiple video stream requests, it's bottlenecks come from the seeking delay caused by the random movement of disk head and from unfair disk access due to disk load unbalance among multiple disks.

This paper presents a novel placement and retrieval policy. The new policy retrieves the requested data through sequential access and maintaining disk load balance so that it can diminish the bottlenecks on retrieving and can provide the real time retrieval services for more users simultaneously. Moreover, the novel retrieval policy introduces the concept of dummy request so that it can simply control the timing for retrieving a data.

1 Introduction

Recent advances in computer and communication technologies have made it possible for us to store and access large quantity of multimedia data over high-speed networks. Of the different media types, video has received the most attention because of its commercial potential in video-on-demand (VOD) applications. An efficient video server primarily acts as an engine reading video streams from disk storage and pumping these to the clients at the proper delivery rate. One of the most important criteria in designing the video server is the maximum number of video streams that can be simultaneously supported. The video server must be able to timely pump the video streams while still supporting a large number of simultaneous clients retrieving the streams from video server. In building the video server, the major parameter that constraints the number of active clients is the data placement and retrieval method that read the streams out of the disk array, which consists of multiple disks. To achieve the high data retrieval requirement, RAID[4] and disk striping scheme [5] for storage system have been used for multiple disks environment.

The video operations such as fast-forward, fast-backward and rewind are important to access the required location of video stream. Because the fast-forward operation does not access disks according to the sequence stored in disk array, it may bring overload to particular disks. If the particular disks are overloaded when supporting many video streams simultaneously, the QOS(Quality-Of-Service) of each video stream may become worse because situations of not retrieving the data inside deadline occur periodically. [2] proposed a data placement scheme for overcoming disk load unbalance problem.

In the disk storage system, sequential access can have approximately two times higher throughput (with block size $\ll$ 100KB per read) than random data access[1]. Because video server must retrieve various video streams to serve a lot of users simultaneously, it generally requires the random data access, which waste disk bandwidth due to seek time and is major origin that decrease disk performance. [1, 3] proposed the data placement scheme for processing data by sequential access.

This paper present a novel data placement and retrieval scheme. The scheme can not only process all video operations such as normal, fast-forward, fast-backward and rewind play through sequential access to disks but also can process data by maintaining the disk load balance among multiple disks in the environment of disk array. So, the new scheme can maximize disk bandwidth so that it can not only minimize waiting time(startup latency) but also support more users.

The rest of this paper is organized as follows. Section 2 describes previous work related with the data placement and retrieval scheme. Section 3 discusses the novel placement policy. In section 4, we discuss the novel retrieval policy. Section 5 concludes this paper.

2 Background

A unit that the video server accesses the video streams is called a segment. That is, the video stream consists of segments and we consider the segment as a unit for placement and retrieval. In this paper, the segment is the GOP of MPEG format, which almost have constant size(70KB). User can demand following operations from video server when the segments of video streams are stored in disk array.

Normal-play : The video server fetches continuous segments within real time constraints forward and transmits them into clients, then the client decodes the segments and displays them.

Fast-forward-play : The video server fetches segments, which are skipped as a constant interval, within real time constraints forward and transmits them into clients, then the client decodes the segments and displays them. The interval skipped is the speed of fast-forward play.

Fast-backward-play : The video server fetches segments, which are skipped as a constant interval, within real-time constraints backward and transmits them into clients, then the client decodes segments and displays them. The interval skipped is the speed of fast-backward play.

Rewind-play : The video server fetches continuous segments within real time constraints backward and transmits them into clients, then the client decodes the segments and displays them.

To provide a lot of users with the video operations simultaneously, video streams is decomposed into segments, which are placed by being scattered over disk array. In the case of RR(Round Robin) scheme, a segment V_i^j of video stream V_i is stored on disk $D_{i+j \bmod X}$ when there are X disks($D_0, D_1, D_2, \ldots, D_{X-1}$). RR scheme maintains regular disk bandwidth only for normal play, but raises the particular disks overloaded when processing fast operations[2, 6]. In particular, because RR scheme retrieves data through random access, it wastes the disk bandwidth due to disk seek time.

VSP(Virtual Sequential Placement) scheme appends the sequential access technique to RR scheme. The VSP partitions each disk into zones, which have the same number of disk blocks[1]. Each segment of each video stream is stored in a zone of a disk by VSP scheme. If we assume that there are X disks and Y zones($Z_0,Z_1,Z_2,...,Z_{Y-1}$) on each disk, a segment V_i^j of video streamV_i is stored on zone $Z_{g \bmod Y}$ of disk $D_{g \bmod X}$ when g is global segment number of a segment V_i^j. The global segment number is counted with segments of other video streams and is counted from 0.

Here, if X and Y are the related prime numbers, disk load balance and zone load balance are maintained[1]. The VSP can process data through sequential access only for normal-play operation but cause random access and the overloaded disks for fast-play operations. Those problems degrade QOS like waiting time or hiccup-free display.

3 novel placement policy

We propose a novel data placement policy, which is called GRP(Going and Returning Placement scheme). GRP is the modified VSP scheme. It can not only process data by sequential access for normal-play and fast(forward or backward)-play operation with constrained speeds but also maintain disk load balance and zone load balance for fast-play operations. To cause forward and backward operations to be processed by sequential access, GRP places segments from inmost zone to outmost zone following the placement from outmost zone to inmost zone. That is, the placement takes the policy that stores with going and returning between inmost zone and outmost zone of disk.

We now describe the GRP policy formally. Like VSP, the GRP partitions each disk into zones, which have the same number of disk blocks. Each segment of each video stream is stored on zones of disks by GRP policy. If there are X disks and Y zones on each disk and g is global segment number of a segment V_i^j of video stream V_i, a segment V_i^j of video stream V_i is stored on zone Z_z of disk D_d based on calculating formulas (6) and (7). The g is global segment number counted with segments of other video streams. The global segment number is counted from 0.

$$C_f = \left(\frac{g}{Y}+1\right)\bmod 2 \tag{1}$$

$$C_b = \left(\frac{g}{Y}\right)\bmod 2 \tag{2}$$

$$D_{interval} = GCD(F_{speed}, X) \tag{3}$$

$$S_{interval} = F_{speed} \cdot \left(\frac{X}{D_{interval}}\right) \tag{4}$$

$$D_{skew} = \left(\frac{g}{S_{int\,erval}}\right) \mod D_{int\,erval} \tag{5}$$

$$d = (g \mod X) + (D_{skew} \mod D_{int\,erval}) \tag{6}$$

$$z = C_f \cdot (g \mod Y) + C_b \cdot (Y - 1 - g \mod Y) \tag{7}$$

The variable C_f and C_b in formulas (1) and (2) need for going and returning placement. The variable $D_{interval}$, $S_{interval}$ and D_{skew} in formulas (3),(4) and (5) are needed in order to avoid overloaded disks when processing fast-play operations. The variable $D_{interval}$ in formula (3) is the greatest common divisor of F_{speed}(speed for fast-operation) and X(number of disks), which is interval between overloaded disks that occur when processing the fast-play operation. The variable $S_{interval}$ in formula (4) is the interval between segments in the overloaded disks when processing the fast-play operation. The variable D_{skew} in formula (5) is a cycle number accessing segments in the overloaded disk repeatedly when processing the fast-play operation. The cycle number is used for reallocating segments by skewing as D_{skew} from the overloaded disks when placing segments in disks for the fast-play operation with a speed.

The GRP provides a constrained speed for a fast-play operation in order to be processed through sequential access. The constrained speeds are *2Y+1, 4Y+1, ...,* *nY+1* when there are X disks and Y zones in each disk(n = X/2−1). Because the constrained speeds depend on the number of zones in each disk, we can adjust the constrained speeds by altering the number of zones in disk. At this time, the number of zones in disk has to be the prime number related to the number of total disks. The smaller the number of zones, the slower the fast-play speeds for sequential processing so that the fast-play operation is more tender but performance of normal play operation may be degraded because of increasing retrieval time in the zone .

4 novel retrieval policy

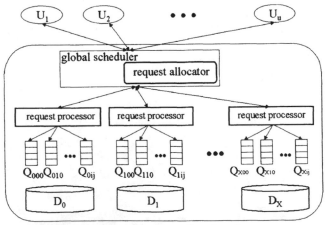

Fig. 1. general structure of retrieval system

Each segment of video streams is stored in each zone of disks by using GRP policy. The segments have to be retrieved through sequential access by retrieval system. Fig.1 shows the general structure of the retrieval system. In Fig.1, U_i denotes users, D_i denotes disks and Q_{ijk} denotes queues in which requests for retrieving segments wait. That is, a queue Q_{ijk} contains the segment requests for the segments which belong to video stream V_k and are stored in zone Z_j of disk D_i. As Fig.1 shows the retrieval system consists of global scheduler and request processors. When a new service request for a video stream arrives, global scheduler considers such the states of system as diskbandwidth etc. and determines whether admitting the service request or not (admission control : this part is out of range of being discussed in this paper).

If the service request is admitted, global scheduler generates the segment requests for retrieving segments of the requested video stream and allocates the segment requests to proper queues in which the segment requests wait to be processed. Request allocator(RA) takes this function of global scheduler. Also, RA inserts dummy segment requests in front of the segment request in order to control the timing of retrieving the segment. Fig.2 describes the procedure of RA.

Procedure of RA
Input:
    V_i // the requested video stream //
    g_I // the global segment number of the initial segment of V_i//
    m // the number of segments of V_i //
Variable
    q // a segment request is added to q-th element of a queue//
    g_k // global segment number of the segment V_i^k of V_i//
    R_i^k // the segment request corresponding to the segment V_i^k of V_i//
    d // the disk #of disk in which a segment was stored //
    z // the zone #of zone in which a segment was stored //
    Y // the number of zones in disk //
    Q_{dzvk} // k-th element of a queue Q_{dzv} that contains the segment requests for retrieving the segments which belong to video stream V_v and was stored in zone Z_z of disk D_d.//
Begin
    $g_0 \leftarrow g_I$
    $q \leftarrow 1$
    for (k = 0 to m)
        calculate d and z for g_k
        add R_i^k to Q_{dzvq}
        insert dummy requests to empty elements in front of Q_{dzvq}
        if g_k mod Y = 0 then $q \leftarrow q + 1$
        end if
    end for
end

Fig. 2. Request Allocator

RPs is allocated to each disk one by one and executed in parallel. A RP_i, which is allocated to disk D_i, serves queues corresponding to own disk D_i in round robin fashion. RP_i serves the requests in the queues one at a time. If segment request is dummy, RP_i waits during τ and maintains retrieval timing of segments(τ is duration during which a segment is transferred). When RP_i being executed, if operation request for a video stream is updated, RP_i fetches the proper element in queue at next round. For example, for only normal play operation, assume that the segment request that will be fetched from queue at next round is k-th request. At this time, if operation request is updated to fast forward play, the segment request that will be fetched from queue at next round is k+2 th request.

5 Conclusion

The video server must support more users while maintaining QOS requested. This needs high speed network environment and storage system with large bandwidth. This paper proposed the novel data placement and retrieval policy which can retrieve the requested video streams through sequential access and by maintaining disk load balance.

Because the proposed policy processes all video operations through sequential access, the diskbandwidth is increased and the average waiting time is decreased in comparison with other schemes. While previous schemes(RR or VSP) raise the overloaded disks for fast operations, the proposed policy(GRP) can maintain the disk load balance because it can forecast the overloaded disks for fast operations and reallocate the segments to disks. Also, because the proposed scheme introduced dummy segment request, it is simple to control the timing for retriveing segments.

However, in order to process fast operations through sequential access, the speed for fast operation is limited to several speeds, which depend on the number of zones in each disk. Though the number of zones influences the performance of normal play operations, it is trivial.

References

1. Gin-Kou Ma, Chiung-Shien Wu, Mei-Chian Liu, and Bao-Shuh P. Lin, "Efficient Real-time Data Retrieval Through Saclable Multimedia Storage", ACM Multimedia '97 Proceedings, pp.165-172, 1997.
2. Taeck-Geun Kwon, Sukho Lee, "Data Placement for Continuous Media in Multimedia DBMS", Proceedings of Multimedia DBMS, August 28-30, pp.110-117, 1995.
3. Sheau-Ru Tong and Yee-Foon Huang, "Study on Disk Zoning For Video Servers", IEEE Multimedia Systems '98, pp86-95, 1998.
4. D.James Gemmel, Harrick M.Vin, Dilip D.Kandlur, P.VenkatRangan, "Multimedia Storage Server: A Tutorial and Survey",IEEE Computer, Vol.28, issue5, pp.40-49, 1995.
5. Steven Berson, Shahram Ghandeharizadeh, "StaggeredStriping in Multimedia Information Systems", ACM SIGMOD, pp.79-90, 1994.
6. Soon M.Chung, Multimedia Information Storage and Management: Placement of Continuous Media In Multi-Zone Disks, Kluwer-Academic Publishers, pp23-55, 1996
7. V.S. Subrahmanian, Sushil Jajodia, Multimedia Database Systems(Issues and Research Directions), Springer, pp237-261, 1996.

A Buffering/Caching Mechanism for Continuous Media Players

Zhiyong PENG

Appliance Family Department, HP Labs Japan
Takatsu Kawasaki 213-0012 Japan

Abstract. In order to reduce the playback discontinuity of a stream of data (audio for example) sent through a packet-switched network, we proposed a buffering/caching mechanism for continuous media players. The stream playback is usually implemented by two parallel processes: receiving and playing. The former receives stream chips from the network while the latter plays the received stream chips and then empties their occupied buffers for the former. Our buffering/caching mechanism makes the receiving process completely independent of the playing process. Thus, the receiving process does not need to wait for the playing process to empty buffers so that the network bandwidth can be used as much as possible. Because the cached stream chips can be played from the local disk, the response latency of the playback control operations such as REPLAY and REWIND can be reduced as well. The mechanism was developed for our hyper audio web system.

1 Introduction

These years, more and more audio and video services[3] emerge on the internet. Unlike the traditional text and graphics transmission, the audio/video content is usually streamed from the server to the client who decodes the received packets in real time, plays the content immediately and then discards the received data. This method enables the user to listen to the content immediately after he has demanded for it. He can also fast-forward and listen to other parts of the content without waiting for the whole file to be downloaded. However, to stream real time audio/video data, the transmission line has to provide the full bandwidth of the stream during the whole transmission period. Concerning the internet, the possible bandwidth is variable. This may lead to drop-outs in the client audio/video output when the actual bandwidth is very low.

Various compression schemas have been developed to improve the playback quality of the audio/video stream. The playback discontinuity can also be reduced by dynamically adapting the amount of transmitted data to the actual capacity of the network connection. To do this, the audio/video data must either be stored in a format that allows dropping parts of the data resulting in a "graceful degradation" or they must be stored in different formats that the server can choose the format best suited for the bandwidth of a given connection. In addition, there are several playback smoothing methods which fall into two main categories: buffer-oriented and bufferless. Buffer-oriented methods preserve play-back continuity by buffering packets at receiver[6] or delaying the playback time of the first received packet[2]. On the other hand, bufferless methods[5] smooth playback through adjusting the source generation rate by means of feedback techniques.

There is still space to reduce effect of network delay variation because we noticed that the network bandwidth may be wasted because the stream receiving process may have to be stopped in order to wait for the stream playing process if their data rates are different. We proposed a circle buffering mechanism which makes the receiving process less dependent on the playing process. Furthermore, by introducing stream caching method, the receiving process can become completely independent of the playing process. Thus, the transmission capability during higher network bandwidth period can be reserved for use during the lower network bandwidth so that the discontinuity resulting from network delay variation can be reduced.

The reminder of the paper is organised as follows. Section 2 and Section 3 discuss stream buffering and stream caching, respectively. Section 4 gives an application example. We conclude the paper in Section 5.

2   Stream Buffering

The continuous media players usually use the technique of double-buffering (a receiving buffer and a playing buffer) to smooth the playback of a stream of data. The receiving buffer is used to receive stream chips from the network, and the playing buffer is used by the playing process. The two operations are performed in parallel. Whenever the playing buffer is consumed and the receiving buffer is full, the two buffers exchange their roles. The process is repeated until the end of the playback.

The double-buffering method requires that the data rates of the receiving and playing process should be the same in order to support continuous playback. However, the internet bandwidth is variable. That means the receiving process may be quicker than the playing process at one time and slower at the other time. With the double-buffering method, the discontinuity may be caused when the receiving process is slower. On the other hand, the higher network bandwidth may not be used enough. For example, at one time the receiving buffer has been filled while the playing buffer has not been consumed completely. The receiving process has to be stopped to wait for the playing process although the network transmission capability at that time can be used. Once the playing buffer has been consumed, the two buffers exchange their roles. If the network bandwidth becomes lower, the playing buffer may have been consumed while the receiving buffer has not been full. Thus, the drop-out of the playback will be resulted in.

If the transmission capability during the higher network bandwidth period can be reserved rather than be wasted, the playback discontinuity during the lower network bandwidth period may be avoided. For this reason, the double-buffering mechanism should be extended with more than two buffers. Thus, although the playing buffer has not been consumed while the receiving buffer becomes full, we have other buffers to receive stream chips. That is, the buffers that are filled during the higher network bandwidth period can be used to compensate for stream chip shortage during the lower network bandwidth period.

We proposed a cycle buffering mechanism, which employs n ($n > 2$) buffers. Initially, n buffers numbered from 0 to n-1 are emptied. Buffer[0] is firstly used to receive stream. When it becomes full, it will be played. Simultaneously the next buffer (Buffer[1]) is used to continue the receiving process. When Buffer[0] has been consumed, it will be emptied and the next buffer (Buffer[1]) will be played if it is full at that time. We define the next buffer of the Buffer[n-1] as Buffer[0] and make the above steps repeat until the end of the stream.

If n is 2, the circle buffering mechanism is actually the double-buffering one. Therefore, the circle buffering mechanism can be regarded as the generalization of the double-buffering one. Among these buffers, two buffers are used for the receiving process and the playing process respectively, the others are used to adjust the difference of the data rate between these two processes. If the data rate of the playing process is greater than the one of the receiving process, there will be more empty buffers ready for receiving. If the data rate of the receiving process is greater than the one of the playing process, there will be more full buffers ready for playing. We can regard all of the full buffers as the playing buffer and all of the empty buffers as the receiving buffer. The number of the full buffers will change according to the network delay. So is the number of the empty buffers. When the network bandwidth is higher, we have more full buffers and less empty buffers. On the other hand, we will have more empty buffers and less full buffers. That is, unlike the double-buffering mechanism, the playing buffer size (the sum of all of the full buffer sizes) need not be equal to the receiving buffer size (the sum of all of the empty buffer sizes). They can be dynamically adjusted according to the actual network bandwidth. Therefore, the circle buffering mechanism can provide more flexibility than the double-buffering one to deal with the network delay variation.

3   Stream Caching

The circle buffering mechanism can make better use of the network bandwidth than the double-buffering one. However, the memory space is limited. If the receiving process is much quicker than the playing process, especially when the playing process is paused by the user, all of buffers may be full so that there will not be any empty buffer that can be used to receive stream. Thus, the receiving process has to be stopped. If the received stream chips are cached into the local disk, the full buffers containing them can be emptied although they have not been played. Thus, the receiving process does not need to be stopped so that the waste of the network bandwidth can be avoided. That means the receiving process becomes completely independent of the playing process. In this way, the network bandwidth can be used as much as possible.

Our stream buffering/caching mechanism is implemented as shown in Fig. 1,

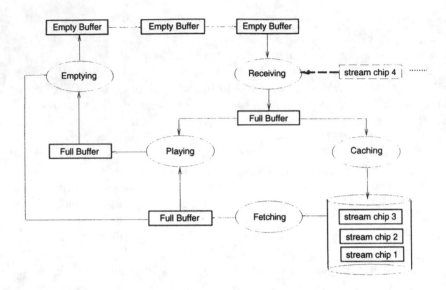

Fig. 1. Stream Buffering/Caching Mechanism

the continuous media content is transmitted in the unit of stream chips of which size is equal to a single buffer size. The stream chips are sequentially numbered. The stream caching mechanism stores the received stream chips at the local disk rather than discarding them after they have been played like the previous buffering mechanisms. There are five processes: receiving, fetching, caching, playing and emptying. They work in parallel. According to the user's content requirement, the set of the stream chips that need to be played is computed. The local disk is firstly checked to see whether there are the required stream chips cached at it. If there are some, they will be fetched into the buffers from the local disk sequencely by the fetching process. The stream chips not existing at the local disk are requested to be transmitted from the remote server and received by the receiving process. The received stream chips are cached at the local disk by the caching process. The stream chips that are fetched from the local disk or received from the network are played by the playing process in the sequence of their number. After a stream chip has been cached and played as well, the buffer containing it will be emptied by the emptying process. In order to guarantee that the receiving process always has an empty buffer to work, the stream caching mechanism may empty full buffers of which contents have been cached but have not been played. If there are two and more such buffers, the one containing the stream chip with the maximal number will be emptied firstly because the stream chips with the smaller number will be played ahead of ones with the larger number.

The user can control the stream playback by operations such as STOP, RE-PLAY, FORWARD, REWIND, PAUSE and RESUME. Some operations such

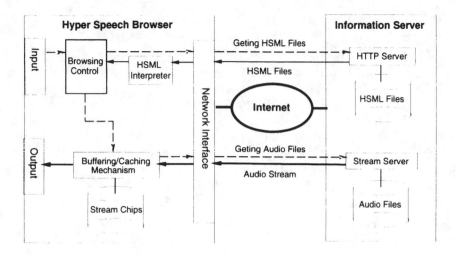

Fig. 2. Hyper Audio Web System

as REPLAY and REWIND require the received stream chips to be played once again. With the stream caching mechanism, these stream chips can be played from the local disk and don't need to be transmitted from the remote server once again. In addition, during the playback of the stream chips from the local disk, the stream chips at the remote server can be prefetched because the receiving process is completely independent of the playing process. Thus, these operations can be responded quickly and the playback of the stream has less discontinuity compared with those without the stream caching supports. Similarly, when the playback is paused, the receiving process does not need to be stopped. The stream chips are received and stored at the local disk. Once the playback is resumed, the prefetched stream chips can be used to restart the playback soon.

4 An Application Example

The stream buffering/caching mechanism was developed for hyper speech browsers which are used to browse hyper audio contents on web. The hyper audio contents consist of two parts. One is the audio files and the other is a text file that defines the playback order of the audio files and the hyper links between them. A hyper speech markup language (HSML)[1] was designed for defining such text files which are called HSML files. The hyper links between audio files are defined by a audio map which uses time intervals to represent hot spots. As we know, the image map in HTML uses areas to represent hot spots. The hot spot is notified by the background beep sound. If the user pushes JUMP button when he hears the background beep sound, the playback of the current audio content will be stopped and the audio content indicated by the link will be played.

As shown in Fig.2, the HSML files and the audio files are respectively serviced by the HTTP-based server and the stream server. The HSML file is first downloaded through HTTP and interpreted by the HSML interpreter, which registers hyper links and asks the stream server to send the stream chips which are not at the local disk. The stream chips in the audio files are transmitted through hyper audio transfer protocol (HATP). The buffering/caching mechanism is used to reduce the discontinuity resulted from network delay variation. The hyper speech browser provides eight buttons (OPEN, JUMP, BACK, REPLAY, FORWARD, REWIND, PAUSE and RESUME) to control the playback and the navigation. The buffering/caching mechanism make these operations be responded quickly compared with the other players such as the real audio players which have not stream caching supports.

5 Conclusion

The cache technique is widely used by the conventional WWW browsers such as Netscape and Internet Explorer. It can reduce the response delay when the downloaded pages are shown once again. The page cache mechanism is designed for the downloading method. That is, the whole page file is transmitted and stored at the local disk. Unlike the page cache mechanism, our stream caching mechanism caches stream chips. The stream chips at the local disk are combined with ones transmitted from the remote server. They are played in their time sequence. To our knowledge, the two commercial streaming systems, Real Audio[4] and Xing Streamworks[7] don't provide players with stream caching supports. We will do performance comparison and analysis with them in the future.

References

1. Makoto J. Hirayama, Taro Sugahara, Zhiyong Peng, Junichi Yamazaki: Interactive Listening to Structured Speech Content on the Internet. Proc. of International Conference on Spoken Language Processing (1998)
2. H. Kanakia, P.Mishra and A. Reibman: An adaptive congestion control scheme for real time packet video transport. IEEE/ACM Transactions on Networking, Vol.3, No.6 (1995) 671-682
3. Karl Jonas, Peter Kanzow, Mathias Kretschmer: Audio Streaming on the Internet Experiences with Real-Time Streaming of Audio Streams. ISIE'97 (1997) 71-76
4. RealAudio by Progressive Networks, http://www.realaudio.com.
5. S.Ramanathan and P.V. Rangan: Feedback techniques for intra-media continuity and inter-media synchronization in distributed multimedia systems. The Computer Journal, Vol.36, No.1 (1993) 19-31
6. W.E. Naylor and L. Kleinrock: Stream Traffic communication in packet switched networks: Destination buffering considerations. IEEE Transactions on Communications, Vol. COM-30, No.12 (1982) 2527-2534
7. Xing Streamworks, http://www.xingtech.com.

An Agent-Based Environment for Remote Diagnosis, Supervision and Control

Reinhold Plösch and Rainer Weinreich

Software Engineering Group, Department of Business Informatics
Johannes Kepler Universität Linz, Austria
{ploesch,weinreich}@swe.uni-linz.ac.at

Abstract. Mobile agent technology has a number of characteristics that make it well suited for distributed information retrieval and monitoring tasks. We present an agent-based environment that provides facilities and tools for remote diagnosis, supervision and control of process automation systems. The environment allows remote and dynamic configuration of diagnosis and supervision tasks, offers a framework for observing and controlling existing (legacy) software, and is also suited for other application domains than process automation.

1.   Introduction and Overview

The term agent is currently being used for a wide variety of software systems. Franklin [3] distinguishes, e.g., adaptive agents, autonomous agents, communicative agents, and mobile agents. The environment described in this paper is based on mobile agents. Mobile agents are software components with a certain degree of autonomy that have the ability to transport themselves from one location in a network to another (see [2], [3], [8]).

The work is part of a research cooperation with Siemens Germany. The major aim of this cooperation is to explore the potential of agent-based architectures for remote diagnosis, supervision and control of steel plant automation systems. The reason for investigation was the realization, that the general problem frame has a number of characteristics including distributed information retrieval, monitoring and notification, as well as parallel processing, which make the problem a typical one suitable for mobile agent technology (see [2], [6] and [7]).

The developed components, frameworks and tools are called RSE (remote supervising environment). The initial focus of RSE was the process automation domain. However, the environment includes general services for dynamic configuration and integration of native system services, which are important for mobile-agent systems in general.

In the next section we describe the primary application domain to provide a general understanding of the problem frame. In Section 3 we outline important requirements on the architecture of our environment and in Section 4 we present the overall architecture with respect to these requirements. Section 5 gives an overview of the provided configuration tools. We conclude by summarizing the main aspects of the presented environment and by describing further work.

2.   Application Domain

RSE is intended to support remote diagnosis as well as continuous supervision and control of steel plant automation systems. A typical steel plant automation system consists of a number of hosts (often with different operating systems), which are connected by a local area network. In *remote system diagnosis* certain aspects of an automation system are observed remotely and the collected data is visualized in order to enable responsible plant supervisors to foresee problems and to timely take adequate actions. The aspects to be monitored depend on the specific automation system and on customer needs. Some requirements on the environment described in the following are the diagnosis of file system capacity, file system integrity, memory and CPU consumption of specified operating system processes and the observation of quality attributes provided by the process control software. A general requirement is a flexible architecture, which enables monitoring of arbitrary aspects of an automation system. To facilitate diagnosis, emphasis is on a convenient presentation of the collected and condensed data in a Web browser using standard presentation techniques (HTML) or using more flexible techniques like Java applets.

While remote system diagnosis aims at long term aspects, *system supervision and control* aims at supervising aspects of an automation system that require instant action in case of problems. To facilitate the supervision and control tasks of plant supervisors, critical aspects (like quality parameters) are supervised continuously. If the specified limits for the supervised aspects are exceeded, autonomous and configurable actions have to be taken by the supervising software. Typical types of actions are automatic notification of plant supervisors, messages to local operators or autonomous changes of parameters for models like temperature or geometry models by the supervising software.

3.   Requirements

A number of different requirements on implementation and design of RSE are imposed by the primary target system(s) and by the described application domain in general. The main requirements are:

(R1)   Portability, since a system may consists of multiple hosts with different operating systems

(R2)   Communication with existing (legacy) systems and usage of dedicated operating system services

(R3)   Dynamic configurability with tool support

(R4)   Visualization of system state

(R5)   Measurement-specific requirements, like support for parallel and continuous measurements

(R6)   Basic distribution issues like security, bandwidth, etc.

As described in Section 2, a typical steel plant automation system consists of multiple hosts which may have different operating systems installed. This means that portability of the supervision and diagnosis software to be installed is important for reducing development and maintenance efforts.

The environment is intended to be used for the supervision and diagnosis of already existing steel plant automation systems. To obtain status information from such a system or to control it from the outside, lower-level communication mechanisms provided for interfacing such systems have to be used. This includes mechanisms like shared memory, files and sockets, in addition to more advanced communication mechanisms like CORBA- or Java-RMI-style remote method invocation. The main communication mechanism used among the components of RSE itself is provided by the underlying agent platform. However, the communication mechanisms used for interfacing with an already existing automation software are often provided by the host operating system. (This has implications on the system design to preserve portability and dynamic configurability as described in Section 4.2.) Another reason for the need of using native operating system APIs is the need for collecting data about the usage of system resources like hard-disk space and memory- or CPU-consumption of certain automation tasks as described in Section 2.

The third main requirement is the need to configure the environment remotely and dynamically (i.e., at run time). This includes dynamic installation and de-installation of system components, and dynamic configuration of component interactions and properties via an Internet connection. Configuring a running system over time may impose versioning problems that have to be handled properly, also. Further, it has to be considered that administration may take place using temporary connections (established, e.g., via a modem) and that the administration node may be a notebook which may even shut down completely. Both temporary connected communication lines and shutdown of the administration host have significant influence on the design of the environment. An example is the issue of transferring code, which cannot be fetched on demand if the connection might be terminated at some point of time in the future.

In addition to remote and dynamic configuration the environment has to provide information about its state to the administrator. This does not mean information about the automation system (which is the central function of RSE anyway), but information about whether subsystems of the automation system are currently supervised or whether some measurement is currently active.

To collect data about the state of the automation system, measurements have to be active either sequentially or in parallel. For example, the system has to be able to measure CPU-consumption of certain automation tasks at multiple hosts at the same time. In addition, since some measurements may be active for hours or days it must always be possible to obtain the results of incomplete measurements and to generate temporary reports. This influences the communication structure of certain parts of the system (e.g., whether communication is synchronous or asynchronous).

The last main requirement concerns basic distribution issues like security and bandwidth use. The administration and configuration of the system via an arbitrary internet connection makes a number of demands on security issues, like ensuring the authenticity of the administrator and preventing the alteration of data and code in transit. Another aspect that has to be taken into consideration is that code and data for system configuration and control sometimes has to be transferred over slow communication lines. Thus reduction of bandwidth use is desired.

4. System Architecture

To provide an understanding of the chosen architecture and of how the requirements listed in the previous section are handled in the current implementation, we will first describe the implementation platform used and then give an overview of the architecture of the two main functional areas, remote diagnosis, and system supervision and control.

4.1 Implementation Platform

The decision for using a mobile agent platform was made before the project was started, because one of the project aims was to investigate the usefulness of agent technology in this domain. The base platform for RSE is IBM's Aglets SDK [6], because of both technical and practical reasons. From a technical perspective, the Aglets system is implemented in Java (see [1] and [4] which offers a certain degree of portability and eases the integration of (Java) third party components because of the standardization provided by the Java platform. Portability is an important requirement (see R1 in Section 3). The agent platform also provides a number of useful security options [5] and, of course, basic functionality for mobile agents, like object migration and code transport.

4.2 Remote System Diagnosis

Figure 1 gives an overview of the architecture of the part of our environment realizing remote system diagnosis. The figure shows two units. A unit is just a collection of hosts, which are usually connected by a local area network.

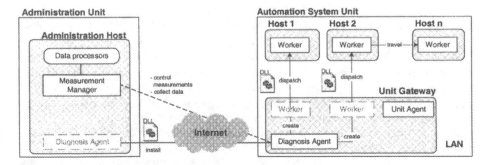

Fig. 1. Architecture for Diagnosis Agents

One host per unit that serves as an entry point for all externally arriving agents is called the unit gateway. The distinguishing feature of the unit gateway is that it hosts a special agent, called the *Unit Agent*, which maintains information about the unit in general and about the installed automation system in particular. For example, the *Unit Agent* knows about the hosts that are part of the automation system and which operating systems are installed on these hosts. The *Unit Agent* is also able to provide information about how to communicate with the automation system, i.e., which (potentially operating system dependent) communication service a diagnosis agent has to use for obtaining measurement data.

An administrator at a remote administration unit, which is connected with the automation system unit via a (potentially temporary) Internet connection, may create and configure a diagnosis agent, and install it at the automation system. Some diagnosis agents may need additional operating-system specific code (see R1 and R2 in Section 3) to perform their diagnosis task. This code has also to be installed at the automation unit. During the installation process, first the agent code and sometimes the code for agents performing subtasks on behalf of the diagnosis agent are transferred from the administration unit to the automation unit. On arrival at the administration unit gateway, the agent determines which platform specific libraries are needed by contacting the responsible *Unit Agent*. Any platform specific native libraries (DLLs) are only transferred from the administration unit if the proper version for a specific operating system is not available at the automation system unit (see R6 in Section 3).

After the installation phase, the connection between the administration unit and the automation system unit can be terminated. The installed diagnosis agent rests in an idle state until it is told to fulfill its measuring task. For starting and terminating measurements and for processing measurement results a tool called *Measurement Manager* is used. The measurement process itself depends on the diagnosis agent. Sometimes data has to be determined at a specific host at a certain point in time and sometimes data has to be collected from several hosts in parallel over a longer period of time (see R5 in Section 3). In the latter case, the diagnosis agent creates a number of worker agents which it sends to each host. Each worker agent carries the proper platform specific library for his target host and immediately starts the measurement after arrival at the target host. Measurement results are sent automatically to all registered measurement managers, which may be located at different units. Data can also be obtained manually (see below). Workers that are not continuously measuring dispose themselves from the target host after measurement is finished. Workers for continuous measurements are supplying the diagnosis agent at predefined rates with temporary results and rest on the target host until measurement is explicitly stopped by the administrator.

An administrator can obtain the collected data from an arbitrary diagnosis agent at any time by means of the *Measurement Manager* tool. If a measurement is not yet complete, temporary results are delivered if available. Each *Measurement Manager* can be configured with data processor components, which are used for analyzing and processing the selected data. We provide data processors that are able to generate HTML-pages for visualizing the results. New data processors, e.g., for performing statistic evaluations or for storing the data in a database can be loaded at run time (see R3 in Section 3).

The system is implemented in a way that the administration unit may be disconnected or may shutdown at any time. Connections with diagnosis agents are regained automatically upon system startup.

4.3 System Supervision and Control

System supervision and control provides facilities for observing critical aspects of the automation system continuously and for automatic reactions in case of problems. Like diagnosis agents, agents for supervision and control are created and configured at a remote administration unit and installed at an automation system unit afterwards. In contrast to diagnosis agents, which may only be installed at the unit gateway, agents for supervision and control may be installed at any host of the automation system as depicted in Figure 2.

After installation *supervision agents* are continuously observing a certain aspect of the automation environment. We have implemented agents for supervising resource consumption (like disk space, memory usage and CPU time) and process control data (like quality parameters). The latter are determined by analyzing log files and by communicating with the automation system via shared-memory segments and sockets. The supervision agents do not initiate any action directly when some critical system state has been detected. Instead, they may be connected to an arbitrary number of *control agents*, which finally perform the specified action.

Control agents are just waiting to be notified about some critical system state by a supervision agent. Examples for control agents are an agent sending emails to plant administrators, an agent for placing a message at local operator's control panel, and an agent switching the process automation task to another (more stable) version. Each supervision agent may be connected to an arbitrary number of control agents and vice versa. The connections between supervision and control agents are either set up remotely using the configuration tool described in Section 5 or negotiated dynamically using a trader agent that is located at every host (see Figure 2).

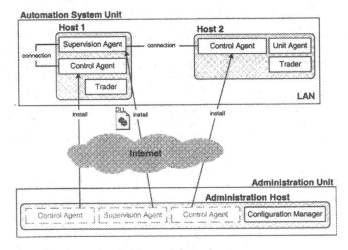

Fig. 2. Architecture for System Supervision and Control

5. Configuration Tools

An important aspect of our system is the ability for remote and dynamic configuration (see R3 in Section 3). We currently provide two tools for the different functional areas described in the sections above. The *Measurement Manager* depicted in Figure 3 is used for controlling (long-term) measurements and report generation. It gives an overview of all diagnosis agents installed at a particular unit and also indicates their current state (see R4 in Section 3), e.g., measurement active or terminated.

Fig. 3. Measurement Manager   **Fig. 4.** Configuration Manager

The units to be controlled—which are different automation plants in our case—are represented by the DNS names of the respective unit gateway hosts, each hosting a number of diagnosis agents. Each of these agents can be selected and asked to start a new measurement, to terminate the currently active measurement or to deliver temporary results of the currently active measurement. The *Measurement Manager* uses data processors for processing measurement results. Data processors may be added or removed dynamically. Most of the data processors that are currently available are HTML generators for reports that are to be displayed in a Web-Browser.

The tool used for managing connections among supervision and control agents remotely and dynamically is called *Configuration Manager* and is depicted in Figure 4. The main window of the *Configuration Manager* displays not only the different units (again represented by the DNS name of the unit gateway) but also all available hosts at each particular unit and all agents at each particular host.

If a supervision agent is selected, its connections to control agents can be modified with the *Connection Manager* also shown in Figure 4. The *Connection Manager* only shows agents that can be connected to the specified supervision agent. In the example above two e-mail agents are connected to an agent signaling significant changes of certain quality parameters. The available connections and views are correctly updated if agents are disposed, new agents are installed, and if an agent changes its location. Both tools use caching strategies for reduced bandwidth use and increased performance.

6. Conclusion and Further Work

The software agents for system supervision and diagnosis are de-coupled from the core automation system, can be designed independently and (de)installed dynamically. Main issues of our environment are the flexible support for interfaces to already existing automation software on different operating systems, frameworks for measurement activities and agent interactions, and tool support for remote and dynamic configuration. Further work includes improved native code management, better management of an agent's user interface code, improved configuration support, and investigation of a minimal set of required security options. We also plan to investigate appropriate monitoring and debugging support for agent-based systems.

Acknowledgements

The work presented has been sponsored and supported by Siemens AG Germany. We would like to thank Christa Schwanninger, Thomas Heimke, Joachim Höhne and Einar Bröse for their cooperation and support.

References

1. Arnold K., Gosling J.: The Java Programming Language, Second edition. Addison-Wesley Longman, Reading, MA, 1998.
2. Cabri G., Leonardi L., Zambonelli F.: Mobile Agent Technology: Current Trends and Perspectives. AICA 98, Napoli, Italy, November 1998.
3. Franklin S., Graesser A.: Is it an Agent, or Just a Program?: A Taxonomy for Autonomous Agents. in Proceedings of the Third International Workshop on Agent Theories, Architectures, and Languages, Springer-Verlag, 1996.
4. Java: Information on Java releases and online documentation can be found at java.sun.com, Sun Microsystems, Inc.
5. Karjoth G., Lange D.B., Oshima M.: A Security Model for Aglets. IEEE Internet Computing, Volume 1, Number 4, July-August 1997.
6. Lange D.B., Oshima M.: Programming and Deploying Java Mobile Agents with Aglets. Addison-Wesley Longman, Reading, 1998.
7. Lange D.B., Oshima M.: Seven Good Reasons for Mobile Agents. Communications of the ACM, Volume 42, Number 3, March 1999, 88-89.
8. White J.: Mobile Agents, in: Software Agents. J. Bradshaw, Editor, MIT Press, 1997, 437-472

The Delivery of Effective Integrated Community Care with the Aid of Agents

Martin D. Beer[1], Trevor J. M. Bench-Capon[1], and Andrew Sixsmith[2]

[1] Department of Computer Science, University of Liverpool,
Chadwick Tower, Peach Street, LIVERPOOL. L69 7ZF United Kingdom.
mdb@csc.liv.ac.uk and tbc@csc.liv.ac.uk
[2] Institute of Human Ageing, University of Liverpool,
PO Box 147, LIVERPOOL. L69 3BX United Kingdom.

Abstract. The INCA (Intelligent Community Support for the Elderly) architecture is based on the integration of a number of autonomous systems; home monitoring, community alarms, care management systems and emergency systems command and control systems using agent technology to build effective co-ordinated care systems.

It is possible, by taking an agent-based approach to allow each of the agencies involved in community care to communicate effectively so that they can co-ordinate care provision by the use of wrappers. In this way, users can use the exiting services, with which they are fully familiar, effectively and are able to take full advantage of the full range of communication facilities without compromising privacy and confidentiality.

1 Introduction

This paper shows that current research into distributed knowledge sharing and intelligent agents [4] can be used to provide a much higher level of support and care than is currently practical. Recent work by the present authors[1] has shown that with proper management of the various conversation classes to provide effective and secure communication with the various support agencies.

Currently individual care providers use their own database, workflow and command and control systems with little or no integration between them. This causes difficulties, not only in the provision of the most effective response to emergencies, but also in the provision of routine care as the older person's requirements change, often quite rapidly.

The move is towards franchising of different aspects of care delivery with the responsible agency preparing a detailed specification, in the form of an Individual Care Plan. It then places contracts to actually deliver the various components of the care, as appropriate. This means that here is now no single agency with the overall authority to manage and monitor the provision of community care.

2 Approach

The provision of care inevitably requires a considerable degree of co-operative activity between individuals and agencies. Each actor is likely to have to interface with a number of different systems and organizational structures, each of which will have its own concept base (or Ontology) [3].

3   The Problem Area Addressed

While community care covers a wide range of activities:

1. The development and updating of an Individual Care Plan developed to meet an assessment of the needs of the individual.
2. The provision of routine care as specified by the Individual Care Plan
3. Emergency support in response to an accident or medical emergency

A number of organisations and individuals play a part in these activities and the interactions between them can then be shown in the form of Use Case diagrams.

3.1   Developing an Individual Care Plan

Before care can be provided effectively, the care co-ordinator has to assess need, and develop an individual care plan. This can be quite difficult, particularly with the severely disabled or those with dementia.

It is also necessary to contact both formal care providers and informal carers to negotiate agreement to deliver the necessary care. The stages in doing this are shown in Figure 1.

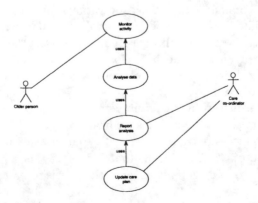

Fig. 1. Individual Care Plan Development Use Case

3.2 Routine Care

The actual delivery of routine care has to be carefully monitored. The objective is to provide the assistance necessary to make up for the disabilities of the individual. The main problem with existing systems is the lack of responsiveness of the services providing it. The INCA system is designed to enhance the responsiveness of the service by:

1. Allowing users to request care directly from care providers and co-ordinators.
2. Providing users with better information about care schedules.
3. Monitoring very disabled people in order to fit care interventions more closely to their patterns of daily activity.

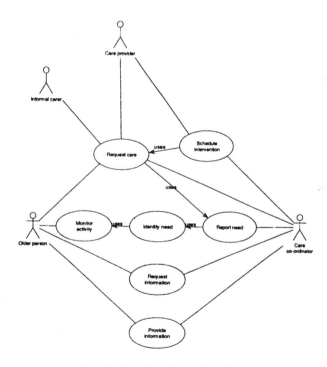

Fig. 2. Routine Care Use Case

3.3 Emergency Support

The case of emergency intervention is rather different. The intention is to provide a proactive alarm system, in addition to the current reactive systems that operate independently of the overall care provision. The primary interface is through the home unit that raises an alert either when some set of environmental conditions is considered out of range, as defined within the individual care plan, or there has been some direct request for help (such as pressing a 'panic button'). These interactions are shown in Figure 3.

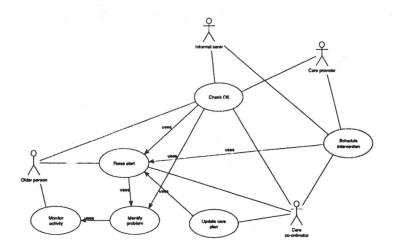

Fig. 3. Emergency Support Use Case

4 The Design of the Conversation Classes

The previous section shows some of the wide range of activities can be supported effectively by the INCA system. Traditional database design techniques have difficulties with this richness, as each scenario contains actors with the same roles performing differently depending on their beliefs and intentions within that scenario. Agent approaches are specifically intended to address these issues.

An alarm condition is raised only when the home unit detects sensor readings outside the normal range. A facilitator is contacted to obtain the address of a suitable service mediator, which is then alerted. This mediator routes the alert to a suitable service provider after adding additional information from the service database. The service provider's mediator determines the appropriate course of action and notifies the necessary carer, possibly via further mediators.

The basic mechanism for the home unit to communicate with service providers is shown diagramatically in Figure 4. This shows the actions required summoning assistance. The actual service provider summoned depends on a number of factors:

1. The type and severity of the problem
2. The service providers able and willing to respond an the anticipated speed of their response
3. The 'cost' of that response in relation to the perceived need

The first is initially controlled by the guard conditions on the conversation class [2] and is determined by information local to the Home Unit. Decisions based on the service provider's ability or willingness to respond require much more general knowledge that is available to the mediator, which can negotiate with a number of service providers. If a service provider is able to do so, then the mediator accepts the most appropriate offer, rejecting all others, and informs the Home Unit.

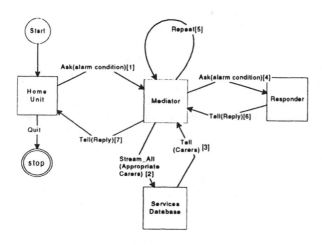

Fig. 4. The Basic Response Conversation Class

5   The Database Perspective

A particular feature of the community care system is that each of the agents involved will typically have its own administrative and scheduling systems that will handle all its activities, not just those using the community care system. It is essential therefore that it interfaces with the existing database systems. This can be done effectively by the provision of Wrappers that map the queries being transmitted within the INCA environment into a form that is understood by the care provider's own systems.

The design of the mapping functions may well cause considerable difficulties, as the different care providers will have very different perceptions of their roles, expressed in the form of different ontologies. These will have to be mapped onto the much more general INCA ontology that has to cover all aspects of care provision. Considerable success has however been achieved by providing mapping functions only for that information required for both sides to perform their intended functions.

6 Discussion

The scenario to be followed is determined by the guard conditions of the relevant conversation class. Each scenario a different service potentially delivered by different service providers using their own information systems and services. For example, the delivery of community care is probably through the local Social Services Department, possibly contracted out to an independent service provider, whereas the delivery of health care would be through the local family doctor, and possibly health visitors. If each has to rely on only its own information valuable time and resources will inevitably be lost in duplicating actions. Even a minimal level of co-ordination can therefore be extremely valuable. It must however be managed effectively to:

1. Maintain the autonomy of all agencies
2. Maintain the privacy of the older person as far as possible
3. Ensure the security and integrity of the information held
4. Link effectively with others involved.

7 Conclusions

The architecture described in this paper allows for the provision of an extremely flexible care package that can be tailored closely to the changing needs of the older person. This is a considerable advance on current arrangements that tend to be quite inflexible because of the difficulties of effective co-ordination. Needs do change, often very rapidly. It is also not always the case that the level of care necessarily has to increase. Current care provision, particularly in the effective response to emergencies, is limited by the lack of co-ordination between the potential responders. An agent-based architecture provides effective answers to these problems by ensuring that the most appropriate information is always used. In this way, help should be provided speedily and effectively when needed.

References

1. Beer, M. D., Bench-Capon, T. J. M. and Sixsmith, A. (1999) 'Some Issues in Managing Dialogues between Information Agents', In Proceedings of Database and Expert Systems Applications 99, Lecture Notes in Computer Science 1677, Springer, Berlin, 1999, pp-521-530.
2. Gray, P.M.D. et al, (1997). 'KRAFT: Knowledge Fusion from Distributed Databases and Knowledge Bases' Database and Expert System Applications (DEXA'97), Toulouse, France, R. Wagner, (Ed.), IEEE Press. pp682-691.
3. Visser, P.R.S., Jones, D.M., Beer, M.D., Bench-Capon, T.J.M., Diaz, B.M., and Shave, M.J.R., 'Resolving Ontological Heterogeneity in the KRAFT Project', In Proceedings of Database and Expert Systems Applications 99, Lecture Notes in Computer Science 1677, Springer, Berlin, 1999, pp 688-697.
4. Wooldridge, M. J., and Jennings, N. R. (1995), 'Intelligent Agents: Theory and Practice', The Knowledge Engineering Review 10(2) 115-152.

Applications of Aglet Technology

Rosane Maria Martins, Magali Ribeiro Chaves, Luci Pirmez and Luiz F. Rust

NCE/UFRJ - Núcleo de Computação Eletrônica
Universidade Federal do Rio de Janeiro
Tel.: +55 21 598-3159 - Caixa Postal: 2324 - Rio de Janeiro RJ Brasil
{rosanemartins, magalichaves}@uol.com.br,
{luci,rust}@nce.ufrj.br

Abstract. The Internet has evolved from an information space to a market space with thousands of electronic storefronts, auctions and other commercial services. This market space is not without problem. A main problem is the difficulty of finding relevant offers. We present two possible solutions to this problem: Bon Marché and Logistics Agents which were developed with IBM's Aglet Workbench – a particular implementation of mobile agents. This paper also surveys the agent technology and discusses the different agent building packages available on the market. Finally, it concludes that the future of local interaction, reduced network loading, server flexibility and application autonomy which are supported by mobile agent technology all help to provide a level agility above distributed problem solving.

Introduction

The current dramatic expansion in network technology and infrastructure, including the explosive growth of the Internet, will soon see an inevitable proliferation of automated, distributed, information agents. With this, advances, opportunities and incentives for the decentralization of design actives are rapidly emerging. This phenomena offers great promise for obtaining and sharing diverse information conveniently, but they also present a serious challenge. The sheer multitude, diversity, and dynamic nature of on-line information source makes finding and accessing any specific piece of information extremely difficult.

To address this problem, several exciting new technologies have been developed. Several groups of Artificial Intelligence (AI) researchers are already actively involved in trying to design Internet assistants that will make easier the filtering or retrieving information from the network and the virtual purchases. Each intelligent assistant is composed by autonomous agents and is based on AI and Distributed Artificial Intelligence (DAI) concepts.

DAI is concerned with all forms of social activity in systems composed of multiple computational agents[1]. An important form of interaction in such systems is cooperative problem solving, which occurs when a group of logically decentralized agents choose to work together to achieve a common goal. The "agent" term is largely used in different areas, such as Distributed Systems or Software Engineering, for this reason, there are almost many definitions for it. However, agent systems present key characteristics which differ them from other softwares.

Agents are autonomous, persistent (software) components that perceive, reason, communicate and act in someone's favour, influencing its environment.

This environment presents many agents which will interact. This interaction is the Multiagent Systems' principal element .

This paper contributes with two applications that emphasize the mobile agents technology as an significant and revolutionary paradigm for distributed problem solving: Bon Marché and Logistics Agents. Both were implemented using IBM's mobile agent framework known as Aglets Software Development Kit (ASDK).

Bon Marché is a mobile and intelligent multiagent auxiliary prototype for the retrieval of distributed structured information in a scenario of several "on-line" bookstores. The proposed system is based on a group of agents trying, simultaneously, to find products of users interest in several virtual places known by them, presenting the results in an homogeneous way.

Logistics Agents is a prototype where users create autonomous agents to buy and sell goods in a context of the automobile components distribution problem. A car assembler looks for suitable supplies to attend the subsidiaries' orders. This commercial transaction is done through the Internet.

This paper is organized as follows. An overview of mobile agent and Aglet concept is given in section 2. Section 3 describes the overall architecture of two applications: Bon Marché and Logistic Agents. Finally, section 4 presents the conclusion and future work.

2 Mobile Agents

Mobile Agents are processes dispatched from a source computer to accomplish a specified task[3,4]. Each mobile agent is a computation along its own data and execution state. In this way, the mobile agent paradigm extends the RCP communication mechanism according to which a message sent by a client is just a procedure call. After its submission, the mobile agent proceeds autonomously and independently of the sending client. When the agent reaches a server, it is delivered to an agent execution environment. Then, if the agent possesses necessary authentication credentials, its executable parts are started. To accomplish its task, the mobile agent can transport itself to another server, spawn new agents, and interact with other agents. Upon completion, the mobile agent delivers the results to the sending client or to another server.

In order for these agents to exist within a system or to themselves form a system they require a framework for implementation and execution. This is known as the agent environment.

2.1 Aglet Technology: A Java based Agent Execution Environment

Developed by the IBM Japan research group, this package is a framework for programming mobile network agents in Java. We can use a few expressions to describe an Aglet[5]: written in pure Java, light-weight object migration , built with persistent support, event-driven. It is easy to understand why JAVA is necessary for WAN application's existence in today's heterogeneous networking environment. Besides providing platform independence, JAVA also provides sandbox security to protect host against malicious attacks from alien applications.

Unlike an applet´s short and boring period of execution, an aglet can exist and execute tasks forever. One of the main differences between an aglet and the simple mobile code of Java applets, is the itinerary that is carried along with the aglet. By having a travel plan, aglets are capable of roaming the Internet collecting information from many places. The itinerary can change dynamically giving the aglet the sense of self-governing and the look of an intelligent agent (that of course is in the hands of the programmer).

An aglet can be dispatched to any remote host that supports the Java Virtual Machine. This requires from the remote host to have preinstalled Tahiti, a tiny aglet server program implemented in Java and provided by the Aglet Framework. A running Tahiti server listens to the host´s ports for incoming aglets, captures them, and provides them with an aglet context (i.e., an agent execution environment) in which they can run their code from the state that it was halted before they were dispatched. Within its context, an aglet can communicate with other aglets, collect local information and when convenient halt its execution and be dispatched to another host. An aglet can also be cloned or disposed.

3 Applications

Two applications based on agent technologies were implemented in this paper: Bon Marché and Logistics Agents.

3.1   Bon Marché – A Group of Mobile Agents for E-Commerce

The agents for electronic commerce considered in this context are those that somehow help the users to shop over the Internet. This type of agent, called shopping agent, may carry out several tasks, such as: to help the user decide what product should be purchased; to make suggestions based on its knowledge of its owner; to find out new things, discounts and special prices; to find stores that sell the desired product or service, among other things.

In order to show the feasibility of the search process for structured and distributed information through the mobile agents technology, this paper proposes the development of a multiagent, mobile and intelligent system called "Bon Marché" in the context of several "on line" bookstores. The goal is to accelerate the retrieval of distributed structured information. This is achieved by improving the phase of the process of data selection, in which the agents run parallel among the servers related to them and at the end returning with all the information requested by the user, without the need to make a call to each one of the servers separately. The information obtained is then presented in a uniform and organized way. Using the information thus presented by the system, it is much easier for the user to choose a product with the most satisfactory characteristics.

Among the possible functions described above, the Bon Marché Agent is intended to help find the stores that sell the desired product and to list the prices of the products found.

The operation of the prototype to achieve this objective is the following:

• user selects the specific product and the desired characteristics of that product (these characteristics will be the restrictions for the search);

• the purchase agent searches for products with the desired characteristics among products of that type;

• as a result of the search, Bon Marché sends an e-mail or shows a screen to the user with a list of products, their respective prices and where they can be found.

3.1.1 Proposed Architecture

The following architecture is proposed to enable the Bon Marché system to have the functionality mentioned above and, in the future, to be applied to many products and stores:

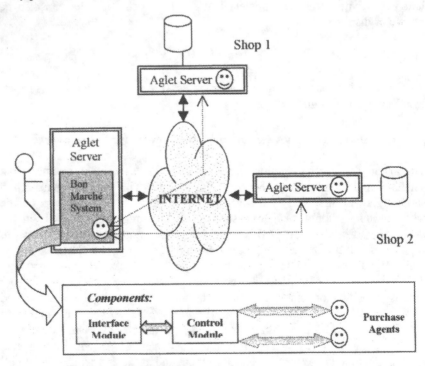

Figure 1 – Overall Architecture of the Bon Marché Purchase Agent

As seen in figure 1, the system presented comprises the following components: Interface Module, Control Module and Purchase Agents. What follows is a detailed list of the system components:

• **Interface Module**: this is the component through which the user contacts the system and places his order. This module is also responsible for presenting the result obtained by the group of agents to the user.

"Title", "author" ,"price range" and "type of itinerary" are the information that the user must provide to the Interface Module so that it may request the Control Module to create and dispatch the purchase agents according to the restrictions imposed by the user.

There are three possibilities of choices for itineraries:

a. *one agent for each server:* According to the quantity of servers registered in the system, one agent is created for each server and dispatched to do its task. When each agent arrives at its destiny, it does its search, send the result as a message to Control Module and "dies".

b. *only one agent that visits all the servers:* It is created only one agent that has in its travel plan the addresses of all servers. It will go to all servers, one by one, do the search, send the result as message to Control Module and "dies" at last visited server.

c. *one agent that goes through the servers until to find the first occurrence*: It is created only one agent that contains in its travel plan the addresses of all servers. But it will travel to next server only if doesn't find any book at former server, that is, the agent travels until to find the first occurence that satisfies the order user.

As soon as the result manager (a component of the control module) compiles all answers received, it sends these answers to the interface module so that they are delivered to the user: on the screen or via e-mail.

• **Control Module**: This module is responsible for the creation and release of purchase agents to begin the search requested by the buyer. This module also aggregates the results found by the different agents. There is a control module for each type of product available in the system, e.g. a control module for books and a different one for CDs.

After receiving the user's requirements from the interface module, the Control Module creates the agents according to such requirements and sends them to the addresses available at a Storage Structure.

Storage Structure is a hash structure that contains the addresses of the various stores associated with the system. There is a storage structure for each type of product researched by the system.

When the Control Module receives a request to send an agent, the latter is created on the "aglet" layer according to user's requirements and travels through the runtime layer, which converts the agent into an array of bytes and such array, on its turn, passes on to the ATP layer – Agent Transfer Protocol, to be sent to its destination. This protocol, then, builds a "bit stream" that contains both general information, such as the system name, and its identification, such as the "byte array" resulting from the runtime layer.

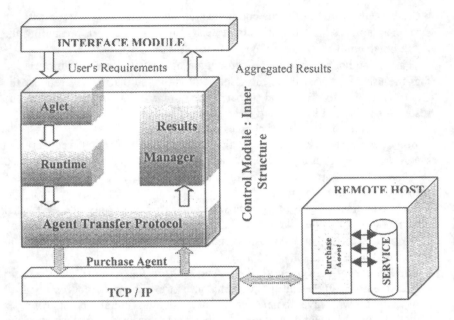

Figure 2 - Control Module - Inner Structure

Upon returning to the server with the information from its search, each purchase agent sends its contents to the Result Manager (Control Module), so that the Results Manager may aggregate all answers obtained and send them to the interface module.

• **Purchase Agents** : Make contact with the stores by accessing their databases, place the order and interpret the answers generated, converting them into a format that is understood by the control module. Before proceeding to their destination, the agents are coded in bit stream: the first segments are general information, such as the agent's identification, and the last segment is the byte array, the agent per se: code and state. The goal of the agents is to check the information found at their destination address, selecting only the information considered relevant and recommended according to the pre-determined rules. Such information shall represent the basis of rules to be used by the agent to make appropriate decisions in the process of evaluation of the items found.

With this architecture, the extension of this system to deal with new products and new stores is simple, although it is necessary to build a control module for each new product.

3.2 Logistics Agents – Solution for a Logistic Problem Applying Multiagent Systems

The Internet has been extensively explored as an environment which brings great ease to integrate clients and suppliers willing to negotiate products and services. Under that light, an area that deserves special attention is the automatic negotiation between clients and suppliers.

The negotiation model presented consists of a system of agents that acts in the process of integration among clients, represented by the subsidiaries of an automaker, and a network of suppliers. This system contributes to the mastering of electronic commerce, since some client agents interact with supplier agents trying to find products and buy products that meet their needs.

The subsidiary which wishes to purchase a product may ask the client agent to initiate the negotiation with a network of supplier agents remotely distributed on the Internet. After a number of interactions with other agents the client agent returns to its original computer and shows the result of its negotiations, i.e. a list of suppliers that best fit its needs in terms of price, freight cost and quantity of product.

As supplier/client agents are created, they are sent from their original computer to an agency, where they will communicate to achieve their overall goal. The Agency, or Meeting Place, is a host computer, where the agents do business. Each agency represents a certain region. In that respect, the client agent will run the network searching for possible suppliers to its demand, and will prioritize agencies located in regions closest to the location of the subsidiary represented by the agent , in order to reduce freight costs.

This section of the paper will try to describe the components forming the model developed and analyze its operation.

3.2.1 Architecture of Model

The architecture of the model is characterized by the exchange of messages among three categories of agents: facilitator agent, supplier agent and client agent.

• **Facilitator Agent:** This Agent is responsible for managing the negotiation between client agents and agency suppliers. The facilitator agent works as an intermediary for such agents. The facilitator records all suppliers with their respective offers and indicates to the client agent the best supplier to establish the negotiation process with. The facilitator agent has an optimization module to carry out that job. That optimization module inquires each supplier able to meet the subsidiary's demand through the "SearchOffer" message and decides which is the most favorable candidate based on which supplier made the best offer (lowest cost).

• **Supplier Agent:** This Agent represents the interests of the supplier. Interests of the supplier means the offer of parts and their respective costs (unit price and freight).

A List of Offer of Material Form is opened when the supplier agent is created. The description of the part, the quantity available for sale and unit price will be typed into the List of Offer of Material.

After confirmation of the information typed in the list of offer of material, the supplier agent will be sent to an agency. At the host computer the agent will make the first contact with the facilitator agent, subsequently requesting to be listed in the database by using the "Register" message.

The supplier agent is responsible for calculating the total cost of the material requested by a subsidiary (price of merchandise, including freight). It is noteworthy that the freight legislation is too wide and this paper is not intended to study all rules and effectiveness in each State. Suppliers hire the service of a shipper, which calculates that cost. This information will be sent to the supplier and will become part of the context of its agent. This case highlights the main advantage of the object-oriented programming: polymorphism. Each class of supplier has a different internal policy to carry out the same method (calculation of freight) and the facilitator agent is not responsible for knowing the procedures of all suppliers. When the facilitator agent inquires the supplier agent in relation to the cost of the material requested by the subsidiary, that agent is not interested in the internal details of that calculation, only in the result. The example shown in Figure 3 shows the table of costs used by a supplier agent. Notice that the cost of freight varies according to the distance. Transportation of a unit of part 0260118 from Manhumirim, MG (supplier's location) to Vila Velha, ES costs R\$116,00 (for conventional shipping) or R\$200 (express shipping). If the same part is shipped to Fortaleza, CE, freight would cost R\$150,00 or R\$256,00, depending on the type of shipping selected.

CD_PC	DEST	CST_PC (R\$)	CFC (R\$)	CFE (R\$)	CFUC (R\$)	CFUE (R\$)	INSURANCE (%)
0260118	ES	500,00	116,00	200,00	11,66	22,00	0,17
0260118	CE	500,00	150,00	256,00	15,00	25,60	0,22

Where :
CD_PC = material code;
DEST = Destination. The client's city;
CST_PC = unit price of the part;
CFC = conventional shipping cost (for a unit of part);
CFUC = conventional shipping cost (when there is more than one unit of part to be shipped);
CFE = express shipping cost (for a unit of part);
CFUE = express shipping cost (when there is more than one unit of part to be shipped);
INSURANCE = cargo insurance;

Figure 3. Table of costs used by a supplier agent

The calculation of freight at both categories is represented by formulae (1) or (3). The cargo insurance is also included in that calculation. This variable is determined according to distance and value of cargo. The Total Cost, represented by formula (4), is found with the result of the calculations of the Cost of Material (1) and the Cost of Conventional (2) or Express Freight (3).

MATERIAL COST = QTDE_REQ * CST_PC $\hspace{3cm}$ (1)

CONVENTIONAL SHIPPING COST = CFC + (QTDE_REQ – 1) * CFUC + $\hspace{1cm}$ (2)
(INSURANCE * MATERIAL COST)

EXPRESS SHIPPING COST = CFE + (QTDE_REQ – 1) * CFUE + (INSURANCE **(3)**
* MATERIAL COST)

TOTAL COST = MATERIAL COST + SHIPPING COST **(4)**

When the entire inventory of the supplier agent has been negotiated, the agent will send a "Unregister" message, requesting to leave the list kept by the facilitator agent. After its exclusion from the database, the supplier will return to its original computer and will show to the user the result of its negotiation with the different client agents that contacted the supplier agent.

• **Client Agent:** This agent represents the interests of a subsidiary. This means the demand for parts that a subsidiary is willing to buy.

A List of Request of Material form is opened when the subsidiary agent is created. That form will contain the subsidiary's identification, description and location entered by the user, as well as the description and quantity of the material requested, later on confirming the information.

After that information is confirmed, the client agent will migrate to an agency searching for the best supplier to meet its demand. After arriving at the agency, the agent will communicate with the facilitator, which will indicate the context of the best suitable supplier. Upon obtaining the answer, the client agent will initiate the negotiation process through the "Negotiate" message. If the client agent does not find the desired supplier, it will go to other agencies searching for new proposals to meet its demand. After making all negotiations, the client agent will return to its original computer and show the result of its interaction with other agents.

4 Discussions and Future Work

We have built two simple prototypes to test the basic concepts and feasibility and conducted some simple experiments.

Nowadays, the Bon Marché system presents a simplified configuration, allowing just one kind of product to be investigated. The selected product to this stage was "book". The purchaser agent is created at the user machine and migrates to the target server. This target server is an aglet server where it may be found the offered service by the supplier.

The results obtained in this initial phase were considered acceptable, due to the information filtering be executed on the server where the resources are located. This circumstance leads to a significant reduced network loading.

The possibility of existence of more than one kind of product to be investigated is a task to be implemented in another phase of this project. An another improvement is an implementation of an intelligent module that permits the Bon Marché system, besides of the conventional search, makes suggestions to the user.

Concerning the Logistics Agents system, a logistic model was implemented to solve the issue of automotive parts distribution. In this case, each subsidiary and supplier creates an agent which shares information seeking for a global solution. From this experimentation, it was obtained good results, once the implementation of mobile agents avoided the overload on the web. In a next stage, it will be developed a sophisticate negotiation scheme for buyers and sellers. We are studying two models : first, involving "price-raise" and decay functions similar to Kasbah's technique [2] and the second, based on computational intelligence, where the agents will be able to make proposals through the experience that they acquired a long their life cycle.

Future works is focused on making smarter agents which are directable at a more natural level for users. Though we have only just scratched the surface in terms of making a truly useful system, we are excited about these works and think they have the chance to essentially change the way people acquire goods and services in the not-too-distant future.

References

1.Bond, A.H.; Gasser , Les.(Eds) **Readings in Distributed Artificial Intelligence**. San Mateo, California: Morgan Kaufmann, 1988.

2.Chavez, A. and Maes, P.: An Agent Marketplace for Buying and Selling Goods, Proceedings of the First International Conference on the Practical Application of Intelligent Agents and Multi-Agent Technology, London, UK, April 1996.

3. Chess, D.; et al. **Itinerant Agents for Mobile Computing.** Journal IEEE Personal Communications, Vol.2, N° 5, October, 1993.

4. General Magic Inc. **Mobile Agents.** http://www.genmagic.com

5.IBM Japan Research Group. **Aglets Workbench.** http://aglets.trl.ibm.co.jp

An Internet-Integrated Manufacturing System Prototype

Stephen Chan[1], Vincent Ng[1], K M Yu[2], and Albert Au[3]

[1] Dept. of Computing, Hong Kong Polytechnic University, Hong Kong
{csschan, cstyng}@comp.polyu.edu.hk
[2] Dept. of Manufacturing Engineering, HK Polytechnic University, Hong Kong
mfkmyu@polyu.edu.hk
[3] Winclient Technologies (HK) LTD, Hong Kong
albertau@poboxes.com

Abstract. A prototype Internet-Integrated Manufacturing (IIM) system has been built based on the Internet, which provides a generic infrastructure and the World-Wide Web, which provides a common user interface. Manufacturing services can be registered with a central server acting as a manager. A user, equipped with only a standard Web browser, can look up various manufacturing services registered with the manager, use a Web-based computer-aided solid design software to interactively collaborate with remote group members to design a product, invoke file format translation services, create a physical model through rapid prototyping, and examine images of the rapidly-produced specimen, without installing any special software, or leaving the office.

1 Introduction

It has been said that 80% of productivity growth is attributed to technological-based advances [1]. The manufacturing industry in Hong Kong used to compete on the basis of inexpensive labor and nimble manufacturers. Since the opening up of China beginning in the late 1970's, however, much of the actual manufacturing activities in Hong Kong have been relocated to southern China to take advantage of the newly-available, even less expensive labor, space, and other resources. In the mean time, costs in Hong Kong have risen significantly. To continue to compete effectively, Hong Kong must increase productivity by increasing the level of technology applied to its manufacturing activities. And one way to do it is to improve the integration of its diverse operations distributed over a wide area, mainly in Southern China, but also overseas. The rapid development of the Internet in recent years offers a golden opportunity for much tighter integration of manufacturing activities on a much wider scope [2] [3] [4].

The IIM system demonstrates the degree in which some of the manufacturing data and services can be accessed through the Internet. The approach taken is the setting up of IIM servers that act as portals to the world of manufacturing services on the

Internet. Internet-accessible manufacturing services register with these portals. Clients seeking to access manufacturing services can then find out what services are available from these portals, and may then access these services in the mode provided. It may occur in the form of sending data as parameters in simple messages or as data files to be processed, to an application running on a remote server. It may be in the form of applets downloaded from a server to be executed on the client machine itself, which will communicate with a remote server, but subsequently be removed upon exiting from the Web page. It may also be in the form of application programs that had to be installed in the client machine in the conventional manner, that can communicate with applications on remote servers through these portals.

2 The IIM/1.0 Architecture

The IIM system consists of manufacturing services, users, IIM managers, and the Internet. Manufacturing services register with the IIM manager dynamically through the Internet. Likewise, users access the IIM manager through the Internet. It can then access the chosen services directly through the Internet, or through the IIM manager. The system setup is illustrated in **Figure 1**.

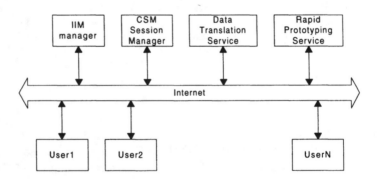

Figure 1. The IIM system architecture.

Services can be classified into different types depending on the manner in which services are provided:
1. Client-server based – users interact with applets download from the service provider. The applets perform most of the services locally on the users' machines, and typically also communicate with the service provider. Alternatively, the client may be installed as a local application permanently.
2. Externally invoked program – Users look up services from the IIM Manager. They then access services by sending requests to the intended service provider through the IIM manager. The IIM manger causes the appropriate program to be executed on a remote server.

3. Message-based –The IIM Manager sends messages to the service on behalf of the users. Results may be returned directly to the users, or routed through the IIM Manager. This is typical of services that cannot be remotely controlled, such as fabrication processes that require attention by a human operator.

In IIM/1.0, three major services are provided: a collaborative solid modeling (CSM) design system, a data format translation service, and a rapid prototyping service. These services enable a product to be completely designed and rapidly manufactured remotely through IIM. A user accesses the IIM manager home page using a common Web browser, which triggers the automatic downloading of an applet (the MainApplet) from the IIM manager to the local computer. The MainApplet (client) communicates with the main IIM manager (server). The MainApplet finds out the services available from IIM manager, and then informs the user by displaying the available services. The user then selects the service, upon which the MainApplet returns a handle to the server that actually provides the service requested, e.g., SessionRequestManager which provides a collaborative solid modeling design system. The MainApplet then communicates with SessionRequestManager directly to access the service. In this manner, new services can be registered with the IIM manager dynamically, without changing any program code and recompiling. Clients of these services, on the hand, can also look up the services available dynamically.

3 The Collaborative Solid Modelling Design System

A collaborative solid modeling CSM system has been integrated into IIM/1.0. The solid modeling functionality supported in CSM has been described in [5] and the extension to provide basic support for multiple users discussed in [6]. Since then we have extended the system to support locking of sub-solids. The CSM system is an interactive and collaborative system deployable on the WWW, employing a client/server architecture. Users can access the CSM system by selecting the "Session Manager" from the IIM Manager. A CSM Session Manager can support more than one design group, each engaging in a design session. A designer can then choose to start a new session, or join an existing session.

All users within a group (in the same session) are working on the same shared object. In reality, each client has its own workspace, and the workspaces belonging to different clients and the server are synchronized. Designers create complex solids by specifying Boolean operations on solids using CSG (Constructive Solid Geometry) [5]. When a client triggers an event, e.g., UNIONing two solids together, the event is processed locally, and information about the event is forwarded to the server. The server does the same operation and also broadcasts the event to all other clients in the same group. The other clients then perform the operation in their local workspaces, synchronizing all workspaces within the group. The data structures representing the solids are not actually passed among the workspaces. Only the name of the event and parameters are passes, reducing network traffic to a minimum. The events are mainly of the following types:

1. Creating or modifying a primitive solid.
2. Performing a Boolean operation on two solids.
3. Replacing a sub-solid with another.

A number of collaboration control methods have been implemented in CSM. One of them is token controlled access [6], in which the user holding the token can view and edit the solid model, while all other users can only view the model. Alternatively a locking scheme can be employed to control access to various components. Users can lock CSG subtrees, which correspond to sub-solids. The root node of a CSG subtree is an interior node in the CSG tree. Locking a CSG subtree A hence implicitly locks all descendant nodes of the root node. If subsequently another user wishes to lock another CSG subtree B which would implicitly lock A, the request to lock B would be rejected.

4 Data Format Translation Service

The CSM system can output the product design in the industry standard product data representation format STEP, as a STEP exchange file [7] file according to the data model defined for AP203 "Application Protocol for Configuration Controlled Design" [8], as illustrated in **Figure 2**.

```
#10=CARTESIAN_POINT('',(36.531708,60.229530,61.000000));
#20=DIRECTION('',(0.000000,0.000000,1.000000));
#30=VECTOR('',#20,1.000000);
#40=LINE('',#10,#30);
#50=CARTESIAN_POINT('',(36.531708,60.229530,61.000000));
#60=VERTEX_POINT('',#50);
#70=CARTESIAN_POINT('',(36.531708,60.229530,19.000000));
#80=VERTEX_POINT('',#70);
#90=EDGE_CURVE('',#60,#80,#40,.T.);
#100=ORIENTED_EDGE('',*,*,#90,.T.);
#110=CARTESIAN_POINT('',(35.500000,58.204681,19.000000));
#120=DIRECTION('',(-0.453989,-0.891007,0.000000));
#130=VECTOR('',#120,1.000000);
#140=LINE('',#110,#130);
#150=CARTESIAN_POINT('',(35.500000,58.204681,19.000000));
```

Figure 2. A Sample STEP data exchange file.

The IIM/1.0 integrates a program, supplied by Unigraphics, for translation from STEP AP203 to the data format for Unigraphics, one of the most popular CAD/CAM systems. The data translation service is provided as an externally executable program on a separate server. Upon selecting this service from the IIM Manager, the user will then be asked to specific the URL for the STEP exchange file to be translated. The translator program will then be executed on the remote server through the Java Native Interface (JNI) with the STEP exchange file as input, which will then be translated into the Unigraphics format and output as a separate file. The URL of the output file will be returned to the user.

5 Rapid Prototyping Service

Rapid Prototyping refers to a group of technologies for converting computer representations of product designs directly into solid objects without human intervention. These technologies are also called "Free Form Fabrication" (FFF) or "Computer Automated Fabrication" (CAF). The machine employed in IIM/1.0 is a Stratasys FDM machine. The FDM (Fused Deposition Modeling) process forms three-dimensional objects from solid or surface models. A temperature-controlled head extrudes thermoplastic material layer by layer. The designed object emerges as a solid three-dimensional part without the need for tooling.

In IIM/1.0, the rapid prototyping service is accessed through electronic mail. Upon selecting the "RP Request" under "services" in the IIM Manager, the user will be asked to supply the URL of the STEP data exchange file containing the solid model definition of the product to be made. The file will then be emailed to the rapid prototyping server for processing. Upon receiving the email request for RP service, an operator converts the STEP data exchange file into the STL format. The STL file is then processed by QuickSlice [9], a slicing program that creates SML (Stratasys Modeling Language) code to drive the FDM system. Quickslice cuts the STL file into horizontal slices. Each slice is extruded as a single layer of material by the FDM hardware to create a physical model. An image of the physical model is then returned to the user through email, as illustrated in **Figure 3**.

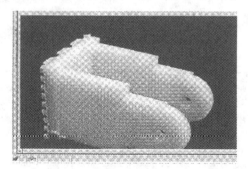

Figure 3. An image of the physical object produced by the rapid prototyping machine.

7 Conclusion and Future Work

A small prototype system supporting several important manufacturing services was successfully implemented. Equipped with only a common Web browser, a number of designers can collaborate interactively to design a solid shape, perform necessary data format translations, and rapidly produce a physical specimen of the product. All the services are provided by remote servers. Some are provided in the form of applets downloaded from the server, some are provided as application programs executed on the remote server but invoked externally, and some are requested through electronically mail, requiring the intervention of an operator, and other physical setups. The IIM/1.0 system, though simple, demonstrates the possibilities made available by the confluence of the infrastructure of the Internet, the standard interface of the World-Wide Web, and Web-friendly programming languages such as Java. The IIM system is undergoing a second phrase of development. In the second phrase, we are focusing on improving the communication infrastructure by employing CORBA, developing a uniform mechanism for invoking remove services through IDL, and providing tighter integration of manufacturing functions to the Internet.

Acknowledgments

The work described in this paper was partially supported by the Hong Kong University Grants Committee, Research Grants Council, Project PolyU 5102/97E.

References

1. Tung, C. H. From Adversity to Opportunity – Address by the Chief Executive at the Legislative Council Meeting, The Hong Kong Special Administrative Region of the People's Republic of China, 7 October, 1998.
2. Erkes, J., Kenny, K., Lewis, J., Sarachan, B., Sobolewski, M., & Sum, R. "Implementing Shared Manufacturing Services on the World-Wide Web", Communications of the ACM, February 1996, Vol. 39, No. 2, pp. 34-45.
3. Deng, Z., Bang, B. & Solvang, B. "Inter-enterprise Collaborative Design and Manufacturing Via WWW/Internet", IFIP TC8/WG8.1 Working Conference on IS in the WWW Environment, 15-17 July 1998, Beijing, China.
4. Roy, U., Bharadwaj, B., Kodkani, S & Cargian, M., "Product Development in a Collaborative Design Environment," *Concurrent Engineering: Research and Applications*, Vol. 5, No. 4., December 1997, pp. 347 - 365.
5. Chan, S., Ng, V. & Au, A., "A Solid Modeling Library for the World-Wide Web," *Computer Networks and ISDN Systems*, V. 30, Issue 20-21, Nov. 1998, pp. 1853 – 1863.
6. Chan, S., Wong, M., and Ng, V. "Collaborative Solid Modeling on the WWW", *Proceedings, 1999 ACM Symposium on Applied Computing*, February 28 – March 2, 1999, San Antonio, Texas, USA.
7. *ISO/IS 10303-21, Product Data Representation and Exchange - Part 21: Clear Text Encoding of the Exchange Structure*, 1994.
8. *ISO/IS 10303-203 Product Data Representation and Exchange - Part 203: Application Protocol: Configuration Controlled Design*, 1994.
9. *QuickSlice Manual Release 6.0*, Stratasys, Inc. 1998.

Example-Based Chinese Text Filtering Model

Lin Hongfei, Zhan Xuegang and Yao Tianshun

(Department of Computer , Northeastern University, Shenyang   China, 110006, hflin@ics.cs.neu.edu.cn)

Abstract: This paper briefly describes the background of text filtering and proposes an example-based Chinese text filtering model. It analyzes the structure of the texts as example, extracts the keywords from the texts by means of the text hierarchical analysis presented in this paper, constructs the user profiles which consist of the keywords above, and then filters the new text collections. Consequently, based on the user feedback, it expands the number of example texts, applies the approach of Latent Semantic Indexing to filter texts, and updates the user profiles to improve the efficiency of text filtering systems.

Keyword: Text filtering, Text Hierarchical Analysis, Latent Semantic Indexing, User Profiles

1   Introduction

With the growth of the information technology, typically the development of the internet and large scale storage media, more and more text information is available, so it is a key problem how to help users get the information which they are interested in and eliminate the noises which are not required by users. Many researchers and organizations make effort to study the information filtering technology on the internet, and various information filtering systems emerge as the times require. In the well-known TREC, information filtering is an important branch of routing task.

Now text filtering technology obtains great progress because the most of the information format on the internet is textual. In addition, text filtering is closely related to text retrieval, text summarization and text categorization.

The basic idea of the Chinese text filtering model is shown as follows: First, example texts are considered as the user's information needs and the features are extracted from them through text hierarchical analysis. Next, text filtering engine starts to run according to the features extracted from example texts. Finally, based on the feedback of users, the model can automatically update the information needs of users and improve its efficiency by means of Latent Semantic Indexing.

2   Example-Based Chinese Text Filtering Model

The procedures of text filtering are basically divided into two tasks: One is the representation technology of information need, namely user profiles; the other is the matching technology of texts and profiles.

The main process of the Chinese text filtering model is described in detail as follows[4,5]. First, it analyzes the structure of the example texts and extracts features from the texts in order to construct user profiles, which are the combination of example texts and their features. In view of the number of example texts being fewer at the beginning of the model, it has to use the keyword-based approach to match profiles and texts from text collection and uses them as the basis of user feedback. As a result, the number of example texts is increased to some extent, and the approach of Latent Semantic Indexing is introduced to improve the performance of text filtering, as the experiment shows, it has remarkable effects.

It should noted that the filtering technology based on keywords extracted from example texts and the filtering technology based on the Latent Semantic Indexing are two independent approaches.

3   Text Structure Analysis and Text Feature Extraction

In Chinese text filtering, the text structure analysis aims at text feature extraction, namely text keywords. Text keywords should have exhaustivity and specificity. Exhausitivity is the degree that the text theme is covered with keywords, and specificity emphasizes that keywords should reveal some content of text. On account of the requirement of exhausitivity, example texts are analyzed by means of the text hierarchical analysis, and then text keywords are extracted from text by hierarchical sequences and ensure the keywords to cover the text theme to the utmost. Owing to the requirement of specificity, it has to eliminate the words in stop list and select the nouns and nouns phrases which possess actual meaning and show the characteristics of the text.

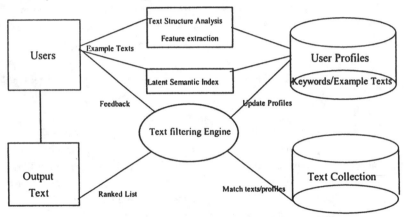

Figure 1.   The Architecture of Text Filtering Model Based on Example

Text structure includes physical structure and logic structure. Text physical structure can express {title, paragraphs, sentences, words}, and it can be easily identified from a text after preprocessing. It essentially represents the composition of a text. As compared with the physical structure, text logic structure can express {theme, hierarchies, paragraphs, keywords}, and it focuses on representing the implied theme of a text and finding out the logic forms of depiction, that is, it not only knows the boundaries of the hierarchies and paragraphs, but also understands their main idea.

It is well known that various types of texts possess various organizational structure. However, the paragraphs in most texts are arranged into hierarchical structure, that is to say that texts have the hierarchical organization[2,6]. Further, it is noted that text hierarchy consists of a sequence of paragraphs and the its boundary has to be determined by readers.

A sequence of paragraphs located in the same hierarchy are very similar in words and their frequency among themselves, because they support the same main idea contained by the hierarchy. Based on this fact, the text hierarchies are segmented by clustering in paragraph order, that is, paragraphs clustering should keep the natural paragraph sequence.

Suppose a text T with n paragraphs and K hierarchies. Let H represent hierarchy and P represent paragraph, then we have the relational expression below.

$$T = H_1 H_2 ... H_K = \{P_{I_1}...P_{I_2-1}\}\{P_{I_2}...P_{I_3-1}\}...\{P_{I_K}...P_{I_{K+1}-1}\}$$

where $i_1 = 1 \le i_2 ..... \le i_K \le i_{K+1} - 1 = n$.($P_1, P_2, ..., P_n$ can be simplified as 1,2, ,n to be convenient for citing and writing.)

The set of keywords of text T is $\{t_1, t_2, ..., t_m\}$, let P_i represent the feature vector of the ith paragraph, where $P_i = (w_{i1}, w_{i2}, ..., w_{im})$, w_{ij} is the weight of t_j in ith paragraph.

Suppose n paragraphs to be divided into K hierarchies, then there are C_{n-1}^{K-1} possible segmenting methods. Let S(n,K) be one of them, where

$$S(n, K) = \{i_1 = 1, i_1 + 1, ..., i_2 - 1\}, ..., \{i_j, i_j + 1, ..., i_{j+1}\}, ..., \{i_K, i_K + 1, ..., i_{K+1} - 1 = n\}$$

the clustering in natural sequences aims at seeking a segmenting method which can make the interior variances of K hierarchies minimal and the exterior variances of K hierarchies maximal, where interior variance is the variance in one hierarchy and exterior variance is the variance among hierarchies. Suppose $D(i_j, i_{j+1} - 1)$ represent the variance of the jth hierarchy, then the total

variance function is $E(S(n, K)) = \sum_{j=1}^{K} D(i_j, i_{j+1} - 1)$.

Seeking the minimum of total variance function E(S(n,K)) can be named after optimal K segmenting method, and its optimization can be implemented as follows. After n paragraphs are divided into $\{i_1 = 1, i_1 + 1, ..., i_{K-1}\}$ and $\{i_K, i_K + 1, ..., i_{K+1} - 1 = n\}$,the former is optimized and get to the optimal K-1 segmentation, the variance of the latter is considered to search the minimum of total variance function E(S(n,K)).

Suppose $S_0(n, K, c_K)$ represent the optimal segmenting method, where c_K is the optimal segmentation i_K , then we have the iterative formula

$$E(S_0(n, K, c_K)) = Min\{E(S_0(i_{K-1}, K-1, c_{K-1}) + D(i_K, n))\}$$

Text logic structure is determined by the boundaries and the number of hierarchies, and the number of hierarchies is determined in two ways. One way is used when a threshold ε is given, then the K that satisfies $\left| E(S(n, K+1)) - E(S(n, K)) \right| \le \varepsilon$ is the optimal number of hierarchies.

The other way is used when K is preset according to general knowledge about the composition and daily experiment, where K is given according to the number of paragraphs, its range is usually from 2 to 6.

After text hierarchical analysis, the principal work is to define the weight functions for keywords and hierarchies, assign the number of keywords for each hierarchy based on the weights of hierarchies, and select the keywords with higher weight in each hierarchy. As a result, the set of keywords is constructed.

It is worthy to focus on the facts below when the weight function of keywords is designed, and they might reveal some heuristics.

The higher paragraph frequency of a keyword, the stronger power for it to represent the theme of text. In addition, short words have higher frequency and richer meanings, therefore they usually are oriented to grammatical function; on the other hand, long words have lower frequency and less meanings, so they usually are oriented to text content. Consequently, enlarging the weight of long words is helpful to enhancing the discriminating power of words, meanwhile, it reduces the unsteadiness of single Chinese words which are generated in the course of word segmenting.

Where do the keywords distribute in the text? First, the text title is fairly related to the text theme. It is reported that in the journals of Chinese natural science the rate which the titles is approximately in accordance with the themes is 98%, and 95% in news reports. Therefore, the keywords in titles are significant. Secondly, the beginning and end of each paragraph include important keywords. It is reported by P.E.Baxendale that 85% of the sentences representing the text theme occur at the beginning of a paragraph and 7% occur at the end of a paragraph, so the keywords at the beginning and the end of a paragraph can be assigned higher weights. Next, the abstract of a text usually includes more keywords, and they have a great deal to do with the theme of a text. Finally, the keywords in the conclusive sentences also obtain higher weight, where the conclusive sentences is the sentences which include such clue words as "it is concluded", "in a word" and so on.

The weight function of keywords :

$$f_w(t_i) = \frac{f_u(t_i)\log_2(1+f_v(t_i))^l}{C\sqrt{\sum_{j=1}^{m}(f_u(t_j)\log_2(1+f_v(t_j))^l)^2}}(1+\alpha)$$

where $f_w(t_i)$ is the weight of t_i £» $f_u(t_i)$ is the frequency of t_i in the hierarchy £» $f_v(t_i)$ is the frequency of t_i in the paragraph £» l is the length of t_i £» C is the proportional coefficient £» if t_i occurs in the conclusive sentences, α equals to 0.5 ,else α equals to 0 ¡ £

In this model, the set of keywords consists of two subsets. One subset is extracted from the header of a text, and the header includes title, subtitles, abstract and keyword list. The other is extracted from the body of a text.

Suppose t keywords are to be selected from a text. First of all, the keywords are selected from the header. The number of the keywords in the header is s and s is less than t, then n stands for the number of the rest keywords and n equals to t - s. Next, they are selected from the hierarchies of the body of text, and the number of keywords extracted from a hierarchy is in proportion to the its weight. Let the feature vector of text be $U = (u_1, u_2, ..., u_m)$ and the feature vector of H_i, that is, ith hierarchy, be $V = (v_{i1}, v_{i2}, ..., vi_m)$, the weight of H_i is defined as:

$$f_h(H_i) = \frac{\sum_{j=1}^{m}u_j v_{ij}}{\sqrt{\sum_{j=1}^{m}u_j^2 \sum_{j=1}^{m}v_{ij}^2}} \quad i = 1,2,...,K. \quad h_i = (f_h(H_i)/\sum_{j=1}^{m}f_h(H_j))*n$$

where K is the number of hierarchies.Then the number of keywords from a hierarchy equal to h_i.

As shown above, the keywords from the header are more significant than that from the body. Furthermore, the keywords from different hierarchy have different weight, so it is necessary to reassign the weight of keywords extracted from a text. The weight of keywords from the header equal to 1.0, the weight of keywords from the first hierarchy equal to 0.8, the weight of keywords from the last hierarchy equal to 0.6, the weight of keywords from the rest hierarchy equal to 0.4. As a result, the user profiles have been constructed with keywords and their weights.

4 Latent Semantic Indexing

Either user profiles or text feature vector is represented using the Vector Space Model (VSM). Its advantage is to transfer the content of text into the vectors which is easy to perform various mathematics calculations. But there are some shortcoming about VSM. The basic hypothesis of VSM is that the words are independent of each other, and it is hard to meet the hypothesis in practical environment, namely skew intersection.

Latent Semantic Indexing is introduced by S. T. Dumais[3]. Its main idea is that there are some relations among words, in another word, there are some latent semantic structures. Therefore, statistical methods are used to search the semantic structures, and the semantic structures can be used to represent the text and words, which can eliminate the relatedness among words to predigest the vector of text.

The Latent Semantic Indexing Algorithm is based on the single value decomposition of a matrix. Let A be the matrix of keywords vs. text, then $A = P\Sigma Q^T$, where P and Q are the orthogonal matrices, Σ is the diagonal matrix and $\lambda_1 \geq \lambda_2 \geq ... \geq \lambda_r > 0$.

$$\Sigma = diag(\lambda_1, \lambda_2, ..., \lambda_r, 0, ..., 0) \qquad PP^T = I \text{ £ <} Q^T Q = I$$

In practice, it is usually adopted to replace the original space by the subspace which is more representative in order to reduce the dimension of vector space. Let $\omega = \sum_{i=1}^{K} \lambda_i / \sum_{j=1}^{r} \lambda_j$, then

choose a proper K to make $\omega \geq \theta$, where θ is selected according to the need £ < for example, θ may be 50%, 55%, 60%, 70%, 75%, ...

$$A = P\Sigma Q^T = (P_K \quad P_\epsilon \quad P_0)\Sigma(Q_K, Q_{\epsilon,} Q_0)^T = P_K \Sigma_K Q_K^T + P_\epsilon \Sigma_\epsilon Q_\epsilon^T \approx P_K \Sigma_K Q_K^T$$

Furthermore, the vectors of the original space are transformed into the vector of the subset by means of the transformation $V_K = \Omega(V) = V^T P_K \Sigma_K^{-1}$.

Latent Semantic Indexing replace the original space with the K dimension orthogonal space, and then words and texts are represented by its point. It can be considered as the conceptual space of latent semantic structure, consequently, it reduces the relatedness among words and the dimensions of vectors. In the less dimensional space, the similarity calculation of words vs words or text vs text make up of these semantic structures. Especially in course of text retrieval and text filtering, it is noted that the its advantage do not depend on whether the keywords occur in a text to judge the their relatedness, so it well reveals the advantage of the conceptualization.

In this Model, based on the keywords filtering, it collects enough example texts to construct the matrix of words vs. text $A = (a_{ij})$, where

$$a_{ij} = \frac{tf_{ij} \log(N/n_j)}{\sqrt{\sum_{k=1}^{n}(tf_{ik})^2[\log(N/n_k)]^2}} \qquad i = 1, 2, ..., m; j = 1, 2, ...n$$

where tf_{ij} is the frequency of t_i in text V_j, N is the number of the text collection, n_j is the text frequency of t_i, that is, the number of texts includes t_i in the text collection.

It is the transformation for the famous formula $tf * idf$ [4] £ < where the factors of length of texts are taken into account, the normalization is applied to the texts.

Let the set of example texts be $V_1, V_2, ..., V_n$ and new text be U, then the conceptual representation of U is obtained by transform Ω.

$(V_1^{(K)}, V_2^{(K)}, ..., V_n^{(K)}) = \Omega(V_1, V_2, ..., V_n)$, that is $U^{(K)} = \Omega(U)$.

When calculating the similarity θ_i of U and $P_1, P_2, ..., P_n$, where P_i is an user profile, θ_i is calculated by cosine coefficient. Then the degree of text U related to the user profiles can be measured by $\theta = Max(\theta_1, \theta_2, ..., \theta_n)$. If $\theta \geq \eta$ £ < where η is the threshold £ < then text U is considered to be in accordance with the requirement of users.

In this model, the maximum number of the example texts is a constant. It always chooses the newest example texts as the original material of Latent Semantic Indexing in order to pursue the newest interests of users.

5 Conclusion

In this paper, the example-based Chinese text filtering model is presented. The approach of keywords-based text filtering is quick and easy to operate, but its precision is not as good as that of Latent Semantic Indexing, because it is influenced by the keywords extracted from example texts. Therefore, the former is used to collect the example texts, after the number of the example texts reaches a certain extent, the latter is applied to filter the text collection. The speed of the latter is lower than that of the former, because the algorithm of the latter is more complicated than the former. In addition, it is not intuitive to users.

The experiment texts are selected from "People's Daily" in 1994. The number of texts is 400 texts, where 100 texts are known as example text, 100 relevant texts and 200 irrelevant texts are adopted as test texts. The two approaches are evaluated in the experiment. One is the approach based on the keywords extracted from example texts by text hierarchical analysis, the other is the approach of Latent Semantic Indexing. The experiment result is showed as follows:

	keywords-based	Latent Semantic Indexing-based	Compared Result
average precision	42%	51%	+9%

Table 1.   The experimental Result

In the beginning, it used the keywords-based text filtering to collect the example texts according to the feedback of users, as the example texts being increased, the number of keywords are also incremental, but the noise is added. Therefore, its precision may be not high. When the number of the example texts is added to a certain extent, it applied the Latent Semantic Indexing to filter texts, and it remarkably improve the precision of text filtering. As a result, it is the final precision of the model.

There is some work to be done in the future. It is necessary to efficiently extract keywords from texts, especially identify the noun phrases and attempt to apply the technology of natural language processing to enhance the exhausitivity and specificity[1]. In addition, it needs to estimate the initial dimensions and the optimal K constant by means of a great deal text collections. Now the initial dimension equals to 100, and the K is determined to satisfy with the conditional expression . Owing to each run against the newest 100 example texts, the efficiency can be guaranteed and operation is easy, but it may be not optimal.

Reference

[1] Tianshun Yao , Natural Language Understanding, TsingHua University Press,1995
[2] G.Salton,J.Allen, Automatic Text Decomposition and Structuring,RIAO94,Paris,6-20
[3] Peter W. Foltz, Latent Semantic Analysis for Text-Based Research, Behavior Research Methods, Instruments and Computers, Vol. 28, No.2 ,1996,197-202.
[4] T.W.Yan and H.Garcia-Molina,SIFT- A tool for wide-area information dissemination, In Proceeding of the USENIX Technical Conference,1995,177-186.,
[5] Qi Lu, Matthias Eichstaedt and Daniel Ford, Efficient profile matching for large scale Webcasting, http://decweb.ethz.ch/WWW7/1923/com1923.htm
[6] Hind, Join, Organizational patterns in discourse, Syntax and Semantics: Discourse and Syntax,Vol.12, Academic Press, New York,1979,135-158.

Navigation-Dependent Web-Views: Defining and Controlling Semantic Unit of Web Pages

Hidenari Kiyomitsu[1] and Katsumi Tanaka[2]

[1] Faculty of Economics, Kobe University, 2-1 Rokkodai, Nada, Kobe, 657-8501 Japan
kiyomitu@econ.kobe-u.ac.jp
[2] Graduated School of Science and Techinology, Kobe University, 1-1 Rokkodai,
Nada, Kobe, 657-8501 Japan
tanaka@db.cs.kobe-u.ac.jp

Abstract. In this paper, we propose an idea of changing the view of web-pages and their link structures by user's link navigation history and predefined *semantic units* of web pages. The major objective of the proposed method is to reflect web page author(creator)'s intention about his/her web data and its linking structures. In our *navigation-dependent web views*, the view of each web page including its hyperlinks is changed according to which link navigation the user took to reach the web page. If user obeys link navigation that is intended by the author, the system will provide necessary and sufficient view of the web-page including all the predefined hyperlinks. Otherwise, our mechanism adds information of unvisited pages to user's view and hides some hyperlinks.

1 Introduction

The notion of the hypertext is a powerful tool to express relationships among documents by hyperlinks with ease. Now, a vast of documents is stored on the Internet sites, and they are connected through the hyperlinks. Hyperlinks are very flexible, and users can freely connect their documents with other documents by establishing hyperlinks.

It is also usual that an author creates his web pages assuming some implicit navigation path that users possibly obey to navigate. For example, when an author creates a page, say A followed by a page B, then the author assumes readers to navigate from page A to page B by following the predefined hyperlink. On the other hand, WWW users can create any hyperlinks from his favorite page to page B directly. In this case, the author's intention is disregarded, and the page A is not always read by users.

In order to prevent such undesirable navigation by users, we suggest the following:

- **Semantic Unit**
  A web document author can specify a collection of related web pages as a *semantic unit*. Within a semantic unit, the readers of the web pages can enjoy full information if they obey the predefined navigation paths. According to

the user's real navigation path, which may not be the same as the author intends, the system dynamically controls the visibility of hyperlinks.

– **Information Complementation**
  If a reader does not obey the predefined navigation paths, the system shows additionally the contents of unvisited pages to him, and/or the system makes some hyperlinks invalid.

2 Semantic Units

Suppose that a web-document author creates his document as three web pages, say A, B, and C. In order to understand the whole contents of his document, he may wish the readers of his web pages to read the pages A, B, and C in this order. In order to reflect the author's intention, he will establish a hyperlink from A to B, and a hyperlink from B to C. In this sense, the aim of these hyperlinks is not only to navigate the three web pages, but also to enforce a kind of *prerequisite* relationship among web pages. That is, the page A should be read before the page B, and the page B should be read before page C in order to comprehend the whole contents of the pages.

Figure1(i) shows a simple web pages and their hyperlinks. There is no restriction on how to navigate the pages A, B, and C. Readers can directly read the page B by specifying the URL of page B directly or by navigating ohter links connected to page B. In the same manner, as shown in figure1(ii), readers can freely access either A, B, or C in an aribitray order, and some readers may read only page B or C independently from page A.

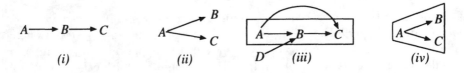

$$(i) \qquad (ii) \qquad (iii) \qquad (iv)$$

Fig. 1. Usual Hyperlinks and Semantic Units

On the other hand, if a hyperlink from page A to page B conveys the prerequisite relationship between page A and B as well as a usual navigation relationship, it is necessary to represent the semantics in a different manner. In this paper,we will denote a collection of hyperlinks having the prerequisite relationships semantics by a box. Each hyperlink contained in a box denotes a prerequisite relationship between two web pages. The nodes and hyperlinks surrounded by a box is called a *semantic unit*. A semantic unit is a meaningful unit of web pages such that the comprehension of the web pages need to navigate all the web pages by navigating predefined links.

For example, the box shown in figure 1(iii) indicates that the links (A, B) and (B, C) constitute a semantic unit, where the understanding of page B needs to read page A, and that the understanding of page C needs to comprehend page B. In the same manner, the box in figure1(iv) indicates that the links (A, B) and (A, C) constitute a semantic unit and that readers are recommended to first read page A, and then to read pages B and C (in either way) to understand the whole contents of the semantic unit.

More formally, a semantic unit is a collection of hyperlinks such that those hyperlinks convey both of usual navigation relationships and prerequisite relationships. For example, semantic units for figure 1(iii) is a set (A,B), (B,C) of hyperlinks. Note that even if we have other hyperlink (A,C) in figure 1(iii), the hyperlink (A,C) may not be always contained in the semantic unit. The meaning of the semantic unit $S = \{(A,B),(B,C)\}$ is as follows:

- The link (A,B) is viable (and so, navigatable) at any time.
- The link (B,C) becomes viable (and so, navigatable) for a user that already read page A and navigated the link (A,B).

Suppose that a user reads page D and that he tries to navigate the link (D,B) in figure 1(iii). Because of the existence of the semantic unit S and the fact that he did not navigate the link (A,B), the link (B,C) does not become viable, and so, he cannot navigate the link (B,C). In other words, the link (B,C) is hidden from the user at that time. Hereafter, in this paper, we assume that the hyperlinks appearing in a semantic unit must compose a connected asyclic graph.

3 Complementation of Information Using Semantic Units

The concept of the semantic units aims not only hiding hyperlinks from any users accessing via undesirable links, but also, providing complementary information with those users. That is, the basic idea is to automatically complement the information of univisited pages to users who are doing undesirable navigations.

Fig. 2. Complementation of univisited pages

Figure 2 shows the example of out complementation mechanism, where an access to an intermediate page C within a semantic unit $S = \{(A, B), (B, C), (C, D)\}$ against the author's intention. Our mechanism in section 3.1 makes the link (C, D) invisible because of the existence of the semantic unit S. This results in the situation that the user cannot navigate the link (C, D) and thus, cannot go to page D.

On the other hand, our notion of *information complementation* is to enforce the user to read pages A and B when he directly enters at the page C. That is, our system tries to guide the user to visit the prerequisite pages by showing the page C together with URLs of pages A and B. This is an example of *positive* usage of our semantic units.

The following is a general procedure to find which information should be complemented when a user clicks a link anchor to navigate a link from an intermediate page p_i to page p_j within a semantic unit. Let S be a semantic unit which contains a link (p_i, p_j). Then, $Reduce(S, (p_i, p_j))$ is a set of links defined as $Reduce(S, (p_i, p_j)) = \{l \mid$ There exists a path $P = l_1 l_2 \ldots l_m (1 \leq m)$ in S such that $l = l_1$ and $(p_i, p_j) = l_m$ the link$\}$

1. Find a collection of semantic units $S = \{S_1, S_2, \ldots, S_n\}$ which include a link (p_i, p_j). If $S = \phi$, then no information complemented, (p_i, p_j) becomes valid, and the algorithm terminates.
2. If there exists at least one semantic unit $S_k (1 \leq k \leq n)$ in which the in-degree of page p_i is zero regarding S_k as a graph. Then the link (p_i, p_j) becomes valid and terminate.
3. For each S_k, if there exists $Reduce(S_k, (p_i, p_j))$ satisfying both of (a) and (b), then output $Reduce(S_k, (p_i, p_j)) - \{(p_i, p_j)\}$ as a candidate of complenmented information.
   (a) $Reduce(S_k, (p_i, p_j))$ includes at least one link whose destination is p_i.
   (b) $Reduce(S_k, (p_i, p_j))$ is a minimal set satisfying (a).

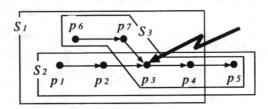

Fig. 3. An example of Complementation

There are three semantic units $S_1 = \{(p_1, p_2), (p_2, p_3), (p_3, p_4), (p_6, p_7), (p_7, p_3)\}$, $S_2 = \{(p_1, p_2), (p_2, p_3), (p_3, p_4), (p_4, p_5)\}$, $S_3 = \{(p_3, p_4), (p_4, p_5), (p_6, p_7), (p_7, p_3)\}$ in figure 3. The thick arrow illustrates a user accesses page p_3 against the author's intention. If the user clicks a link anchor to page p_4, the complementation procedure will work.

$$Reduce(S_1, (p_3, p_4)) = \{(p_1, p_2), (p_2, p_3), (p_3, p_4), (p_6, p_7), (p_7, p_3)\}$$
$$Reduce(S_2, (p_3, p_4)) = \{(p_1, p_2), (p_2, p_3), (p_3, p_4)\}$$
$$Reduce(S_3, (p_3, p_4)) = \{(p_3, p_4), (p_6, p_7), (p_7, p_3)\}$$

Since $Reduce(S_2, (p_3, p_4))$ and $Reduce(S_3, (p_3, p_4))$ are minimal among above three, our argolithm outputs $\{(p_1, p_2), (p_2, p_3)\}$ and $\{(p_6, p_7), (p_7, p_3)\}$ as candidetes of complemented information.

4 Implementation and Examples

It is an important problem how to implement the semantic units and information complementation function in usual web environment. Recently, hypertext languages have been given some facilities for specifying active links that are embedded procedures and many user agents can purse their facilities. But, it is still difficult to obtain users' navigation histories from clients. Because there is no hypertext language (including XML) to carry out to store and manipulate user's navigation history. The Netscape Navigator can store user navigation history at a file "/.netscape/history.db"on UNIX platform, but permission of this file prevents any accesses from getting user's history data. Therefore, it is difficult to get user's history from client side. Our example for implementing the semantic units and information complementation is to use Server Side Includes(SSI). Any page in some semantic units has a procedure to store and check user's visiting history and to suggest next pages or some complements at clicking a link anchor to next page. But, the way of visualization for the complemented information depends on author's objective and his implementation. Because of using HTML as a hypertext language in this implementation, links are embedded in visited page as in-line links.

At the server side, the link visualization proceeds according to user's link navigation. When a user accesses a page in semantic units, this server gets environment variables such as ENV. An element of ENV indicates an IP address as a symbol 'REMOTE_ADDR'. Our implementation uses IP address for identifying the user. This is why e-mail address of the user or user ID is not always sent in issuing "http get" from client. Therefore user visiting history data is a file enumerating IP addresses. First, the system evaluates IP address sent of a client whether it exists at the file storing user-visiting page as behavor of client. Then, the system returns one or more hyperlinks to next pages or complements.

5 Conclusions

In this paper, we proposed the idea of *navigation-dependet web views*, which can change the view of web-pages and their link structures based on the notions of *semantic units* and *information complementation*. It should be noted that our ideas can be implemented without any sacrifice of restricting the freedom of web access mechanism. In our *navigation-dependent web views*, the view of each web page including its hyperlinks is changed according to which navigation path the user took to reach the web page. If user obeys a link navigation that is intended by the author, the system will provide necessary and sufficient view of the web-page including all the predefined hyperlinks. Otherwise, our mechanism adds information of unvisited pages to user's view and hides some hyperlinks. We have shown the ways to add information and to hide hyperlinks based on the notion of sematic units. Recently, similar ideas were proposed by Stotts and Cabarrus[1] and by Réty[2]. Stotts and Cabarrus regards web as an automaton, and the hyperlink navigation is controlled by a user's state (which is determined by the user navigation history). Réty also adopts the same approach, and the visibility (or the navigationability) of hyperlinks are controlled by previously-visited pages. Especially, constraints concerned with the link visibility is represented by PROLOG-like logic programs. These two approaches are the same as our work in spirit, but, neither of them introduced the notion of *semantic units* and complementation. Our *semantic units* can be also expressed in those approach, but we focus flexibility for changing link structure because the link structure of Web changes frequently.

One more direction of related researches is concerned with how to *find* semantic units in web graph. Tajima et al. proposed a way to discover querying units in graph-structured data such as web, netnews, and E-mails[3]. Hatano et al.[4] and Li et al.[5] showed a way to find a semantic information unit, that is a subgraph of web, for a given query. Clearly, their approaches are different from ours because our work assumes that semantic units are determined apriori by their authors. But, our notions of link visualization and information complementation can be applied to those semantic information units found by their approaches. Finally, the following issues are to be further studied:

- General formalization of semantic units and related issues.
- Developemnt of more effective presentations of complemented information.
- Implementation of navigation dependent web views for XML environment.

Acknowledgement

Thanks are due to Dr. Keishi Tajima, Dr. Kazutoshi Sumiya, and other members of Tanaka Lab. of Kobe University for their useful discussions. This research is partly supported by Research for the Future Program of Japan Society for the Promotion of Science under the Project: Researches on Advanced Multimedia Contents Processing.

References

1. P. David Stotts, Cyrano Ruiz Cabarrus, "Hyperdocuments as Automata: Verification on Trace-Based Browsing Properties by Model Checking" *ACM Transaction of Information Systems*, Vol. 16, No. 1, pp. 1-30, 1998.
2. Jean-Hugues Réty, "Structure Analysis for Hypertext with Conditional Linkage", *Proc. of Hypertext '99*, pp. 135-136, 1999.
3. Keishi Tajima, Yoshiaki Mizuuchi, Masatsugu Kitagawa, and Katsumi Tanaka, "Cut As a Querying Unit for WWW, Netnews, and E-mail", *Proc. of Hypertext '98*, pp. 235-244, June 1998.
4. Kenji Hatano, Ryouichi Sano, Yiwei Dan and Katsumi Tanaka, "An Interactive Classification of Web Documents by Self-Organization Maps and Search Engines", *Proc. of DASFAA '99*, pp. 19-25 1999.
5. Wen-Syan Li and Yi-Leh Wu, "Query Relaxation by Structure for Web Document Retrieval with Progressive Processing", *Proc. of Advanced Database Symposium '98*, pp. 19-25, Dec. 1998.

An Efficient Chinese Word Segmentation Algorithm for Chinese Information Processing on the Internet

P.K. Wong

Department of Computing Studies, Hong Kong Institute of Vocational Education
(Sha Tin), Hong Kong Vocational Training Council, Sha Tin, N.T., Hong Kong,
pkwong@vtc.edu.hk

Abstract. A Chinese word segmentation algorithm based on forward maximum matching and word binding force is proposed in this paper. To support this algorithm, a text corpus of over 63 millions characters is employed to enrich an 80,000-words lexicon in terms of its word entries and word binding forces. As it stands now, given an input line of text, the word segmentor can process on the average 210,000 characters per second when running on an IBM RISC System/6000 3BT workstation with a correct word identification rate of 99.74%. The proposed word segmentation algorithm can be applied to process the huge amount of Chinese information on the Internet.

1 Introduction

In this world, over one fifth of people know Chinese. In recent years, the amount of Chinese information processing by computers increases dramatically. As long as computer becomes more popular, this situation will be more so in the 21th century. Nowadays, the Internet has been an important channel for information exchange. A huge amount of Chinese information is transmitting through the Internet at every second. Chinese is different to English in many ways, so particular algorithms should be introduced to process Chinese information on the Internet. One of the major difference between Chinese and English is that a Chinese sentence is a sequence of Chinese characters without any explicit word boundaries. The basic semantic unit in Chinese is word instead of character. In most of the time, a Chinese sentence should be segmented into words before searching a word in it, or before analying its structure or meaning. Hence, word segmentation is an important step in Chinese information processing. On the other hand, when the amount of Chinese information being processed is very huge, the speed of the applied word segmentation algorithm is very critical.

About 5,000 characters are being used in modern Chinese and they are the building blocks of all words. Almost every character is a word and most words are of one or two characters long but there are also abundant words longer than two characters. Before it is segmented into words, a line of text is just a sequence of characters and there are numerous word segmentation alternatives. Usually, all but one of these alternatives are syntactically and/or semantically incorrect. This is the case because unlike texts in English, Chinese texts have no word markers.

Word segmentation algorithms belong to one of two types in general, viz., the structural [6] and the statistical type [4][3][5] respectively. A structural algorithm resolves segmentation ambiguities by examining the structural relationships between words, while a statistical algorithm compares the usage frequencies of the words and their ordered combinations instead. Both approaches have serious limitations.

2   Maximum Matching Method for Segmentation

Maximum matching [2] is one of the most popular structural segmentation algorithms for Chinese texts. This method favours long words and is a greedy algorithm by design, hence, sub-optimal. Segmentation may start from either end of the line without any difference in segmentation results. In this paper, the forward direction is adopted. The major advantage of maximum matching is its efficiency while its segmentation accuracy can be expected to lie around 95%.

3   Word Frequency Method for Segmentation

In this statistical approach in terms of word frequencies, a lexicon needs not only a rich repertoire of word entries, but also the usage frequency of each word. To segment a line of text, each possible segmentation alternative is evaluated according to the product of the word frequencies of the words segmented. The word sequence with the highest frequency product is accepted as correct. This method is simple but its accuracy depends heavily on the accuracy of the usage frequencies. The usage frequency of a word differs greatly from one type of documents to another, say, a passage of world news as against a technical report. Since there are tens of thousands of words actively used, one needs a gigantic collection of texts to make an accurate estimate, but by then, the estimate is just an average and it may not be suitable for any type of document at all. In other words, the variance of such an estimate is too great making the estimate useless.

4   The Lexicon

Most Chinese linguists accept the definition of a word as the minimum unit that is semantically complete and can be put together as building blocks to form a sentence. However, in Chinese, words can be united to form compound words, and they in turn, can combine further to form yet higher ordered compound words. As a matter of fact, compound words are extremely common and they exist in large numbers. It is impossible to include all compound words into the lexicon but just to keep those which are frequently used and have the word components united closely. A lexicon was acquired from the Institute of Information Science, Academia Sinica in Taiwan. There are 78410 word entries in this lexicon, each associated with a usage frequency. A corpus of over 63 million characters of news lines was acquired from China. Due to cultural differences of the two societies, there are many words encountered in the corpus but not in the lexicon. The latter must therefore be enriched before it can be applied to perform the lexical analysis. The first step towards this end is to merge a lexicon published in China into this one, increasing the number of word entries to 85,855.

5 The Proposed Word Segmentation Algorithm

The proposed algorithm of this paper makes use of a forward maximum matching strategy to identify words. In this respect, this algorithm is a structural approach. Under this strategy, errors are usually associated with single-character words. If the first character of a line is identified as a single-character word, what it means is that there is no multi-character word entry in the lexicon that starts with such a character. In that case, there is not much one can do about it. On the other hand, when a character is identified as a single-character word β following another word α in the line, one cannot help wondering whether the sole character composing β should not be combined with the suffix of α to form another word instead, even if that means changing α into a shorter word. In that case, every possible word sequence alternative corresponding to the subsequence of characters from α and β together will be evaluated according to the product of its constituent word binding forces. The binding force of a word is a measure of how strongly the characters composing the word are bound together as a single unit. This force is often equated to the usage frequency of the word. In this respect, the proposed algorithm is a statistical approach. It is as efficient as the maximum matching method because word binding forces are utilized only in exceptional cases. However, much of the word ambiguities are eliminated, leading to a very high word identification accuracy. Segmentation errors associated with multi-character words can be reduced by adding or deleting words to or from the lexicon as well as adjusting word binding forces.

6 Structure of the Lexicon

Words in the lexicon are divided into 5 groups according to word lengths. They correspond to words of 1, 2, 3, 4, and more than 4 characters with group sizes equal to 7025, 53532, 12939, 11269, and 1090 respectively. Since most of the time spent in analyzing a line of text is in finding a match among the lexicon entries, a clever organization of the lexicon speeds up the searching process tremendously. Most Chinese words are of one or two characters only. Searching for longer words before shorter ones as practised in maximum matching means spending a great deal of time searching for non-existent targets. To overcome this problem, the following measures are taken to organize the lexicon for fast search:

- All single character words are stored in a table of 32768 bins. Since the internal code of a character takes 2 bytes, bits 1-15 are used as the bin address for the word.
- All 2-character words are stored in a separate table of 65536 bins. The two low order bytes of the two characters are used as a short integer for bin address. Should there be other words contesting for the same bin, they are kept in a linked list.
- Any 3-character word is split into a 2-character prefix and a 1-character suffix. The prefix will be stored in the bin table for 2-character words with clear indication of its prefix status. The suffix will be stored in the bin table for 1-character words, again, with clear indication of its suffix status. All duplicate entries are combined, i.e., if α is a word as well as a suffix, the two entries are combined into one with an indication that it can serve as a word as well as a suffix.
- Any 4-character word is divided up into a 2-character prefix and a 2-character suffix, both stored in the bin table for 2-character words, with clear indications of their respective status. Each prefix points to a linked list of associated suffixes.
- Any word longer than 4 characters will be divided into a 2-character prefix, a 2-character infix and a suffix. The prefix and the infix are stored in the bin table for 2-character words, with clear indications of their status. Each prefix points to a linked list of associated infixes and each infix in turn, points to a linked list of associated suffixes.

Maximum matching segmentation of a sequence of characters "...abcdefghij..." at the character "a" starts with matching "ab" against the 2-character words table. If no match is found, then, "a" is assumed a 1-character word and maximum matching moves on to "b". If a match is found, then, "ab" is investigated to see if it can be a prefix. If it cannot, then "ab" is a 2-character word and maximum matching moves on to "c". If it can, then one examines if it can be associated with an infix. If it can, then one examines if "cd" can be an infix associated with "ab". If the answer is negative, then the possibility of "abcd" being a word is considered. If that fails again, then "c" in the table of 1-character words is examined to see if it can be a suffix. If it can, then "abc" will be examined to see if can be a word by searching the 1-character suffix linked list pointed at by "ab". Otherwise, one has to accept that "ab" is a 2-character word and moves on to start matching at "c". If "cd" can be an infix preceded by "ab", the linked list pointed at by "cd" as an infix will be searched for the longest possible suffix to combine with "abcd" as its prefix. If no match can be found, then one has to give up "cd" as an infix to "ab".

7 Training of the System

Despite the fact that the lexicon acquired from Taiwan has been augmented with words from another lexicon developed in China, when it is applied to segment 1.2 million character news passages in blocks of 10,000 characters each randomly selected over the text corpus, an average word segmentation error rate (μ) of 2.51% was found with a standard deviation (σ) of 0.57%, mostly caused by uncommon words not included in the enriched lexicon. Then it is decided that the lexicon should be further enriched with new words and adjusted word binding forces over a number of generations. In generation i, n new blocks of text are picked randomly from the corpus and words segmented using the lexicon enriched in the previous generation. This process will stop when μ levels off over several generations. The $100(1 - \alpha)\%$ confidence interval of μ in generation i is $\pm t_{0.5\alpha, n-1}\sigma/\sqrt{n}$ where σ is the standard deviation of error rates in generation $i - 1$, and n is the number of blocks to be segmented in generation i. $t_{0.5\alpha, n-1}$ is the density function of $(0.5\alpha, n - 1)$ degrees of freedom[1]. Throughout the experiments below, n is always chosen to be 20 so that the 90% confidence interval (i.e., $\alpha = 0.1$) of μ is about $\pm 0.23\%$.

8 Experimental Results

The lexicon has been updated over six generations after being applied to word segment 1.2 million characters. The vocabulary increases from 85855 words to 87326 words. The segmentation error rates over seven generations of the training process are shown in the table below:

Lexicon Generation Number	Error Rate μ over a text of 200,000 Characters	
	Max. Mat.	Max. Mat. & Word Bind. Force
0	5.71%	2.32%
1	5.20%	2.16%
2	4.66%	1.88%
3	4.98%	1.62%
4	2.60%	0.43%
5	2.47%	0.30%
6	2.44%	0.26%

Most of these errors occur in proper nouns not included in the lexicon. They are hard to avoid unless they become popular enough to be added to the lexicon. The CPU time used for segmenting a text of 1,200,000 characters is 5.7 seconds on an IBM RISC System/6000 3BT computer.

9 Conclusion

Lexical analysis is a basic process of analyzing and understanding a language. The proposed algorithm provides a highly accurate and highly efficient way for word segmentation of Chinese texts. Due to cultural differences, the same language used in different geographical regions and different applications can be quite different causing problems in lexical analysis. However, by introducing new words into and adjusting word binding forces in the lexicon, such difficulties can be greatly mitigated.

References

1. Jay L. Devore: Probability and statistics for engineering and sciences. Duxbury Press (1991) 272–276
2. Yuan Liu, Qiang Tan, and Kun Xu Shen: The word segmentation rules and automatic word segmentation methods for Chinese information processing (in Chinese). Qing Hua University Press and Guang Xi Science and Technology Press (1994) 36
3. Kim-Teng Lua and Kok-Wee Gan: An application of information theory in Chinese word segmentation. Computer Processing of Chinese and Oriental Languages 8-1 (1994) 115–123
4. K.T. Lua: From character to word – an application of information theory. Computer Processing of Chinese and Oriental Languages 4-4 (1990) 304–313
5. Richard Sproat and Chilin Shih: A statistical method for finding word boundaries in Chinese text. Computer Processing of Chinese and Oriental Languages 4-4 (1990) 336–349
6. Liang-Jyh Wang, Tzusheng Pei, Wei-Chuan Li, and Lih-Ching R. Huang: A parsing method for identifying words in mandarin Chinese sentences. Processings of 12th International Joint Conference on Artificial Intelligence (1991) 1018–1023 Sydney Australia

Push-Based News Delivery with CORBA

Gary Yat Chung WONG and Andy Hon Wai CHUN

City University of Hong Kong
Department of Electronic Engineering
Tat Chee Avenue
Kowloon, Hong Kong
e-mail: ycwong@ee.cityu.edu.hk, eehwchun@cityu.edu.hk

Abstract. In today's fast paced world, information and data changes far too rapidly. The capability to get updated information and news is an important and decisive factor in business and finance. With Internet's popularity, more and more people are getting their news from the Internet instead of from hardcopy newspapers. In the near future, most personal digital assistant (PDA) and cellular phones will be Internet-enabled. In the coming 21 century, it will be trivial to read news from portable devices while travelling to work! It is predictable that demand for news will no longer be only once or twice a day but immediate – the minute after the event occurred. This paper describes a "true" push model to deliver news using the Common Object Request Broker Architecture (CORBA). Our model supports instant and dynamic news delivery. A generalised design pattern of our model is also presented that is applicable to other applications that also require this form of real-time information delivery.

1 Introduction

The use of Internet has increased dramatically in the past few years. With the rapid growth of technology, most of the PDAs and cellular phones will be able to connect to Internet. Using PDAs and cellular phones to retrieve *fresh* news for decision making in business and investment will be trivial in the near future. However current technologies for news delivery, such as via e-mail, surfing newspaper Web-sites or client polling servers for news (e.g. Web browser channels, PointCast and EntryPoint), are not so suitable for rapid changing information (e.g. stock market information). Those method are too slow and too late (e-mail and manual surfing) or demand a lot of client and network resources (information channels). The user will also need to manually filter out irrelevant information. We therefore propose a model for news delivery that is based on "true" push. Information is sent directly to clients only when there is updates. Clients can subscribe (or connect, more technically) to fine-grained news channels (event channels) that offers precise types of information services. These channels are different from current browser channels as they actually push data to clients. Furthermore, the model is highly scalable as it can make use of IP multicast capabilities in the Internet.

CORBA [5] is an open architecture that allows objects written in different program languages[1] to be shared across different platforms and networks on the Internet. Furthermore, the CORBA Event/Notification Services [4] provide a standard interface to perform publish-and-subscribe mode of push. Some CORBA vendors have extended their CORBA services to work on top of IP Multicast for scalability [3, 8]. To take advantage of these features, CORBA is the core infrastructure of our design.

The next Section summaries the basics of CORBA in a nutshell. This is followed by the system architecture and the design of our push model for news delivery. The paper closes with a generalised design pattern for push-based information delivery.

2 Background

This section introduces some basic CORBA terminology that will be used in this paper. CORBA is an object-oriented architecture for distributed computing that allows objects written in different languages and running on different platforms over a LAN or Internet to communicate and share data and services. Distributed objects communicate via the CORBA Object Request Broker (ORB) [5] bus. Distributed objects are identified by their Interoperable Object Reference (IOR) [5]. Server objects (servants) are accessible by other objects through a program language-independent interface – the CORBA Interface Definition Language (IDL) [5]. An IDL pre-compiler creates skeleton and stub code for server and client respectively according to the CORBA standard language mapping. After server instantiated an object adapter, clients can access servants through the ORB and object adapter. CORBA also defines a set of Common Object Services (COS) [4] that provide infrastructure supporting services, such as security, naming, transactions, etc. Currently 15 services have been identified. The model presented in this paper makes use of the CORBA Naming and Event services.

3 System Architecture

The core of our Push-based News Delivery System (PNDS) uses the CORBA Event Service. There are three main roles in CORBA Event Service [4]– supplier, consumer and event channel. Event channel is the middleman between supplier and consumer. Depending on whether a push or pull model is used, the supplier can be client (push) or servant (pull), the consumer can also be client (pull) or servant (push), and the event channel is both client and servant. In the following, we will describe the flow of the push model.

There are seven OMG-specified IDLs in the CORBA Event Service to support push: *EventChannel, PushSupplier, ProxyPushSupplier, PushConsumer, ProxyPushConsumer, SupplierAdmin* and *ConsumerAdmin*. The *PushSupplier* gets a *SupplierAdmin* by via *EventChannel*. *ProxyPushConsumer* represents a subscribed

---

[1] Object Management Group (OMG) [2] defines different language mapping for CORBA, include C, C++, Java, COBOL, ADA and SmallTalk

PushConsumer and can be obtained from the *SupplierAdmin*. After *PushSupplier* connected to *ProxyPushConsumer*, the supply-side registration procedure is complete. On the consumer side, *PushConsumer* obtains a *ConsumerAdmin* via *EventChannel*. After that, the *ProxyPushSupplier,* which represents suppliers can be obtained from the *ConsumerAdmin*. *PushConsumer* connects to *ProxyPushSupplier* and the consume-side registration completes. After initialisation, *PushSupplier* can now push information implicitly to all *PushConsumers* via *ProxyPushConsumer,* without needing to know all *PushConsumers* locations, i.e., communication is decoupled.

Our PNDS consists of News Client, System Administrator Client, Reporter/Editor Client and News Server objects. News Client is built using JDK 1.1.6 [7] with HotJava HTML Component [7]. Besides basic Web browsing capabilities, it is also retrieves a list of channels from the News Server, subscribes to desire channels and receives news updates through subscribed event channels. Reporter/Editor Client is a news supplier responsible for notifying subscribed News Clients of fresh news. System Administrator Client is responsible for channel management such as creating and removing event channels. Servant objects reside on News Server can be located using Naming Service. In our implementation of PNDS, we used the ORBacus [6] ORB with COS support.

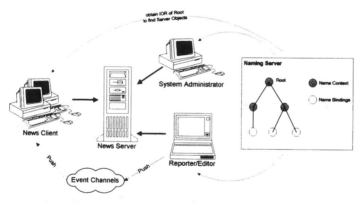

Fig. 1. PNDS System Architecture

After starting the News Server, the System Administrator Client adds channels to the server. News clients can then connect to the News Server and subscribe to desired news channels. Editors can publish articles and notify news clients immediately through the Reporter/Editor Client on their PCs. For urgent news, reporters can post articles to Web Servers directly and can instantly notify all news clients via the Reporter/Editor Client on their Internet-enabled laptop or PDA. Compared with traditional news delivery on Internet, push-based news delivery is instantaneous.

4 Design of PNDS

This Section describes how we make use of the push model in PNDS. Since the design and implementation of PNDS is totally object-oriented, the OMG-standard Unified Modelling Language (UML) [1] notations will be used to describe our design.

In PNDS, there are two types of supplier and consumer pairs. *SystemConsumer* and *ChannelSupplier* are responsible for broadcasting messages to all clients; messages can be announcing new news channels for example. *NewsConsumer* and *NewsSupplier* are used to broadcast news events. News Client contains a *ChannelManager* responsible for subscribing to desired channels. *ChannelManger* may contain several *NewsConsumer*, depending on the number of channels subscribed. Besides news channels, the channel manager also contains a *SystemConsumer* to receive system broadcast messages. When the News Client starts, it connects to a *NewsServer* servant using Naming Service and obtains the current list of channels. The client *ChannelManager* then selects desired event channels (defined as IOR) to connect to. When *NewsConsumer* or *SystemConsumer* receives messages from the supplier, the client user interface takes action and displays the message or loads the appropriate Web page.

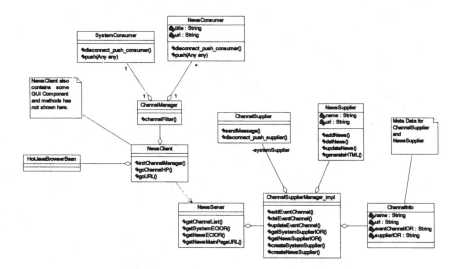

Fig. 2. UML Class diagram of News Client and Server

On the server side, besides the *NewsServer* servant, there are Channel Supplier Manager, Channel Supplier and News Supplier Servant responsible for channel management, publishing system messages and publishing news, respectively. System Administrator Client (SA Client) can connect to channel supplier manager via Naming Service and obtain list of suppliers (IORs) through channel supplier manager. Therefore the SA Client can create, delete and update event channels and also send message to news clients. Information related to channels created by SA Client is stored in *ChannelInfo*. Reporter/Editor Client can notify News Clients by first obtaining *NewsServer* and *channel supplier manager* servants from Naming Service, it then gets a list of news channels from the NewsServer for reporters to select which channel to publish news to. After uploading HTML files to the Web Server and specifying the added title and links, news channel main Web page will be generated (with the added links). Then the appropriate supplier object reference of the required channel is obtained. The *addNews* method in *NewsSupplier* will be invoked and push a string to client for fresh news and cause clients to update their screens.

5 Generalise Design Pattern for Push Model

Our model can also be used in other applications such as stock market prices delivery, software component update, meeting scheduler, etc. In this Section, we present a generalised design pattern of our model for reuse in other applications.

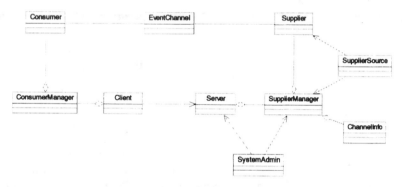

Fig. 3. Generalised architecture for most push-based applications

Consumer is an object that implements the *PushConsumer* IDL defined by the Event Service. It receives messages from Supplier through EventChannel. In PNDS, message is stored as a CORBA Any object. "Any" is an IDL type to represent any CORBA objects. If necessary, Supplier can pass any suitable object type to Consumer. Consumer is also responsible for extracting information from server and taking action. **ConsumerManager** contains a set of consumers; the responsibility of consumer manager is channel filtering.

Client connects to Server and obtains a list of available channels. After Consumer Manager selects appropriate channels, IORs of channels are obtained from Server for Consumer to connect to. It is also responsible for retrieving initial information for consumers. (If pull model is also implemented, consumer can obtain initial information from supplier directly by calling *ProxyPullSupplier*'s pull method during initialisation.)

Server provides information to clients, such as channel list, event channel objects or object references, and initial information for consumers.

SupplierManager is responsible for creating, deleting and updating event channels and suppliers. **ChannelInfo** is created when event channels are created and is implicitly associated with that channel and supplier by storing their object references. Clients can obtain those object references through *SupplierManager*.

Supplier is an implementation of the *PushSupplier* interface defined by the Event Service. It receives requests from *SupplierSource* clients and pushes messages to consumers through event channels.

SystemAdmin is a client that calls *SupplierManager* to create, delete or update channels and suppliers. In some cases, it may obtain a list of channels from server to perform conflict checking such as to avoid creating an existing channels or deleting non-existing channels.

SupplierSource obtains Supplier from *SupplierManager* and sends messages to interested clients through that Supplier.

For example, in a stock information system, clients can be the graphic user interface to plot stock price graphs. After client obtains a list of available stock information, consumer manager may select the stocks that the client is only interested in and create a consumer to received stock prices from the event channel. On server side, server provides stock list and event channel object references to clients. Supplier manager creates stock event channels and suppliers according to a stock database using *SystemAdmin*. When stock information has been updated, *SupplierSource* is responsible for pushing the new information (the latest stock price) to supplier and supplier pushes the price information to consumer on client side at once.

6   Conclusion

In this paper, we described the object-oriented design and architecture of our CORBA-compliant PNDS. A prototype of our system has been successfully implemented. As the need for up-to-the-second information becomes more and more critical, we predict more information sources will be using a similar push-based model of deliver. This paper also provided a generalised design pattern that other developers can use to develop their own push-based application.

References

1. Grady Booch, James Rumbaugh, Ivar Jacobson: The Unified Modeling Language User Guide. Addison Wesley (1999)
2. Object-Management Group: The OMG Home Page- http://www.omg.org
3. Object-Oriented Concept: The OOC Home Page- http://www.ooc.com
4. OMG document: CORBAservices: Common Object Services Specification (98-07-05)
5. OMG document: The Common Object Request Broker: Architecture and Specification, Revision 2.2 (98-07-01)
6. OOC: ORBacus For C++ and Java (User Guide)
7. Sun Microsystems: Sun Microsystems Java Technology Home Page- http://www.javasoft.com
8. TAO CORBA ORB: http://www.cs.wustl.edu/~schmidt/TAO.html

Mutual Synergy between Web Caches

Ahmed Mokhtar[1], Gerardo Rubino[2]

[1] Cnet Rennes, 4 Rue Clos Courtel, 35512 Cesson Sevigne, France
ahmed.mokhtar@cnet.francetelecom.fr
[2] IRISA, Campus de Beaulieu, 35042 Rennes Cedex; France
rubino@irisa.fr

Abstract. This paper, which consists of two parts, studies different kinds of what we call 'synergy between caches'. The first part defines the synergy term in our context. Then, we propose to define three different kinds of synergy: local synergy, global synergy and mutual synergy. Local synergy concerns the cooperation between caches in the local domain. Global synergy results from the cooperation between a local cache and non local caches. Mutual synergy concerns the relation between local and global synergy. This study explains how cooperative caching may result in mutual synergy. The paper introduces an example of a complete and simple architectural solution to obtain mutual synergy. Such a solution increases the Quality of Service (QoS) with no major modification to the network configurations. The second part of the paper introduces the specifications of the Mutual Synergy Machine (MSM). The mutual synergy machine is a virtual machine implementing a "universal translator" between Web caches. The paper shows the rule of MSM in enhancing the performance of cooperative caches.

1 Introduction

Caching is an old technique used by many different applications, both software and hardware. Now, it is also used in the World Wide Web as a method to increase QoS and, in particular, to decrease latency. At first, caching was deployed in a simple fashion. We mean by this that only single caches were used (with no cooperation at all with other caching systems). The performance of a single cache depends on the storage media size, the platform (hardware and software), the replacement policy and the management policy. As far as single caching is concerned, the more the capacity of the hard disk, the better the performance. The replacement policy varies depending on the characteristics of data requested by the users. The most commonly used replacement policies are: First In First Out (FIFO), Last In First Out (LIFO) and Least Recently Used (LRU). The management policies are concerned with data types and domains. After recognizing the importance of caches, the idea of having cooperation between them appeared. Cooperative cache performances depend on the factors we mentioned for single caches but in different manners. Besides, the performance is affected by new factors as, for example, the protocol in use and the architecture of the whole system. We propose to use the term *cache synergy* to refer to the power that the cache gains from the cooperation with other caches. Such power is non controllable but observable. To deal with an operational concept, we differentiate three categories of synergy, which we call *local synergy*, *global synergy* and *mutual synergy*. As we will see, there are examples of the first two categories in the Web, while the third one is a new scheme proposed here. Local synergy is only obtained by first level caching. Global synergy can be reached by both first and higher level caching. Mutual synergy merges the two levels of synergy to improve the total quality of service. We can identify another kind of synergy which is *destructive* (we call this one *reversed synergy*), referring to the fact that latency increases and global quality of service degrades. This results, in general, from bad configurations or misplacing components in the caching hierarchy.

2 Local Synergy

Theoretically, if two local single caches cooperate based on a preparatory protocol, synergy appears, either constructive or destructive. Destructive synergy means that the cooperation between caches results in a lack of performance and decreases the quality of service. Constructive synergy usually appears when proper protocols are used, like Cache Array Routing Protocol (CARP) and Web Cache Control Protocol (WCCP). CARP is a Microsoft invention while WCCP is a CISCO one. Local synergy may also be obtained by users' clustering and redirection between caches. The following points show the general scheme for local synergy. The synergy is said to be local if the following conditions are satisfied:

1. The generating caches are managed locally.
2. No data redundancy occur between the generating caches.
3. The universe of addresses is divided between the caches.
4. A fault tolerance technique must exist between the caches.

The following section explains the CARP mechanism as an example of caches that provides local synergy.

2.1 Local Synergy In Carp

Cache Array Routing Protocol (CARP) is appropriate for a group of proxy servers that serve the same audience of downstream clients or proxies. The idea behind CARP is to provide load balancing, reliability, and to eliminate redundant data from the caches. To achieve such objectives, there should be a CARP manager in each member of the array. Such a manager performs two major functions. Firstly, it applies a hashing function to each requested URL and maps it onto the right cache array member. Secondly, it maintains the array membership table [2]. The cache array member receives the HTTP request and resolves the URL. Applying the hashing function, the cache member identifies the proper cache member for the request. When the proper cache member receives the request, it searches for the requested object locally. If it does not exist, the proper array member forwards the HTTP request to the origin server, retrieves the data, reserves a copy for itself and sends the response back to the user. The performance of CARP within large organizations depends mainly on the infrastructure of the organization. The link data rate between the different sites where the members are located is a key factor in utilizing such a protocol. Figure 1 shows the data flow process in CARP.

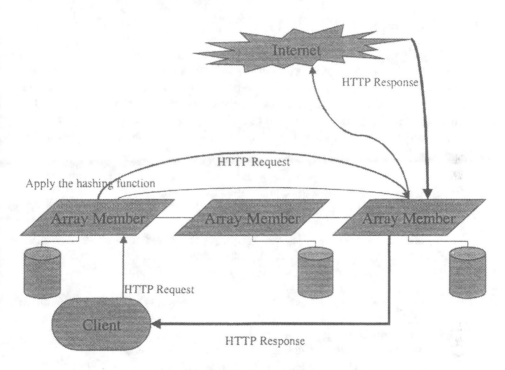

Fig. 1. CARP data flow

Here, the user fires an HTTP request that will be directed to the array member that is coupled to his site (nearest array member). The array member applies the hash function and directs the request to the proper caching array member that supposed to have the object requested in the URL. If the proper caching array member has the object, it will forward it directly to the user over an HTTP connection. If not, the proper caching member will fire a new HTTP request to the origin server (We assume any HTTP request that is fired to the Web is to the origin server). The answer from the origin server is then forwarded to the user with a copy reserved in the proper caching array member. Using CARP in such a case will provide load balancing and eliminate data redundancy. On the other hand, if the object does not exist locally, it will forward the HTTP request to the origin server, which may thus result in performance degradation.

3 Global Synergy

The synergy is said to be global if the caches producing such synergy are not managed locally. The best example for producing global synergy is ICP. The following section explains the ICP process.

3.1 Global Synergy In ICP

The idea behind the use of such a protocol is to locate the data (object) requested by a client within a group of proxy caches that have a cooperative relation with the local one. The term local cache refers to the proxy cache that receives the first HTTP request from the client. The sequence of the data retrieval process is as follows: The client fires an HTTP request to the local cache. This local cache will answer with the requested data object if it has it and if it is still valid to use. If not, the local cache will fire the ICP request after ensuring the following conditions:

1. The HTTP request is not targeting a local server (a local server is any nearby server). The local server should be predefined for the cache.
2. The request method used is the GET method and not any other ones like POST, PUT, ...
3. There are no restrictions for that request according to the cache server configuration. As an example, the requested data should have no match in the 'hierarchy_stoplist' configured by the proxy administrator [1].

When the proxy fires such an ICP request, it expects the answer within a predefined delay. If the answer is delayed more than the predefined delay, the request will be forwarded directly to the origin server. The hierarchy of the caching mesh using ICP deploys parents and siblings. The major difference between parents and siblings appears in handling the requests. While parents can reply with either hits or misses, siblings will only reply if they get a cache hit. The parent can forward the requests if they do not match any of its cached objects while the sibling cannot. The parent can be shown as an upper level caching, while the sibling is at the same level. Figure 2 shows the data flow between siblings, parents and a local cache. It is normal to have many siblings. Care should be taken when configuring more than one parent to avoid infinite loops. The local caches may act as siblings to other caches. Regional caches are parents of many local caches and may be siblings of other regional caches. The national caches are parents of regional caches, and as they are the third level caches, they should not have parents, but they may have siblings. The disadvantages of ICP are data redundancy and the lack of management of groups of caches which may be located in different places under different operating systems and different policies of control. That is, the ICP requests are directed to some caches with non-controlled performance and configuration. Experts may be able to avoid many of the disadvantages if the right configuration decisions are made. Data redundancy with siblings is very hard to avoid. The normal scenario is the following. The user sends the HTTP request to the caching proxy coupled to his site. The caching proxy then searches for the requested object in the local cache after applying the verification process to the request. If the object does not exist, it will fire an ICP request to its siblings and parent. When it receives an answer, it will forward it to the user while reserving a copy for itself. We should mention here that the process will not be that straightforward, as the configuration of the proxy can play a major role. A bad configuration may result in major problems in both performance and operation. In this case, the use of ICP will introduce some data redundancy as well as internal ICP traffic into the level of the organization. Obviously, this may not be needed. On the other hand, if the object does not exist inside the organization, it may be found nearby inside the region without the need for further connection to the origin server. The average performance enhancement by using ICP is usually about 30%. The performance measurement in both cases is based on bandwidth consumption and the Quality of Service (mainly latency). We assume that the percentage of requests served by the caches (cache hits) represents increased performance.

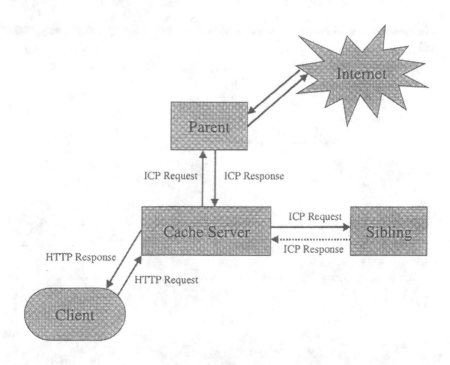

Fig. 2. ICP Data Flow

4 Mutual Synergy

As mentioned beforehand, mutual synergy results from the interaction between both global and local synergy. Such an interaction might be either constructive or destructive. The following section explains the constructive synergy results from CARP as a local synergy producer and ICP as a global synergy producer.

4.1 ICP Over CARP

The change of the cache mesh for using ICP over CARP will provide the major advantage of keeping the load balancing performance offered by CARP while benefiting from the advantage of ICP in locating non existing objects in the neighborhood caches for some other organizations without the need to access the origin server. Here, if the object does not exist, all the requests will be directed to the top level proxy that uses ICP, as shown in figure 3. The top level proxy will act this time as a transparent engine that generates ICP requests to find objects in the neighborhood. When it finds the object, it will return it to the proper array member without reserving a copy for itself. As shown, there is no need for disk space because the proxy that runs ICP will not save any object for itself. Besides, it will not need verification for the objects or the method as these factors will have been handled within the first level cache, performed by CARP. When we tested this approach it resulted in a 30% increase in performance compared to the use of CARP only [3]. The use of such an approach does not need any modification in either protocols, and saves disk space and bandwidth with an increase in the QoS.

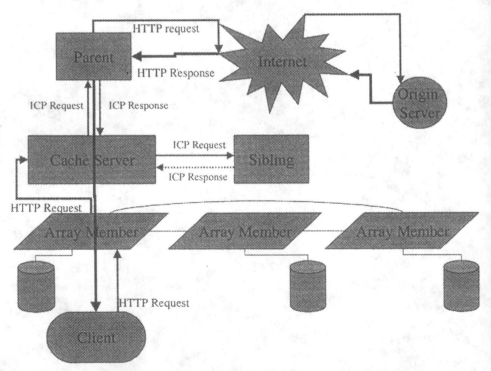

Fig. 3. ICP over CARP

To apply such an approach we need to configure the local caching array members to be connected through another proxy. In this proxy, ICP is deployed. As the requests generated (or forwarded) by the caching array members are HTTP requests, the upper level proxy will handle them normally. Moreover, the second level ICP proxy can be configured to skip all the verification processes concerning the method and local access. All the changes in this approach are contained in the configuration without any need for core modifications.

One of the applications of this approach that may be of interest would be to build a specific machine for the purpose of firing ICP requests and handling the responses. Such a machine would need no disk space for caching data objects (eliminating redundancy) and would skip the request verifications mentioned in section 3.1, as those verifications would have already been made in the first level caching (CARP level). This proposal is developed in the next section.

4.2 MSM

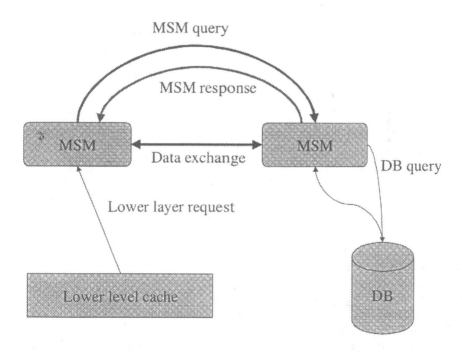

Fig. 4. MSM Data Flow

The Idea behind the MSM is to have a machine dedicated to mutual synergy more than caching. As we showed in the previous section, by using ICP over CARP, we can eliminate many processes. Moreover, we may not cache any data in the second level caching (ICP). In this case, we may replace the ICP machine in the second level caching by the MSM that will function as a simplified ICP protocol. An MSM could be storage free. The OS might be loaded over the network and the caching protocol embedded in the OS. MSM runs SCPMS which stands for Simplified Caching Protocol for Mutual Synergy. The MSM receives the HTTP request from the lower layer caching and resolves it to get the Requested URL, then fires a light weight request to the other machines. When an MSM receives a query for a specific URL, it accesses the lower layer caches' database and check the availability of the requested object. If available, the MSM will answer with a marked response which indicates the availability and the exact place to find the data. When an MSM receives a further request, it checks the signature. If it matches one of the predefined signatures for it, the request will be directly forwarded to the right place to find the requested object. Figure 4 illustrates the operation between two MSM machines. The MSM query is a very simple one just asking for a specific URL. If the requested data is not found, no answer will be sent. If further request is sent, it will be automatically ignored.

5 Conclusions

We introduced new terms in the context of Web caching, namely the synergy concept, and its variations called local, global and mutual. The goal is to help us to present a new proposal to implement cooperation techniques at different levels of a global caching system. More generally, we think that this terminology can help in understanding the behavior of this part of the Web architecture, in order to make better designs and thus, to get better QoS.

The paper showed that we can benefit from integrating both local and global synergy. To achieve this objective, we introduced the concept of Mutual Synergy Machine (MSM). Our study proposes a simple scenario for interacting between two mutual synergy machines. The MSM has two major advantages: first, it simplifies the cooperation between caches and, second, it allows us to benefit from the advantages of different types of caching at the same time.

References

[1] Claffy K. and Wessels D., "Internet Caching Protocol (ICP), version2". IETF RFC2186, 1997.
[2] Valloppillil V. and Rossj K.W., "Cache Array Routing Protocol v1.0", IETF Drafts.
[3] Mokhtar A. and Moufah H, "Cooperative Caching Based on ICP and CARP Interaction". SCSC'99 Proceedings, p. 141, 1999.

Architecture of Object Web

Gary Yat Chung WONG and Andy Hon Wai CHUN

City University of Hong Kong
Department of Electronic Engineering
Tat Chee Avenue
Kowloon, Hong Kong
e-mail: ycwong@ee.cityu.edu.hk, eehwchun@cityu.edu.hk

Abstract. It is quite remarkable how widespread and popular the Internet is nowadays. The use of Web browsers is no longer restricted to only the scientific and academic communities. With increased popularity, users also demand more interactive and timely form of Web browsing. Information sources on Internet are no longer static and isolated; instead information has become distributed and dynamic. A typical example is stock market information. Tokyo, Hong Kong, and Singapore stock markets are located in different places and the prices are quite dynamic. It would be nice if the user can view "live" consolidated data from multiple sources at the same time on the same browser screen. However for backward compatible reason, current browser technologies built on top of existing protocols and infrastructures cannot satisfy these needs. On the other hand, the Common Object Request Broker Architecture (CORBA) and its Object Web vision enables this type of real-time distributed browsing. In this paper, we present a new type of browser, which we call the Object Web Browser that browses not only HTML pages but also objects in the Intergalactic Object Web.

1 Introduction

As Internet becomes more popular, users become more sophisticated and demanding. They want their Web browsing experiences to be more interactive and dynamic, and the content up-to-the-second. The nature of information on the Web has also become more distributed. Technologies such as CGI, Servlet, NSAPI, ISAPI, ASP, JSP, etc. were invented to compensate for deficiencies of the current HTTP mode of Web browsing – slow interaction, "faked" client-server, and not suited for a distributed environment. Unfortunately, these new technologies are basically "patches" and cannot go too far. It is evident that the next big wave of Web browsing technologies will be built on top of IIOP and the Object Web. The term "Object Web" (OW) describes the vision that millions to billions of CORBA compliant objects that live on machines on the Internet can freely communicate with each other to share data and services. This paper proposes extensions to current Web browsers to capitalize on the potential advantages offered by the Object Web architecture. Before going into details of our proposal, let us look at an example scenario of how future Web browsing might be like:

An investor wants to check stock information in several active markets. He starts up an "Object Web Browser" and types in the "object names" of stock objects to display (see Section 3). An Object Web Browser (OWB) is a term we will use in this paper to describe a browser that is IIOP-enabled and knows how to communicate with CORBA-compliant objects using a standardized IDL interface – the OWB API. After entering the object names, the OWB automatically locates the machines these objects live in. A login window pops up for authorization and the user information is sent to the server or servers that the objects live in through a secure protocol. After verification, the user is registered with those stock objects and a spreadsheet of stock information is displayed. Each spreadsheet cell is connected to a distributed object located somewhere within the Object Web. Information displayed on a single OWB screen may come from different machines on the Internet and can be updated dynamically with CORBA Event/Notification Services. Up-to-the-second updates can be "pushed" onto the screen without the need for the user to refresh or reload. In addition, the user can redirect the spreadsheet data to a graph-plotting object also located on the Object Web to produce a graph of stock prices over a specified period. After the user logs out, service charges for the use of the intergalactic objects may be billed to the user, which he/she can, of course, pay with e-cash.

The above example illustrates how future Web browsing on the Object Web can show dynamic changing data potentially from many machines distributed over the Internet all on the same page. For simple static text, HTTP may be good enough, but for critical business needs, Object Web-based browsing seems to be the only solution.

However, for the above scenario to work, several extensions to the current Web infrastructure are needed. For instances, data should no longer be stored in HTML pages but in CORBA objects, which we will call Document Objects. Document Objects are any CORBA-compliant objects that implement the OWB Interface. These Document Objects will have CORBA Properties to facilitate precise query and search (see Section 5) using CORBA Trading Service, instead of current manual trial-and-error. Properties can be defined by the Document Object owner/author or generated dynamically using Artificial Intelligence (AI) techniques such as frame-like demon [4]. Properties can also be used to filter objects for access control.

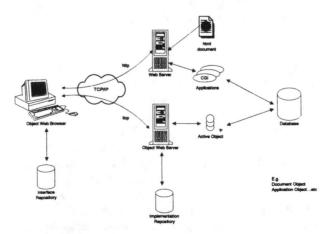

Fig. 1. Architecture of the proposed Object Web Browser

2 Architecture of the Object Web Browser

CORBA is a very suitable core framework for the Object Web because of its open architecture, high interoperability, the availability of Common Object Services (COS) [2], and the Object Management Architecture (OMA) [3], which provides the backdrop for Intergalactic object interaction.

For Object Web browsing, we propose two types of Document Objects – static and dynamic. Static Document Objects (SDO) contains static information typical of current HTML pages. The content of a SDO is obtainable through the OWB API. It also contains a list of CORBA Properties to describe its content. An OW Browser can obtain the SDO content through the OWB API and display on browser screen with appropriate layout. Dynamic Document Object (DDO) contains dynamically changing data and can be implemented as Shippable Places Compound Documents [6] or JavaBeans components on the client-side. As DDO communicates with client objects directly via IIOP, this mechanism is more interactive than existing technologies and is truly client-server. We call Web servers that supports our Object Web browsing – Object Web Servers (OWS). OWS is a servant defined with IDL and registered to our Extended Naming Context (see Section 3). OWS activates objects via information in the Implementation Repository and returns object information such as IOR, etc.

3 Extended Naming Service

The Object Web may contain millions to billions of objects; locating them can be a difficult task if not impossible. The CORBA Naming Service [2] is typically used to locate objects. It is a tree structure of naming contexts and name bindings. Searching a directory of all the objects in the Object Web is of course impossible. Using federated Naming Services can solve some of these problems by distributing the load across many machines. To be even more efficient, we are proposing an Extended Naming Service, which is similar DNS [5]. The Extended Naming Service uses a URL-like structure:

```
iiop://objectweb.cityu.edu.hk/pathname/objectname

iiop                      - Internet Inter-ORB Protocol
objectweb.cityu.edu.hk - compound name in CORBA Naming Service
pathname/objectname:      - object location w.r.t. web server
```

For compatibility, our new Extended Naming Service IDL inherits from current Naming Service IDL. There may be many naming servers; any node in the naming tree structure can be a naming server.

Searching the extended tree can be in both directions. Both searches execute in a recursive way until object is found or timeout. To increase the search speed, each naming server can cache compound name-IOR pairs. When a naming server is required to search, it starts a thread to search IOR cache and another thread to perform two-way search. If required IOR is in the cache, a "stop" request will propagate along the search tree to halt the search. If the cached IOR becomes invalid, client can force naming server to search without using cache.

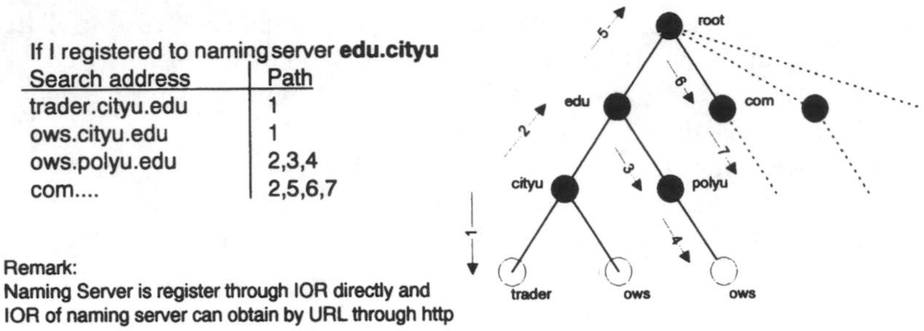

If I registered to naming server **edu.cityu**

Search address	Path
trader.cityu.edu	1
ows.cityu.edu	1
ows.polyu.edu	2,3,4
com....	2,5,6,7

Remark:
Naming Server is register through IOR directly and
IOR of naming server can obtain by URL through http

Fig. 2. Architecture of Extended Naming Service

4 Object Web Proxy Server

It is clear that network bandwidth needed to support Object Web-styled computing is much higher than current Internet. Therefore, we propose the concept of an "Object Web Proxy Server" (OWPS) to reduce traffic in ways similar to a Web Proxy Server. Traffic in Object Web browsing is different from current Web browsing. Current traffics are mainly request and return of text and binary such as pictures via HTTP. In Object Web, traffics are mainly marshaled parameters and return data during object communication via IIOP. Our proposed Static Document Objects will probably generate more data traffic with page contents than Dynamic Document Objects, which send mainly dynamic data. However, since the SDO do not change with time or change infrequently, they can be cached. DDO are dynamic and may contain application objects and have connections to persistent data sources, they are not suitable for caching. Therefore, our proposed OWPS will cache only SDO.

The OWPS will be CORBA-compliant with its own IDL. Within OMA, OWPS can defined as a set of CORBA Application Objects [3], which provide CORBA objects (more specifically, SDO) caching. The following is a sketch of the Object Web Proxy Server IDL.

ProxyStore contains *findProxyBinding* and *findProxyBindings* methods to locate a *ProxyBinding* or bindings (return *ProxyIterator*) respectively from given URL-like locator (Section 3). The later method retrieves objects in the same directory, which might be related.

ProxyBinding stores location-object pair. Objects can be stored using either CORBA Persistent Object Services or CORBA Externalization Service [2]. The *getType* method indicates the storage type and *getDate*, *setDate*, *getRef* and *increaseRef* methods are used for replacement policy. *ProxyIterator* provides access to a set of proxy bindings.

ProxyFactory is an interface to create proxy binding and *ProxyAdmin* provides method to access and modify the proxy size also replacement policy.

Our OWPS operates similarly to a regular Web Proxy Server. Location and persistent/externalized object pairs are cached when clients contact objects the first time through the OWPS. When cache is full, objects are deleted according to replacement policies such as Least Recent Used (LRU) or Least Frequent Used (LFU). When an object is requested, *ProxyStore* returns *ProxyBinding* or *ProxyBindingIterator* if object found in the cache, else a binding not found exception is thrown and object will be obtained from the Internet via Object-by-Value. When binding is referenced, *setDate* and *increaseRef* methods are invoked to support the replacement policies. If needed, CORBA Event Services can be used to notify OWPS when objects become invalid or have changed.

5   Searching the Object Web

Searching for objects in the Intergalactic Object Web is not easy. One approach is to use the CORBA Trader Service that allows clients to locate objects based on a set of user-specified properties. Web brokers is definitely the future trend. Instead, of manually searching of information a broker helps search and consolidate information. CORBA Trader Service is one way to implement a broker. HP is providing e-service software that is also similar.

Properties may be static or dynamic. Static properties are fixed while dynamic properties are those that may be added or deleted from time to time. Trader Service *DynamicPropEval* interface can dynamically discover properties on-the-fly. Servers register with a trader using its object reference, service type and properties of service. Clients can then obtain a list of matching servers using specified policies, constraints and preferences through the Trader *Lookup* interface.

The magic that allows the trader to search within the large Intergalactic Web space is the fact that a trader can be linked to many other traders via a federation. Although clients might be connected to only one trader, clients are actually searching across many traders.

Current Web searches are done using keyword matching. Trader Service uses properties associate with Document Objects to make the search more precise and accurate. To further enhance the search, intelligent mobile agents [1] may be used to categorise document by means of AI techniques such as Frames [4], Semantic Networks, Pattern Matching, etc. Mobile agents may search through many trader servers to find more and accurate results overnight and notify user when they turn on the machine the next day! To be able to search intelligently and precisely will be one of the major achievements in future Object Web-based browsing.

6   Transition to Object Web

We cannot transition to a new Object Web-style browsing overnight. A lot of research and development work lies ahead. On the client side, OW Browsers need to be developed that are backward compatibility and also HTML documents. The development of OW Browser should go in parallel with the development of Object Web Server technologies. Static Document Objects is probably a good place to start and will mimic current HTML-style of browsing. To read static document, the OW

Browser should able to download SDO IDL and access to server objects through client stub [3] generated by IDL. To search through the intergalactic space, better forms of naming service is needed, like the Extended Naming Service described in Section 3. The Object Web Server will need to be registered with the new extended naming service. At the same time, there is still a lot of work to be done in federated Trader Service (Section 5) to make search more efficient. To allow mobile agents to travel and search through Object Web, Object Web Servers must provide mobile agents services with adequate access rights [1]. Research on Object Web Proxy Server and Dynamic Document Objects with other COS such as licensing, translation, security, etc. can starts after Static Document Object browsing technology matures and stables.

7 Conclusion and Future Works

As the need for distributed and dynamic real-time information increases, current form of Internet Web browsing via HTTP is not sufficient. This paper describes a CORBA-based architecture to be built on top of the Object Web that can provide highly interactive Web browsing of highly distributed and dynamic information sources in an efficient manner – we call this Object Web Browsing. Besides describing the architecture of the Object Web Browser, a simple extended Naming Service for intergalactic naming is proposed. In order to reduce traffic in the Object Web, a design of an Object Web Proxy Server was described. We propose to encapsulate information sources as Document Objects instead of flat HTML files, which allows efficient and precise search to be performed. Search will make use of the CORBA Trader Service and CORBA-compliant mobile agents. We further described research and development steps to take to achieve our vision. The Object Web architecture is a clear direction that the Internet community will be heading. However, we desperately need open standards to be defined quickly.

References

1. Danny B. Lange and Mitsuru Oshima: Programming and Deploying Java Mobile Agents with Aglets. Addison Wesley (1998)
2. OMG document: CORBAservices: Common Object Services Specification (98-07-05)
3. OMG document: The Common Object Request Broker: Architecture and Specification, Revision 2.2 (98-07-01)
4. Patrick Henry Winston: Artificial Intelligence Third Edition. Addison Wesley (1992) pp.209-230
5. Pau Albitz and Cricket Liu: DNS and BIND. O'REILLY (1998)
6. Robert Orfali, Dan Harkey, Jeri Edwards: Instant CORBA. Addison Wesley (1997)

JWeb: An Innovative Architecture for Web Applications

Mario Bochicchio [1], Roberto Paiano[1], Paolo Paolini[2]

[1]Telemedia Lab, University of Lecce, Italy
{bomal,rpaiano}@ingle01.unile.it
[2]Hypermedia Open Center, Politecnico di Milano, Italy
paolo.paolini@elet.polimi.it

Abstract. The recent diffusion of WWW technology and the widespread need of producing high quality WWW applications in a cost-effective manner have made important to improve the quality and the efficiency of the engineering process for WWW sites. In this paper we argue that the first ingredient needed for a well-organized process is a design model, able to describe the structural and navigational properties of WWW applications. The second ingredient is a suitable set of tools supporting the design and the development of the applications. Assuming HDM as design model, we present JWeb, a suite of tools supporting several activities: initial conceptual design, development of supporting database to store data, insertion of data, customization of design for specific applications, prototyping of applications etc.

1 Introduction and background

Web applications were, at the very beginning, hand-coded HTML pages: the information handled by each page was structured "ad-hoc" and the links among pages were set "manually". This production method was acceptable until a few pages had to be produced, but it became rapidly unmanageable when applications of several hundreds or thousands of pages had to be linked and maintained.

In a good WWW application, in fact, the reader should be able to effectively exploits the potential information managed by the application: i.e. he/she should be able to quickly locate the objects of his/her interest, to understand the inner structure of the objects, to easily move (navigate) from one object to another, to easily accomplish complex access sessions. Summarizing: a good application should be usable [1-3].

Several factors concur to the achievement of this goal, and one of the most important factors is to have a good structuring of the information objects and a good structuring of the navigation patterns. Several authors and several communities have recently proposed the adoption of design models [4-8], and design patterns [9-12] in order to improve the quality and usability of hypermedia applications, at least for those aspects concerning structure and navigation. Design models provide, in fact, the primitives that allow to structure the information objects and the corresponding navigation patterns along regular and systematic features, improving consistency, predictability (for the user), robustness of the design, and therefore improving usability.

The ancestor of these models can be traced to the Hypermedia Design Model (HDM), developed in 1993 [13] and evolved to its actual definition through various theoretical refinements [5,10,14] and through the application to many real projects (e.g. [15-17]). While HDM was evolved, it was clear that a number of modeling and implementation activities (e.g. schema design, content production, application prototyping, dynamic pagination etc.) could be automated and supported by software.

JWeb is a set of tools based on HDM and exploiting that idea [18]. In particular, JWeb supports the design and the implementation of multiple hypermedia applications, both on-line (Inter/extra/intranets) and off-line (CD, DVD, ...), from a dynamic set of contents, for a given application field.

The overall architecture of JWeb is the subject of the remaining of this paper: in section 2 we point out the general problems concerning design and implementation support; in section 3 we describe the architecture and the components of JWeb; in section 4 we draw the conclusions and describe future work.

2 General Problems

In our experience, the main problems concerning the design and the implementation of WWW applications, independently from a specific development strategy, can be summarized in the following four points:

1. Modeling

   Design involves the definition of the general properties of the application and of its details considering several "dimensions": information structures, navigation patterns, interaction and multimedia control, interface, etc. Several models have been proposed to describe information structures and navigation [4-8]. Various ISO standards are also available to describe and implements multimedia control and interaction (e.g. HyTime, PREMO, MHEG, ...). Finally, the design of the man-machine interface (visual design) is a frequent cause of confusion and problems among technicians (with its "bits and tags" problems) and "interface creators" (with its "click everywhere to do everything" philosophy). The choice of the proper model for describing each part or set of features of the application is a crucial aspect of organizing the overall design process.

2. Content's production

   In general, contents are the "primary reason of existence" of hypermedia applications, in fact the author's message for the application readers (if any) is in multimedia contents. For that reason, in the ideal hypermedia application the budget resources should be focused as much as possible on contents production.

   However the related production process is complex and difficult to manage, in fact contents are rapidly changing, especially for WWW sites; they are heterogeneous (multi-language for localization, multi-target to support various kind of readers, multi-media, ...); they are subject to encoding (JPEG, GIF, BMP, PNG, ...), trans-coding (AVI→MPEG, TXT→RTF, ...), editing, versioning and testing; proper naming and placement conventions must be defined for the media files etc. etc.

   For all these reasons the creation and the maintenance of contents must be supported by an editorial repository (DBMS) provided with suitable software tools.

3. Content's reuse

Contents should be reused for at least two reasons: to expand the audience (Internet, CD, DVD, wireless terminals, ...), and to share the high (in percentage) production costs of contents among various projects.

For example, a company could reuse the same media files for a promotional CD, for various e-catalogs (final users, resellers, fairs, expositions, ...), for the company's Web site, for intra/extranet purposes etc.

Obviously, the contents should be "re-configured" and adapted to the various purposes. This basically means that the various applications are based on a common structural model, then each application is "derived" from the common model by identifying the portion of logical design that must be kept and/or changed, and by integrating it with additional definition and/or media slots.

4. Software production and reuse

In the hypermedia communication process, authors and readers are connected over the space (on-line: Web applications) or over the time (off-line: CD/DVD applications). In this scenario the supporting software implements the "communication channel": it is effective if it is "transparent". This means that the run-time software should be flexible and powerful, to support naïve users as well as "experienced navigators"; moreover it should be developed and tested before contents, because contents, in real projects, are released very late; obviously, it should be robust and error-free; and finally it should be inexpensive with respect to contents, because contents are the focus of the production effort.

For all these reasons the run-time software must be contents independent and application independent; in fact it can be complex enough and flexible enough only if its development costs can be shared over a large number of (different) projects.

To solve problems 2 to 4, various commercial development tools, such as FrontPage, from Microsoft, or Cold Fusion, from Allaire, are available, to build dynamic pages from (normal or multimedia) databases.

In our opinion this is only a partial solution, because the tools, in itself, are unable to dominate the peculiar complexity of hypermedia applications. For example, for the application designer, the links between the data model, used to store multimedia objects in the database, and the application features, such as the navigation control or the history management, are not clear at all. Moreover the visual interface design is based on technical considerations rather than on communication effectiveness (or, at least, usability), and we could continue with other problems.

What we say is that problems 2 to 4 cannot be successfully solved without solving problem 1, because a right modeling is essential in any good engineering process.

3 JWeb Architecture

The JWeb project takes into consideration most of the issues described in the previous section, with special emphasis on the HDM modeling phase. The overall goal is the creation of an integrated environment, to support the design, the prototyping and the implementation of families of sophisticated hypermedia applications, either on-line (Internet, Mobile, ...) or off-line (CD-ROM, DVD-ROM, ...). The architecture of JWeb, shown in fig. 1, is based on six components:

- JWEdit, the schema editor, to define/modify the HDM conceptual model of the application;
- JWData, the schema mapper, to create/maintain the environment repository and the related data structures;
- JWFeed, the instance editor, to insert/edit/delete the multimedia contents and the visual interface elements in the repository;
- JWXdef, the application configurator, to derive multiple application variants (e.g. multi-language, multi-target, ...) from the same main conceptual schema;
- JWXport, the application generator, to pack the application (multimedia data + navigational structure + presentation interface) in an executable format;
- JWEngine, to execute an application.

JWeb is strongly based on XML, in fact all the schemas are described in XML, and in this format they are exchanged across tools; all the pieces of content can be "exported" as XML files, and exchanged across tools; finally, all the multimedia information items (pictures, sounds, films, Java applets, HTML/XML pages, Shockwave animations, RealVideo streams,...), created with standard tools, can be easily integrated within the applications.

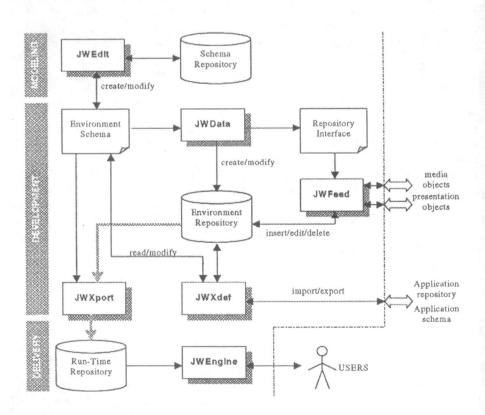

Fig. 1. JWeb Environment

The life cycle of a simple hypermedia application, in JWeb, is the following:

1. the conceptual schema for the given application domain is developed (using JWEdit), either from scratch, or "readapting" a previously created schema.
2. The environment repository is created (using JWData) on the basis of the conceptual schema.
3. The pieces of content are created, using standards authoring tools, and inserted in the repository according to the HDM schema, also creating all the needed links.

While the previous steps are shared among all applications belonging to a given family, the following ones refer, instead, to the development of each specific application (family member):

4. The conceptual schema is completed with additional access structures [14] and other application-specific details.
5. The visual style of the presentation is defined, using JWXdef. The visual style, in term of editorial masks, is defined by page templates in HTML/XML format or in Shockwave format (created with Macromedia Director).
6. The presentation objects (buttons, backgrounds, Java applets, ...), specific to the application, are collected in the repository. The definition of the visual style and the creation of the presentation objects are performed externally to JWeb, by using the tools preferred by the authors. The visual style of the presentation can gradually evolve from a simple, schematic form, useful for rapid prototyping purposes, up to the final layout;
7. The content and the interface elements are extracted and prepared for the execution by packaging them (using JWXport) in a suitable run-time format,
8. The application is executed by an application-independent interpreter (JWEngine), driven by the schema and the data stored in the run-time repository.

All or some of the above steps can be repeated if change or evolution of the application becomes necessary. Most of the changes can be automatically handled. A manual intervention is required when new presentation objects (e.g. a new interactive timeline or a searchable index with a new visual layout) are added to the application.

The current JWeb implementation has already been used for a family of e-catalogs for the fashion industry [18]. It has also been used to design and implement a configurable multimedia tutorial for a consortium of IT enterprise [19] and to develop a number of prototypes for research projects. In addition the current version of JWeb is being used to teach hypermedia design techniques at three universities (Politecnico di Milano, University of Lecce and University of Italian Switzerland), with a total of nearly 300 students per year.

In the following of this section, more details will be provided on the tools:

- JWEdit: it allows the designer to create or modify the schema of an application, using HDM modeling primitives. Beside the modeling aspects, a number of powerful features have been added to the editor to better support the design process:
  - a schema already defined can be stored and classified according to application areas (e.g. "museum information point" or "fashion catalog"). The saved schemas can act as "template" allowing a designer to start a new job by recovering a design already developed and modifying it. Such a "reuse" of conceptual design is very effective, above all in the early stage of the design activity; also it is a powerful training tool.

- Features have been added, to deal with "incomplete design" situations, allowing the designer to take later the incomplete parts and refine them.
- JWEdit can save and export a conceptual schema, using XML and a specific DTD. This allows easy exchanges of schemas across different teams of designers and also with other tools of the JWeb chain.
- JWData: it is the tool that builds and manages the Environment Repository. The repository is implemented as a relational database. Most of its structures can be automatically derived from the WWW conceptual schema. A human expert must manually provide a few decisions and a few parameters only. Multimedia information items are not stored within the relational database, but as external files to guarantee the independence of the adopted multimedia formats from the DBMS handling policies. JWData is also able to populate the DB with some trial data for fast prototyping purposes. This is a key feature for a number of jobs, such as training, interface and content development, design brainstorming etc.
- JWFeed: it is a generic data entry application that can be used to insert information in the Environment Repository in a "model driven" way.
- JWXdef: it allows the definition of a specific application, out of a large conceptual schema. A number of operations are possible:
  - Entity types and link types can be selected. New entity types or new link types can be defined. Special versions of existing entity/link types can be also defined. The selected (entity and link) types and the new definitions will be part of the conceptual schema of the specific application.
  - Specific information items can be selected (for inclusion) and/or added. In the latter case the new information items will be available only for the specific application being designed, not for the other applications of the same family. Also the localization process[1] can be favored by adding a complete set of new slots to take care of different languages and cultural adaptations.
  - Existing collections can be selected or new ones can be defined.
  - Externally-created style-sheets or hand-made HTML templates can be imported;
- JWXport: it is used to create the run-time repository (see fig. 1).
- JWEngine: it is an interpreter that performs "on the fly" the composition of the application pages requested by the user. This operation requires several steps:
  - the interpretation of the user request, according to the application schema;
  - the selection of the proper interface template, for the presentation;
  - the fetching of the data from the repository;
  - the merging of the data within the template.

The logical structure of JWEngine is depicted in fig.2.

The Event Manager, EM, detects the user requests and sends a parametric URL to the Main Server Engine, MSE. This component performs the parameters decoding and asks the Navigation Engine, NE, to evaluate it. The Navigation Engine resolves the names of the hypermedia objects needed to create the requested page. The DBEngine, DBE, retrieves the needed objects from the run-time repository, passing them to the Presentation Engine, PE. The Presentation Engine is in charge of properly inserting the retrieved objects in the presentation template. The Session Manager, SM, is responsible for detecting and storing the session parameters selected by the user

---

[1] I.e. the adaptation of an application to foreign markets

(language, sound volume, ...). The History Manager, HM, keeps track of the navigation steps performed by the user, for later usage.

The current implementation, for on-line purposes, is based upon a client-server architecture. The server-side is implemented as a Java Servlet and includes the MSE, the NE, the DBE, and part of the PE.

The client-side is implemented as a Java applet and includes the EM, the SM, the HM and the remaining of the PE.

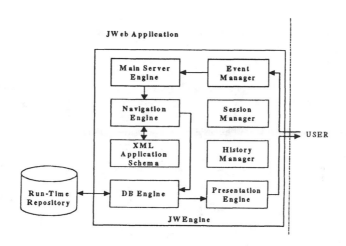

Fig. 2. JWEngine: internal structure

4 Conclusions and future work

The main use of JWeb will be to support design and prototyping of sophisticated WWW applications. For such a reason the main trust of our current work is to improve the number of modeling features supported by JWEdit and JWXdef. Our desire is to be able to support very advanced design features, including all those that can be found in the best WWW sites.

A suitable documentation generator will be added to JWEdit, to better support the modeling phase (that is of paramount importance).

The prototyping capabilities of JWeb will be improved, both for advanced design (e.g. for testing different alternatives) and training (e.g. for visualizing the implication of an attempted design).

In order to balance the different and sometimes conflicting requirements between hypermedia training and real application design we are planning two different JWeb versions:

- a full size version for sophisticated design;
- a light version, favoring simplicity and speed over completeness, for training.

As far as actual implementation of the applications is concerned, we still maintain that it is not our main goal. It is true, however, that in some cases, the applications resulting from the JWeb chain could be delivered as final implementation, and in some cases we have successfully done it even with the current version of the tools.

In our plan the new version of the tools will be released before December '99

References

1. F.Garzotto, M.Matera, "A Systematic Method for Hypermedia Usabilty Inspection", In *The New Review of Hypermedia and Multimedia*, 3, 1997
2. J, Nielsen,R.L.Mack, "Usabilty Inspection Methods", John Wiley & Sons, New York 1994.
3. F.Garzotto, M.Matera and P.Paolini, "Abstract Tasks for Hypermedia Usability Evaluation", Dept. of Electronics and Information, Polytechnic of Milan, Tech. Report No.03-99, 1999.
4. F.Garzotto, L.Mainetti and P.Paolini, "Hypermedia Application Design: A Structured Approach", In J.W.Schuler, N.Hannemann and N.Streitz Eds., "Designing User Interfaces for Hypermedia", Springer Verlag, 1995.
5. D.Schwabe, G.Rossi, The Object-Oriented Hypermedia Design Model, Communications of the ACM, Vol. 38, N. 8, pp.45-46, Aug. 1995
6. T.Isakowitz, E.A.Stohr, P.Balasubramanian: "RMM: a methodology for structured hypermedia design", Communications of the ACM Vol.38, No.8, Aug. 1995, pp. 33-44.
7. G.Mecca, P.Atzeni, A.Masci, P.Merialdo, G.Sindoni: "The Araneus Web-Base Management System". SIGMOD Conference 1998. Pp. 544-546.
8. Fraternali P., Paolini P.-" The Autoweb System"; submitted for publication
9. E. Gamma, R. Helm, R. Johnson and J. Vlissides. Design Patterns. Elements of Reusable Object-Oriented Software. Addison-Wesley, 1996
10. F. Garzotto, P.Paolini, D. Bolchini, S. Valenti "Modeling-by-patterns of web applications" In World-Wide Web and Conceptual Modeling - Proc. Int. workshop WWWCM'99 - in conjunction with the 18th Int. Conference on Conceptual Modeling (ER'99), Paris, France, Stephen W. Liddle (ed.), Springer Verlag - to appear
11. M. Nanard, J. Nanard and P. Kahn. "Pushing Reuse in Hypermedia Design: Golden Rules, Design Patterns and Constructive Templates". In Proc. of the ACM International Conference on Hypertext '98, ACM Press, 1998, pp. 11-20.
12. G. Rossi, D. Schwabe and F. Lyardet, "Improving Web Information Systems with Design Patterns". In Proc. of the 8th International World Wide Web Conference, Toronto (CA), May 1999, Elsevier Science, 1999
13. F.Garzotto, P.Paolini and D.Schwabe, "HDM - A Model Based Approach to Hypermedia Application Design", ACM Transactions on Information Systems, 11, 1 (Jan. 1993), 1-26
14. Franca Garzotto, Luca Mainetti, Paolo Paolini, "Adding Multimedia Collections to the Dexter Model". ECHT 1994: 70-80
15. Hytea Projects reports, available from Politecnico di Milano and from Siemens corporate research center in Munich (Germany).
16. MINERS Projects reports, available from Politecnico di Milano and from EDS-Italy corporate research center in Rome (Italy).
17. U.Cavallaro, F.Garzotto, P.Paolini and D.Totaro, "HIFI: Hypertext Interface for Information Systems", IEEE Software 10, 6 (Nov. 1993), 48-51.
18. M. A. Bochicchio,R. Paiano, P. Paolini " JWeb: an HDM Environment for fast development of Web Applications" - ", Proceedings of Multimedia Computing and Systems 1999 (IEEE ICMCS '99), Vol.2 pp.809-813
19. M. A. Bochicchio, P. Paolini, "An HDM Interpreter for On-Line Tutorials", Proceedings of MultiMedia Modeling 1998 (MMM '98), pp.184-190, Ed. N. Magnenat-Thalmann and D. Thalman, IEEE Computer Society, Los Alamitos, Ca, USA, 1998.

XML Arouse the WEB Architecture Revolution

Chai Xiaolu, Cao Jing, Gao Yongqing, Shi Baile

Shanghai International Database Research Center,

Computer Science Department, Fudan University, Shanghai, China

{972404, cgao, 972465}@fudan.edu.cn

Abstract In this paper, a brand-new web architecture model based on XML is presented. First, an open framework of browser is provided which can add in new XML-based markup language support easily by plugging a browser extension. In this framework, we use browser extension to access the XML document via DOM interface and to manipulate the visualized page via VPOM (Visualized Page Object Module) interface. On the other hand, to support the client requirement, an XML repository should be built. It can manage XML objects storage/access as well as support XML queries with high performance. This repository should be capable of inter-operating with other repository, which is compliant with our repository access interface standard.

1 Introduction

With the amount and variety of information sources increasing, the information/media species that need to be presented in web are more and more abundant. As for the semantic presentation and information management, current web server provides comparative limited supports. On the other hand, the browser is lack of an information presentation mechanism, which can present kinds of information uniformly and efficiently with high security and extendibility.

To a web project with the current browser/server architecture, which treats the HTML as the information presentation core, it's not easy to transfer the traditional software engineering in normal information systems to web engineering in web information systems. The models, such as Object Model, are hard to be combined with HTML.

The web architecture needs to be changed to accommodate the new Internet application environment. In this paper, we present brand-new open web architecture as well as some relative technologies. The XML [2] is the core of this architecture.

The rest is organized as follows. Section 2 scans related work. In section 3, we describe the open web architecture. In section 4, prospective remarks are offered.

2 Related Works

XML is a data description language standardized by the World Wide Web Consortium (W3C). XML emphasizes description of information structure and content instead of its presentation. The data structure and its syntax are defined in DTD (Document Type Definition) specification. In addition to XML, XSL, XPointer, XLink, XPath are also in the process of standardization which is a specification to define styles, anchors, links and paths within XML documents. Thus, XML has great potential as an exchange format of many kinds of structured and semi-structured data.

XML is widely accepted in the Web community now. An important ability of XML is to define a special format for information description. Current applications includes CDIF (Case Data Interchange Format), UIML (User Interface Markup Language), UXF (UML Exchange Format) [10], RDF (Resource Description Framework), and many other XML applications.

To support the XML information retrieval, it is expected that XML Repository should be established to store mass XML documents. Dirk [9] analyze the requirement and foundation of the repository via comparing the realization with flat files, RDB and OODB. Registry and Repository Technical Specification of OASIS [8] is under writing. It seeks to specify operation of a registry for XML-related entities, including but not limited to DTDs and schemas, with appropriate interfaces, that enable searching on the contents of a repository of those entities. This is compliant with the specification and responsive to requests for entities by their identifiers.

3 Open Web Architecture

3.1 Browser/Server Architecture Today

Within more than ten-year, the range of web application became more and more wide. However, the browser's architecture is not changed in essence. It analyzes and presents HTML, interprets JavaScript/VBScript, partly support XML. The browser is lack of ability to easily support other markup languages, although we can use JAVA, ActiveX and Plug-In. With these technologies, we will encounter some problems: to support other markup languages, especially for XML-based markup languages, we have to write a quite large program to contain a XML parser. Nevertheless, this parser should be shared for all XML-based markup language interpreters. Java applet's running efficiency is a problem for mass processing. The security problem makes ActiveX and Plug-In not be accepted widely. Moreover, under this architecture, the markup language interpreters are hard to be reused and integrated uniformly.

One of our objectives is to construct a browser to support as many markup languages and provide internet-user as abundant information form as possible. This browser should be of Security, Extendibility, Efficiency and Facility.

In order to support the XML-based browser, today web server based on flat files or relational database can't work efficiently. For it is not able to represent full features of XML, we need to re-build the web server architecture to be based on XML repository. The new architecture can lead the today web to a new XML web age.

3.2 Open Framework for Browser

Our Open Framework model can be described as below:

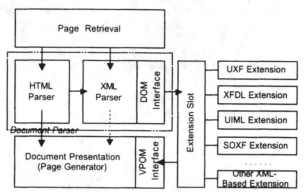

Fig. 1. The Open Framework for Browser

Page Retrieval: Retrieve XML/HTML documents from Internet/intranet web-site or other XML Repository and send them to Document Parser.

Document Parser: In this model, the parser can process such nested HTML and XML document. The type identifier of XML section (or document) should be indicated in the first tag of this XML section.

According to the section type, XML section will be processed by the corresponding BROWSER EXTENSION via DOM interface that is plugged in Extension Slot, and HTML section will be directly processed by Document Presentation.

Document Presentation: The functions of this module include visual presentation of HTML document, visual presentation of normal XML document that uses XSL and VCL access interface. VCL (Visual Component Library) is a component library including all of components. The VCL access interface named VPOM (Visualized Page Object Module) is for the Browser Extension to manipulate and build visualized page.

Extension Slot: Extension Slot is the extended slot of the browser with open framework. All Browser Extension will be plugged in the Extension Slot. Extension Slot will dispatch the embedded XML sections to relative XML Browser Extension.

Browser Extension: A particular BROWSER EXTENSION interprets a particular XML-based markup language and presents the part of document via VPOM which is a XML-tree parsing script program. In the browser extension, two browser objects are used: Document Object and Visualized Page Object. Programmers can use Document Object (corresponding to DOM) to manipulate XML document and use Visualized Page Object (corresponding to VPOM) to manipulate and build visualized page.

DOM: DOM [5] is a platform- and language-neutral interface. The Document Object Model provides a standard set of objects for representing XML and HTML documents, and a standard interface for accessing and manipulating them.

VPOM: VPOM (Visualized Page Object Module) is an interface for the visualized page's manipulation. Use VPOM interface, we can create each kind of media element and control these elements in the visualized page.

3.3 Open XML Repository

XML Repository is a special purpose database that can manage XML objects in a native format, allowing the developer to focus entirely on business logic instead of database design and programming. A XML Repository should include features, such as:

– XML document import/export and authoring/processing support
– Scheme definition, generation and maintenance for XML document
– Query support for XML elements
– Programming API to implement application server

To store XML documents with high efficiency, we classify the XML documents according its semantics-rich level. We call it semantic classification. XML documents can be classified into three types:

– Raw XML documents without DTDs or with poor DTDs which will be directly stored as a full document or be decomposed into several glancing elements
– Well-formed XML documents with well-defined DTDs from which we can generate fine schema and decompose them into precise elements.
– Semantics-rich XML documents with precise and intact DTDs (maybe with XML Schema definitions additional). With this type, we can generate excellent schema that even is an OO model, and decompose them into XML objects.

Aiming at the local storage situation, we can classify XML documents into four types on the other hand:

– The schema and document (which will decompose into elements or objects according its semantics-rich level) are stored both locally.
– Schema is stored locally, but the document itself is in the remote repository or exists as an external file.
– The document is stored in local repository while we can't generate any schemas for it due to its low semantics-rich level.
– Both schema and document are stored in remote repository or existed as an external file. We just have a link or pointer to them.

We called it distribution classification.

To support the basic features and the types of XML documents above, we design the architecture of XML Repository based on relational database and some additional external indexes. The architecture can be described as Fig.2.

Next, we describe the detail of every modules of repository:

Access Interface: It is a user/program access interface. It includes programming interface for application server implementation, document interface for document import/export and authoring, query interface for XML query.
Document Manager: Document Manager includes the functions as document import which analyze document's structure, converts DTDs to schema and decompose the document into elements or objects, document export, which recompose the XML objects and elements of an XML document needed.

View Definition and Management: This module is for remote/external XML query. Views can be defined by remote/external XML query. Thus further query can be based on the view definition. In addition, the virtual view can be materialized, and it need increment update.

XML Query: The main function of this module is to convert between XML query and SQL query. It decomposes the XML query into subquery, which can be converts to canonical SQL query and implements them. On the other hand, it retrieves partial results from the search engine and recomposes them into an XML result.

Core Schema/Object Management: This is one the core modules of the repository. It manages of the schemas, metadata, indexes and objects in the repository.

Data Resistance: In this module, conversion between active objects (schemas, metadata, elements and objects) and relational database objects are retained. Moreover, it provides a mechanism to access physical XML index.

Repositories Schema/Data Exchange: It is a vital module featured by open and distribution. If heterogeneous repository have a compatible interface with the same standard, they also can be interoperable.

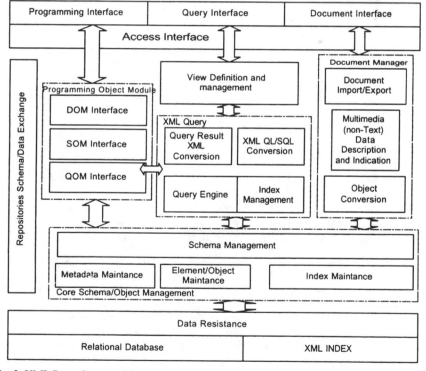

Fig. 2. XML Repository Architecture

3.4 Features

We can gain these features in web application building and web engineering:

- Inherent XML information storage and presentation ability
- Abundance information species supported
- Software engineering models applied in web engineering such as OO-model
- Query with high performance in XML Repository
- High performance in XML elements/objects processing
- Open thin-browser, special information extension plug-and-play with high security, efficiency
- Standard Repository Objects with DCOM technology makes application server building easily
- Interoperate repository access interface provides abilities seamless combination of repositories

4 Prospect

We wish that this XML-based open web architecture be applied in future web application. In browser, More kinds of information can be gotten with high efficiency and security. With open framework for browser, we can extend the browser's ability to application. In server, application server can fully utilize the features from open XML repository to realize rare complex web application simply. XML no doubt gives us a chance to arouse a web revolution.

References

1. Chai Xiaolu, Gao Yongqing, Cao jing, XML: Lead Browser to Be an Open Framework, XML/SGML Asia Pacific' 99, Oct., 1999
2. T.Bray, J.Paoli, and C.M. Sperberg-McQueen, eds, Extensible Markup Language (XML) 1.0, W3C
3. D.Beech, et.al, XML Schema Part 1: Structures, *W3C*, Working Draft 6-May-1999
4. Murray Altheim, et.al, Modularization of XHTML, *W3C*, Working Draft 06-April-1999
5. L. Wood, et.al, Document Object Model (DOM) Level 1 Specification Version 1.0, *W3C*, 1-October-1998
6. Jayavel Shanmugasundaram, Kristin Rufte, Gang He, et.al., Relational Databases for Querying XML Documents: Limitations and Opportunities, VLDB' 99
7. Deutsch, M. Fernandez, D. Florescu, A. Levy, D. Suciu, XML-QL: A Query Language for XML, http://www.w3.org/TR/NOTE-xml-ql
8. OASIS Registry and Repository Technical Specification (Draft), www.oasis-open.org, 1999
9. Dirk Bartels, A Scalable XML Repository, SGML World 1997
10. Junichi Suzuki and Yoshikazu Yamamoto, Managing the Software Design Documents with XML, ACM SIGDOC 1998.

Knowledge Beads – Approach for Knowledge Representation and Market Place Negotiations for Internet Agents

Simon Fong and Chin Kok Poh

School of Applied Science, Nanyang Technological University, Singapore
asccfong@ntu.edu.sg   chin_kp@mindless.com

Abstract: Knowledge Representation can be modeled using rule-based semanntics with self-learning capabilities based on given feedback. There are 3 approaches expounded in this paper to achieve this model – a) knowledge-bead b) bill-of-knowledge and c) self learning knowledge mapping. Knowledge-Bead is the fundamental building blocks for rule-based systems that allow for synchronised attribute analysis and comparisons in an agent driven negotiation process. The bill of knowledge is the structure for collections of knowledge-beads that will allow inheritance of rules and attributes. This approach allows probabilistic weightage based knowledge maps so that an infinite level of states can be modelled. This model fits well with the negotiation process is made up of continuous non-binary states. We are also proposing alternative modesl for market place negotiations using Sensing Agent.

1   The Design Principles of Knowledge Beads (KBds)

We propose a new generic architecture for building information agents that do data matching. The matching is powered by a hierarchical and inheritable rule-based system with knowledge mapping. Such a knowledge representation system is driven by Knowledge Beads. The aims of knowledge beads are as follow.

- Provide a concise and standard method to exchange *descriptive knowledge* between agents during negotiations. It focuses on what the agents want to achieve rather than how the agent decides on the quality of the deal.
- Use the approach of exchanging knowledge through *data-centric* and *structural* approach instead of the free form practice by emerging standards such as KIF.
- Knowledge Beads focuses on the *semantics* of the knowledge exchanged rather than the pragmatics of knowledge exchanged. That will be handled by other available methods such as KQML.
- Knowledge Beads by design inherently exhibits characteristics of inheritance of attributes and rules, associative-semantics, structured knowledge slots, operators based rules and time-sensitive knowledge representations.

In doing electronic negotiations, we can further classify the types of knowledge that are specific to this. *Descriptive Knowledge* is the portion that deals with what you want to buy and what your expectations (goals) are based on product definition, price, quality, modes of payments, logistical arrangements, etc. In the implementation of KBds, we are going to focus on descriptive knowledge. We chose a *data-centric and structured* approach because with a disciplined semantics description environment, less data resources (e.g. storage and network bandwidth) is needed. However to allow more flexibility, we advocated that this approach also supports a limited set of meta-knowledge capabilities that can be expanded later if needed.

2 Knowledge Exchange between Agents

For an agent-based negotiation to be successful, these principles are recommended:

    1.   Principle 1: Using agreed Points of References.

    2.   Principle 2: Definitions can evolve over time.

    3.   Principle 3: Alternate Definitions.

    4.   Principle 4: Compound definitions can be built.

    5.   Principle 5: Conditions/Goal are weighted.

2.1 Standardise Agreed Points of References

We shall see that as the atomic definitions are the same it does not matter how the knowledge/conditions are structurally defined. As long as the same points of reference are used, we can effectively communicate and negotiate.

In our implementation these atomic level (read points of references) are known as *attribute beads*. We shall cover the definition of an attribute bead later when we discussed the implementation of Knowledge Beads method.

$$(\forall x)(MASTER\_REFERENCE(x)) \rightarrow STANDARD\_REFERENCE.$$

2.2 Time Phased Evolution of Definitions

We need to be able to change our definitions of what we need over time. This scenario below is a typical situation. EXAMPLE: I am will need to use a copper connector this month but next month I will need to use a carbon connector. In this case, I will need to let the seller agent know about my intention to change the type of connector.

$(\exists xt1t2)(RULE(x)$ & $TIME\_GT(t1, start\_time)$ & $TIME\_LT(t2, end\_time)) \rightarrow$ GOAL_MET(xt1t2) where start_time is the starting time and end_time is the ending time for the effectivity of the rule.

2.3 Alternate Definitions

I am sure all of us understand the need to have a primary definition. But 'alternate definitions', what is that ? An alternate definition can be viewed (as the name suggests) as another set of points of references that can be used in the rules.

- PRIMARY DEFINITION OF MY PERFECT 'CAR'
  RULE(1) – The car must be RED.
  RULE(2) – The make must be ALFA ROMEO.
- ALTERNATE DEFINITION OF MY PERFECT 'CAR'
  RULE(1) – The car must be RED.
  RULE(2) – The make must be BMW.

This way when my buyer agent goes to the marketplace, it can look for my perfect 'car' based on these 2 sets of criteria. The operating principle of the alternate definitions can be summarised as: $(\exists x)(PRIMARY(x) \mid ALTERNATE_1(x) \mid ... \mid ALTERNATE_n(x)$ where n >= 1) $\rightarrow$ GOAL_MET(x)

2.4 Compound Definition – Inheritance

We are trying to establish here that with inheritance of attributes, it will help enable **a consistent process of defining the shared/common knowledge.** Inheritance will help consistency because the rule needs only to be defined once and then it can be 'inherited' by another rule as part of its criteria. This is what we have done here:

$(\exists x)(FAVOURITE\_THINGS(x) \rightarrow COLOR(red)$

With inheritance, we have essentially done the definition in 2 steps:

$(\forall x)(FAVOURITE\_COLOUR(x)) \rightarrow COLOR(red)$

$(\exists x)(FAVOURITE\_OBJECT(x) \bullet FAVOURITE\_COLOUR(x)) \rightarrow (FAVOURITE\_THINGS(x))$

2.5 Weighted Goals – Hierarchy of weighted criticality

Let's deal with HIERARCHY now. We need it because when we discuss inheritance, it implies that we need hierarchy. It is an implied condition. Also with a hierarchical structure we can do proper weighted criticality calculation.

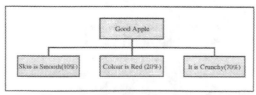

Figure 1: Choose a Good Apple

If we can only meet 2 of the 3 criteria, a red crunchy apple that has rough skin is preferred because 'crunchiness' has the highest marks(percentages). This concept reinforces the need to have hierarchy and weighted criticality. This answers the question that we do need to have inheritance and hierarchy.

$$\text{Weighted Criticality} = \sum_{n=1}^{n} Goal(n)_{boolean\_value} \times \text{Weightage}(n)$$

3 Implementing Knowledge Beads

3.1 Structure of Knowledge Beads

At the atomic level is what we call the attribute bead. An attribute bead will have 2 characteristics, it will define what is the attribute_type and what is the attribute_value. A *simple* Knowledge Bead will consists of a collection(s) of attribute bead(s). A *complex* Knowledge Bead will consist of at least an attribute bead and another simple (or complex) Knowledge Bead.

3.2 Standardising Points of Reference for Knowledge Beads

Attribute comparison is the process where values of similar attributes have their values compared. This allows the same points of references need to be used during the comparison. A Knowledge bead helps define the collection of attribute type(s) and attribute value(s). A Knowledge bead can also be based on another knowledge bead that will ultimately allow it be exploded to a collection of attribute types and attribute values. An attribute bead consists of the attribute type and the attribute value. These attribute types and values need to be 'registered' with a central attribute librarian.

Attribute Type	Legal Values for Attributes	Legal UOM
Colour	RED, BLUE,GREEN	
Weight	Number	KG
Shape	String	
Age	Number	MONTHS
Things	SHIRT, PHONE, CUP,CAR	

Table 1– A sample of a registered Attribute Table.

To allow complex attribute definitions, we will be able to define relationships between attributes in a single knowledge bead. A knowledge bead may consists of a collection of attribute types and values that may have relationship defined for the collection of attribute_type and attribute_value. So ultimately when comparisons are made, they are all using the same points of reference although the conditions could be complex.

3.3 Defining the Bill-of-Knowledge

The bill-of-knowledge is a data definition structure that allows us to build rules that are time-phased and also allows inheritance. It attempts to provide a 'world-view'[5] of things. The defined structure a record element of Bill-of-Knowledge are:

Field Name	Data Type	Description
RESULTING_KBDS	A_Type or KBd	The Knowledge Bead (KBd) that will result from the collection of inherited KBd(s) or Attribute Type (A_Type).
INHERITED_KBDS	A_Type or KBd	The KBd or A_Type that will be used to build the resulting KBd.
INHERITED_WEIGHT	Number	The weightage allocated for the KBd or A_Type.
WEIGHT_OPERATOR	Weight_Operator	When the A_Val_Operator defines a range of values, the weight_operator can be in binary mode or ratio mode.
ATTRIBUTE_VALUE	A_Val	A valid registered attribute value for the attribute type.
A_VALUE_OPERATOR	A_Val_Operator	Implemented Value BOOLEAN Operators LT, LE, EQ, GT, GE.
KB_EFFECTIVE_DATE	Date	Date the Knowledge Bead action definitions will be effective.
KB_ACTION_CODE	KB_Action	Implemented Knowledge Beads Actions Codes: (A)dd, (D)elete, (G)roup
KB_ACTION_LEVEL	Integer	The indication of the priority in which the group definitions will be interpreted.
KB_ACTION_NUMBER	String	A label to identify items that are grouped together.
KB_COMPULSORY	Boolean	To state if the requested attribute type and attribute value pair is a compulsory condition.

Table 2 – Record Definition for the bill of knowledge

4 Market Place Models

A successful market place will have to support these capabilities (1) Standardised Definitions and Points of Reference, (2) Business Brokering and (3) Facility for Agent Negotiations.

4.1 Standardised Definitions and Points of Reference

We will apply use the Master Librarian for this purpose. The Master Librarian is a collection attribute types and attribute values From the controlled tables of the Master Librarian that is referred to by the Internet agents, the common ground for definitions can be established.

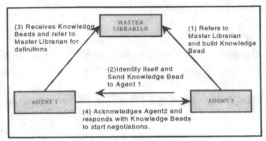

Figure 2 - Master Librarian standardising definitions

4.2 Business Brokering

The Master Librarian can facilitate the business brokering process. It need not be a dynamic business brokering where the agents needs to be physically present in the Master Librarian's domain, although this can be done. The advantage of static business brokering is that it is a very efficient on resource requirement. Dynamic brokering requires the agents to be active and present in the master librarian's domain and it will constantly advertised its presence. This model is shown below.

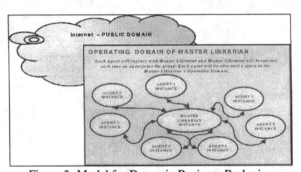

Figure 3- Model for Dynamic Business Brokering

The static business brokering process is a 2 step process. First the agent needs to register itself with the Master Librarian. When it want to negotiate, it will request the list of relevant agents that it could negotiate with.

4.3 Facility for Agent Negotiations

There are a few models we can use for the market place. The are as follows:
- Centralised Execution-mode Market Agent (CExMA): This is where the agents programme instance is running in the Master Librarian's operating domain. There is a risk of the agent programme wreaking havoc in the master librarians operating domain, known as the Alan Turing's Halting Problem[1]. Also we need to take care of agent privacy so that proprietaty methods of negiotiation is not hacked.

- Distributed Execution-mode Market Agent (DExMA): This is slight variation of the CExMA method in that it run's in the on the agent's operating domain instead of the Master Librarian's domian. The danger here is that the both the agent negotiation methodology can be hacked and deciphered directly.
- Sensing-mode Market Agent (SenMA): This is different model where all agents runs in their own respective domain. Only data of knowledge beads are exchanges. There is no execution of program in another domain. This mode l allows to make use of the current Internet technology which is stateless. This follows along the lines of client server methods.

	Master Librarian's Program Instance	Agent1 Program Instance	Agent2 Program Instance
Master Librarian Operating Domain	CExMA , DexMA, SeMA		
Agent1 Operating Domain	CExMA	DexMA, SeMA	
Agent2 Operating Domain	CExMA	DExMA	SeMA

Table 3- Matrix of Program Instance vs. Operating Domain of various Negotiation Models

5 Conclusion

With a properly designed bill of knowledge and knowledge beads which serve as the basic building blocks of a given information and applying the basics of demand supply matching, the challenge of matching will be overcome. In the information analysis example, the search criteria are actually the demand side of the knowledge beads and the documents are actually the supply side of the knowledge beads. Basically what is proposed is nothing more that using knowledge beads as the basis to do demand supply matching. Once we are able to build the knowledge beads, determine the demand side and determine the supply side, matching will come naturally.

References

[1] A.K. Caglayan, "Agent Sourcebook", WILEY COMPUTER PUBLISHING, pp.179, 1997, ISBN: 0-471-15327-3.

AOM: An Agent Oriented Middleware Based on Java

Kwang-Jin Paek and Tai-Yun Kim

Multimedia Network Lab.
Dept. of Computer Science & Engineering, Korea University
1, 5-ga, Anam-dong, Sungbuk-gu, Seoul, 136-701, Korea
pkj@netlab.korea.ac.kr

Abstract. Agents are the next significant software abstraction, especially for distributed systems. Mobility is an orthogonal property of agents – that is, not all agents mobile. An agent can just sit there and communicate with its surroundings by procedure calling and messaging. In this paper, we provides an agent oriented middleware system based on Java, AOM. The AOM aims to develop a new middleware paradigm that exploits the computational advantages of mobile agent paradigm that reduces network load, minimize response time and makes load-balance in distributed environment.

1 Introduction

The purpose of a distributed communications framework is to provide a good way for the parts of a distributed system to communication. The distributed object-oriented frameworks that get the most attention are those that model messaging as method calls. CORBA and RMI are two excellent examples of this type of framework. These systems are often called remote procedure call systems. The magic of these systems is that they make remote procedure (or method) calls appear to be local procedure calls (LPCs). Mobile agent technology extends this model by including mobile processes, i.e., processes which can autonomously migrate to new hosts.

In this paper, we assume that an agent is a computer program whose purpose is to help a user perform some jobs. Mobile agents are defined as active objects (or clusters of objects) that have behavior, state and location. Mobile agents provide certain advantages compared to traditional approaches as the reduction of communication costs, better support of asynchronous interactions, or enhanced flexibility in the process of software distribution. The question what real advantages mobile agents offer has been subject of various papers (e.g. 1,2,3) and ongoing discussions in mobile agent mailing lists. Since agents consist of program code and the associated internal state, we can envision mobile agents that can move between computers in a network. A typical definition of the term 'mobile agent' looks like "some kind of a program, fulfilling autonomously a task on behalf of a user, roaming the net" [6].

The goal of our AOM is to provide the prototype of next generation middleware that support synchronous and asynchronous communication mechanism and flexible mobility of agents. We test the performance and advantages of AOM against other middlewares. We implement AOM, an extension of Java programming environment that provides a flexible substrate for adaptive mobile programs. Since mobile programs are scare, we developed a AOM test bed for our experiments. To evaluate if AOM can take advantage of mobile agent paradigm, we examined the performance of AOM, RPC, and MOM test bed. Eventually, we confirmed that the AOM system provides many practical benefits.

The rest of this paper is structured as follows: Section 2 will describe middleware, namely RPC, MOM, and RP. In section 3, we present an Agent Oriented Middleware (AOM). In section 4, we implement our prototype of AOM and evaluate its performance. Finally, The paper concludes with a result of evaluation and a summary of the article's essential issues and future work.

2 Distributed Communication & Middleware Segmentation

Middleware is an enabling layer of software that resides between the business application and the networked layer of heterogeneous platforms and protocols. Middleware encompasses a wide range of services and products, including message-queuing, application development environments (ADEs), object development environments, database access, distributed transaction processing, messaging communications, and RPC-based communications [4]. We present representative RPC, MOM, and remote programming. In addition, we compare these middlewares in various points of views. Especially, we review the potential of mobile agent paradigm.

2.1 Remote Procedure Call (RPC)

The remote procedure call (remote method invocation) is an action oriented, synchronous communication mechanism. It "transfers" the control flow (including some arguments) from the caller to the called until the request is served and the result returned. In the agent system, the RPC is available as a communication mechanism between agents. With its help, an agent may call any public method of another agent. If a method of an agent is called by another agent, the method is executed concurrently to the normal control flows in the called agent. While an RPC is executed, the called agent mustn't migrated [9].

The salient characteristic of remote procedure calling is that each interaction between the user computer and the server entails two acts of communication, one to ask the server to perform a procedure, and another to acknowledge that the server did so. Thus ongoing interaction requires ongoing communication[5].

In order to access the remote server portion of an application, special function calls, RPCs, are embedded within the client portion of the client/server application program. Because they are embedded, RPCs do not stand alone as a discreet middleware layer. When the client program is compiled, the compiler creates a local stub for the client portion and another stub for the server portion of the application. These stubs are invoked when the application requires a remote function and typically support synchronous calls between clients and servers [7].

The RPC introduces overhead due to marshalling, transmission, and unpacking and has a typical latency of a few milliseconds. Like the local procedure call, the RPC is synchronous; the client process suspends, maintaining the entire process state, until it receives the return RPC from the server. Secure RPCs add authentication and encryption facilities to the client-server communication, but introduce significant overhead [8].

2.2 Message Oriented Middleware (MOM)

Messages are a data oriented communication mechanism, generally used to transfer data between processes. Messages are either asynchronous or synchronous. Messaging is emerging as a popular alternative to RPC for client-server communication. It is an outgrowth of both electronic mail systems and earlier distributed computing schemes in which applications communicated via files or pipes. The client application composes a message, typically composed of tagged or structured text, which is to be delivered to an appropriate software processor for the type of message.

MOM is an enabling software layer residing between the business applications and the network infrastructure that supports high performance interoperability of large scale distributed applications in heterogeneous environments. It supports multiple communication protocols, languages, applications, and hardware and software platforms. The strength of RPC lies in its high efficiency and low latency. The strength of messaging lies in its robustness, particularly over wide-area networks [1].

Messages are put into queues (which can be memory or disk based) for either immediate or subsequent delivery. This allows programs to run independently, at different speeds, and without a logical connection between them.

2.3 Remote Programming (RP)

An alternative to remote procedure calling is remote programming. The RP approach views computer-to-computer communication as enabling one computer not only to call procedures in another, but also to supply the procedures to be performed. Each message that the network transports comprises a procedure that the receiving computer is to perform and data that are its arguments. The salient characteristic of remote programming is that a user computer and a server can interact without using the network once the network has transported an agent between them. Thus, ongoing interaction does not require ongoing communication. The implications of this fact are far reaching.

Fig. 1 shows the mobile agent paradigm. The agent can migrate between two agent systems, e.g. an agent system on the mobile device and an agent system at a server in the network. While executing at an agent place, the agent can access a system agent, which offers him a dedicated functionality provided by the underlying host system.

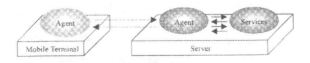

Fig. 1. The Mobile Agent Paradigm

A mobile agent is a piece of software together with its current execution state that is able to migrate between places. A system agent is a specialized agent that is allowed to access the system resources of the host of the agent system. Mobile agents communicate with other mobile agents and with system agents while execute their tasks. An agent system contains additional system services that help mobile agents to perform their tasks [8]. For a full-fledged migration, the program, the data (object attributes) and the execution state of the agent has to be transformed into a transport representation. The big advantage of the described migration mechanism is the fact, that it can be implemented in Java without any change to the interpreter (including the Java object serialization) is available [9].

Here are seven good reasons to start using mobile agents. They are 1)reduce the network load, 2)overcome network latency, 3)encapsulate protocols, 4)execute asynchronously and autonomously, 5)adapt dynamically, 6)naturally heterogeneous, 7)robust and fault-tolerant. We surveyed five middlewares. AOM is another new middleware technology. RPC, CORBA, TCP, MOM, and AOM are five overlapped architectural concepts, as shown in **Fig. 2**. AOM provides higher abstraction and more communications flexibility.

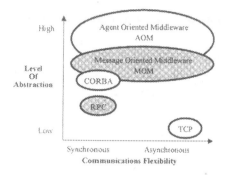

Fig. 2. Overlapped design space of RPC, CORBA, MOM, TCP, and AOM

Although mobile agent technology sounds exciting, our interest in mobile agents should not be motivated by the technology per se but rather by the benefits agents using mobile agents.

3   AOM: An Agent Oriented Middleware

AOM provides the clear-cut and potential architecture that consists of three components, AOM server, AOM client, and AOM semantic router. AOM server is composed of four modules that are user agent manager, location manager, service agent manager, and message manager. AOM semantic router is a kind of MOM message server. Message manager of AOM client and server is a kind of MOM message manager. In AOM, a mobile agent is migrated as MOM message.

Java is an object-oriented, network-savvy programming language. Here are agent characteristics of Java: benefits. They are Platform Independence, Secure Execution, Dynamic Class Loading, Multithread Programming, Object Serialization and Reflection. Fig. 3 shows the architecture of AOM. There is three component.

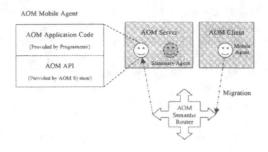

Fig. 3. Architecture of AOM

AOM semantic router makes load balance for AOM servers. Mobile agents are routed based on it's own contents by semantic router which monitoring loads of AOM servers.

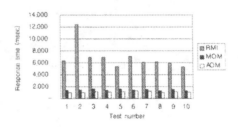

Fig. 4. Test results of response time

4   Implementation and estimation of AOM

AOM prototype system was made of pure Java, JDK1.2. All components of AOM can run any platform. AOM supports two modes, synchronous and asynchronous mode. To transmit mobile agents, we use Java object serialization API. AOM system consists of AOM server, AOM client, and AOM semantic router. In addition, AOM provides AOM API as Java packages for AOM applications.

We simulated AOM with the connection that established far across the distance between Pusan and Seoul is 455Km. Java Remote Method Invocation (RMI) is a distributed object model for the Java language that retains the semantics of the Java object model, making distributed objects easy to implement and to use. RMI, MOM, and AOM are made with pure Java language.

MOM is employed as an infrastructure of AOM communication. In a sequence of interactions, an alternating sequence of remote procedure calls and agent migrations performs better than a pure sequence of remote procedure calls or messages. This result was confirmed by measurements (see **Fig. 4**) on a prototype implementation of AOM. Sequentially packet loss rates are 22%, 29%, 14%, 12%, 9%, 11%, 11%, 5%,

12%, 10%. In this result, We find that high packet loss rate and low bandwidth made more different response time.

Distributed systems often rely on communications protocols that involve multiple interactions to accomplish a given task. The result is a lot of network traffic. Mobile agents allow us to package a conversation and dispatch it to a destination host, where the interactions can take place locally.

Mobile agents are also useful when it comes to reducing the flow of raw data in the network. When very large volumes of data are stored at remote hosts, these data should be processed in the locality of the data rather than transferred over the network. The motto is simple: move the computations to the data rather than the data to the computations.

5   Conclusion and future work

Mobile agents is a promising technology moving towards the vision of usable distributed heterogeneous open networks. In this paper, we proposed AOM: new middleware paradigm combining agent technology and middleware technology.

AOM also suitable to mobile computing environment that is low bandwidth and high packet lose rate. Conclusively, We make confirm that AOM is new middleware paradigm for the next generation, and mobile computing.

In addition, we will support cryptographic component for secure Internet applications.

References

1. C. G. Harrison, D. M. Chess and A. Kershenbaum, "Mobile Agents: Are they a good idea? IBM Research Report," 1995.
2. Joachim Baumann, Fritz Hohl, Nikolaos Radouniklis, Kurt Rothermel and Markus Straber, "Communication Concepts for Mobile Agent Systems," IPVR, University of Stuttgart, Germany, 1996.
3. Eckerson, Wayne W., "Three Tire Client/Server Architecture: Achieving Scalability, Performance, and Efficiency in Client Server Applications", Open Information Systems, 1995.
4. Message Oriented Middleware Association (MOMA), A Middleware Taxonomy, 1998. (URL: http://www.moma-inc.orgdeucation/ taxonomy.html)
5. General Magic, Inc., White Paper: Mobile Agents While Paper, 1998. (URL: http://www.genmagic.com/technology/ techwhitepaper.html)
6. A. Lingnau, O. Drobnik, P. Dvmel, "An HTTP-based Infrastructure for Mobile Agents", Proc. of the 4th International WWW Conference, Boston, USA, 1995. (URL: http://www.w3.org/pub/Conferences/WWW4/Papers/150/).
7. Steinks, Steve, "Middleware Meets the Network", LAN: The Network Solutions Magazine 10, 13, December 1995.
8. Ernu Kovacs, Klaus Ruhrle, and Matthias Reich, "Mobile Agents On The Move – Integrating an Agent System into the Mobile Middleware", the Proceedings of the ACTS Mobile Summit 1998, Greece, 1998.
9. M. StraBer, J. Baumann and F. Hohl, "Mole – A Java Based Agent System", Proc. 2nd ECOOP Workshop on Mobile Object Systems, dpunkt-Verlag, 1996.

CORBA-based Open Authentication Support Service of Electronic Commerce

Kyung-Ah Chang, Byung-Rae Lee, Tai-Yun Kim

Dept. of Computer Science & Engineering, Korea University,
1, 5-ga, Anam-dong, Sungbuk-ku, Seoul, 136-701, Korea
{gypsy93, brlee, tykim}@netlab.korea.ac.kr

Abstract. In this paper, based on CORBA security service specification[4] which OMG defined, we propose the open authentication support service for subjects of electronic commerce, providing the authentication of object level and the authenticated key exchange. This proposed service, by Kerberos[5] for the authentication and the authenticated key exchange, assures not only the identification of a partner but also the confidence of origin of business item for negotiations between subjects of electronic commerce. Since our deployed Kerberos is extended to the open authentication support service based on CORBA platform, it is efficient for security administration to manage the information such as a key management in the heterogeneous distributed computing environment.

1 Introduction

Recently, much research is being undertaken to provide the open and comprehensive solutions to securing commerce over the Internet and other public information networks. As in a physical marketplace, the main purpose[11] in an electronic marketplace is to bring potential a Merchant and a Buyer together;

- A Merchant offers his goods and a Buyer orders his goods; Both of these are mutual negotiations, sometimes ending with an agreement.
- Both a Merchant and a Buyer might need certain certificates; A Buyer can buy goods from a trusted Merchant, a Merchant can deliver goods to a trusted Buyer.
- A Merchant delivers his goods and a Buyer makes payments; Both of these are fairness of mutual exchanges.
- A Buyer or a Merchant might be dissatisfied with what has happened so far; several exception handlers and dispute handlers may exist.

To realize these requirements for Electronic Commerce(EC), we need a powerful middleware system that can integrate non-interoperable distributed computing. CORBA[2, 3] is a standard middleware supporting heterogeneous networks, designed as a platform-neutral infrastructure for inter-object communication.

This paper consists of four parts: CORBA security service for EC, open authentication support service, performance and conclusion. Section 2 gives the CORBA security service associated with electronic commerce. Section 3 shows the structure of the open authentication support service based on Kerberos[5] with CORBA[4]. Finally, Sections 4 and 5 give a performance and conclusion, respectively.

2 CORBA-based Security Service

2.1 CORBA Security Services

The CORBA security services provide interfaces[4] for the following:

- Authenticating and generating credentials for principals, including the delegation of credentials to intermediary principals
- Performing secure transactions between objects
- Auditing secure transactions for later review
- Non-repudiation facilities that generate evidence of transactions, to prevent principals involved in a secure transaction from denying the previous action

All these and their interfaces are specified in an implementation of independent manner[3]. So the interface of security service is independent of the use of symmetric or asymmetric keys, and the interface of a principal's credential is independent of the use of a particular certificate protocol.

2.2 Current View of CORBA-based Model

In 1996, RFP tackled the problem of interoperability between ORBs in the security implementations. It asked for an extension to the current IIOP[3] standard that could establish secure connections between the Clients and the Servers implemented using different ORBs. These ORBs would, of course, require the same security mechanism.

IONA[14]'s immediate plans for security incorporate a DCE-based implementation of the CORBA level 1[4], and the SSL into Orbix and OrbixWeb. However, with U.S. export restrictions, OrbixSSL provides RSA with 1024 bit keys, which are allowed to U.S. citizens only. Recently, the OMG's Electronic Commerce Domain Task Force(ECDTF) together with CommerceNet is working jointly on the standardization and development of a framework for open electronic commerce services[12]. Considering the specification of requirements and the architecture for EC, this joint submission "sets a higher bar" by requiring features that are superset of those features included in the CORBA security specification. The eCo system[13], nearly 20 CommerceNet members, has developed proprietary payment solutions. However, this system does not yet provide the integrity of message level, the authentication nor the authorization of principles that are currently specified in the CORBA security specification.

3 Open Authentication Support Service of Electronic Commerce

3.1 Description of EC Support Model

The architecture of EC described in this paper is structured in layers[10]; commerce layer, exchange layer, supporting services layer. In general, the commerce layer provides services that directly implement applications of EC, which handle the Client's registration, offering, ordering, and various payments, etc. The exchange layer provides services for handling and packaging business items as well as transfer and fairness of mutual exchanges. The basic items can be bundled in CORBA objects. The security attributes stored in each type of these objects determine the label of privilege that is required for the exchange.

In this paper, we concentrate on the credential service block of exchange layer which receive parsed messages by the exchange manager. This block handles a credential of each participant, thereby performing all secure invocations between a Merchant and a Buyer. This block contains authentication service, authorization service, and session identifier service. The exchange manager obtains a security feature by requesting 'get_service_information' to the ORB. Information returned includes the security functionality level, the options supported, and the version of the security specification to which it conforms.

3.2 Specification of Open Authentication Support Service

The credential service block will enable the combined security service based on principal's credential to support the authentication for peer entities to perform the mutual negotiations, and authorization for the Providers to control the domain accesses. In this section, we propose a mechanism for the open authentication support service based on Kerberos[5] and a rule of label-based access control.

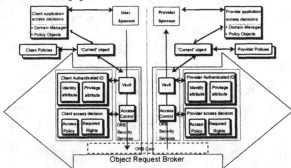

Fig. 1. CORBA-based Mechanism for Subjects of EC

Once authenticated with Fig. 1, the user sponsor is associated with a credential object, which contains information about its authenticated identity and the access rights under this identity. These credentials are then used in secure transactions, to verify the access privileges of the parties involved, and to register identities for actions that are audited or carried out in a non-repudiation mode. The Client requests the Provider through a local reference. The Client's credentials are attached to the request by the security services present in the ORB, and sent along with the request over the transport mechanism in use. The provider sponsor receives the request through its ORB, along with the Client's credentials. The provider sponsor can decide whether to honor the request or not, based on the access rights of the Client's identity.

The authenticate() method looks up the identification information for a login name in the principal profile storage. If this matches the supplied identification information, we create the Session IDentifier(SID_{azs}, SID_p) by encrypting the Principal name(ID_U) and returns it to the Client. Otherwise we throw the exception 'NotAuthenticated'.

The method authorize() handles three parameters: a Session IDentifier(SID_{azs}), the Provider(ID_P) which the Client wants to access, and the name of the operation to invoke. If the name of the Provider(ID_P) the Client wants to invoke is among these, this is allowed to proceed.

Table 1. Open Authentication Support Service based on Kerberos[5]

(a) Authentication Service Exchange : to obtain Session Identifier
(1) US → AS : Options $\|$ ID_U $\|$ $Domain_U$ $\|$ ID_{azs} $\|$ Times $\|$ $Nonce_1$
(2) AS → US : $Domain_U$ $\|$ ID_U $\|$ SID_{azs} $\|$ E_{Ku} [$K_{u,azs}$ $\|$ Times $\|$ $Nonce_1$ $\|$ $Domain_{azs}$ $\|$ ID_{azs}]
$\quad\quad SID_{azs} = E_{Kazs}$ [Flags $\|$ $K_{u,azs}$ $\|$ $Domain_U$ $\|$ ID_U $\|$ Times]
(b) Authorization Service Exchange : to obtain peer-supporting another Session Identifier
(3) US → AZS : Options $\|$ ID_P $\|$ Times $\|$ $Nonce_2$ $\|$ SID_{azs} $\|$ $Authenticator_U$
(4) AZS → US : $Domain_U$ $\|$ ID_U $\|$ SID_P $\|$ $E_{Ku,azs}$[$K_{U,P}$$\|$Times$\|$$Nonce_2$$\|$$Domain_P$$\|$$ID_P$$\|$$SID_P$]
$\quad\quad SID_{azs} = EK_{azs}$ [Flags $\|$ $K_{U,azs}$ $\|$ $Domain_U$ $\|$ ID_U $\|$ Times]
$\quad\quad SID_P = E_{Kp}$ [Flags $\|$ $K_{U,P}$ $\|$ $Domain_U$ $\|$ ID_U $\|$ Times]
$\quad\quad Authenticator_U = E_{Ku,azs}$[$ID_U$ $\|$ $Domain_U$ $\|$ TS_1]
(c) Fairness of Mutual Exchanges : to obtain service
(5) US → PS : Options $\|$ SID_P $\|$ $Authenticator_U$
(6) PS → US : $E_{Ku,p}$ [TS_{2+1} $\|$ Subkey $\|$ Seq#]
$\quad\quad SID_P = E_{Kp}$ [Flags $\|$ $K_{U,P}$ $\|$ $Domain_U$ $\|$ ID_U $\|$ Times]
$\quad\quad Authenticator_U = E_{Ku,p}$ [ID_U $\|$ $Domain_U$ $\|$ TS_2 $\|$ Subkey $\|$ Seq#]

US : User Sponsor, AS : Authentication Service Block, AZS : Authorization Service Block, SID_{azs} : Session Identifier to access Authorization Service Block, SID_P : Session IDentifier to access Provider, $Domain_U$: Domain ID of Principal

This proposed service has reflected an actual Internet scheme and activated when the Clients make a connection to Web page with a login name. The current object represents the current execution context for both the Client and the Provider. The current object supports the secure current interface, which gives access to the secure information. This current object supports DII[2] interface, which reflects a dynamic update of credential information on mutual exchanges for peer entities, between a Merchant and a Buyer.

Both the user sponsor and the provider sponsor transfer Session IDentifiers(SID_p) before mutual exchanges occur. This sequence makes it possible for a Merchant and a Buyer to apply security policies to the open authentication support service before exchange.

4 Security and Analysis

4.1 Security Analysis of Proposed Schemes

In open distributed computing, the DCE[6] and the SESAME[8] are the well known security systems, based on Kerberos[5], of the Client/ Server architecture. As seen in the Table 2, our proposed authentication support service shows better security features like the authentication for peer entities to perform the mutual negotiations and the fairness of exchange. Therefore it has the good advantages of interoperability with other security services.

Table 2. Security Analysis of Proposed Schemes

	DCE[6, 7]	SESAME[8]	Open Authentication Support Service
Access control level	Application	Application	Application/ System
Authentication	Unilateral	Unilateral	Unilateral/ Mutual
Authorization policy	ACL based	ACL based	Label based Rule
Fairness of exchange	No	No	Yes
Flag of privilege type	Positive	Positive/ Negative	Positive
Grant/ Revoke privileges	Controlled by Server	Controlled by Server	Label based Rule
Privilege type	User ID/ Group	User ID/ Role	User ID/ Group/ Role/ Domain
Scalability	Average	Average	High
Security policy domain	Server's domain	Server's domain	System Imposed
Service execution	Application Server Side	Application Server Side	Application Server/ Client Side
Suitability	Stable User base	Stable User base	Mandatory Controls

4.2 Feature Comparison with Middleware Schemes

Table 3. Performance Analysis with Middleware Schemes

	DCE[6]	DCOM[9]	CORBA[1]
Interoperability	O	△	O
Market position	X	O	O
Network transparency	O	X	O
Openness	△	X	O
Platform independence	O	X	O
Scalability	X	O	O
Separation of interfaces and implementations	△	O	O
Supporting for broad range of languages	△	O	O
Supporting multi-vendor	O	X	O
Supporting legacy system	O	X	O
Supporting services	X	O	O

X : non-supported, △ : weakly supported, O : well-supported

From both a historical and technological viewpoint, three of the most important middleware technologies are the Distributed Computing Environment(DCE)[6], the Distributed Component Object Model(DCOM)[9], and the Common Object Request Broker Architecture(CORBA)[1]. As described in Table 3, the CORBA is the most predominated middleware compared with other systems.

5 Conclusion and Future works

The open authentication support service that proposed in this paper is very critical in EC, since it provides the identification of a partner, and the confidence of origin of business item for negotiation. The goal of our system is to offer the open and comprehensive solutions for secure commerce over the Internet and other distributed computing. Our architecture of EC is reflected in the layered structure; The exchange layer handles transfers and fair exchanges of items. The commerce layer provides methods for downloading certified commerce services and the necessary trust management. It supports a mutual authentication between EC subjects, reliability of information integrity and technologic neutral way of open distributed object space with large scalability.

Research should be made on the efficiently distributed object system to support a mutual distributed security for EC and other Internet services. In addition, for a key management, a perfect synchronization of session keys should be considered.

References

1. Object Management Group: CORBA 2.2/ IIOP Specification, OMG (1998)
2. Robert Orfali, Dan Harkey: Client/ Server Programming with JAVA and CORBA, John Wiley & Sons (1997)
3. Andreas Vogel: Java Programming with CORBA, 2nd Ed., John Wiley & Sons (1998)
4. Object Management Group: CORBA services: Common Object Security Specification (1997) 15-1 ~ 15-294
5. John T. Kohl, B. Clifford Neuman, Theodore Y. Ts'o: The Evolution of the Kerberos Authentication Service, EurOpen Conference (1991)
6. Mannix, Frank: OSF/DCE : Introduction to Open Software Foundations Distributed Computing Environment, Digital Services (1992)
7. G. White and U. Pooch: Problems with DCE Security Services, Computer Communication Review, Vol. 25, No. 5 (1995)
8. T. Parker, D. Pinkas: SESAME V4 Overview, SESAME Issue1 (1995)
9. Mark Roy, Alan Ewald: Inside DCOM, DBMS Magazine (1997)
10. Matthias Schunter, Michael Waidner: Architecture and Design of a Secure Electronic Marketplace, Proceedings JENC 8 (1997)
11. M. Waidner: Development of a Secure Electronic Marketplace for Europe, ESORICS '96 (1996)
12. Stephen McConnell: The OMG/CommerceNet Joint Electronic Commerce Whitepaper, OSM (1997)
13. Jay M. Tenenbaum: eCo System: CommerceNet Architectural Framework for Internet Commerce, CommerceNet Inc. (1997)
14. IONA Technologies: OrbixSecurity White Paper (1998)

A Publish / Subscribe Framework:
Push Technology in Electronic Commerce

Edward C. Cheng[1]

OCT Research Laboratory. Birkbeck College, University of London
3 WatersPark Dr., #215, San Mateo, CA 94403

Abstract Publish/Subscribe (P/S) technology, conceptually divides resource managers (RM) and applications within a transaction tree into two categories: resource producers and resource consumers. Publishers enqueue information and the P/S system pushes it to the subscribers. Applying the P/S paradigm to the Internet-based Electronic Commerce (sometimes known as *Webcasting*), the RM's that produce and consume information can be real people. In this case, customers subscribe voluntarily or unknowingly to provide merchants their own information. Based on these customer profiles which may include information about their household or buying patterns, companies make decisions to push products and marketing messages to the relevant prospects electronically.

In this paper, OMM, an object-oriented organizational model, is presented as an underlying model to support P/S in E-Commerce. Firstly, it allows companies to flexibly model both the consumers and the materials to be consumed. Secondly, it allows users to specify business policies in SQL-like queries to match the consumers with the materials. Every time a new material is published, OMM automatically pushes it to the right audiences. The paper also discusses our experience of applying the research prototype, OMM/PS, to support the E-Commerce strategy of a commercial insurance firm.

1. Introduction

Electronic Commerce applications aim to conduct business over the electronic network. Although electronic business transactions evolved from EDI protocols will continue to play a major role in E-Commerce, the rapid growth of the Internet (in 1998, 2+ million new users are added to the Internet every quarter [4]) has pushed companies to expand the scope of E-Commerce applications to cover the full range of business activities which include marketing, negotiation, fulfillment and follow-up, all on the Web. Publish/Subscribe (P/S), a form of push technology, plays a significant role in E-Commerce by ensuring high volume, high performance and reliable processing of data as well as transactions over a number of RM's [1,2,3]. P/S typically divides *agents* into two categories: publishers and subscribers. Publishers produce resources and the P/S system pushes them to the subscribers, which consume the resources. A subscriber may in turn generate resources and become a publisher. With P/S, subscribers do not need to know *what, when* and *where* the information is; the P/S system is responsible for finding the subscribers every time when a new material is published. In the Internet-based E-Commerce environment, publishers are the agents representing the merchants while subscribers are the customers and business prospects. Applying the P/S paradigm to the Internet-based E-Commerce environment has helped electronic marketing and customer services to propagate large amount of information to their consumer base. Some even suggest with the maturing of push technology, the age of finding products through Web browsing will soon be over [5].

---

[1] cheng@db.stanford.edu

Unfortunately, P/S implementations have historically focused on technologies around data delivery options, delivery mechanism, reliable queues and transactional behavior [1,2,3,8]. Although many companies have attempted to automate P/S on the Internet by in-house development, there is no formal model proposed in this area. For most businesses, the large amount of information regarding the subscribers are stored in RDBMS or corporate directories, but the connections between the publishers and the subscribers are handled in a rather ad-hoc manner. Furthermore, the produced materials such as products, promotion plans, Web pages, news items, marketing messages, and service contracts are not modeled into the P/S system formally. As a result, it requires excessive human-intervention to sort and match the materials with the subscriber-base, thus fails to support very high volume push of relevant and just-in-time information.

This paper discusses an organizational model, namely OMM (Organization Modeling and Management), to support two aspects of P/S. Firstly, it provides an object-oriented reference model to flexibly model both the publisher and the subscriber. To model the publisher means to include all kinds of materials that are produced by the publisher. To model the subscriber means to capture the customer profiles. Secondly, it allows users to define business policies in SQL-like queries to match between the consumers and the produced materials. The next section covers the related research work in P/S and organization modeling. Section 3 describes the OMM conceptual and reference model for enterprise modeling. OMM does not assume a particular process or application architecture. With this generic approach, OMM is able to map its object types to other organizational data schemes and to present an integrated multi-dimensional view of different organizational resources. Section 4 presents the P/S concept in E-Commerce and discusses a Java-based prototype, OMM/PS. The paper will conclude in section 5 with a summary and our future research direction.

2. Related Work

Push technology has been around in various forms for many years. Early work of using computer networks for pushing data was performed in the 1980's [1]. The Boston Community Information System at MIT [6] and the Datacycle database system [7] are examples that incorporate some form of push technology. Their focus is mainly on broadcasting large amount of data with very high throughput, but none of these systems focuses on doing business on the Web, and none addresses the issue of P/S matching.

The P/S work initiated by Tibco and Oracle Corporation focus exclusively on supporting low level transactions [3,8]. Although the Advanced Queueing (AQ) in Oracle 8 allows users to build P/S system to support Internet-based push technology, it lacks the relationship model to automate the matching of publisher and subscriber. As a result, it fails to support high-volume and just-in-time push of relevant information.

Others has proposed organization models and methodologies mainly to support workflow systems. Representative works include M*-OBJECT [12], ORM [13], SAM* [14], and ObjectFlow [15,16]. They all start from the process view and tightly couple the organization model with the role model, and some even with the process model. Among the list, ORM [13] is the closest to support P/S modeling. ORM is a standalone client-server database application to support organization modeling in WorkParty, a workflow system by SIEMENS [17]. ORM has an application programming interface

(API) and a graphical user interface to allow users to define and populate the organizational database. Although ORM separates the organization model from the process model, it did not separate the organization model from the role model; the two are still integrated. Also, the organization definition and the role definition of ORM are still static like other prior arts, and it suffers from lack of a dynamic relationship model. The OVAL work by MIT supports easy modeling of organizations but it only has a static relationship model to define links between objects [24,25].

Overall, the existing approaches of P/S and the modeling of various P/S objects and the associated connections suffer from the following common weaknesses:

- Focus exclusively on supporting push mechanism and transactions. We need to apply the P/S paradigm to support Internet-based E-Commerce applications, which requires pushing of large amount of *just-in-time* information to only *relevant* audiences.

- Lack of a conceptual organization reference model. We need a generic solution so that we can apply the model to different electronic business environment.

- Support only some predefined resource types. Network DS focuses on machine nodes, users and applications; messaging DS on user addresses; and BPR organization sub-components on users, groups and roles. To model the consumer base as well as the different types of materials to be pushed in E-Commerce, the P/S system must be extensible and flexible in order to define the characteristics of various resource types which include customers, employees, marketing materials, products, promotion packages, news briefs, and others.

- Assume only static and hardwired relationships between resources. In reality, consumers and their demands are rapidly changing, that means their interests of receiving certain type of information also change.

- Lack a flexible matching model to automate the push of information. Most in-house implementations of P/S today embed the matching mechanism in the programming logic. As a result, adding new types of resources into the automated P/S system is rather difficult.

3. The OMM Organization Model

As discussed, most organizational modeling systems exist to serve only the associated workflow engine. The organization model of these systems naturally integrates with the role model. Contrary to existing systems, OMM methodology separates the organization model from the role model of the BPM system [10,11,17,20,21]. With the OMM approach, organizations are modeled separately from the business processes and applications [10]. Role definitions are done through the organizational modeling and management interface [11]. Abstracting the organization component from the workflow program allows us to get rid of the constraints from the workflow system and be flexible in modeling the enterprise. In addition, the organization component becomes a stand-alone application, which is now able to support more than just workflow [9] but also other aspects of E-Commerce such as P/S in this case.

The OMM employs a generic reference model, which can be applied flexibly to define different resource types and their inter-relationships. Resource types are user-defined;

they may include customers, employees, products, services, marketing materials, documents, new briefs, URL's and others. Modeling of an enterprise involves defining these classes of resources and the dynamic relationships between these resource objects. A P/S system is interested in pushing either a piece of newly published material to a subset of customers, or a subset of readily available materials to a new or changed customer. For example, an insurance company will be interested to publish and push the news item regarding travel safety in Uganda to all commercial clients who has branch offices in East Africa. Similarly, a client who has updated his profile through the web to indicate that the company has grown beyond 10 employees should receive the information about a new worker's compensation insurance policy.

There are three fundamental entities in the OMM model, namely the *organizations*, *members*, and *virtual links*.

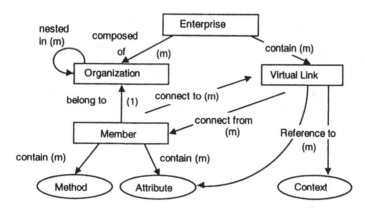

Figure 1. The OMM Organization Model

An enterprise is composed of a number of OMM organizations. Each *organization* represents a class of resources such as customers, employees, departments, products or news articles. Each *member* object within an organization maps to an actual entity of the corporation. Members of the same class share a common set of attributes and methods that is extensible by the user. A member can relate or link to other members through *virtual links*. Contrary to static connections, a virtual link only has a relationship definition, which is evaluated and resolved at runtime. Figure 1 uses an E-R diagram to show the OMM model. We shall discuss each of the OMM objects in greater detail.

3.1 Organizations

An enterprise is composed of a number of OMM organization objects. OMM organizations are created to map to the different dimensions and components of a company. Each organization has a unique identifier across the global enterprise. Using the OMM organizations, resources can be partitioned both *vertically* and *horizontally*; vertically into different dimensions or resource types, such as people, products, services and so on. Horizontal partitioning can be applied to break components of the same type into smaller units, such as breaking people into engineers, sales and marketing, and temporary workers.

For instance, an OMM organization may be defined to represent the people of the company, another to represent the different products, even another to represent the marketing publications, and so on. This creates a view of vertical partitioning of the corporation. Each partition keeps the organization information of a particular dimension. In addition, we can further divide an organization within the same dimension horizontally. For instance, people belonging to the engineering department may be included in one organization class, while people in the marketing department are placed in another. In other words, vertical partitioning helps to define the different types of resources within the enterprise, while horizontal partitioning allows users to logically divide resources of the same dimension into smaller sub-components.

3.2 Members and the Information Model

OMM uses an object-oriented model to capture its member information. An enterprise has a main member class which is the super-class containing a list of system-defined attributes and methods. All user-defined member classes are subclasses of the main member class and inherit the properties of the super-class. Figure 2 shows the class hierarchy.

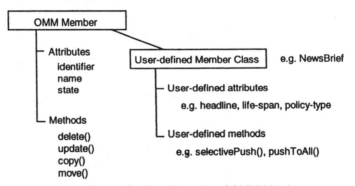

Figure 2. Class Hierarchy of OMM Member

The identifier attribute is unique for each member across the entire enterprise. Each member object has a name that is given by the user and is unique only within an OMM organization.

From the class definition point of view, the OMM model is similar to the *Object Class* in the directory model of X.500 [18]. OMM members are different from the members of X.500 in that they support class inheritance, method extension, and object life cycle. The latter captures the dynamic behavior of a resource within an actual corporation. It also allows the P/S system to properly reduce amount of traffic by eliminating inactive resources from the pool of communication. Furthermore, the OMM model is unique in that objects may relate dynamically to one other through *virtual links*.

3.3 Virtual Links and the Relationship Model

As collaborative effort exists between company resources, it is necessary to model relationships between them [22,23]. OMM uses *virtual links* to define dynamic relationships between member objects. Virtual links are rules constructed based on the member attributes and contextual variables. The OMM engine evaluates the rules to identify roles and relationships that resources have in the company. In OMM, a relationship is established from one resource to another, and as such it can be represented as a directed edge. If a bi-directional relationship (such as supervisor-subordinate relationship) is desired, it can be modeled as two relationships; one as a *reverse* relationship of the other. In this respect, resource objects are like nodes while virtual links are the directed edges in a graph. The syntax to define virtual links can be found in Cheng [10].

With virtual links, the connection between resources is dynamic and virtual because the relationship is defined with a regular expression over the attributes rather than a pair of static resource IDs. There may be a predefined owner of a relationship, or the owner can be assigned at runtime. When a virtual link is resolved on an owner, a member object, the relationship expression is evaluated over all the members in the organization scope, and there may have any number of resources satisfying the criteria indicating a relationship with the *owner* in question. An example of a relationship can be:

```
Owner:                 null
Relationship Name:     match_region_news
Expression:            ($X.region = $owner.region) OR
                       ($X.interestedRegion = $owner.region)
Organization Scope:    customer
```

When a news item is created, the user specifies the values of its attribute. In this example, the news item has an attribute called *region* which represents the region of the world that this news is concerned; the customer class has two attributes, namely *region* which indicates the location of the customer, and *interestedRegion* which the customer declares in his profile that he is interested in those regions for future expansion. When the user publishes the news item, OMM resolves the virtual link, *match_region_news*, over that news item. The news item becomes the *owner* of this resolution instance. The *region* attribute value of the news item is retrieved from the OMM database. For this example, let us assume the value is 'East Africa'. The virtual link expression now becomes:

```
($X.region = 'South Africa') OR ($X.interestedRegion = 'East Africa')
```

The P/S system now calls OMM to resolve this expression over the customer class. All customers whose profiles indicate their *region* or *interestedRegion* to be 'South Africa' are the candidates to receive the news item, and the P/S system will push the actual article or a URL link of the article to them through Internet Email. We will cover the detailed *Push* mechanism in section 4.

Note that a link may or may not be *transitive* in nature. When a transitive relationship r_1 is defined, and if member m_1 relates to member m_2 in r_1, and m_2 relates to m_3 in r_1, it follows that m_1 also relates to m_3 in r_1. For example, if a customer updates his profile and triggers P/S to evaluate a relationship *policy_document* which is defined as:

Expression:	($X.policy = $owner.holdingPolicy) OR
	($X.parentPolicy = $owner.policy)
Organization Scope:	document

In the first instance of evaluation, the updated customer is the *owner*. All those documents with *policy* type matching the *holdingPolicy* of the owner will be returned. If transitive relationship is to be evaluated, each document selected will become the owner of a second round evaluation of the relationship. All documents which identify the *owner* document as their *parentPolicy* will be returned. The evaluation tree will go on until no more document is returned. Obviously there is a cost associated with resolving transitive relationships; they should therefore be used with care.

When defining a relationship type, a *reverse* relationship can be specified. For example, if relationship types r_1 and r_1' are defined as reverse relationships to each other, and if member m_1 relates to m_2 in r_1, then m_2 relates to m_1 in r_1'.

A virtual link may also be defined between a member and an organization. When an OMM organization object is part of a relationship, all member objects within that organization are involved in it. For instance, if *message A* is an merge-and-acquisition announcement to all the customers, then all people in the customer class will receive the pushed information.

4. Conclusion

In our study, we found that push technology is playing a more and more significant role in E-Commerce. Although the statement of web browsing will be replaced totally by *web casting* is clearly overstated [5], we see that publish/subscribe is becoming a major vehicle in E-Commerce for companies to expand market size and enhance customer relationship.

Further research with OMM/PS includes giving a weight factor to attributes such that the system can have more intelligence to filter audience. We are also working on using different push mechanisms than simply e-mail and attachments. One specific example is to change the content of a customer's personal Web page when the profile is updated.

References

[1]   Franklin, M., Zdonik, S. "Data In Your Face": Push Technology in Perspective, *Proceedings of SIGMOD '98*, Seattle, WA, 1998.

[2]   Hal Berghel. The New Push for Push Technology, *netWorkers*, 2(3):28-36, June, 1998.

[3]   Transactional Publish/Subscribe: The Proactive Multicast of Database Changes. *Proceedings of SIGMOD '98*, Seattle, WA. 1998.

[4]   Internet Trak, 2nd Quarter, 1998. *Ziff-Davis Publishing* July, 1998. http://www.zd.com/marketresearch/IT2Q.htm.

[5]   Push! Kiss your browser goodbye. *Wired magazine*. March, 1997.

[6]   Gifford, D.   Polychannel Systems for Mass Digital Communication, *CACM*, 33(2), February, 1990.

[7]   Herman, G., et al.   The Datacycle Architecture for Very High Throughput Database Systems. *Proceedings of SIGMOD '87*, San Francisco, CA. 1987.

[8]   Cheng, E., et. al. An Open and Extensible Event-based Transaction Manager, *Proceedings of USENIX Conference*, 1991.

[9]   Cheng, E. Re-engineering and Automating Enterprise-wide Business Processes, *Proceedings of International Working Conference on Information Industry*, Bangkok, Thailand, April, 1995.

[10]   Cheng, E. A Rule-Based Organization Modeling System to Support Dynamic Role-Resolution in Workflow. *Proceedings of the 11th International Conference on Parallel and Distributed Computing Systems*. September, 1998.

[11]   Cheng, E. An Object-Oriented Organizational Model to Support Dynamic Role-based Access Control in Electronic Commerce Applications, *Proceedings of HICSS'99*, Maui, Hawaii, January, 1999.

[12]   Di Leva, A., Giolito, P., Vernadat, F. The M*-OBJECT Organisation Model for Enterprise Modelling of Integrated Engineering Environments. *Concurrent Engineering - Research and Applications*. 5(2):183-194, 1997.

[13]   Rupietta, W.   Organization Models for Cooperative Office Applications. *Database and Expert Systems Applications*. *Proceedings of the 5th International Conference, DEXA '94*, Athens, Greece, 1994.

[14]   Su, S. Modeling Integrated Manufacturing Data with SAM-*. *Computer*, 19(1):34-49, 1986.

[15]   Hsu, M. An Execution Model for an Activity Management System, *Digital Technical Report*, April, 1991.

[16]   Hsu, M., Kleissner, C. Objectflow - towards a process management infrastructure. *Distributed and Parallel Databases*. 4(2):169-194, 1996.

[17]   Bussler, C. Analysis of the Organization Modeling Capability of Workflow Management Systems. *Proceedings of the PRIISM '96 Conferenc*,. Maui, Hawaii. January, 1996.

[18]   *CCITT Recommendation X.500 to X.521: Data Communication Networks, Directory*. Blue Book. Also ISO/IEC Standards ISO 9594-1 to ISO 9594-7, 1988.

[19]   Berio, G., et. al. The M*-OBJECT Methodology for Information System Design in CIM Environments. *IEEE Transactions on Systems, Man, and Cybernetics*. 25(1):68-85, 1995.

[20]   Mertins, K., Heisig, P., Krause, O. Integrating business-process re-engineering with human-resource development for continuous improvement. *International Journal of Technology Management*. 14(1):39-49, 1997.

[21] Bussler, C. Enterprise Process Modeling and Enactment in GERAM. *Proceedings of the 3rd International Conference On Automation, Robotics and Computer Vision (ICARCV '94)*, Singapore, November, 1994.

[22] Willcocks, L., Smith, G. IT-enabled BPR - organizational and human-resource dimensions. *Journal of Strategic Information Systems*. 4(3):279-301, 1995.

[23] Roos, H., Bruss, L. Human and Organization Issues, *The Workflow Paradigm*, pp. 35-49, Future Strategies Publishing, 1994.

[24] Malone, T.W., Lai, K.-Y. and Fry, C. Experiments with Oval: A Radically Tailorable Tool for Cooperative Work. *ACM Transactions on Information Systems*, 13(2):177-205. April, 1995.

[25] Malone, T.W., et. al. Tools for inventing organizations: Toward a handbook of organizational processes. *Proceedings of the 2nd IEEE Workshop on Enabling Technologies Infrastructure for Collaborative Enterprises*, Morgantown, WV, April, 1993.

SemNet: A Semantic Network for Integration of Databases

Jeong-Oog Lee and Doo-Kwon Baik

Software System Lab., Dept. of Computer Science & Engineering, Korea University,
1, 5-ka, Anam-dong, Sungbuk-gu, SEOUL, 136-701, KOREA
{ljo, baik}@swsys2.korea.ac.kr
http://swsys2.korea.ac.kr/index.html

Abstract. A multidatabase system provides integrated access to heterogeneous, autonomous component databases in a distributed system. In
order to gain integrated access to a multidatabase system, semantic heterogeneities have to be detected and resolved. That is, the multidatabase
system must interpret and integrate the meaning of the information and
identify semantically equivalent or related objects.

The approach presented in this paper uses WordNet as linguistic knowledge to represent and interpret the meaning of the information, to integrate the information, and to give users efficient access mechanism to
the integrated information.

1   Introduction

A multidatabase system provides integrated access to heterogeneous, autonomous
component databases in a distributed system. An essential prerequisite to achieving interoperability in multidatabase systems is to be able to identify semantically equivalent or related items in component databases. Another problem in
multidatabase systems is allowing users to handle information from different
databases that refer to the same real-world entity.

As linguistic theories evolved in recent decades, linguists became increasingly
explicit about the information a lexicon must contain in order for the phonolog-
ical, syntactic, and lexical components to work together in the everyday production and comprehension of linguistic messages. WordNet is an electronic lexical
system developed at Princeton University and organized by semantic relations
such as synonymy, antonymy, hyponymy, and meronymy [2]. The noun portion
of WordNet is designed around the concept of synset which is a set of closely
related synonyms representing a word meaning.

The approach presented in this paper uses WordNet as linguistic knowledge
to represent and interpret the meaning of the information, to integrate the information, and to give users efficient access to the integrated information. The
basic idea is to make a semantic network for each component database and to use
WordNet to providing mapping between the semantic networks. Using WordNet
and the descriptions of the database objects, we construct a semantic network for
each component database. Then, a global semantic network can be created with

the semantic relations in WordNet and the semantic networks. A global semantic network provides semantic knowledge about a distributed environment.

The rest of this paper is organized as follows. In section 2, we address the problem of semantic heterogeneity and define the types of schema conflicts. Section 3 presents the process of constructing a semantic network. Section 4 shows how we can detect semantic heterogeneity based on the semantic networks and the semantic relations in WordNet. Finally, in section 5, we offer our conclusion.

2 Semantic Heterogeneity

In order to gain integrated access to the multidatabase, semantic heterogeneities have to be detected and resolved. Semantic heterogeneities include differences in the way the real world is modeled in the databases, particularly in the schemas of the databases [3].

Since a database is defined by its schema and data, semantic heterogeneities can be classified into schema conflict and data conflict [5]. Schema conflicts mainly result from the use of different structures for the same information and the use of different names for the same structures. Data conflicts are due to inconsistent data in the absence of schema conflicts. Figure 1 shows an example to illustrate semantic heterogeneities.

Component Database 1 (CDB₁)

```
Undergraduate (sid, name, sex, address, advisor#)
Graduate (sid, name, sex, address, advisor#)
FullProfessor (pid, name, sex, office)
AssociateProfessor (pid, name, sex, office)
AssistantProfessor (pid, name, sex, office)
```

Component Database 2 (CDB₂)

```
Student (sid, name, gender, advisor#)
Address (sid, street, city, state)
Professor (pid, name, sex, position, office)
```

Component Database 3 (CDB₃)

```
Student (pid, name, female, male, street, city, state, advisor#)
Faculty (fid, name, office)
```

Fig. 1. An Example of database schemas

As our focus is only on the schema conflicts, we assume that data conflicts such as different representations for the same data are already conformed. Focusing on schema conflicts, we define the types of conflicts which are considered in this paper as follows.

Entity versus entity structure conflicts (EESC) occur when component databases use different numbers of entities to represent the same information. **Entity versus attribute structure conflicts (EASC)** occur if an attribute of some component databases is represented as an entity in others. **Entity versus value structure conflicts (EVSC)** occur when the attribute values in some component databases are semantically related to the entities in other component databases. **Attribute versus attribute structure conflicts (AASC)** occur when component databases use different numbers of attributes to represent the same information. **Attribute versus value structure conflicts (AVSC)** occur when the attribute values in some component databases are semantically related to the attributes in others. **Entity versus entity name conflicts (EENC)** arise due to different names assigned to the entities in different component databases. **Attribute versus attribute name conflicts (AANC)** are similar to EENC and arise due to different names assigned to the attributes in different component databases.

3   Semantic Networks

To integrate information from multiple component databases, users must represent the meaning of the information in each component database in a unified way. At each component database (CDB), to represent the information, a local database administrator (DBA) makes descriptions of database objects. In making descriptions, we make reference to ISO/IEC 11179 [6]. Using descriptions and WordNet, users create a representation table. Then, a semantic network for the component database can be created according to the representation table. All the semantic networks in component databases shall be integrated into a global semantic network for a multidatabase system.

3.1   Principles for Making Descriptions

The following are principles that must be used to make descriptions in order to represent the meaning of the information in a component database. A description can be formed with syntactic and semantic rules. Semantic rules govern the source and content of the words used in a description and enable meaning to be conveyed. Syntactic principles specify the arrangement of components within a description.

Semantic Rules. Semantics concerns the meanings of description components. The components are entity terms, property terms, key terms, and qualifier terms. An entity term is a component of a description which represents an activity or object in real world. For example, in a description **Student Last Name**, the component **Student** is entity term. A set of property terms must consist of terms which are discrete and complete. For example, in the description **Student Last Name**, the component **Last Name** is property. A key term is a component of a description for a database object, which describes the form of representation of the database object. For example, in **Student Last Name**, the component **Name** is key term. Qualifier terms may be attached to entity terms, property terms, and key terms if necessary to uniquely identify a description.

Syntactic Principles. The entity term shall occupy the first (leftmost) position in the description. Qualifier terms shall precede the component qualified. The property term shall occupy the next position. And, the key term shall occupy the last position. No abbreviations are allowed. For example, a description **Student ID** is not allowed. It must be **Student Identification Number**. Furthermore, All descriptions shall be unique within a component database.

Data Types. Every attribute value belongs to some data type. Although various database systems may support different data types, most support at least numeric, character, and boolean data type. Some database systems may also use a coding scheme to represent an attribute. For example, in figure 2, CDB_2 represents the attribute **position** as 1 for full professor, 2 for associate professor, and 3 for assistant professor. In such a case, during making a description, users must describe the meaning of the codes.

3.2 Constructing Semantic Networks

After descriptions are created according to the above rules, the descriptions are decomposed into unit terms. A unit term means a word or a phrase that can be found in WordNet. For example, as a compound noun, 'phone number', can be found in WordNet, it is treated as a unit term. The result for this decomposing process is a representation table. A representation table consists of object type, object name, data type, description, and a set of unit terms. Figure 2 depicts an example of a representation table.

Rec#	Object_Type	Object_Name	Data_Type	Description	Unit_Terms
1	E	Professor		professor	\<professor\>
2	A	pid	n	professor identification number	\<professor\> \<identification number\>
3	A	nm	s	professor name	\<professor\> \<name\>
4	A	sex	b	professor gender /M=male I F=female	\<professor\> \<gender\> /\<male\> I \<female\>
5	A	position	c	professor position /1=full professor I 2=associate professor I 3=assistant professor	\<professor\> \<position\> /\<full professor\> I \<associate professor\> I \<assistant professor\>
6	A	salary	n	professor salary	\<professor\> \<salary\>
7	A	office	n	office room number	\<office\> \<room\> \<number\>

Fig. 2. An example of a representation table

In making a representation table, the component database administrator must cope with synonymy and polysemy. To identify unit terms related by synonymy automatically, we use synsets in WordNet. However, to acquire correct meaning of a unit term, the component database administrator must deal with its polysemy manually, For example, when the local DBA inputs a unit term 'client' into WordNet, he/she must choose one among many different meanings.

Given a set of unit terms of a component database, each unit term is connected with a word (or a phrase) in WordNet. The output for this process is a semantic network. A semantic network provides mapping between words in WordNet and unit terms in a component database.

4 Semantic Detection and a Global Semantic Network

A multidatabase system must interpret the meaning of the information and identify semantically equivalent or related objects. Once semantic networks are constructed, they are integrated into a global semantic network. In integrating semantic networks, a multidatabase system can detect semantic heterogeneity based on them.

4.1 Semantic Detection using Semantic Networks and WordNet

The following are examples that show how we can detect semantic heterogeneity based on the semantic networks and the semantic relations in WordNet. The examples are explained with schemas in figure 1. The results of detection process can be used to resolve semantic heterogeneity in information retrieval.

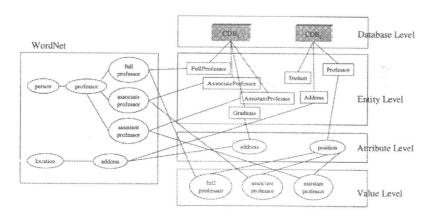

Fig. 3. A partial state of merging two component databases, CDB_1 and CDB_2

Detection of EESC. According to the hyponymy semantic relation in Word-Net, we can find that *professor* is a hypernym of *full professor, associate professor*, and *assistant professor* (figure 3). Therefore, the entity **Professor** in CDB_2 is semantically equivalent to a set of entities, {**FullProfessor, AssociatePro-fessor, AssistantProfessor**}, in CDB_1.

Detection of EASC. In the figure 3, both the attribute **address** in CDB_1 and the entity **Address** in CDB_2 are linked to a word *address* in WordNet. Therefore, the attribute **address** is semantically equivalent to the entity **Address**.

Detection of EVSC. CDB_2 uses a coding scheme to represent the attribute **position** as 1 for full professor, 2 for associate professor, and 3 for assistant professor. These values are linked to entities in CDB_1, respectively (figure 3). Therefore, the values of **position** are semantically equivalent to the entities, **FullProfessor**, **AssociateProfessor**, and **AssistantProfessor**, in CDB_1.

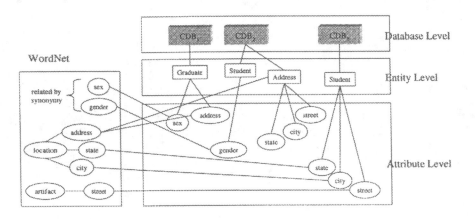

Fig. 4. A partial state of merging three component databases, CDB_1, CDB_2 and CDB_3

Detection of AASC. We already explained that the entity **Address** in CDB_2 is semantically equivalent to the attribute **address** in CDB_1. And all the attributes of **Address** in CDB_2 are equal to a set of attributes, {**state**, **city**, **street**}, in **Student** in CDB_3 (figure 4). Therefore, the attribute **address** is semantically equivalent to the set of attributes, {**state**, **city**, **street**}.

Detection of AANC. In the figure 4, as *sex* and *gender* are synonymous in WordNet, we can interpret that the meaning of the two attributes, **sex** in CDB_1 and **gender** in CDB_2, are the same.

Detection of AVSC. CDB_3 uses a coding scheme to represent the attribute **sex** as F for female, M for male. These values are linked to the attributes in CDB_1, respectively (figure 5). Therefore, the values of **sex** are semantically equivalent to the attributes, **female** and **male**, in CDB_2.

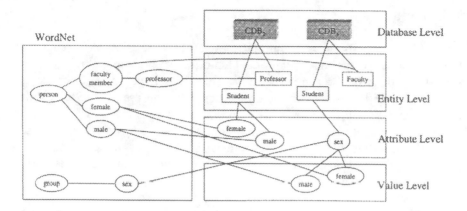

Fig. 5. A partial state of merging two component databases, CDB_2 and CDB_3

Detection of EENC. According to the hyponymy semantic relation in Word-Net, we can find that *faculty member* is a hypernym of *professor* (figure 5). Therefore, the entity **Professor** in CDB_2 is semantically equivalent to the entity **Faculty** in CDB_3.

The output for merging phase is a global semantic network. A global semantic network provides a multidatabase system with necessary knowledge for integrated access to component databases.

4.2 The Role of a Global Semantic Network

A multidatabase system can provide a uniform interface to a multitude of component databases. Consider the knowledge a multidatabase system would need to answer the following question:

"Find those professors whose salary is over $50,000."

To answer this question, the system must have several kinds of knowledge as follows.

- A multidatabase system must know where to find the relevant information on the component databases (**access knowledge**).
- A multidatabase system must know which entities, attributes, or values in the component databases meet the semantics in the query (**semantic knowledge**).

To acquire this knowledge, we develop a global semantic network, which specifies the semantic relations among entities, attributes, and value domains in component databases. Once a global semantic network is constructed, we can resolve semantic heterogeneity based on it.

5 Conclusion

The traditional approach to a multidatabase system focuses on procedures to merge individual component database schemas into a single global schema. The disadvantage of this approach is that a user must re-engineer the global schema whenever any of the sources change or when new sources are added. Multi-database language approach eliminates problems of creating and maintaining the global schema, but presents a more complex global interface to the user. In several researches [1][4], an information mediator has been developed for integrating of information in dynamic and open environments. One issue that is common to all of those approaches using an information mediator is how to scale these systems to large numbers of information sources in a way that is both computationally tractable and natural to the developers of new applications.

In our approach, user's descriptions for database objects are crucial for integrating of component databases. Weak and wrong descriptions may degrade the multidatabase system, which shall be a drawback of our approach. However, if users make descriptions according to our guidelines, the multidatabase system frees users from the tremendous tasks of finding the relevant component databases and interacting with each component database using a particular interface. Furthermore, our approach has the advantage of source independence by describing the meaning of the information in terms of general linguistic knowledge, which means that the multidatabase system can efficiently update the global semantic network when the component databases are changed, added, or deleted. Overall, our approach provides a simple, efficient, and effective mechanism for integrating autonomous, heterogeneous component databases.

References

1. Craig A. Knoblock, Yigal Arens, and Chun-Nan Hsu: Cooperating Agents for Information Retrieval, Proceedings of the second International Conference on Cooperative Information Systems (1994)
2. G. A. Miller, R. Beckwith, C. Fellbaum, D.Gross, and K. Miller: Five Papers on WordNet, CSL Reort 43, Cognitive Systems Laboratory, Priceton Univ. (1990)
3. M. Garcia-Solaco, F. Saltor, and M. Castellanos: Semantic Heterogeneity in Multidatabase Systems, Object-Oriented Multidatabase Systems: A Solution for Advanced Applications, Edited by Orman A. Bukhres, Ahmed K. Elmagarmid, Prentice Hall Inc. (1996) 129-202
4. R. Bayardo, W. Bohrer, et al: InfoSleuth: agent-based semantic integration of information in open and dynamic environments, ACM SIGMOD Record, Vol. 26, No. 2 (1997)
5. W. Kim, J. Seo: Classifying Schematic and Data Heterogeneity in Multidatabase Systems, IEEE Computer, Vol. 24, No. 12 (1992) 12-18
6. Specification and standardization of data elements, ISO/IEC 11179

Reliable Communication Service for Mobile Agent Based on CORBA

Byung-Rae Lee, Kyung-Ah Chang, and Tai-Yun Kim

Dept. of Computer Science & Engineering, Korea University,
1, 5-ga, Anam-dong, Seongbuk-ku, Seoul, 136-701, Korea
{brlee, gypsy93, tykim}@netlab.korea.ac.kr

Abstract. Mobile agents[1] are active entities, which may migrate to meet other agents and access the place's services. For mobile agent collaboration in distributed environment, mobile agents should be able to exchange messages with each other, even if they are moving across a network. The ability to send messages to a moving agent is important mechanism for agent collaboration. In this paper, we propose reliable messaging mechanism with notification messages based on CORBA[2]. This mechanism allows messages in flight when a mobile agent moves, and messages sent based on an out-of-date IOR[3], to be forwarded directly to the mobile agent's new location.

1 Introduction

The CORBA has been established as an important standard, enhancing the original Remote Procedure Call (RPC) based architectures by allowing relatively free and transparent distribution of service functionality[4,5]. Besides mobile agent technology has been proved to be suitable for the improvement of today's distributed systems. Thus, an integrated approach is desirable, combining the benefits of both client/server and mobile agent technology[6].

The purpose of the MASIF[1] is to achieve a certain degree of interoperability between mobile agent platforms of different manufactures. Two interfaces are specified by the MASIF standard: the MAFAgentSystem[1] interface provides operations for the management and transfer of agents, whereas the MAFFinder[1] interface functions as a dynamic name and location database of agents, places, and agent systems.

In this paper, we propose CORBA-based reliable communication service with notification messages in distributed agent environment. This mechanism allows messages in flight when a mobile agent moves, and messages sent based on an out-of-date IOR binding, to be forwarded directly to the mobile agent's new location. Proposed service works with MASIF naming services, preserving interoperability.

The remainder of this paper will proceed as follows. In Section 2, naming services in distributed agent environment is discussed. In section 3, CORBA-based proposed reliable communication scheme is presented. Notification messages used in proposed service are explained. In Section 4, we show the performance analysis of proposed reliable communication service. Finally, in section 5, we discuss current status of this work and the future directions that this work may take.

2 Mobile Agent and CORBA

The CORBA naming services are designed for static objects. When CORBA naming services are applied to mobile agents, they may not handle all cases as well.

A mobile agent gets a new IOR after each migration. In this case, the IOR that is kept by the accessing application becomes invalid. Following three solutions for this problem are specified in MASIF.

1. The first solution is that the ORB itself is responsible for keeping the IOR of moving objects constant. The mapping of the original IOR to the actual IOR of the migrated agent is managed by a corresponding proxy object, which is maintained by the ORB.
2. The second solution is to update the name IOR associated to the mobile agent after each migration, i.e. to supply the naming service with the actual agent IOR. In this case the application contacts the Naming Service in order to get the new agent IOR. A disadvantage of this solution is that the MAFFinder must be contacted by the migrating agent after each migration step in order to retrieve the new IOR to which each message must be sent[1].
3. When a mobile agent migrates for the first time, the original instance remains at the home agent system and forwards each additional access to the migrated instance at the new location. One disadvantage of this solution is that the proxy agent must be contacted by the migrating agent after each migration step in order to retrieve the new IOR to which each access request must be forwarded. Another disadvantage is that the home agent system must be accessible at any time. If the home agent system is terminated, the agent cannot be accessed anymore, since the actual IOR is only maintained by the proxy agent[1].

In MASIF, messages in flight to the old location when the mobile agent moved are likely to be lost and are assumed to be retransferred if needed. To avoid risk of message losses, proposed scheme provides a means for allowing message in flight to the previous agent system to be forwarded to the new location.

3 Reliable Communication Service

In this section, we propose reliable communication service to allow messages can be delivered from a source agent to a target mobile agent without message losses or delivery failure. Proposed mechanism supports the second and third solution of MASIF, MAFFinder and home agent based concepts, because MASIF doesn't rely on the first solution, ORB-based approach.

3.1 Reliable Communication

MASIF naming service allows transparent interoperation between mobile agents and their correspondents mobile agents.but the MAFFinder or home agent system plays a key role in supporting location transparent communication service. To provide reliable communication service, considerations should be made to support flying messages in addition to the MAFinder or home agent system failure.

Proposed reliable communication service provides means for agent systems to record the IOR of a mobile agent and to then forward their own messages to the current location indicated in that binding. Using proposed mechanism, as a side effect of these communication to a mobile agent, the original sender of the message may be informed of the mobile agent's current IOR, giving the sender an opportunity to record the current IOR.

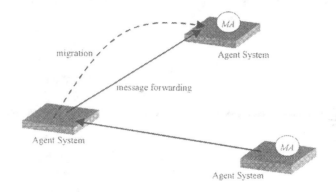

Fig. 1. Message Forwarding Mechanism

Messages in flight to the old location when the mobile agent moved are likely to be lost and are assumed to be retransferred if needed. To avoid risks of message losses, proposed mechanism provides means for the mobile agent's previous foreign agent system to be reliably notified of the mobile agent's new mobility binding allowing messages in flight to the mobile agent's previous foreign agent system to be forwarded to its new location as shown in figure 1.

3.2 Message Queue

Proposed system provides support for reliable transmission of messages across the network via use of an underlying message queuing subsystem. The message queue in agent system serves as a transmission buffer for the request in this manner. This feature of the message queuing subsytem is a natural fit to the disconnected operational mode of the mobile agent paradigm because it provides "store and forward" mechanism.

Flying message can be stored on the message queue of an intermediate agent system while a target mobile agent migrating. When the target mobile agent arrives at the destination, the agent system would then forward the message to the target mobile agent.

A message queuing subsystem can provide additional reliability by maintaining a copy of the messages to be transmitted an on-disk queue until the recipient of this message transmission has acknowledged its receipt via the notification messages.

3.3 IOR Update Mechanism

Following notification messages are defined to provide a flexible mechanism for agent systems to update their IOR entries, associating the mobile agent's unique name with its new IOR. It is the mechanism by which mobile agent request forwarding services after migration, keeping agent systems' mobility bindings be up-to-date information.

- *Binding Warning* message: An agent system will receive a *Binding Warning* message if an agent system maintaining an IOR entry for one of the agent system's mobile agent uses an out-of-date entry.
- *Binding Request* message: A *Binding Request* message is to request a mobile agent's current mobility binding from the mobile agent's home agent system.
- *Binding Update* message: A *Binding Update* message is used for notification of a mobile agent's current mobility binding. It should be sent in response to a *Binding Request Message* or a *Binding Warning* message.
- *Binding Acknowledge* message: A *Binding Acknowledge* message is used to acknowledge receipt of a *Binding Update* message.

The mobile agent need to transfer a *Binding Update* message to its previous foreign agent system until the matching *Binding Acknowledge* message is received. As shown in figure 2, previous foreign agent system can forward messages to the destination agent system using the information from the *Binding Update* message.

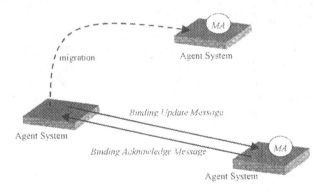

Fig. 2. IOR Update Mechanism

3.4 Using the Binding Table

Proposed communication service provides a means for agent systems to record the IORs of mobile agents in the binding table and to then send their own messages directly to the current location indicated in that binding., without contacting MAFFinder or bypassing the home agent system.

Agent system maintains a binding table to keep track of recently associated mobile agents.

If the sender agent system has an IOR entry in the binding table, it can send messages directly without contacting the MAFFinder or home agent system. This service is useful in case of network failure.

If the sender agent system has illegal binding, it may receive *Binding Warning* message. After receiving *Binding Warning* message, it should send *Binding Request* message to the MAFFinder or home agent system of target mobile agent.

An agent system may create or update a binding table entry for a mobile agent only when it has received the mobile agent's mobility binding. In addition, an agent system may use any reasonable strategy for managing the space within the binding table. When a new entry needs to be added to the binding table, the agent system may choose to drop any entry already in the table, if needed, to make space for the new entry.

4 Performance Analysis

Table 1 shows the performance analysis of other mobile agent platforms and proposed CORBA-based reliable communication service.

Table 1. Performance Analysis with Mobile Agent Platforms

	Ara[7]	Aglet[8,9]	Voyager [10,11]	Proposed Service
Reliability	×	×	△	- Forwarding - Message Queue - Binding Table
Interoperability	×	×	×	O

× : not supported, △: weakly supported, O: well supported

Ara only support simple control messages to be transferred remotely. Its remote messaging system does not allow messages in flight when agent moves. Aglet does not care about message losses because of incorrect location information. Proposed service allows an agent to send messages to other agents, even if they are moving and regardless of where they are in the network based on MASIF solutions. Only proposed mechanism is MASIF compliant. Although Voyager is CORBA enabled, it does not conform to MASIF.

Table 2. Performance Analysis with MASIF

	MASIF	Proposed Service
Reliability	No specification	- Forwarding - Message Queue - Binding Table

Table 2 shows performance enhancements of proposed service with the IOR table comparing with MASIF submissions. MASIF does not care about message losses or network failure. Proposed service provides reliable communication via a binding table. If binding is not correct, transferred messages will be forwarded to the target mobile agent.

5 Conclusion and Future works

We proposed reliable communication service based on CORBA, which provides means for any agent system to maintain a binding table. Proposed mechanism allows a mobile agent to send messages to other mobile agents, even if they are moving and regardless of where they are in the network. If the binding table doesn't have a target agent entry, the original MASIF messaging mechanism can be used instead.

Proposed reliable communication service can be applied to Electronic Commerce (EC). Mobile agents can migrate to many EC related hosts gathering information (e.g. lowest prices). Another applicable area is where requiring fast message delivery capabilities. For example, Intrusion Detection System (IDS)[12] need reliable notifications and responses. We are also considering security enhanced messaging system. Because messages can be routed through several agent systems, message integrity and confidentiality should be provided by some cryptographic means[13].

References

1. OMG: Mobile Agent System Interoperability Facilities Specification, November (1997)
2. OMG: The Common Object Request Broker: Architecture and Specification (1998)
3. OMG: CORBA Service: Common Object Services Specification (1998)
4. Andreas Vogel and Keith Duddy: JAVA™ Programming with CORBA, Wiley (1998)
5. Robert Orfail, Dan Harkey and Jeri Edward: Client/Server Survival/Guide, 3rd Ed., Wiley (1999)
6. T. Magedanz, K. Rothermel, S. Krause: "Intelligent Agents: An Emerging Technology for Next Generation Telecommunications?, Proceedings of IEEE INFOCOM '96, pp. 464-472, IEEE Press (1996)
7. Peine. H., Stolpmann. T: "The Architecture of the Ara Platform for Mobile Agents", Lecture Notes in Computer Science, No. 1219, pp.50-61, Springer Verlag, April (1997)
8. IBM Tokyo Research Labs: Aglets Workbench: Programming Mobile Agents in Java, http://www.trl.ibm.co.jp/aglets/ (1999)
9. Danny B. Lange Mitsuru Oshima: Programming and Deploying Java™ Mobile Agents with Aglets™, Addison Wesley (1998)
10. ObjectSpace: ObjectSpace Voyager CORBA Integration Technical Overview (1997)
11. ObjectSpace: Voyager Core Package Technical Overview (1997)
12. Aurobindo Sundaram: An Introduction to Intrusion Detection, Crossroads, ACM, October (1998)
13. W. M. Farmer, J. D. Guttman, V. Swarup: Security for Mobile Agents: Issues and Requirements, 19th National Information Systems Security Conference (NISSC 96) (1996)

Technology of Image Coding for Cell Losses in ATM Transmission

Jian CONG, Suo CONG, Zaimin LI, Gansha WU, Wen JIN

102 Lab, Institute of Communication
University of Electronic and Technology
Chengdu,Sichuan
P.R.China
congjian@fudan.edu

Abstract. This paper considers the model of a layered image coding when some of the cell are lost and a new technology for image reconstruction in receiver is proposed. Experiment results have shown that compared with the other theme of image coding in ATM network, the algorithm proposed here improves the quality of image details with the same cell loss rate and no effect to coding efficiency and can easily be implemented.

Index Terms. Layered Image Coding, Image Reconstruction

1.Introduction

Nowadays the VBR (Variant Bit Rate) service and corresponding flow control mechanism that ATM-based networks can provide make them a widely accepted solution in video and image communication fields. Nevertheless for the reason that ATM-based networks resort to TDM(Time Division Multiplex) mode to manage bandwidth resources, cell-loss cases come into existence when congestion can't be avoided. We count on two solutions to improve the image quality of communication in ATM environments. The first, the native congestion control mechanism of ATM-based networks can relax the congestion-originated cell loss. On the other side we can go off from the image coding, whose soul is to better the steadiness of source-end coding scheme, design the coding algorithm insensitive to cell loss, and adopt some backward processing techniques at the receiver-end to reconstruct the lost cells. In this domain, H.Tominaga put forward a DPCM-based and layered VBR coding algorithm, but it's at the cost of coding efficiency [1]。 Another ELC（Edge Location Complementation） algorithm utilizing sub-band division and VPIC technique to reconstruct the lost high frequency sub-band of the images.

This paper focuses on the cell loss of ATM-based networks to put forward a layered image coding solution and corresponding receiver-end image reconstruction algorithm. What's different to the traditional layered coding solution is that we no longer resort to the frequency components of an image as the only criteria to evaluate the importance of information, but higher the transmission priority of high frequency.

Under the same channel condition and cell loss rate, this solution can provide better-detailed quality of images than others and won't hurt the coding efficiency even a bit. The layered coding scheme is given in the second section, then in the third section we'll discuss the receiver-end lost cell reconstruction algorithm, the experiment simulation result appears in the last section.

2.The Layered Coding Scheme of Image in ATM-based networks

According to the flow control mechanism of ATM-based networks, some cells will be discarded to relieve the ponderance of congestion when it unavoidably occurs. So the fortunately survived cells can arrive at the receiver's end. In the same way, the selective discarding solution is applied to the image transmission in the ATM environments, which, combined with relative image coding scheme and backward processing technique, can reduce the influence of cell loss to image quality. Now we come to layered coding because the above-discussed selective discarding of cells in image communication is implemented by it. Commonly used layered coding techniques include subband-based, predictive coding-based، transformation coding-based and H.261-based variant bit rate layered coding algorithm[2]. What we suggest in this essay is transposition coding-based.

During the transformation coding, the property of HVS (Human Vision System) plays an important role: high frequency information which reacts slightly to humans' vision can be transmitted via low priority cells, whereas the low frequency information is given high priority. This layered scheme starts off from the visual property of human beings assumed that even all the low priority cells have lost, the quality of the main body of images still can be guaranteed. But because this scheme hasn't counted in the statistical characteristic of the image signals, the quality of detailed information can't be satisfying. From the statistical view, the pertinence between high frequency components is dramatically low than that of low frequency ones. Our one choice is to reconstruct the lost low frequency information from the low frequency components of adjacent regions, while another is to reconstruct the high frequency information using adjacent high frequency components. Obviously the former outgoes the latter in practical effect. We ground on both the visual property of human eyes and statistical property of image signals to provide a new layered coding method.

We adopt a two-layered coding method. Assume f: $N \times N$ as the input image. At the first step of this transformation encoding scheme, f is divided into $M \times M$ blocks, named $f_B = \{f_B(i, j), i, j = 1, 2, \ldots\ldots, N/M\}$. We divide f into two layers in space domain according the following procedure: retrieve the quincunx blocks of f_B into two subsets: f_B^o and f_B^e, transform them into F_B^o and F_B^e each, then divide F_B^o and F_B^e prospectively into two sub-layers according to the traditional layer scheme, i.e. according to the variety of transform coefficient frequency, so we get the following four sub-layers: $F_B^o(H)$ 、 $F_B^o(L)$ 、 $F_B^e(H)$ and $F_B^e(L)$, which echoes to four priorities, where $F_B^o(L)$ and $F_B^e(L)$ correspond to the highest and lowest priority individually.Fig.1 gives the system framework of image layered coding scheme in ATM-based communications.

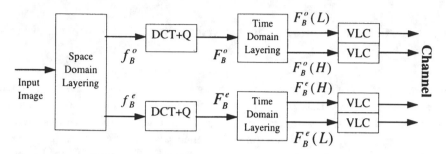

Fig. 1. Layered coding scheme in ATM-based communication

In the ATM specifications, only one bit indicates the priority of cell——CLP（Cell Loss Priority）, for instance, the cells whose CLP is 1, i.e. with low priority, will be discarded when congestion occurs. During the image source coding, cells are classified into two categories: basic cell CLP0 and minor cell CLP1. Therefore the above two-layered coding method introduces two schemes to set the priority of image cell: Static and dynamic.

In the static scheme, cells are classified by fixed criteria, that's to say that the priority setting of cells will not be adjusted according to the diversification of network status in the service procedure. For example, cells belonged to $F_B^o(H)$ 、 $F_B^o(L)$ 、 $F_B^e(H)$ are marked as high priority, viz CLP0; and $F_B^e(L)$ -typed cells, low priority, are marked as CLP1. During congestion, CLP1 cells are discarded, then at the receiver's end backward reconstruction algorithm provided in this essay can be expected to restore the images with good quality of detail.

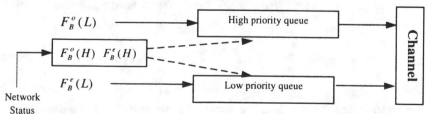

Fig. 2. Cell priority dynamic adjustment scheme

Image/video service, as the highest speed service, will be a great relief to network congestion if it can achieve relatively high cell loss enduring rate under controlled quality. Thereby this essay brings forward a scheme that can adjust cell priority dynamically as Fig.2, which is expected to heighten the cell loss enduring rate further in image transmission. So when utilizing backward processing algorithm of Section 3 at the receiver's end the quality of restored image can be controlled in definite scope. In accordance to the evaluation of experiment simulated results, even under the worst condition, the subjective quality of restored images still can be retained above category 4~3.

3. Reconstruction method of lost cell information at the receiver's end

Note that the variety of luminance in native images is not very abrupt but transitional. So we can assume the variety of pixel luminance between the damnified area and its adjacent normal area is flat enough[3]. So our reconstruction algorithm is grounded on this assumption. Let f represent the image signals whose domain is Area S, and C is another area within S and more strictly $C \subset S$, the border of which is C^r. Corresponding we have $f_C = \{f(x) / x \in C\}$、 $f_{Cr} = \{f(x) / x \in C^r\}$ representing the image signals of Area C、C^r. If $F_C = L(f_C)$ indicates the image(not the "image" referring to picture) of f_C in the transformation domain, where L(.) represents reversible mapping from space domain to transformation domain. So the reconstruction criteria of image information within f_C is to treat f_{Cr} as transcendent evaluation of information, $\hat{F}_C$, and the derivation $\hat{f}_{Cr}$ from $\hat{F}_C$ approaching f_{Cr} according to Frobenius norm, see Formula (1).

$$\hat{F}_C = E\left(F_C \Big/ f_{Cr}\right) \qquad s.t. \qquad \min \left\| \hat{f}_{Ci} - f_{Cr} \right\|_2 \tag{1}$$

If arranging the elements of $\hat{F}_C$ and f_{Cr} into column vector and still named $\hat{F}_C$ and f_{Cr}, the dimensions of each are 4N-4×1 and $N^2 \times 1$. So it is undetermined to estimate $\hat{F}_C$ from the border information f_{Cr}, that's to say that $\hat{F}_C$ is not the only optimized solution. We will demonstrate how to educe the optimized solution of $\hat{F}_C$ with the conformance to Formula(2), and assert that this solution is determined by the choice of the orthogonal bases of the Hilbert space on which f_{Cr} projects. This space is spanned by the boundary components of the transform field. For the reason that orthogonal base has still several choices, the optimized solution is not exclusive.

Let $\{\phi_{u,v}(x, y)\}$ $u, v = 0, 1, \ldots\ldots N-1$ be the base signals of the transformation domain that $F_C(u, v)$ corresponds to. Fetch the signal component of each base signal on the border of blocks and normalize them to $\psi_{u,v}(l)$, then we get Formula (2) as the following:

$$\hat{f}_{Cr}(l) = \sum_{u} \sum_{v} \hat{F}_C(u,v)\psi_{u,v}(l) \tag{2}$$

We can know from Formula (1)、(2) and the projection theorem that $\hat{f}_{Ci}$ equals to the projection that f_{Cr} projects on the space which is spanned linearly by one group of the base vectors of the $\psi_{u,v}(l)$ and $\hat{F}_C(u,v)$ acquire the optimum solution under this group of base vectors when the base vector of $\psi_{u,v}(l)$ is complete to the f_{Cr}. So it is important to analyze the features of the $\psi_{u,v}(l)$ u, v=0,1, ... , N-1. In the following part, we draw the conclusion by analyzing the features of the 2-D discrete cosine base signal's components on the edge of the sub-blocks of the image.

1) If $u1 \neq u2$ _and_ $v1 \neq v2$, then we have $\langle \psi_{u1,v1}(l), \psi_{u2,v2}(l) \rangle = 0$.

2) If $u1 = u2$, then when v1+v2 is odd or when $v1 = v2$ and u1+u2 is odd, we have that $\langle \psi_{u1,v1}(l), \psi_{u2,v2}(l) \rangle = 0$.

3) Let $P = (N-2)/2$, then we can combine the remainder vectors linearly and normalize them to produce another group of vectors that are orthogonal each other based on formula (3).

$$\sum_{i} \left(\psi_{ui,v}(l) - \psi_{v,ui}(l) \right) \quad \forall \psi_{ui,v}(l) and \psi_{v,ui}(l) \notin \Psi^1, ui+uj = even, i = 0,1,......, P-1-v \tag{3}$$

From the conclusion 1) and 2), we can determine one group of vectors that are orthogonal each other and the number of vectors in this group is 2N. This group of vectors is denoted as Ψ^1. Among the remainder elements of the $\{\psi_{u,v}(l)\}$, some elements can produce another group of vectors Ψ^2 that are orthogonal each other by combining those elements linearly according some definite rules. It can be proved that Ψ^2 and Ψ^1 are orthogonal each other. The Ψ^2 is defined in conclusion 3).

From conclusion 3), we can conclude that there are 2N-4 vectors which are orthogonal each other in the Ψ^2. If we define $\Psi = \Psi^1 \cup \Psi^2$, then the rank of Ψ is 4N-4 and the dimension of f_{Cr} is 4N-4 x 1. Because Ψ is complete to f_{Cr}, so based on the Parseral theorem, we can draw conclusion that f_{Cr} is superposed fully with its projection on Ψ and acquire the formula (4).

$$\hat{f}_{Cr}(l) = \sum_{i=0}^{4N-5} < \Psi(i), O_f(l) > \Psi(i) = f_{Cr}(l) \tag{4}$$

So, while $\psi_{u,v}(l) \in \Psi^1$, we can compute $\hat{F}_C(u,v)$ by formula $\hat{F}_C(u,v) = \langle \psi_{u,v}(l), f_{Cr}(l) \rangle$. And we can calculate $\hat{F}_C(u,v)$, which is according to Ψ^2, via usingformula (3). In the standard JPEG or MPEG algorithm, the image is divided into 8x8 sub-blocks. Then based on the conclusion upwards, there are 4x8-4 =28 bases in Ψ. Among them, there are 16 bases in Ψ^1 which are selectedfrom $\{\psi_{u,v}(l)\}$ directly but the choice is not unique.

0	1	16	17	16	17	16	17
2	3	18	19	18	19	18	19
16	18	4	5	20	21	20	21
17	19	6	7	22	23	22	23
16	18	20	22	8	9	24	25
17	19	21	23	10	11	26	27
16	18	20	22	24	26	12	13
17	19	21	23	25	27	14	15

Fig. 3. One Choice of the selection of the orthogonal bases for 8x8 sub-block in DCT transformation

The bases in Ψ^2 are produced by linearly combining and normalizing the elements in $\{\psi_{u,v}(l)\}$. In figure 3, we give one choice of the 28 bases while the size of the sub-block is 8x8. In this figure, the number 0-27 represents the location of the transform coefficients, which are corresponding to these bases.

4.Performance Analysis

If K transform coefficient of sub-block $F_C(u,v)$ is lost in transmission, the boundary discontinuity of block $F_C(u,v)$ is defined by $D_{ir}' = \left\| f_i'(l) - f_r(l) \right\|_2$ and the SNR is

$$SNR_1 = \left(\sum F^2(u,v) - \sum_K F^2(ui,vi) \right) \Big/ \sum_K F^2(ui,vi).$$ With processed by the

algorithm proposed in this paper, the block discontinuity of the post-processed block $F_C(u,v)$ is $\hat{D}_{ir} = \left\| \hat{f}_i(l) - f_r(l) \right\|_2$,if only coefficients in Ψ^1 is lost, we can get formula (5) as the following.

$$\hat{D}_{ir} = \left\|\hat{f}_i(l) - f_r(l)\right\|_2 \geq \left\|\hat{f}_i(l) - f_i(l)\right\|_2 - \left\|f_i(l) - f_r(l)\right\|_2 \qquad (5)$$

$$= \left\|\sum_i \left(\hat{F}(ui,vi) - F(ui,vi)\right)\psi_{ui,vi}(l)\right\|_2 + \left\|f_i(l) - f_r(l)\right\|_2 = \sum_i \left(\hat{F}(ui,vi) - F(ui,vi)\right)^2 + \left\|f_i(l) - f_r(l)\right\|_2$$

$$\sum_i \left(\hat{F}(ui,vi) - F(ui,vi)\right)^2 \leq \hat{D}_{ir} + \left\|f_i(l) - f_r(l)\right\|_2 \approx \left\|f_i(l) - f_r(l)\right\|_2$$

The gain of SNR is then obtained by.

$$G = \sum_i F^2(ui,vi) \Big/ \sum_i \left(\hat{F}(ui,vi) - F(ui,vi)\right)^2 \geq \sum_i F^2(ui,vi) \Big/ \left\|f_i(l) - f_r(l)\right\|_2 \qquad (6)$$

5.Experiment Simulated Results

During the experiment, we choose a LENA image ,a GIRL image and a BABOON image of 8 BIT、256×256 as the source image. Encode them into four sub-layers as above, and list the restored results of the two images in Fig. 4, in which we adopt Fourth-layer loss (in the second column) and Third & Fourth sub-layer loss (in the third column) individually.

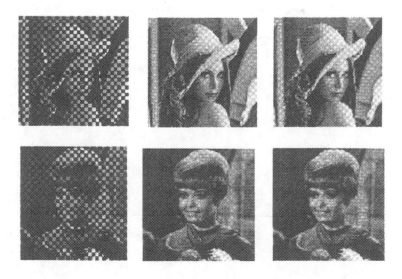

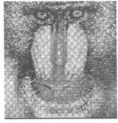

Fig. 4. The reconstruction effect of the LENA,GIRL and BABOON images under the losses of different layer coefficients.

6.Conclusion

We have proposed a model of layered image coding and a new homologous method for image reconstruction. From a computational viewpoint, the proposed method is simple as well since the computational complexities is O(n). The performance was shown to be very effective even with high-frequency dominant images such as baboon.

7.References

1. Tominaga H, et al. A video coding method considering cell losses in ATM-based networks. Signal Processing: Image communication , 1991,3(4):291-300
2. M. Ghanbari, Two-layer coding of video signals for VBR networks, IEEE J. Select Areas Commun., vol. 7, pp. 771-781, June 1989.
3. Byeungwoo Jeon , Jechang Jeong . Blocking artifacts reduction in image compression with block boundary discontinuity criterion. IEEE Trans. on Circuits and System for Video Technology. Vol. 8, No 3, June 1998

Author Index

Lecture Notes in Computer Science

For information about Vols. 1–1668
please contact your bookseller or Springer-Verlag

Vol. 1702: G. Nadathur (Ed.), Principles and Practice of Declarative Programming. Proceedings, 1999. X, 434 pages. 1999.

Vol. 1703: L. Pierre, T. Kropf (Eds.), Correct Hardware Design and Verification Methods. Proceedings, 1999. XI, 366 pages. 1999.

Vol. 1704: Jan M. Żytkow, J. Rauch (Eds.), Principles of Data Mining and Knowledge Discovery. Proceedings, 1999. XIV, 593 pages. 1999. (Subseries LNAI).

Vol. 1705: H. Ganzinger, D. McAllester, A. Voronkov (Eds.), Logic for Programming and Automated Reasoning. Proceedings, 1999. XII, 397 pages. 1999. (Subseries LNAI).

Vol. 1706: J. Hatcliff, T. Æ. Mogensen, P. Thiemann (Eds.), Partial Evaluation – Practice and Theory. 1998. IX, 433 pages. 1999.

Vol. 1707: H.-W. Gellersen (Ed.), Handheld and Ubiquitous Computing. Proceedings, 1999. XII, 390 pages. 1999.

Vol. 1708: J.M. Wing, J. Woodcock, J. Davies (Eds.), FM'99 – Formal Methods. Proceedings Vol. I, 1999. XVIII, 937 pages. 1999.

Vol. 1709: J.M. Wing, J. Woodcock, J. Davies (Eds.), FM'99 – Formal Methods. Proceedings Vol. II, 1999. XVIII, 937 pages. 1999.

Vol. 1710: E.-R. Olderog, B. Steffen (Eds.), Correct System Design. XIV, 417 pages. 1999.

Vol. 1711: N. Zhong, A. Skowron, S. Ohsuga (Eds.), New Directions in Rough Sets, Data Mining, and Granular-Soft Computing. Proceedings, 1999. XIV, 558 pages. 1999. (Subseries LNAI).

Vol. 1712: H. Boley, A Tight, Practical Integration of Relations and Functions. XI, 169 pages. 1999. (Subseries LNAI).

Vol. 1713: J. Jaffar (Ed.), Principles and Practice of Constraint Programming – CP'99. Proceedings, 1999. XII, 493 pages. 1999.

Vol. 1714: M.T. Pazienza (Eds.), Information Extraction. IX, 165 pages. 1999. (Subseries LNAI).

Vol. 1715: P. Perner, M. Petrou (Eds.), Machine Learning and Data Mining in Pattern Recognition. Proceedings, 1999. VIII, 217 pages. 1999. (Subseries LNAI).

Vol. 1716: K.Y. Lam, E. Okamoto, C. Xing (Eds.), Advances in Cryptology – ASIACRYPT'99. Proceedings, 1999. XI, 414 pages. 1999.

Vol. 1717: Ç. K. Koç, C. Paar (Eds.), Cryptographic Hardware and Embedded Systems. Proceedings, 1999. XI, 353 pages. 1999.

Vol. 1718: M. Diaz, P. Owezarski, P. Sénac (Eds.), Interactive Distributed Multimedia Systems and Telecommunication Services. Proceedings, 1999. XI, 386 pages. 1999.

Vol. 1719: M. Fossorier, H. Imai, S. Lin, A. Poli (Eds.), Applied Algebra, Algebraic Algorithms and Error-Correcting Codes. Proceedings, 1999. XIII, 510 pages. 1999.

Vol. 1720: O. Watanabe, T. Yokomori (Eds.), Algorithmic Learning Theory. Proceedings, 1999. XI, 365 pages. 1999. (Subseries LNAI).

Vol. 1721: S. Arikawa, K. Furukawa (Eds.), Discovery Science. Proceedings, 1999. XI, 374 pages. 1999. (Subseries LNAI).

Vol. 1722: A. Middeldorp, T. Sato (Eds.), Functional and Logic Programming. Proceedings, 1999. X, 369 pages. 1999.

Vol. 1723: R. France, B. Rumpe (Eds.), UML'99 – The Unified Modeling Language. XVII, 724 pages. 1999.

Vol. 1725: J. Pavelka, G. Tel, M. Bartošek (Eds.), SOFSEM'99: Theory and Practice of Informatics. Proceedings, 1999. XIII, 498 pages. 1999.

Vol. 1726: V. Varadharajan, Y. Mu (Eds.), Information and Communication Security. Proceedings, 1999. XI, 325 pages. 1999.

Vol. 1727: P.P. Chen, D.W. Embley, J. Kouloumdjian, S.W. Liddle, J.F. Roddick (Eds.), Advances in Conceptual Modeling. Proceedings, 1999. XI, 389 pages. 1999.

Vol. 1728: J. Akoka, M. Bouzeghoub, I. Comyn-Wattiau, E. Métais (Eds.), Conceptual Modeling – ER '99. Proceedings, 1999. XIV, 540 pages. 1999.

Vol. 1729: M. Mambo, Y. Zheng (Eds.), Information Security. Proceedings, 1999. IX, 277 pages. 1999.

Vol. 1730: M. Gelfond, N. Leone, G. Pfeifer (Eds.), Logic Programming and Nonmonotonic Reasoning. Proceedings, 1999. XI, 391 pages. 1999. (Subseries LNAI).

Vol. 1732: S. Matsuoka, R.R. Oldehoeft, M. Tholburn (Eds.), Computing in Object-Oriented Parallel Environments. Proceedings, 1999. VIII, 205 pages. 1999.

Vol. 1733: H. Nakashima, C. Zhang (Eds.), Approaches to Intelligent Agents. Proceedings, 1999. XII, 241 pages. 1999. (Subseries LNAI).

Vol. 1734: H. Hellwagner, A. Reinefeld (Eds.), SCI: Scalable Coherent Interface. XXI, 490 pages. 1999.

Vol. 1564: M. Vazirgiannis, Interactive Multimedia Documents. XIII, 161 pages. 1999.

Vol. 1591: D.J. Duke, I. Herman, M.S. Marshall, PREMO: A Framework for Multimedia Middleware. XII, 254 pages. 1999.

Vol. 1735: J.W. Amtrup, Incremental Speech Translation. XV, 200 pages. 1999. (Subseries LNAI).

Vol. 1736: L. Rizzo, S. Fdida (Eds.): Networked Group Communication. Proceedings, 1999. XIII, 339 pages. 1999.

Vol. 1738: C. Pandu Rangan, V. Raman, R. Ramanujam (Eds.), Foundations of Software Technology and Theoretical Computer Science. Proceedings, 1999. XII, 452 pages. 1999.

Vol. 1740: R. Baumgart (Ed.): Secure Networking – CQRE [Secure] '99. Proceedings, 1999. IX, 261 pages. 1999.

Vol. 1742: P.S. Thiagarajan, R. Yap (Eds.), Advances in Computing Science – ASIAN'99. Proceedings, 1999. XI, 397 pages. 1999.

Vol. 1745: P. Banerjee, V.K. Prasanna, B.P. Sinha (Eds.), High Performance Computing – HiPC'99. Proceedings, 1999. XXII, 412 pages. 1999.

Vol. 1746: M. Walker (Ed.), Cryptography and Coding. Proceedings, 1999. IX, 313 pages. 1999.

Vol. 1747: N. Foo (Ed.), Adavanced Topics in Artificial Intelligence. Proceedings, 1999. XV, 500 pages. 1999. (Subseries LNAI).

Vol. 1749: L. C.-K. Hui, D.L. Lee (Eds.), Internet Applications. Proceedings, 1999. XX, 518 pages. 1999.